THE GOSPEL
ACCORDING TO JOHN

VOLUME 29

THE ANCHOR BIBLE is a fresh approach to the world's greatest classic. Its object is to make the Bible accessible to the modern reader; its method is to arrive at the meaning of biblical literature through exact translation and extended exposition, and to reconstruct the ancient setting of the biblical story, as well as the circumstances of its transcription and the characteristics of its transcribers.

THE ANCHOR BIBLE is a project of international and interfaith scope. Protestant, Catholic, and Jewish scholars from many countries contribute individual volumes. The project is not sponsored by any ecclesiastical organization and is not intended to reflect any particular theological doctrine. Prepared under our joint supervision, THE ANCHOR BIBLE is an effort to make available all the significant historical and linguistic knowledge which bears on the interpretation of the biblical record.

THE ANCHOR BIBLE is aimed at the general reader with no special formal training in biblical studies; yet, it is written with the most exacting standards of scholarship, reflecting the highest technical accomplishment.

This project marks the beginning of a new era of co-operation among scholars in biblical research, thus forming a common body of knowledge to be shared by all.

William Foxwell Albright
David Noel Freedman
GENERAL EDITORS

THE ANCHOR BIBLE

THE GOSPEL
ACCORDING TO
JOHN
(i–xii)

INTRODUCTION, TRANSLATION, AND NOTES

BY

RAYMOND E. BROWN, S.S.

Doubleday & Company, Inc.
Garden City, New York

NIHIL OBSTAT
Myles M. Bourke, S.S.L., S.T.D.
Censor Librorum

IMPRIMATUR
✠ Terence J. Cooke, D.D.

February 24, 1966
New York

ISBN: 0-385-01517-8
Library of Congress Catalog Card Number 66–12209
Second Edition
Twentieth Printing
1983

PREFACE

Volume 29 of The Anchor Bible is the first part of a three–volume translation of and commentary on John and the Johannine Epistles. It contains an introduction to the whole Gospel and a treatment of chs. i–xii, or the Johannine account of the public ministry of Jesus (the Gospel itself has a break at the end of ch. xii). The second volume (vol. 29A) will contain a treatment of chs. xiii–xxi of the Gospel, or the account of the Last Supper, the passion of Jesus, and the appearances of the risen Jesus. The third volume (vol. 30) will introduce and comment on the three Johannine Epistles. The two Gospel volumes (29 and 29A) should be of about the same length, and indexes to the whole will appear at the end of vol. 29A.

The tremendous amount of scholarly work on John in the last few years and a notable change in the direction of Johannine studies (see Introduction, Part I) have made necessary a somewhat longer and more detailed commentary than has hitherto been the custom in the Anchor Bible series. However, we trust that the reader will not begrudge the greater expenditure of time and effort required by these volumes, for the Fourth Gospel is more than worthy of all the time and effort we can give to it. A. Harnack once remarked that this Gospel is one of the great enigmas of the early history of Christianity, and more recently C. H. Dodd has made the claim that if we can understand John, we shall know what early Christianity really was. It is easy to understand that such a work, which is both enigma and keystone, requires extensive explanation. A translation with brief notes would serve no purpose here, for the many important commentaries on John already in existence would, by comparison, immediately expose with brutal clarity the superficiality of an inadequate treatment.

Only with considerable hesitation has the present writer undertaken this project of another commentary on John, precisely because there are already many excellent commentaries in English and in German. However, the brilliant originality of these commentaries and of the abundant periodical literature on John has provided Johannine studies with an embarrassment of riches. It is often only by working through several commentaries, each with a view all its own, that the interested student can get a true appreciation of the problems in John and the possible solutions. Thus, the one factor above all others that has contributed to this writer's decision to produce these volumes has been a conviction that the time has come to gather the fruit of the brilliant but isolated contributions of his predecessors and to make a synthesis of what is of value in their very divergent approaches to the Gospel. The author has no idea whether or not his fellow scholars will agree that the correct approach to such a synthesis lies in the direction he has chosen, namely, in a moderately critical theory of the composition of the Gospel, combined with the conviction that the Gospel is rooted in historical tradition about Jesus of Nazareth. Nevertheless, the fact that the views both of the more adventurous critics and of those inclined to a traditional evaluation of the Gospel find an honest (one hopes) and appreciative hearing in the same commentary may be of considerable value to the student.

Fortunately we live at a time when a considerable degree of objectivity has been reached in biblical scholarship, so that a commentator can profit from the serious work of scholars of all religious communions. What has contributed most in this direction has been the establishment of the clear difference between the thoughts of the various biblical authors (which are the concern of a biblical scholar) and the subsequent use and development of those thoughts in divergent theologies (which are the concern of a theologian). The second point is important, for the majority of those who read Scripture are believers for whom the Bible is more than an interesting witness to past religious phenomena. Nor can it be neglected by the biblical scholar without peril of religious schizophrenia. Nevertheless, as we have come to realize, sincere confessional commitment to a theological position is perfectly consonant with a stubborn refusal to make a biblical text say more than its author meant it to say. There is no reason why scholars of different denominations cannot agree on the literal meaning of Scripture, even though they may disagree on the import of certain passages in the evolution of theology. The Anchor Bible is committed to this thesis, and the writer has composed his volumes in this spirit.

The translation strives for a correct but thoroughly contemporary style. There is no attempt to produce prose of formal literary beauty—the writer would not be capable of this—but only an attempt to render the simple, everyday Greek of the Gospel into the ordinary American English of today. The borderline between good modern usage and usage that is too colloquial for a written work is not sharp or easy to define, although there has been a serious effort in the translation to avoid what would border on slang. The interplay of conversations and arguments in the Gospel is the area in which the problem of proper usage is the most delicate.

Occasionally the choice of a truly apt English word has yielded to the necessity of preserving theological terms important to the evangelist. Thus, for example, in ii 4 "time" would represent contemporary English usage better than "hour" (as the Goodspeed translation has recognized), but the notion of "the hour" is too crucial in the thought of the Gospel to be sacrificed. In xix 30 "he died" would be a smoother reading than "he handed over the spirit" but would obscure the Johannine theme that Jesus, once lifted up (in crucifixion and resurrection), communicates the Spirit.

Third person pronouns referring to God the Father have been capitalized in the translation as a visible means of distinguishing between references to the Father and references to Jesus. For the sake of consistency this principle of distinction has been carried over into the NOTES and COMMENT. It has not always been easy to decide what should go into the NOTES and what should go into the COMMENT, but the desire to obtain simplicity and consecutive thought in the COMMENT has been a guiding factor. The student will find much of interest in the NOTES; the more general reader may be content with the COMMENT, which deals with the broad ranges of the Gospel's thought and composition.

The General Selected Bibliography on p. CXLV contains only general works frequently cited. In making references to them, we shall use the author's name and the page number, thus, Bultmann, p. 12[5]—the elevated number refers to a footnote. At the end of each part of the Introduction, the COMMENT on major segments of the text, and units in the Appendixes, an appropriate sectional bibliography is provided. Most of the references in the unit are to that sectional bibliography—thus, Bultmann, *art. cit.*, refers to an article by Bultmann cited in the following sectional bibliography.

The writer is grateful to all those—too many to name—who have helped him in one way or another with this volume. Particularly valuable was the assistance by way of checking and proofreading rendered by the seminarians of St. Mary's Seminary, Baltimore, especially by Mr. John Kselman. The co-operation of Mr. Eugene Eoyang and the staff at Doubleday was outstanding.

By chance this volume has a publication date which falls very close to the seventy-fifth birthday of Professor William F. Albright, born May 24, 1891. The writer remembers that his first article on John was the product of one of the Professor's seminars at the Johns Hopkins University. And so he would like to take this occasion to acknowledge frankly his debt to the scholarship, example, and generosity of this great biblical scholar. *Ad multos annos.*

CONTENTS

I. PROLOGUE

II. THE BOOK OF SIGNS

PART ONE: THE OPENING DAYS OF THE REVELATION OF JESUS

PART TWO: FROM CANA TO CANA

PART THREE: JESUS AND THE PRINCIPAL FEASTS OF THE JEWS

PRINCIPAL ABBREVIATIONS

1. BIBLICAL AND APOCRYPHAL WORKS

Besides the standard abbreviations of books of the Bible used in the series:

Deuterocanonical Books of the OT:

Tob	Tobit
Judith	Judith
I & II Macc	I & II Maccabees
Sir	Sirach or Ecclesiasticus
Wis	Wisdom of Solomon
Bar	Baruch

Apocryphal Books related to the OT:

Jub	Jubilees
En	Enoch or Henoch
II Bar	II Baruch
I & II Esd	I & II Esdras
Ps Sol	Psalms of Solomon

2. PUBLICATIONS

AASOR	Annual of the American Schools of Oriental Research
AER	American Ecclesiastical Review
APCh	*Apocrypha and Pseudepigrapha of the Old Testament in English* by R. H. Charles (2 vols.; Oxford: Clarendon, 1913)
ATR	Anglican Theological Review
BA	The Biblical Archaeologist
BAG	W. Bauer (as translated by W. F. Arndt and F. W. Gingrich), *A Greek-English Lexicon of the New Testament* (University of Chicago, 1957)
BASOR	Bulletin of the American Schools of Oriental Research
BCCT	*The Bible in Current Catholic Thought*, ed. J. L. McKenzie, in honor of M. Gruenthaner (New York: Herder & Herder, 1962)

BDF   F. Blass and A. Debrunner (as translated by R. W. Funk),
             *A Greek Grammar of the New Testament and Other Early
             Christian Literature* (University of Chicago, 1961). Refer-
             ences to sections
Bib   Biblica
BibOr   Bibbia e Oriente
BJRL   Bulletin of the John Rylands Library (Manchester)
BNTE   *The Background of the New Testament and Its Eschatology*,
             eds. W. D. Davies and D. Daube, in honor of C. H. Dodd
             (Cambridge, 1956)
BVC   Bible et Vie Chrétienne
BZ   Biblische Zeitschrift
CBQ   Catholic Biblical Quarterly
CDC   Cairo Genizah Document of the Damascus Covenanters (the
             Zadokite Documents)
CINTI   *Current Issues in New Testament Interpretation*, eds. W. Klassen
             and G. F. Snyder, in honor of O. A. Piper (New York:
             Harper, 1962)
CSCO   Corpus Scriptorum Christianorum Orientalium (Louvain)
CSEL   Corpus Scriptorum Ecclesiasticorum Latinorum (Vienna)
DB   H. Denzinger and C. Bannwart, *Enchiridion Symbolorum*, rev.
             by A. Schönmetzer, 32 ed. (Freiburg: Herder, 1963). Ref-
             erences to sections
DBS   Dictionnaire de la Bible—Supplément
ECW   *Early Christian Worship* by Oscar Cullmann (see General Se-
             lected Bibliography)
EstBib   Estudios Bíblicos (Madrid)
ET   Expository Times
ETL   Ephemerides Theologicae Lovanienses
EvJean   *L'Evangile de Jean* by M.-E. Boismard *et al.* (Recherches
             Bibliques, III; Louvain: Desclée de Brouwer, 1958)
EvTh   Evangelische Theologie (Munich)
GCS   Die Griechischen Christlichen Schriftsteller (Berlin)
HTR   Harvard Theological Review
IEJ   Israel Exploration Journal
IMEL   *In Memoriam Ernst Lohmeyer*, ed. W. Schmauch (Stuttgart:
             Evangelisches Verlag, 1951)
Interp   Interpretation (Richmond, Virginia)
JBL   Journal of Biblical Literature
JeanThéol   *Jean le Théologien* by F.-M. Braun (see General Selected Bibli-
             ography)
JG   *Johannine Grammar* by E. A. Abbott (London: Black, 1906).
             References to sections
JJS   Journal of Jewish Studies
JNES   Journal of Near Eastern Studies
JohSt   *Johannine Studies* by A. Feuillet (New York: Alba, 1964)

JPOS	Journal of the Palestine Oriental Society
JTS	Journal of Theological Studies
LumVie	Lumière et Vie
MD	La Maison-Dieu
NovT	Novum Testamentum
NRT	Nouvelle Revue Théologique
NTA	New Testament Abstracts
NTAuf	*Neutestamentliche Aufsätze,* eds. J. Blinzler, O. Kuss, and F. Mussner, in honor of J. Schmid (Regensburg: Pustet, 1963)
NTE	*New Testament Essays* by Raymond E. Brown (Milwaukee: Bruce, 1965; reprinted New York: Doubleday Image, 1968)
NTPat	*Neotestamentica et Patristica,* in honor of O. Cullmann (SNT, VI)
NTS	New Testament Studies (Cambridge)
PG	Patrologia Graeca-Latina (Migne)
PL	Patrologia Latina (Migne)
1QH	Qumran Hymns of Thanksgiving
1QpHab	Qumran Pesher on Habakkuk
1QM	Qumran War Scroll
1QS	Qumran Manual of Discipline
RB	Revue biblique
RecLC	*Recueil Lucien Cerfaux* (3 vols.; Gembloux, 1954–62)
RHPR	Revue d'histoire et de philosophie religieuses
RivBib	Rivista Biblica (Brescia)
RSPT	Revue des sciences philosophiques et théologiques
RSR	Recherches de science religieuse
RThom	Revue Thomiste
SacPag	*Sacra Pagina,* eds. J. Coppens, A. Descamps, E. Massaux (Louvain, 1959)
SBT	Studies in Biblical Theology (London: SCM)
SC	Sources Chrétiennes (Paris: Cerf)
ScEccl	Sciences Ecclésiastiques (Montreal)
SFG	*Studies in the Fourth Gospel,* ed. F. L. Cross (London: Mowbray, 1957)
SNT	Supplements to Novum Testamentum (Leiden: Brill)
StB	H. L. Strack and P. Billerbeck, *Kommentar zum Neuen Testament aus Talmud und Midrasch* (5 vols.; Munich: Beck, 1922–55)
StEv	*Studia Evangelica* (Papers from the Oxford International Congresses of NT Studies; published at Berlin, Akademie–Verlag)
TalBab	The Babylonian Talmud, English ed. by I. Epstein (London: Soncino, 1961)
TalJer	The Jerusalem Talmud
TD	Theology Digest
ThR	Theologische Rundschau (Tübingen)
TLZ	Theologische Literaturzeitung

TNTS   *Twelve New Testament Studies* by John A. T. Robinson (SBT,
          No. 34; London: SCM, 1962)
TS   Theological Studies
TWNT   *Theologisches Wörterbuch zum Neuen Testament,* ed. G. Kittel
          (Stuttgart: Kohlhammer, 1933–   )
TWNTE   Same work translated into English by G. W. Bromiley (Grand
          Rapids: Eerdmans, 1964–   )
TZ   Theologische Zeitschrift (Basel)
VD   Verbum Domini
VigChr   Vigiliae Christianae
VT   Vetus Testamentum
ZDPV   Zeitschrift des Deutschen Palästina-Vereins
ZGB   M. Zerwick, *Graecitas Biblica* (4 ed.; Rome: Pontifical Biblical
          Institute, 1960). References are to sections; these are the same
          in the English translation of the 4 ed. by J. Smith (Rome:
          1963)
ZKT   Zeitschrift für katholische Theologie
ZNW   Zeitschrift für die neutestamentliche Wissenschaft und die Kunde
          der älteren Kirche
ZTK   Zeitschrift für Theologie und Kirche

3. Versions

KJ   The Authorized Version of 1611, or the King James Bible
LXX   The Septuagint
MT   Masoretic Text
NEB   The New English Bible (New Testament, 1961)
RSV   The Revised Standard Version, 1946, 1952
SB   La Sainte Bible—"Bible de Jérusalem"—traduite en français
          (Paris: Cerf). D. Mollat, *L'Evangile de saint Jean* (2 ed.,
          1960)
Vulg.   The Vulgate

4. Other Abbreviations

NT   New Testament
OT   Old Testament
Aram.   Aramaic
Boh.   Bohairic (Coptic)
Eth.   Ethiopic
Gr.   Greek
Heb.   Hebrew
OL   Old Latin

OS	Old Syriac (OS^{cur}; OS^{sin} denote the Curetonian and Sinaiticus mss. respectively)
Sah.	Sahidic (Coptic)
App.	Appendixes in the back of the volume
P	Papyrus
par.	parallel verse(s)
*	Asterisk after a manuscript indicates the original hand of the copyist, as distinct from later correctors
[ ]	Brackets in the translation indicate a textually dubious word or passage

INTRODUCTION

I. THE PRESENT STATE OF JOHANNINE STUDIES

In this century an enormous literature has been devoted to the Fourth Gospel. Indeed, the most instructive introduction to the study of the Gospel is to read one of the surveys of the literature on John—for instance, that of Howard, or the shorter article of Collins. The ephemeral character of some of the positions taken merits sober reflection. The most valuable analysis of Johannine literature is found in French in the writings of Menoud, whose own very competent and balanced opinions emerge from his criticism of the works of other scholars. His bibliographies are most helpful. Haenchen's German survey is also remarkably complete.

In particular, in the decade after the Second World War there emerged a number of major contributions to the study of John. The commentaries of both Hoskyns (1940) and Bultmann (1941) may be included in this group since they had no wide circulation until after the War. In addition, Dodd's *Interpretation* (1953) and the commentaries of Barrett (1955) and Lightfoot (1956) come immediately to mind. The difference of approach in these various works caused much discussion, as evidenced by the articles of Grossouw, Käsemann, and Schnackenburg.

Even a cursory acquaintance with this literature reveals that the trend in Johannine studies has passed through an interesting cycle. At the end of the last century and in the early years of this century, scholarship went through a period of extreme skepticism about this Gospel. John was dated very late, even to the second half of the 2nd century. As a product of the Hellenistic world, it was thought to be totally devoid of historical value and to have little relation to the Palestine of Jesus of Nazareth. The small kernel of fact in its pages was supposedly taken from the Synoptic Gospels which served as a basis for the author's elaborations. Needless to say, few critics thought that the Gospel according to John had the slightest connection with John son of Zebedee.

Some of these skeptical positions, especially those regarding authorship and the source of influence on the Gospel, are still maintained by many reputable scholars. Nevertheless, there is not one such position that has not been affected by a series of unexpected archaeological, documentary, and textual discoveries. These discoveries have led us to challenge intelligently the critical views that had almost become orthodox and to recognize how fragile was the base which supported the highly skeptical analysis of John. Consequently, since the Second World War there has emerged what Bishop John A. T. Robinson calls a "new look" in Johannine studies—a new look that shares much with the look once traditional in Christianity. The dating of the Gospel has been moved back to the end of the 1st century or even earlier. A historical tradition underlying the Fourth Gospel similar to the traditions underlying the Synoptic Gospels is being posited by some. In fact, the author of the Gospel is gradually having his status as an orthodox Christian restored, after long languishing in the dungeons of Gnosticism to which he had been relegated by many critics. And perhaps strangest of all, some scholars are even daring to suggest once more that John son of Zebedee may have had something to do with the Gospel. This reversal of trend, however, does not mean that all the intervening critical scholarship has been in vain. Scholarship cannot return to pre-critical days, nor should it ever be embarrassed by the fact that it learns through mistakes. Indeed, it is the admirable honesty of biblical criticism and its ability to criticize itself that has led to a more conservative estimation of the historical value of the Fourth Gospel.

In the vast body of literature on John, the Germans and the British have been the most fruitful contributors. The Germans have been more adventurous in their theories of the origins, composition, and sequence of the Gospel. The British, tending less to reconstructions, have done more to draw a theology from the Gospel as it now stands. Surprisingly enough, neither of these great approaches to Johannine exegesis has been markedly influenced by the other. The individualism of the leading scholars has been conspicuous, and in a few instances it would seem that opposing views were deliberately ignored. As the bibliographies indicate, this commentary has profited from writers of all schools.

BIBLIOGRAPHY

Surveys of Literature on John

Braun, F.-M., "Où en est l'étude du quatrième évangile," ETL 32 (1956), 535–46.

Collins, T. A., "Changing Style in Johannine Studies," BCCT, pp. 202–25.

Grossouw, W., "Three Books on the Fourth Gospel," NovT 1 (1956), 35–46.

Haenchen, E., "Aus der Literatur zum Johannesevangelium 1929–1956," ThR 23 (1955), 295–335.

Howard, W. F., and Barrett, C. K., *The Fourth Gospel in Recent Criticism and Interpretation,* 4 ed. (London: Epworth, 1955).

Käsemann, E., "Zur Johannesinterpretation in England," *Exegetische Versuche und Besinnungen,* II (Göttingen: Vandenhoeck, 1964), pp. 131–55.

Menoud, P.-H., *L'Evangile de Jean d'après les recherches récentes* (Neuchâtel: Delachaux, 1947).

———"Les études johanniques de Bultmann à Barrett," EvJean, pp. 11–40.

Montgomery, J. W., "The Fourth Gospel Yesterday and Today," *Concordia Theological Monthly* 34 (1963), 197–222.

Robinson, James M., "Recent Research in the Fourth Gospel," JBL 78 (1959), 242–52.

Schnackenburg, R., "Neuere englische Literatur zum Johannesevangelium," BZ 2 (1958), 144–54.

Stanley, D. M., "Bulletin of the New Testament: The Johannine Literature," TS 17 (1956), 516–31.

The "New Look" in Johannine Studies

Hunter, A. M., "Recent Trends in Johannine Studies," ET 71 (1959–60), 164–67, 219–22.

Mitton, C. L., "The Provenance of the Fourth Gospel," ET 71 (1959–60), 337–40.

Pollard, T. E., "The Fourth Gospel: Its Background and Early Interpretation," *Australian Biblical Review* 7 (1959), 41–53.

Robinson, John A. T., "The New Look on the Fourth Gospel," StEv, I, pp. 338–50. Now in Robinson's TNTS, pp. 94–106.

II. THE UNITY AND COMPOSITION
OF THE FOURTH GOSPEL

A. THE PROBLEM

Is the Fourth Gospel as it now stands the work of one man? (We shall exclude from this discussion the Story of the Adulteress in vii 53–viii 11 which is not found in the earliest Greek witnesses; see § 30.) The solution commonly accepted before the advent of biblical criticism was that this Gospel was the work of John son of Zebedee, written shortly before his death. We shall discuss the identity of the author in Part VII below; but, even if we lay aside the question of identity, there are features in the Gospel that offer difficulty for any theory of unified authorship. Too often—as Teeple, *art. cit.*, has pointed out—difficulties have been created by not respecting the intention of the author, and complicated hypotheses have been constructed where simple explanations were available. Still, making every allowance for this, we find these major difficulties:

First, there are differences of Greek style in the Gospel. We refer the reader to the discussion of ch. xxi (in The Anchor Bible, vol. 29A), which differs from the rest of the Gospel in small stylistic details that betray difference of authorship. The Prologue is written in a carefully constructed, interlocking poetic pattern found but rarely in the Gospel proper. Moreover, the Prologue employs important theological terms not found elsewhere in the Gospel, for example, *logos* ("Word" personified), *charis* ("grace" or "covenant love"), *plērōma* ("fullness").

Second, there are breaks and inconsistencies in sequence. Too much has been made of the geographical and chronological "jumps" in John, whereby without any indication of a transition one chapter may be situated in a different locale from that of the previous chapter. Such jumps would be crucial only if the Gospel were an attempt to give us a complete account of the ministry of Jesus, but xx 30 and xxi 25 state specifically that the account in the Gospel is incomplete. Yet, even if we are careful not to impose upon the evangelist our modern passion for chronology, there are still seeming contradictions in the present order of the Gospel. In xiv 31 Jesus concludes his remarks at the Last Supper and gives the command to depart; yet this is followed by three more chapters of discourse and the departure does not seem to take place until xviii 1. In xx 30–31 we are given a clear conclusion to the Gospel: the evangelist sums up his narration and explains the purpose he had in writing; yet this is followed by another, seemingly independent chapter with another conclusion. There also seems to be a twofold conclusion to the public ministry in x 40–42 and xii 37–43 (see discussion in § 37, p. 414), although here the evidence is not as clear. The disciples of John the Baptist who were present when the Baptist identified Jesus and explained his mission in i 29–34 do not seem to understand anything about Jesus in iii 26–30. After his first sign at Cana (ii 11), Jesus works signs in Jerusalem (ii 23); yet his next miracle at Cana is apparently designated as his second sign (iv 54), as if there were no signs intervening. In vii 3–5 his brothers speak as if Jesus had never worked signs in Judea, despite the Jerusalem signs just mentioned and another miracle in ch. v. At the Last Supper Peter asks Jesus where he is going (xiii 36, also xiv 5); yet in the same setting in xvi 5 Jesus complains that no one has asked him, "Where are you going?" Throughout ch. iii Jesus has been at Jerusalem, which is in Judea; yet in mid-chapter (iii 22) we are suddenly told that he came into Judea. One or the other of these difficulties may be explained away, but not all of them. It appears that in John we have on the one hand the elements of a planned and cohesive outline (Part X below), and on the other, elements that seem to indicate alterations, insertions, or re-editings. On the one hand there are dramatic scenes that betray minute editorial care (ch. ix, and the trial before Pilate in xviii–xix); on the other there are scenes that lack finish and organization (chs. vii–viii).

Third, there are repetitions in the discourses, as well as passages that clearly do not belong to their context. At times, the evangelist's economy of style is truly impressive, but at other times what has been said seems to be repeated over again in only slightly different terms. This repetition is not pedagogic but appears to be the result of two different traditions of the same words (a phenomenon akin to what we find in the traditions of the Pentateuch). For example, what is said in v 19–25 with an emphasis on realized eschatology (Part VIII below) appears again and, in part, almost verbatim in v 26–30 with an emphasis on final eschatology. What is said and what happens in vi 35–50, where Jesus presents his revelation as the bread of life, is almost the same as what is said and what happens in vi 51–58, where Jesus presents his body as the bread of life (p. 288). What is said in the Last Discourse in xiv 1–31 is largely said all over again in xvi 4–33. In addition to these duplications, there are sections of discourse that do not belong to their context. Who is speaking in iii 31–36, John the Baptist or Jesus? The context would indicate John the Baptist, but the words are appropriate to Jesus. Another discourse that is probably not in its original sequence is xii 44–50, where we find Jesus making a public proclamation when we have just been told that he went into hiding (xii 36).

B. POSSIBLE SOLUTIONS

Difficulties such as we have sampled above have caused many scholars to abandon the traditional picture of the composition of the Gospel by one man from memory. With much oversimplification, we shall group below modern alternative explanations under three headings. We stress, however, that these solutions are not necessarily mutually exclusive; they may be, and often are, combined.

(1) *Theories of Accidental Displacements*

Perhaps the simplest solution to the difficulties found in John is to rearrange parts of the Gospel. From the time of Tatian (ca. 175) to the present day, scholars have thought that by moving passages around they could put John into consecutive order. Their usual presupposition has been that some accident displaced passages and destroyed the original order, thus creating the confusion that we now find in the Gospel. Since there is absolutely no evidence in any of the textual witnesses for any other order than that which we now possess, it must be assumed that this accidental displacement happened before the Gospel was published. And generally it is assumed that it took place after the death or in the absence of the evangelist; for were he available, he could easily have restored his original order.

The amount of rearrangement that has been proposed varies considerably. Many scholars who do not otherwise favor rearrangement, for example, Wikenhauser, will at least support a reversal of order between chs. v and vi in order to obtain better geographical sequence. (Unfortunately, we have no proof that the evangelist shared this geographical interest.) Bernard in his commentary supports a fairly extensive rearrangement, affecting not only v and vi, but also the whole of xv and xvi in the Last Discourse, and parts of iii, vii, x, and xii. Bultmann carries rearrangement even further, so that individual verses and parts of verses are affected; for example, in one part of his rearrangement, the order of verses is ix 41, viii 12, and xii 44. Wilkens and Boismard are others who tend toward frequent rearrangement.

There is no doubt that rearrangement does solve some problems of the Gospel. That it does not solve them all means that often it has to be combined with another explanation of the composition of the Gospel, for example, the source or edition theories to be discussed below. It is important to note, however, that there are serious objections to any theory of displacement and rearrangement:

First, there is a danger that the rearrangements will reflect the interests of the commentator, which may not be the same as the interests of the evangelist. It is possible that the rearrangements will destroy a sequence that was intended, at least by the final editor of the Gospel. For instance, if the section on John the Baptist in iii 22–30 (§ 11) seems to break up what might be a better sequence between iii 1–21 and 31–36 (so Bernard), may one not argue that the passage was inserted in its present location precisely to remind the reader of the baptismal significance of the words in iii 1–21, a significance which might otherwise be missed? Geographically ch. vi does go better before v, but the evangelist might have intended the bread theme of vi to be followed immediately by the water theme in vii (37–38) in order to echo the story of the Exodus where God gave Israel bread from heaven and water from the rock. If one comments on the Gospel as it now stands, one is certain of commenting on an ancient Gospel as it really existed at the final moment of its publication. If one indulges in extensive rearrangement, one may be commenting on a hybrid that never existed before it emerged as the brain child of the rearranger. One can exaggerate this objection; for instance, Bultmann has unfairly been accused of commenting on the Gospel according to Bultmann, rather than on the Gospel according to John. The very title of his commentary, moreover, *Das Evangelium des Johannes* (rather than the more usual *nach Johannes* or *Johannesevangelium*) has been interpreted by some to indicate Bultmann's firm assurance that he has found the real Gospel *of* John behind the Gospel as it has been transmitted to us. But this is to read too much into a perfectly acceptable title.

Second, rearrangements are based on the thesis that the Gospel does not make satisfactory sense as it now stands; but many commentators, like Hoskyns, Barrett, and Dodd, are convinced that the present order does make sense. Generally, if we respect the evangelist's limited purpose, the Gospel is an intelligible document in its present form; and we can reasonably assume that this form of the Gospel made sense to the one who had the final responsibility for the Gospel's appearance. But we must reckon with the possibility that while this editor put the Gospel in the order that seemed best to him, he was not in a position to know the original order of the manuscript and had to settle for what he has given us. The real question is whether with our modern scientific tools almost 1900 years later we are able to establish a more original order than was possible for a contemporary editor. That no great assurance marks this task is clearly demonstrated in the sharp differences between the proposed elaborate rearrangements.

Third, theories of displacement do not always offer an adequate explanation of how the displacement took place. If the Gospel was written out on a scroll, any theory of displacement is difficult. Rolls tend to lose their outmost leaves, but confusion of leaves within the roll is not plausible. It has been suggested that a scroll came apart into separate sheets when the joints where the sheets were glued together came loose. But we must remember that often in such rolls the columns of writing overlap the joints, and if a joint comes apart, the sheets can be easily matched.

More recently scholars have suggested that the original form of the Gospel was a codex or book, a form in which detached sheets are a greater hazard. But even if sheets became detached, the original order could have easily been restored for those sheets that did not both begin with a new sentence and end at the conclusion of a sentence (because incomplete sentences would provide a clue to the sequence of the sheets). Only pages that were units in themselves would pose a problem. This observation has led the advocates of the displacement theory to calculate how many letters would be on the *recto* and *verso* of a codex leaf. Units that became displaced would have to be of such a length or a multiple thereof. Bernard, I, pp.

xxviii ff., does a creditable job of computing this for the displacements he proposes in John, and F. R. Hoare has given a strong exposition of the possibilities of this approach. One might ask, however, how great would be the mathematical likelihood of finding in a manuscript of John such a large number of units that would not overlap on to other leaves. One might also ask in how many proved cases in antiquity did such large-scale, accidental displacements take place before the work was published.

If a theory of displacement of regular units has at least some plausibility, one cannot say the same for a theory of displacement of lines. That Bultmann never explains how the displacement he posits could have taken place is, as Easton, *art. cit.*, has noted, a great weakness. His rearrangement is supposed to be so patently better than the existing order of the Gospel that the dislocations may be said to have been demonstrated exegetically. But many will not be so easily convinced. Was the Gospel written on small bits of papyrus, often containing no more than a sentence? This seems to be the only way to explain the dislocations that Bultmann posits. Any theory of damage to a scroll or a codex would leave us with broken sentences that became detached, but in Bultmann's theory the displacements are always composed of complete sentences.

In summary, the theory of accidental displacement seems to create almost as many problems as it solves. The solution to our problem would appear to lie in the direction of a more deliberate procedure.

(2) *Theories of Multiple Sources*

If the fourth evangelist combined several independent sources, some of the stylistic differences, as well as the lack of sequence and the presence of duplications, can be accounted for. In the recent forms of the source theory it is customarily supposed that the evangelist composed none of the sources himself but received them from elsewhere. It is also usually proposed that these sources were written, for oral sources would have been rendered in the evangelist's own style and thus be more difficult to discern. (We may note, however, that Noack has been a strong proponent of a theory in which the entire Gospel arose from oral tradition.) Frequently a theory that conceives of the Gospel as the composite of a combination of sources has been joined with a theory that views the Gospel as having undergone several editions or redactions—but such a composite theory can become quite complicated. For instance, in the early part of this century one German scholar arrived at six combinations of sources and redactions. A complete history of the source theories may be found in the surveys of Johannine literature listed at the end of Part I of the Introduction; the names of Wendt, Spitta, Faure, and Hirsch have been associated with such theories.

One interesting modern example is that of Macgregor and Morton. On the basis of statistical analysis, they have proposed that the Gospel was composed by joining two sources, J^1 and J^2. The former, the longer source, is characterized by short paragraphs; the latter has long paragraphs. Although both sources belong to the same general sphere of theological persuasion, there is some stylistic evidence that they are from different hands (*op. cit.,* p. 71). J² contains ch. iv, most of vi, ix–xi, xiv–xvi 24, and xvii. Such a breakdown of the material does not in itself solve the principal problems mentioned above, and so Macgregor also introduces the theory of multiple editings. The validity of dividing sources on the basis of paragraph length has been questioned. Perhaps all that the statistical analysis has done is to separate the better edited sections of the Gospel.

The most influential form of the source theory proposed today is that of Bultmann, and we shall discuss this in detail. Bultmann distinguishes three *principal* sources.

(*a*) *The* Semeia-Quelle *or Sign Source:* John narrates a select number of Jesus' miracles, and these constitute the main narrative sections in the first part of the Gospel (chs. i–xii). Bultmann suggests that these were excerpted from a larger collection of signs attributed to Jesus. The indication of borrowing from a source is found in the enumeration of signs in ii 11 and iv 54, and in the mention of various signs in xii 37 and xx 30. The latter passage states that Jesus performed many other signs not written down in this Gospel. Bultmann thinks that the story of the call of the disciples in i 35–49 may have constituted the introduction to the Sign Source. This source was written in a Greek that betrays strong Semitic affinities (verb before subject, absence of connective particles, etc.). Since Bultmann does not believe in the miraculous, and since he finds this source somewhat more developed than the Synoptic narrative material, he attributes to this source little real historical value for reconstructing the career of Jesus of Nazareth. The Greek text of the reconstructed Sign Source may be found in Smith, pp. 38–44.

(*b*) *The* "Offenbarungsreden" *or Revelatory Discourse Source:* It was from this source that the evangelist drew the discourses attributed to Jesus in the Gospel. The source began with the Prologue and contained poetic discourses written in Aramaic. The Syriac *Odes of Solomon* is a surviving example of the type of literature that this source resembled. The theology of this source was an early Oriental Gnosticism as professed by a group like the followers of John the Baptist and later by the Mandean writings (see Part IV below). The source was translated into Greek either by the evangelist himself or by another, but the poetic format was maintained. The main task of the evangelist was to Christianize and to demythologize the discourses: he placed them on the lips of Jesus and thus gave them a historical setting. What was once said by the Gnostic figure of Original Man is now said by Jesus the Revealer; what once referred to any son of perdition now refers to Judas (xvii 12); no longer does xii 27 refer to a general conflict with the demonic lower world, but to the passion of Jesus. Additions and changes introduced into the source material are betrayed by their departure from the poetic format. A Greek text of the reconstructed Revelatory Discourse Source is found in Smith, pp. 23–34, and an English text in Easton, pp. 143–54.

(c) *The Passion and Resurrection Story:* Although this narrative had much in common with the passion story underlying the Synoptic Gospels, Bultmann insists that the fourth evangelist drew on non-Synoptic material. The style of this source is not clearly defined, but it was written in a Semitizing Greek. For the reconstructed Greek text see Smith, pp. 48–51.

In Bultmann's theory the evangelist wove these three sources together with ingenuity, making them the vehicle of his own thought. He himself had belonged to a Gnostic group of disciples of John the Baptist and had converted to Christianity. His Greek, as evidenced in the additions and connecting passages, shows less Semitic influence than that of his sources. (For the details of his style see Smith, pp. 9–10.) However, in some way the work of the evangelist fell into disorder; the lines of the discourses were mixed up, and a great number of displacements resulted.

Therefore Bultmann posits a final stage in the evolution of the Gospel, namely, the work of the Ecclesiastical Redactor. This figure had both a literary and a theological task. First, he tried to put the work of the evangelist back into proper order. He succeeded in part, but he still left many displacements. (To some extent, Bultmann himself has finished the task of the Redactor by moving verses around to restore the original order.) The second task of the Redactor was the more important theological one. The evangelist's work was still too Gnostic to be accepted by the Church at large. For instance, it made no mention of the sacraments or of the second coming. The Ecclesiastical Redactor, a type of primitive *censor librorum,* added sacramental references, like the one to water in iii 5, the one to the Eucharist in vi 51–58, and the one in xix 34b–35 referring symbolically to both Baptism and the Eucharist. He added references to final eschatology and the last day in passages like v 28–29 and xii 48. In historical details the Redactor tried to harmonize John with the Synoptic tradition. Thus he won acceptance by the Church for the Fourth Gospel.

The evaluation of Bultmann's theory as representative of the source theories is difficult. Many of the weak points in such a reconstruction of John are personal to Bultmann's own form of the source theory; other shortcomings are common to all source theories. Among the former are the postulated Gnostic influence, the presupposed non-sacramental character of the evangelist's work, and his exclusive interest in realized eschatology; these contentions shall be examined later. We have already pointed out the difficulties facing the elaborate displacement hypothesis advanced by Bultmann. The portrait of the Ecclesiastical Redactor is particularly subject to doubt. It seems at times that the additions credited to him have been determined by a form of circular reasoning where one rather arbitrarily decides what fits the theological outlook of the evangelist and attributes what is left to the Redactor.

But aside from these peripheral difficulties, what are we to say about the Sign Source and the Revelatory Discourse Source? The quasi-poetic format of the Johannine discourses has been accepted by many (see Part IX below); one need not pattern it on a collection of Gnostic poems, for it resembles the discourse style of personified Wisdom in the OT. The enumeration of signs in several Gospel passages is an impressive argument. However, whether such an enumeration reflects an earlier and simpler (oral?) stage of the Gospel outline where iv 54 was the second sign after the Cana sign of ii 1–11 or whether there was a truly independent Sign Source is not to be decided without other evidence.

Four major difficulties militate against a source theory of the Bultmann type:

(a) In John signs and discourses are closely woven together. Dodd, *Interpretation*, has shown impressively that the discourses which accompany the signs are the interpretations of the signs. Chapter vi is a perfect example of this, for the Bread of Life Discourse interprets the multiplication of the loaves. This is such a consistent feature of chs. ii–xii that it seems incredible that the signs and discourses came from totally independent sources. An exception may be claimed, however, for the two Cana signs which are not accompanied by interpretative discourses (but see p. 198 on iv 46–54). These two signs remain the best argument for the existence of some sort of Sign Source. See below, p. 195.

(b) Embedded in the discourses are sayings of Jesus which, by comparison with those in the Synoptics, have every reason to be considered as belonging to a primitive tradition of the words of Jesus. Dodd, *Tradition*, has shown this, and we shall insist on it in the commentary. This means that, in part at least, the discourses consist of traditional sayings and explanatory developments. The supposed pre-Christian collection of poetic Revelatory Discourses then becomes somewhat superfluous.

(c) The stylistic differences among the various sources are not verifiable. E. Schweizer, *op. cit.*, isolated thirty-three peculiarities of Johannine style. His work was supplemented by Jeremias and Menoud, and has been brought to its fullest development by Ruckstuhl, whose list has reached fifty. These Johannine peculiarities appear in material from all three of the sources posited by Bultmann, as well as in the material attributed to the evangelist himself, and even in some of the material attributed to the Ecclesiastical Redactor (although Ruckstuhl has pressed his arguments too far here). Now, we grant that in incorporating the sources into one work, the evangelist would introduce common elements of style. However, if we remember that, according to Bultmann's hypothesis, one of the sources was originally in Aramaic poetry and another was in Semitizing Greek, and the evangelist himself wrote in a less Semitized Greek, the commonness of Johannine peculiarities in all three is inexplicable. As P. Parker, p. 304, has remarked, "It looks as though, if the author of the Fourth

Gospel used documentary sources, he wrote them all himself." Smith's sympathetic study of Bultmann (p. 108) concludes that the arguments of Schweizer and Ruckstuhl present obstacles that Bultmann's answers have not removed.

(*d*) There are no really convincing parallels in antiquity for the types of sources that Bultmann has postulated. We have nothing like the proposed Sign Source. The *Odes of Solomon* has been proposed as a parallel to the Revelatory Discourse Source, but the similarity of this collection of hymns is more to the Prologue than to the discourses. Of course, Bultmann joins the Prologue and the discourses as one source, but the poetry of the Prologue is quite different from that of the discourses. Hans Becker, *op. cit.,* has sought parallels for the Discourse Source from a wider field of Gnostic literature. That parallels for isolated portions of John may be found in individual passages in the Mandean and Hermetic literature (see Part IV below) is true. But this does not mean that there is a good example of a collection of discourses such as Bultmann proposes.

There seems to be a strong reaction among Bultmann's own pupils, for example, Käsemann, against the source theory in its strict formulation. We cannot help but judge that the theory suffers from almost insuperable difficulties.

(3) *Theories of Multiple Editions*

The pattern common to these theories is that one basic body of Gospel material has been edited several times to give us the present form of John. There is no agreement on the number of editions or on whether the editions were all done by the same man; but generally at least two editors are posited, and one of them is often identified with the writer of the Johannine Epistles. E. Schwartz and Wellhausen were among the earlier proponents of this approach. We may divide the modern proponents into two camps, one which posits a rather complete rewriting of the Gospel, another which posits minor editing.

First, the theory of an editing that consists in a radical rewriting borders on a source theory. It stands to reason that if there was an original document to which a great deal of material was subsequently added, even to the point of giving the original work a totally new orientation, we are not far from the combination of two sources. (Thus the Macgregor-Morton hypothesis of J^1 and J^2 could really be listed here.) Only when the additional material has come from the same author as the original work do we get a decisive variation, a variation that frees the editing theory from the objections about stylistic consistency that undermine the source theory.

A good example of an editing theory which attributes rewriting to the same author (the Beloved Disciple) is that of W. Wilkens. He proposes three stages. (*a*) The *Grundevangelium* consisting of the narratives of four Galilean signs and three Jerusalem signs—thus like a book of signs (xx 30). (*b*) The evangelist added seven discourses to the signs. These discourses had their own prehistory for which the evangelist was responsible. (c) This collection of signs and discourses was turned into a Passover Gospel by the transposition of three stories from Passover week into an earlier setting (ii 13–22, vi 51–58, xii 1–7), thereby extending the Passover motif throughout the Gospel. Then there was a considerable rearrangement of verses and breaking up of discourses. These editions represented the work of the evangelist's whole lifetime; a final redactor made some additions, for example, in ch. xxi.

There are some important contributions in Wilkens' theory, of which we have given but the barest outline. The suggestion (originally his father's) about the transposition of scenes from Passover has a certain validity, as we shall point out in the commentary. Moreover, this theory which accepts the authorship of the Beloved Disciple (see Part VII below), who was an eyewitness, is more adaptable to the presence of historical tradition than is Bultmann's theory. However, one of the objections to Bultmann's theory is valid here as well; namely, the difficulty of explaining the close harmony between sign and discourse. Also, in Wilkens' theory the process of editing consisted in adding material and rearranging it but never in rewriting what was originally written; that does seem to be a curious way of editing one's own work.

Second, there are other theories of editing that are less radical. Parker, for instance, suggests two editions of John. The second would have involved the addition of passages like ii 1–12, iv, vi, and xxi, excerpts concerned largely with Galilee. Thus, Parker arrives at a first edition that was a Judean gospel, in harmony with his theory that the evangelist was a Judean disciple. Boismard has his own variation of an edition theory: John son of Zebedee was responsible for the central plan of the Gospel and for its tradition. He either wrote or supervised the writing of the basic Gospel and was responsible for two or more re-editions which introduced slight changes of plan and different formulations of the same material. Then there was a final redaction by Luke, who gathered together all the strands of Johannine material into the Gospel as we now know it. Boismard seeks to prove this identification of the redactor from the Lucan characteristics he finds in the style of ch. xxi and in the additions to the Prologue. We shall give an example of Boismard's theory of editing in our treatment of i 19–34 (pp. 67–71) and compare it with Bultmann's theory.

In judging the theories of various editions, we must abstract from the individual peculiarities—for example, Parker's division along geographical lines, Boismard's identification of the final redactor as Luke. By itself a theory of editing can account for the breaks of sequence in the present form of the Gospel—caused by the editor's insertion of new matter into the original outline. Such a theory can also explain repetitions, for the editor may have included variant forms of the same words. Unattached portions of discourse might be explained by a desire to preserve a morsel of tradition without being able to find an ideal place to insert it. The stylistic objections against the source theories are not applicable here where the material used in the various editions has come from the same man. Those passages of the Gospel where the Greek style does betray a difference of hand, for example, ch. xxi, can be explained by positing a final redaction by another hand.

Perhaps the chief fault of the theories of editing is the temptation to reconstruct too exactly the history of the editions. The problems in John are obvious, and it is possible that various editings caused these problems; but we must preserve our skepticism about any commentator's attempt to tell us down to the half verse what belongs to what edition.

C. The Theory Adopted in This Commentary

We shall comment on the Gospel in its present order without imposing rearrangements. Some object to this procedure on the ground that such an approach attains only to the meaning given to passages in the final edition of the Gospel, and hence perhaps only to the meaning of a subordinate editor rather than to the meaning of the evangelist. Yet, if one thinks of the final editor as someone loyal to the evangelist's thought, there will be very few times when editing has completely changed the original meaning of a passage. We prefer rather to run this risk than—by ingenious rearrangement—run the much greater risk of imposing on passages a meaning they never had. Naturally, where there is reason to suspect that in the formative history of the Gospel a passage had another setting and meaning, we shall mention it with proper qualifications as to the certainty with which the original position can be reconstructed. But we shall give primary consideration to the passage as it now stands.

We posit five stages in the composition of the Gospel. These, we believe, are the minimal steps, for we suspect that the full details of the Gospel's prehistory are far too complicated to reconstruct. Here we shall simply describe the stages; the reasons for positing them will become apparent in the following parts of the Introduction, and the practical impact of the various stages will be seen in the commentary on the translation. Naturally, the difficulties mentioned at the beginning of this part have guided what we propose here, and the previous solutions mentioned have all contributed to our tentative solution.

Stage 1: The existence of a body of traditional material pertaining to the words and works of Jesus—material similar to what has gone into the Synoptic Gospels, but material whose origins were independent of the Synoptic tradition. (We know, of course, that the Synoptic Gospels were dependent on several traditions, but we shall use the singular, "Synoptic tradition," when drawing general comparison between these Gospels and John.) We shall discuss this stage in Part III of this Introduction, and the question of whether or not the material came from an eyewitness in Part VII.

Stage 2: The development of this material in Johannine patterns. Over a period lasting perhaps several decades, the traditional material was sifted, selected, thought over, and molded into the form and style of the individual stories and discourses that became part of the Fourth Gospel. This process was probably accomplished through oral preaching and teaching, if we can draw any analogy from what we know of the formation of the other Gospels. B. Noack has rendered Johannine studies a service in stressing the influence of oral tradition on the Gospel, although his conclusions may be somewhat exaggerated. C. Goodwin, JBL 73 (1954), 61–75, has noted interesting indications that some of John's citations of the OT are from memory, a conclusion which also points toward oral transmission. Yet, toward the end of this second stage, written forms of what was preached and taught took shape.

This stage was decisively formative for the material that ultimately went into the Gospel. Some of the stories of Jesus' miracles, probably those most used in preaching, were developed into superb dramas, for example, ch. ix. (See E. K. Lee, "The Drama of the Fourth Gospel," ET 65 [1953–54], 173–76.) The sayings of Jesus were woven into lengthy discourses of a solemn and poetic character, much like the discourses of personified Wisdom in the OT (see Part VIII below). All the techniques of Johannine storytelling, like misunderstanding and irony (Part IX below), were introduced or, at least, developed in the way we now know them. Various factors contributed to the welding of sign and interpretative discourse. This was not necessarily an artificial joining, for even in Stage 1 a miracle had often carried with it words of explanation. But now the needs of preaching and perhaps, in some scenes (ch. vi), the needs of incipient liturgy demanded longer explanation and a more unified arrangement.

That this preaching and teaching was the work of more than one man is suggested by the existence of units of Johannine material, like ch. xxi, that are different in style from the main body of material. There may have been many such units that did not survive. However, what has gone into the Gospel seems to stem in large part from one dominant source. Since the general traits of Johannine thought are so clear, even in the units that betray minor differences of style, we should probably think of a close-knit school of thought and expression. In this school the principal preacher was the one responsible for the main body of Gospel material. Perhaps, too, in such a school we may find the answer to the problem of other Johannine works, like the Epistles and Revelation, which share common thoughts and vocabulary, but betray differences in style.

Stage 3: The organization of this material from Stage 2 into a consecutive Gospel. This would be the first edition of the Fourth Gospel as a distinct work. Since we have posited in Stage 2 a dominant or master preacher and theologian who gave shape to the main body of surviving Johannine material, it seems logical to suppose that it was he who organized the first edition of the Gospel; in this commentary it is to him that we refer when we use the term "evangelist." It is impossible to say whether he physically wrote the Gospel himself or used the services of a scribe. Most probably this first edition was in Greek and not in Aramaic (see Part IX below).

As the outline of the Gospel (Part X below) will show, there is a cohesiveness in the over-all plan of the work as it has come down to us, and we suspect that this basic cohesiveness was present in the first edition of the Gospel. Thus, we part company from a theory such as that of Wilkens, which would see in the first edition only a collection of signs. We would also differ from Parker, who posits a first edition that has no Galilean ministry. We doubt that any substantial edition of a Gospel that is based ultimately on a historical tradition of the works and words of Jesus could have ignored the ministry in Gallilee, which was so much a part of Jesus' life. If the plan of the first edition of the Gospel had the theme of Jesus' replacing the various feasts of the Jews, as does the present Gospel outline in chs. v–x, then the Galilean scene in vi would have been part of the first edition, for that chapter has Jesus replacing the manna associated with the Exodus and Passover time.

The organization of the first edition of the Gospel meant selection, and not all of the Johannine material stemming from the evangelist's preaching would have been included. If the evangelist had preached over a number of years, he had probably phrased the tradition of Jesus' words in different ways at different times. Thus, there would have been in circulation different versions of discourses, adapted to varying needs and audiences. We shall see the importance of this point in Stage 5.

Stage 4: Secondary edition by the evangelist. It is possible that the evangelist re-edited his Gospel several times in his lifetime, as Boismard has suggested; but most of the features that seem to require a secondary editing can be explained in terms of *one* re-editing. When we discuss the purpose for which the Fourth Gospel was written (Part V below), we shall see that it was intended to answer the objections or difficulties of several groups, for example, the disciples of John the Baptist, Jewish Christians who had not yet left the Synagogue, and others. We suggest that the adaptation of the Gospel to different goals meant the introduction of new material designed to meet new problems. For instance, the parenthetical passage ix 22–23 seems to represent an adaptation of the story of the blind man to the new situation in the late 80s or early 90s which involved the excommunication from the Synagogue of Jews who believed in Jesus as the Messiah. In our discussion of i 19–34, we shall note the traces of editing there (§ 2, § 3). However, we frankly admit that it is not always possible to distinguish between what belongs to the second editing of the Gospel and what belongs to the final redaction—which is our next stage.

Stage 5: A final editing or redaction by someone other than the evangelist and whom we shall call the redactor. We think that the most likely supposition is that the redactor was a close friend or disciple of the evangelist, and certainly part of the general school of thought to which we referred in Stage 2.

One of the principal contributions of the redactor to the Gospel was to preserve all the available Johannine material from Stage 2 that had not been previously inserted into editions of the Gospel. This material would in part be material stemming from the preaching days of the evangelist himself and would therefore not differ in style or vocabulary from the rest of the Gospel. The fact that this material was added at the last stage of the Gospel does not mean that it is any less ancient than material that found its way into the earlier additions. Thus, the age of the material is not a criterion that will always enable us to detect additions by the redactor; the awkwardness of an intrusive passage in the sequence of the Gospel is a much more reliable criterion. That some of this material represents a variant duplicate of material already in the Gospel is another criterion and, indeed, is the reason for assuming that the final redactor was not the evangelist himself. The evangelist would have reworked the material into a consonant whole; but the redactor, not feeling free to rewrite the Gospel as it came to him, simply inserted the duplicate discourses, often side by side with the form of the discourse that existed in the earlier edition, for example, vi 51–58 next to vi 35–50. With some discourses that had no setting, the redactor chose to add them at the end of an appropriate scene rather than to interrupt the scene, for example, iii 31–36 and xii 44–50.

In particular, the redactor seems to have made a large collection of Johannine material in which Jesus was portrayed as speaking to his disciples. Such a collection was added to the Last Supper Discourse of Jesus in chs. xv–xvii. That this addition was the work of the redactor and not of the evangelist seems likely from the fact that the original ending of the Last Discourse in xiv 31 was not tampered with or adapted to the new insertion. Among the material thus added was xvi 4–33, a variant duplicate of the discourse in ch. xiv.

The redactor was also probably responsible for adding the material in chs. xi and xii to the Gospel outline. In the commentary (p. 414) we suggest that the original ending of the public ministry came in x 40–42, and we point out the historical problem caused by the presentation of the Lazarus story in xi as the chief cause for Jesus' execution. If chs. xi and xii do represent a late addition of Johannine material, it is not impossible that this addition was made in the second edition of the Gospel (Stage 4). However, the use of the term "the Jews" in xi–xii differs from that of the rest of the Gospel, a fact that is less difficult to reconcile if the Lazarus story had an independent history and was added by the redactor.

The insertion of the Lazarus motif of chs. xi–xii into the account of the last days before Passover seems to have caused the redactor to shift the incident of the cleansing of the Temple, originally associated with Jesus' entry into Jerusalem, to another section of the Gospel (now in ch. ii). Liturgical interest seems to have been a factor in shifting eucharistic material associated with Jesus' words over the bread and wine at the Last Supper from that locale to vi 51–58. In this suggestion of relocation of material we are close to Wilkens, although we do not find compelling the motive that he attributes to such shifts; namely, to spread the theme of Passover throughout the Gospel. Rather, it is quite likely that Passover was already mentioned in ii and vi, and that the redactor was simply shifting material from one Passover feast in Jesus' life to another. Since we shall comment on these passages in their present sequence, we shall also be able to point out theological themes in that sequence which prompted the relocation.

Some of the material that the redactor added seems to be stronger in its reference to sacraments than the rest of the Gospel. *Pace* Bultmann, however, we do not believe that the redactor's purpose was to insert sacramental references in a non-sacramental Gospel, but rather to bring out more clearly the latent sacramentalism already in the Gospel (Part VIII below). We believe that sacramentalism can be found in all the stages we have posited for the Gospel formation, but the explicit sacramental references may belong predominantly to the final redaction.

The redactor added to the Gospel Johannine material that had not come from the evangelist. We have already pointed to ch. xxi as an example. It was probably also the redactor who added the Prologue to the Gospel, if we are correct in interpreting the Prologue as a once-independent hymn composed in Johannine circles.

We remain uncertain as to whether the final redactor was also responsible for the introduction into John of some parallels to the Synoptic tradition. As will be seen in Part III, we believe that the major part of Johannine material with parallels in the Synoptic tradition does not come directly from the Synoptic Gospels or from their sources, but from an independent tradition of the works and words of Jesus which has inevitable similarities with the traditions behind the Synoptics. Yet, there are a few passages where, for instance, John is so similar to Mark (vi 7, xii 3, 5) that we cannot exclude the possibility that the final redactor introduced minor elements directly taken from the Synoptics (with Mark as the most likely source). But we do insist that such close parallels can also be explained in terms of dependence on similar early traditions, and so we find no absolutely compelling reason to posit Johannine dependence on the Synoptics even on this rather superficial level of borrowing incidental details. There are editorial remarks, like iii 24, which show awareness of details about the life of Jesus that have not been mentioned in the Gospel proper, but again this is no clear proof of dependence on the Synoptics.

To sum up, although we have spelled out this theory of the five stages of the composition of the Gospel at some length, we would stress that in its basic outlines the theory is not really complicated and fits in rather plausibly with what is thought about the composition of the other Gospels. A distinctive figure in the primitive Church preached and taught about Jesus, using the raw material of a tradition of Jesus' works and words, but shaping this material to a particular theological cast and expression. Eventually he gathered the substance of his preaching and teaching into a Gospel, following the traditional pattern of the baptism, the ministry, and the passion, death, and resurrection of Jesus. Since he continued to preach and teach after the edition of the Gospel, he subsequently made a second edition of his Gospel, adding more material and adapting the Gospel to answer new problems. After his death a disciple made a final redaction of the Gospel, incorporating other material that the evangelist had preached and taught, and even some of the material of the evangelist's co-workers. A theory of two editions and a final redaction by a disciple would not be extraordinary among the theories of the composition of biblical books—a very similar theory is proposed for the Book of Jeremiah.

We believe that the theory we have proposed solves most of the difficulties discussed above. It explains why Schweizer and Ruckstuhl find a rather uniform style throughout the Gospel, for in Stages 2, 3, and 4, one dominant figure has shaped, phrased, and edited the material, and even in 5 much of the added material stems from this same figure. Yet, while preserving the substantial unity of the Gospel, this theory explains the various factors that militate against unity of authorship. The redaction in Stage 5 accounts for the presence of Johannine material of different style and also for the presence of duplicate discourses, the insertions that seem to interrupt, the seeming rearrangement of some scenes (without, however, positing elaborate displacements).

There remain many inadequacies and uncertainties in such a theory. In Stage 2, where the material from Stage 1 was developed in Johannine patterns, how much personal contribution did the evangelist make? What precisely was in the first edition of the Gospel, and what was added in the second? How can one infallibly distinguish between the hand of the re-editing evangelist and the hand of the redactor? We make no pretense to facile answers to such questions. All that we pretend to have done is to have given a working hypothesis for the study of the Gospel, a hypothesis that combines the best details of the various theories narrated at the beginning of this discussion, and avoids the more obvious difficulties.

BIBLIOGRAPHY

Becker, H., *Die Reden des Johannesevangeliums und der Stil der gnostischen Offenbarungsreden* (Göttingen: Vandenhoeck, 1956).

Boismard, M.-E., "Saint Luc et la rédaction du quatrième évangile," RB 69 (1962), 185–211.

Easton, B. S., "Bultmann's RQ Source," JBL 65 (1946), 143–56.

Hoare, F. R., *The Original Order and Chapters of St. John's Gospel* (London: Burns and Oates, 1944).

Käsemann, E., "Ketzer und Zeuge, zum johanneischen Verfasserproblem," ZTK 48 (1951), 292–311.

Láconi, M., "La critica letteraria applicata al IV Vangelo," *Angelicum* 40 (1963), 277–312.

Macgregor, G. H. C. and Morton, A. Q., *The Structure of the Fourth Gospel* (Edinburgh: Oliver and Boyd, 1961).

Noack, B., *Zur johanneischen Tradition, Beiträge zur Kritik an der literarkritischen Analyse des vierten Evangeliums* (Copenhagen: Rosenkilde, 1954).

Parker, P., "Two Editions of John," JBL 75 (1956), 303–14.

Ruckstuhl, E., *Die literarische Einheit des Johannesevangeliums* (Freiburg: Paulus, 1951).

Schulz, S., *Komposition und Herkunft der Johanneischen Reden* (Stuttgart: Kohlhammer, 1960).

Schweizer, E., *Ego Eimi* (Göttingen: Vandenhoeck, 1939).

Smith, *The Composition and Order of the Fourth Gospel* (see General Selected Bibliography).

Teeple, H. M., "Methodology in Source Analysis of the Fourth Gospel," JBL 81 (1962), 279–86.

Wilkens, W., *Die Entstehungsgeschichte des vierten Evangeliums* (Zollikon: Evangelischer Verlag, 1958).

III. THE TRADITION BEHIND THE FOURTH GOSPEL

In the theory of composition that we have proposed, Stage 1 involves the existence of a body of traditional material pertaining to the works and words of Jesus. We shall now discuss the likelihood of the existence of such tradition and of its relation to the traditions underlying the Synoptic Gospels. For the moment the question concerns the primitive character of the tradition behind John and thus whether this tradition is of a status comparable with that of the Synoptic traditions. The further question of the degree to which such a primitive tradition of the Christian community represents the deeds and *ipsissima verba* of Jesus will be taken up at the end of this discussion.

The very fact that John is classified as a Gospel presupposes that John is based on a tradition similar in character to the traditions behind the Synoptic Gospels. Even those commentators who treat the Fourth Gospel simply as a work of theology devoid of historical value must be impressed by the fact that this theology is written in a historical cast. Paul too was a theologian, but he did not write his theology in the framework of Jesus' earthly ministry. Indeed, some would regard the Fourth Gospel as an attempt to prevent the kerygmatic preaching of the Church from being mythologized and divorced from the history of Jesus of Nazareth.

Form criticism has established that the outline of Jesus' ministry seen in the Synoptic Gospels is an expansion of the basic kerygmatic outline of the deeds of Jesus used by the earliest preachers. Dodd and others have shown that in its fundamental details the outline in Mark is the same as that found in the Petrine sermons in Acts, especially Acts x 34–43. This kerygmatic outline is not dissimilar to the outline of the ministry in John, as the articles of Dodd and Balmforth affirm (also Barrett, pp. 34–35). If the Marcan kerygma begins with the baptism of Jesus by John the Baptist, so does John. In the Synoptic kerygma the baptism is followed by a long ministry in Galilee in which Jesus heals and does good; this is found in John too but more briefly (iv 46–54, vi). After the Galilean ministry, in both the Synoptics and John, Jesus goes to Jerusalem, where he speaks in the temple precincts; then follow the passion, death, and resurrection. Where John differs significantly from the Synoptic outline is in the report of a much longer Jerusalem ministry, but is this an essential variation from the outline? After all, Luke too has its variations, for example, in the journey to

Jerusalem, which takes some ten chapters. We may grant then that John has basically kerygmatic features in its outline; but even with this recognition we must ask whether the kerygmatic features stem from a primitive tradition, for they could conceivably represent an artificial imitation of Gospel style.

To answer this question we shall first evaluate the information unique to John. If what is found only in John proves to be factual, then we have good grounds for suspecting that John has its roots in a primitive tradition about Jesus. Secondly, we shall examine the material that is shared by John and the Synoptics to see if John draws from the Synoptic Gospels or from the traditions behind them. If John does not, then again we would have reason for positing an independent, primitive tradition behind John.

A. THE VALUE OF THE INFORMATION FOUND ONLY IN JOHN

Today there is a growing tendency to take very seriously the historical, social, and geographical details peculiar to narratives found only in the Fourth Gospel; the works cited in the bibliography to this discussion by Albright, Higgins, Leal, Pollard, and Stauffer are among the many examples of this tendency. Modern investigations of antiquity, especially through archaeology, have verified many of these details. We refer the reader to the commentary for specific elaboration, but here we may mention the following instances as the most striking:

- In ch. iv John's references to the Samaritans, their theology, their practice of worshiping on Gerizim, and the location of Jacob's well all seem to be accurate.
- In ch. v the very precise information about the pool of Bethesda is perfectly accurate as to name, location, and construction.
- The theological themes brought up in relation to Passover (ch. vi) and the Feast of Tabernacles (vii–viii) reflect an accurate knowledge of the festal ceremonies and of the synagogue readings associated with the feasts.
- Details about Jerusalem seem to be accurate, for example, the references to the pool of Siloam (ix 7), to Solomon's Portico as a shelter in winter time (x 22–23), and to the stone pavement of Pilate's Praetorium (xix 13).

From such accuracy we may say that the Fourth Gospel reflects a knowledge of Palestine as it was before its destruction in A.D. 70, when some of these landmarks perished. Of course, this does not mean that the Johannine information about Jesus has been verified, but at least the setting in which Jesus is placed is authentic.

For the egregious blunders about Palestine once attributed to John, there is often a perfectly reasonable explanation. We shall try to show in the commentary that theological purpose—not necessarily a naïve assumption about the duration of the priestly office—guided the reference to the "high priest that year" (xi 49). The exaggerated role of the Pharisees seems to be more a question of simplified emphasis than of an erroneous concept of their role in government. Anachronistic terminology like "the Jews" for Jesus' opponents and Jesus' use of "your Law" (viii 17, x 34) are more reflections of the apologetic tendencies of the Gospel than ignorant blunders.

Of the anachronisms once urged against John, the most serious was the abstract language the evangelist attributed to Jesus. The dualistic references to light and darkness, truth and falsehood, which are not found in the Synoptics, seemed clearly to reflect the language and thought of a later time and another place than the time and place of the ministry of Jesus. The Johannine Jesus seemed to walk in the Hellenistic world of the 2nd century. But we know now that the language attributed to Jesus in John was perfectly at home in the Palestine of the early 1st century. The Dead Sea Scrolls found at Qumran from 1947 on have given us the library of an Essene community whose span of existence covered the period from ca. 140 B.C. to A.D. 68. These documents offer the closest ideological and terminological parallels yet discovered for the dualism and the peculiar vocabulary of the Johannine Jesus (see Part IV below). Of course, the discovery does not prove that Jesus himself spoke in this abstract language, since the evangelist familiar with such language may have merely reinterpreted Jesus in its terminology. (After all, Bultmann suggests that the evangelist was a member of a Gnostic sect of disciples of John the Baptist who reinterpreted Jesus against a Gnostic background.) And we must still face the problem of why Jesus speaks differently in the Synoptic Gospels. Yet, at the least, we may say that the abstract language used by Jesus in John is no longer a conclusive argument against the Johannine use of historical tradition.

Let us turn for a moment to material which is not exclusive in John, that is, to material treated both in John and in the Synoptics, but where John's treatment is noticeably different. We think chiefly of geographical and chronological details. Unlike the Synoptics, John has: a ministry of baptizing by Jesus in the Jordan valley; a two or three year public ministry; frequent journeys to Jerusalem; clashes with the Jerusalem authorities that extend over a long period of time; Roman connivance in the arrest of Jesus; a role attributed to Annas in the interrogation of Jesus; Passover eve, and not Passover day, as the date of Jesus' death. In our opinion, as shall be seen in the commentary, a defense can be made for every one of these Johannine details, and in some of them the Johannine picture is almost certainly more correct than the Synoptic picture. For instance, passages like Luke xiii 34 (several attempts to win over Jerusalem) and Mark xiv 13–14 (Jesus has acquaintances in Jerusalem) are difficult to reconcile with the Synoptic outline wherein during his ministry Jesus goes only once to Jerusalem, in the last days of his life. Again, there is the well-known difficulty of reconciling the activities that the Gospels describe as taking place on Good Friday with the Synoptic dating of that day as Passover.

B. THE QUESTION OF DEPENDENCY UPON THE SYNOPTIC GOSPELS

We now turn to the material that John shares in common with the Synoptic Gospels. With regard to narrative this would include: part of the ministry of John the Baptist; the cleansing of the Temple (ii 13–22); the healing of the royal official's son (iv 46–54); the sequence centered on the multiplication of the loaves (vi); the anointing of Jesus and the entry into Jerusalem (xii); and the general outline of the Last Supper, the passion, death, and resurrection. With regard to the sayings of Jesus this would include many isolated verses.

The earliest stage of theory about the relation of John to the Synoptics was the supposition that John was written to supplement the Synoptic picture of Jesus' life and personality. Today this view is almost universally abandoned, for the relatively few points of direct contact between the outline of John and that of the Synoptics really create more chronological and historical problems than they solve. There is nothing in the Fourth Gospel that gives any indication that the author intended to supplement the Synoptic Gospels and nothing that would give us any guide or assurance in using John in this way.

In the era of criticism the theory gained ground that in all common material John was dependent on the Synoptic Gospels. Indeed, even Johannine scenes that had no parallel in the Synoptic tradition were sometimes explained as an amalgamation of Synoptic details. For instance, the story of Lazarus and his two sisters in ch. xi was thought to be a combination of one of the Synoptic stories about the raising of a dead person, of the Lucan parable about Lazarus (see Luke xvi 31), and of the Lucan story about Martha and Mary (Luke x 38–42).

This theory has by no means been discarded. Mendner, *art. cit.*, strongly insists that John vi is dependent on the Synoptic account of the multiplication (although for the connected scene of Jesus' walking on the water, the influence is in the opposite direction!). Lee, *art. cit.*, argues for John's dependence on Mark, as does Barrett in his commentary. Bailey, *op. cit.*, contends that John knew Luke's Gospel. A variation of this theory is that the fourth evangelist knew the traditions behind the Synoptics rather than the Synoptic Gospels themselves. For example, see the discussions of the theories of Borgen and Buse in our discussion of John xviii–xix (in The Anchor Bible, vol. 30). Parker, Osty, and Boismard are among the scholars who believe that such a relationship existed between the Gospels of John and Luke.

On the other hand there is an increasing number of scholars who think that John was dependent neither on the Synoptic Gospels nor on any of their written sources (as far as these sources can now be reconstructed). Gardner-Smith was very influential in this trend, and Dodd's *Tradition* is an exhaustive defense of Johannine independence.

To decide the question one must study each of the scenes and sayings shared by the two traditions to see wherein John and the Synoptics are the same and wherein they differ. One must also observe whether John consistently agrees with any *one* of the Synoptic Gospels in material peculiar to that Gospel, or with any significant combination of the Synoptic Gospels, for example, with the material proper to Matthew and Luke. In such a study the differences are even more significant than the similarities; for if one posits Johannine dependency, one should be able to explain every difference in John as the result of a deliberate change of Synoptic material or of a misunderstanding of that material. (Various motives might guide such changes; for example, better sequence, theological emphasis.) Goodwin, *art. cit.*, argues that the fourth evangelist cited the OT freely from memory and that he could have done the same with the Synoptics. However, any explanation of Johannine differences that must appeal as a principle to numerous capricious and inexplicable changes really removes the question from the area of scientific study.

In the commentary we have given particular attention to a comparison of John and the Synoptics. Our over-all conclusion regarding *similarities* is that John tends to agree with Mark and with Luke more frequently than with Matthew, but over a series of scenes John does not agree in a consistent way with any one Synoptic Gospel. If one were to posit dependency on the basis of similarities alone, one would have to suppose that the fourth evangelist knew all three Gospels and chose in an eclectic manner, now from one, now from another. However, even this suggestion does not hold up when one examines the *dissimilarities*. In parallel scenes, most of the details peculiar to John, some of which make the story more difficult, cannot be explained as deliberate changes of the Synoptic tradition. If one cannot accept the hypothesis of a careless or a capricious evangelist who gratuitously changed, added, and subtracted details, then one is forced to agree with Dodd that the evangelist drew the material for his stories from an independent tradition, similar to but not the same as the traditions represented in the Synoptic Gospels.

In the commentary we have also given attention to the possibility that the fourth evangelist drew on one or more of the sources that seem to lie behind the Synoptic Gospels, for example, on "Q" (the source that supplied the material common to Matthew and Luke). Another example has been advanced by I. Buse, who suggests that in the account of the passion John is dependent on one of the two pre-Marcan sources isolated by Taylor. This is obviously a more difficult question, since one is dealing with a reconstructed source and not with an extant work. Without being absolute on the question, we tend to come to the same solution as above, namely Johannine independence, for once again there are many differences that cannot be explained without resorting to non-Synoptic material. Yet here we must face the difficulty that the Synoptic sources are only imperfectly represented in the final Gospels, and therefore a source may actually have contained material that John drew on and the Synoptics did not. To settle the Johannine differences on this principle, however, is once more to remove the solution from any real scientific control. From the evidence available, it seems best to accept the general solution of an independent tradition behind John.

We stress that this is a *general* solution; it means that the main body of material in John was not drawn from the Synoptic Gospels or their sources. However, earlier (Part II) we reconstructed a long history for the composition of the Fourth Gospel; it is very possible that during that history there was minor cross-influence from the Synoptic tradition. Unless we are to presuppose that the Johannine community was isolated from other Christian communities (a suggestion that does not harmonize with the proposal that John was written at Ephesus or at Antioch), it is hard to believe that this community would not sooner or later have become familiar with the Gospel tradition accepted by other communities.

Perhaps we can illustrate with some possible instances of cross-influence. We may begin with Mark. In discussing John vi, we shall show serious reasons for believing that John's narrative of the multiplication of the loaves rests on independent tradition. Yet it is striking that only John and Mark (vi 37) mention the sum of two hundred denarii in reference to the price of the bread needed to feed the crowd. Another striking example is the very strange Greek expression "perfume made from real nard" which is used in John xii 3 and Mark xiv 3. The sum of three hundred denarii appears only in John xii 4 and Mark xiv 5 as a detail in the accounts of the anointing of Jesus. It is almost impossible to decide whether such minor parallels represent cross-influence or simply betray the fact that the independent tradition behind John had many features in common with the admittedly primitive tradition behind Mark.

The important parallels between John and Matthew are relatively few (see discussion of xiii 16, 20, xv 18 ff.). There are some interesting contacts between John and the Petrine material peculiar to Matthew (see discussion of i 41–42, vi 68–69, xxi 15–17). Moreover, one should not forget the saying phrased in Johannine style that appears in Matt xi 25–30 (Luke x 21–22). Yet few scholars posit direct contact between Matthew and John.

In many ways the possibility of cross-influence on John from Luke is the most interesting. In scenes shared by John and several Synoptics, the parallels between John and Luke are usually not impressive. Rather, it is with the peculiarly Lucan material that John has the important parallels. The following is by no means an exhaustive list (see Osty, Parker, Bailey), but it does show that the parallels lie both in minute details and in the broad sweep of narrative and ideas.

- One multiplication of loaves and fish.
- Mention of figures like Lazarus; Martha and Mary; one of the Twelve, named Jude or Judas (not Iscariot); the high priest Annas.
- No night trial before Caiaphas.
- Double question put to Jesus concerning his messiahship and divinity (Luke xxii 67, 70; John x 24–25, 33).

▪ Three "not guilty" statements by Pilate during the trial of Jesus.
▪ Post-resurrectional appearances of Jesus in Jerusalem; the similarity here is very strong if verses like Luke xxiv 12 and 40 are original.
▪ A miraculous catch of fish (Luke v 4–9; John xxi 5–11).

How are we to evaluate such parallels? Personally we find nothing in them to prove Boismard's contention that Luke was the final redactor of the Fourth Gospel. Some of the parallels may best be explained by assuming that the independent tradition behind John had features also found in the peculiar Lucan sources, even though these features did not appear the same way in both traditions, for example, John does not tell the same story concerning Martha and Mary that Luke tells. But this supposition will not explain all the parallels. For instance, in the account of the anointing of the feet in xii 1–7 (§ 41) John is dependent on details that come from a peculiar Lucan development of the basic narrative, and it is hard to see how the fusion of details found in both Luke and John could have happened independently. On the other hand, there are incidents in Luke which may well have arisen through cross-influence from some stage of the Johannine tradition, for example, the second ending of the parable about Lazarus (Luke xvi 27–31) which mentions the possibility of Lazarus' coming back from the grave. Thus, in the relations between Luke and John cross-influence is possible in both directions. Since such cross-influence does not express itself in identical wording, it may well have taken place at an oral stage in the history of Gospel composition.

To summarize, then, in most of the material narrated in both John and the Synoptics, we believe that the evidence does not favor Johannine dependence on the Synoptics or their sources. John drew on an independent source of tradition about Jesus, similar to the sources that underlie the Synoptics. The primitive Johannine tradition was closest to the pre-Marcan tradition but also contained elements found in the sources peculiar to Matthew (e.g., Petrine source) and to Luke. In addition to the material drawn from this independent tradition, John has a few elements that seem to suggest a direct borrowing from the Synoptic tradition. During the oral formation of the Johannine stories and discourses (Stage 2), there very probably was some cross-influence from the emerging Lucan Gospel tradition. Perhaps, although we are not convinced of this, in the final redaction of John (Stage 5) there were a few details directly borrowed from Mark. There is no evidence, however, *pace* Bultmann, that such borrowing, if it did take place, was for the purpose of making the Fourth Gospel acceptable to the Church at large.

C. THE VALUE OF JOHN IN RECONSTRUCTING JESUS' MINISTRY

It has been a commonplace in the critical investigation of the historical Jesus that no reliance can be placed on the material found in John. Even the "new quest" of the historical Jesus among the post-Bultmannians, especially Bornkamm and Conzelmann, neglects John. This question deserves reconsideration in view of the conclusions reached above; namely, that within the material proper to John there is a strong element of historical plausibility, and that within the material shared by John and the Synoptics, John draws on independent and primitive tradition.

But in reopening the question of whether or not the Fourth Gospel can be a witness to the historical Jesus, we must proceed with care. In Part II we posited five stages in the composition of John, with each stage representing a step further away from the primitive tradition. We cannot ignore the implications of such a development, for it limits the ability of the final form of the Gospel to give a scientifically accurate portrait of the Jesus of history. Let us examine the implications in each stage of Johannine development.

(*a*) The tradition of Jesus' works and words that underlies John (Stage 1) resembles the traditions behind the Synoptic Gospels. In short, these traditions give us variant forms of the narratives about what Jesus did and said. Now, the development of such variants took time. If we ask which of these traditions is the earliest, we are asking a question that admits of no simple answer. Even within the Synoptic family of traditions, one cannot give a blanket rule as to which form of a saying is always to be preferred, the "Q" form or the Marcan form. So too in comparing John and the Synoptics, we find that sometimes the material underlying John's account seems to be more primitive than the material underlying the Synoptic account(s), for example, the story of Jesus' walking on the water in John vi 16–21. At other times, just the opposite is true. Thus, a critical judgment is necessary *for each instance.*

Perhaps we may take this occasion to insist that when in the commentary we do analyze a Johannine narrative or saying and discover that there is primitive tradition underlying it, we are perfectly aware that we are using "primitive" in a relative sense, for the primitive tradition may already represent ten or twenty years of development from the time of Jesus. In general, where possible, we shall try to trace the origins of Johannine material back to Stage 1, and then to show what implications this *may* have for the historical ministry of Jesus. But we make no pretense to try or to be able to decide with any consistency precisely how much scientific history underlies each Johannine scene. Similarly, in pointing out Synoptic parallels for Johannine stories and sayings, we make no presupposition that the Synoptic parallels are necessarily exact historical echoes of what Jesus did and said. Rather, we take for granted some knowledge of the history of the Synoptic tradition. The purpose in presenting such parallels is to show that John's Gospel is not as different as might first seem.

(*b*) Stages 2 and 3 in our theory of the composition of John saw the dramatic and theological reshaping of the raw material from the Jesus tradition and the weaving of such reshaped stories and sayings into a consecutive Gospel. This same process, *mutatis mutandis,* also took place in the formation of the Synoptic Gospels. At one time John the Evangelist was spoken of as *the Theologian*, almost with the implication that only in the Fourth Gospel did we have a theological view of the career of Jesus. Today we recognize that each Gospel has a theological view, and that the fourth evangelist is one theologian among the other evangelist-theologians. Nevertheless, it is still true that the fourth evangelist is the theologian par excellence. In particular, the formation of the sayings of Jesus into the Johannine discourses represented a profound theological synthesis. It seems true, for instance, that behind John vi there lies a core of traditional material, containing not only the multiplication of the loaves but also a misunderstanding of what was meant by the scene and the consequent explanation of the bread by Jesus. Yet the formation of this material into the magnificent structure that we now have in John vi represents a unique theological grasp of the ultimate implications of Jesus' deeds and words. The less-developed Synoptic accounts of the scene are not of the same theological quality or mastery. Naturally, in any attempt to use John as a guide to the historical Jesus, such theological development must be taken into account. We are not suggesting that the Johannine theological insight has not been loyal to Jesus of Nazareth; rather it has often brought out implications found in a scene, however far back that scene can be traced. But subsequent development, no matter how homogeneous, is something that is refractive when one's purpose is to establish scientifically the exact circumstances of the ministry of Jesus. And so, although we think that the Fourth Gospel reflects historical memories of Jesus, the greater extent of the theological reshaping of those memories makes Johannine material much harder to use in the quest of the historical Jesus than most Synoptic material.

Even beyond the development that went into the formation of Johannine units is the development that took place when these units were welded into a Gospel. Selection and highlighting were required to make possible the organization now visible in John. Thus, in the first edition of John there came to the fore themes that were probably quite obscure in the hustle and bustle of the actual ministry. It is quite plausible, for instance, that Jesus may have spoken publicly on the occasion of Jewish feasts and may have directed his remarks to a contrast between his own ministry and the theme of the feast. But the systematic replacement of feasts spelled out in John v–x is the product of much reflection by the author, in an attempt to capture the significance of Jesus and his ministry.

If all of this means that John (and this is true of the other Gospels as well) is somewhat distant from a history or biography of Jesus, John xx 30–31 has made it clear that the author's intention was to produce a document not of history but of faith. Yet Sanders, *art. cit.*, is quite right in insisting that John is deeply historical—historical in the sense in which history is concerned not only with what happened but also with the deepest meaning of what happened.

(*c*) The final redaction of the Gospel, Stage 5 of the composition, places still more obstacles to the use of John in reconstructing the ministry of

Jesus. The extra Johannine material that was inserted in the Gospel narrative was not necessarily arranged in any chronological order; and indeed, according to our hypothesis, the addition of material caused the displacement of such scenes as the cleansing of the Temple. Thus, an unqualified acceptance of the present arrangement of the Gospel as truly chronological is not possible.

John mentions at least three Passovers (ii 13, vi 4, xi 55) and therefore implies at least a two-year ministry. Biographers of Jesus have used this indication to form an outline of the ministry, dividing the material found in the Gospels into the activities of the first and second (and third) years. For instance, we may be told that the Sermon on the Mount (Matt v–vii) took place in the first year of the ministry, shortly after Passover (John ii 13). Such a procedure is invalid. Not only does it ignore the fact that the Synoptic material itself is not chronologically ordered (e.g., the Sermon on the Mount, as it now stands, is a composite of words spoken on various occasions), but also it ignores the fact that the Gospels themselves give no real indications for such synchronization of Johannine and Synoptic data. Properly evaluated, the Synoptic tradition and the Johannine tradition are not contradictory; at times they illuminate each other through comparison, as Morris, *art. cit.,* has pointed out. However, the fact that neither tradition shows a scientific interest in chronology betrays itself when we seek to combine them into a consecutive picture. Even the few points of possible chronological contact between the two traditions offer difficulty. For instance, in the early part of the ministry described in John, Jesus makes several journeys into Judea and returns again to Galilee, but it is very hard to match any one of the return journeys with the Synoptic tradition of a return to Galilee after the baptism by John the Baptist. The multiplication of the loaves found in all four Gospels might seem to offer possibility of synchronization, but the issue is confused by the presence of *two* multiplication accounts in Mark-Matthew.

Even were there possibility of synchronization, however, a theory of a two- or three-year ministry as a framework for dividing Jesus' activities ignores the problem created by the purpose for which the Fourth Gospel was written. Since John xx 30 specifically states that the Gospel is not a complete account of Jesus' activities, there is no way of knowing that the three Passovers mentioned were the only Passovers in that ministry. There is no real reason why one cannot postulate a four- or five-year ministry. Furthermore, since the first Passover mentioned in John is intimately connected to the scene of the cleansing of the Temple, a scene which has probably been displaced, some have questioned the value of the reference to this first Passover as a chronological indication.

From all these remarks it should be clear why we must be very cautious about the use of John in scientifically reconstructing in detail the ministry of Jesus of Nazareth, even as we must be careful in so using the other Gospels. We do believe that John is based on a solid tradition of the works and words of Jesus, a tradition which at times is very primitive. We believe that often John gives us correct historical information about Jesus that no other Gospel has preserved, for example, that, like John the Baptist, Jesus had a baptizing ministry for a period before he began his ministry of teaching; that his public ministry lasted more than a year; that he went several times to Jerusalem; that the opposition of the Jewish authorities at Jerusalem was not confined to the last days of his life; and many details about Jesus' passion and death. Yet, in evaluating the Johannine picture of Jesus, we cannot neglect the inevitable modifications made in the various stages of Johannine composition.

BIBLIOGRAPHY

The Historical Value of John

Albright, W. F., "Recent Discoveries in Palestine and the Gospel of John," BNTE, pp. 153–71.

Brown, R. E., "The Problem of Historicity in John," CBQ 24 (1962), 1–14. Also in NTE, Ch. IX.

Dodd, C. H., "Le kérygma apostolique dans le quatrième évangile," RHPR 31 (1951), 265–74.

Higgins, A. J. B., The Historicity of the Fourth Gospel (London: Lutterworth, 1960).

Leal, J., "El simbolismo histórico del IV Evangelio," EstBib 19 (1960), 329–48. Digested in TD 11 (1963), 91–96.

Pollard, T. E., "St. John's Contribution to the Picture of the Historical Jesus." The Inaugural Lecture at Knox College, Dunedin, New Zealand.

Potter, R. D., "Topography and Archeology in the Fourth Gospel," StEv, I, pp. 329–37.

Sanders, J. N., "The Gospel and the Historian," The Listener 56 (1956), 753–57.

Stauffer, E., "Historische Elemente im Vierten Evangelium," Homiletica en Biblica 22 (1963), 1–7.

John and the Synoptics

Bailey, J. A., The Traditions Common to the Gospels of Luke and John (SNT VII, 1963).

Balmforth, H., "The Structure of the Fourth Gospel," StEv, II, pp. 25–33.

Brown, R. E., "Incidents that are Units in the Synoptic Gospels but Dispersed in St. John," CBQ 23 (1961), 143–60. Also in NTE, Ch. XI.

Gardner-Smith, P., Saint John and the Synoptic Gospels (Cambridge: 1938).

Goodwin, C., "How Did John Treat His Sources," JBL 73 (1954), 61–75.

Haenchen, E., "Johanneische Probleme," ZTK 56 (1959), 19–54.

Lee, E. K., "St. Mark and the Fourth Gospel," NTS 3 (1956–57), 50–58.

Mendner, S., "Zum Problem 'Johannes und die Synoptiker,'" NTS 4 (1957–58), 282–307.

Morris, L., "Synoptic Themes Illuminated by the Fourth Gospel," StEv, II, pp. 73–84.

Osty, E., "Les points de contact entre le récit de la passion dans saint Luc et dans saint Jean," Mélanges J. Lebreton (RSR 39 [1951]), 146–54.

Wilkens, W., "Evangelist und Tradition im Johannesevangelium," TZ 16 (1960), 81–90.

IV. PROPOSED INFLUENCES ON THE RELIGIOUS THOUGHT OF THE FOURTH GOSPEL

We have commented on the depth of the theological perspective in the Fourth Gospel. In many ways it is a unique perspective, quite different from the mildly divergent theological outlooks found in the Synoptic Gospels. The figure of Jesus who walks through the pages of John differs in many ways from the figure presented in the Synoptics. Not only is there a different manner of speaking, but also the majestic timelessness of divinity stands forth more clearly. The Johannine Jesus presents himself before men with the solemn "I am" formula (see App. IV). He has come into a world of darkness as the light, into a world of falsehood and hatred as the truth; and his presence divides men into two camps as they either come to the light or turn away from it, as they either believe in the truth or refuse to hear. How much of the evangelist has gone into this portrait of Jesus? Some will say that because the evangelist was attuned to his subject he was able to see in Jesus more than others saw and his genius enabled him to express it. Others will think of the portrait of Jesus as almost entirely the evangelist's creation. In any case, to some degree, perhaps indefinable, the evangelist's own outlook and insight is echoed in the Gospel. How can we explain the peculiar characteristics of the evangelist's thought? What influenced him?

Throughout the commentary we shall caution against exaggerating the differences between John and the Synoptics in their portraits of Jesus, and shall try to show that even the most characteristically Johannine elements have some parallel in the Synoptic tradition. Yet, having stated this caution, we must still recognize a characteristic Johannine cast of thought and seek to account for it. The three most frequently suggested influences on the evangelist are Gnosticism, Hellenistic thought, and Palestinian Judaism.

A. GNOSTICISM

The theory of Gnostic influence on John has been popularized by the History of Religions School (Bousset, Reitzenstein), so prominent in the early decades of this century. The theory has had important proponents in W. Bauer and Bultmann. On the other hand, Büchsel, Percy, and E. Schweizer have thoroughly questioned the theory.

The matter is unusually difficult because, as J. Munck, CINTI, p. 224, has put it, Gnosticism is "a scientific term that has no generally accepted scientific definition." All can recognize common patterns in developed Gnosticism: for example, ontological dualism; intermediary beings between God and man; the agency of these beings in producing the evil, material world; the soul as a divine spark imprisoned in matter; the necessity of knowledge gained through revelation in order to free the soul and lead it to light; the numerical limitation of those capable of receiving this revelation; the saving revealer. But which of these elements are essential for a movement to be truly called Gnostic?

(1) *John and Christian Gnosticism*

Classic Gnosticism, as we know it through the hostile comments of the Church Fathers, was a movement which appeared fully developed in the 2nd century A.D. Therefore, if we date the Gospel ca. 90–100 (see Part VI below), it can scarcely have been influenced by this Gnosticism. But there has been a tendency to postulate an earlier form of Gnosticism, or at least to trace the components of Gnosticism to an earlier date. Scholars speak of pre-Christian Gnosticism, Jewish Gnosticism, and even apply the term to the theology of Qumran. Part of the difficulty is that until recent times there was very little extant Gnostic literature of the early centuries, and thus the field was wide open to hypothesis. Scholars were understandably wary of reconstructing Gnostic thought from a patristic apologetic directed against it.

The discovery at Chenoboskion in Egypt in 1947 of a group of Gnostic documents in Coptic has changed the whole picture. As regards John, we are now able to compare this Gospel with Christian Gnosticism of the 2nd century. One of the Gnostic works, the *Gospel of Truth,* is a Coptic translation of a Greek work from the school of Valentinian Gnosticism and perhaps was composed by Valentinus himself. Quispel and Barrett in their articles and Braun, JeanThéol, I, pp. 111–21, have compared the thought and vocabulary of this document with that of John. They find the two Gospels far apart. If there were common points of origin, there has been a considerable and divergent development. The present writer has devoted an article to a comparison between John and another Chenoboskion work, the *Gospel of Thomas.* The Gnosticism in this work is not as developed as that of the *Gospel of Truth,* and *Thomas* might better be described as incipiently Gnostic. Yet, there is still a considerable distance between John and *Thomas,* for characteristically Johannine terms are used in *Thomas* in a manner quite different from Johannine usage. If there is any dependence of one on the other, it is quite indirect; and the direction of the dependence would be *Thomas* on John.

Thus, as far as we can determine, John would be out of place among the Gnostic works found at Chenoboskion. We do not mean that John could not have been used by the 2nd-century Gnostics (see Part VI), but that it is not a typical 2nd-century Gnostic composition.

(2) *John and the Reconstructed Pre-Christian Gnosticism*

Turning now to the postulated earlier forms of Gnosticism, let us examine Bultmann's proposal that the Revelatory Discourse Source was Gnostic in its tendency, and that the evangelist was an ex-Gnostic. (For a concise treatment of Bultmann's ideas on Gnosticism, see his *Primitive Christianity* [New York: Meridian, 1957], pp. 162–71.) Since the evangelist has demythologized and Christianized his source, Bultmann undoes the work of the evangelist in order to reconstruct this Gnosticism. He classifies it as early Oriental Gnosis, in distinction to the later, more Hellenized Gnosis of which we have been speaking above. There is, for instance, in the reconstructed Gnosticism a dualism of light and darkness, but no speculation about the origins of darkness and evil. In the sphere of light there are supernatural beings besides God, for example, angels; but this Gnosticism posits no complicated theories of emanation. Moreover, since this Gnosticism is an offshoot of Judaism or has been influenced by Judaism, its dualism has been modified by the OT tenet of God's supremacy even over the sphere of evil. Thus, the creation of the world involved no battle between darkness and light, as in Iranian or Zoroastrian dualism.

Perhaps the most important single doctrine in Bultmann's reconstruction of this Gnosticism is the redeemer myth. As seen in later Gnostic documents, this myth supposes the existence of an *Urmensch*, an Original Man, a figure of light and goodness, who was torn apart and divided into small particles of light. These particles, as human souls, were seeded in a world of darkness, and it has been the task of the demons to make them forget their heavenly origins. Then God sends His Son in corporeal form to waken these souls, liberate them from their bodies of darkness, and lead them back to their heavenly home. He does this by proclaiming the truth and by giving souls the true knowledge (*gnōsis*) which will enable them to find their way back. Bultmann finds traces of such a myth underlying the discourses in John. The figure now historicized as Jesus was once the Gnostic redeemer and heavenly revealer. In the Revelatory Discourse Source this redeemer was the pre-existent (John i 1) who became flesh (i 14) and ultimately returned to God. He was the light who came into the world (i 9, viii 12); he was the way to God (xiv 6). The Paraclete is another facet of the Gnostic myth (see App. V in The Anchor Bible, vol. 29A).

The charge of circular reasoning has been hurled against Bultmann; namely, that he presupposes that there was a Gnosticism in the background of John, and then uses John as his main source for reconstructing this Gnosticism. However, Bultmann claims to have other evidence of this pre-Christian Gnosticism in the traces of it that have survived in the *Odes of Solomon* (see p. 21) and particularly in the Mandean writings. The Mandeans are a baptizing sect still extant in Mesopotamia. The researches of Lidzbarski and Lady Drower have enabled scholars to reconstruct some of their past history and thought; for a summary see Dodd, *Interpretation*, pp. 115–130. Their theology, when it appears in full bloom, is a highly syncretistic mixture of Jewish lore, Gnostic myth, and Nestorian and Syrian

Christianity. Their legends tell how they fled to Babylonia under persecution from false prophets (like Jesus) and false religions (Judaism and Christianity). Their great revealer, Manda d'Hayye, whose name means "Knowledge of life," was baptized by John the Baptist. He taught a way of salvation which would enable men to pass over to the world of light.

The oldest forms of Mandean theology known to us are to be dated relatively late in the Christian era, and there is no possibility that John was influenced by this thought as we now know it. We should note, too, that there is no Mandean work like John; nor is there a Mandean work that exactly resembles the Revelatory Discourse Source posited by Bultmann. But Bultmann supposes that the Mandean thought represents a later derivative of the very type of Gnosticism that he postulates in the NT era among the disciples of John the Baptist and which served as a background for John. Hence he cites parallel symbols, thought patterns, and phrases in John and the Mandean writings; and he looks on them as echoes of pre-Christian Gnosticism.

How are we to evaluate Bultmann's theories about the Mandeans? The latest investigation is that of K. Rudolph, *Die Mandäer* (Göttingen: Vandenhoeck, 1960), and he suggests that the Mandeans may well be correct in tracing their roots to Palestine in the early Christian era. And, of course, there probably was continuity between the earliest stage of their thought and the later stage known to us. As for the origins of Mandean Gnosticism, the contention is gaining ground that the Gnostic layers in Mandean thought and writing are relatively early.

However, the whole problem of pre-Christian Gnosticism remains difficult. When Gnosticism appears in the 2nd century A.D., it is an amalgamation of different strains of thought, and certain of these strains are truly ancient. But were they really *joined* in the pre-Christian era? For it was the joining of the strains that produced Gnosticism. As A. D. Nock, "Gnosticism," HTR 57 (1964), 255–79, has pointed out, the Chenoboskion finds have reaffirmed the patristic picture of Gnosticism as a Christian heresy. The figure of Christ seems to have been the catalyst that prompted the shaping of proto-Gnostic attitudes and elements into definable bodies of Gnostic thought.

In particular, the latest researches on the Gnostic redeemer myth by C. Colpe (1961) and H. M. Schenke (1962) cast serious doubts on whether the ancient but heterogeneous elements that went into that myth were already joined in the pre-Christian or early Christian period. Schenke has argued that the oft-made identification of the Gnostic redeemer with "the Son of Man" is a post-Christian development. Another fact that casts doubt on Bultmann's theory is that the thought of the Qumran community does not resemble Bultmann's reconstruction of what a Palestinian baptizing sect in the 1st century was thinking about. And yet this community has undeniably close geographical and theological affinities with John the Baptist, and so might have been expected to be somewhat similar to the Gnostic sectarians of John the Baptist posited by Bultmann. At Qumran there is a

modified dualism; there are proto-Gnostic elements, but there is no redeemer myth and there is no developed Gnosticism.

In summation, one cannot claim that the dependence of John on a
postulated early Oriental Gnosticism has been disproved, but the hypothesis
remains very tenuous and in many ways unnecessary. We hope to show
below that OT speculation about personified Wisdom and the vocabulary
and thought patterns of sectarian Judaism, like the Qumran community, go
a long way toward filling in the background of Johannine theological
vocabulary and expression. Since these proposed sources of influence are
known to have existed, and the existence of Bultmann's proto-Mandean
Gnostic source remains dubious, we have every reason to give them preference.

B. HELLENISTIC THOUGHT

In raising the question of Greek influence on John, we must make an important distinction. There was a strong Hellenistic element already present
in the Judaism of NT times, both in Palestine and Alexandria. Therefore,
if John was dependent on contemporary Judaism, there was inevitably a
Hellenistic influence on Johannine thought. We have just spoken of personified Wisdom speculation; in deuterocanonical books like Sirach and
Wisdom of Solomon this speculation has been colored by Hellenistic
thought. We have also just spoken of Qumran, and there was strong
Hellenistic influence on such Jewish sects. Josephus draws an analogy between the thought of the Essenes (we consider the Qumran group to have
been Essenes) and that of the neo-Pythagoreans, attributing to the Essenes
an anthropology with clear Hellenistic features. Braun, JeanThéol, II, pp.
252–76, points out affinities between the *Hermetica* and Essene thought as
it is found in Josephus and the Qumran scrolls. Cullmann has attempted
to draw together the Qumran Essenes, the Samaritans, and the Hellenists
(Acts vi 1) under the banners of a non-conformist Judaism sharing an opposition to the Temple and a predilection for Hellenistic thought.

We take for granted, therefore, a Greek strain within Judaism which had
an influence on Johannine vocabulary and thought. But the question we
ask here is whether there was another Hellenistic influence on John that did
not come through Judaism but came from without. Was the evangelist particularly familiar with Greek thought so that he reinterpreted the Gospel
message in Hellenistic terms? Three strains of Greek thought have been
offered as possible explanations for the peculiarities in Johannine theological
expression: a popular form of Greek philosophy, Philo, and the *Hermetica*.
We shall discuss each in turn, but it is perhaps well to stress that we are
seeking *formative* influence on the evangelist's thought. A slightly different
problem is whether or not the evangelist has given the Gospel a veneer
of Hellenistic phraseology in order to convert the Greek world. This
question is more closely related to the purpose of the Gospel which we
shall discuss in Part V.

(1) *John and Greek Philosophy*

Some of the older commentators on John, for example, E. A. Abbott, W. R. Inge, stressed Johannine borrowings from the schools of Greek philosophic thought, especially from Platonism or Stoicism.

First we may consider Platonism. In John there are contrasts between what is above and what is below (iii 31), between spirit and flesh (iii 6, vi 63), between eternal life and natural existence (xi 25–26), between the real bread from heaven (vi 32) and natural bread, between the water of eternal life (iv 14) and natural water. These contrasts may be compared to a popular form of Platonism where there is a real world, invisible and eternal, contrasted with the world of appearances here below. The similarity is impressive, but we should note that popular Platonism had already infiltrated Judaism. As we shall see in Part VIII, beside the horizontal, linear distinction between the present age in the history of Israel and the age to come after divine intervention, there was also in the Jewish thought of this period a vertical distinction between the heavenly and the earthly. A contrast between spirit and flesh is not unknown in the OT (Isa xxxi 3), and Qumran offers a contrast between what is on the level of flesh and what is from above (1QH x 23, 32). Even the contrast between real bread and natural bread is foreshadowed in a passage like Isa lv 1–2 where the bread of God's teaching is contrasted with what is not bread. Thus, the affinities to popular Platonism that have been proposed for John are quite explicable in the light of Palestinian Judaism. Sometimes they are only seeming affinities which are explicable in terms of the OT; sometimes they are real affinities but stem from Greek thought that had already become a part of the Jewish background.

A parallel to Stoicism has been suggested by the use of *logos,* "the Word," in the Prologue, for this was a popular term in Stoic thought. Our treatment of this term in App. II will show that the Johannine usage is quite different from that of the Stoics. Moreover, the hymn which is the Prologue had its own history within Johannine circles, and it is risky to argue from terminological parallels in the Prologue to influence on the whole Gospel. Thus, there is no real reason to suppose that the Gospel was influenced by any more Greek philosophy than what was already present in the general thought and speech of Palestine.

(2) *John and Philo*

A dependence of John upon Philo of Alexandria has been suggested. A contemporary of Jesus, Philo represented in his work an attempt to combine Judaism and Greek thought. We have no clear evidence that Philo's work was known in early 1st-century Palestine; and so if the evangelist was dependent on Philo, this familiarity probably was gained outside Palestine. Once again the use of *logos* in the Prologue is a key argument, for Philo employed this term (see App. II). Argyle, *art. cit.,* attempts to show a wider dependence of John upon Philo because some of the biblical imagery used by John (Jacob's ladder, brazen serpent, vision of Abraham) is also used by Philo, precisely in connection with the doctrine of the *logos*. Perhaps we miss the point of the argument; but the very fact that, unlike Philo, John does not use this imagery in connection with "the Word" and the fact that in the total Gospel "the Word" has only a minor role would seem to weaken the case for dependency on Philo.

Wilson's cautious article on the subject is quite instructive. He observes that while we know Philo's work, most of the work of his predecessors has not survived. The Philonian reflections on the *logos* are probably the culmination of a long history of such thought. Moreover, both Philo and John draw on the OT, and in the concept of *logos* they both draw on the Wisdom Literature of the OT. It is not surprising, therefore, that at times their thought develops along parallel lines. But when one comes to essential methodological procedure, Philo and John are far apart. The overwhelming philosophical coloring found in Philo does not appear in John, and the elaborate Philonian allegories have little in common with the Johannine use of Scripture. Dodd, *Interpretation*, p. 133, has said that Philo, along with Rabbinic Judaism and the *Hermetica*, remains one of our most direct sources for the background of Johannine thought. Personally, we believe that the evidence points rather toward a common background shared by both Philo and John. Perhaps Braun, JeanThéol, II, p. 298, has phrased it best: if Philo had never existed, the Fourth Gospel would most probably not have been any different from what it is.

(3) *John and the* Hermetica

Still other scholars who posit Hellenistic influence on John turn to a higher, philosophical religion such as that of the *Hermetica*. In Egypt, in the 2nd and 3rd centuries A.D., a body of Greek literature grew up centered on Hermes Trismegistus, a legendary sage of ancient Egypt believed to have been deified as the god Thoth (=Hermes). The thought expressed in this literature is a syncretism of Platonic and Stoic philosophy with the religious tradition of the Near East. The various books of the literature, largely independent of each other, were for the most part written after the Fourth Gospel, although there are early elements contained in them. The critical edition of this corpus of writing, which constitutes the *Hermetica*, has been edited by Nock and Festugière. Cast in the form of dialogues between Hermes and his sons, these writings proclaim a lofty concept of God and of man's ethical obligations. The perfect man possesses the knowledge of God, and salvation is through this revealed knowledge (see John xvii 3). Elements of semi-pantheism and of Gnosticism can be found in the *Hermetica*.

In comparing these writings to John, scholars have found some very interesting parallels of thought and vocabulary (both Braun and Dodd give lists). Most would not posit direct dependence of John upon the *Hermetica*, but Dodd is impressed with the value of the *Hermetica* in interpreting John. Kirkpatrick, *art. cit.*, has stressed that the similarities between the two literatures should not be overemphasized. Some of the theological terms that are the most important in the *Hermetica* are totally absent from John, for example, *gnōsis, mystērion, athanasia* ("immortality"), *dēmiourgos* ("demiurge"). A statistical comparison of vocabulary is also interesting. There are 197 significant words in John beginning with the one of the first four letters of the Greek alphabet; 189 of these appear in LXX; only 82 of them appear in the *Hermetica*. Thus John is far closer to the language of the Greek OT than to that of the *Hermetica*. Braun issues another caution. There are indications that some of the authors of the *Hermetica* knew Christianity and even wrote against it. Braun detects the presence of a scribe who may have had some knowledge of John. If this is true, the direction of parallels between John and the *Hermetica* would have to be seriously examined.

Thus, once again we are dealing with a literature that is later than John, but whose hypothetical early stages are used to explain the thought of the fourth evangelist. A better explanation might be that in the similarities the two literatures share (e.g., vocabulary like "light," "life," "word") they are both dependent on a theological terminology more ancient than either of them; namely, the terminology that sprang from the combination of Oriental speculation on Wisdom and Greek abstract thought. Such a combination is already exemplified in the pre-Christian period in the deuterocanonical Book of Wisdom. That this common basis was built upon in two such different ways as we now see in the *Hermetica* and John suggests that the two literatures had little to do with each other in the formative stages. Thus, we would agree with Kirkpatrick that we can evaluate the *Hermetica* on the same level as the Mandean writings and as other evidences of Gnosticism, that is, as constituting no significant part of the background of the Gospel.

C. Palestinian Judaism

A large number of scholars are coming to agree that the principal background for Johannine thought was the Palestinian Judaism of Jesus' time. This Judaism was far from monolithic, and its very diversity helps to explain different aspects of Johannine thought. We shall consider the OT, rabbinic Judaism, and the Judaism of the Qumran sectarians.

(1) *John and the Old Testament*

John has fewer direct OT citations than have the other Gospels. The Nestle Greek text indicates only 14, all from books in the Palestinian canon of the OT. In the Westcott-Hort list of OT references used in the NT, only 27 passages are listed for John, as compared with 70 for Mark, 109 for Luke, and 124 for Matthew. The infrequency of Johannine *testimonia* is deceptive, however, as Barrett has shown in his article on the subject. Many of the themes of the Synoptic *testimonia* have been woven into the structure of the Fourth Gospel without explicit citation of the OT. Unlike Mark vii 6, John does not cite Isa xxix 13 to the effect that the hearts of the people of Israel are far from God although they honor Him with their lips; yet this theme goes all through Jesus' arguments with "the Jews" in the Fourth Gospel.

More important, as Braun has shown in JeanThéol, II, John reflects even more clearly than the Synoptic Gospels the great currents of OT thought. Jesus is presented as the Messiah, the Servant of Yahweh, the King of Israel, and the Prophet—all figures in the gallery of OT expectations. Many of the allusions to the OT are subtle, but quite real. Hoskyns, *art. cit.*, has shown how Genesis influenced John, even though John never explicitly cites it. The narrative of the first days of creation and of the first man and woman is the backbone of John i 1–ii 10, and the theme of mother Eve returns as Jesus hangs on the cross in xix 25–30. There are references to Abraham (viii 31 ff.), Isaac (iii 16), and Jacob (iv 5 ff.).

The whole story of Moses and of the Exodus is a very dominant motif, as Glasson has shown in great detail. Some scholars have even suggested that the whole organization of the Fourth Gospel was patterned on Exodus. Enz, *art. cit.*, compares each section of John to a section of Exodus; R. H. Smith, *art. cit.*, compares Jesus' signs as reported in John with Moses' signs in bringing the plagues on Egypt. Inevitably such elaborate equivalences are forced in some details, although we do agree with Smith that a very important factor in the Johannine concept of the "sign" was the use of "sign" for Moses' miracles (App. III). Without making ourselves dependent on this quest for the same structural pattern in Exodus and John, we may still point out the numerous Johannine references to Moses (i 17, v 46, etc.) and to the events of the Exodus (the manna in vi 31 ff., the water from the rock in vii 38, the bronze serpent in iii 14, the Tabernacle in i 14). The speeches of Moses in Deuteronomy have often been suggested as offering a parallel in the psychology of their composition to the discourses of Jesus in John, that is, both represent a reworking of traditional material into the format of discourse. The Deuteronomic concept of commandment is close to the Johannine concept. There are also references to other events in the subsequent history of Israel (to the Judges in x 35; to the theme of the royal shepherd in x 1 ff.).

Half of John's explicit citations are from the prophets (five from Isaiah; two from Zechariah). Griffiths, *art. cit.*, has offered Deutero-Isaiah as a good OT parallel to John, for both of these reinterpret previous traditions with considerable originality. It is to Deutero-Isaiah that we must go for the background of the Johannine usage of *egō eimi*, "I am," (App. IV) and for some elements of the universality attributed to Jesus' mission. The last part of Zechariah seems to lie behind John's reflections on the feast of Tabernacles and on the stream of living water (vii 37–38). Vawter, *art. cit.*, suggests that Ezekiel may offer background for certain features in the Johannine theology of the Son of Man and of the Paraclete.

The Wisdom Literature is also important for an understanding of John. As in the other Gospels, so also in John the Book of Psalms is a frequent source for *testimonia*. We shall show in Part VIII that the most decisive influence on the form and style of the discourses of Jesus in the Fourth Gospel comes from the speeches of divine Wisdom in books like Proverbs, Sirach, and Wisdom of Solomon.

It may be legitimately asked whether such dependence on the OT shows that the ambiance of John's thought was *Palestinian* Judaism, for the LXX was known outside Palestine. Some scholars have argued that at least some of the explicit citations of the OT that appear in John seem to be directly translated from the Hebrew and do not come from the LXX (so Braun, JeanThéol, II, pp. 20–21); this would modify Goodwin's suggestion that John's variations from the LXX arise from the fact that the evangelist cited freely and from memory. A more interesting possibility is that in passages like iii 14, iv 6, 12, vii 38, and xii 41, John may be citing the Palestinian Targums (the local Aramaic translations of Scripture) rather than the Hebrew Bible. The implications for the background of the Gospel are obvious.

(2) John and Rabbinic Judaism

These reflections lead us to the question of the relation between the Fourth Gospel and the rabbinic documents. The latter are notoriously hard to date. They were written in the Christian era and often quite late, but frequently they preserve very early material going back to the time of Jesus and even before. (The reader is served notice, however, that while we shall cite rabbinic parallels, it is often impossible to prove that this parallel reflects the thought of 1st-century Judaism.) Since the work of the rabbis is the continuation of the Pharisaic Judaism of Jesus' time, it is of great importance for NT study.

Scholars like Schlatter and Strack and Billerbeck have pointed out many parallels between Johannine and rabbinic thought, as we shall see in the commentary. More recently, Dodd, *Interpretation,* pp. 74–97, and D. Daube, *The New Testament and Rabbinic Judaism* (London University, 1956) have come up with interesting insights into John gained from rabbinic literature. Concepts like that of the hidden Messiah (see p. 53), and speculations on the creative role of the Torah (which John adapted to "the Word"—see App. II) and on the nature of life in the world to come are all important for understanding Johannine developments.

Miss Guilding has maintained that the discourses that Jesus utters on the occasion of great feasts are closely related to the themes of the readings assigned to be read in the synagogues at these feasts (see p. 278). In ch. vi, Borgen has pointed out how similar the format of Jesus' Discourse on the Bread of Life is to the homiletic pattern of the rabbinic *midrashim* (or free interpretations of Scripture passages). Others have found in ch. vi parallels to the Jewish Passover *Haggadah* in the Seder service. Such strong Jewish influence on the Fourth Gospel could most plausibly be explained if it had its origins in Palestine or if its author was familiar with Palestinian Judaism. This would also explain the accurate knowledge of Palestinian details mentioned in Part III above.

(3) *John and Qumran*

Until the discovery of the Dead Sea Scrolls little was known of sectarian Judaism in Palestine. The rabbinic documents preserved the spirit and thought of the Pharisees; but the Sadducees were (and remain) poorly known, and even less was known of the Essenes, who were mentioned briefly in Josephus, Philo, and Pliny. It is the life and thought of the latter group that have been unfolded for us through the manuscript and archaeological discoveries at Qumran on the northwest corner of the Dead Sea. The fact that the Essene community at Qumran was destroyed in A.D. 68 means that with rare exception its documents antedate Christian literature and that, unlike the case of the Mandean literature and the *Hermetica,* we do not have to reconstruct a pre-Christian theology from later documents.

Since both the Qumran literature and the NT are dependent on the OT, the only parallels of thought and vocabulary that can be really significant for determining influence are those that are not also found in the OT. Articles on the relation between John and Qumran (Brown, F.-M. Braun, Kuhn) have singled out modified dualism as one of the most important parallels. In the Qumran literature there are two principles created by God who are locked in struggle to dominate mankind until the time of divine intervention. They are the prince of lights (also called the spirit of truth and the holy spirit) and the angel of darkness (the spirit of perversion). In John's thought Jesus has come into the world as the light to overcome the darkness (i 4–5, 9), and all men must choose between light and darkness (iii 19–21). Jesus is the truth (xiv 6), and after his death the struggle to overcome the evil force is carried on by the Spirit of Truth (or the Holy Spirit: xiv 17, 26). It will be noted that not only the dualism but also its terminology is shared by John and Qumran. This dualism is not found in the OT, and Kuhn may be right in suggesting that its ultimate roots are in Zoroastrianism (where, however, it is a question of the absolute dualism of opposed, uncreated principles—a possible exception is the Zervanite form of Zoroastrianism in which the two principles are subordinate to a supreme deity). Several of the apocrypha also reflect this dualism; for example, the Testaments of the Twelve Patriarchs: usually these are works that are in some way related to the Qumran group. The recent study by O. Böcher, *Der johanneische Dualismus im Zusammenhang des nachbiblischen Judentums* (Gütersloh: Mohn, 1965) insists that Johannine dualism is far closer to the dualism of Jewish apocalyptic and sectarian thought than it is to anything in the Hellenistic and Gnostic sources.

Another significant point shared by John and Qumran is the ideal of love of one's brother within the community. While some passages in the Synoptic Gospels stress the Christian's duty to love all men, John's stress is on the love of one's fellow Christian (xiii 34, xv 12). Qumran's concept of love as a positive command is more developed than in the OT, but always the emphasis is on the love of one's fellow sectarians, even to the extent of hating others. The relation between water and the giving of the spirit, a symbolism dear to John (iii 5, vii 37–38), may also be hinted at in the Qumran literature. We shall document these observations in the commentary.

In our judgment the parallels are not close enough to suggest a direct literary dependence of John upon the Qumran literature, but they do suggest Johannine familiarity with the type of thought exhibited in the scrolls. (We must allow the possibility that this thought and vocabulary were not the exclusive property of the Qumran Essenes.) Now, of course, John is a Christian document; and the centrality of Jesus in Johannine thought makes it quite different from the theology of Qumran, which is centered on the Law. For instance, whereas for Qumran the prince of lights and the spirit of truth are titles for the same angelic being, for John the light and the Spirit of Truth are two distinct agents of salvation. We expect such differences in any comparison between a Christian and a non-Christian literature, and it is an annoying oversimplification to think that because of these obvious differences, there can be no relation between John and Qumran. Thus, Teeple, *art. cit.*, makes an important point of the fact that there are theological concepts and terms that are found often in the Qumran literature but not in John, and vice versa. This means nothing unless one is trying to show that the Qumran literature was the only and direct source of John's thought. Nor is it really significant that one can take some of the most important parallels of vocabulary between John and the Qumran scrolls and find a single or an occasional occurrence of such vocabulary elsewhere in Jewish literature. The real question is whether the other occurrences give evidence of the emphasis that is shared by John and Qumran. For instance, in the OT there are many references to light as something spiritually good; Ps xxvii 1 says, "Yahweh is my light." (M. Dahood, The Anchor Bible, vol. 16.) But that is not the same as the dualistic opposition between light and darkness that is a *major factor* in the theology of Qumran and of John. We have said that both Qumran and John have roots in the OT; but if these two literatures have capitalized on relatively insignificant OT terms and have developed them in much the same way, then we have significant parallels.

What can be said is that for *some* features of Johannine thought and vocabulary the Qumran literature offers a closer parallel than any other contemporary or earlier non-Christian literature either in Judaism or in the Hellenistic world. And, in fact, for such features Qumran offers a better parallel than even the later, post-Johannine Mandean or Hermetic writings.

In sum, then, we suggest that into Johannine theological thought patterns has gone the influence of a peculiar combination of various ways of thinking that were current in Palestine during Jesus' own lifetime and after his death. The Christian preachers interpreted Jesus the Christ against the background of the OT, and the preaching behind the Fourth Gospel was no exception. However, the Fourth Gospel has done this not so much by explicit citation as by showing how OT themes were implicitly woven into Jesus' actions and words. In particular, this Gospel has gone much further than the Synoptics in interpreting Jesus in terms of the OT figure of personified Wisdom. Some of the background of Jesus' thought is to be found in the presuppositions of the Pharisaic theology of his time, as these are known to us from the later rabbinic writings. It is no accident that Jesus is called a rabbi more frequently in John than in any other Gospel. Moreover, in John the thought of Jesus is expressed in a peculiar theological vocabulary that we now know to have been used by an important sectarian Jewish group in Palestine.

Does all this mean that the fourth evangelist took Jesus' simple message and reinterpreted it in terms of the OT Wisdom Literature and of Pharisaic and sectarian thought, perhaps because the evangelist himself was particularly familiar with that thought? Or were such elements already in Jesus' own outlook and expression, and were they to some extent lost in the Synoptic tradition of his works and words? A nuanced answer would, in part, include both suggestions. On the one hand, it is time to liberate ourselves from the assumption that Jesus' own thought and expression were always simple and always in one style, and that anything that smacks of theological sophistication must come from the (implicitly more intelligent) evangelists. On the other hand, we must recognize in the fourth evangelist a man of theological genius who has put something of himself and of his own outlook into the composition of the Gospel. In Greek literature does not one have a similar problem in the dialogues of Plato in distinguishing what is of Socrates and what is of Plato, even though the Socrates of Xenophon speaks differently from the Socrates of Plato? Perhaps *one* key to this problem in the Gospel is the Gospel's own claim to be dependent on the testimony of a disciple who was particularly loved by Jesus (xxi 20 and 24, xix 35—see Part VII below). If this is true, a certain connaturality of thought between disciple and master might be presumed.

BIBLIOGRAPHY

John and Gnosticism

Barrett, C. K., "The Theological Vocabulary of the Fourth Gospel and of the Gospel of Truth," CINTI, pp. 210–23.

Brown, R. E., "The Gospel of Thomas and St. John's Gospel," NTS 9 (1962–63), 155–77.

Dodd, *Interpretation*, pp. 97–114.

Quispel, G., "Het Johannesevangelie en de Gnosis," *Nederlands Theologisch Tijdschrift* 11 (1956–57), 173–203.

John and Philo

Argyle, A. W., "Philo and the Fourth Gospel," ET 63 (1951–52), 385–86.

Dodd, *Interpretation*, pp. 54–73.

Wilson, R. McL., "Philo and the Fourth Gospel," ET 65 (1953–54), 47–49.

John and the Hermetica

Braun, F.-M., "Hermétisme et Johannisme," RThom 55 (1955), 22–42, 259–99.

————"Appendices II et III," in JeanThéol, II, pp. 253–95.

Dodd, *Interpretation*, pp. 10–53.

Kilpatrick, G. D., "The Religious Background of the Fourth Gospel," SFG, pp. 36–44.

John, the Old Testament, and Rabbinic Judaism

Barrett, C. K., "The Old Testament in the Fourth Gospel," JTS 48 (1947), 155–69.

Braun, JeanThéol, II: *Les grandes traditions d'Israël*.

Dodd, *Interpretation*, pp. 74–96.

Enz, J. J., "The Book of Exodus as a Literary Type for the Gospel of John," JBL 76 (1957), 208–15.

Glasson, *Moses*.

Griffiths, D. R., "Deutero-Isaiah and the Fourth Gospel," ET 65 (1953–54), 355–60.

Hoskyns, E. C., "Genesis i–iii and St. John's Gospel," JTS 21 (1920), 210–18.

Smith, R. H., "Exodus Typology in the Fourth Gospel," JBL 81 (1962), 329–42.

Vawter, B., "Ezekiel and John," CBQ 26 (1964), 450–58.

Young, F. W., "A Study of the Relation of Isaiah to the Fourth Gospel," ZNW 46 (1955), 215–33.

John and Qumran

Braun, F.-M., "L'arrière-fond judaïque du quatrième évangile et la Communauté de l'Alliance," RB 62 (1955), 5–44.

Braun, H., "Qumran und das Neue Testament," ThR 28 (1962), especially pp. 192–234.

Brown, R. E., "The Qumran Scrolls and the Johannine Gospel and Epistles," CBQ 17 (1955), 403–19, 559–74. Reprinted in *The Scrolls and the New Testament,* ed. K. Stendahl (New York: Harper, 1957), pp. 183–207. Also in NTE, Ch. VII.

Kuhn, K. G., "Johannesevangelium und Qumrantexte," NTPat, pp. 111–21.

Teeple, H. M., "Qumran and the Origin of the Fourth Gospel," NovT 4 (1960), 6–25.

V. THE DESTINATION AND PURPOSE
OF THE FOURTH GOSPEL

Commentators on John have suggested many motives that may have prompted the writing of the Gospel. Perhaps there should be a caution against exaggerating the need for finding specific aims in the Gospel. If John is based on historical tradition and genuine theological insight, then one of the principal reasons for writing the Gospel may have been to preserve this tradition and insight. But once we have observed this caution, the question arises of immediate aims which may have guided the choice of the material and the orientation the author gave to it.

Many have found an apologetic or a missionary motif in the Fourth Gospel. The proposed groups to whom the argumentation may have been directed include the sectarians of John the Baptist, "the Jews," and various heretical, Gnostic, or Docetic groups. Other scholars stress that John was written to confirm Christians in their faith. Schnackenburg has wisely pointed out that a besetting fault has been the attempt to interpret everything in the Gospel in terms of one of these goals, and the failure to recognize that the various editions of the Gospel may represent the adaptation of the central message to a new need. Thus, it is perfectly legitimate to speak of the several aims of the Gospel. We shall treat four.

A. APOLOGETIC AGAINST THE SECTARIANS OF JOHN THE BAPTIST

At the end of the last century Baldensperger, insisting that the Prologue was the key to the understanding of John, pointed out the unfavorable contrast between John the Baptist and Jesus in the Prologue. He suggested that one of the chief purposes of the Gospel was to refute the claims of the sectarians of John the Baptist who were exalting their master at the expense of Jesus. That Baldensperger had recognized one of the Gospel's aims was accepted by most of the succeeding commentaries. As we have mentioned, Bultmann has even posited that the evangelist had been one of the Gnostic sectarians of John the Baptist and that the Prologue was once a hymn in praise of John the Baptist. More recently, however, Schnackenburg, in "Johannesjünger," and others have reacted against exaggerations in the emphasis given to this apologetic motif. We should note the following points.

Our evidence about the sectarians of John the Baptist is very limited. In Acts xviii 5–xix 7, Luke speaks of a group of about twelve disciples at Ephesus (the traditional site for the composition of the Fourth Gospel) who had been baptized with John's baptism and did not know of the Holy Spirit. It is generally thought that they were followers of John the Baptist who had maintained their identity and circulated in the Greek world. But the passage could mean simply that they were primitive disciples of Jesus who had been baptized with water during Jesus' ministry (John iii 23) before the Spirit was given (vii 39), for these disciples show no opposition toward accepting full Christian initiation from Paul.

Our other most important source of information is the Pseudo-Clementine *Recognitions,* a 3rd-century work drawn from earlier (probably 2nd-century) sources. At the time the *Recognitions* were composed, it was known to the author that the sectarians of John the Baptist claimed that their master and not Jesus was the Messiah (see below, pp. 46–47). Thus, these sectarians must have survived well into the Christian era and become opponents of Christianity. We cannot be absolutely certain, however, that the 1st-century sectarians were already making such claims about John the Baptist. Indeed, the Syriac and Latin forms of the *Recognitions* differ significantly on the reading of at least one of the passages where John the Baptist is called the Messiah—a difference which may indicate a developing theology on this point which only gradually found its way into the literature. At any rate, we have not many guidelines for interpreting the thought of the sectarians at the time when John was written.

There is no certain evidence that the early sectarians of John the Baptist were Gnostic, and the Pseudo-Clementines give no evidence of this. It is true that Gnosticism appears among the Mandeans, who may well descend from one group of the sectarians, but there is every suspicion that the Gnosticism was a later element added through Mandean syncretism rather than part of the heritage from the sectarians. (In general, the Mandean literature shows respect for John the Baptist and mentions that he baptized the heavenly revealer, Manda d'Hayye.) A better indication of a possible Gnostic element in the theology of the sectarians of John the Baptist is the patristic tradition that traces the origins of Gnosticism to Samaria, where John the Baptist was probably active (see NOTE on iii 23). The founding fathers of Gnosticism, Simon Magus and Dositheus of Shechem, were identified in patristic writings as followers of John the Baptist. We shall discuss below the possible anti-Gnostic features in John, but whether these should also be considered as directed against the followers of John the Baptist remains dubious.

It is reasonable to suspect that *some* of the negations about John the Baptist in the Fourth Gospel were intended as refutations of claims that the sectarians of John the Baptist made about their master. A guide may be supplied here by the claims made by the later sectarians of John the Baptist in the 3rd-century *Recognitions.* Thus, apologetic motifs may be found in i 8–9 which states that Jesus, not John the Baptist, was the light; in i 30 which states that Jesus existed before John the Baptist and is greater

than he; in i 20 and iii 28 which stress that John the Baptist is not the
Messiah; in x 41 which says that John the Baptist never worked any
miracles. It may well be as part of the apologetic against the sectarians
of John the Baptist that John gives no emphasis to John the Baptist's
ministry of preaching and baptizing such as we find described in Matt
iii 1–12. John presents John the Baptist only as a witness to Jesus. The
addition of the final redactor in iv 2 refutes any claim that Jesus was a
baptizer on the same level as John the Baptist (a claim that might find
support in iii 22, 26), and that idea may also lie behind I John v 6. Perhaps
the most telling line in any discussion of the relative merits of John the
Baptist and of Jesus is found in John iii 30 where John the Baptist speaks
of his own decreasing importance in face of Jesus. (See further B. W.
Bacon, JBL 48 [1929], 40–81.)

The commentary will mention other possible instances of this apologetic.
It should be clear, however, that it is impossible to interpret the whole Gospel
against the background of the theology of the John the Baptist sectarians.
Many scholars see a connection between John the Baptist and Qumran:
John the Baptist lived at the same time and in the same region of Judea as
the Qumran sectarians, and his thought and vocabulary have many Qumran
affinities. On this basis it has been suggested that the followers of John the
Baptist would be sympathetic to Qumran thought, and that it is because
the Fourth Gospel is addressed to them that it has so many Qumran affinities.
In other words, John has portrayed Jesus in Qumran dress in order to win
over the sectarians of John the Baptist. This is possible, but somewhat
simplistic, and very hypothetical. At most it can explain a small part of the
Gospel.

The Prologue deserves special consideration, for in passages like i 6–9, 15,
there is a strong apologetic against any exaggeration of the role of John the
Baptist. It is not wise to use the Prologue as a key to the whole Gospel if, as
we believe, it was once an independent hymn which has been adapted to
serve as the introduction to the Gospel. Moreover, the attention given to
John the Baptist in the Prologue is in part accidental. The commentary
will suggest that when the Prologue was added, it caused a displacement of
the opening lines of the Gospel which naturally concerned John the Baptist.
The insertion of these displaced lines into the heart of the Prologue was
guided in part by the practical desire of not losing them and in part by
apologetic motif. (This leads us to suspect that the apologetic against the followers of John the Baptist belongs to one of the latest strata of Gospel
composition.) The literary history of the lines about the Baptist inserted
into the Prologue precludes interpreting other parts of the Prologue in
the light of this apologetic. For instance, just because the Prologue identifies
Jesus as the Word, there is no reason to believe that the sectarians
thought that John the Baptist was the Word.

Although it may have passages directed against the exaggerations of these
sectarians, the Fourth Gospel gives a place of honor to John the Baptist
himself. It is true that John does not record the saying found in Matt xi 11

and Luke vii 28 in which Jesus identifies John the Baptist as the greatest among those born of women. Nevertheless, for John the role of John the Baptist was very important: he was sent by God (i 6) to reveal Jesus to Israel (i 31, iii 29), and was one of the major witnesses to Jesus, to be ranked alongside the Scriptures and the miracles (v 31–40). If Jesus was the light, John the Baptist "was the lamp, set aflame and burning bright" (v 35). Thus, the view of John the Baptist in the Fourth Gospel is no less complimentary than that of the Synoptics.

B. ARGUMENT WITH THE JEWS

In a Gospel that contains historical tradition we would expect to find some memory of Jesus' struggle with the Pharisees. Since Jesus addressed himself primarily to the people of Israel and tried to bring them to believe that the kingdom of God was present in his own ministry, we naturally expect to find this element preserved in the Gospels either in the form of missionary appeal to Israel or in terms of an apologetic to answer the Jewish rejection of Jesus. There are instances of this in Matthew; but in setting up a contrast between Christian and Jew, John may well be the strongest among the Gospels.

For instance, John emphatically insists that Jesus is the Messiah, the very claim that the Jews rejected. John uses the Greek form of this title (*christos*) more frequently than does any other Gospel and is the only Gospel to use the transliterated form *messias* (i 41, iv 25). John identifies Jesus with figures featured in OT and Jewish apocalyptic expectations: the Servant of God (see COMMENT on i 29, 34); the apocalyptic lamb (i 29); the King of Israel (i 49); the Holy One of God (vi 69). A glance at the Outline of the First Book of the Gospel (p. CXL) shows the importance given to the theme of Jesus' replacement of Jewish institutions like ritual purification, the Temple, and worship in Jerusalem (chs. ii–iv) and of Jewish feasts like the Sabbath, Passover, Tabernacles, and Dedication (chs. v–x). Now, plausibly some of this stems from Jesus' own outlook on his ministry, but why this emphasis in John? We shall suggest two tendencies in the Johannine stress on the Jews and their theology.

(1) Justification of Christian Claims against Jewish Unbelief

The strongest impression that one gains from reading the Fourth Gospel's treatment of the Jews is of its polemic attitude. There is an attack here against the religious position of Judaism—Jesus is the Messiah, and in his presence and face to face with what he has done, Judaism has lost its pre-eminence. Moreover, the Gospel's attitude is stronger than that warranted by the attempt of Christianity to justify its own status; there is a pointed argument here. John resorts to a rabbinic style of arguing in passages like x 34–36 in order to defend Jesus' right to be called Son of God.

The Gospel calls on Jewish legal principles (v 31 ff., viii 17) in order to justify Jesus' testimony on his own behalf. The bitter character of the polemics can easily be seen in passages like viii 44–47, 54–55. The disciples of Moses and the disciples of Jesus (ix 28) are locked in struggle.

The polemic attitude of the Fourth Gospel toward Judaism is seen in the use of the term "the Jews," which occurs seventy times in John as compared with five or six occurrences in each Synoptic Gospel. Grässer, *art. cit.,* has questioned the reliability of the use of this term as an index of Johannine attitude, since the term has various shades of meaning in the Gospel—a true observation. For instance, when Jesus is speaking to a foreigner, as to the Samaritan in iv 22, he uses the Jews as no more than a religious, nationalistic designation (see also xviii 33, 35). In passages that speak of the feasts or the customs of the Jews (ii 6, 13, vii 2), there may be nothing opprobrious in the use of the term. Moreover, there is one stratum of Johannine material, particularly evident in xi–xii, where the term the Jews simply refers to Judeans and thus covers both Jesus' enemies and those who believe in him. (There is evidence that this portion is a later insertion into the original plan of the Gospel and, therefore, may have had its own history within the Johannine tradition; see also the COMMENT on viii 31.) Leaving aside these exceptions, some of which are obvious, others of which are explicable in terms of literary criticism, the Fourth Gospel uses "the Jews" as almost a technical title for *the religious authorities, particularly those in Jerusalem, who are hostile to Jesus.*

This understanding of the term may be substantiated in three ways. *First,* it is quite clear that in many instances the term "the Jews" has nothing to do with ethnic, geographical, or religious differentiation. People who are ethnically, religiously, and even geographically Jews (even in the narrow sense of belonging to Judea) are distinguished from "the Jews." For instance, in ix 22 the parents of the blind man, obviously Jews themselves, are said to fear "the Jews," that is, the Pharisees who are investigators. The former cripple, a Jew himself, is pictured in v 15 as informing "the Jews" that Jesus was his benefactor. *Second,* in some passages the Gospel speaks interchangeably of "the Jews" and of the chief priests and the Pharisees. In xviii 3 the police are supplied by the chief priests and the Pharisees, while in xviii 12 they are the police of "the Jews." In viii 13 the interrogators are called Pharisees, while in viii 18 ff. they are "the Jews." *Third,* this understanding is borne out by a comparison with the Synoptics. In John xviii 28–31 "the Jews" bring Jesus before Pilate, while in Mark xv 1 the Sanhedrin has this task. See also John ii 18 and Mark xi 27–28.

Now, how can this peculiar use of the term be explained, for obviously it is anachronistic in the ministry of Jesus? It has often been remarked that in John many of the classes and divisions of people so prominent on the Synoptic scene have disappeared: for example, the Sadducees, Herodians, Zealots, tax collectors, scribes, sinners, righteous, poor, rich, etc. To some extent this is due to the dualism of the Gospel which levels class distinction: there are now only good and bad, sons of light and sons of darkness, the truthful and the liars. But in another way the disappearance of these groups is the work of simplification and the change of historical perspective. The Gospel was written, we believe, after A.D. 70 when many of the religious distinctions and groupings of Jesus' time no longer had meaning; the destruction of the Temple had simplified Judaism. Thus, only the chief priests and the Pharisees remain in John—the chief priests because their role in the Sanhedrin and the trials of Jesus was too essential a part of the story to be forgotten, the Pharisees because they are precisely that Jewish sect which survived the calamity of 70. The Judaism of the time in which the Gospel was written was Pharisaic Judaism.

It is this situation in which the Gospel was written that explains the use of the term "the Jews." The era of large Christian missionary inroads into Judaism has passed. Jesus had been preached to the Jews both in Palestine and the Diaspora, and the decision had been made for or against Jesus. For the most part, the Jews who had accepted Jesus were now simply Christians and part of the Church, so that when Christians spoke of the Jews without qualification they were referring to those who had rejected Jesus and re-mained loyal to the Synagogue. We find exactly this use of the term in Matt xxviii 15. Thus, in an era when there were ill feelings between the Church and the Synagogue, "the Jews" was a term used with a connotation of hostility to Christians. In the Fourth Gospel, then, the evangelist uses the term with the meaning that it had in his own time. For him, "the Jews" belong to "the world," that is, they are part of that division of men who are in dualistic opposition to Jesus and refuse to come to him as the light. (John is not anti-Semitic; the evangelist is condemning not race or people but opposition to Jesus.)

This does not mean that the evangelist has forgotten the true circum-stances of Jesus' ministry in the anachronistic use of "the Jews." By this term he indicates his belief that the Jews of his own time are the spiritual descendants of the Jewish authorities who were hostile to Jesus during the ministry. He regards the attitude of these authorities as the typical Jewish attitude as he knows it in his own time. Unlike the Synoptic Gospels, John does not attack the Pharisees or the Jews for hypocrisy or for their moral and social behavior; the whole attack on them centers on their refusal to believe in Jesus and their desire to kill him. This is because the struggle be-tween the Church and the Synagogue in the evangelist's time is not based on morals but on the acceptance of Jesus as the Messiah. Even the question of the observance of the Law which so engaged Paul's energies has disappeared in John. John does not treat the Law as either a problem for Christians or as an enemy; it is simply something that has been superseded by the great act of divine covenant love in Jesus Christ (i 17). The Law is something that affects Jews, not Christians; and so Jesus speaks of it to the Jews as *"your* Law" (viii 17, x 34, also xv 25—notice the similar use of "your synagogues" in Matt xxiii 34).

Still another aspect of the Johannine attitude is seen in the distinction between "the Jews" and "Israel." The latter is a favorable term describing the real succession to the OT heritage. John the Baptist came that Jesus might be revealed to *Israel* (i 31). Nathanael who promptly accepts Jesus is not a Jew but a genuine Israelite (i 47), a man without guile replacing the old Jacob-Israel in whom there was guile. Even the emphasis on Jesus as a rabbi in the Fourth Gospel may reflect Johannine polemics. The term is not clearly an anachronism as once assumed (see NOTE on i 38), but the Johannine emphasis on the title may be by way of contrasting Jesus with the great rabbis of the Jewish assembly at Jamnia in the last quarter of the 1st century. The contrast between the disciples of Moses and the disciples of Jesus in ix 28 is more of the same. It will be noted, however, that John does not react to Jewish claims about Moses by any denigration of Moses; for in Johannine thought, if the Jews truly believed in Moses, they would believe in Jesus (v 46).

(2) *Appeal to Jewish Christians in the Diaspora Synagogues*

If the polemic against the Synagogue is an important motif in the Fourth Gospel, we should recognize that this battle is probably not being fought in Palestine. The Gospel in its present form is written in Greek and takes care to explain Hebrew or Aramaic words like Messiah, Rabbi, Siloam—terms that would scarcely need an explanation in Palestine. Nor would an aside like iv 9 be needed for a Palestinian audience. Of course, it is not impossible that the first edition of John was directed to the Palestinian scene and the subsequent edition(s) adapted for an audience living outside Palestine. Nor, since we believe that the Gospel was also directed to Gentiles, is it impossible that some of these explanations were included for Gentile readers. (This seems to be true in ii 6 and xix 40, where general Jewish customs are explained.) Nevertheless, the most plausible theory is that even those passages which contain polemic against the Synagogue contemplate the situation outside Palestine. In vii 35 there is a sarcastic reference by the crowds to what Jesus will do: "Surely he isn't going off to the Diaspora among the Greeks?" This is an example of Johannine irony where the truth is unwittingly proposed by Jesus' adversaries. The Gospel is proof that through his preachers Jesus has gone into the Diaspora.

Now, as we have stressed, John's attitude toward "the Jews" is not missionary but apologetic and polemic. The violence of the language in ch. viii, comparing the Jews to the devil's brood, is scarcely designed to convert the Synagogue, which in Johannine thought is now the "Synagogue of Satan" (Rev ii 9, iii 9). It is no accident that some of the discussions in John between Jesus and the Jews anticipate the classic apologetic that Justin addressed to Trypho in the middle of the 2nd century. Thus, along with Schnackenburg, "Messiasfrage," we reject, at least in part, the thesis of John A. T. Robinson and Van Unnik that the main and almost exclusive purpose of John was to serve as a missionary handbook to convert Diaspora Jews. If the language of the Johannine argument against the Jews serves as a guide, the purpose must have been one of countering Jewish propaganda rather than of persuading the Jews with a hope of mass conversions.

Yet, there may have been one group of Jews that the Gospel addressed with a certain hopefulness; namely, the small group of Jews who believed in Jesus but as yet had not severed their relationship with the Synagogue. In the 80s and 90s of the 1st century these Jewish Christians were going through a crisis.

In the first years after Jesus' death his disciples met opposition from the Jerusalem rulers, even as Jesus had met opposition. Acts preserves memories of conflicts between the Christian leaders and the Sanhedrin (iv 1–3, v 17–18). The decision of Gamaliel in Acts v 33–40 seems to have marked a turning point for the Jewish Christian community of Jerusalem and to have initiated a period of more peaceful relationships between it and the Sanhedrin. It is true that Acts viii 1 reports a persecution of the Church in Jerusalem, but those who were scattered were the Hellenist Christians who antagonized the Jewish authorities by their opposition to the Temple. In subsequent years there were isolated acts of violence, like Herod's execution of James son of Zebedee and imprisonment of Peter (Acts xii 2–3), but otherwise the Jerusalem community seems to have lived at peace with the Jewish authorities. There is no hint of persecution in A.D. 49, when the council of Jerusalem was held. James was very careful to enjoin observance of some basic points of Mosaic ritual on all Christians, even Gentiles, in the territory of Palestine and Syria (Acts xv 22 ff.), probably with the intent of avoiding friction with Judaism. In 58, when Paul came to Jerusalem (Acts xxi 18 ff.), it was still customary for Jewish Christians to offer sacrifice in the Temple. The subsequent execution of James in the 60s at the command of the high priest marked the opening of a new period of hostility.

However, as Carroll, *art. cit.*, has pointed out, it was only the beleaguered Judaism of the days after the destruction of the Temple that thought it absolutely necessary to cut off the Jews who believed in Jesus. Danger of extinction usually forces a religion to become more rigidly orthodox in order to survive, and Judaism was no exception. With Temple and sacrifice gone, devotion to the Law was the principal factor that held Judaism together. Paul's attitude toward the Law and, indeed, Jesus' own freedom of behavior would have been well known; and therefore, in the perilous situation facing Judaism after 70, the Jews who believed in Jesus were looked on as a possibly subversive factor as regards the all-important question of the Law. Throughout the 80s there was an organized attempt to force the Christian Jews out of the synagogues. We see an echo of this in the *Shemoneh Esreh* or *Eighteen Benedictions* recited by the Jews as the chief prayer in the synagogues. The reformulation of these benedictions took place after 70; and the twelfth benediction, ca. 85, was a curse on the *minim* or heretics, primarily Jewish-Christian. (See W. D. Davies, *The Setting of the Sermon on the Mount* [Cambridge: 1964], pp. 275–76.) Since this curse had to be recited by the Jews in the synagogues, a Jew who believed in Jesus would be forced to curse himself or else to admit his belief publicly by refusing to say the curse. Around 90, while Rabbi Gamaliel II was president of the Jamnia assembly, formal excommunication came into more frequent use as a weapon against dissenters.

We have explained this sequence of events in detail because of its importance for dating the Fourth Gospel (see Part VI below). There are rather clear indications that the Fourth Gospel makes an appeal to these Jews who believed in Jesus and who were torn between their faith and a natural desire not to desert Judaism. The generally hostile attack on "the Jews" would not apply to them, for it was precisely the Jews hostile to Jesus who were making trouble for the Jews with Christian leanings. The heavy emphasis on Jesus as the Messiah (especially xx 31) would be designed to strengthen their faith in this crucial confession which had become the testing stone of continued admission to the synagogues. The theme of Jesus' replacement of Jewish institutions and feasts would be an encouragement to them, for they would have to leave such practices behind if they withdrew from the synagogues.

More specifically: on three occasions (ix 22, xii 42, xvi 2), John mentions excommunication from the Synagogue. Twice John refers to those who believe in Jesus but do not have the courage to confess their faith. In xii 42–43 this reference is combined with biting sarcasm; in xix 38 Joseph of Arimathea is brought forward as an example of one who overcame this fear and publicly acknowledged his following of Jesus. The excommunication theme is strongest in ch. ix; and in this narrative, as Allen, *art. cit.*, has shown, the hero is a man who comes to believe in Jesus even at the cost of his expulsion from the Synagogue. John is inviting the Jewish Christians in the Diaspora synagogues to follow his example.

C. ARGUMENT AGAINST CHRISTIAN HERETICS

A tradition going back to the 2nd century and Irenaeus (*Adv. Haer.* III 11:1; SC 34:179–80) says that the Gospel of John was written against Cerinthus, a heretic of Asia Minor with Gnostic leanings. We do not know much of Cerinthus' thought, but Irenaeus (*ibid.*, I 26:1; PL 7:686) says that Cerinthus considered *Jesus* to be the son of Joseph, while *Christ* was a celestial aeon who descended on Jesus for a while at the time of his baptism and left him before his death. If this is a correct picture of Cerinthus' doctrine, there is little in the Gospel designed to refute such a theory. The real refutation of this type of thought comes in I John with its strong insistence that Jesus is the Christ come in the flesh and that Jesus cannot be severed (iv 2–3). Perhaps all that Irenaeus' information tells us is that in the Johannine literature there was an attack on Cerinthus. It may be that Cerinthus also held that the world was created by a demiurge rather than by God. In this case, John i 3 would be significant, for it insists that all creation was effected by the Word of God. But this is scarcely a major emphasis in the Gospel.

Jerome (*In Matt. Prolog.;* PL 26:19) mentions that the Gospel of John was directed to Ebion along with Cerinthus. Ebion was probably not a real person but an eponymous hero of the Ebionites, a Jewish Christian group. Irenaeus first mentions Ebion in the same passage where he mentions Cerinthus (*Adv. Haer.* I 26:2; PL 7:686—perhaps this is why Jerome assumes that the Gospel was also directed to Ebion). The thought that the Fourth Gospel was written to confute Christians like the Ebionites, who had not abandoned their Jewish practices, is somewhat akin to the proposal made above that it was written in part as an address to the Jewish Christians in the synagogues. The Ebionites had features of theological thought, for example, dualism, which are also found at Qumran (see J. Fitzmyer, TS 16 [1955], 335–72). Thus, what we said above about possible Qumran features in the theology of the sectarians of John the Baptist might also be applied here. The fourth evangelist may have chosen language like that of Qumran to appeal to groups who shared similar language and thought. In summary, while we do not deny that certain features that appear in later Ebionite theology correspond to features in John, so that the Gospel might be usefully read by those with incipient Ebionite tendencies, nevertheless we do not believe there is sufficient evidence that the Gospel was directed to the Ebionites specifically. It may be mentioned that Victorinus of Pettau, ca. 300, joins the Gnostic Valentinus to Ebion and Cerinthus as another target against whom the Gospel was supposedly directed (*In Apoc.* XI 1; CSEL 49:97).

It has also been suggested that the Fourth Gospel was directed against Docetism. Docetism was not so much a heresy by itself as it was an attitude found in a number of heresies. Its central contention was that Jesus Christ did not truly come in the flesh, for his flesh was only an appearance—he only seemed to be a man. Some of the remarks of Ignatius of Antioch, ca. 110, seem to be directed against such an error, so this heretical thought may well have been in circulation when John was written. Wilkens' theory of various editions of the Gospel (see Part II above) sees an increasing polemic against Docetism in the later editions of the Gospel. Certainly there are passages in John that may have an anti-docetic thrust. "The Word became flesh" (i 14) springs to mind immediately. The scene in xix 34 would be shattering to the docetic cause, for the realism of the blood and water pouring from the side of the wounded Jesus militates against any theory that he was a phantasm. That this is an important scene in John is underlined by the editorial parenthesis in the next verse (35) which claims eyewitness verification. However, there are many theological motifs in xix 34, for example, sacramentalism, fulfillment of vii 38–39; and it is not possible to be sure which motif was being underlined by the editor. The Docetists seem to have neglected the Eucharist and to have denied that it was the flesh of Jesus (Ignatius *Smyrnaeans* vii 1). Therefore, the eucharistic realism of John vi 51–58 may also have been anti-docetic in tendency. The difficulty is that all these passages are perfectly understandable even without the anti-docetic interpretation. An honest judgment would be that an anti-docetic motif is possible and even probable in the Gospel, but it has no great prominence. If it exists, its best attestation is found in passages that belong to the latest stage of Johannine editing. By contrast, the First Epistle offers more verses capable of anti-docetic interpretation than does the much longer Gospel.

Not one of the suggestions that John was written against early Christian heretics is without difficulty. The Gospel does not seem to support the thesis that this motive was particularly strong in the evangelist's mind.

D. ENCOURAGEMENT TO BELIEVING CHRISTIANS, GENTILE AND JEW

John A. T. Robinson and Van Unnik maintain that John shows little interest in the Gentiles. It is pointed out that xx 31 specifies the purpose of the Gospel in these words: ". . . that you may [continue to] have faith that Jesus is the Messiah," and that Messiah or *Christos* was not a meaningful religious title to the Gentiles. First of all, however, there is a question of whether this verse refers to those who are to come to belief or to those who are already believers. Secondly, we must not forget that the Christian preachers carried over to the Gentiles much Jewish religious terminology. Gentiles who became interested in the message about Jesus would soon have to learn some OT background (a good example is Paul's argument from the OT addressed to the Gentile converts in Galatia) and have to learn what Messiah meant. Thus, there is no contradiction in addressing a Gospel to Gentiles in order to persuade them that Jesus is the Messiah. Thirdly, the whole of John xx 31 should receive attention; it says the Gospel was written ". . . that you may [continue to] have faith that Jesus is the Messiah, *the Son of God.*" As Schnackenburg, "Messiasfrage," emphasizes, there is no doubt that the second title would appeal to a Gentile religious background where the gods had sons.

If there is nothing to exclude attention to the Gentiles in the Fourth Gospel, there are on the positive side clear statements of universalism. Jesus comes into the world as a light for *every man* (i 9). Jesus takes away the sins of the *world* (i 29); he has come to save the *world* (iii 17). When he is lifted up on the cross and in resurrection, he draws *all men* to himself (xii 32). Besides these statements which implicitly include the Gentiles, there are specific references. In unconscious irony the Jews in vii 35 incredulously foretell that Jesus will go to the Diaspora and teach the Greeks. The public ministry comes to a climactic finale in xii 20–21 when the Greeks or Gentiles ask to see Jesus—a sign that all men have begun to come to Jesus and that therefore it is now the time (or "the hour") for his return to the Father in crucifixion, resurrection, and ascension. (Robinson, TNTS, p. 112[7], thinks that "Greeks" in vii 35 means Greek-speaking Jews, but we think that the role of xii 20 in the plan of the Gospel cannot be explained unless "Greeks" means Gentiles.) In x 16 Jesus stresses that he has other sheep who do not belong to this fold but must be brought and made part of the one sheep herd under the one shepherd. That this refers to the conversion of the Gentiles receives support from xi 52; there we are told that Jesus died not only for the Jewish nation, but also to gather together the dispersed children of God and make them one. In iv 35 Jesus sees the field of the Samaria mission ripe for the harvest; and while the Samaritans are not precisely Gentiles, they are outside the mainstream of Judaism. These same Samaritans hail Jesus in iv 42 as "the Saviour of the *world*." Finally, it is not impossible that the homage done to Jesus in mockery by the Romans in xix 1–3, 19–22, is meant in Johannine irony to predict that one day these Gentiles will truly accept Jesus as king. Thus, it seems quite clear that the Gentiles have a role in the perspective of the Fourth Gospel.

Perhaps, however, we may best say that much of the Gospel is addressed to the Christian believer without distinction of whether his derivation is Jewish or Gentile. This is a Gospel designed to root the believer deeper in his faith. The stated purpose of the Gospel in xx 31 is probably not primarily missionary, and a good case can be made for understanding this verse in the sense of the reader's *continuing* to have faith that Jesus is the Messiah, the Son of God. The Gospel wants to make this faith something alive, and thus in Jesus' name to bring life to the reader. Certainly the believer is in focus throughout chs. xiii–xvii (chapters which Van Unnik, p. 410, finds difficult for his thesis that the Gospel is primarily a missionary work directed to the Jews). A new people has appeared, a people coming from both the Jewish fold and outside (x 16), a people whose earthly origins are of little importance since they are begotten from above (iii 3). It is true that, by way of apologetic against the Jews, the evangelist stresses that Jesus came to his own and his own people did not accept him (i 11). But much more does the evangelist speak to those who did accept him and thus became God's children, begotten not by human desire but by God (i 12–13).

In Part VIII we shall discuss some of the decisive theological emphases in the Gospel, but we would anticipate here by pointing out that all these emphases are directed to crises within the believing Church rather than to the conversion of non-believers. If the Gospel stresses realized eschatology, it is to lead the believer away from any overemphasis on the anticipated glories of the future coming of Jesus. The evangelist wishes the believer to realize that he already possesses eternal life, that he is already a son of God and has already met his judge. If the Gospel has a strong sacramental tone, its purpose is to root Baptism and the Eucharist in what Jesus said and did, lest the believer lose a sense of contact with the earthly Jesus and thus Christianity devolve into a mystery religion. If the evangelist brings forward the figure of the Paraclete (App. V, The Anchor Bible, vol. 29A), his purpose is to reassure the believer that with the passing of the apostolic generation the memory of Jesus is not to be extinguished, for Jesus' Spirit remains in the Christian, keeping alive that memory. The major purpose of the Gospel, then, is to make the believer see existentially what this Jesus in whom he believes means in terms of life. Bultmann has not done Johannine studies a disservice in pointing out some of the existential qualities of the Fourth Gospel. Much more than Bultmann, however, we believe that the evangelist rooted this existential goal in a picture of Jesus that had not only historic but also historical value.

BIBLIOGRAPHY

Allen, E. L., "The Jewish Christian Church in the Fourth Gospel," JBL 74 (1955), 88–92.

Bowker, J. W., "The Origin and Purpose of St. John's Gospel," NTS 11 (1964–65), 398–408.

Carroll, K. L., "The Fourth Gospel and the Exclusion of Christians from the Synagogues," BJRL 40 (1957–58), 19–32.

Grässer, E., "Die Antijüdische Polemik im Johannesevangelium," NTS 11 (1964–65), 74–90.

Jocz, J., "Die Juden im Johannesevangelium," *Judaica* 9 (1953), 129–42.

Robinson, John A. T., "The Destination and Purpose of St. John's Gospel," NTS 6 (1959–60), 117–31. Also in TNTS, pp. 107–25.

Schnackenburg, R., "Das vierte Evangelium und die Johannesjünger," *Historisches Jahrbuch* 77 (1958), 21–38.

——"Die Messiasfrage im Johannesevangelium," NTAuf, pp. 240–64.

van Unnik, W. C., "The Purpose of St. John's Gospel," StEv, I, pp. 382–411.

VI. THE DATE OF THE FINAL WRITTEN FORM
OF THE GOSPEL

It is now time to raise the question of the date to be attributed to the *final written form* of the Gospel. It should be stressed that we are not asking when the historical tradition behind the Fourth Gospel took shape, or when the Gospel was first written down and edited—in other words we are not primarily concerned here with the dating of Stages 1–4 in our theory of the composition of the Gospel, for, after all, these stages are hypothetical. The question here concerns the date of the only stage of the Gospel that is clearly not hypothetical, namely, the final form that has come down to us, including ch. xxi.

A. THE LATEST PLAUSIBLE DATE

The range for the dating of John has been greatly narrowed in the last thirty years. Most scholars today regard as impossibly high the dates once suggested by H. Delafosse (A.D. 170) and A. Loisy (150–160—his opinion in 1936). Barrett, p. 108, sets A.D. 140 as the latest possible date for the publication of the Gospel, but even this is rather high. (Note, however, that Barrett is speaking of publication, not of writing.) The general opinion fixes 100–110 as the latest plausible date for the written composition of John. Let us discuss some of the factors that have helped to determine this *terminus ante quem*.

The classic argument used to support a very late dating for John was the development of theology. F. C. Baur put the Synoptics, Paul, and John into the framework of Hegelian thesis, antithesis, and synthesis, with John representing a period that had gone far beyond Pauline theology. Although Baur still has his admirers, for example, Mary Andrews, the theory of linear development of NT theology has been successfully refuted. If we remember that Paul's writings antedated the Synoptic Gospels, a developed christology becomes a precarious chronometer, as Goodenough has pointed out. The view that Johannine sacramentalism, for example, vi 51–58, is too developed to have been formulated in the 1st century reflects some antiquated ideas about the origins of sacramental thought in the Church. Basically we have another example of the argument from the development of theology in the claim that the Fourth Gospel must be late because it is by the same author as the Johannine Epistles, and the latter are late because they reflect late Church organization. However, the common authorship of the Gospel and the Epistles is something that must be examined and not assumed; and also the parallels of organization between the Dead Sea Scroll community and the Lucan portrait of the Church in Acts have caused serious rethinking about the supposed lateness of Church organization. Thus, it may be said that, while most scholars still think of John as the latest of the four Gospels, it is very difficult to fix the date of the Gospel on the basis of a theory of theological development. There is nothing in the theology of John that would clearly rule out final composition in the 1st century.

Another argument used to demonstrate the necessity of dating John in the late 2nd century was the claim that there is no evidence of the use of John by early 2nd-century writers. It is quite clear that in the last part of the 2nd century, after 170, the Fourth Gospel was known to Tatian, Melito of Sardis, Theophilus of Antioch, Irenaeus, and others. Yet, a close examination of the early writers in this century led Sanders, followed by Barrett, to maintain that there is no satisfactory proof for the use of the Gospel before 150. This evidence has been exhaustively re-examined by Braun, JeanThéol, I, who finds ample reason to affirm that John was accepted in orthodox circles in Egypt, Rome, Syria, and Asia Minor, even from the early years of the 2nd century. For instance, Braun, arguing against Sanders and Barrett, thinks it certain that Ignatius of Antioch, ca. 110, was dependent on John, even though he does not cite the Gospel *ad litteram*. Maurer's full-scale treatment of the problem comes to the same conclusion. From a careful study of one passage in Justin Martyr, ca. 150, Romanides, *art. cit.*, maintains that this apologist knew the Fourth Gospel; and this is Braun's conclusion as well. Tarelli and Boismard believe that Clement of Rome, A.D. 96, used the Fourth Gospel, but this is very difficult to establish. In this instance, the evidence at most seems to show that Clement had a knowledge of theological thought and vocabulary similar to that found in John.

Thus, on the point of the early patristic use of John there remains much difference of opinion among competent scholars. Personally, we find Braun's study attractive, for his judgments about the use of John by various writers are carefully qualified. An objective evaluation would seem to indicate that the argument for the late dating of John because the Gospel was not used in the early 2nd century has lost whatever probative force it may have had. On the other hand, we remain uncertain about any conclusive argument for a precise dating of the Gospel drawn from the supposed use of it by Clement or by Ignatius. Even if Ignatius did know Johannine tradition, how can we be sure from what stage of the composition of the Gospel his knowledge stems? There is no possible proof that Ignatius knew the final form of the Gospel, as it has come down to us.

Still another argument for the late dating of John has been the evident affection for this Gospel among 2nd-century Gnostic circles. Von Loewenich (1932) put forward the thesis that John was first circulated in heterodox

Gnostic circles before it was admitted to the Church at large; and Sanders and Barrett contend that the Gnostics are the first to show definite traces of the use of John. The force of this argument for the dating of the Gospel depends to some extent on the date that one assigns for the emergence of Gnosticism. If Gnosticism is a 2nd-century phenomenon and John originates in Gnostic circles, then it is logical to date John in the 2nd century. But, if in the manner of Bultmann one postulates a pre-Christian Gnosticism, then the Gnostic use of John is not decisively significant for dating the Gospel. We have already discussed the latter hypothesis in Part IV:A.

Braun's study of the 2nd century had the problem of the Gnostic use of the Gospel in mind, and he came to the conclusion that the orthodox use of the Gospel was both earlier and more faithful to the Gospel than the Gnostic use. As long as we had practically no representative works of 2nd-century Gnosticism, it was possible to postulate the existence of a mildly aberrant Christian Gnosticism quite unlike the heresy described by the Fathers—a Gnosticism of which John would be representative. As we have mentioned in Part IV:A, the discovery at Chenoboskion of documents representing 2nd-century Gnosticism has shown that John has little in common with works like the *Gospel of Truth* and the *Gospel of Thomas*. Wherever these gospels and John have developed a common theme, the Gnostic documents stand at a much greater distance from the primitive gospel message than does John. Thus, it seems clear that 2nd-century Gnosticism as it is known to us from Chenoboskion is post-Johannine.

The thesis that John was dependent on the Synoptic Gospels has favored a late dating, especially if Matthew and Luke are dated in the 80s. But, as we saw in Part III:B, this dependency is now rejected by many scholars. The opposite view which posits an independent historical tradition behind John tends to lower the dating of the Fourth Gospel. If there is in John a correct tradition of Palestinian places, situations, and customs, it seems logical to maintain that such a tradition took shape before the destruction of 70 or, at least, shortly after 70 when there was still a witness who could remember the Palestinian scene as it was. It is very unlikely that one could return to Palestine in the 80s and compose a reliable tradition of the works and words of Jesus on the basis of untapped local traditions, for the Roman ravaging of the land and the exile of the Christian community in the 60s constituted a formidable barrier to the continuity of tradition. Now, if we accept the probability (which is a near certainty) that the historical tradition behind the Gospel, our Stage 1, was formed before 70, the subsequent stages of Gospel composition cannot be prolonged much beyond 100. That such a tradition could have survived well into the 2nd century before taking final form is very hard to credit.

The most conclusive argument against the late dating of John has been the discovery of several 2nd-century papyri texts of John. In 1935 C. H. Roberts published Rylands Papyrus 457 (P^{52}), an Egyptian codex fragment of John xviii 31–33, 37–38. The dating of this papyrus to 135–50 has been widely accepted; and the latest attempt to date NT papyri by K. Aland, NTS 9 (1962–63), 307, assigns to P[52] a date at the "beginning of the 2nd cent." More recently, two late 2nd-century or early 3rd-century (175–225) witnesses to the Fourth Gospel have been published as Bodmer Papyri II and XV (P[66], P[75]), giving us very substantial sections of John. Another Egyptian witness to John is Papyrus Egerton 2 (treated in an addendum to the COMMENT on ch. v), a composite work from ca. 150 drawing on both John and the Synoptics. That this "Unknown Gospel" is dependent on John and not vice versa is widely accepted today; and it is important that both this papyrus and Tatian's *Diatessaron,* or harmony of the Gospels, written ca. 175, give to John an equal status with the Synoptic Gospels. One can scarcely imagine such an evaluation if John had just been composed.

Thus, it is quite clear that John circulated in many copies in Egypt in the period 140–200. The theory that John was composed in Egypt has had little support. If, as is generally supposed, it was composed in Asia Minor (or even Syria), we must allow time for it to have reached Egypt and to have passed into common circulation there. Moreover, the Bodmer Papyri reflect partially different textual traditions of the Gospel, that is, P[66] is close to the text we later find in Codex Sinaiticus; P[75] is almost the same as the text of Codex Vaticanus. The development of such variation must have required time.

To sum up, the positive arguments seem to point to 100–110 as the latest plausible date for the writing of the Gospel, with strong probability favoring the earlier limit of 100.

B. The Earliest Plausible Date

In some ways the *terminus post quem* is not so easy to establish as the *terminus ante quem.* Again let us mention the factors that bear on this question, with the reminder that we are primarily concerned with the final written form of the Gospel.

We pointed out above that the historical tradition that we have posited behind the Fourth Gospel was most likely formed before 70, and that several decades probably elapsed between the formation of this tradition (Stage 1) and the final redaction of the Gospel (Stage 5). The traditions that underlie the Synoptic Gospels are usually dated to the period between 40 and 60. Some would wish to date the tradition underlying John later; but, as we have insisted, no over-all judgment can be passed that pre-Johannine tradition is more developed than pre-Synoptic tradition. In stories and sayings shared by the two traditions, a judgment has to be made in each instance, and sometimes that judgment favors the antiquity of John. Thus, personally we would be willing to assign the same date to the tradition behind John that is assigned to the Synoptic sources, and to date Stage 1 of the composition of the Gospel to the period between 40 and 60.

Nevertheless, even with the Synoptic Gospels, there was a lapse of time between the formation of the sources behind the Gospels and the actual writing of the Gospels. For instance, Matthew and Luke are often dated to the period between 75 and 85. According to our hypothesis, John underwent several editions and a final redaction. We think it quite possible that the *first* edition of John is to be dated to the same general period as Matthew and Luke.

We have advised against recklessly fixing the date of NT works on the basis of the comparative development of their theologies. Yet, when confined to a single form of literature, this method has a certain validity. It is licit to compare the four Gospels in order to decide in general which is the most primitive and which the most developed. On the whole, we believe that the precritical judgment that John is the most theologically developed and the latest of the Gospels is essentially sound. In our opinion, Matthew, probably the latest of the Synoptic Gospels (ca. 85?), offers John the most rivalry in theological development.

However, others, for example, Goodenough, have used comparative theology to argue for a very early date for John. For instance, it is remarked that John does not report the institution of the Eucharist at the Last Supper, and therefore it is claimed that John represents a period before the Pauline account of the institution came to dominance. Such an argument reflects the highly questionable assumption that the account of the institution stems from Paul and not from the earliest tradition. Moreover, it fails to recognize that John vi 51–58 may well enshrine the *adapted* Johannine account of the institution, moved here from the account of the Last Supper. Another argument from silence is that John, like Mark and Paul, is ignorant of the Virgin Birth, and so is earlier than Matthew or Luke. However, the possibility must be left open that in John vii 42 the observation about Jesus' birth is left unanswered, not because of the ignorance of the evangelist, but as an instance of Johannine irony, an irony that implies that the evangelist did know the true story of the birth of Jesus. (However, other interpretations of the irony are possible, and so the argument is not certain.) Certainly, John evinces an interest in what preceded the baptism of Jesus in the Jordan; only the Johannine quest, unlike that of Matthew and Luke, does not touch on the human origins of Jesus but on his pre-existence. If the final editor of John chose to preface the Gospel with a community hymn to Jesus as the Word, this does not mean that he was ignorant of all infancy narratives. Quite plausibly, he is simply reflecting the local usage in Asia Minor where people sang "hymns to Christ as to a God," while Matthew and Luke are reflecting the mentality of Palestine where popular traditions of the birth of Jesus were preserved. In judging the attempt of Goodenough and others to argue for an early date from comparative theology, we must admit that we find nothing in John that would demand a date before 70 for the final written form of the Gospel.

There is a reasonably precise indication for the *terminus post quem* for the dating of John in the theme of excommunication from the synagogues which, as we saw in Part V:B, plays an important role in the Gospel. The problem does not seem to have been acute before 70; and the datable incidents like the formulation of the twelfth blessing in the *Shemoneh Esreh* and the use of formal excommunication at Jamnia belong to the period 80–90. This evidence makes unlikely a date before 80 for the final written composition of the Gospel, and indeed makes the 90s the probable era. Justin's *Dialogue against Trypho,* ca. 160, represents an accumulation of the Jewish-Christian polemic which had developed throughout the 2nd century. It often seems to stand in direct continuity with the polemic against the Synagogue in John, and this offers another reason for not dating the final form of John too early in the 1st century. We have noted already and will point out further in the commentary that the sections in John that refer specifically to excommunication seem to belong to the final stages of Gospel editing. This may mean that the first edition of the Gospel took shape in the 70s or early 80s before the excommunication question flared up.

Chapter xxi 18–19 gives symbolic but relatively clear witness to the fact that Peter had died by crucifixion, an event which took place in the late 60s. Moreover, if the Beloved Disciple is a historical figure (and this, in our opinion, is virtually dictated by the evidence—see Part VII below), then, seemingly at a considerable interval after Peter's death, a long-lived eyewitness of the ministry of Jesus passed away—an eyewitness who was intimately connected with the Fourth Gospel. The discussion in the COMMENT on xxi 22–23 is really intelligible only in these terms; for why would there arise a problem about this disciple's dying before the return of Jesus if the disciple were alive and healthy? The intricate reasoning around the more obvious interpretation of Jesus' statement is a patently desperate attempt to justify what is a *fait accompli.* Indeed, the tone of crisis in the chapter would seem to indicate that this disciple's death marks the end of an era in the Church and the close of the period of the eyewitnesses. Once again a date much earlier than 80 makes all of this implausible, and a date in the 90s seems more likely. It may be noted that another NT work that is concerned with the same problem of the passing of the apostolic generation, namely II Peter (iii 3–4), is generally considered by critics, Protestant and Catholic, to be one of the latest of the NT works (although we think that there is no compelling reason for dating II Peter later than ca. 125).

In Part VIII we shall present our understanding of the basic theological problems of the Gospel; these problems, as we understand them, demand a date after 70. The realized eschatology which dominates the Gospel seems to be an answer to the indefinite delay in the Parousia. As it appeared before 70, the problem of the Parousia was subject to rather facile answer—Jesus would come again soon, but the exact time could not be set.

If I Peter is to be dated before 70, we have an eloquent witness that the immediacy of the Parousia was still very much a part of Christian expectation right up to the fall of Jerusalem (I Pet iv 7). The radical reinterpretation of the question in John which puts the major emphasis on realized eschatology (without excluding a continued but indefinite expectation of a final coming) seems to belong to a later period. Similarly, as we hope App. V (in vol. 29A) will show, the whole doctrine of the Paraclete as the continued presence of Jesus in his Church seems to be called forth by the passing of the apostolic period and the severance of the human links with Jesus of Nazareth. The sacramentalism of the Gospel, aimed at rooting the sacraments in the ministry of Jesus, seems directed to an age where the relationship between Church life and the historical life of Jesus has grown dim.

In sum, then, we believe that the span of time during which the final form of the Fourth Gospel may have been written is, at its outermost limits, A.D. 75 to 110, but the convergence of probabilities points strongly to a date between 90 and 100. The testimony given about 200 by Irenaeus (Eusebius *Hist.* III 23:1–4; GCS 9^1:236–38), our most important early witness to the Fourth Gospel, says that John, the disciple associated with the Gospel, lived on at Ephesus into the reign of Trajan (98–117). If one accepts this early attribution of the Gospel (see Part VII below) and combines it with the implication in John xxi 20–24 that the disciple responsible for the Gospel is dying or has died, one might settle on a plausible date of ca. 100 for the *final redaction* of the Gospel. If the historical tradition underlying the Gospel goes back to 40–60, and the first edition of the Gospel is dated somewhere between 70 and 85 (a dating which is very much a guess), then the five stages we have posited in the composition of the Gospel would cover over forty years of preaching and writing.

BIBLIOGRAPHY

General

Andrews, Mary E., "The Authorship and Significance of the Gospel of John," JBL 64 (1945), 183–92.

Goodenough, E. R., "John a Primitive Gospel," JBL 64 (1945), 145–82.

Turner, G. A., "The Date and Purpose of the Gospel of John," *Bulletin of the Evangelical Theological Society* 6 (1963), 82–85.

John and 2nd-Century Writers

Boismard, M.-E., "Clément de Rome et l'Evangile de Jean," RB 55 (1948), 376–87.

Maurer, Christian, *Ignatius von Antiochien und das Johannesevangelium* (Zürich: Zwingli, 1949).

Romanides, J. S., "Justin Martyr and the Fourth Gospel," *Greek Orthodox Theological Review* 4 (1958–59), 115–34.

Sanders, J. N., *The Fourth Gospel in the Early Church* (Cambridge: 1943).

Tarelli, C. C., "Clement of Rome and the Fourth Gospel," JTS 48 (1947), 208–9.

VII. THE IDENTITY OF THE AUTHOR AND THE PLACE OF COMPOSITION

It is notorious that many biblical scholars are also passionate readers of detective stories. These two interests come together in the quest to identify the author of the Fourth Gospel. Before we discuss the evidence, it may be wise to clarify the concept of "author." In the terminology of modern literary criticism "author" and "writer" are often synonymous terms; when they are not, it is customary to identify the literary collaborator as well as the main author. Antiquity did not share this fine sense of proper credits, and frequently the men whose names were attached to biblical books never set pen to papyrus. Therefore, in considering biblical books, many times we have to distinguish between the *author* whose ideas the book expresses and the *writer*. The writers run the gamut from recording secretaries who slavishly copied down the author's dictation to highly independent collaborators who, working from a sketch of the author's ideas, gave their own literary style to the final work. That some distinction between author and writer may be helpful in considering the Fourth Gospel is suggested by the existence of several NT Johannine works which betray differences in style. The question of stylistic differences between John and I John will be discussed in the introduction to the commentary on the Epistles; but the necessity of positing different writers for John and Revelation is indeed obvious.

Even if we confine authorship to responsibility for the basic ideas that appear in a book, the principles that determine the attribution of authorship in the Bible are fairly broad. If a particular author is surrounded by a group of disciples who carry on his thought even after his death, their works may be attributed to him as author. The Book of Isaiah was the work of at least three principal contributors, and its composition covered a period of over 200 years. Yet it is not simply a miscellaneous anthology; for it has similarities of theme and style which reflect a school of thought and which, in the broad biblical sense of authorship, justify the attribution of the book to Isaiah. In an even wider application of authorship, Solomon is spoken of as the author of the Wisdom Literature (Proverbs, Ecclesiastes, Wisdom of Solomon) because his court offered an atmosphere in which formal wisdom literature could develop and thus he served as the patron of the wisdom writers. In a similar way David is spoken of as author of the Psalms, and Moses as author of the Pentateuch, even though parts of these works were composed many hundreds of years after the traditional author's death. As we now turn to the early testimonies about the authorship of the

Fourth Gospel, we must keep before us the broad content of the ancient conception of authorship, lest we tend to make these testimonies say more than they were meant to say. Sometimes the "author" of a book is simply a designation for the *authority* behind it.

A. THE EXTERNAL EVIDENCE ABOUT THE AUTHOR

This evidence consists in the statements of early Christian writers and is conveniently available in the commentaries of Bernard and Barrett. It has been thoroughly discussed by Nunn. We shall offer only a summary here. Irenaeus (ca. 180–200) in *Adv. Haer.* III 1:1 (SC 34:96) says that, after the writing of the other Gospels, John, the disciple of the Lord who reclined on his bosom (John xiii 23, xxi 20), published his Gospel at Ephesus. Stemming from the same period, there are other early witnesses to authorship by John the disciple of the Lord (Barrett, pp. 96–97; Bernard, I, pp. lvi–lix): the Muratorian Fragment (ca. 170–200); the Latin anti-Marcionite Prologue (ca. 200); and Clement of Alexandria as cited in Eusebius *Hist.* VI 14:7 (GCS 9²:550). If this tradition of authorship was well established by the end of the 2nd century, it seems probable that the authors of these testimonies were identifying "John the disciple" as John son of Zebedee, one of the Twelve (even though Sanders, *art. cit.,* challenges this). Irenaeus does not state that he is speaking of the son of Zebedee (but see Eusebius *Hist.* VII 25:7 [GCS 9²:692] and the Leucian *Acts of John* [ca. 150]). Yet even if we accept the evidence that the ancient writers were speaking of the son of Zebedee, another question remains, namely, whether they were right in so identifying this John to whom the Gospel was customarily attributed—a question which we shall discuss below.

The first question that must be asked, however, concerns the value of the tradition that the Fourth Gospel came from *John,* a disciple of the Lord. The Gospel itself speaks of the Beloved Disciple who rested on the Lord's bosom: was Irenaeus simply guessing that this unnamed disciple was John? There is a good indication that he was not, for according to Eusebius *Hist.* IV 14:3–8 (GCS 9¹:332), Irenaeus got his information from Polycarp, bishop of Smyrna, who had heard John. If a chain of tradition from John to Polycarp to Irenaeus can be established, then Irenaeus' testimony to authorship is very valuable indeed. But the correctness of the chain of tradition has been contested on several scores.

a. Irenaeus places John at Ephesus, and there is no NT evidence that John son of Zebedee was ever at Ephesus. It is true that Revelation (i 9) purports to have been written at Patmos near Ephesus by a John, but was this John the son of Zebedee? In Rev xviii 20 and xxi 14 the author refers to the Twelve as if he were not one of their number—scarcely a conclusive objection, but one worth considering. As for the career of the son of Zebedee, he seems to have been active in the Jerusalem and Palestine area at least until A.D. 49 (Acts iii 1, viii 14; Gal ii 9). Neither in Paul's address to the elders of Ephesus in 58 (Acts xx 18 ff.) nor in the Epistle to the Ephesians (63?) is there any indication of John's presence at Ephesus. To the theory that John went to Ephesus at the time of the revolt in Palestine (66–70) it may be objected that in Ignatius' *Letter to the Ephesians* (ca. 110) the work of Paul at Ephesus is mentioned, but nothing of John. Papias who writes from Asia Minor ca. 130 does not seem to mention John's stay in Asia. That Polycarp of Smyrna in his short letter to the Philippians (ca. 135) does not mention John is not surprising, but we should note that the somewhat legendary life of Polycarp by Pionius does not refer to Polycarp's having known John, a detail which is basic to Irenaeus' evidence.

No argument from negative evidence is, of course, conclusive, and there is some impressive evidence that John the son of Zebedee was actually at Ephesus. Justin, at Ephesus ca. 135, speaks of John, one of the apostles of Christ, as having resided there (*Trypho* LXXXI 4; PG 6:669; with Eusebius *Hist.* IV 18:6–8; GCS 9^1:364–66). Could a spurious tradition have developed so soon? The apocryphal *Acts of John*, written ca. 150 by Leucius Charinus, mentions the ministry of John at Ephesus. Polycrates, bishop of Ephesus, writing to Pope Victor about 190 (Eusebius *Hist.* v 24:3; GCS 9^1:490), claims that John was buried at Ephesus. Excavations at Selçuk, a hill near Ephesus, beneath the basilica later built in honor of John, have shown the existence of a mausoleum from the 3rd century; and Braun, JeanThéol, I, p. 374, thinks that this confirms the testimony of Polycrates. Thus, the objection to Irenaeus' tradition on the grounds that John was never at Ephesus is scarcely conclusive.

b. There is a tradition that John son of Zebedee died as a young man. Both summarized evidence drawn from Philip of Side (430) and George Hamartolus (9th century) attribute to Papias the tradition that John was killed by the Jews along with his brother James (who died in the 40s). Two martyrologies from Edessa and Carthage (5th–6th centuries) have the same tradition. A full discussion can be found in Bernard, I, pp. xxxvii–xlv, but the reliability of these sources is not particularly impressive. In part the tradition probably results from a confusion of John the Baptist with John son of Zebedee, and in part from an overliteral interpretation of Mark x 39, where Jesus predicts that the sons of Zebedee will share his suffering. This argument against Irenaeus' tradition is very weak.

c. It has been suggested that Irenaeus was wrong about Polycarp's relation to John, as seemingly he was wrong in other instances. In *Adv. Haer.* v 33:4 (PG 7:1214) he says that Papias heard John; but this contradicts Papias' own evidence, as Eusebius (*Hist.* III 39:2; GCS 9^1:286) was quick to point out. If Papias knew John only through intermediaries, and Irenaeus was simplifying the relationship between Papias and John, how do we know that he was not simplifying the relationship between Polycarp and John? Of course, Irenaeus says that he knew Polycarp personally, while he does not claim to have known Papias. Nevertheless, the fact that Irenaeus would have been very young at the time he claims to have known Polycarp makes confusion at least a possibility.

d. It has been suggested that there was at Ephesus another John who was the author of the Gospel, and that Irenaeus and other early writers confused this John with the son of Zebedee who was a disciple of the Lord. (This proposal is somewhat different from the suggestion already noted that, in speaking of John the disciple of the Lord, Irenaeus did not mean the son of Zebedee; yet many of the points made below will be relevant to both suggestions.) Several candidates have been proposed for this other John of Ephesus.

First, we may mention John Mark who figures in Acts as a relative of Barnabas and a part-time companion of Paul. That John Mark was at Ephesus is mentioned in II Tim iv 11. No real difficulty is offered by the tradition that associates John Mark with the see of Alexandria rather than of Ephesus, for this tradition does not appear until the 4th century (Eusebius *Hist.* II 16:1 and 24:1; GCS 9[1]:140, 174). Moreover, in two very interesting articles Bruns has shown that there was confusion in antiquity between John son of Zebedee and John Mark. In commenting on Acts xii 12, Chrysostom seems to have thought that the John mentioned there was John the disciple, when it is commonly agreed that it was John Mark (Bruns, "John Mark," p. 91). A 5th-century Egyptian witness identifies John Mark as the unnamed disciple of John i 35. A 6th-century tradition from Cyprus says that Jesus met John Mark when he performed the miracle at the pool of Bethesda, a miracle narrated only in the Fourth Gospel, and speaks of the presence of this John at Ephesus. Spanish church writers of the 6th–8th centuries identify John the disciple as a relative of Barnabas. A 10th-century Arabic work, drawing on earlier fragments, identifies John Mark as one of the servants who handled the water-made-wine at Cana, another miracle found only in the Fourth Gospel. All of this information may be reinforced when Morton Smith publishes his recently discovered letter of Clement of Alexandria which pertains to a secret gospel of Mark, a gospel that seems to narrate or echo Johannine stories.

This material indicates a possibility of confusion in antiquity, although some of the references are clearly worthless. It must be noted that there is not thus far any ancient testimony which identifies John Mark as the author of the Fourth Gospel. When John Mark is identified as an evangelist, he is associated with the Gospel of Mark (3rd-century Monarchian Prologue to the Second Gospel). If any persuasive argument can be made for John Mark's authorship of the Fourth Gospel, it stems from internal evidence and will be discussed below.

Second, we may mention John the Presbyter, named by Papias, bishop of Hierapolis in Asia Minor. Writing ca. 130 (Eusebius *Hist.* III 39:4; GCS 9[1]:286), Papias tells us how he sought after Christian truth in this out-of-the-way town: "If, then, anyone came who had been a follower of the elders [*presbyteroi*], I inquired into the sayings of the elders—what Andrew, or what Peter said, or what Philip, or Thomas, or James, or JOHN, or Matthew, or any of the other disciples of the Lord said; and the things which Aristion and the elder [*presbyteros*] JOHN, disciples of the Lord, were saying." In this statement Papias seemingly mentions two groups of men, both of whom he calls "disciples of the Lord," and there is a John in each group. The first group contains the names of the Twelve who from the past tense of the verb ("said") would appear to have been dead, and thus one may identify the John in the first group as the son of Zebedee. The second group contains two men, Aristion and John, who perhaps were among the larger number of Jesus' disciples outside the Twelve (see Luke x 1); from the present tense of the verb, they would seem to have still been alive when Papias made his inquiries. Some scholars have objected that eyewitness disciples of the Lord could scarcely still have been alive in A.D. 130, and have proposed that this second group consisted of disciples of the Apostles and thus of second generation disciples ("presbyter" can have this meaning). It must be pointed out, however, that while Papias may have been writing ca. 130, he speaks of past inquiries, perhaps made many years before and at a time when disciples of the Lord could have still been alive.

Thus, it seems that besides speaking of the son of Zebedee, Papias speaks of another John who was in a position to communicate information about Jesus, whether or not he was an eyewitness himself. (The attempts of Zahn and others to maintain that Papias speaks twice of the same John seem forced.) Papias does *not* say that this John lived at Ephesus or that he wrote anything. That this John did live at Ephesus is supposed by later writers. The 4th-century *Apostolic Constitutions* VII 46 (Funk ed., pp. 453–55), in mentioning bishops at Ephesus, speaks of a John appointed by John, seemingly John the Presbyter appointed by John the Apostle. Eusebius *Hist.* III 39:6 (GCS 9¹:288) cites a report that there were two tombs or funerary monuments at Ephesus bearing the name "John." Both this passage and also Dionysius of Alexandria whom Eusebius quotes (*Hist.* VII 25:6–16; GCS 9²:694–96) suggest literary activity for John the Presbyter, namely, that he was the visionary author of Revelation. Such a suggestion is aimed at freeing the son of Zebedee from responsibility for the millenarianism of that book.

Once again, then, there is not the slightest positive evidence in antiquity for making John the Presbyter the author of the Fourth Gospel. Indeed, the evidence after Papias that mentions John the Presbyter affirms that John son of Zebedee was also at Ephesus and was the author of the Gospel. That the evangelist was John the Presbyter is a modern theory. It has been observed that the author of II and III John calls himself a presbyter, and that one may make a case for having this same presbyter as author of I John and of the Gospel. However, the common authorship of Gospel and Epistles is disputed; and even if it is admitted, the title "presbyter," found in II and III John, would be applicable to John son of Zebedee. We have evidence in I Pet v 1 that the term "presbyter" was used for members of the

Twelve; and indeed the statement of Papias with which we began this discussion seems to use the term "elders" or "presbyters" for the first group of men mentioned who are definitely members of the Twelve. Consequently, we may observe that there is certainly very little evidence to support John the Presbyter as the author of the Fourth Gospel, but the presence of two Johns does create the possibility of confusion in the later patristic evidence as to who wrote the Gospel.

e. A final factor that has caused some to doubt the evidence of Irenaeus is the existence in antiquity of groups who denied that the Fourth Gospel was written by John son of Zebedee. Irenaeus, *Adv. Haer.* III 11:9 (SC 34:202), mentions those erroneous teachers who, in their anxiety to combat the false Montanist charismatics and prophets, refused to admit the gift of the Spirit. This forced them to reject the Gospel according to John in which the Lord had promised to send the Paraclete. Tertullian, *Adv. Marcion* IV 2 (CSEL 47:426), hints at an uneasiness about the Fourth Gospel because of the difficulty of harmonizing its chronology with that of the Synoptics. In his *Adv. Haer.* LI (GCS 31:248 ff.) Epiphanius (ca. 375, but drawing on the earlier work of Hippolytus of Rome, a pupil of Irenaeus) mentions that the Alogoi attributed both Revelation and John to the heretic Cerinthus. The name Alogoi, reflecting the Greek for "no *logos*," seems to be a sobriquet made up to designate those who rejected the Gospel which begins with a Prologue concerning the *logos*. Hippolytus is supposed to have written a book in defense of the Fourth Gospel. Scholars will argue that such opposition to the Gospel could scarcely have developed if the Gospel were commonly attributed to an Apostle. However, we cannot overlook the fact that these fringe groups, who for their own theological purposes rejected the Fourth Gospel, were looked on as heretics; and the audacity of heretical groups in their scriptural views, for example, the Marcionites, should not be underestimated. It does not seem that there is real evidence of a widespread doubt in the early Church about Johannine authorship.

Thus, it is fair to say that the only ancient tradition about the authorship of the Fourth Gospel for which any considerable body of evidence can be adduced is that it is the work of John son of Zebedee. There are some valid points in the objections raised to this tradition, but Irenaeus' statement is far from having been disproved.

B. THE INTERNAL EVIDENCE ABOUT THE AUTHOR

Both explicitly and implicitly the Fourth Gospel tells us something about its author. Let us begin by concentrating on the explicit evidence. Two passages identify the source of the tradition which is found in the Gospel. In xix 35 we are told that one who had seen the piercing of Jesus' side during the crucifixion had given testimony and his testimony was true. The eyewitness at Calvary is not clearly identified, but just before this passage, in xix 26–27, we hear of the presence of the disciple whom Jesus loved at the

foot of the cross. A clearer passage is found in xxi 24 where we are told of
the disciple whom Jesus loved: "It is this same disciple who is the witness for
these things; it is he who wrote these things; and his testimony, we know, is
true." It is not certain from this verse whether the disciple in question
physically wrote these things or caused them to be written. "These things"
might refer only to the events in ch. xxi; but since this is obviously a
reference to the same eyewitness as in xix 35, the disciple in question is being
proposed as the source for the whole Gospel narrative. It will be noted that
the statement in xxi 24 clearly distinguishes the disciple from the writer of
ch. xxi (the "we").

How are these two passages to be evaluated? Chapter xxi is an addition to
the Gospel and belongs to the final redaction. The other passage, xix 35,
is a parenthesis, probably added in the editing of the Gospel. Therefore, we
cannot be certain that in the first edition of the Gospel there was such an
attribution of the Gospel tradition to an eyewitness disciple. Nevertheless,
even if this attribution belongs to the latest pre-publication stage of the
Gospel, it would seem to represent the view prevalent in Johannine circles
at the end of the 1st century. It is true that such an attribution may have
been added to the Gospel as an attempt to clothe an anonymous work with
the mantle of apostolic authority, but an attribution without a personal
name does not seem specific enough for that purpose. At any rate, before
any such concession is made, the first task is to see if the attribution can be
taken at face value.

Who is this disciple whom Jesus loved? There are three types of references
to anonymous disciples in the Fourth Gospel:

(a) In i 37–42 two disciples of John the Baptist follow Jesus. One is
named: Andrew; the other is unnamed. In the immediate context other
disciples appear: Simon Peter, Philip, and Nathanael.

(b) There are two passages that mention "another disciple" or "the other
disciple":

▪ xviii 15–16: Peter and another disciple follow Jesus, who has been taken
  captive, to the palace of the high priest. The other disciple is known
  to the high priest and gets Peter into the palace.

▪ xx 2–10: Mary Magdalene runs to Peter and to the other disciple (the one
  whom Jesus loved) to tell them that Jesus' body is not in the tomb. The
  other disciple outruns Peter to the tomb. Peter enters first; then the other
  disciple enters, sees, and believes.

(c) There are six passages that mention the disciple whom Jesus loved
(the verb "to love" is *agapan* in all the instances except xx 2 where *philein*
is used):

▪ xiii 23–26: The disciple whom Jesus loved leans back against Jesus' chest
  during the Last Supper, and Simon Peter signals to him to ask Jesus about
  the betrayer.

▪ xix 25–27: The disciple whom Jesus loved stands near the cross, and Jesus
  gives Mary to this disciple as his mother.

▪ xx 2–10: The "other disciple" mentioned under (b) above is parenthetically identified as "the one whom Jesus loved." For the content of the scene see above.

■ xxi 7: The disciple whom Jesus loved is in a fishing boat with Simon Peter and the other disciples; he recognizes the resurrected Jesus standing on the shore and tells Peter.

■ xxi 20–23: The disciple whom Jesus loved is following Peter and Jesus; the writer parenthetically reminds us that he is the same disciple spoken of in xiii 23–26. Peter turns and sees the disciple and asks Jesus about him. Jesus says that possibly the disciple will remain alive until he himself returns. The writer says that this statement of Jesus created confusion among the Christians who began to believe that the disciple would not die. Reading between the lines, we may assume that the disciple has died, whence the need of explanation.

■ xxi 24: The writer tells us that this disciple is the source of the things that have been narrated.

In comparing these types of references, we find that xx 2 identifies the Beloved Disciple (henceforth BD) with the other disciple mentioned in the second passage of (b). It is not clear whether or not the BD is also to be identified with the other disciple in the first passage under (b); but an affirmative answer is suggested by the fact that the disciple in this scene (xviii 15–16) is associated with Peter, an association which seems to be a mark of the BD. There is nothing that would clearly identify the unnamed disciple in (a) as the BD, although Peter is once more in the context, albeit less directly. Thus, it is to be noted that at least in the second passage under (b) and in (c) we have the same anonymous disciple who is known in two different ways, as "the other disciple" and as "the disciple whom Jesus loved." If modesty was what led this eyewitness not to refer to himself by name in reporting traditional stories about Jesus, it is difficult to believe that he would constantly call attention to the special love that Jesus had for him. A plausible solution is that the eyewitness disciple referred to himself simply as "the other disciple," and that it was his own followers who referred to him as the BD. This suggestion receives some confirmation from xx 2 where "the one whom Jesus loved" is obviously a parenthetical addition to identify "the other disciple." Let us now discuss the various solutions proposed for the identity of the BD.

First, it has been proposed that the BD is not a real figure but a symbol. For Loisy, p. 128, he is the perfect Christian disciple, close to Jesus at the Last Supper and the hour of death, the first to believe in the risen Christ. For Kragerud, the BD is the symbol of the Johannine school of thought. For Bultmann, pp. 369 ff., in several scenes the BD represents the Hellenistic branch of the Christian Church. In xix 26 Jesus leaves his mother (=Jewish Christianity) in the care of the BD (=Hellenistic Church). In xx 2–10 the BD (Hellenistic Church) outstrips Peter (Jewish Church) in believing. Actually this is a revival of ancient symbolism; Gregory the Great (*Hom. in Evang.* II 22; PL 76:1175) found the same symbolism that

Bultmann finds, only in reverse order, for the BD in Gregory's thought represents the Synagogue and Peter represents the Church.

That the BD has a figurative dimension is patent. In many ways he is the exemplary Christian, for in the NT "beloved" is a form of address for fellow Christians. Yet this symbolic dimension does not mean that the BD is nothing but a symbol. One may accept a symbolic dimension for Mary and Peter, as Bultmann does; but that does not reduce these characters to pure symbols. The obvious import of the passages in John that describe the BD is that he is a real human being whose actions are important on the Gospel scene. And so we do not believe that the recognition of the secondary, symbolic dimension of the BD obviates the quest for his identity.

Second, Lazarus is the one male figure in the Gospel of whom it is specifically said that Jesus loved him. *Philein* or *philos* is used of Lazarus in xi 3, 11, 36; *agapan* is used in xi 5. (We note that usage of verbs in reference to the BD is just the opposite, for there *agapan* is more frequent.) Filson, *art. cit.,* argues that the Gospel was meant to be self-intelligible to its readers, who would have no recourse to a 2nd-century tradition identifying the author as John son of Zebedee, and hence the BD should be interpreted by the Gospel's own reference to Jesus' love for Lazarus. (His argument is valid only if the readers were not well aware of the identity of the author even before they started the Gospel, and they may well have been aware of this if the author was a famous Apostle.) Eckhardt, *op. cit.,* goes even further by suggesting that Lazarus was a pseudonym for John son of Zebedee after he had been brought back from the dead by the power of Jesus! Sanders, *art. cit.,* p. 84, thinks that the basis of the Fourth Gospel was a work written in Aramaic by Lazarus (which was then edited by John Mark, who was the evangelist). It is worth noting that all the passages about the BD occur after the resurrection of Lazarus. It has been (facetiously?) suggested that the reason why the BD was the first to recognize the risen Christ in xxi 7 was because he was Lazarus who had gone through the same experience himself.

Yet it is hard to believe that the same person is spoken of anonymously in chs. xiii–xxi and is mentioned by name only in chs. xi and xii. It is true that chs. xi–xii may well represent Johannine material inserted at the later stage of Gospel editing or of final redaction, and this may account for the different usage in those chapters. But are we to suppose that the final redactor would have left such a glaring inconsistency and would not have introduced the designation of the BD into those chapters as well? We recognize, of course, that this objection is not insuperable: after all, in the Servant songs of Deutero-Isaiah the Servant is anonymous, while in other chapters the Servant is identified as Jacob-Israel. However, we wonder if it is not more logical to suppose that the BD is someone who is not named in the Gospel but was known to the readers.

Third, John Mark is another possible candidate for the role of the BD. Parker and Sanders have identified the author of the Fourth Gospel as John Mark (for Sanders the evangelist is not the same as the BD who is

Lazarus), a view maintained years ago by Wellhausen. There are a number
of factors that seem to support this and to make John Mark a good
candidate:

- John Mark's home was in Jerusalem (Acts xii 12), and most of the
  Fourth Gospel is centered on Jesus' ministry in Jerusalem. The correct
  geographical information peculiar to this Gospel pertains largely to the
  Jerusalem area.
- John Mark seems to have had relatives in the priestly class. His cousin
  Barnabas was a Levite (Col iv 10; Acts iv 36). Indeed, there are some
  ancient references to John Mark as a priest. The Fourth Gospel shows
  an interest in the Temple and feasts; and if the disciple of xviii 15
  was the BD, then he was known to the high priest.
- Through Paul, Mark seems to have been acquainted with Luke (Philem
  24), and this would account for cross-influence between the Lucan and
  the Johannine tradition.
- John Mark seems to have had contact with Peter (Acts xii 12; I Pet v 13),
  and the BD is constantly associated with Peter. The Fourth Gospel gives
  Peter a very important role.

Other arguments have been advanced, but these are the most striking.
There immediately springs to mind the objection that traditionally John
Mark is thought to have been the author of the Second Gospel, not of
the Fourth. However, as Bruns, "John Mark," p. 90, has pointed out, the
2nd-century witnesses to the Gospel of Mark never identify John Mark
with Mark the evangelist. It is worth noting that in Acts Luke never refers
to John Mark simply as Mark, and many patristic writers did not recognize
that the Mark of the Pauline letters was the John Mark of Acts.

A more basic objection may be offered to the thesis that John Mark was
the BD, namely, that it would seem logical that the BD was one of the
Twelve. His closeness to Jesus seems to have given him a position along
with Peter as one of the most important figures in the ministry. These are
the first two disciples to be informed of the empty tomb in xx 2. The position
of the BD next to Jesus at the Last Supper is another indication, for the
Synoptic Gospels describe this meal as one that Jesus shared with the
Twelve (Mark xiv 17; Matt xxvi 20). How then could the BD have been
John Mark (or for that matter, Lazarus), who is never mentioned in the
Synoptic account of the ministry? This would mean that the disciple who
was closest to Jesus was not even remembered in the lists of his specially
chosen disciples! The whole Christian world was waiting in expectation
for Jesus to return before the death of the BD (John xxi 23); yet if the
BD was John Mark, the Christian records do not even recall that Jesus
ever knew the man.

Fourth, John son of Zebedee seems to meet many of the basic requirements for identification as the BD. He was not only one of the Twelve, but,
along with Peter and James, one of the three disciples constantly selected
by Jesus to be with him. The close association with Peter posited in the
description of the BD would fit no other NT figure as well as it fits John

son of Zebedee. In the Synoptics, John appears with Peter more often than does any other disciple; and in the early history described in Acts, John and Peter are companions in Jerusalem (chs. iii–iv) and in the mission to Samaria (viii 14). The latter mission is very important in the light of what the Fourth Gospel says about a mission among the Samaritans (see p. 184).

An extremely important factor in discussing the identity of the BD is that the Fourth Gospel claims to preserve his memories of Jesus. If these are truly his memories, they survived even though they were often quite unlike the memories that went into the Petrine kerygma that underlies Mark and, through Mark, influenced Matthew and Luke. In other words, John's historical tradition is somewhat of a challenge to the general tradition shared by the Synoptics. Does it not seem likely that the man behind it would have had to be a man of real authority in the Church, a man of a status not unlike Peter's? In this respect John son of Zebedee would be a more likely prospect than a minor figure like John Mark.

There are other minor points that favor John son of Zebedee. It is quite possible that he was related to Jesus. In the NOTE on xix 25 we shall point out the reasons why it has been suggested that Salome was the mother of John and also the sister of Mary the mother of Jesus. If John was Mary's nephew, this would explain why Jesus entrusted his mother to John (xix 25–27). It might also explain one of the great problems about the BD; namely, that if "the other disciple" of xviii 15–16 was the BD, then the BD was known to the high priest. To explain how a Galilean fisherman like John would have had an "in" at the high priest's home, some would make John a purveyor of fish by appointment to the sacerdotal palace! Others fall back on the information of Polycrates of Ephesus (ca. 190) that John the BD was a priest who wore the priestly golden plate (Eusebius *Hist.* v 24:3; GCS 9¹:490). While the information of Polycrates that John was at Ephesus may warrant some confidence, the information about John's priesthood may well be a deduction from the passage we are considering. The same report was made in antiquity of James and Mark (of all three, Bernard, II, p. 594, takes this information seriously, pointing out that their priestly rank may explain why James and John, along with Peter, were important in the Jerusalem church according to Gal ii 9). But, if we leave aside Polycrates' report about John's priesthood, the possibility that John was Mary's nephew may help to explain his priestly connections, for Mary had relatives in the priestly family according to Luke i 5, 36 (although the historicity of this Lucan information is not accepted by all).

The most complete list of objections to the identification of John son of Zebedee as the BD is found in Parker's "John the Son of Zebedee," an article written to oppose the hypothesis, gradually returning to favor, that John was the author of the Gospel. In our personal judgment, some of the many objections he brings forward are unconvincing. For instance, the fact that the Fourth Gospel does not mention John's mother Salome or his brother James would not seem hard to understand; if John did not mention himself for reasons of anonymity, he might have extended this anonymity to his family. The following arguments are the ones that offer real difficulty:

- John was a Galilean, but this is a Gospel which gives dominant attention to the Jerusalem ministry of Jesus. The usual explanation is that, as one of Jesus' chosen three, John accompanied him on his various trips to Jerusalem. If John was a nephew of Mary, we may also recall that Mary had relatives in Judea (Luke i 39). The reason why the Fourth Gospel centers attention on Jerusalem is partly theological; there is no necessary implication that the author did not know of the extended Galilean ministry.
- Acts iv 13 describes the son of Zebedee as "illiterate and ignorant," scarcely attributes of the fourth evangelist. However, authorship, as we mentioned at the beginning of this part, does not necessarily mean that John physically wrote the Gospel or gave it its relatively smooth Greek phrasing. The Gospel claims that the BD was the source of its tradition, and that is what concerns us here.
- Two of the principal scenes of which John was a witness, the Transfiguration and the Agony in the Garden, are not mentioned in this Gospel. This is strange, unless we are to accept the somewhat forced suggestion that the BD's passion for anonymity caused him to omit scenes that could not be described without self-identification. It will be noted, however, that elements that appear in the Synoptic descriptions of the Transfiguration and the Agony also appear in the Fourth Gospel (see COMMENT on xii 23, 27–28); and, in *some* ways, as we hope to show, the treatment of that material in the Fourth Gospel may be more original than the Synoptic treatment.

There are, then, quite clearly, difficulties to be faced if one identifies the BD as John son of Zebedee. However, in our personal opinion, there are even more serious difficulties if he is identified as John Mark, as Lazarus, or as some unknown. When all is said and done, the combination of external and internal evidence associating the Fourth Gospel with John son of Zebedee makes this the strongest hypothesis, if one is prepared to give credence to the Gospel's claim of an eyewitness source.

C. CORRELATION OF THE HYPOTHESIS OF JOHN AS AUTHOR WITH A MODERN THEORY OF COMPOSITION

Does the Gospel's claim to have an eyewitness as source bear up under a modern critical analysis of the tradition underlying the Gospel? How can the claim that John son of Zebedee was the author be reconciled with the process of composition of the Gospel proposed in Part II? Would John have been responsible only for the historical tradition behind the Gospel (Stage 1)? This would seem to be the minimal proposal that one could make and still attribute authorship (in the ancient sense of "author"=authority) to John. Or does the evidence allow John to have been author in a more immediate way, in the sense that John was the preacher and theologian who shaped the historical material into the stories and discourses of the Gospel (Stages 2 and 3) and even edited the Gospel (Stage 4)?

Before attempting to answer these questions, we should recall that it cannot be maintained that John was the final redactor of the Gospel (Stage 5), because the "we" of xxi 24 is distinct from the BD, and also because the BD was probably dead when ch. xxi was written (xxi 22–23). This means that someone else besides John was involved in the Gospel; and, indeed, the ancient evidence does not attribute to John the undivided authorship of the Gospel, for almost every account of the composition associates others with John. Clement of Alexandria (Eusebius *Hist.* VI 14:7; GCS 9^2:550) says that John was encouraged by his disciples or companions. The Muratorian Fragment (ca. 170) also speaks of the instigation of John's fellow disciples and bishops, and says that John related "all things in his own name, aided by the *revision* of all." The Latin Preface to the Vulgate of John speaks of John's calling together his disciples in Ephesus before he died. The Latin anti-Marcionite Prologue (ca. 200) speaks of Papias' writing the Gospel at John's dictation. There is a 4th-century tradition that Marcion was the scribe of John; and in the 5th-century *Acts of John,* Prochorus, a disciple of John, claims to have been the scribe to whom John dictated the Gospel at Patmos. These attributions are legendary; but, taken as a whole, they constitute an ancient recognition that the disciples of John contributed to the Gospel as scribes or even as editors.

Turning now to the questions raised above, we may begin by asking whether the historical tradition behind the Fourth Gospel (Stage 1) reflects the testimony of an eyewitness. Of course, the very fact that we do posit historical tradition at least leaves it possible that John stands behind this Gospel, but there are still difficulties. Dodd is probably the greatest modern champion of an independent historical tradition underlying the Gospel, and yet he does not regard Johannine authorship as probable (*Tradition,* p. 17[1]). The basic difficulty is that, while in some instances the form of a story or saying underlying the Johannine account is more primitive than the form underlying the Synoptic account, in other instances it is more developed. How can such development be reconciled with the theory that the form stems from an eyewitness who presumably would remember exactly what happened?

In dealing with the Synoptic Gospels, where there is also marked development in the underlying historical tradition, critics stress that the evangelists themselves were not eyewitnesses and that the traditions they used stood, for the most part, at some distance in time and maturity from eyewitness testimony. In Mark, however, there appear with frequency scenes that have seemingly direct eyewitness characteristics, presumably because in these instances Mark is drawing on Peter's eyewitness. Some of the features in the historical tradition underlying John do betray memories that may have come without change from an eyewitness (see Part III:A above). But if one is to attribute the whole historical tradition to an eyewitness, then one must posit that this eyewitness exercised considerable freedom in adapting and developing his memories of what Jesus said and did. This does not seem improbable if we remember that the one who is presumed to have been the eyewitness, John son of Zebedee, was also an Apostle commissioned to preach Jesus to men. He would necessarily have had to adapt to his audience the tradition of which he was a living witness. The conception of the apostolic eyewitness as an impartial reporter whose chief interest was the detailed accuracy of the memories he related is an anachronism. (On this question the statement of the Catholic Pontifical Biblical Commission of April 21, 1964, is of interest, for it makes quite clear that the apostolic eyewitnesses were not passive channels of tradition: "They interpreted his words and deeds according to the needs of their listeners.")

In summation, then, the question of whether the historical tradition underlying John came from an eyewitness like John son of Zebedee can be answered scientifically only in terms of probability. On the one side of the scale is the fact that this tradition shows development. This is not an insuperable obstacle, and personally we believe that it is outweighed by the ancient tradition and the Gospel's own claim that it does represent the testimony of an eyewitness. Thus, we do not think it unscientific to maintain that John son of Zebedee was probably the source of the historical tradition behind the Fourth Gospel.

We may now turn to the question of whether an eyewitness (John) was also responsible for Stages 2 through 4 of the composition of the Gospel, where the historical tradition was formed into dramatic and polished narratives and into long discourses and finally into a carefully edited Gospel. Here the difficulties are more formidable. For instance, is it really conceivable that an eyewitness was responsible for the *final* form of the story of how Mary anointed Jesus (xii 1–7)? If modern criticism has any validity, then the anointing of Jesus' feet represents an amalgamation of diverse details from two independent stories, in one of which a woman anointed Jesus' head and in the other of which a sinful woman wept and her tears fell on his feet. Thus, in this and in many other instances there is a considerable distance between what is now in the Gospel and what critical investigation would reconstruct as the actual scene or saying in the ministry of Jesus—a distance that involves simplification, amplification, organization, dramatization, and theological development. Scholars will vary in estimating this distance, but all will agree that there *is* a distance. The process responsible for such development can only with the greatest difficulty be attributed to an eyewitness.

Here, in our opinion, probabilities favor another solution, for we may make use of the ancient evidence that the disciples of John played a role in the composition of the Gospel. Above we favored the suggestion that John son of Zebedee was the source of the underlying historical tradition which had already undergone some development in his own preaching. It is quite possible that his disciples, imbued with his spirit and under his guidance and encouragement, preached and developed his reminiscences even further, according to the needs of the community to which they ministered. Since the Gospel seems to imply that the BD lived longer than most of the other eyewitnesses, we need not suppose that the source of the historical tradition was closed off at the beginning of the disciples' preaching, for they could return to their master and share in more of his insights into the ministry of Jesus. (In part, this may explain the fact that some of the Johannine stories show greater polish and development than do other stories.) In particular, we would posit *one principal disciple* whose transmission of the historical material received from John was marked with dramatic genius and profound theological insight, and it is the preaching and teaching of this disciple which gave shape to the stories and discourses now found in the Fourth Gospel. In short, this disciple would have been responsible for Stages 2 through 4 of the composition of the Gospel, as we have posited them. An analogy has been suggested by P. Gaechter (ZKT 60 [1936], 161–87): the relation between the disciple who wrote the Fourth Gospel and the eyewitness who was his source is not unlike the relation between Mark and Peter. (Needless to say, this analogy would have to be qualified.) We give no name to the disciple-evangelist of the Fourth Gospel, although some may be attracted by the hypothesis of John the Presbyter.

The objection may be raised that, if John son of Zebedee was only the source of the historical tradition, then the disciple-evangelist was the real author of the Gospel; and the Gospel is not really the Gospel according to John. The very analogy of Mark and Peter may be used against our theory, for after all the Second Gospel did come out as the Gospel according to Mark, not as the Gospel according to Peter. There are two points that may be made in answer to this objection.

First, in the early Christian mentality the apostolic roots of a work were really more worthy of notice than the contributions of those who actually composed and wrote a work. Scholars differ in their judgments about NT authorship, but *some* would call upon such a principle to explain the attribution of II Peter to Peter and the Pastorals to Paul. The fact that the Second Gospel was attributed to Mark and not to Peter is probably not to be solved in terms of how much or how little Mark worked over Peter's tradition, but in terms of the fact that Mark was known in the early Church as a companion of Paul, Barnabas, and Peter. (Thus, we assume the modern identification of Mark with John Mark of Acts to be correct, even though that identification seems to have been ignored in the 2nd century.) The First Gospel reflects a situation that is just the opposite. The relation of the first evangelist to Matthew was probably far more tenuous than the dependence of Mark upon Peter; but the first evangelist was not a well-known figure, and so his Gospel came to be named after his somewhat distant apostolic source. The fact that the disciple-evangelist of the Fourth Gospel was not famous was probably a factor in the naming of that Gospel.

But there is a *second* and more important consideration. We suggest that John's relationship to his disciples was much closer than Peter's relationship to Mark (who in his earlier days was closer to Paul), and that the Fourth Gospel is truly in the spirit of John. Admittedly we are speculating here, but the ancient references to John's disciples do seem to imply a closeness between the master and those who gathered around him. And so when we speak of disciples, we are thinking of men thoroughly formed in John's own thought patterns. In our personal understanding of the Gospel, it would not be exact to say that John's influence was confined to supplying the historical tradition, for the development of this material in Stages 2 through 4 is a continuation along the lines of the development already found in Stage 1. (And that is why it is often very difficult to be certain whether a particular aspect of a story or exposition of a saying of Jesus belongs to the historical tradition or is part of subsequent interpretation.) After all, the Gospel does seem to imply, at least in ch. xxi, that the BD remained alive as a continuing influence throughout the period when the Gospel was being written, so that it can be said (xxi 24): "It is he who wrote these things" (i.e., caused them to be written—see NOTE). On the other hand, this does not mean that the disciple-evangelist can be reduced to the role of John's secretary, but rather that the disciple's real formative contribution to the Gospel closely reflected his master's outlook.

As we mentioned in Part II, some evidence for this theory may be found in the fact that there are several Johannine works (Gospel, Epistles, Revelation) which share a distinctive theological milieu but betray differences of style and development. Barrett, p. 113, has suggested that the different pupils gathered around John were responsible for the three works (although the Epistles may be further subdivided). He thinks that Revelation is the work that is most directly John's, and with that we agree fully. Indeed, even the Greek of Revelation could have come from John, for it is far more primitive and Semitic than the more polished style of the Epistles and Gospel. If one is inclined to posit different writers for the Gospel and the Epistles, their closeness would seem to indicate that their writers belonged to the same school of thought; and thus the suggestion that they were different disciples of John is quite plausible. (We shall leave to the Introduction to the Epistles [The Anchor Bible, vol. 30] a thorough discussion of this question and an exposition of our own views.) And, of course, we find the hand of another disciple of John, and probably one closely associated with the evangelist, in the final redaction of the Gospel (Stage 5).

Once again, in order to be perfectly clear, we have no illusions that the theory of authorship advanced in this discussion has been, or can be, proved. It is an *ad hoc* theory, formulated with the intent of doing as much justice as possible to the ancient evidence, the witness of the Gospel itself, and the clear demands of critical scholarship. It will not satisfy anyone who is convinced that only one of these three sources of knowledge about the authorship of the Gospel need be taken seriously.

D. The Place of Composition

The early traditions about the composition of John mention Ephesus, and we shall mention below the internal evidence in favor of Ephesus. But first let us consider the other candidates.

Alexandria has had a certain following (Stather Hunt, Broomfield, J. N. Sanders for a while). The wide circulation of John in Egypt, as attested by the papyri, is a factor here. However, caution is demanded, for one reason why there are Egyptian papyri of any work is that the climate of Egypt was more favorable than that of the other Christian centers for the survival of papyri. The fact that Alexandria was the home of Philo, of the authors of the Hermetic Corpus, and of the Gnostic Valentinus has had some importance in the thinking of scholars who maintain that the Gospel was influenced by one or the other of these schools of thought.

Antioch or Syria is another candidate, and one upheld by W. Bauer and Burney. The possibility that Ignatius of Antioch draws on John is an important factor here. Whether or not there is direct literary dependence, the fact that there are similarities in Ignatius' theology to Johannine themes is enough to raise the question of whether they come from the same region. There is evidence of a tradition among Latin writers that Ignatius was a disciple of John (paraphrases by Rufinus of Eusebius *Hist.* III 36:1–2 [GCS 9¹:275] and by Jerome of Eusebius *Chronicle* [GCS 47:193–4]). For Syriac evidence of the same tradition in the 4th–6th centuries see C. F. Burney, *The Aramaic Origins of the Fourth Gospel* (Oxford: Clarendon, 1922), p. 130. Others draw an argument from the relations between I John and Matthew, since the latter is generally thought to have been a Gospel from Syria. The lack of close parallels between John and Matthew, however, render this argument dubious. Still another argument is based on resemblances between John and the *Odes of Solomon,* a Syrian work. In general, whatever is valid in these arguments can be explained if some Johannine thought made its way to Syria; there is really nothing here that would convince us that the Gospel was written in Syria.

Ephesus still remains the primary contender for identification as the place where John was composed. Besides the almost unanimous voice of the ancient witnesses who speak of the subject, we have an argument from the parallels between John and Revelation, for the latter work clearly belongs to the area of Ephesus. The anti-synagogue motif in the Gospel (see Part VI above) makes sense in the Ephesus region, for Rev ii 9 and iii 9 attest bitter anti-synagogue polemics in this area of Asia Minor. If there is in the Gospel a polemic against the disciples of John the Baptist, the NT mentions disciples baptized with John's baptism at only one place outside Palestine—Ephesus (Acts xix 1–7). If there are parallels between John and the Qumran scrolls, is it an accident that Qumran parallels are most visible in Colossians and Ephesians, epistles addressed to the Ephesus region? Any incipient anti-docetic and anti-Gnostic polemic would also have been at home on the Ephesus scene.

The question of the place of the Gospel's composition is not an extremely important one; but there is nothing in the internal evidence to give major support to any other theory than that which has ancient attestation; namely, that the Gospel was composed at Ephesus.

BIBLIOGRAPHY

Bruns, J. E., "John Mark: A Riddle within the Johannine Enigma," *Scripture* 15 (1963), 88–92.

————"The Confusion between John and John Mark in Antiquity," *Scripture* 17 (1965), 23–26.

Eckhardt, K. A., *Der Tod des Johannes* (Berlin: De Gruyter, 1961). See review in CBQ 24 (1962), 218–19.

Filson, F. V., "Who Was the Beloved Disciple?" JBL 68 (1949), 83–88.

Kragerud, A., *Der Lieblingsjünger im Johannesevangelium* (Oslo University, 1959). See review by M.-E. Boismard, RB 67 (1960), 405–10.

Nunn, H. P. V., *The Authorship of the Fourth Gospel* (Oxford: Blackwell, 1952).

Parker, P., "John and John Mark," JBL 79 (1960), 97–110.

————"John the Son of Zebedee and the Fourth Gospel," JBL 81 (1962), 35–43.

Sanders, J. N., "St. John on Patmos," NTS 9 (1962–63), 75–85.

VIII. CRUCIAL QUESTIONS IN JOHANNINE THEOLOGY

Obviously, a commentary does not give scope for a long treatment of Johannine theology. However, the approach that one takes to certain disputed questions in Johannine theology helps to determine one's whole outlook on the purpose and composition of the Gospel. These select questions will be treated briefly here.

A. ECCLESIOLOGY

The question of whether there is a theology of the Church in John has become a burning issue in Johannine studies. For Bultmann the evangelist was a converted Gnostic and one of the basic sources of the Gospel was Gnostic; therefore the Fourth Gospel cannot be expected to show a real sense of tradition, Church order, salvation history, or the sacraments (*Theology*, II, pp. 8–9, 91). In John (iv 23) the Church is a collection of individuals joined by personal faith to Jesus, rather than the people of God descended from Israel. There is no stress in John on the organic unity of the Church. E. Schweizer, *art. cit.*, does not share Bultmann's Gnostic preoccupations, but his conclusions about Johannine ecclesiology are not very different. On the other hand, for Barrett, p. 78, the fourth evangelist is more aware than any other evangelist of the existence of the Church. O. Cullmann, "L'évangile johannique et l'histoire du salut," NTS 11 (1964–65), 111–22, vigorously challenges Bultmann's contention that John has lost the perspective of salvation history.

Before we broach the problem, we must raise some methodological considerations. The argument from silence (i.e., an argument based on significant omission) plays an important role in the minimal views of Johannine ecclesiology. A tacit principle seems to be that what John does not mention, John is opposed to, or, at least, considers of minimal importance. Such a presupposition is not without its dangers, as we hope to show.

As our *first* example of the argument from silence, we may mention the claim that many ecclesial terms are not found in John. The Catholic scholar, D'Aragon, *art. cit.*, observes that we do not find in John descriptions of the Christian community as "church," or as "people of God," or as "body of Christ." There is no imagery of the community as a building. Other ecclesial terms occur but seldom: "bride" (iii 29); "kingdom of God" (iii 3, 5); "flock" (x 16). But how is such silence to be evaluated?

The terms cited are *NT* ecclesial terms; but, with the exception of "kingdom of God," they are not really *Gospel* terms. How would the Synoptic Gospels fare if this criterion of ecclesiology were applied to them? In these three Gospels, the term "church" in the strict sense occurs only in Matt xvi 18 (see Matt xviii 17). In Mark, only in one passage (ii 19–20) is there any use of the imagery of the bride/bridegroom to describe the relation of Jesus to his disciples, and Mark does not use the concept of the "people of God." Is not the real difficulty here that John's ecclesial terminology is being compared with that of works which are not Gospels, for example, the Pauline Epistles? The tacit assumption seems to be that if John were interested in the Church, John would be just as free as the Pauline Epistles in the use of later ecclesial vocabulary. However, if there is validity in the contention that John was dependent on a historical tradition of the words of Jesus, then there were rather narrow limits imposed on the vocabulary used in the Gospel. Certainly, Johannine thought represents a development and an expansion of what Jesus had taught during his ministry, but the format of a Gospel made it imperative to express this development in a way that was reasonably faithful to the vocabulary of Jesus. We cannot expect to find the evangelist placing flagrant anachronisms on the lips of Jesus—for example, to find the Johannine Jesus talking about his body which is the Church.

The *second* methodological consideration about the argument from silence concerns comparisons made between John and the other Gospels. It is noted that John fails to record some of the ecclesial expressions and scenes recorded in the Synoptic Gospels. For instance, Schweizer, p. 237, says of John: "He does not mention either the election (Mark 3:13 ff.) or the sending forth of the disciples (Mark 6:7 ff.)." As we shall see below, other scholars characterize John as non-sacramentalist because the Fourth Gospel omits the scenes pertaining to the Eucharist and Baptism which are found in the Synoptics. Yet the selection of Gospel scenes was very much determined by the purpose of the evangelist, and it is not to be expected that all the Gospels would express their ecclesiology in the same way. Does John really ignore the apostolic mission of the disciples? True, John gives no list of the Twelve and has no scene by the Sea of Galilee where the disciples are called to leave their fishing and follow Jesus. But is not the scene in i 35–50 the Johannine equivalent of the election of disciples? This election is presupposed in vi 70, xiii 18, and xv 16. A mission of the disciples is reflected in xv 16, xvii 18, xx 21, and is acted out in xxi 1–11. Thus, the idea of the mission of the Twelve is not lacking in John but is expressed in a way that is different from its presentation in the Synoptic Gospels. Similarly, it would not be true to state that John had no sense of a covenant with a new people of God because John failed to record the words of Jesus about the blood of the covenant (Mark xiv 24). The covenant theme appears in another form in John xx 17, "I am ascending . . . to my God and your God." This saying adapts to the new

Christian situation the covenant formula of Lev xxvi 12 and Exod vi 7: "I will be your God."

At times, the argument from silence can be turned around; for it may be that certain things are not mentioned in John, not because the evangelist disagrees with them but because he presupposes them. If the Gospel was written to show the Christians that their life in the Church was rooted in Jesus' own ministry, then, quite logically, we may suspect that the evangelist was presupposing the existence of ecclesiastical institutions and order and felt no need to prove the importance of the Church in Christian living. If the evangelist stressed the individual's union with Jesus, this need not have been because the evangelist was opposed to the intermediary aspect of the Church and the sacraments, but perhaps because he was opposed to the formalism which is the inevitable danger of established institutions and practices. Not the bypassing of these institutions but an attempt to ensure their meaningfulness may well have been the evangelist's purpose. His may not have been a disdain of the Church but a fear that the Church would gradually come to be thought of as an entity independent of the historical Jesus. Thus, one must be extremely careful in inferring the evangelist's motive from his silence.

In particular, Bultmann's approach to the Gospel leaves itself open to methodological objections on the question of ecclesiology (and of the sacraments). Bultmann recognizes that in the Gospel as it now stands there are clear references to the sacraments and to salvation history, but he regards these as the additions of the Ecclesiastical Redactor who imposed ecclesiology on the original Gospel. Sometimes there are solid reasons drawn from literary criticism for attributing such passages to the final redaction of the Gospel; but in other instances, as we shall see in the commentary (e.g., xix 34), one suspects that a passage is attributed to the redactor precisely because it is sacramental. Moreover, as we have insisted, the concept of the redactor as one who corrects the evangelist's theology is far from proved. If we are right in thinking of the redactor as a disciple of John and fellow disciple of the evangelist, then the more obvious ecclesiology of scenes added by the redactor may be simply a clarification and amplification of the evangelist's own outlook.

This leads us to the final methodological observation. Just as Acts is used along with the Gospel of Luke in a study of Lucan theology, so also must the other works of the Johannine school, Epistles and Revelation, be consulted before generalizing about the Johannine view of the Church. Feuillet and Schnackenburg have done this in their studies; and their interpretation of Johannine ecclesiology is, in our opinion, far more satisfactory than that of scholars who seem to posit a necessary opposition among these works, even though "the Johannine writings" have so much in common by way of style, ideology, and terminology. The limitations imposed on a Gospel by its format and its purpose warn us that a Gospel will necessarily be an incomplete index to its author's thoughts. Now, if John, I–III John, and Revelation stem from different writers within the

Johannine school, it is to be expected that these writers would not agree on every point. Nevertheless, quite often these other writings should be able to help us fill in points in Johannine theology on which the Gospel has been silent. Recourse to other Johannine works is in many instances far less risky than those speculative reconstructions of the evangelist's thought which have as their basis what he did *not* say.

With these cautions in mind, let us now turn to some of the disputed points in Johannine ecclesiology. The question of whether or not John has lost the perspective of salvation history will be treated under eschatology. But we may say here that there should be some qualification of the claim made by Schweizer, p. 240, that John does not picture the Church as a people based on an act of God in history. For John no Christian life is possible without the death, resurrection, and ascension of Jesus, for that salvific act of God in history is the source of the Spirit, which is the principle of the Christian life. John may not use the term "people" to describe those whose Christian status is dependent on this act of God; but, as we shall now see, that does not rule out other possible ways of indicating unity among believers.

(1) *The Question of Community.* Does the stress in John on an individual relationship with Jesus obviate the concept of community that is essential to ecclesiology? For instance, it has been claimed that the fourth evangelist took the vineyard, the OT symbol for the nation of Israel, and adapted it to the figure of a vine which represents Jesus and branches which represent Christians. Not collectivity but dependence on Jesus is now the thrust of the symbol. However, the symbolism of the vine and the branches is not that simple. As we shall point out in the COMMENT on ch. xv (The Anchor Bible, vol. 29A), the LXX in Ps lxxx 14–15 had already identified the vine with the "son of man," and so the identification of the vine as Jesus may have had roots, as it were, in an older tradition. The fact that in Dan vii a "son of man" is a human figure who represents the whole of God's people, and is thus a corporate person, warns us against too facilely cataloging the Johannine use of the vine and the branches as exclusively individualistic.

To the claim that John stresses unity with Jesus at the price of community, we should note the prayer of Jesus in xvii 22: ". . . that they may be one." In addition, we may question whether in the NT mind there was a sharp distinction between personal union with Jesus and community. It is interesting that at Qumran, for instance, the word *yahad,* which is the name for the community, emphasizes the unity of the members. A very important factor in this unity is the acceptance of a particular interpretation of the Law. *Mutatis mutandis* the same idea would be applicable to the Christian community and the adherence of the members to Jesus. One of the lessons of the symbol of the vine and the branches is that if one is to remain as a branch on the vine, one must remain in the love of Jesus (xv 9). Yet this love must be expressed in love for one's fellow believer (xv 12). No Gospel stresses as much as John does, the point that Christian love is a love of one's fellow disciples of Jesus, and thus a love within the Christian community.

Nor is the vine the only metaphor in the Gospel relevant to the Johannine concept of community. There is also the imagery of the flock and the sheep-fold in ch. x. Some have objected that in this parable "flock" or "sheep herd" is mentioned only once (x 16). But the imagery of the fold that implicitly runs throughout is also symbolic of community. In the larger body of Johannine literature, we find a strong stress on Christian community. I John ii 19 describes the anti-christs as those who have cut themselves off from the Christian community. Revelation xix 6–8 and xxi 2 use the imagery of the bride of Christ (also John iii 29); and Rev xxi 3 refers to the people of God, implicitly presenting the Christians as the heirs to Israel of old. It is true that in the Fourth Gospel there is no stress on blood continuity with Israel, a problem that bothered Paul. For John the true Israelite is Nathanael (i 47) who believes in Jesus. The true Israelite is not born of carnal lineage (i 13) but begotten of water and Spirit (iii 5); he is a child of God, not because Israel is God's child, but because he is a believer (i 12). But these believers are knit into community through faith in Jesus and their love for one another, and they are gathered from the whole world into one (xi 52).

(2) *The Question of Church Order.* The Johannine figure of the vine is often contrasted with the Pauline ecclesial imagery of the body. It has been pointed out (e.g., Schweizer, p. 236) that, while both figures portray Jesus as the source of life, there is no emphasis in John's symbol on the different functions of the various members of the community. For John what is important is that the members are united to Jesus, and there is no emphasis that some branches are the channels through which life passes from Jesus to others. By an argument from silence, this might imply that there is no sense of Church order in John. (Schweizer, p. 237, says of the Johannine picture of the Church: "It has no priests or officials. There is no longer any diversity of spiritual gifts. . . . There is no church order at all.") But is this a valid deduction? All our cautions above about the argument from silence apply here. From the symbolism of the vine and the branches, for instance, one may conclude that the evangelist wishes to stress union with Jesus, and this emphasis fits the purpose of the Gospel. But to go beyond that and posit that the evangelist is opposed to or indifferent to a structured Church is risky indeed.

Actually, there are passages in John that imply an order among those who believe in Jesus. In the Johannine treatment of the disciples there is a double aspect. Often they are the model for all Christians. As Via, p. 173, says, "For John the disciples represent the Church or are the Church in miniature, so that what he says about the disciples he understands about the Church." However, in some passages where Jesus speaks of the future, the disciples take on the aspects of Church leaders. In John xxi 15–17 Peter is entrusted with pastoral care over the flock. In iv 35–38 and xiii 20 it is implied that the disciples have a role in the Christian mission, and xx 23 gives them an authoritative power to absolve or hold fast men's sins. The other works of the Johannine school show a sense of Church order. I John ii 24 implies an authoritative teaching. Rev xxi 14 describes the heavenly Jerusalem as built upon the foundations of the Twelve Apostles. The description of the heavenly court in Rev iv may well reflect the seating arrangement of ecclesiastical authorities in the earthly liturgy of the writer's time. The fact, however, that the references just given come from different strains in the Johannine literature does make it difficult to make an over-all judgment on the evangelist's concept of Church order.

(3) *The Question of the Kingdom of God.* The omission in John of the formula *basileia tou theou,* "kingdom of God [or of heaven]," except for iii 3, 5, is a difficult problem, although not so formidable an obstacle to Johannine ecclesiology as it might first seem. The Synoptic emphasis on the *basileia* making itself felt in Jesus seems to have become in John an emphasis on Jesus who is *basileus* ("king") and who reigns. John refers to Jesus as king fifteen times, almost double the number of times that this reference occurs in any of the other Gospels. Moreover, the parables that the Synoptics associate with the *basileia* seem to give way in John to figurative speech centered about the person of Jesus. If the Synoptic *basileia* is like leaven working in a mass of dough, the Johannine Jesus is the bread of life. If there is a Synoptic parable of the shepherd and the lost sheep, the Johannine Jesus is the model shepherd. If the Synoptics record a parable where the *basileia* is like the vineyard which shall be handed over to others (Matt xxi 43), the Johannine Jesus is the vine.

To a certain extent this change of emphasis means that in John there is less apparent reference to collectivity than there is in the Synoptic concept of *basileia*. But we must not exaggerate. If Jesus is the king of Israel, he has an Israel of believers to rule over; if Jesus is the shepherd, he has a flock that has to be gathered; if Jesus is the vine, there are branches on the vine. Moreover, in comparing the symbolism of the Synoptics and of John on this point, we must have a precise understanding of what is meant in the Synoptic Gospels by *basileia tou theou*. The primary stress in this phrase is on God's reign or rule, and not on His kingdom—something active is meant, not something static; not a place or institution, but the exercise of God's power over the lives of men. Thus, the *basileia tou theou* is not simply the Church, and the rarity of the phrase in John does not necessarily reflect a lack of appreciation for the Church. In stressing the role of Jesus as *basileus* and in using parabolic language of Jesus himself (rather than of "the reign of God"), perhaps John brings out more clearly than do the Synoptics the role of Jesus in the *basileia tou theou*. But such a clarification is quite understandable in terms of the purpose of the Gospel.

In summation, there are passages in John which give a picture of a community of believers gathered by those whom Jesus sent out. This community is structured, for some are shepherds (at least Peter according to xxi 15–17) and others are sheep. That such ecclesiology does not receive major stress in the Gospel is quite intelligible if the evangelist was taking for granted the existence of the Church, its life and institutions, and attempting to relate this life directly to Jesus. That this was the case and that the evangelist was not opposed to an organized Church is suggested by the other Johannine works. In I John we find an orthodox and righteous community from which heretics are excluded; in Revelation we find a strong sense of the continuity between the Christian Church organized upon the Twelve Apostles and the Israel of the OT stemming from the twelve tribes.

B. SACRAMENTALISM

Perhaps on no other point of Johannine thought is there such sharp division among scholars as there is on the question of sacramentalism. On the one hand, there is a group of Johannine scholars, including both Protestants (Cullmann, Corell) and Catholics (Vawter, Niewalda), who find many references to the sacraments in John. This sacramental evaluation of the Fourth Gospel has been popularized in France by Bouyer's commentary on John, and in America by D. M. Stanley in a series of articles in the Catholic liturgical magazine *Worship*. In general, the British commentaries by Hoskyns, Lightfoot, and Barrett have shown themselves decidedly favorable to Johannine sacramentalism. Barrett, p. 69, states: ". . . there is more sacramental teaching in John than in the other Gospels." All of these scholars tend to see symbolic references to Baptism in Johannine passages which mention water, and to the Eucharist in Johannine passages dealing with meals, bread, wine, and vine. An even broader range of sacramental reference has been proposed by the Catholic writers, for example, to Matrimony at Cana, and to Extreme Unction in the scene of the anointing of the feet (xii 1–8). In our article on the subject, pp. 205–6, we give a list of some twenty-five proposed sacramental references in John! Almost all of these proposed sacramental references are by way of symbolism. The explanation of why the evangelist presented the sacraments through symbolism seems to lie in this principle: the recognition that OT prophecy had a fulfillment in the NT created a Christian sensitivity to typology; therefore, it was intelligible to present Jesus' words and actions as prophetic types of the Church's sacraments. Cullmann stresses that Baptism and the Eucharist were familiar to the early Christian communities, and that therefore symbolic references to them would be easily recognized. By associating Baptism and the Eucharist with Jesus' own words and actions, John is once more trying to show the roots of Church life in Jesus himself.

On the other hand, there is another group of Johannine scholars who see no references to the sacraments in John. For some of these, the original Gospel was anti-sacramental. Among those who take a minimal view of Johannine sacramentality one may list Bornkamm, Bultmann, Lohse, and Schweizer, noting however that their views vary widely. In general, they base their case on the lack of overt references to Baptism and the Eucharist in John. John narrates neither the eucharistic action of Jesus at the Last Supper nor an explicit baptismal command like Matt xxviii 19. Moreover, some would insist that in centering salvation on personal acceptance of Jesus as the one sent by God, John has created a theological atmosphere that would obviate material intermediaries like the sacraments. The emphasis in John is on word, not on sacrament. We have already called attention to Bultmann's attribution to the Ecclesiastical Redactor of what he considers the three clearly sacramental references in the Gospel (see p. xxx above). As for the symbolic references to the sacraments, these scholars of the non-sacramentalist school would simply regard the uncovering of much of this symbolism as eisegesis.

How are we to judge such radically opposed views? There are valid points made by each side. Let us begin with the more explicit Johannine references to the sacraments, those which Bultmann relegates to the Ecclesiastical Redactor. It will be seen in the COMMENT on vi 51–58 that we agree with Bultmann and Bornkamm that there are valid reasons for thinking that these verses were added to ch. vi. By not considering the valid literary arguments for such a view, some of the sacramentalist interpreters of John have weakened their case. But even if a more explicit reference to a sacrament, like vi 51–58, is an addition, the question must still be asked if this addition was designed to correct the evangelist's theology or to make his thought more explicit. Köster, *art. cit.*, pp. 62–63, is perfectly correct, for instance, in insisting that there was already a cultic and sacramental element present in ch. vi even without 51–58. Therefore, the recognition that some of the explicit sacramental references belong to the final redaction does not mean any acceptance of the theory that the original Gospel was non-sacramental or anti-sacramental. It is a question of seeing different degrees of sacramentality in the work of the evangelist and that of the final redactor.

When we turn to the implicit, symbolic Johannine references to the sacraments, we believe that many of the sacramentalist interpreters have not used truly scientific criteria in determining the presence of sacramental symbols. Their guiding principle seems to be that since a passage can be understood sacramentally, it was intended sacramentally. Not only Bultmann, but more conservative scholars like Michaelis and Schnackenburg have detected the danger of eisegesis here. For some of the sacramental references proposed by Cullmann and Niewalda, there is no evidence in the context that the evangelist so intended the passage. Faced with this difficulty, Niewalda has thrown aside as impractical the search for internal indications of the author's sacramental intent. He falls back on external evidence, namely, an indication in the early centuries that a passage of John was understood as a symbolic reference to a sacrament. For this purpose he consults the patristic writings, the liturgy, catacomb art, etc.

In the *art. cit.* we have presented a detailed exposition of our personal views on the necessary criteria for accepting symbolic sacramental references in John. In brief, we would accept the external evidence proposed by Niewalda as a *negative* criterion. If there is no evidence in the early Church that a passage of John was understood sacramentally, then one should be very suspicious of modern attempts to introduce a sacramental interpretation. We make the fundamental supposition that the evangelist intended his implicit references to the sacraments to be understood, and that some trace of that understanding would probably have survived in the early Christian use of the Gospel. The sacraments of Baptism and the Eucharist were popular themes among Christian writers and artists, and it is unlikely that they would have overlooked a Gospel passage that was generally understood to be a sacramental reference.

However, external evidence alone is insufficient as a *positive* criterion of sacramental reference. Many of the early Christian writers were not exegeting the Gospel but using it freely as a catechetical tool. Therefore, even though they may use a Johannine story, like that of the healing in ch. v, as an illustration of Christian Baptism, this is not a sufficient guarantee that the evangelist so intended the story. Often a considerable period of time separates the Gospel from the pertinent liturgical, literary, and artistic reference that would find a sacramental use for a passage of the Gospel. In that time a symbolism may have developed which was not part of the original Gospel.

And so, in addition to the negative check supplied by external evidence, we must have a positive indication within the text itself that the evangelist intended a reference to the sacraments. Of course, in determining what constitutes a positive indication, exegetes will disagree. Michaelis, for instance, in rejecting virtually all of Cullmann's examples, seems to demand from the evangelist the type of indication that we might expect in a 20th-century writer. This is to be overcritical, for the symbolism taken for granted in the 1st century may not seem at all obvious to the modern mind, much less attuned to symbolism. Who would have dared to see in the lifting up of the bronze serpent on the pole a symbol of the crucified Jesus if the evangelist himself had not indicated this (iii 14)? From the symbols that the Gospel itself has identified (for another example, see xxi 18–19), it is obvious that the evangelist's mentality was not at all the same as the mentality of the modern interpreter. As an example of what we would regard as adequate positive indication that the evangelist intended a sacramental reference, the reader may consult the COMMENT on the story of the healing of the blind man in ch. ix and of the washing of the feet in xiii 1–11.

Thus, the necessary criterion for recognizing symbolic references to the sacraments is found in the combination of internal indication and external, early Christian evidence. This criterion is not foolproof; but it does reduce considerably the dangers of eisegesis, while not exposing the Gospel to a minimalist exegesis. Using this criterion of combined evidence, we find that, in addition to the more explicit references to the sacraments, some of which may come from the final redactor, there is in the very substance of the Gospel a broad sacramental interest; and in this respect John is quite in harmony with the Church at large.

What then of the omission in John of sacramental passages found in the Synoptics? The absence of the scene often thought to represent the institution of Baptism (Matt xxviii 19) is not really a problem, since that scene is not found in Mark or Luke either. (And it should be noted that the classical theologians are not in agreement that the scene describes the institution of Baptism. There are some, for example, Estius, who would associate the institution with the Nicodemus scene found only in John. In any case this is a post-NT problem.) The omission of the eucharistic scene at the Last Supper is more difficult; but if the hypothesis in the commentary is correct, echoes of this scene have been incorporated into vi 51–58.

What a comparison with the Synoptics does show is that, while John may treat of Baptism and the Eucharist, this Gospel does not associate these sacraments with a single, all-important saying of Jesus uttered at the end of his life as part of his departing instructions to his disciples. The Johannine references to these two sacraments, both the more explicit references and those that are symbolic, are scattered in scenes throughout the ministry. This seems to fit in with the Gospel's intention to show how the institutions of the Christian life are rooted in what Jesus said and did in his life.

Moreover, among the four Gospels it is to John most of all that we owe the deep Christian understanding of the purpose of Baptism and the Eucharist. It is John who tells us that through baptismal water God begets children unto Himself and pours forth upon them His Spirit (iii 5, vii 37–39). Thus Baptism becomes a source of eternal life (iv 13–14), just as the Eucharist too is an indispensable means of transmitting God's life to men through Jesus (vi 57). In a symbolic way John shows that the eucharistic wine means a new dispensation replacing the old (the Cana scene, and the description of the vine in ch. xv) and that the eucharistic bread is the real bread from heaven replacing the manna (vi 32). Finally, in a dramatic scene (xix 34) John shows symbolically that both of these sacraments, baptismal water and eucharistic blood, have the source of their existence and power in the death of Jesus. This Johannine sacramentalism is neither merely anti-docetic nor peripheral, but shows the essential connection between the sacramental way of receiving life within the Church at the end of the 1st century and the way in which life was offered to those who heard Jesus in Palestine. If symbolism is used, it is because only through symbolism could the evangelist teach his sacramental theology and still remain faithful to the literary form of Gospel in which he was writing. He could not interpolate sacramental theology into the Gospel story by anachronistic and extraneous additions, but he could show the sacramental undertones of the words and works of Jesus that were already part of the Gospel tradition.

C. ESCHATOLOGY

There is an enormous body of literature dealing with NT eschatology, and the problem is so complicated that here we can touch lightly only the ramifications of the problem in John. Although almost every point about eschatology is disputed, including its definition, perhaps we can best approach Johannine eschatology under two headings.

(1) The "Vertical" and the "Horizontal" View of God's Salvific Action

If we use spatial terminology, we may characterize the general biblical view of salvation as "horizontal," for while God acts from above, He acts in and through the sequence of history. From the time of creation God has guided the world and men inexorably forward to a climax, a climax which is often seen in terms of divine intervention in the linear course of history. Thus, salvation lies either in history or as a climax to history. Opposed to this is a "vertical" view which sees two worlds coexistent, one heavenly, one earthly; and the earthly world is but a shadow of the heavenly. Earthly existence is fallen existence, and history is a prolongation of the meaningless. Salvation is made possible through escape to the heavenly world, and this can occur only when someone or something comes down from the heavenly world to set men free from earthly existence. Obviously these are simplified pictures of the two views, but we shall have to ask toward which view of history and salvation the Fourth Gospel inclines.

In many ways this Gospel betrays a vertical approach to salvation. The Son of Man has come down from heaven (iii 13), the Word has become flesh (i 14), with the purpose of offering salvation to men. The culmination of his career is when he is lifted up toward heaven in death and resurrection to draw all men to himself (xii 32). There is a constant contrast in John between two worlds: one above, the other below (iii 3, 31, viii 23); a sphere that belongs to Spirit, and a sphere that belongs to flesh (iii 6, vi 63). Jesus brings the life of the other world, "eternal life," to the men of this world; and death has no power over this life (xi 25). His gifts are "real" gifts, that is, heavenly gifts: the real water of life, as contrasted with ordinary water (iv 10–14); the real bread of life, as contrasted with perishable bread (vi 27); he is the real light that has come into the world (iii 19). These characteristics betraying an atemporal and vertical approach to salvation have constituted one of Bultmann's main arguments for advancing the hypothesis of Gnostic influence on John.

But there is also much of the horizontal approach to salvation in John. The Prologue, which describes the descent of the Word into human flesh, does not ignore salvation history which begins with creation. If the coming of Jesus represents the era of the dominance of Spirit over flesh, so that all men worship God in Spirit, Jewish history has been the preparation for this climactic era (iv 21–23). The whole of the Scriptures which record salvation history points to Jesus (v 39). The "hour" of which we hear so much in John (ii 4, viii 20, xii 23, etc.), the hour of Jesus' passion, death, resurrection, and ascension, is the culminating hour in the long history of God's dealing with men. Jewish customs, feasts, and religious institutions find their fulfillment in Jesus (see Outline in Part X).

Nor does history stop with this hour. It has been remarked that instead of writing a Gospel and a Book of Acts, the fourth evangelist has concentrated within the Gospel not only the eschatological hour of the ministry but also the whole "time of the Church." And thus it might be thought that with the intervention of Jesus there could be nothing more. But the evangelist, as we have suggested above, is presupposing the existence of a Church. His problem is not whether there will be a "time of the Church," but how this is related to Jesus. He presupposes Christian missionary activity (iv 35–38, xx 21), a conflict of Christianity with the world (xvi 8), an influx of those who will come to believe through the preaching of the word (xvii 20), and a gathering of them into a flock to be shepherded (xi 52, x 16, xxi 15–17). That we are correct in insisting that Johannine thought is not devoid of a horizontal outlook on salvation is also suggested in the Book of Revelation, which is concerned precisely with a salvation that is to come at the end of history. Undoubtedly Revelation and John betray different emphases on this question, but we should be wary about assuming that their positions are contradictory.

Thus, the Johannine view of salvation is both vertical and horizontal. The vertical aspect expresses the uniqueness of the divine intervention in Jesus; the horizontal aspect establishes a relationship between this intervention and salvation history. This is why no Gnostic interpretation of the Fourth Gospel can do justice to its full teaching. The blending of the vertical and the horizontal may be said (perhaps too facilely) to represent a blending of the Hellenistic and the Hebrew approaches to salvation, but such a blending occurred long before the Fourth Gospel was written. It was already present in the deuterocanonical Book of Wisdom. Dodd, *Interpretation*, pp. 144 ff., has shown that early rabbinic thought reflects two different aspects of the "future life." One borders on the horizontal, for it posits two ages in which the life of the age to come replaces the life of the present age; the other borders on the vertical, for its posits a life beyond the grave, differing from the life of men upon this earth. Of course, Christian theology has made a similar synthesis of the vertical and the horizontal in positing immortality of the soul as well as the final resurrection of the dead.

(2) *Realized Eschatology and Final Eschatology*

This topic is related to the preceding, but has a slightly different modality. In Jesus' preaching about the *basileia tou theou* and in his attitude toward his own ministry, there is clearly an eschatological outlook, for he presents himself as in some way having introduced the definitive moment in human existence. But in what precise way?

The advocates of final, apocalyptic eschatology, for example, A. Schweitzer, maintain that in speaking of the coming of the *basileia,* Jesus was speaking of that dramatic intervention of God which would bring history to a conclusion. In their interpretation, Jesus expected that intervention in his own ministry or in the immediate future so that it would come about through his death. When his hopes were disappointed and the *basileia* did not come, the Church eventually solved the problem by projecting the final coming of Jesus into the distant future. On the other hand, the advocates of realized eschatology, for example, C. H. Dodd, maintain that Jesus proclaimed the presence of the *basileia* within his own ministry, but without the apocalyptic trimmings usually associated with the event. His presence among men was the one and only coming of God. But his followers were the heirs of an apocalyptic tradition which spoke of a coming in might and majesty, and so they could not believe that all had been realized in Jesus' ministry. To satisfy their expectations they projected a second, more glorious coming in the future—at first, in the near future; then, in the distant future. Between these extreme views of Gospel eschatology there is a whole range of intermediate views. A view, once common, is now losing popularity, namely, that the *basileia tou theou* established as the result of Jesus' ministry was the Church. Perhaps the most widely accepted intermediate view is that the eschatological reign of God was present and operative in the ministry of Jesus, but in a provisional way. The establishment or realization of the *basileia* is yet to come, and the Church is oriented toward that future *basileia.*

In many ways John is the best example in the NT of realized eschatology. God has revealed Himself in Jesus in a definitive form, and seemingly no more can be asked. If one points to OT passages that seem to imply a coming of God in glory, the Prologue (i 14) answers, "We have seen his glory." If one asks where is the judgment that marks God's final intervention, John iii 19 answers, "Now the judgment is this: the light has come into the world." In a figurative way Matt xxv 31 ff. describes the apocalyptic Son of Man coming in glory and sitting on the throne of judgment to separate the good and the bad. But for John the presence of Jesus in the world as the light separates men into those who are sons of darkness, hating the light, and those who come to the light. All through the Gospel Jesus provokes self-judgment as men line up for or against him; truly his coming is a *crisis* in the root sense of that word, where it reflects the Gr. *krisis* or "judgment." Those who refuse to believe are already condemned (iii 18), while those who have faith do not come under condemnation (v 24—see the discussion of the Johannine concept of judgment on p. 345). Even the reward is realized. For the Synoptics "eternal life" is something that one receives at the final judgment or in a future age (Mark x 30; Matt xviii 8–9), but for John it is a present possibility for men: "The man who hears my words and has faith in Him who sent me *possesses* eternal life. . . .

he has passed from death to life" (v 24). For Luke (vi 35, xx 36) divine sonship is a reward of the future life; for John (i 12) it is a gift granted here on earth.

Yet there are also passages in John which reflect a future element in their eschatology. We may distinguish between those which are simply futuristic and those which are apocalyptic. For instance, one prominent futuristic element is that the full gift of life does not come during the ministry of Jesus but only afterward through the resurrection. When Jesus speaks of a present opportunity to receive life, we should realize that in the intention of the evangelist Jesus is actually speaking through the pages of the Gospel to a post-resurrectional Christian audience. These Christians are the ones who have the chance to obtain life through faith in Jesus, through Baptism (iii 5), and through the Eucharist (vi 54). The life-giving factor is the Spirit (vi 63, vii 38–39), and that Spirit is given only after Jesus is lifted up to the Father (vii 39, xvi 7, xix 30, xx 22). The full faith in Jesus which brings life to men is possible only after the resurrection, when men confess him as Lord and God (xx 28). Only then do they understand what he means when he says, "I AM" (viii 28). The eucharistic food is a future gift from the viewpoint of the public ministry (vi 27, 51).

There is another futuristic element in Jesus' attitude toward what happens after death. Although Jesus insists that "eternal life" is offered here below, he recognizes that physical death will still intervene (xi 25). This death cannot destroy eternal life, but obviously there must be an aspect of completeness to eternal life after death that is lacking in those who have yet to pass through physical death. Moreover, after death there is no longer the possibility of losing eternal life through sin. Another indication of future reward is the statement that Jesus passes through death and resurrection so that he may prepare dwelling places in his Father's house to which he will bring those who believe in him (xiv 2–3). If men see the glory of Jesus on this earth, there is a future vision of glory to be granted when they shall join Jesus in the Father's presence (xvii 24).

Most scholars will admit at least the futuristic elements mentioned thus far; the real problem concerns final or apocalyptic elements in the eschatology of John. Is there to be a second coming, a resurrection of the dead at the end of time, and a final judgment? There are clear passages that speak in this manner (v 28–29, vi 39–40, 44, 54, xii 48). How are these passages to be treated and reconciled with what we have seen of realized eschatology? For Bultmann they are the additions of the Ecclesiastical Redactor, adapting Johannine theology to the theology of the Church at large. That this is not a satisfactory view even on purely literary grounds has often been remarked, for some of the passages do not seem to be additions (see Smith, pp. 230–32). That it is not true to the over-all picture of Johannine theology is suggested by another work, Revelation, which is the book of the NT that treats of apocalyptic eschatology *ex professo*. On the other hand, even if we believe, against Bultmann, that there is a strain of apocalyptic eschatology in genuine Johannine thought, there is little doubt that Van Hartingsveld's attempt to refute Bultmann by putting the emphasis in John on future eschatology swings the pendulum too much in the opposite direction.

Stauffer has suggested that the evangelist is a reformer in the sense that by his emphasis on realized eschatology and the hidden Messiah (p. 53 below) he is stripping off the vulgar apocalyptic elements that have entered Christian thought since the death of Jesus. His view is not far from Dodd's contention that Johannine realized eschatology is close to Jesus' original thought. Boismard, however, thinks that the passages dealing with final apocalyptic are the earlier passages in the development of Johannine thought, and those dealing with realized eschatology represent later insight.

We cannot discuss all these suggestions; but from the NT evidence we suggest as a workable hypothesis the following general development of NT eschatology. Within Jesus' own message there was a tension between realized and final eschatology. In his ministry the reign of God was making itself manifest among men; and yet, as heir of an apocalyptic tradition, Jesus also spoke of a final manifestation of divine power yet to come. The obscurity of the Gospel references would indicate that Jesus had no clear teaching on how or when this final manifestation would take place. There are some statements which seem to refer to its coming in the near future (Mark ix 1, xiii 30; Matt x 23, xxvi 64); others seem to suppose a lapse of time (Luke xvii 22) and no fixed date (Mark xiii 32–33). It is a dubious procedure to excise one or the other group of statements in order to reconstruct a consistent eschatological view held by Jesus. The recognition that there were both realized and final elements in Jesus' own eschatology means that in the subsequent developments seen below, the NT writers were not creating *ex nihilo* theories of realized or of final eschatology, but were applying to a particular situation one or the other strain already present in Jesus' thought. And we may add that there were strains of both types of eschatology in the Judaism contemporary with Jesus. The *War Scroll* (1QM) shows Qumran's expectations of final divine intervention. Yet at the same time the sectarians believed that they already shared in God's heavenly gifts, were delivered from judgment, and enjoyed the companionship of the angels. See J. Licht, IEJ 6 (1956), 12–13, 97.

Confusion about eschatology is a mark of early Christian thought. Acts ii 17 ff. portrays Peter as proclaiming that the last day has arrived in the resurrection of Jesus and the outpouring of the Spirit. Thus, the first emphasis in eschatological expectation seems to have been that all things were accomplished by and in Jesus Christ and that only a short interim would be granted by God to allow the eschatological proclamation to be made to men. The rejection of this proclamation by many brought to the fore another strain of thought stemming from Jesus which spoke of a coming of the Son of Man in judgment on the wicked, a picture that was naturally colored by apocalyptic elements from the preachers' own background. The gradual passing of the years raised more acutely the problem of how soon this coming would take place, a problem that caused anguish for Paul in his correspondence with the Thessalonians and Corinthians. (That Paul's expectation of a second coming did not prevent him from having a strong realized eschatology is seen in his attitude toward the Church in the Captivity Epistles.) Written perhaps in the 60s, I Pet iv 7 could still proclaim, "The end of all things is at hand."

The destruction of Jerusalem in 70 was a watershed in the development of NT eschatological thought. It is clear from passages like Luke xxi 20 and Rev iv–xi that some theologians saw the destruction of Jerusalem as the (partial) fulfillment of Jesus' words describing the coming of the Son of Man in wrath to punish the wicked. But what of the glorious establishment of the *basileia?* Some seem to have kept their hopes of an immediate parousia alive as long as there was a representative of the apostolic generation alive. The reactions to the passing of this last tangible sign of immediate parousia are found in the cynicism which is the target of II Pet iii 4 and the disappointment which is the target of John xxi 22–23.

Others turned toward a more positive answer. Leaving aside the question of when Jesus would return, they emphasized all that the Christians had already received in Jesus Christ. There need be no excessive worry about final judgment, for the reaction of men to Jesus in faith or in disbelief was already a judgment. There need be no excessive longing for the blessings the parousia would bring, for divine sonship and eternal life, the two greatest gifts, were already in the possession of Christians through faith in Jesus and through Baptism and the Eucharist. For those who died in Jesus there was no indefinite agony of waiting till the last day and the resurrection of the dead, for after death there was a continuation of the eternal life that they already possessed—a continuation that death could not affect and a continuation that constituted even closer union with Jesus and his Father. From time to time persecution and trial would revive the passionate yearning for the immediate return of Jesus and divine deliverance. We see this in Rev xii–xxii where Roman persecution acts as a catalyst for apocalyptic hopes. But the ordinary Christian teaching was more and more phrased in terms of realized eschatology. This combination of a dominant realized eschatology with admixtures of apocalyptic expectation has continued as a standard Christian outlook even until the present day.

Positing as we do a long development in the composition of the Fourth Gospel from the stage of historical tradition until the stage of final redaction (Stages 1–5), *a priori* we may expect to find in John traces of the swinging to and fro of eschatological expectation in the 1st century. Bultmann, Dodd, and Blank are, we believe, correct in insisting that the main emphasis in the Gospel is on realized eschatology, for the Gospel proper was written in the period after the fall of Jerusalem when hopes of an immediate parousia quickly faded. One of the purposes of the Gospel was to teach Christians what a gift they had received in Jesus who was the source and basis of their life in the Church. The Gospel very clearly regards the coming of Jesus as an eschatological event which marked the change of the aeons. If the Gospel begins with "In the beginning," it is because the coming of Jesus will be presented as a new and definitive creation. Jesus' breathing on the disciples in xx 22 as he communicates to them the life-giving Spirit is like God's breathing on dust when He first created man (Gen ii 7), but now through His Spirit God has recreated men as His own children (i 12–13).

The passages in John that treat of apocalyptic eschatology are a remembrance that this theme was found in Jesus' own preaching. They took their formation at a period in the development of Johannine thought when final eschatology was an important motif. Was this an early period as Boismard thinks, or a late period as Bultmann thinks? As we shall see in the commentary, these passages are often doublets of other passages where the same words of Jesus are interpreted in terms of realized eschatology; for example, compare v 26–30 (apocalyptic) with v 19–25 (realized). In such instances, Bultmann may be correct in attributing the addition of the passage with final eschatology to the final redactor (or at least, one might suggest, to the second edition of the Gospel—Stage 4).

However, there are two cautions. *First,* since we do not believe that the redactor was a censor but rather one who preserved Johannine material and who tried to make the Gospel as complete a collection of this material as possible, the material pertaining to final eschatology that was added to the Gospel was not necessarily late material. Boismard may be correct in thinking that these added passages were early interpretations; perhaps they took shape in the period before 70 when final eschatology was more vivid. In this case, the redactor would have been adding early material that was not incorporated into the first edition of the Gospel. However, since there were also moments after 70 when apocalyptic eschatology revived, as we mentioned in reference to Revelation, it is very difficult to make any absolute statements about the relative antiquity of such passages.

A *second* caution concerns the presumed purpose of the redactor (or editor) in adding to the Gospel passages wherein final eschatology was proposed. There is no real proof that this was done in an attempt to make the Gospel more orthodox and acceptable to the Church. In part the redactor's intention may have been to preserve Johannine material that would have otherwise been lost. If the final redaction of the Gospel took place in the late 90s, perhaps shortly after the period when Revelation was written, the redactor was living in a period of persecution when an emphasis on final eschatology would have encouraged the readers of the Gospel. Or one might even theorize that he did not wish the intensive realized eschatology of the Gospel to crowd out the expectation of the second coming and thus give a false picture of the total thought of John son of Zebedee and of the evangelist. In any case, the final form of the Gospel with its twofold eschatology is not, in our opinion, an unfaithful mirror of the several strains in Jesus' own attitude toward eschatology.

D. WISDOM MOTIFS

One aspect that immediately sets the Fourth Gospel apart from the other Gospels and gives it peculiar force is its presentation of Jesus as incarnate revelation descended from on high to offer men light and truth. In discourses of quasi-poetic solemnity, Jesus proclaims himself with the famous "I am" formula, and his divine and celestial origins are apparent both in what he says and in the way he says it. His otherworldliness is visible in the way that he can treat with majestic disdain the plots against him and the attempts to arrest him. He is best described in his own words: "In the world but not of it." We suggest that in drawing this portrait of Jesus, the evangelist has capitalized on an identification of Jesus with personified divine Wisdom as described in the OT. (Obviously this is not the only factor that has contributed to the portrait, but here we wish to draw attention to the strength and number of the Wisdom motifs.) Just as the NT writers found in Jesus the antitype of elements in the historical books of the OT (e.g., of the Exodus, Moses, David) and the fulfillment of the words of the prophets, so the fourth evangelist saw in Jesus the culmination of a tradition that runs through the Wisdom Literature of the OT.

The Wisdom Literature covers a wide spectrum of material and is one of the most cosmopolitan sections of the OT, sharing much in common with the writings of sages in Egypt, Sumeria, and Babylon. This ecumenism of the wisdom movement showed itself in a later period in the openness of the biblical sages to Hellenistic influence, for it was in works like Ecclesiastes and the Wisdom of Solomon that Greek philosophic thought and vocabulary made its greatest inroads into the Bible. Almost half of the deuterocanonical literature, preserved in the canon of Alexandria, is of a sapiential character. The blend of Oriental mysticism and mythology with Greek philosophy, found in the Wisdom Literature, had an influence that continued even after the biblical period, and traces of it can be found in Egyptian Gnosticism and Hermeticism.

In the NT, James represents a Christian wisdom book, illustrating that part of sapiential writing which deals with practical ethics. Some of the more mystical trends in wisdom thought had ramifications in Colossians and Ephesians. The Gospel of John, supposedly from the same section of the world as that addressed in these two epistles, also betrays this influence. In App. II we shall show the background that the Wisdom Literature offers for the concept of "Word" or *logos;* here we shall be more concerned with the Johannine portrait of Jesus.

Although references to personified divine Wisdom (a female figure, since the Hebrew word for wisdom, *ḥokmā,* is feminine) are scattered widely in the OT, our chief sources here will be the poems dedicated to Wisdom and found in Job xxviii; Prov i–ix; Bar iii 9–iv 4; Sir i, iv 11–19, vi 18–31, xiv 20–xv 10, xxiv; Wis vi–x.

According to these descriptions, Lady Wisdom existed with God from the beginning even before there was an earth (Prov viii 22–23; Sir xxiv 9; Wis vi 22)—so also the Johannine Jesus is the Word who was in the beginning (i 1) and was with the Father before the world existed (xvii 5). Wisdom is said to be a pure emanation of the glory of the Almighty (Wis vii 25)—so also Jesus has the Father's glory which he makes manifest to men (i 14, viii 50, xi 4, xvii 5, 22, 24). Wisdom is said to be a reflection of the everlasting light of God (Wis vii 26); and in lighting up the path of men (Sir l 29), she is to be preferred to any natural light (Wis vii 10, 29)—in Johannine thought God is light (I John i 5); and Jesus who comes forth from God is the light of the world and of men (John i 4–5, viii 12, ix 5), ultimately destined to replace all natural light (Rev xxi 23).

Wisdom is described as having descended from heaven to dwell with men (Prov viii 31; Sir xxiv 8; Bar iii 37; Wis ix 10; James iii 15)—so also Jesus is the Son of Man who has descended from heaven to earth (i 14, iii 31, vi 38, xvi 28). In particular, John iii 13 is very close to Bar iii 29 and Wis ix 16–17. The ultimate return of Wisdom to heaven (En xlii 2) offers a parallel to Jesus' return to his Father.

The function of Wisdom among men is to teach them of the things that are above (Job xi 6–7; Wis ix 16–18), to utter truth (Prov viii 7; Wis vi 22), to give instructions as to what pleases God and how to do His will (Wis viii 4, ix 9–10), and thus to lead men to life (Prov iv 13, viii 32–35; Sir iv 12; Bar iv 1) and immortality (Wis vi 18–19). This is precisely the function of Jesus as revealer, as portrayed in numerous passages in John. In accomplishing her task, Wisdom speaks in the first person in long discourses addressed to her hearers (Prov viii 3–36; Sir xxiv)—so also Jesus takes his stand and addresses men with his discourses, often beginning with "I am . . ." (App. IV). The symbols that Wisdom uses for the instruction that she offers are symbols of food (bread) and drink (water, wine), and she invites men to eat and drink (Prov ix 2–5; Sir xxiv 19–21; Isa lv 1–3 [God offering His instruction])—so also Jesus uses these symbols for his revelation (John vi 35, 51 ff., iv 13–14).

Wisdom is not satisfied simply to offer her gifts to those who come; she roams the streets seeking men and crying out to them (Prov i 20–21, viii 1–4; Wis vi 16)—so also we find the Johannine Jesus walking along, encountering those who will follow him (i 36–38, 43), searching out men (v 14, ix 35), and crying out his invitation in public places (vii 28, 37, xii 44). One of the most important tasks that Wisdom undertakes is to instruct disciples (Wis vi 17–19) who are her children (Prov viii 32–33; Sir iv 11, vi 18)—so also in John those disciples who are gathered around Jesus are called his little children (xiii 33). Wisdom tests these disciples and forms them (Sir vi 20–26) until they love her (Prov viii 17; Sir iv 12; Wis vi 17–18) and they become friends of God (Wis vii 14, 27)—so also Jesus purifies and sanctifies his disciples with his word and truth (xv 3, xvii 17) and tests them (vi 67) until he can call them his beloved friends (xv 15, xvi 27). On the other hand, there are men who reject Wisdom (Prov i 24–25;

Bar iii 12; En xlii 2)—so also we see in John many who will not listen when Jesus offers them the truth (viii 46, x 25). For those who reject Wisdom death is inevitable; truth is unattainable; and their pleasure in the things of life is transitory. (Bruns, *art. cit.*, has pointed out that the bleak outlook caused by the bankruptcy of human wisdom in Ecclesiastes is not unlike that envisaged in John vi 63, where it is said that the flesh is useless and only the Spirit can give life.) Thus the coming of Wisdom provokes a division: some seek and find (Prov viii 17; Sir vi 27; Wis vi 12); others do not seek and when they change their minds, it will be too late (Prov i 28). The same language in John describes the effect of Jesus upon men (vii 34, viii 21, xiii 33).

Besides these comparisons between the career of Wisdom and the ministry of Jesus, another parallel to Wisdom may be found in the Spirit-Paraclete which teaches men to understand what Jesus told them (App. V, The Anchor Bible, vol. 29A). Also the post-resurrectional inhabitation of Jesus within those who believe in him (xiv 23) may be compared to Wisdom's power to penetrate men (Wis vii 24, 27).

This short treatment should help to support our contention (Part IV above) that the Wisdom Literature offers better parallels for the Johannine picture of Jesus than do the later Gnostic, Mandean, or Hermetic passages sometimes suggested. (It may be noted also that what John shares in common with these latter bodies of literature often represents a common but independently received heritage from the Jewish Wisdom Literature.) However, John has noticeably modified details of the presentation of Wisdom by introducing a much sharper historical perspective than is found in the OT poems. If Jesus is incarnate Wisdom, this incarnation has taken place at a particular place and time, once and for all. But even this demythologizing of the Wisdom concept by incorporating it into salvation history is not totally new, for one encounters the same tendency in the very late Wisdom Literature. Sirach xxiv 23 and Bar iv 1 would identify Wisdom with the Law given on Sinai, and Wis x illustrates the activity of Wisdom in the lives of the patriarchs from Adam to Moses. (It is interesting to note that John's references to the OT are largely references to men like Abraham, Moses, and Isaiah who have given testimony to Jesus and foreseen his days, and thus have been witnesses of divine wisdom—v 46, viii 56, xii 41.) John carries this further by seeing in Jesus the supreme example of divine Wisdom active in history, and indeed divine Wisdom itself.

Is the presentation of Jesus as divine Wisdom a peculiarly Johannine development, or can it be traced back into the early tradition of the other Gospels? Some information pertinent to this understanding of Jesus may be found in all the Gospels. For instance, although at times Jesus wore the mantle of the prophet, he also betrayed certain characteristics of the wisdom teacher. (See A. Feuillet, RB 62 [1955], 179 ff.) He was addressed as "Teacher"; he gathered disciples; he answered questions about the Law; he spoke in proverbs and parables. In the later Gospels there is a tendency to highlight the sapiential character of Jesus' pronouncements. Matthew and Luke generalize sayings of Jesus once directed to a particular situation and make them wisdom sayings with a universal application (for examples, see Davies, *Setting*, pp. 457–60). Scholars differ on how much of this sapiential character was found in "Q" (the source common to Matthew and Luke), but the fact that "Q" has at least some wisdom features means that the sapiential emphasis goes back to a relatively early stage in the formation of the Gospel tradition. However, one must note that in general the sapiential strain in the Synoptic tradition does not develop in exactly the same way that it develops in John. In the Synoptics, Jesus' teaching shows a certain continuity with the ethical and moral teachings of the sages of the Wisdom Literature; in John, Jesus is personified Wisdom.

However, there are a few passages in the Synoptics that are much closer to the sapiential strain in John. In Luke xxi 15 Jesus promises to give his disciples wisdom which will enable them to speak. In Luke xi 49 a saying is attributed to "the Wisdom of God" which Matt xxiii 34 attributes to Jesus himself. The enigmatic saying, "Wisdom is justified by [all] her children [or deeds]," is found in both Matt xi 19 and Luke vii 35 in a context which might lead the reader to identify Jesus as the "Wisdom" of the saying. In another "Q" passage (Luke xi 31; Matt xii 42) Jesus is exalted over the wisdom of Solomon. In Mark x 24 Jesus addresses his disciples as "Children," a form of address which, as we saw above, both personified Wisdom and the Johannine Jesus employ. The theme of Jesus coming into the world to call men is found in all three Synoptics (Mark ii 17 and par.). In Luke vi 47 (but not in Matt vii 24) Jesus says: "Everyone who *comes to me* and hears my words . . ."—a saying in the style of personified Wisdom and typical of the Johannine Jesus (v 40, vi 35, 45).

The most important passage in the Synoptic Gospels reflecting the theme of personified Wisdom is the "Johannine logion" (Matt xi 25–27; Luke x 21–22), a "Q" saying wherein Jesus is presented as a revealer, as the Son who enables men to know the Father. Davies, *Setting*, p. 207, suggests that the original emphasis in this revelation may have been more eschatological than sapiential. Nevertheless, we do have here a saying of markedly Johannine type which goes back to early tradition. The saying that follows it in Matt xi 28–30, wherein Jesus invites men to come to him to find rest, closely echoes the appeals of Wisdom in Sir xxiv 19 and li 23–27.

The Synoptic evidence is not overwhelming, but there is enough of it to make one suspect that the identification of Jesus with personified Wisdom was not the original creation of the Fourth Gospel. Probably here, as with other Johannine themes like "the hour," and the "I am" sayings, John has capitalized on and developed a theme that was already in the primitive tradition.

■ ■ ■

By way of evaluation, then, how are we to estimate the place of Johannine theology in the spectrum of NT theology? As we have already cautioned (Part VI:A), little credence can be given to the older view which placed the Synoptics, Paul, and John in a Hegelian sequence of thesis, antithesis, and synthesis. By way of reaction to such artificially smooth sequences, the more recent tendency has been to treat Johannine theology as if it stood out of sequence—either in the sense that the evangelist stood so far apart from orthodox Christian thought that his work needed censorship in order to be accepted, or in the sense that he was an unconscious prophet of an existential approach to Jesus who cut through the externalism of Church and sacraments and placed each Christian in a direct "I–thou" relationship to Jesus. Still another suggestion is that John represents thought which circulated in a "backwater" community, cut off from the Church at large.

Personally, we find no major difficulty in fitting John into the mainstream of Christian thought; it is another facet of the manifold Christian understanding of Jesus. Of course, John's theology is not the same as that of Paul, or that of James, or that of any of the Synoptic writers. Although all of these writers shared an essential unity in belief that made them Christians, they also exhibited a notable diversity in theological approach and emphasis (see our remarks in NovT 6 [1963], 298–308). Such diversity is well illustrated in the various NT treatments of the problems just discussed—ecclesiology, sacraments, and eschatology. We do not believe that there is convincing evidence that any NT writer regarded the Church, the sacraments, or the parousia as irrelevant; but they certainly gave expression in very different ways to the relevancy of these topics, and this expression was greatly guided by factors of time, place, and individual understanding. Certainly, through comparison we can find traces of development and sequence, but there is no all-embracing linear development in NT thought. To recognize this makes more understandable the place of highly individual theological thought like John's.

That John has much in common with other NT works has been emphasized in recent comparative articles. Besides the studies of John and the Synoptics mentioned in Part III, there have been studies on John and Paul, for example, A. Fridrichsen, in *The Root of the Vine* (New York: Philosophical Library, 1953), pp. 37–62; and P. Benoit, NTS 9 (1962–63), 193–207 (summarized in English in TD 13 [1965], 135–41). These articles find many underlying similarities between Johannine and Pauline thought, despite the very different articulation. When we consider the Prologue, we shall point out that this seemingly unique Johannine hymn has definite parallels with the Pauline hymns in Colossians and Philippians.

In his exhaustive commentary on the Epistle to the Hebrews, C. Spicq (Paris: Gabalda, 1952), I, pp. 109–38, devotes a very interesting study to some sixteen parallels in thought between John and Hebrews. And now one could add to this list the Qumran affinities found in both works. Spicq, I, p. 134, remarks that from these contacts it seems that Hebrews represents a link between the theological elaborations of Paul and John. A long list of parallels between John and the Catholic Epistles, especially I Peter, could also be drawn up. Thus, while the fourth evangelist may be *the Theologian,"* he was neither as solitary nor as out-of-step as many would have us believe.

BIBLIOGRAPHY

Ecclesiology

Corell, Alf, *Consummatum Est: Eschatology and Church in the Gospel of St. John* (London: SPCK, 1958).

Dahl, N. A., "The Johannine Church and History," CINTI, pp. 124–42.

D'Aragon, J.-L., "Le caractère distinctif de l'Eglise johannique," in *L'Eglise dans la Bible* (Paris: Desclée de Brouwer, 1962), pp. 53–66.

Feuillet, A., "Le temps de l'Eglise d'après le quatrième évangile et l'Apocalypse," MD 65 (1961), 60–79. Summarized in English in TD 11 (1963), 3–9.

Schnackenburg, R., *The Church in the New Testament* (New York: Herder and Herder, 1965), especially pp. 103–17.

Schweizer, E., "The Concept of the Church in the Gospel and Epistles of St. John," in *New Testament Essays in Memory of T. W. Manson,* ed. A. J. B. Higgins (Manchester University, 1959), pp. 230–45.

van den Bussche, H., "L'Eglise dans le quatrième Evangile," *Aux origines de l'Eglise* (Recherches Bibliques, VII: Louvain: Desclée de Brouwer, 1965), pp. 65–85.

Via, D. O., "Darkness, Christ, and the Church in the Fourth Gospel," *Scottish Journal of Theology* 14 (1961), 172–93.

Sacramentalism

Braun, F.-M., "Le baptême d'après le quatrième évangile," RThom 48 (1948), 347–93.

Brown, R. E., "The Johannine Sacramentary Reconsidered," TS 23 (1962), 183–206. Also in NTE, Ch. IV.

Bultmann, R., *Theology of the New Testament* (New York: Scribner, 1955), II, pp. 3–14.

Clavier, H., "Le problème du rite et du mythe dans le quatrième évangile," RHPR 31 (1951), 275–92.

Craig, C., "Sacramental Interest in the Fourth Gospel," JBL 58 (1939), 31–41.

Cullmann, ECW.

Köster, H., "Geschichte und Kultus im Johannesevangelium und bei Ignatius von Antiochien," ZTK 54 (1957), 56–69.

Lohse, E., "Wort und Sakrament im Johannesevangelium," NTS 7 (1960–61), 110–25.

Michaelis, W., *Die Sakramente im Johannesevangelium* (Bern: 1946).

Niewalda, P., *Sakramentssymbolik im Johannesevangelium* (Limburg: Lahn, 1958).

Schnackenburg, R., "Die Sakramente im Johannesevangelium," *SacPag,* II, pp. 235–54.

Smalley, S., "Liturgy and Sacrament in the Fourth Gospel," *Evangelical Quarterly* 29 (1957), 159–70.

Vawter, B., "The Johannine Sacramentary," TS 17 (1956), 151–66.

Eschatology

Blank, Josef, *Krisis: Untersuchungen zur johanneischen Christologie und Eschatologie* (Freiburg: Lambertus, 1964).

Boismard, M.-E., "L'évolution du thème eschatologique dans les traditions johanniques," RB 68 (1961), 507–24.

Stählin, G., "Zur Problem der johanneischen Eschatologie," ZNW 33 (1934), 225–59.

Stauffer, E., *"Agnostos Christos:* Joh. ii. 24 und die Eschatologie des vierten Evangeliums," BNTE, pp. 281–99.

van Hartingsveld, L., *Die Eschatologie des Johannesevangeliums* (Assen: van Gorcum, 1962).

Wisdom Motifs

Braun, F.-M., "Saint Jean, la Sagesse et l'histoire," NTPat, pp. 123–33. See JeanThéol, II, pp. 115–50.

Bruns, J. E., "Some Reflections on Coheleth and John," CBQ 25 (1963), 414–16.

Moeller, H. R., "Wisdom Motifs and John's Gospel," *Bulletin of the Evangelical Theological Society* 6 (1963), 92–100.

Ziener, G., "Weisheitsbuch und Johannesevangelium," Bib 38 (1957), 396–418; 39 (1958), 37–60.

IX. THE LANGUAGE, TEXT, AND FORMAT OF THE GOSPEL—AND SOME CONSIDERATIONS ON STYLE

A. THE ORIGINAL LANGUAGE OF THE GOSPEL

It is probable that Jesus' ordinary conversation was in Aramaic, although there are some scholars who think that he normally spoke Hebrew. The fact that the Dead Sea Scrolls are largely in Hebrew means that Hebrew was preferred as a sacred and a literary language and that spoken Hebrew remained in use among the educated of Judea longer than was formerly thought. But this evidence really does little to prove that a Galilean prophet like Jesus would speak to the people in Hebrew, although Jesus may have known Hebrew for synagogue use.

Such an Aramaic background naturally had an effect on the quality of the Greek in which the remembrance of Jesus' words has been preserved by the Gospels. Moreover, there was further Semitic influence on this Greek, for the early apostolic preachers who brought the message of Jesus into the Greek world were also Semites for whom Greek was, at most, a secondary language. Probably, too, several of the evangelists were Jews whose imperfect mastery of Greek has to be taken into allowance. Still another factor is that the Christian message in the Greek world was first preached in the diaspora synagogues and consequently was phrased in the religious vocabulary of Greek-speaking Judaism—a Greek which was influenced by the Semitized style of the LXX, the Greek OT. Therefore, from all these channels Aramaisms, Hebraisms, and Semitisms (i.e., constructions abnormal in Greek, but normal in Aramaic, in Hebrew, or in both these Semitic languages) made their way into the Gospels. It must be clear that the presence of such features is not sufficient to prove that a Gospel was first written in one of the two languages; at most it may prove that certain sayings once existed in Aramaic or Hebrew, or that the native language of the evangelist was not Greek.

Is it possible that the Fourth Gospel was originally written in Aramaic in whole or in part, and what would indicate this? The possibility can scarcely be denied, for it does seem that some gospel material was written in Aramaic. For instance, Papias reports that Matthew composed the words (of the Lord) in the "Hebrew dialect," that is, presumably Aramaic. A *Gospel according to the Hebrews* or "written in Hebrew letters," was known as late as Jerome's time. Among the modern scholars who have suggested that, in whole or in part, John was first written in Aramaic are Burney, Torrey, Burrows, Macgregor, De Zwaan, Black, and

Boismard; and we remember that Bultmann supposes an Aramaic original for the Revelatory Discourse Source. The following arguments have been proposed:

(a) the presence of Aramaisms, but not Hebraisms—Torrey considers this conclusive, but Burney does not;

(b) the presence of mistranslations, that is, the confused state of a Greek passage is thought to have resulted from an error in rendering into Greek an obscure Aramaic phrase, and the true sense of the passage is apparent with retroversion into Aramaic—Burney depends heavily on this;

(c) the existence of Greek manuscript variants which may represent two different possible translations into Greek of the Aramaic original— Black and Boismard have brought forward numerous examples, and we shall call attention to their suggestions in the commentary;

(d) the fact that some of John's OT citations seem to be drawn directly from the Hebrew (Burney) or from the Targums, the Aramaic translations of the OT used in the Galilean synagogues (Boismard);

(e) the possibility of retroverting the "poetry" of the discourses or of the Prologue into good Aramaic poetry (Burney)—we remember that Bultmann suggests the parallel of the *Odes of Solomon*, which are in Syriac (a later form of Aramaic).

These arguments are not of equal value. We have already called attention to the insufficiency of (a) as a proof. The mistranslations mentioned in (b) are more persuasive, but there is always an element of subjectivity in deciding that the Greek makes no sense as it now stands. With (d) we have always to face the possibility that the evangelist was really citing the Greek OT, but freely and from memory. Even the citation of the OT from the Aramaic Targums may simply reflect Jesus' own usage, without proving that the Gospel was written in Aramaic. Thus, no one argument is sufficient, and it is more a question of convergence of probabilities. The difficulty of the problem is indicated by the ever increasing caution of the proponents of an Aramaic original. Burney was more cautious than Torrey; and Black and Boismard are more cautious still than Burney.

Personally, we tend to agree with the majority of scholars who do not find adequate evidence that a complete edition of the Gospel according to John (Stage 3) ever existed in Aramaic. It is possible, however, that bits of the historical tradition underlying John were written in Aramaic, especially if the source of this tradition was John son of Zebedee. But even this possibility lies beyond proof. If there are mistranslations into Greek or alternate translations, these may have arisen in the oral transmission and translation of the historical material before Stage 1, especially since Greek would not have been John's native language. How early alternate Greek translations found their way into different manuscript traditions of the Fourth Gospel is not easy to explain, but this phenomenon is not without difficulty, no matter when it occurred.

B. The Greek Text of the Gospel

The science of textual criticism is a difficult one; a full discussion of the textual presuppositions behind our translation would be complicated for the ordinary reader, and somewhat unnecessary for the scholar. As with most of the other NT works, the basic Greek text of John is determined by a comparison of the great codices of the 4th and 5th century: Vaticanus, Sinaiticus, and the Greco-Latin Codex Bezae. In general, Vaticanus represents an "Eastern" textual tradition popular in Egypt, particularly at Alexandria, while Bezae represents a "Western" textual tradition, also found in the early translations into Latin (OL) and Syriac (OS). While elsewhere Sinaiticus is close to Vaticanus, for the first seven chapters of John it is closer to Bezae.

One must evaluate the different readings of these and other Greek textual witnesses, plus the evidence of the early versions in Latin, Syriac, Coptic, and Ethiopic. The citations of John in the early Church Fathers are also important. Where there are different readings of any real importance, we shall present them with an evaluation; but we make no attempt to give the complete list of witnesses behind every reading. We have no desire to freight our notes with all the references and sigla that one finds in the footnotes of a critical Greek NT.

We should give some attention here to the recent papyri discoveries that affect the text of John, for these are of major importance. We now have more papyri copies of John (seventeen) than of any other NT book. The Greek papyri from the Bodmer collection published in the last ten years are the most remarkable because of their antiquity. They are major textual witnesses for the Gospel some 150 years older than the great codices mentioned above. It is quite clear that P[75] agrees more closely with Codex Vaticanus than with any other manuscript. P[66], however, has a text that stands somewhere between Vaticanus and Sinaiticus, perhaps somewhat closer to the latter. When these two papyri agree, they give very strong evidence for a reading, and we have made liberal use of them in our translation. Nevertheless, we have not hesitated to reject their evidence when the laws of textual criticism seem to point to another reading found in a later witness as the more original. After all, the very fact that P[66] and P[75] do not always agree means that even by A.D. 200 many copyists' changes and mistakes had already crept into the copies of the Gospel text.

Another development worthy of note in the textual study of John has been the work of Boismard, who is seeking to establish readings more primitive than those preserved in any of the Greek witnesses. His chief tools are the early versions, the citations found in the Church Fathers, and the *Diatessaron* of Tatian (harmony of the Gospels written about 175, probably in Greek, but preserved only in later commentaries and translations). He points out that the patristic readings, for example, those of John Chrysostom, are often significantly shorter than the readings found in the codices, and brevity is frequently a sign of a more original reading. Recently J. N. Birdsall has shown the possibility that the divergent patristic text reconstructed by Boismard was still available in Photius' time (9th century). Boismard's contentions have had considerable influence on the French translation of John for the "Bible de Jérusalem," La Sainte Bible (abbr. SB). In the NOTES to our translation we shall mention some of the more impressive examples brought forward by Boismard; but where his readings are entirely dependent on the versions and the patristic citations, and have no support in the Greek manuscript witnesses, we are very hesitant. The Fathers often presented a short form of a passage because they were interested in only part of the citation; they often adapted for theological purposes; and so they have their limitations as guides to the exact wording of the passages of Scripture.

Even with the use of all the latest evidence and the application of the rules of textual criticism, scholars will not always agree on the original Greek readings of some disputed passages. We have preferred in these instances to use brackets to make this uncertainty immediately obvious to the reader.

C. THE POETIC FORMAT OF THE GOSPEL DISCOURSES

That the Johannine prose of the discourses of Jesus is uniquely solemn has been recognized by many. Some have suggested that this prose is quasi-poetic and should be printed in poetic format. This would offer one more point of similarity between the Johannine Jesus and personified Wisdom, for Wisdom speaks in poetry. What would be the basis for considering the Johannine discourses as quasi-poetic?

The fundamental principle in OT poetry is parallelism, and occasionally parallelism appears in the words of Jesus as reported by John. Synonymous parallelism, where the second line repeats the idea of the first, is exemplified in John iii 11, iv 36, vi 35, 55, vii 34, xiii 16. Antithetic parallelism, where the second line offers a contrast with the first, is found in iii 18, viii 35, ix 39. There is an interesting example in iii 20 and 21 where one whole verse is balanced against another. Synthetic parallelism, where the sense flows on from one line to another, is well illustrated in viii 44. A particular form of this, "staircase" parallelism, where one line picks up the last principal word of the preceding line, is found in the Prologue, in vi 37, viii 32, xiii 20, xiv 21. The presence of parallelism, however, while frequent in John, is not the dominant characteristic of the discourses. We may also note that parallelism is not peculiar to the Fourth Gospel. Burney, *Poetry*, pp. 63–99, shows that the same forms of parallelism are found in the words of Jesus recorded by the Synoptics.

Rhyme is not very frequent in Semitic poetry, but it does occur. In

Poetry, pp. 174–75, Burney retroverts John x 1 ff. into Aramaic and shows a pattern of rhyme. Not only is the retroversion quite speculative, but also there are relatively few sections of the Gospel which lend themselves to a pattern of rhyme, even when retroverted.

If the discourses of Jesus in John are to be printed in poetic format, the basis of the quasi-poetic style lies in rhythm. Some would propose a rhythm of accentual beats. To some extent at least such delineation of ictus is calculated on a hypothetic Aramaic original. For instance, Burney finds lines of four beats each in xiv 1–10; lines of three beats in iii 11 and iv 36; and the sorrowful *Qinah* meter of three beats in the first line and two in the second in xvi 20. Gächter has been the most thoroughgoing in his quest for a rhythm of stressed syllables in John. He works with Greek text, although occasionally he will reconstruct the Aramaic original. He prefers short lines of two beats each, and does not believe that the poetic division of a line must necessarily constitute a sense unit—the line is one of stress rhythm and need not convey a complete thought. This feature makes Gächter's reconstruction of the poetry quite unique and gives it very little resemblance to the wisdom poetry of the OT. Gächter also insists on a highly complicated system of strophic arrangement.

As we have mentioned, Bultmann maintains that the Greek form of the discourses in John has for the most part preserved the poetic format of the original Revelatory Discourse Source. D. M. Smith's isolation and printing of the material which Bultmann attributes to this source (see *Composition*, pp. 23–34) shows at first glance how good a case can be made for casting John in poetic format. And we suggest that this holds true even if we do not resort to putative Aramaic originals or even to counting off accentual beats. In the various discourse sections of the Gospel there is a constant rhythmic effect of lines of approximately the same length, each constituting a clause. Possibly this does reflect a stress rhythm in an Aramaic original, but the general pattern is quite observable in the Greek. Two features of Bultmann's arrangement are more open to question. He joins the Prologue with the rest of the discourse material, but the "staircase" parallelism of the Prologue represents a far more carefully worked out poetic style than any passage of length in the discourses. In our opinion, the Prologue was a hymn, while the discourses were not. Secondly, in his reconstruction of the poetic format, Bultmann is rather arbitrary in his excision of glosses which he attributes to the final redactor. We are not certain that the poetic format is so fixed or strict that awkward lines can be treated as additions.

In his translation of John for the French "Bible de Jérusalem," D. Mollat has given us the discourses in a poetic format—one of the few modern attempts to do this in a Bible intended for the general public. He never formulates his principles for dividing lines; but, as with Burney and Bultmann, his divisions are into sense lines. At times, in his struggle to present balanced lines in the French translation, Mollat sacrifices the balance of the Greek lines. Bultmann did not have to face this translation problem, for he prints the Gospel verses in Greek. Mollat has adopted a block form for his poetic lines, while Bultmann indents subordinate lines.

It is a very interesting exercise to make a comparative study of these various attempts at setting the Johannine discourses in a poetic format. Perhaps two thirds of the time Bultmann and Mollat will be in agreement on the number of lines into which a verse should be divided. Yet, even with one-third variation, they are much closer to one another than to Gächter. To take but one example, in vi 35 both Mollat and Bultmann have three lines, while Gächter has five.

It is difficult to give any conclusive proof that a poetic format is justified. Perhaps all that can be said is that, when one has worked with the material for a while, searching to find a format, one does get caught up into the pattern. And so, with some hesitation, we have decided to use poetic format in our own translation in order to offer the English reader an opportunity to judge for himself whether or not there is a rhythmic balance in the Johannine lines. But we must issue a caution. Our division of English lines remains faithful to the division in the Greek (with occasional inversion of lines); and so, since several English words may be required to translate one Greek word, an appearance of balance between English lines will not always be possible. To obtain more even English lines it would be necessary to ignore the Greek balance, as Mollat has done from time to time. We have printed as a line of poetry the double "Amen" (for translation see NOTE on i 51), used so often by the Johannine Jesus to introduce a discourse. Strictly it is not part of the poetry, but it did not seem worth while to maintain a special format for the one line.

We have not hesitated to consult the reconstructions by Bultmann, Mollat, and Burney, nor have we hesitated to disagree with their division of lines where we believed another division was justified. In some difficult lines, one commentator's guess is as good as another's, and recourse to a hypothetical Aramaic original is not really decisive. Sometimes the division of lines has to be determined by the division one finds in the context. For instance, what we now have as the first four lines of xii 26 could really be printed as two lines:

> If anyone would serve me, let him follow me;
> and where I am, my servant will also be.

However, we are inclined to break this up and treat the adverbial clauses as separate lines on the analogy of the conditional clauses in xii 24. Actually at one time these were probably independent sayings, and so the force of the analogy is not certain. Again, iii 15, which we have rendered as two lines, could easily stand as one line. However, it is an obvious contrast with the last part of iii 16 which really has to be broken into two lines, and this contrast has determined our usage in iii 15. In turn, both of these verses have guided our present division of iii 20–21. In the context of the Prologue we have printed the inserted vs. 15 as prose, for it does not match the careful poetry of this hymn. But when the same words appear in the Gospel proper, they are worthy of the poetic format of the discourses (i 30). Thus, the principles of division are flexible.

Perhaps it is worth while to insist once more that the use of poetic format means only that there is a quasi-poetic balance to the prose of the discourses. We do not believe that one can consistently find rhyme, strict parallelism, or exact stress patterns. If the prose is solemn, it is far from lyrical. The language of the discourses achieves a monotonous grandeur by repetition of simple words and not by the use of highly literary vocabulary. For that reason we have translated these discourses into ordinary English (and indeed we would not have the literary capacity to create a true poetry for them, were that justified).

D. NOTABLE CHARACTERISTICS IN JOHANNINE STYLE

(1) *Inclusion.* At the end of a passage the Gospel will often mention a detail or make an allusion which recalls something recorded in the opening of the passage. This feature, well attested in other biblical books, for example, the Wisdom of Solomon, can serve as a means of packaging a unit or a subunit by tying together the beginning and the end. Note the references to the two Cana miracles in ii 11 and iv 46, 54; the references to the Transjordan in i 28 and x 40; the implicit references to the paschal lamb in i 29 and xix 36.

(2) *Chiasm* or inverted parallelism. In two units which share a number of parallel features, the first verse of I corresponds to the last verse of II, the second verse of I corresponds to the next to the last verse of II, etc.

$$
\begin{array}{ccc}
\text{I} & & \text{II} \\
\text{vs. 1} & = & \text{vs. 7} \\
\text{vs. 2} & = & \text{vs. 6} \\
\text{vs. 3} & = & \text{vs. 5} \\
& \text{vs. 4} &
\end{array}
$$

Good examples may be seen in vi 36–40 (p. 276) and in the organization of the trial before Pilate (xviii 28–xix 16).

(3) *Twofold or Double Meaning.* The Gospel often plays on the double meanings of words, whether in Aramaic or Greek, for example: in iii 3 ff. on *anōthen* as "from above" and "again"; in iv 10–11 on the twofold meaning "living" and "flowing" to describe the water; in vii 8 on the ambiguity of "going up" (to Jerusalem or to the Father?).

(4) *Misunderstanding.* This feature is sometimes the counterpart to the preceding; in other instances it is related to the symbolic language of Jesus. When Jesus is speaking on the heavenly or eternal level, his remarks are often misunderstood as referring to a material or earthly situation. The water and bread that he employs to symbolize his revelation are not understood as symbols by the audience (iv 10 ff., vi 32 ff.). His body is the

Temple to be destroyed and raised up, but the hearers think of the Jerusalem Temple (ii 19–22). In part this may be a studied literary technique, for the misunderstanding usually causes Jesus to explain himself more thoroughly and to unfold his doctrine. However, since this symbolism is the Johannine equivalent of the parabolic language of the Synoptics, this misunderstanding is the Johannine equivalent of the failure to understand that greets the parables in the Synoptic tradition (Mark iv 12). It represents the world's inability to see the truth.

(5) *Irony*. The opponents of Jesus are given to making statements about him that are derogatory, sarcastic, incredulous, or, at least, inadequate in the sense they intend. However, by way of irony these statements are often true or more meaningful in a sense they do not realize. The evangelist simply presents such statements and leaves them unanswered (or answered with eloquent silence), for he is certain that his believing readers will see the deeper truth. Good examples are iv 12, vii 35, 42, viii 22, xi 50.

(6) *Explanatory Notes*. In the Gospel we often find explanatory comments, inserted into the running narrative of the story. They explain names (i 38, 42), and symbols (ii 21, xii 33, xviii 9); they correct possible misapprehensions (iv 2, vi 6); they remind the reader of related events (iii 24, xi 2) and reidentify for him the characters of the plot (vii 50, xxi 20). Tenney has counted some fifty-nine such notes; and if it would not lead to confusion, they might well be placed at the bottom of the page as footnotes, as E. V. Rieu does in his NT translations. However, this creates a problem of versification; and so we have adopted the reasonable compromise of using parentheses, except for the occasional note that we have been able to work smoothly into the narrative. These notes are often indicative of the editing process at work in the composition of the Gospel.

BIBLIOGRAPHY

Brown, Schuyler, "From Burney to Black: The Fourth Gospel and the Aramaic Question," CBQ 26 (1964), 323–39—good bibliography.
Gundry, R. H., "The Language Milieu of First-century Palestine," JBL 83 (1964), 404–8.

Greek Text

1. The Bodmer Papyri:

P[66] or Bodmer Papyrus II, dating from ca. 200, was published by V. Martin, with chs. i–xiv appearing in 1956 and the rest in 1958. For corrections of the 1956 ed., see Teeple and Walker in JBL 78 (1959), 148–52; and Fee in JBL 84 (1965), 66–72. For a good bibliography see NTA 2 (1958), ⌗322. A revised ed. of P[66] was published by Martin and J. W. Barns in 1962. For subsequent corrections see Barns in *Muséon* 75 (1962), 327–29.

P[75] or Bodmer Papyrus XV, dating from ca. 200, was published by Martin and R. Kasser in 1961.

In a continued article K. Aland has analyzed the relations of these two papyri and collated their readings: NTS 9 (1962–63), 303–13; NTS 10 (1963–64), 62–79, dealing particularly with P[66]; NTS 11 (1964–65), 1–21, dealing particularly with P[75].

Clark, K. W., "The Text of the Gospel of John in Third-century Egypt," NovT 5 (1962), 17–24.

Porter, C. L., "Papyrus Bodmer XV (P[75]) and the Text of Codex Vaticanus," JBL 81 (1962), 363–76.

Zimmermann, H., "Papyrus Bodmer II und seine Bedeutung für die Textgeschichte des Johannesevangeliums," BZ 2 (1958), 214–43.

In 1958 R. Kasser published Papyrus Bodmer III, a 4th-century Boh. (Coptic) version of John rendered directly from the Greek. In an article in *Muséon* 74 (1961), 423–33, Kasser studies this manuscript in relation to the other Coptic witnesses to John.

2. Patristic Citations:

Birdsall, J. N., "Photius and the Text of the Fourth Gospel," NTS 4 (1957–58), 61–63.

Boismard, M.-E., "Critique textuelle et citations patristiques," RB 57 (1950), 388–408.

———"Lectio Brevior, Potior," RB 58 (1951), 161–68.

———"Problèmes de critique textuelle concernant le quatrième évangile," RB 60 (1953), 347–71.

Poetic Format

Burney, C. F., *The Poetry of Our Lord* (Oxford: Clarendon, 1925).

Gächter (Gaechter),* P., in a series of articles, has treated individual passages:

John i 1–18	ZKT 60 (1936), 99–111;
v 19–30	NTAuf, pp. 65–68;
v 19–47	ZKT 60 (1936), 111–20;
vi 35–58	ZKT 59 (1935), 419–41;
viii 12–59	ZKT 60 (1936), 402–12;
x 11–39	ZKT 60 (1936), 412–15;
xiii–xvi	ZKT 58 (1934), 155–207.

Characteristics of Style

Clavier, H., "L'ironie dans le quatrième évangile," StEv, I, pp. 261–76.

Cullmann, O., "Der johanneische Gebrauch doppeldeutiger Ausdrücke als Schlüssel zum Verständnis des vierten Evangeliums," TZ 4 (1948), 360–72.

Léon-Dufour, X., "Trois chiasmes johanniques," NTS 7 (1960–61), 249–55.

Lund, N. W., "The Influence of Chiasmus upon the Structure of the Gospels," ATR 13 (1931), 27–48, 405–33.

Tenney, M. C., "The Footnotes of John's Gospel," *Bibliotheca Sacra* 117 (1960), 350–64.

* Both spellings are used by the author in his own published works.

X. THE OUTLINE OF THE GOSPEL

A. The General Outline of the Gospel

The following division is suggested by the Gospel itself:

i 1–18: THE PROLOGUE

An early Christian hymn, probably stemming from Johannine circles, which has been adapted to serve as an overture to the Gospel narrative of the career of the incarnate Word.

i 19–xii 50: THE BOOK OF SIGNS

The public ministry of Jesus where in sign and word he shows himself to his own people as the revelation of his Father, only to be rejected.

xiii 1–xx 31: THE BOOK OF GLORY*

To those who accept him Jesus shows his glory by returning to the Father in "the hour" of his crucifixion, resurrection, and ascension. Fully glorified, he communicates the Spirit of life.

xxi 1–25: THE EPILOGUE*

An added account of post-resurrectional appearances in Galilee.

It is quite clear that the end of ch. xii and the beginning of xiii specifically mark a break in the narrative. In xii 37–43 there is a summary description and analysis of Jesus' public ministry and its effect on the people; xii 44–50 are the last words of Jesus directed to the people in general. In xiii 1–3 there is a shift in emphasis, marked by the words, "It was before the Passover feast, and Jesus was aware that the hour had come for him to pass from this world to the Father." All Jesus' words in chs. xiii–xvii are directed to "his own" (xiii 1), his disciples whom he loves and who have come to believe in him. The spirit of these two main divisions of the Gospel is summed up in two verses of the Prologue (i 11–12) which contrast his own people who did not accept him and those who did accept him, thus becoming God's children. The second division of the Gospel comes to an end in xx 30–31, a conclusion which comments on the content and purpose of the Gospel. The reasons for treating ch. xxi as an Epilogue will be explained in our second volume.

We have designated in 19–xii 50 as "The Book of Signs" because these

* These divisions appear in vol. 30.

chapters largely concern Jesus' miracles, referred to as "signs," and discourses which interpret the signs. By contrast, the word "sign" occurs in the second division of the Gospel only in the summary statement of xx 30. The second division, which narrates what happened from the Thursday evening of the Last Supper until Jesus' appearance to his disciples after the resurrection, has all through it the theme of Jesus' return to his Father (xiii 1, xiv 2, 28, xv 26, xvi 7, 28, xvii 5, 11, xx 17). This return means the glorification of Jesus (xiii 31, xvi 14, xvii 1, 5, 24), so that the resurrected Jesus appears to his disciples as Lord and God (xx 25, 28)—whence our title "The Book of Glory." The signs of the first book anticipated the glory of Jesus in a figurative way for those who had the faith to see through the signs to their significance (ii 11, xi 4, 40), but many greeted these signs with only limited perception and inadequate belief. The action of the second book, directed to those who believed in the signs of the first, accomplishes in reality what was anticipated by the signs of the first book, so that the Prologue can exclaim: "We have seen his glory, the glory of an only Son coming from the Father" (i 14).

B. The General Outline of the Book of Signs

We propose to divide this book into four parts; the detailed outline of each part will be given at the beginning of our treatment of the part. On the next two pages we shall give simply a general outline of the whole book with the main subdivisions, so that the reader may intelligently follow our discussion of the principles for dividing the Book of Signs.

What are the indications within the Gospel itself that can serve as a guide for subdividing the Book of Signs? That the indications are not absolutely clear is suggested by the many disputes between scholars about how this book of the Gospel should be divided. After the Prologue, there is a relatively continuous narrative from i 19 to xii 50. The Gospel gives us some indications of the passing of time, for example, the three Passovers mentioned in ii 13, vi 4, and xi 55; but these are merely by way of setting for a particular narrative, and there is nothing to suggest that they are signposts for a division of the Gospel. The idea of dividing Jesus' ministry into two or three years does not come from the Gospel itself.

If we speak of a Book of Signs, it is not impossible that the *signs* may represent a key to the division of the book. The following miraculous signs are narrated in some detail:

(1) Changing water to wine at Cana (ii 1–11)
(2) Curing the royal official's son at Cana (iv 46–54)
(3) Curing the paralytic at the pool of Bethesda (v 1–15)
(4) Multiplication of the loaves in Galilee (vi 1–15)
(5) Walking upon the Sea of Galilee (vi 16–21)
(6) Curing a blind man in Jerusalem (ix)
(7) Raising Lazarus from the dead at Bethany (xi)

DIVISION OF THE BOOK OF SIGNS
(i 19–xii 50)

Part One: The Opening Days of the Revelation of Jesus (i 19–51, plus ii 1–11)

A.   i 19–34   The Testimony of John the Baptist:
     (19–28)   Concerning his role in relation to the one to come;
     (29–34)   Concerning Jesus.

B.   i 35–51   The Baptist's Disciples come to Jesus as he manifests himself:
     (35–42)   a. Two disciples—Jesus acknowledged as rabbi;
                    b. Simon Peter—Jesus as Messiah;
     (43–51)   a. Philip—Jesus as fulfillment of Law and prophets;
                    b. Nathanael—Jesus as Son of God and King of Israel;
                  —A Saying about the Son of Man.

(ii 1–11 The Disciples Come to Believe in Jesus as He Manifests His Glory at Cana—this scene both closes Part One and opens Part Two)

Part Two: From Cana to Cana—various responses to Jesus' ministry in the different sections of Palestine (ii–iv)

A.   ii 1–11   The First Sign at Cana in Galilee—water to wine.
        12   Transition—Jesus goes to Capernaum.

B.   ii 13–22   Cleansing of the Temple in Jerusalem.
     23–25   Transition—Reaction to Jesus in Jerusalem.

C.   iii 1–21   Discourse with Nicodemus in Jerusalem.
     22–30   The Baptist's final Witness to Jesus.
     31–36   Discourse of Jesus completing the preceding.
     iv 1–3   Transition—Jesus leaves Judea.

D.   iv 4–42   Discourse with the Samaritan Woman at Jacob's Well.
     43–45   Transition—Jesus enters Galilee.

E.   iv 46–54   The Second Sign at Cana in Galilee—healing the official's son; the household become believers.
                    (This scene both closes Part Two and opens Part Three)

Part Three: Jesus and the principal feasts of the Jews
(v–x, introduced by iv 46–54)

(iv 46–54 Jesus gives life to the official's son at Cana)

A.   v 1–47   THE SABBATH—Jesus performs works that only God can do on the Sabbath:
    (1–15)   Gift of life [healing] to the man at Bethesda pool in Jerusalem;
    (16–47)   Discourse explaining the giving of life and his work on the Sabbath.

B.   vi 1–71   PASSOVER—Jesus gives bread replacing the manna of the Exodus:
    (1–21)   Multiplication of the loaves; walking on the sea;
    (22–24)   Transition—The crowd comes to Jesus.
    (25–71)   Discourse explaining the multiplication.

C. vii 1–viii 59   TABERNACLES—Jesus replaces the water and light ceremonies:
    vii (1–13)   Introduction: Will Jesus go up to the feast?
    (14–36)   Scene 1: Discourse on the middle day of the festal week;
    (37–52)   Scene 2: The last day of the feast:
        [vii 53–viii 11 The Adulteress—
        a non-Johannine interpolation]
    viii (12–59)   Scene 3: Miscellaneous discourses.

    ix 1–x 21   Aftermath of Tabernacles:
    ix (1–41)   Healing of the man born blind—Jesus as the light;
    x (1–21)   Jesus as sheepgate and shepherd.

D.   x 22–39   DEDICATION—Jesus, the Messiah and Son of God, is consecrated in place of the temple altar:
    (22–31)   Jesus as the Messiah;
    (32–39)   Jesus as the Son of God.
    40–42   Apparent Conclusion to the public ministry.

Part Four: Jesus moves toward the hour of death and glory (xi–xii)

A.   xi 1–54   Jesus gives men life; men condemn Jesus to death:
    (1–44)   Jesus gives life to Lazarus—Jesus as the life;
    (45–54)   The Sanhedrin condemns Jesus to die; withdrawal to Ephraim.
    55–57   Transition—Will Jesus come to Jerusalem for Passover?

B.   xii 1–36   Scenes preparatory to Passover and death:
    (1–8)   At Bethany Jesus is anointed for death;
    (9–19)   The crowds acclaim Jesus as he enters Jerusalem;
    (20–36)   The coming of the Greeks marks the coming of the hour.

Conclusion: Evaluation and summation of Jesus' ministry (xii 37–50):

    xii (37–43)   An evaluation of Jesus' ministry to his own people;
    (44–50)   An unattached discourse of Jesus used as a summary proclamation.

Even a cursory glance at the distribution of these signs throughout the chapters of John indicates that they scarcely form an adequate basis for the division of the Gospel. And indeed we should emphasize that these are not the only signs mentioned in the Book of Signs, for there are passing (sometimes implicit) references to signs in ii 23, iv 45, vii 4, xii 37 (and see xx 30). The fact that there are *seven* signs narrated at length has fascinated some, for a pattern of sevens is clear in another work of the Johannine school, Revelation. Boismard, *art. cit.*, has perfected to a fine art the discovery of sevens in the Fourth Gospel: seven miracles, seven discourses, seven similes used by Jesus, seven titles in ch. i, seven days in i–ii, seven periods in Jesus' life, etc. But a closer look leads one to suspect that this ingenuity is being imposed on the evangelist, who never once gives the slightest indication that he has such numerical patterns in mind and never uses the word seven (contrast Revelation). For instance, does the evangelist intend (4) and (5) above to be treated as two separate signs?

Dodd, *Interpretation,* divides Book One into seven episodes, which form a somewhat more satisfactory apportionment than the seven signs:

(1) The New Beginning (ii 1–iv 42)
(2) The Life-giving Word (iv 46–v 47)
(3) The Bread of Life (vi)
(4) Light and Life (vii–viii)
(5) Judgment by the Light (ix 1–x 21) and Appendix (x 22–39)
(6) The Victory of Life over Death (xi 1–53)
(7) Life through Death (xii 1–36)

Dodd's general principle of joining sign with interpretative discourse is valid, and the brilliance of his analysis of many of these units should leave a permanent mark on Johannine studies. But there is a problem of over-all apportionment. There is a certain unity in chs. ii–iv, but is this "unit" to be put on an equal footing with a single chapter like xi? Chapters ii–iv are composed of at least five different stories set in different locales; ch. xi consists substantially of one well-knit narrative. Has not Dodd too been hypnotized by a desire to find a pattern of seven in the Gospel?

We propose our own division with hesitancy, realizing the danger of imposing insights on the evangelist. But we do claim that there are certain indications in the Gospel itself for the broad lines of this division. For instance, the theme of John the Baptist and his disciples who become Jesus' disciples holds together i 19–ii 11, our Part One. The Gospel itself makes the connection between the first sign at Cana and the second sign at Cana, the two scenes which are the demarcation of our Part Two. The emphasis on feasts as the occasion and indeed subject matter of Jesus' discourses is underlined by the evangelist in chs. v–x, our Part Three. And not only the theme of Lazarus, but also certain stylistic peculiarities bind together chs. xi–xii, Part Four.

There is, moreover, in this division an earnest effort to respect the fluidity of the Gospel's thought. In Revelation it is quite clear that the last member of one series of seven items is at the same time the beginning of the next series, for example, in Rev viii 1 the seventh seal opens the seven trumpets. While we are reluctant to transfer features that are peculiar to Revelation as a book of apocalyptic (e.g., numerical patterns) to the different literary form of the Gospel, nevertheless, we suggest that this feature of overlapping thought may help in dividing the Gospel as well. For instance, the evangelist clearly ties the Cana scene to what has preceded by stressing the role of the disciples (ii 2, 11); yet by emphasizing that this was the first of Jesus' signs the evangelist also looks forward to what is to follow. The same problem faces us with the second Cana miracle (iv 46–54) which looks backward in recalling the first Cana miracle, and yet looks forward with its theme of life, which is taken up in ch. v. The endless arguments about how to place such scenes in a division of the Gospel may find a solution if we recognize that these scenes have a double role of concluding one part and opening the next.

The Themes of the Individual Parts of the Book of Signs

Part One: The themes here are obvious in our table of division. The added question of whether the part is held together by the theme of the seven days of the new creation will be discussed in relation to ii 1–11.

Part Two: There are at least two principal themes that run through this part. While the evangelist suggests these themes rather clearly, one cannot find them worked out consistently in every subdivision; and the desire for logical development has led interpreters to force these themes beyond the expressed intention of the Gospel. The first theme is that of replacing Jewish institutions and religious views:

In A: the replacement of the water for Jewish purifications
In B: the replacement of the Temple
In D: the replacement of worship at Jerusalem and Gerizim

However, in C there is no clear reference to replacement; the suggestion that Jesus is replacing birth into the Chosen People by begetting from above is forced. Possibly, in E one might find a replacement of inadequate faith in signs, but this is scarcely a particularly Jewish religious view.

The second theme is that of the different reactions of individuals and groups to Jesus:

In A: the disciples believe at Cana in Galilee
In the Transition of ii 23–25, many at Jerusalem believe inadequately in his signs
In C: Nicodemus at Jerusalem believes inadequately
In D: the Samaritan woman believes with doubts (iv 29); the Samaritan populace believes more fully (iv 42)
In the Transition of iv 43–45, many of the Galileans believe inadequately in his signs
In E: the royal official and his household come to believe on the basis of Jesus' word and sign

The temptation is to find a logical development in this sequence. One that has been suggested is a growth of faith from Nicodemus, a Jew, through the

CXLIV INTRODUCTION

Samaritan woman (a half-Jew) to the royal official, a Gentile. However, the designation of the official as a Gentile is on the basis of his identification with the Synoptic centurion; John does not mention it, and the evangelist can scarcely have expected the readers to guess it. Other scholars see a geographical progression: faith gets stronger as Jesus moves away from Jerusalem through Samaria into Galilee. But the faith of the Galileans in iv 43–45 is the same as the faith of those at Jerusalem in ii 23–25; and there is no significant difference of faith between the Samaritan populace of iv 42 and the official's household of iv 53. We must beware of being more ingenious than the evangelist himself.

Part Three: This is dominated by Jesus' actions and discourses on the occasion of great Jewish feasts. However, the relation of what is said to a theme of the feast is less obvious in some cases than in others. Subdivisions B and C are the clearest, but in D the reference to the theme of Dedication is subtle and confined to only one verse (x 36). There are subthemes: the Exodus symbolism of manna and of water from the rock uniting vi and vii; opposition to the Pharisees uniting ix and x. The theme of light illustrated in ix is matched in the next part by an enactment of the theme of life in xi, and there are many parallels between these two chapters.

Part Four: The theme of life and death that dominates this part is centered around Lazarus. We shall discuss in the commentary the details of literary criticism that suggest that this part had its own peculiar history.

BIBLIOGRAPHY

Boismard, M.-E., "L'Evangile à quatre dimensions," LumVie 1 (1951), 94–114.
Feuillet, A., "Essai sur la composition littéraire de Joh. ix–xii," *Mélanges Bibliques rédigés en l'honneur de André Robert* (Paris: Bloud et Gay, 1957), pp. 478–93. Now in English in JohSt, pp. 129–47.
van den Bussche, H., "De Structuur van het vierde Evangelie," *Collationes Brugenses et Gandavenses* 2 (1956), 23–42, 182–99.

XI. GENERAL SELECTED BIBLIOGRAPHY

No attempt has been made to give a complete Johannine bibliography; only works actually used are cited—recent works receive the most attention. For method of reference to this bibliography see p. VII.

Barrett, C. K., *The Gospel According to St. John* (London: SPCK, 1956).
Bernard, J. H., *A Critical and Exegetical Commentary on the Gospel According to St. John*, ed. A. H. McNeile, 2 vols. (Edinburgh: Clark, 1928).
Black, M., *An Aramaic Approach to the Gospels and Acts* (2 ed.; Oxford: Clarendon, 1954).
Blinzler, J., *The Trial of Jesus* (Westminster: Newman, 1959).
Braun, F.-M., *Jean le Théologien* (abbr. JeanThéol), I: *Jean le Théologien et son Evangile dans l'Eglise ancienne*, 1959; II: *Les grandes traditions d'Israël*, 1964; III: *Sa théologie: Le mystère de Jésus-Christ*, 1966 (Paris: Gabalda).
Bultmann, R., *Das Evangelium des Johannes* (16 ed. with Suppl.; Göttingen: Vandenhoeck, 1959).
Cullmann, O., *Early Christian Worship* (abbr. ECW), trs. A. S. Todd and J. B. Torrance (SBT, No. 10; London: SCM, 1953).
Dodd, C. H., *The Interpretation of the Fourth Gospel* (Cambridge, 1953).
——————*Historical Tradition in the Fourth Gospel* (Cambridge, 1963).
Glasson, T. F., *Moses in the Fourth Gospel* (SBT, No. 40; London: SCM, 1963).
Guilding, Aileen, *The Fourth Gospel and Jewish Worship* (Oxford: Clarendon, 1960).
Hoskyns, E., *The Fourth Gospel*, ed. F. N. Davey (2 ed.; London: Faber, 1947).
Lagrange, M.-J., *Evangile selon Saint Jean* (8 ed.; Paris: Gabalda, 1948).
Lightfoot, R. H., *St. John's Gospel*, ed. C. F. Evans (Oxford: Clarendon, 1956).
Loisy, A., *Le Quatrième Evangile* (1 ed.; Paris: Picard, 1903—2 ed.; Paris: Nourry, 1921). References to 2 ed. unless otherwise indicated.
Macgregor, G. H. C., *The Gospel of John* (Moffatt Commentaries; New York: Doubleday, 1929).
Mollat, D., *Introductio in exegesim scriptorum sancti Joannis* (Rome: Gregorian, 1961).
Richardson, A., *The Gospel According to Saint John* (Torch Commentaries; London: SCM, 1959).
Schlatter, A., *Der Evangelist Johannes* (3 ed.; Stuttgart: Calwer, 1960).
Schürer, E., *A History of the Jewish People in the Time of Jesus Christ*, 5 vols. (Edinburgh: Clark, 1890).
Smith, D. M., *The Composition and Order of the Fourth Gospel* (Yale, 1965).
Strathmann, H., *Das Evangelium nach Johannes* (10 ed.; Göttingen: Vandenhoeck, 1963).
Taylor, V., *The Gospel According to St. Mark* (London: Macmillan, 1953).

Thüsing, W., *Die Erhöhung und Verherrlichung Jesu im Johannesevangelium* (Münster: Aschendorff, 1960).

van den Bussche, H., *L'Evangile du Verbe,* 2 vols. (Brussels: Pensée Catholique, 1959 and 1961).

Westcott, B. F., *The Gospel According to St. John,* reissued by A. Fox (London: Clarke, 1958 [original 1880]).

Wikenhauser, A., *Das Evangelium nach Johannes* (2 ed.; Regensburg: Pustet, 1957).

Wiles, M. F., *The Spiritual Gospel* (Cambridge, 1960).

I. THE PROLOGUE

An early Christian hymn, probably stemming from Johannine circles, which has been adapted to serve as an overture to the Gospel narrative of the career of the incarnate Word.

1. THE INTRODUCTORY HYMN
(i 1–18)

First Strophe

I
1 In the beginning was the Word;
the Word was in God's presence,
and the Word was God.
2 He was present with God in the beginning.

Second Strophe

3 Through him all things came into being,
and apart from him not a thing came to be.
4 That which had come to be in him was life,
and this life was the light of men.
5 The light shines on in the darkness,
for the darkness did not overcome it.

(6 There was sent by God a man named John 7 who came as a
witness to testify to the light so that through him all men might believe—8 but only to testify to the light, for he himself was not the
light. 9 The real light which gives light to every man was coming into
the world!)

Third Strophe

10 He was in the world,
and the world was made by him;
yet the world did not recognize him.
11 To his own he came;
yet his own people did not accept him.
12 But all those who did accept him
he empowered to become God's children.

That is, those who believe in his name—13 those who were begotten,
not by blood, nor by carnal desire, nor by man's desire, but by God.

Fourth Strophe

14 And the Word became flesh
and made his dwelling among us.
And we have seen his glory,
the glory of an only Son coming from the Father,
filled with enduring love.

(15 John testified to him by proclaiming: "This is he of whom I said,
'The one who comes after me ranks ahead of me, for he existed before
me.'")

16 And of his fullness
we have all had a share—
love in place of love.

17 For while the Law was a gift through Moses, this enduring love came
through Jesus Christ. 18 No one has ever seen God; it is God the only
Son, ever at the Father's side, who has revealed Him.

15: *testified*. In the historical present tense.

NOTES

i 1. *In the beginning*. In the Hebrew Bible the first book (Genesis) is named
by its opening words, "In the beginning"; therefore, the parallel between the
Prologue and Genesis would be easily seen. The parallel continues into the next
verses, where the themes of creation and light and darkness are recalled from
Genesis. John's translation of the opening phrase of Gen i 1, which is the
same as that of LXX, reflects an understanding of that verse evidently current
in NT times; it does not necessarily give us the original meaning intended by
the author of Genesis. E. A. Speiser (The Anchor Bible, vol. 1) translates:
"When God set about to create heaven and earth . . ."
beginning. This is not, as in Genesis, the beginning of creation, for creation
comes in vs. 3. Rather the "beginning" refers to the period before creation and is
a designation, more qualitative than temporal, of the sphere of God. Note how
the Gospel of Mark opens: "The *beginning* of the Gospel of Jesus Christ [the
Son of God] . . ."
was the Word. Since Chrysostom's time, commentators have recognized that
each of the three uses of "was" in vs. 1 has a different connotation: existence,
relationship, and predication respectively. "The Word was" is akin to the "I am"
statements of Jesus in the Gospel proper (see App. IV). There can be no
speculation about how the Word came to be, for the Word simply was.
in God's presence. We attempt here and in vs. 2 a rendering that will capture
the ambiguity of the Gr. *pros ton theon*. Two basic translations have been
proposed: (a) "with God"=accompaniment. BDF, § 239[1], points out that
although *pros* with the accusative usually implies motion, it is sometimes used
in the sense of accompaniment, according to the general weakening in Hellenistic

Greek of the distinction between prepositions of motion and of localization, e.g., between *eis* and *en*. The idea of pre-creation accompaniment appears in John xvii 5: "that glory which I had *with you* [*para*] before the world existed." See the alternate reading of vii 29. **(b)** "towards God"=relationship. In an article in Bib 43 (1962), 366–87, De la Potterie has argued strongly that the dynamic sense of *eis* and *pros* is not lost in John's Greek. He insists that when John uses *pros* and the accusative, it does not mean accompaniment. He points (pp. 380 ff.) to vs. 18, which forms an inclusion with vs. 1, and the expression found there *eis ton kolpon* (literally, "into the Father's bosom," or as we translate, "ever at the Father's side"). The argument that he draws from vs. 18 for the dynamic interpretation of the *pros* in vs. 1, however, depends on the dynamic use of *eis* in vs. 18, and this is disputed. An argument is also drawn from I John i 2, ". . . this eternal life such as it was in the Father's presence [*pros ton patera*]." Yet, since the subject of this sentence is "life," communion rather than relationship seems to be implied. Comparisons between John and I John on the basis of vocabulary present difficulty, for the same words appear in the two works with slightly different nuances. Our own view is that there is a nuance of relationship in John i 1b, but without the precision of that relationship between the Word and God the Father that some would see, e.g., filiation.

God's presence. The article is used with *theos* here. When the Father, Jesus, and the Holy Spirit are involved, *ho theos* is frequently used for God the Father (II Cor xiii 13). Verse 18, the inclusion with vs. 1, speaks of the Father, as does the parallel just mentioned in I John i 2. By emphasizing the relationship between the Word and God the Father, vs. 1b at the same time implicitly distinguishes them.

was God. Vs. 1c has been the subject of prolonged discussion, for it is a crucial text pertaining to Jesus' divinity. There is no article before *theos* as there was in 1b. Some explain this with the simple grammatical rule that predicate nouns are generally anarthrous (BDF, § 273). However, while *theos* is most probably the predicate, such a rule does not necessarily hold for a statement of identity as, for instance, in the "I am . . ." formulae (John xi 25, xiv 6—with the article). To preserve in English the different nuance of *theos* with and without the article, some (Moffatt) would translate, "The Word was divine." But this seems too weak; and, after all, there is in Greek an adjective for "divine" (*theios*) which the author did not choose to use. Haenchen, p. 313[38], objects to this latter point because he thinks that such an adjective smacks of literary Greek not in the Johannine vocabulary. The NEB paraphrases the line: "What God was, the Word was"; and this is certainly better than "divine." Yet for a modern Christian reader whose trinitarian background has accustomed him to thinking of "God" as a larger concept than "God the Father," the translation "The Word was God" is quite correct. This reading is reinforced when one remembers that in the Gospel as it now stands, the affirmation of i 1 is almost certainly meant to form an inclusion with xx 28, where at the end of the Gospel Thomas confesses Jesus as "My God" (*ho theos mou*). These statements represent the Johannine affirmative answer to the charge made against Jesus in the Gospel that he was wrongly making himself God (x 33, v 18). Nevertheless, we should recognize that between the Prologue's "The Word was God" and the later Church's confession that Jesus Christ was "true God of true God" (Nicaea), there was marked development in terms of philosophical thought and a different problematic. See COMMENT.

3. *all things came into being.* From the 2nd century on, this has been taken as a reference to creation. Pollard, *art. cit.,* sees it as a wider reference to all God's external actions, including salvation history, because the Fourth Gospel is not interested in cosmology. However, we shall see that the Prologue had a history independent of the Gospel and does not necessarily have the same theology as the Gospel. In any case, "all things" is a wider concept than "the world," the sphere of man, which will be mentioned in vss. 9–10. The verb "came into being" is *egeneto,* used consistently to describe creation in the LXX of Gen i.

apart from him. Boismard, p. 11, insists that "without him" is not an adequate translation, for not only causality but also presence is implied.

3b–4. These lines are sometimes divided in another way, thus: "3b and apart from him there came to be not a thing which came to be. / 4 In him was life." In such a division, the clause "which came to be"—instead of beginning vs. 4—completes vs. 3. This alternate division is found in the Clementine Vulg.; and according to Mehlmann, "De mente," it was Jerome's own division (except for one instance). But De la Potterie, "De interpretatione," insists that Jerome changed to this division only about A.D. 401 for apologetic reasons. Most modern commentators use the division we have chosen in our translation; Barrett and Haenchen are exceptions. In an attempt to prove that our division is the most ancient Boismard, p. 14, gives an impressive list of patristic writers who used it; and he suggests that the above alternate translation was introduced only in the 4th century as anti-Arian apologetics. The Arians used our division, "That which had come to be in him was life," to prove that the Son had undergone change and therefore was not truly equal to the Father. To counter this the orthodox Fathers preferred the alternate translation, which removed the basis of the Arian interpretation. Not all scholars, however, accept such an explanation of the origin of the alternate division. Mehlmann, "A Note," tries to show that it was pre-Arian; and Haenchen suggests that *our* punctuation arose among the Gnostics. Be this as it may, the poetry of the Prologue favors our division, for the climactic or "staircase" parallelism of the lines requires that the end of one line should match the beginning of the next. In our division the "came to be" at the end of vs. 3 matches the "had come to be" at the beginning of 4. Moreover, there is an interesting parallel at Qumran for 3b which helps to confirm our reading (1QS xi 11): "And by His knowledge all has come to be, and by His thought, He directs all that is and *without Him not a thing is done* [or made]." See De la Potterie for an exhaustive discussion of the whole problem.

4a. *That which had come to be in him was life.* There are five very difficult problems in this line: **(a)** "That which *had come to be.*" The Prologue shifts from the aorist *egeneto,* "came to be," which was used twice in vs. 3, to a perfect *gegonen,* "had come to be." Some believe that this is an attempt to give a generic idea of created being: *"all* that which had come to be." Normally, however, the emphasis in the perfect tense is on duration: something took place in the past but still has effect at the time of speaking. **(b)** "In him" or "in it"? Van Hoonacker in 1901 and Loisy in 1903 suggested a possibility that had not been recognized by earlier commentators; namely, that this phrase should be translated "in it" and considered to be a *casus pendens* resuming "that which had come to be." The resultant translation, "That which had come to be, in it was life," offers serious difficulties. If a resumptive were intended, *en toutō* ("in this") would be more normal; also the word "life" has no article and should be a predicate, not a subject. That "life" in 4a should be a predicate is also suggested by the "staircase" parallelism, since what would then be a predicate in 4a would be a subject in 4b. There is a variant of the "in it" translation that is opted for by Mollat in SB: "That which had come to be, in it he was life." This translation avoids some of the difficulties just mentioned; but it introduces as subject the pronoun implied in the verb, and there is no other example of this in vss. 1–5. See Lacan, pp. 67–69. (c) If we accept the reading "in him," to which group of words do we associate it? There are two possible readings: "That-which-had-come-to-be was life in him" and "That-which-had-come-to-be-in-him was life."

Many modern scholars accept the first reading, "was life in him," and thus join Eusebius, Cyril of Alexandria, Augustine, and most of the Latin Fathers. This translation usually entails that the subject, "that-which-had-come-to-be," be taken in the same sense as the "all things" which came into being of vs. 3; namely, that it refer to the whole of creation. However, 4b ("this life was the light of men") seems to indicate that not all creation but only living creatures or, more likely, men are meant by "that-which-had-come-to-be" in 4a. A further difficulty in this translation is the awkwardness of the verb, and many have to paraphrase: "found life" or "was alive." Even the tense of the verb is difficult since we would expect a present tense: "is alive in him." For these reasons recent treatments by Lacan and Vawter find this translation too awkward. If the author of the Prologue wished to express the sentiments of the hymn in Col i 17, "In him all things subsist," he chose a very obscure way to do so.

Origen, Hilary, Ambrose, and the older Greek Fathers accepted the second reading: "That-which-had-*come-to-be-in-him* was life." This would be the reading normally indicated by the position of the phrase "in him" in Greek. The clause "that-which-had-come-to-be-in-him" has nothing to do with a change within the Word or with the pre-existence of divine ideas in the Word. Rather, following vs. 3, the clause represents a narrowing down of creation; vs. 4 is not going to talk about the whole of creation but a special creation in the Word. (d) "was life" or "is life"? There is respectable textual evidence for reading a present tense in vs. 4a; however both Bodmer papyri support the imperfect. The same tense is required in both lines of 4, and the evidence for the imperfect in 4b is overwhelming (even though Boismard, p. 12, would correct it and read the present in both lines). We suggest that the imperfect was original in 4a, but some scribes changed it to the present because it fitted better with the reading mentioned above: "That-which-has-come-to-be *is* life in him." (e) "life"—does this mean natural life or eternal life? If the subject of line 4a is taken to be the whole of creation, then eternal life would be singularly inappropriate. But if, as we suggest, a special aspect of creation is meant, i.e., creation in the Word, then eternal life is quite appropriate. The word for "life" (*zōē*—see App. I:6) never means natural life in John or the Johannine Epistles. The identification of this life with the light of *men* in the next line makes us think that eternal life is meant. In the Prologue to I John (i 2) "life" is specified as "eternal life."

4b. *this life was the light*. Some would reverse subject and predicate: "the light of men was this life"; they point to viii 12, "the light of life." (See discussion in Boismard, pp. 18–19.) Once again "staircase" parallelism suggests that "light" is the predicate since it is the subject of 5a. The symbolism of light is related to Gen i.

5. *shines on*. Bultmann's suggestion, p. 26[4], that this verb was originally imperfect has no textual support.

did not overcome. Does this aorist refer to a specific attempt of the darkness to overcome the light? Or is it a complexive aorist summing up a series of attempts (BDF, § 332)? Or is it a gnomic aorist indicating that darkness is always trying to overcome light (BDF, § 333)? If, as we think, this is a reference to the sin in Gen iii, then the normal meaning of the aorist as a single past action is suitable.

overcome. The Greek verb *katalambanein* is hard to translate, and we can distinguish four tendencies among translators: (a) "to grasp, to comprehend." Cyril of Alexandria, the Latin tradition, Lagrange, Macgregor, Braun are among the many who interpret the verb as a reference to intellectual comprehension. If "the light" is a reference to the incarnate Word, this meaning is quite intelligible; for then the line is saying that men did not perceive the light brought by Jesus during his ministry (iii 19). The best argument for this translation is found in the parallels in vss. 10, 11: "yet the darkness did not comprehend it . . . yet the world did not recognize him . . . yet his own people did not accept him." Note that if in vs. 5b we accept "comprehend," the initial *kai* should be translated as "yet," and not as "for." (b) "to welcome, receive, accept, appreciate." Dupont, Bultmann, and Wikenhauser are among those who prefer this meaning, which matches the meaning of *paralambanein* ("accept") in vs. 11. Although Black, p. 10, does not regard "receive" as an adequate translation of the Greek, he suggests that the original Aramaic was *la qabblēh qablâ*, "the darkness did not receive it." (The Aramaic play between *qablâ*, "darkness," and *qabblēh*, "receive it," is obvious.) Other proponents of an Aramaic original for the Prologue reconstruct the original verb otherwise. Burney thinks of an original *'aqbēl*, "darken," misread as *qabbēl*, "receive"; Schaeder abandons wordplay and suggests *'aḥad*, "overcome"; Nagel, *art. cit.*, points out that the root *qbl* in later Aramaic (Syriac) has a note of opposition, and he makes other suggestions that can mean both "grasp" and "overcome." The Aramaic evidence is scarcely conclusive. (c) "to overtake, overcome [grasp in a hostile sense]." Origen, the majority of the Greek Fathers, Schlatter, Westcott, and Boismard are among those who accept this meaning. *Katalambanein* has this meaning in its only other use in John (xii 35): "the darkness will come over you." The opposition between light and darkness in Johannine dualistic thought seems to demand such a verb to describe their encounter. As we shall see, the concept of the Word in the Prologue is similar to that of personified Wisdom in the OT. It is worth noting that Wis vii 29–30 compares Wisdom to a light that darkness cannot *supplant*, for wickedness does not prevail over Wisdom. Another parallel is in the *Odes of Solomon* xviii 6: "That the light may not be overcome by the darkness." The *Acts of Thomas* 130 speaks of a "light that has not been overcome." These reasons and parallels cause us to accept "overcome" for vs. 5b, but we admit that reading 5b as the reason for 5a (*"for* the darkness did not overcome it") destroys the parallelism with 10c and 11b. (d) "to master." This is Moffatt's attempt to capture the two meanings of "understand" and "overcome." Another ambiguous translation might be "absorb." Finally, we should mention the possibility that *katalambanein* had one meaning when the verse stood as part of an independent hymn, and took on another meaning when the hymn became the Prologue of the Gospel.

6. *There was.* This is not the *ēn*, "was," used of the Word in vss. 1–2, but the *egeneto* used of creation in vss. 3–4. John the Baptist is a creature.

sent by God. In i 33 John the Baptist will speak of "the one who *sent* me to baptize"; in iii 28 he says, "I am *sent* before him."

7. *all men.* The concern has shifted from the "all things" of vs. 3 to the sphere of men. Some see here a view of John the Baptist's role that contradicts i 31, where it is said that John the Baptist came that Jesus might be revealed *to Israel*. But the idea is that ultimately John the Baptist's message would touch all men, just

as Jesus' message, spoken in Israel, would touch all men. The Fourth Gospel stresses more the role of John the Baptist as a witness than as a baptizer.

8. *not the light.* In v 35 Jesus calls John the Baptist a lamp; but Jesus himself is the light (iii 19, viii 12, ix 5).

9. Some would take this verse as poetry continuing vs. 5, thus:

> He was the real light
> that gives light to every man;
> he was coming into the world.

Line 9a can mean, "The real light was," or, if we supply a subject from the verb form, "He was the real light." The meaning must in part be determined by what is done with 9c where the verbal form is simply a participle ("coming into the world"), probably modifying "light." If we read 9a as "He was the real light," then the separated participle in 9c is very awkward; notice how it has to be artificially avoided above by supplying another "he was" in 9c. If we read 9a as "The real light was," then the participle of 9c is the periphrastic continuation of the verb: "The real light was . . . coming into the world." Periphrastic circumlocution is known in classical Greek, but its frequency in the NT may be under Aramaic influence (BDF, § 353). The periphrastic use of *einai* ("to be") plus a present participle as a circumlocution for the imperfect occurs nine times in John. The special difficulty in i 9 is that the verb "was" is separated from the participle by a clause, although we have examples of similar separation in i 28; Mark xiv 49; Luke ii 8 (see ZGB, § 362). Perhaps the motive behind the separation in vs. 9 was to end the verse on the theme of "the world" which would be picked up in vs. 10. Further, if on the basis of BDF, § 353[1] one wishes to stress that in such cases of separated periphrasis there is a certain independence granted to the main verb, then the idea is that there *was* a real light and it was *coming* into the world.

Along with Bernard, Gächter, Käsemann, and others, we think that the evidence is strongly against considering vs. 9 as part of the poetry of the Prologue. It does not have the conjunctive particle *kai* which is so common in the poetic parts of the Prologue; it uses subordination which they do not. The "light" is the subject of vs. 9; and this subject is not taken up in vs. 10. Rather the masculine pronoun in vs. 10 ("light" is neuter) indicates that its subject is the Word, the same subject that is prominent in the opening lines of the other stanzas (vss. 1, 3, 14). The periphrasis that we have postulated for vs. 9 would be strange in poetry, and quite unlike the use of "was" in vss. 1–2. Verse 9 is a contrast with vs. 8—the real light is Jesus, not John the Baptist—and belongs to the same level of the Prologue's literary history as vs. 8, namely, the level of final redaction. Curiously enough, Schnackenburg considers only 9c to be editorial.

real light. "Real" reflects *alēthinos;* see App. I:2.

gives light. Some think that this does not mean the light of revelation, but the spotlight of judgment, the pitiless, all-revealing light not to be avoided. Verse 7, however, seems to imply a light that one believes in.

to every man. If John the Baptist's witness was for all men, the sphere of enlightenment from the real light can scarcely be less.

coming into the world. There are two possible words for the participle to modify: (a) "man"="The real light which gives light to every man coming into the world." This is the interpretation of the early versions (OL, Vulg., OS, Boh.), the Greek Fathers (Eusebius, Cyril of Alexandria, Chrysostom), and many modern scholars (Burney, Schlatter, Bultmann, Wikenhauser). It creates a redundancy, for in rabbinic literature "they who come into the world" is an expression for men. On this basis Bultmann, p. 31[6], thinks that we should simply excise "man" in vs. 9 as a gloss. (b) "light"="The real light . . . was coming into the world." This interpretation is supported by the Sahidic, the Latin Fathers (Tertullian and Cyprian), and by most modern commentators (Lagrange, Braun, Dupont, Westcott, Macgregor, Bernard, Boismard, etc.). It fits the context better, for in vs. 10 the stress is on the Word (=the light) as being in the world. We note too that "coming into the world" is not used in John to describe men, but is used to describe Jesus the light; e.g., iii 19: "The light has come into the world" (also xii 46). It seems, finally, that the contrast of vs. 9 with vs. 8 also demands this interpretation: John the Baptist was not the light; the real light was coming into the world.

10. *He was.* The Word, not the light.

the world. See App. I:7. This is part of the creation of vs. 3, but only that part of creation that is capable of response, the world of men. This is seen clearly in iii 19: "The light has come into *the world,* but *men* have preferred darkness to light."

was made. Or "came to be"—the *egeneto* of creation in vs. 3.

not recognize. In the question of whether this verse refers to the OT or the NT presence of God's Word among men, we might remember that in the OT the basic sin is the failure to obey Yahweh, while for John the basic sin is the failure to know and believe in Jesus. (Naturally, knowledge of Jesus would also imply repentance and a new life in his service.)

11. *To his own.* The expression is neuter; it occurs again in xix 27 where the disciple takes Mary *to his own* (to his own home, into his care). In vs. 11a the idea seems to be what was peculiarly his own in "the world," i.e., the heritage of Israel, the Promised Land, Jerusalem.

his own people. Here the expression is masculine. Those who think that this hymn was originally in Aramaic point out that *dîlēh* ("his own"—without differentiation of gender) would have been found in both 11a and 11b. They are hard put to explain why the Greek translator chose two different genders to express it. The reference is clearly to the people of Israel; according to Exod xix 5, Yahweh said to Israel: "You shall be *my own possession* among all the peoples." Bultmann, p. 35, rejects this and sees a cosmological reference, rather than a reference to salvation history. His interpretation flows from his presupposition that the Prologue was originally a Gnostic hymn.

12. Do lines 12a–b belong to the original hymn, or are they prose comment? Bernard, De Ausejo, Green, Haenchen, Robinson, Schnackenburg do *not* accept them as part of the hymn. In part the position taken will depend on whether or not one regards this stanza as referring to the historical career of the incarnate Word. If one does, it seems odd to end the stanza on the negative note of vs. 11. If poetic format is the absolute guide, however, then these lines are cast differently from the preceding verses.

all those who did accept him. This clause in the nominative is an expansion of the indirect object of "empower" (literally "he empowered *them*") in vs. 12b. It is an example of the *casus pendens* construction where a word or phrase is taken out of its normal place in the sentence and put first. The construction occurs 27 times in John, compared with 21 times in all three Synoptics. However, the phrase thus moved is usually the expansion of a nominative or an accusative, rarely of a dative as here. The construction is Semitic but is also found in colloquial Greek of non-Semitic origin.

empowered. Literally "gave power" (*edōken exousian*), or, if we wish to trans-

late the Gr. *exousia* more exactly, "gave authority or right"—Dodd, *Interpretation,*
p. 270[1], characterizes "power" as a most misleading translation. However, to
make of this a semi-judicial pronouncement whereby the Word gave men the *right*
to become God's sons is to introduce an element strange to Johannine thought:
sonship is based on divine begetting, not on any claim on man's part. Bultmann,
p. 36[1], and Boismard, pp. 42–43, are probably correct in seeing the Greek as an
awkward attempt to render the idea behind the Semitic expression, "he gave
[*nathan*] them to become."

God's children. "Children"=*tekna* (also xi 52); *huios,* "son" is used in John
only for Jesus. Contrast Matt v 9, which uses *huioi* for men: the peacemakers
shall be called God's sons; also Paul in Gal iii 26. Yet, while John preserves a
vocabulary difference between Jesus as God's son and Christians as God's
children, it is in John that our *present* state as God's children on this earth
comes out most clearly; I John iii 2: "Beloved, we are God's children now."

That is, those who believe in his name. This clause also explains the indirect
object of "empowered," just as vs. 12a; only while 12a is in the nominative, 12c is
in the dative. (We have tried to capture the better agreement of 12c by introducing it with "That is.") That 12a and 12c really say the same thing has left its
mark in the copying of the text. Some of the Latin, Greek, Syriac Fathers and
the *Diatessaron* seem to omit 12c, while a few Latin Fathers, Philoxenus of
Mabbug, and an Ethiopic witness omit 12a. Boismard, RB 57 (1950), 401–8,
argues that the present text of John is a conflation of alternate readings. However,
the fact that 12c is in typical Johannine language and thought pattern makes it
possible that 12c is an editorial expansion of the hymn. It may have been added to
stress that not only the original acceptance of Jesus (aorist in 12a), but also
continued belief in him (present in 12c), entitled men to become God's children.

believe in. See App. I:9 on *pisteuein eis,* a typically Johannine construction.

in his name. This is also typically Johannine (ii 23, iii 18; I John v 13). Belief
in the name of Jesus is not different from belief in Jesus, although the former
expression brings out clearly that to believe in Jesus one must believe that he
bears the divine name, given to him by God (xvii 11–12). For the possibility that
this name may be "I AM" see App. IV.

13. Is vs. 13 part of the original poetic hymn, or part of the editorial comment?
Bernard, Gaechter, Green, Haenchen, Jeremias, Käsemann, Robinson, Schnackenburg, and Wikenhauser are among those who think of it as editorial expansion.
Certainly the style is different from the clearly poetic stanzas of the hymn. The
apologetic motif is strong in 13, and this is not true of the poetic verses. Verses
1–5, 9–12, and 14 sing of the Word's activities, while vs. 13 tells of those who
believe in him. There is really only one serious objection to considering both 12c
and 13 as editorial additions: 12c is dative, 13 is nominative (like 12a—we have
tried to express the difference by the dash). Could it be that we are encountering
additions made by different hands? However, on the level of ideas, 12c and 13 can
go together, for in Johannine thought those who believe and those begotten
by God are equivalent: "Everyone who believes that Jesus is the Messiah is begotten by God" (I John v 1).

those who were begotten. The textual evidence for reading a plural is overwhelming, with not a single Greek ms. supporting the singular. The singular,
"he who was begotten," is read by one OL witness, perhaps by the OS[cur]; and
the text is applied to Jesus by a number of Fathers (Justin?, Irenaeus, Tertullian)
and by some early writings (*Liber Comicus, Epistula Apostolorum*). On this
rather slender evidence the singular has been supported by a considerable num-

ber of scholars: Boismard, Blass, Braun, Burney, Dupont, Mollat (SB), Zahn, and others. The patristic evidence for the singular is difficult to evaluate because it may be that the text is simply undergoing adaptation to Jesus in order to support the virgin birth. One can imagine an *a fortiori* argument: if it is true that Christians are not begotten by blood, by carnal desire, etc., how much more true was this of Jesus. The Latin evidence also has pitfalls, for the Latin *qui* is both singular and plural and the difference between *qui natus est* and *qui nati sunt* is only in the verb. Three arguments seem conclusively to favor the plural. *First,* both the ancient Bodmer papyri read a plural. *Second,* texts in the process of transmission tend to become more, not less, christological. Is it logical to suppose that scribal tradition on such a large scale would dilute a valuable reference to the virgin birth of Jesus if the singular were the original reading? *Third,* John and I John never describe Jesus as having been begotten by God (I John v 18 is dubious); but they do speak thus of those who follow Jesus (iii 3–8; I John iii 9, iv 7, v 1–4, v 18a). Recently J. Schmid has discussed the problem thoroughly, only to opt for the plural, as do Barrett, Bultmann, Lightfoot, Wikenhauser, and others.

The only argument *against* the plural is the relationship of vs. 13 to 12b. Boismard, p. 37, asks how can the Word empower men *to become* God's children if they were already begotten by God? But this is to impose too exact a logic on the sequence. Verse 13 explains what is meant by God's children; it explains that those who accepted Jesus were those who were granted to Jesus by the Father (vi 37, 65); they were not the ones begotten from below, but the ones begotten from above (iii 31).

begotten. Although this verb can mean "born" (as of a female principle—see NOTE on iii 3), the idea of agency implied in "begotten" is clearly more appropriate. In I John iii 9 the seed of God is mentioned.

not by blood. The word for "blood" is plural. This is curious against a background of Hebrew mentality, for there the plural of "blood" means bloodshed. Bernard, I, p. 18, suggests a background of Greek physiology where the embryo was thought to be made of the mother's blood and the father's seed. In this interpretation the three negatives in the verse rule out woman, lust, and man. Such an interpretation eliminates any use of the text to prove the virgin birth of Jesus. Others suggest that we are to think of the "blood" of vs. 13b and the "flesh" of 13c as a unit, the Hebrew "flesh and blood," equivalent to "man" (Matt xvi 17; I Cor xv 50). This explanation is ruled out by the fact that "blood" is a plural, and by the order "blood, flesh"; moreover, 13c speaks not of the "flesh" but of the "desire of the flesh." Boismard, p. 44, mentions the possibility that "blood" might be a dignified way of speaking of seed. Such euphemism seems unlikely since there is no hesitation of speaking about seed in the Johannine writings (I John iii 9).

nor by carnal desire. Literally "the desire of the flesh." The word "desire" is omitted in some Ethiopic mss. and in some of the Fathers, perhaps in order to bring the text more into conformity with the "flesh and blood" idiom mentioned above. *Thelēma*, "will, desire," appears for "lust" in some of the Greek papyri of this period. "Flesh" here is not a wicked principle opposed to God. Rather, it is the sphere of the natural, the powerless, the superficial, opposed to "spirit," which is the sphere of the heavenly and the real (iii 6, vi 63, viii 15).

nor by man's desire. Man was looked on as the principal agent in generation; some considered the woman's role no more than that of a vessel for the embryo. This clause is omitted in Vaticanus, ms. 17, and some Fathers. Boismard, RB 57

(1950), 401–8, suggests that the redundancy in these clauses and the evidence for the omission of one or the other point to the fact that we have a conflation of alternate readings.

14. Does vs. 14 belong to the poetry of the Prologue? De Ausejo thinks that 14a–b form a two-line strophe or stanza by themselves; and he puts 14c–e with 16 and 18 as another strophe. Schnackenburg eliminates 14c–d as an addition and retains only 14a–b,e as the original poetry. Green regards just 14e as an addition. For Käsemann the whole verse is an addition. On the basis of poetic format it may be noted that the *kai* pattern appears in the first three lines. The last line cannot be easily excised from the poetry since it ties in so closely with 16. It seems best to accept the whole of 14 as poetry, and this is the view of the majority of the critics.

became flesh. "Flesh" stands for the whole man. It is interesting that even in the unsophisticated christological terminology of the 1st century it is not said that the Word became *a* man, but equivalently that the Word became man.

made his dwelling. Skēnoun, related to *skēnē,* "tent," is literally "to pitch a tent." In the NT it is found only here and in Revelation; see COMMENT for OT background.

among us. Literally "in us"; compare Rev xxi 3: "Behold the dwelling of God is with men; He will dwell with them." Here, the first person makes its appearance in the Prologue; "us" refers to mankind.

we. This is a more confined use of the first person, for the "we" is not mankind but the apostolic witnesses, as in the Prologue of I John. It is this shift of meaning reflected in "us" and "we" that makes some think of vs. 14c–d as being an addition.

seen. For *theasthai* see App. I:3. Compare I John i 1: ". . . something we have seen [*hōran*] with our own eyes; something we actually looked at [*theasthai*], and felt with our own hands." De Ausejo, pp. 406–7, thinks that this is a reference to seeing the resurrected Christ, but such a jump from the Incarnation is rather abrupt.

glory. For *doxa,* see App. I:4.

of an only Son. Literally "*as* of an only Son"; the versions (OS, Copt, Eth.) and Tatian seem to have read the "as" earlier in the line: "as the glory of an only Son." Kačur, *art. cit.,* thinks this is the original reading. However, the versions would not be precise on a point like this; moreover, it may have been theologically desirable to avoid the reading "as of an only Son," lest someone interpret it to mean, "as if he were an only Son." The meaning of "as" is, of course, not "as if" but "in the quality of."

only Son. For a complete treatment of this term *monogenēs* see D. Moody, JBL 72 (1953), 213–19. Literally the Greek means "of a single [*monos*] kind [*genos*]." Although *genos* is distantly related to *gennan,* "to beget," there is little Greek justification for the translation of *monogenēs* as "only begotten." The OL correctly translated it as *unicus,* "only," and so did Jerome where it was not applied to Jesus. But to answer the Arian claim that Jesus was not begotten but made, Jerome translated it as *unigenitus,* "only begotten," in passages like this one (also i 18, iii 16, 18). The influence of the Vulg. on the KJ made "only begotten" the standard English rendition. (Actually, as we have insisted, John does not use the term "begotten" of Jesus.) *Monogenēs* describes a quality of Jesus, his uniqueness, not what is called in Trinitarian theology his "procession." It reflects Heb. *yāhîd,* "only, precious," which is used in Gen xxii 2, 12, 16, of

Abraham's son Isaac, as *monogenēs* is used of Isaac in Heb xi 17. Isaac was Abraham's uniquely precious son, but not his only begotten.

coming from the Father. "Coming" is not in the Greek but is supplied from the context. What word does this phrase modify: "Son" (W. Bauer, Boismard, Bultmann, Westcott) or "glory" (Braun, Dupont, Lagrange)? In v 44 Jesus attacks the Jews for not seeking that glory which comes from the One God. Thus there is a Johannine parallel for glory coming from the Father, but not exactly in the sense meant here. See also xvii 22 where it is said implicitly that Jesus has been given glory by the Father. There are also Johannine parallels for the application of the phrase "from [*para*] the Father" to the Son (vi 46, vii 29, ix 16, xvi 27), and two other uses of the "only Son" (iii 15–17; I John iv 9) mention the Father's sending of the Son into the world. There is no major difference in meaning no matter which word the phrase modifies. If we read "an only Son coming from the Father," the reference is to the mission of the Son, not his procession within the Trinity; the "we have seen" makes this certain.

filled with. What does this adjective modify: the Word, the glory, or the Son? The nominative masculine singular form would make agreement with "the Word" of 14a the most regular construction, and this is the understanding of the Latin translations. (This is another reason why some scholars regard 14c–d as an addition.) However, as BDF, § 137[1], points out, this adjective is sometimes treated as indeclinable; hence it could modify "glory" (so Codex Bezae, Irenaeus, Athanasius, Chrysostom) or "only Son." There is no major difference in meaning.

enduring love. Literally two nouns, *charis* and *alētheia;* for Boismard the construction of the adjective "full" followed by two determinatives is a proof that Luke edited the Prologue, for there are five examples of such a construction in Acts. *Charis,* "grace," appears in John only here; it is found 25 times in Luke-Acts, and in Paul it is quite common for God's gift of redemption. For *alētheia,* "truth," see App. I:2. However, these two words are used here in a unique way reflecting the famous OT pairing of *ḥesed* and *'emet.* God's *ḥesed* is His kindness or mercy in choosing Israel without any merit on Israel's part and His expression of this love for Israel in the covenant. Suggested translations are: "covenant love," "merciful love," "kindness," "loving-kindness." For the Qumran Essenes their community was a covenant of *ḥesed.* God's *'emet* is His fidelity to the covenant promises. Suggested translations are: "fidelity, constancy, faithfulness." In Exod xxxiv 6 we hear this description of Yahweh as He makes the covenant with Moses on Sinai: "The Lord, a God merciful and gracious, slow to anger, and rich [*rab*] in *ḥesed* and *'emet.*" See also Pss xxv 10, lxi 7, lxxxvi 15; Prov xx 28. Kuyper, *art cit.,* gives a complete treatment.

The real objection to seeing the Prologue's *charis* and *alētheia* as a translation of *ḥesed* and *'emet* is that *ḥesed* is normally rendered in LXX by *eleos,* "mercy," not by *charis.* However, John's use of Scripture is often not faithful to LXX. J. A. Montgomery, "Hebrew Hesed and Greek Charis," HTR 32 (1939), 97–102, has shown that *charis* is an excellent translation for *ḥesed.* The Syriac translates both the *ḥesed* and *'emet* of the OT and the *charis* and *alētheia* of John i 14 by the same words (*taibūtâ* and *qushtâ*). The Christian Syro-Palestinian dialect renders *charis* by *ḥasdâ* (=*ḥesed*). As for *alētheia,* in a passage like Rom xv 8 it clearly represents the covenant fidelity of the OT. It is interesting to note that the Word of God who comes down from heaven in Rev xix 11–13 is called "faithful and true [*pistis . . . alēthinos*]," which is probably another reflection of the *ḥesed* and *'emet* motif.

15. John the Baptist makes this statement of Jesus in i 30. It is agreed today that this verse is an addition to the original hymn, an addition of the same type as vss. 6–8(9), awkwardly breaking up vss. 14 and 16.

testified. Literally, historical present, although Haenchen, p. 353, treats it as a real present in the sense that John the Baptist is now giving witness along with the community. The use of a present for an aorist tense in vivid narrative is common in the NT. Some regard it as a sign of Aramaic influence, but it is found in classical writers as well. Black, p. 94, says there is nothing especially Semitic about its use, although it is overdone in Mark and John. It is probably to be regarded as an example of less polished writing. We shall note the historical presents in the textual notes to the translation.

by proclaiming. Literally perfect tense: "and has proclaimed": the perfect here has simply the value of a present tense (BDF, § 341). The present of the verb *krazein* is rare, and the perfect is used in its place (BDF, § 101). John the Baptist's witness to Jesus and proclamation of him is looked on as still in effect against the claims of the sectarians.

I said. Even in i 30 the reference to a previous statement by John the Baptist is awkward; here it is illogical and the sure sign of editing.

16. A few commentators (Bernard, Käsemann) would exclude this verse from the original hymn. On the one hand, vs. 16 is closely tied in to 14, with 16a picking up the theme of fullness (not quite in "staircase" fashion, however), and 16c picking up the theme of love. Perhaps (see below) the introductory *kai* is present. On the other hand, the poetry of 16 is not of the same quality as that of the rest of the hymn. If 16 was an addition, then we have to accept two stages of editing, for it would not make sense to say that the same editor at the same time added both 15 and 16 (16 expands 14; 15 is an interruption). It is perhaps best to opt for simplicity and accept 16 as part of the hymn.

And. Verse 16 begins with *hoti* ("that, because, for") in the best witnesses, including the Bodmer papyri. However, there is respectable Greek evidence for *kai*—also in the versions and the Fathers, but they would not necessarily be precise witnesses in an instance like this. The best argument for *hoti* is the possibility that *kai* was introduced in imitation of the initial *kai* found throughout the poem. Boismard, pp. 59–60, and Bultmann, p. 51[6], argue, on the other hand, that *hoti* may be an insertion reflecting the Alexandrian exegesis of Origen's time wherein it was thought that John the Baptist was still speaking: "He existed before me *because* of his fullness we have all [even I] had a share." The suggestion that *hoti* represents a misunderstanding of the Aramaic relative *de* (Burney; Black, p. 58) is too speculative. If *hoti* is original, then vs. 16 is a proof that the Word who became flesh was in truth filled with enduring love, *for* of that fullness we were all able to have a share.

fullness. Plērōma, occurring only here in the Johannine writings, is an important Pauline theological term; it appears in the hymn of Col i 19: "And in him God was pleased for all the *plērōma* to dwell." Its exact connotation in the Prologue depends to some extent on what "filled with" in vs. 14 modifies.

we. This refers to mankind as did the "us" in 14b; see NOTE on "we" in vs. 14c.

in place of. The preposition *anti* does not occur again in the Johannine writings; perhaps this is an argument against considering vs. 16 as editorial, for we would expect the editor to use typical Johannine vocabulary. Several meanings are possible for it here: (a) "Love in place of love." This idea of *replacement,* as held by the Greek Fathers (Origen, Cyril of Alexandria, Chrysostom), connotes the *ḥesed* of a New Covenant in place of the *ḥesed* of Sinai. Verse 17 seems to support this. The objection that John would not have considered the giving of the Law on Sinai as *ḥesed* because of the Johannine opposition to "the Jews" seems to overlook the fact that John never denies the role of Israel. In iv 22 we hear: "Salvation is from the Jews [=Israel, on a foreigner's lips]." (b) "Grace upon grace" or "grace after grace": *accumulation.* Many modern commentators (Lagrange, Hoskyns, Bultmann, Barrett) support this reading on the basis of a text in Philo (*De Posteritate Caini* 145) where *anti* clearly has this meaning. Normally, however, accumulation would be expressed by *epi,* while *anti* implies opposition or substitution. The translation of *anti* as accumulation is strongly supported by Spicq in *Dieu et l'homme* (Paris: Cerf, 1961), pp. 30–31, citing W. Hendriksen's specialized study of *anti* in the NT. (c) "Grace for grace" or "grace matching grace": *correspondence.* The idea behind this translation is that the grace that constitutes our share corresponds to the grace of the Word. Bernard, J. A. T. Robinson, and Lacan support this translation which is close to a recognized meaning of *anti,* "in return for." Joüon compares *anti* to Heb. *keneged* in Gen ii 18, 20, "a helper matching him"; see RSR 22 (1932), 206. The translation of *charis* as reflecting *ḥesed* fits in with translation (*a*) more easily than with the other two translations, but it is not impossible in (*b*) and (*c*).

17. That this verse does not belong to the original hymn is maintained by Bernard, Bultmann, De Ausejo, Käsemann, Schnackenburg, and others. Among its peculiarities is the mention of historical figures (e.g., Moses), a feature not found in the Pauline hymns; yet Heb i 1 mentions the prophets. Bultmann says that the contrast in this verse between Law and grace (*charis*="love") belongs more to Pauline theology; however, see below. There is no *kai* connective. It is perhaps best to see in vs. 17 an editorial explanation of 16c.

was a gift. "To give a law" is not a Greek expression, but is typically Semitic.

this enduring love. Once again this represents the two nouns *charis* and *alētheia.* The articles before the nouns indicate a reference to the "enduring love" already spoken of in vs. 14, whence our translation as "this." If one accepts the translation of 16c as "love *in place of* love," then one understands the gift of the Law through Moses as an instance of *ḥesed* and *'emet,* an understanding that truly reflects the OT outlook. The theory that vs. 17 contrasts the absence of enduring love in the Law with presence of enduring love in Jesus Christ does not seem to do justice to John's honorific reference to Moses (i 45, iii 14, v 46). Rather vs. 17 contrasts the enduring love shown in the Law with the supreme example of enduring love shown in Jesus. It is true that in the Gospel Jesus speaks derogatively of "your Law"; yet this reflects opposition not so much to the Law as given to Moses as to the Law interpreted and used by the Jewish authorities against Jesus and Christianity. There is no suggestion in John that when the Law was given through Moses, it was not a magnificent act of God's love. A contrast similar in spirit to that of John i 17 is found in Heb i 1: "God spoke of old to our ancestors through the prophets, but in these last days He has spoken to us through His Son." Boismard, pp. 62–64, argues that enduring love is not so much a divine attribute but a reference to qualities inherent in man and planted there by Jesus Christ. The distinction is probably too subtle.

18. Some scholars who regard vs. 17 as editorial accept 18 as part of the original poem, e.g., De Ausejo and Bernard. It might be set up in four lines of poetry, thus:

> No one has ever seen God;
> it is God the only Son,
> ever at the Father's side,
> who has revealed him.

Bernard, however, sets it up in three lines, combining 18b–c in one line. In either case there are no *kai's;* the co-ordination is poor; and there is *casus pendens*—indications that we are not dealing with hymnic poetry.

God the only Son. This phrase is set off by itself in *casus pendens* and then resumed in the last clause of vs. 18 by *ekeinos* ("that one") as the subject of "revealed," thus: "God the only Son ... that one has revealed Him." The textual witnesses are not in agreement on the reading; there are three possibilities: (a) [*ho*] *monogenēs theos,* "God the only Son." This is supported by the evidence of the best Greek manuscripts, including the Bodmer papyri, by the Syr., by Irenaeus, Clement of Alexandria, and Origen. This reading is suspect as being too highly developed theologically; yet it is not anti-Arian polemic, for the Arians did not balk at giving this title to Jesus. Some object to the strangeness of the statement that only God can reveal God, and the implication that only God has seen God. (b) *monogenēs huios,* literally "the Son, the only one." This combination appears in three of the other four uses of *monogenēs* in the Johannine writings (iii 16, 18; I John iv 9), and its appearance here may have resulted from a scribal tendency to conform. This reading is attested by the versions (Latin, OS^cur), by the later Greek witnesses, and by Athanasius, Chrysostom, and the Latin Fathers. (c) *monogenēs,* "the only Son." While this is the simplest reading, it may have resulted from conformity with vs. 14. One could explain reading (*b*) as an expansion of this. It has the poorest attestation of the three readings: Tatian, Origen (once), Epiphanius, Cyril of Alexandria. Boismard accepts it, but the complete lack of Greek textual support makes it suspect.

ever at the Father's side. Literally "the one who is in[to=*eis*] the bosom of the Father." For *eis* see NOTE on "in God's presence" in vs. 1; De la Potterie would stress the dynamic force of the preposition as indicating an active and vital relationship. "Bosom" connotes affection. Does the use of the present participle ("the one who is") imply that the earthly Jesus, the Word-become-flesh, was with the Father at the same time that he was on earth? Thüsing, p. 209, and Windisch, ZNW 30 (1931), 221 ff., argue against such an interpretation; Haenchen, p. 324[75], points out that *einai* has no past participle and maintains that the present participle here has a past connotation, "the one who was." If one wishes to support simultaneity in earth and in heaven, however, one may invoke iii 13 where Jesus speaks of himself as "the Son of Man who is in heaven," and viii 16, "I have at my side the One who sent me." Others think that the reference to the Son at the Father's side is a reference to the Ascension. Thus the whole career of the Word is sketched in the Prologue: the Word with God; the Word come into the world and become flesh; the Word returned to the Father. This great cycle of descent and ascent is prominent in the Gospel, e.g., xvi 28. No conclusive decision about these various interpretations seems possible.

revealed Him. The "Him" is not expressed but is demanded if we translate the verb as "reveal." The verb *exēgeisthai* means "to lead" but is not attested in this meaning in the NT or in early Christian literature (BAG, p. 275); there it means "to explain, report," and especially, "to reveal [divine secrets]." In the article he has devoted to this verse (also *Prologue*, pp. 66–68), Boismard defends the meaning "lead" here, connecting the verb with the phrase "into the Father's bosom," thus: although no one has ever seen God, the only Son who is with the Father has led men into the Father's bosom. And so, the Word who was with God has become man and led men back up to God. This suggestion works against Boismard's other thesis that it was Luke who adapted the hymn to the Gospel of John as a Prologue, for it is precisely in the Lucan writings that the verb does not mean "to lead."

COMMENT: GENERAL

If John has been described as the pearl of great price among the NT writings, then one may say that the Prologue is the pearl within this Gospel. In her comparison of Augustine's and Chrysostom's exegesis of the Prologue, M. A. Aucoin points out that both held that it is beyond the power of man to speak as John does in the Prologue. The choice of the eagle as the symbol of John the Evangelist was largely determined by the celestial flights of the opening lines of the Gospel. The sacred character of the Prologue has been reflected in a long-standing custom of the Western Church to read it as a benediction over the sick and over newly baptized children. Its former place as the final prayer of the Roman Mass reflects its use as a blessing. Indeed, it took on a magical character when it was used in amulets worn around the neck to protect against sickness. All these attestations of sublimity, however, do not remove the fact that the eighteen verses of the Prologue contain for the exegete a number of bewildering textual, critical, and interpretative problems.

Problem of the Relation of the Prologue to the Gospel

In the estimation of some, the Prologue has little to do with the substance of the Gospel but represents a phrasing of the Christian message in Hellenistic terms to catch the interest of Greek readers. For others, the Prologue is a preface to the Gospel—an overture, an outline, or a summary. Yet, as the opening of a Gospel, the Prologue has a certain uniqueness. In Jewish and Hellenistic literature the normal opening of a book that recounts a story is either a lapidary summary of contents (Luke, Revelation) or the heading of the first chapter (Mark). Such a poetic opening as the Prologue can be matched only in epistles like I John and Hebrews. As for content, although two other Gospels, Matthew and Luke, have a preface before they begin the account of Jesus' public ministry, these prefaces take an entirely different approach from that of the Prologue. They move the story of Jesus back to his conception, but John's poetic opening takes it back before creation. The Prologue is not concerned with the earthly origins of Jesus but with the heavenly existence of the Word in the beginning.

If we grant that the concept behind the Prologue is unique, we notice relationships between it and the body of the Gospel. Verses 11 and 12 seem to be a summary of the two main divisions of John. Verse 11 covers the Book of Signs (chs. i–xii), which tells how Jesus came to his own land through a ministry in Galilee and Jerusalem and yet his own people did not receive him. Verse 12 covers the Book of Glory (chs. xiii–xx), which contains Jesus' words to those who did receive him and tells how he returned to his Father in order to give them the gift of life and make them God's children. J. A. T. Robinson, p. 122, insists on the number of themes shared by the Prologue and the rest of the Gospel: pre-existence (i 1=xvii 5); the light of men and of the world (i 4, 9=viii 12, ix 5); opposition between light and darkness (i 5=iii 19); seeing his glory (i 14=xii 41); the only Son (i 14, 18=iii 16); no one, save the Son, has seen God (i 18=vi 46). And, of course, the two interruptions about John the Baptist are related to what the Gospel will say about him (i 7 is picked up in i 19; i 15=i 30). Thus, at least in its present form, the Prologue cannot be said to be totally extraneous to the Gospel.

Nevertheless, there are some differences between the Prologue and the Gospel which must be accounted for. There are highly poetic lines in the Prologue, exhibiting a climactic or "staircase" parallelism whereby a word prominent in one line (often the predicate or last word) is taken up in the next line (often as subject or first word). This parallelism, while found both in the OT (Ps xcvi 13) and elsewhere in John (vi 37, viii 32), never attains the perfection illustrated in vss. 1–5 of the Prologue. In John, Jesus' discourses have a solemnity and phrasing that goes beyond ordinary prose, but there is nothing of length in the Gospel to match the poetic structure of the Prologue. (That is why, although vs. 15 is the same as vs. 30, we set up vs. 15 as prose, for it does not match the poetic style of the Prologue; yet we set up vs. 30 in the semi-poetic format of the solemn pronouncements.)

In addition to a difference of format, there are also theological concepts and terms in the Prologue that have no echo in the Gospel. The central figure of the Prologue is the Word, a term which does not occur as a christological title in the Gospel. The important terms *charis*, "covenant love," and *plēroma*, "fullness," of vss. 14, 16 do not occur in the Gospel; and *alētheia*, "endurance, fidelity," has a different meaning ("truth") in the Gospel. The picture of Jesus as the Tabernacle ("tent dwelling") in vs. 14 does not occur in the Gospel, where Jesus is the Temple (ii 21).

The confusing combination of similarities and dissimilarities between Prologue and Gospel has been interpreted in different ways. Ruckstuhl is convinced by the similarities that the same hand composed both Prologue and Gospel, while J. A. T. Robinson is persuaded that the same author wrote the Prologue after he had written the Gospel. Schnackenburg, convinced by the dissimilarities that the Prologue was not originally the work of the evangelist, rejects as secondary additions any lines of the Prologue that have Johannine characteristics. Today many authors are moving toward positing an originally independent poem that has been adapted to the Gospel. This may explain the Johannine features in the non-poetic lines, but does not explain the Johannine features in the original poem. If one takes any of the many critical reconstructions of the original poem (see below), even Schnackenburg's, where there has been a systematic attempt to rule out Johannine features, one is still left with a poem that is more at home in the Johannine writings than anywhere else in the NT. This is easily seen by comparing it with the Prologue to I John and to Rev xix 13 where Jesus is called the Word of God. Therefore, while it is perfectly reasonable to recognize that the evidence points to the composition of the Prologue as independent of that of the Gospel, it seems also reasonable to posit that the Prologue was composed in Johannine circles. The similarities between the *poetry* of the Prologue and the Gospel are thus accounted for.

De Ausejo's study of the hymns of the NT suggests that the solution lies in seeing that the original poem underlying the Prologue was a hymn of the Johannine church. Hymns to Christ are mentioned in the NT in Eph v 19 and perhaps also in Col iii 16. Pliny, writing to Trajan ca. A.D. 111 (*Epist.* x 96:7), describes the Christians of Bithynia in Asia Minor as saying "a hymn to Christ as to a God." Eusebius (*Hist.* v 28:5; GCS 9^1:500) cites a testimony that speaks of psalms and hymns which from the beginning were sung to Christ as the Word, divinizing him. It is interesting that these references to hymns have some connection with Asia Minor; thus the conjecture that the original of the Prologue was a hymn of the Johannine church at Ephesus has a claim to likelihood. To test the hypothesis let us first compare the Prologue with some of the known NT hymns.

If we analyze Philip ii 6–11, we find a sequence not unlike that of the Prologue. Philippians begins the hymn with Christ Jesus being in the form of God, as the Prologue begins by telling us that the Word was God. Philippians says that Jesus emptied himself and took on the form of a servant, becoming [or being born] in the likeness of man; the Prologue says that Word became flesh. Philippians says that God has exalted Jesus so that every tongue will proclaim that Jesus is the Lord, to the glory of the Father; the Prologue ends on the theme of God the only Son being ever at the Father's side, and vs. 14 speaks of the glory of an only Son coming from the Father. In both instances the exaltation or glory is witnessed by men.

An analysis of Col i 15–20 also shows similarities to the Prologue (see J. M. Robinson, JBL 76 [1957], 278–79). In Colossians we hear that the Son is the image of the invisible God; in the Prologue he is the Word of God. In Colossians all things are created in, through, and unto the Son; in the Prologue all things are created through, in, and not apart from the Word. In Colossians the Son is the beginning; in the Prologue, "In the beginning was the Word." In Colossians all the fullness dwells in the Son and all things are reconciled through him; in the Prologue we have all had a share in the fullness of the Word-become-flesh.

Even a short hymn like that of I Tim iii 16 shows parallels to the Prologue. There we hear, "He was manifested in the *flesh* . . . he was taken up in *glory*." The opening verses of Hebrews form a short hymnic prologue resembling the Johannine Prologue. Heb i 2–5, without using the expression "the Word," says that God *"spoke* to us by a Son . . . through whom also He *created the world*. He reflects *the glory* of God . . . upholding the universe by his word [*rēma*] of power. When he had made purification for sins, he sat down *at the right hand of the Majesty* on high." Later on, Heb iv 12 speaks of "the word of God," but the exegesis that sees this as a personal reference to Jesus is dubious.

Support for seeing traces of an original hymn in the Prologue is found in the collection of 2nd-century Christian semi-Gnostic hymns known as the *Odes of Solomon*. See Braun, JeanThéol, I, pp. 224–51, for the relation of these *Odes* to the *Gospel of Truth* and the Dead Sea Scrolls. These hymns have a certain relation in style and vocabulary to the Prologue, especially Nos. vii, xii, xvi, xix, and xli. Ode xli 13–14 says that the Son of the Most High has appeared in the perfection of his Father: "A light has gone out from the Word which was in him from the beginning . . . he was designated before the creation of the world." Ode xviii 6 says that the light was not conquered by the darkness. Thus we have Johannine themes preserved in hymnic style. We may mention, however, that the existence of such Christian semi-Gnostic hymns really does nothing to prove Bultmann's contention that the Prologue hymn was originally part of the Revelatory Discourse Source and originally a Gnostic hymn written in praise of John the Baptist. The few passages cited in the *Odes* are possibly dependent on John. In the early Gnostic literature there are few, if any, good parallels *of length* for the format that Bultmann finds in the Prologue. More specifically, there is not the slightest evidence that the Baptist sectarians ever referred to John the Baptist as the Word. The strong anti-Gnostic features in the Prologue (vss. 3, 14) also militate against this suggestion.

The Formation of the Prologue

If we accept the evidence that the basis of the Prologue consisted of a hymn composed in the Johannine church, what verses belonged to this hymn and how was it joined to the Gospel? There is no agreement on either question. In the latter question some think that there were two stages of editing the hymn to adapt it to the Gospel; some think that there was one, and this was done by the final redactor. Gaechter suggests that the adaptation was made by the translator who worked with John and put his thought into Greek. Boismard thinks that Luke redacted this hymn because he finds Lucan expressions in vss. 14 and 17; the similarities with the Pauline hymns are also traced through Luke.

In the former question concerning what belonged to the original hymn there is even more debate. We give below a cross section of scholarly opinion. All those cited regard vss. 6–8, and 15 as secondary additions; and many would add vss. 9, 12–13, 17–18. The only general agreement is on vss. 1–5, 10–11, and 14 as parts of the original poem. The principal criterion is the poetic quality of the lines (length, number of accents, co-ordination, etc.).

However, as Haenchen has pointed out against the strict adherents to this criterion (Gaechter, Bultmann, Käsemann, Schnackenburg), the type of regularity they demand is not found in most of the Pauline hymns. Moreover, if the poetic criterion is set on the basis of a hypothetical *Aramaic* original, we are on very subjective grounds. Another criterion in determining the lines of the original is thought pattern, for example, the exclusion from the poem of the apologetic lines written against the Baptist sectarians. However, when a scholar rather arbitrarily forms a set of presuppositions about the original import of the poem (the Gnostic theory), and then proceeds to eliminate lines that do not agree with his hypothesis, this criterion becomes very subjective.

Bernard	accepts:		1–5,	10–11,	14,		18.
Bultmann	"		1–5,	9–12b,	14,	16.	
De Ausejo	"		1–5,	9–11,	14,	16,	18.
Gaechter	"		1–5,	10–12,	14,	16, 17.	
Green	"	1,	3–5,	10–11,	14a–d,		18.
Haenchen	"		1–5,	9–11,	14,	16, 17.	
Käsemann	"	1,	3–5,	10–12.		(uncertain of 2)	
Schnackenburg	"	1,	3–4,	9–11,	14abe,	16.	

Once the original lines have been determined, there is the problem of breaking them up into stanzas or strophes. Matching length is a criterion here, although De Ausejo completely ignores it. Strict mathematical proportion, however, is not to be demanded, as it is not found in the Pauline hymns. The development of thought can also be an important criterion, but there is much disagreement on the development in the Prologue.

In the NOTES we have advanced the reasons for and against the various theories about individual lines. With great hesitancy we suggest the following outline of the formation of the Prologue, emphasizing its tentative nature. The original hymn:

First strophe:	vss.	1–2.	The Word with God.
Second strophe:		3–5.	The Word and Creation.
Third strophe:		10–12b.	The Word in the World.
Fourth strophe:		14, 16.	The Community's Share in the Word.

To this hymn have been added two sets of additions:

1. Explanatory expansions of the lines of the hymn:
   vss. 12c–13, added at the end of the third strophe, to explain how men become God's children;
   vss. 17–18, added at the end of the fourth strophe, to explain "love in place of love."

2. Material pertaining to John the Baptist—perhaps originally the opening verses of the Gospel, displaced when the Prologue was prefaced to the Gospel by the final redactor:
   vss. 6–9, added at the end of the second strophe, before the treatment of the Incarnation;
   vs. 15, added in the middle of the third stanza.

We see no way of being certain whether these two sets of additions were the work of one man and done at the same time.

There are several questions that we make no attempt to settle. Burney, Black, and Bultmann argue strongly for an Aramaic original for the hymn; the evidence is not conclusive. Lund and Boismard see a pattern of chiasm in the final form of the Prologue (see Introduction, Part IX:D). Lund's arrangement, *art. cit.*, is spectacularly intricate. Boismard's is simpler, and is supported by some valid observations (the concluding vs. 18 picks up the theme of the opening vs. 1; and vs. 15 matches vss. 6–8). However, the parallels Boismard finds between vss. 3 and 17 and between vss. 4–5 and 16 are highly imaginative. We remain in doubt on the applicability of a chiasm pattern to the Prologue.

The question of where the Prologue begins to speak of the incarnate career of the Word as Jesus Christ will be discussed below. However, we should mention the novel theory of De Ausejo that the whole hymn refers to the Word-become-flesh. He correctly insists that the Pauline hymns tend to refer to Jesus Christ throughout. Philippians, for example, is speaking of Jesus Christ even when it speaks of his being in the form of God before he emptied himself and took on the form of a servant. This way of speaking is strange to Christian theology in the aftermath of Nicaea; for before the Incarnation one speaks of the Second Person of the Trinity and it is insisted that Jesus Christ came into being at the moment of the Incarnation. But the NT made no such precise distinction in its terminology, and De Ausejo may well be right. At least one may say that even in its opening verse the Prologue does not conceive of a Word that will not be spoken to men.

COMMENT: DETAILED

First Strophe. *The Word with God* (vss. 1–2)

If it is unusual to open a Gospel with a hymn, the praise of the Word is not an unfitting opening to the written account of the apostolic kerygma. In v 24 and xv 3 Jesus characterizes his message as a "word"; the Prologue shows that the messenger himself was the Word. We may have a hint of such a contrast in the Gospel itself in x 33–36 where there seems to be a contrast between God's *word*, which is addressed to men and makes them gods, and God's Son, who is sent into the world and is called God (="The Word was God"). Since the first words of the Prologue opened Genesis, they are peculiarly fitting to open the account of what God has said and done in the new dispensation.

The description of the Word with God in heaven before creation is remarkably brief; there is not the slightest indication of interest in metaphysical speculations about relationships within God or in what later theology would call Trinitarian processions. The Prologue is a description of the history of salvation in hymnic form, much as Ps lxxviii is a poetic description of the history of Israel. Therefore, the emphasis is primarily on God's relation to men, rather than on God in Himself. The very title "Word" implies a revelation—not so much a divine idea, but a divine communication. The words "In the beginning," although they refer to pre-creation, imply that there is going to be a creation, a beginning. If this poem was going to concentrate on God Himself, there would be no beginning. The Prologue says that the Word was; it does not speculate *how* the Word was, for not the origins of the Word but what the Word does is important. The Prologue does not proceed in the direction of its Qumran parallel cited in the NOTE on vss. 3b–4. There in good Hellenistic fashion God's knowledge is stressed as a creative factor; here in the manner of the OT God's Word is stressed. We shall discuss the background of the concept of "the Word" in App. II, but we may emphasize here that the whole cast of the hymn as salvific history removes it a distance from the more speculative Hellenistic world of thought. As Dodd, *art. cit.*, p. 15, points out, no Hellenistic thinker would see a climax in the Incarnation, just as no Gnostic would triumphantly proclaim that the Word had become flesh.

As mentioned in the NOTE on 1c, the Prologue's "The Word was God" offers a difficulty because there is no article before *theos*. Does this imply that "God" means less when predicated of the Word than it does when used as a name for the Father? Once again the reader must divest himself of a post-Nicene understanding of the vocabulary involved. There are two considerations.

The NT does not predicate "God" of Jesus with any frequency. V. Taylor, ET 73 (1961–62), 116–18, has asked whether it ever calls Jesus God, since almost every text proposed has its difficulties. See our article treating all the pertinent texts in TS 26 (1965), 545–73. Most of the passages suggested (John i 1, 18, xx 28; Rom ix 5; Heb i 8; II Pet i 1) are in hymns or doxologies—an indication that the title "God" was applied to Jesus more quickly in liturgical formulae than in narrative or epistolary literature. We are reminded again of Pliny's description of the Christians singing *hymns* to Christ as God. The reluctance to apply this designation to Jesus is understandable as part of the NT heritage from Judaism. For the Jews "God" meant the heavenly Father; and until a wider understanding of the term was reached, it could not be readily applied to Jesus. This is reflected in Mark x 18 where Jesus refuses to be called good because only God is good; in John xx 17 where Jesus calls the Father "my God"; and in Eph iv 5–6 where Jesus is spoken of as "one Lord," but the Father is "one God." (The way that the NT approached the question of the divinity of Jesus was not through the title "God" but by describing his activities in the same way as it described the Father's activities; see John v 17, 21, x 28–29.) In vs. 1c the Johannine hymn is bordering on the usage of "God" for the Son, but by omitting the article it avoids any suggestion of personal identification of the Word with the Father. And for Gentile readers the line also avoids any suggestion that the Word was a second God in any Hellenistic sense.

There is a further consideration, however. We have mentioned the suggestion by the Catholic scholar De Ausejo that the Word throughout the Prologue means the Word-become-flesh and that the whole hymn refers to Jesus Christ. If this is so, then perhaps there is justification for seeing in the use of the anarthrous *theos* something more humble than the use of *ho theos* for the Father. It is Jesus Christ who says in John xiv 28, "The Father is greater than I," and who in xvii 3 speaks of the Father as "the only true God." The recognition of a humble position for Jesus Christ in relation to the Father is not strange to early Christian hymns, for Philip ii 6–7 speaks of Jesus as emptying himself and not clinging to the form of God.

Because vs. 2 repeats vs. 1 some scholars ascribe it to the secondary editing of the hymn. If we regard vss. 1–2 as a strophe, however, then vs. 2 may be an inclusion: the strophe begins and ends on the theme of "the beginning." Lund claims it as an example of chiasm since the ideas of vs. 2 are in inverse order from 1a,b. Bultmann, p. 17, is probably correct when he insists that the repetition is far from otiose. The great danger for any Hellenistic community in reading that the Word was God would be polytheism, and vs. 2 insists again on the relationship between the Father and the Word.

Second Strophe. *The Word and Creation* (vss. 3–5)

With the appearance of "came into being" (*egeneto*) in vs. 3 we are in the sphere of creation. All that is created is intimately related to the Word, for it was created, not only through him, but also in him. We find the same idea in the hymn of Col i 16: "For in him were all things created . . . all things were created by him and in him." The same unity that exists between the Word and his creation will be applied in John xv 5 to Jesus and the Christian: "Apart from me you can do nothing."

The fact that the *Word* creates means that creation is an act of revelation. All creation bears the stamp of God's Word, whence the insistence in Wis xiii 1 and Rom i 19–20 that from His creatures God is recognizable by men. Moreover, the Word's role in creation means that Jesus has a claim on all; as vs. 10 will poignantly insist, the world rejected this claim. The expression "all" (*panta*) in vs. 3 is a quasi-liturgical formula which captures the fullness of God's creation. Notice its use in Rom xi 36: "For from Him and through Him and to Him are *all things*. To Him be glory forever. Amen." See also I Cor viii 6 and the appearance of *panta* in the hymn of Col i 16.

Boismard, pp. 102–5, asks what type of causality does the Word exercise in creation: efficient or exemplary causality? In Appendix II we shall point out that the creative word of God in the OT seems to be the efficient cause of creation. Yet personified Wisdom and the Torah (which are also part of the background of the Prologue's use of the Word) seem to exercise in creation the causality of a model or exemplar. Therefore there may be elements of both types of causality in creation through and in the Word. Boismard states: "It is therefore probable that for St. John also the Word of God plays a part in creation because it is the pronouncement of an idea, and not because it is endowed, as such, with effectiveness." However, there is nothing in the Prologue to stress that the Word is the pronouncement of a divine idea, and such speculation belongs more to the Greek world and later theology.

We note finally that in saying that it is through the Word that all things came into being, the Prologue is at a distance from Gnostic thought whereby a demiurge and not God was responsible for material creation, which is evil. Since the Word is related to the Father and the Word creates, the Father may be said to create through the Word. Thus the material world has been created by God and is good.

The interpretation of vs. 4 depends on how one solves the difficult problem of its translation (see NOTE). In the translation accepted it marks a progression over vs. 3 in two ways. First, the fact of creation (that all things came to be) is no longer in view; emphasis has shifted to *what* had come to be. Second, the focus is on a special aspect of what had come to be, namely what had come to be in the Word—the special creation of the Word. It is true that for some scholars the Prologue has at this point passed from creation to the Incarnation (Spitta, Zahn, B. Weiss, Vawter). They point out that the gift of life which is mentioned in vs. 4 is associated in the Gospel with the coming of Jesus (iii 16, v 40, x 10). Yet, a jump from creation in vs. 3 to the coming of Jesus in 4 seems exceedingly abrupt, especially when the "that which had come to be" in 4 is a link to "came to be" in 3. If vss. 4–5 refer to the coming of Jesus, then the clearer reference to his coming in 9 and 10 seems tautological. Also the editor of the Prologue has inserted a reference to John the Baptist *after* vs. 5, and one can scarcely imagine that the editor would introduce John the Baptist after describing the ministry of Jesus and its effect. Clearly the editor thought that the references to the coming of Jesus began in vs. 10; he put the coming of John the Baptist in vss. 6–8 before the coming of Jesus, and used vs. 9 to connect John the Baptist to the moment of that coming. Of course, the editor could have misunderstood the import of vss. 4–5, but he was much closer to the original hymn than we are. This objection also militates against the theory of Käsemann, who sees a reference to the coming of Jesus, not in vs. 4, but in 5, which he joins to 10, and against the theory of Bultmann, who begins the work of the revealer in history with vs. 5, which he joins to 9.

We suggest that the meaning of vss. 4–5 lies much closer to that of vs. 3. From the opening words of the hymn there has been a deliberate parallel to the opening chapters of Genesis. This carried into vs. 3 with its use of *egeneto* (see NOTE); and now it carries into 4–5 with the mention of light and darkness, for light was God's first creation (Gen i 3). "Life" is also a theme of the creation account in Gen i 11 ("living creatures" in i 20, 24, etc.). Of course, in its first chapter Genesis is speaking of natural life while the Prologue is speaking of eternal life. Yet, eternal life is also mentioned in the first chapters of Genesis, for ii 9 and iii 22 speak of the tree of life whose fruit, when eaten, would make man live forever. Man was shut off from this life by his sin; but, as we see in Rev xxii 2, the eternal life of the Garden of Eden prefigured the life that Jesus would give to men. In John vi Jesus will speak of the bread of life which a man may eat and live forever—a bread, therefore, which has the same qualities as the fruit of the tree of life in Paradise. John viii 44 mentions man's loss of the opportunity for eternal life in Paradise when it describes the devil as a murderer from the beginning and the father of lies (the serpent lied to Eve). And so we suggest that in vs. 4 the Prologue is still speaking in the context of the creation narrative of Genesis. That which had especially come to be in God's creative Word was the gift of eternal life. This life was the light of men because the tree of life was closely associated with the tree of the knowledge of good and evil. If man had survived the test, he would have possessed eternal life and enlightenment.

Verse 5 may also be interpreted against this background. There was an attempt by darkness to overcome the light—namely the fall of man. Notice that the aorist, "overcame," thus receives its normal meaning as referring to a single past action. But the light shines on, for although man sinned, a ray of hope was given to him. Gen iii 15 says that God put enmity between the serpent and the woman and that the serpent was not destined to overcome her offspring. In particular, the seed of the woman, which for the NT was Jesus, would be victorious over Satan. (We emphasize that we are dealing here with the Christian and, perhaps, late Jewish understanding of Gen iii 15, not the understanding of the original author of the passage.) That Johannine circles capitalized on Gen iii 15 we see in Rev xii, where the victory of Jesus over the devil is pictured in terms of the victory of the woman's child over the serpent.

Parenthesis: *John the Baptist's Witness to the Light* (vss. 6–9)

If the second strophe dealt with the creation by the Word and the Word's initial gift of life and light and the attempt by the darkness to overcome the light, the third strophe will deal with the Word's own coming into the world to defeat the darkness. Between the two strophes an editor has inserted four verses dealing with John the Baptist and his role of preparing men for the coming of the Word and the light.

Boismard and others have made an interesting suggestion about the origin of vss. 6–7: that they were the original opening of the Gospel which was displaced when the Prologue was added. The first words of vs. 6, "There was sent by God a man named John," would be a normal opening for a historical narrative. Judg xiii 2 opens the Samson narratives with: "And there was a man of Zorah of the Danites" (also xix 1; I Sam i 1). Moreover, if at least the substance of 6–7 came before i 19, there would have been a good sequence: 7 says that John the Baptist came as a witness to testify, and 19 ff. presents his testimony and the circumstances under which it was given. In such circumstances the strange expression "to testify to the light" makes more sense. Ordinarily light can be seen and there is no need for someone to testify to it; but in 19 ff. it is a question of testifying before those who are hostile and who have not yet seen Jesus.

Verse 8 has a motif of its own. We have mentioned in the Introduction (Part V:A) that one of the goals of the Fourth Gospel was a refutation of exaggerated claims made by the sectarians of John the Baptist. The Prologue in vs. 8 subordinates John the Baptist to Jesus. Is the refutation even more specific? Did the sectarians think of John the Baptist as the light? It has been suggested that the *Benedictus,* the hymn of Zachary in Luke i 68–79, was once a hymn to John the Baptist, subsequently adapted to Christian use. Verses 78–79 connect the ministry of John the Baptist with that moment when the day dawns from on high to give light to those who sit in darkness. Thus it *may* be that the sectarians claimed the title of light for John the Baptist.

Seemingly vs. 9 is the transition that the editor has made to adapt vss. 6–8 to their present place in the Prologue. The stress on real light picks up the theme of 8; the stress on coming into the world prepares for 10. J. A. T. Robinson, p. 127, thinks that all four verses (6–9), as well as 15, were part of the original opening of the Gospel; really, however, only 6–7 read well before 19. The picture of light coming into the world to enlighten men is a messianic one taken from the OT, particularly from Isaiah. In the description of the messianic prince of peace Isa ix 2 announces: "The people who walked in darkness have seen a great light; light has shone on those who dwelt deep in the land of darkness." In the second part of Isaiah (xlii 6) Yahweh proclaims of His servant: "I have given you as a covenant to the people, a light to the nations . . . to bring out from prison those who sit in darkness." In the third part of Isaiah (lx 1–2) we hear the clarion call to Jerusalem: "Arise, shine, for your light has come, and the glory of the Lord has risen upon you. For behold, darkness shall cover the earth; and thick blackness, the peoples; but the Lord will rise upon you . . . and nations shall come to your light." The Prologue associates the witness of John the Baptist, the Isaian voice in the wilderness, with the prophetic proclamation of the coming of the light. The Fourth Gospel was not alone in adapting to Jesus the OT prophecies pertaining to light; Matt iv 16 applies Isa ix 2 to the ministry of Jesus.

We may mention in passing that H. Sahlin, *art. cit.,* has attempted to show that vss. 6–9 belonged to the original form of the Prologue and were applied to the Word. For example, he reads, "He [the Word] became man, sent by God. He came as a witness to testify to the light . . ." Sahlin suggests that under the influence of Synoptic parallels like Mark i 4 the verses were mistakenly applied to John the Baptist. This is ingenious but completely beyond the range of proof.

Third Strophe. *The Word in the World* (vss. 10–12b)

The third strophe of the original hymn seems to deal with the Word incarnate in the ministry of Jesus. However, many scholars do not share this view. Westcott, Bernard, and Boismard suggest that the reference to the Word's presence in the world in vss. 10–12 is to be interpreted in terms of the activity of the divine word in the OT period; and Schnackenburg, p. 88, thinks of the presence of Wisdom in the world and in Israel. The period between Adam and Moses has been suggested for vs. 10; the Sinai covenant and the subsequent infidelity of Israel for 11; and the faithful remnant of Israel for 12.

Of course, this view means that the editor of the Prologue misunderstood the hymn in inserting the reference to John the Baptist before vs. 10. Moreover, it runs against the fact that most of the phrases found in 10–12 appear in the Gospel as a description of the ministry of Jesus. If the Word is in the world (10a), Jesus says that he has come into the world (iii 19, xii 46), that he is in the world (ix 5); and frequently these statements are in juxtaposition to the theme of his being the light, just as i 10 follows i 5 with its theme of light. The presence of the Word in the world is rejected, for the world does not recognize the Word (10c). In like manner the presence of Jesus in the world meets rejection (iii 19), for men do not recognize who Jesus is (xiv 7, xvi 3; I John iii 1). The particularly poignant rejection of the Word by his own people (11b) is also matched in the ministry of Jesus as he is rejected in Galilee (iv 44) and by the Jewish people in general (xii 37). The phrase "did not accept" (*paralambanein* in 11; *lambanein* in 12) is used of Jesus in iii 11 and v 43 (*lambanein*). Indeed, as we have pointed out, vss. 11 and 12 are really short summaries of the two parts of the Gospel: the Book of Signs and the Book of Glory. The opening line of the Book of Glory (xiii 2) announces: "Having loved *his own* who were in the world, he now showed his love for them to the very end." In other words, in place of the Jewish people who had been his own (i 11), he now has formed around himself a new "his own," the Christian believers (i 12).

The conclusive argument that vss. 10–12 refer to the ministry of Jesus is, in our opinion, found in 12. Schnackenburg has no difficulty with 12 since he rejects that verse from the original hymn; but any commentator who accepts 12 as part of the hymn must reckon with the statement that the Word's career in the world empowered men to become God's children. It seems incredible that in a hymn coming out of Johannine circles the ability to become a child of God would have been explained in another way than in terms of having been begotten from above by the Spirit of Jesus (iii 3, 5; see COMMENT on xx 17 in The Anchor Bible, vol. 29A; I John iii 9). If the revelation of the OT empowered men to become God's children, the whole conversation with Nicodemus is unintelligible. Dodd, *Interpretation*, p. 282, argues that before the coming of Jesus there were children of God and cites xi 52 about the dispersed children of God. But does John mean that these dispersed people are already children of God without having heard of Jesus and being begotten from above? Or does John not mean that these are people who have been called by God to be his children and to accept Jesus as their shepherd?

Thus we agree with Büchsel, Bauer, Harnack, Käsemann, and others that the third strophe of the hymn refers to the earthly ministry of Jesus. We note that the hymn of Philip ii 6–11 passes from Jesus in the form of God directly to Jesus in the form of a servant, from heaven to the ministry of Jesus, without any description of God's work in the OT period. In the hymn in Col i 15–20 the thought passes from the Son as the image of God and the first-born of all creation to the death of Jesus.

A few remarks may be made on the individual verses. As we shall point out in App. II, the rejection of the Word by men in vs. 10 is quite similar to the rejection of Wisdom by men in En xlii 2: "Wisdom came to make her dwelling place among the children of men and found no dwelling place." This is a reflection of the Johannine theology that Jesus is personified Wisdom. Verse 11 is not synonymous with 10 (*pace* Bultmann), but marks a narrowing down of the activity of the Word to Israel. It represents the sentiment expressed in Matt xv 24 that Jesus was sent only to the lost sheep of the house of Israel. In John xii 20–23 when the Gentiles come to Jesus, this is a sign that the ministry is over and the hour is at hand. To some the contrast between non-acceptance in vs. 11 and acceptance in 12 seems too sharp; nevertheless, exactly the same contrast is found in iii 32–33: "He testifies to what he has seen and heard, but *no one accepts his testimony. Whoever does accept* his testimony has certified that God is truthful." Such sharp contrasts are found in early Christian hymns, for example, I Tim iii 16, "He was manifested in the flesh, justified in the Spirit."

Verses 12c–13. The reason for the evaluation of these verses as editorial comment on vs. 12 has been advanced in the NOTES, where we found it necessary to explain the verses in order to justify our translation. The editor has made his addition between strophes.

Fourth Strophe. *The Community's Share in the Word-become-flesh* (vss. 14 and 16)

The last strophe of the hymn introduces the community and gives poetic expression to what the career of the Word means in the life of the community. In particular, vs. 14a,b summarizes and gives more vital expression to what was said in 10–11; 14c–e and 16 expand on the idea of becoming God's children from 12 by showing how we share in the fullness of God's only Son. This is the last strophe of the hymn, and it forms an inclusion with the first strophe. Verses 14 and 1 are the only two verses in the hymn that mention "the Word" specifically.

Vs. 1. The Word was   matching   Vs. 14. The Word became
       (*ēn*)   (*egeneto*)
  1. The Word in God's
     presence   matching   14. The Word among us
  1. The Word was *God* matching   14. The Word became *flesh*

Thus the eternal being of the Word in the opening strophe is contrasted to the temporal becoming of the Word in the last strophe. Only when one understands the summary quality of the last strophe, which captures the activity of the preceding verses of the hymn and deliberately contrasts it to the theme of the first strophe, can one see that there is no contradiction to suggest that the third strophe deals with the ministry of Jesus and still 14a is a clear reference to the Incarnation. Verse 14a,b offers a summary of the Word's activity for community admiration and praise, since community participation is to be expected in a hymn. When the hymn was adapted to serve as Prologue for the Gospel, this summary verse could also point ahead to the career of Jesus to follow.

Verse 14a describes the Incarnation in strongly realistic language by stressing that the Word became *flesh*. The word "flesh" seems to have been associated with the Incarnation from the earliest days of Christian theological expression. Rom i 3 describes God's Son who was descended from David according to the flesh; and Rom viii 3 catches even better the element of scandal in this when it speaks of God's "sending His own Son in the likeness of sinful flesh." The hymn in I Tim iii 16 contrasts manifestation in the flesh with vindication in the Spirit. Does the mention of flesh in John i 14 represent a kenotic element comparable to what we find in the hymn of Philip ii 7: "He emptied himself, taking on the form of a servant, becoming in the likeness of man"? De Ausejo in his article on "flesh" in John (EstBib 17 [1958], 411–27) stresses this. Since in his opinion the whole hymn has been in praise of the incarnate Jesus, the statement in vs. 14a that the Word became flesh must have a special emphasis of weakness and mortality. Käsemann, p. 93, however, insists that the scandal consists in the presence of God among men and not in the becoming flesh—not the how, but the fact. For Käsemann 14a says no more than 10a, "He was in the world." The parallelism between 14a and 14b gives support to Käsemann's contention.

Is there a polemic intent in vs. 14a? Certainly its theology would not have been compatible to Gnostic or Docetic strains of thought. No line in the hymn gives sharper expression to the difference between the Prologue's concept of the Word and that of the Stoics and of the *Corpus Hermeticum*. The Greek who admired the *logos* as formulating the orderliness of the world aspired to be joined with God in His universe. The suggestion that the ultimate encounter with the *logos* of God would be when the *logos* became flesh would have been unthinkable. The Prologue does not say that the Word entered into flesh or abided in flesh but that the Word *became* flesh. Therefore, instead of supplying the liberation from the material world that the Greek mind yearned for, the Word of God was now inextricably bound to human history. Yet, while 14a would not be acceptable to some of the schools of philosophical or theological thought in the Hellenistic world, we cannot be certain that it was written against such views. The Johannine Epistles are more clearly polemic, as in I John iv 2–3: "Every spirit that acknowledges Jesus Christ *come in the flesh* belongs to God, while every spirit that severs Jesus does not belong to God" (also

II John 7). There *may* be an element of polemic on this point in the Gospel in passages like vi 51–59 and xix 34–35. We may note finally that the hymn's stress on flesh in vs. 14a is somewhat different from the attitude in the editorial comment on the hymn in 13, where it is emphasized that God's children were not begotten by the desire of the flesh.

Let us turn now to the attitude toward revelation implied in "The Word became flesh." The title, "the Word," was appropriate in vs. 1 because the divine being described there was destined to speak to men. When the title is used for the second time in vs. 14, this divine being has taken on human form and has thus found the most effective way in which to express himself to men. Thus, in becoming flesh the Word does not cease to be the Word, but exercises his function as Word to the full. In commenting on this verse Bultmann, p. 42, formulates one of the theses that runs through his thought-provoking commentary, namely, that contact with the Word-become-flesh is contact with revelation itself, for Jesus brings no teaching and is not a guide to heavenly mysteries such as found in the Gnostic picture of teachers descended from heaven. The contrast with the Gnostic picture is valid: Jesus is incarnate Wisdom or revelation itself. But does not Bultmann make too much of a revealer without a revelation? Perhaps this is by way of over-reaction to an older view where Jesus was thought to proclaim revelation in a series of ordered propositions. First, it is true that throughout John the stress is on accepting Jesus, and much of the time this means accepting his claim to be sent from God. But, as Käsemann, pp. 95–96, insists, if the fact that Jesus was sent is all important, this is in itself a tremendous revelation of "the one thing that is necessary." It is a revelation that the Creator is here present to his creatures; and the Creator does not come with empty hands, for he gives light and life and love and resurrection. Second, there remains a considerable amount of teaching in what Jesus says. For instance, there is teaching about his Father's salvific love for men (iii 16–17), about the Holy Spirit, the Paraclete, about the Law and its obligations (v 16–17, vii 19–23), about the duties of love among Christians (xiii 12–17, 34), about Baptism (iii 5), and about the Eucharist (vi 51–58—of course, Bultmann rejects the sacramental passages as additions of the Ecclesiastical Redactor). Much of the teaching that Matthew puts in the Sermon on the Mount is found in John, scattered at times, and in variant forms, but nevertheless present. Therefore, we may say that if the Word became flesh, it was not only to be encountered but also to speak.

Verse 14b and the succeeding lines show that, if the Word has become flesh, he has not ceased to be God. In 14b this is given expression in the verb *skēnoun* ("make a dwelling; pitch a tent") which has important OT associations. The theme of "tenting" is found in Exod xxv 8–9 where Israel is told to make a tent (the Tabernacle—*skēnē*) so that God can dwell among His people; the Tabernacle became the site of God's localized presence on earth. It was promised that in the ideal days to come this tenting among men would be especially impressive. Joel iii 17 says, "You will know that

I am the Lord your God who makes his dwelling [*kataskēnoun*] in Zion."
At the time of the return from the Babylonian Exile Zech ii 10 proclaims:
"Sing and rejoice, O daughter of Zion, for look, I come and will make
my dwelling [*kataskēnoun*] in your midst." In the ideal Temple described
by Ezekiel (xliii 7) God will make His dwelling in the midst of His people
forever, or as the LXX has it: "*My name* shall dwell in the midst of the
house of Israel forever." (The latter is interesting in view of the Johannine
interest in *the name*.) When the Prologue proclaims that the Word made
his dwelling among men, we are being told that the flesh of Jesus Christ is
the new localization of God's presence on earth, and that Jesus is the
replacement of the ancient Tabernacle. The Gospel will present Jesus as the
replacement of the Temple (ii 19–22), which is a variation of the same
theme. In Rev vii 15 the verb *skēnoun* is used of God's presence in
heaven, while in xxi 3 the great vision of the heavenly Jerusalem echoes
the promise of the prophets, "He will dwell [*skēnoun*] with them, and they
shall be His people." Thus, in dwelling among men, the Word anticipates
the divine presence which according to Revelation will be visible to men
in the last days.

As an intermediary between the pentateuchal and prophetic use of
"tenting" and the use of "tenting" in the Prologue we may call attention
to passages in the Wisdom Literature where Wisdom is said to tent or
make her dwelling among men (see App. II). In the hymn of Sir xxiv,
Wisdom sings: "The Creator of all . . . chose the spot for my tent, saying,
'In Jacob make your dwelling [*kataskēnoun*], in Israel your inheritance.'"
Thus, in making his dwelling among men, the Word is acting in the manner
of Wisdom.

There is another aspect of the divine presence suggested in vs. 14b. The
radicals *skn* which underlie the Greek verb "to tent" resemble the Hebrew
root *škn* which also means "to dwell" and from which the noun *shekinah*
is derived. In rabbinic theology *shekinah* was a technical term for God's
presence dwelling among His people. For instance, in Exod xxv 8 where
God says, "Let them make me a sanctuary that I may dwell among them,"
the Targum or Aramaic translation has, "I shall cause my *shekinah* to
reside among them." Like the use of *memra* discussed in App. II, the use of
shekinah as a surrogate for Yahweh in His dealings with men was a way of
preserving God's transcendence. The Targum of Deut xii 5 has God's
shekinah dwell in the sanctuary rather than His name. The threat in Hos
v 6 that Yahweh will withdraw from Israel becomes in the Targum a
threat that He will cause His *shekinah* to ascend to heaven and depart
from men. Even the omnipresence of God which no sanctuary can compass
is called His *shekinah* in the Talmud. Though some of these works stem
from a period later than the 1st century A.D., the theology of the *shekinah*
was known at that time; and it is quite possible that in the use of
skēnoun the Prologue is reflecting the idea that Jesus is now the *shekinah*
of God, the locus of contact between the Father and those men among

whom it is His delight to be. See L. Bouyer, "Le Schékinah, Dieu avec nous," BVC 20 (1957–58), 8–22.

The thought of the divine presence in Jesus who now serves as the Tabernacle and perhaps as the *shekinah* overflows into vs. 14c: "We have seen his glory." In the OT the *glory* of God (Heb. *kābôd;* Gr. *doxa*—see App. I:4) implies a visible and powerful manifestation of God to men. In the Targums "glory" also became a surrogate, like *memra* and *shekinah,* for the visible presence of God among men, although its use was not as frequent as that of the other surrogates. (If in Exod xxiv 10 we are told that Moses and the elders saw the God of Israel, in Targum Onkelos we hear that they "saw the glory [Aram. *y͏eqar*] of the God of Israel.") However, what we are primarily interested in is the constant connection of the glory of God with His presence in the Tabernacle and the Temple. When Moses went up Mount Sinai (Exod xxiv 15–16), we are told that a cloud covered the mountain and the glory of God settled there while God told Moses how to build the Tabernacle. When the Tabernacle was erected, the cloud covered it and the glory of God filled it (Exod xl 34). The same phenomenon is reported when Solomon's Temple was dedicated (I Kings viii 10–11). Just before the destruction of the Temple by the Babylonians, Ezek xi 23 tells us that the glory of God left the city; but in the vision of the restored Temple Ezekiel saw the glory of God once more filling the building (xliv 4). Thus, it is quite appropriate that, after the description of how the Word set up a Tabernacle among men in the flesh of Jesus, the Prologue should mention that his *glory* became visible.

Do lines 14c,d refer to a particular manifestation of the glory of the incarnate Word? We have mentioned in the NOTE that "we have seen" seems to be a reference to apostolic witness, like the "we" of the Prologue to I John. Many suggest, therefore, that the hymn is referring to the moment when Peter, *John,* and James witnessed the Transfiguration of Jesus, a scene not recorded in John but found in the Synoptics and II Pet i 16–18. On that occasion Luke ix 32 says that they saw his *glory.* And just as the Prologue speaks of the glory of an only Son, so at the Transfiguration the heavenly voice proclaimed Jesus as "my beloved Son" ("beloved" has the connotation of "only"). The account of the Transfiguration in II Peter may throw some light on the problem mentioned in the NOTE, whether in vs. 14d "coming from the Father" modifies "glory" or "Son." In II Pet i 16–17 the author speaking as Peter says, ". . . we had been eyewitnesses of his majesty. *He received from God the Father* honor and *glory . . .*" (Bo Reicke, The Anchor Bible, vol. 37); here clearly it is glory that comes from the Father. A reference to the Transfiguration would fit in well with the Tabernacle theme we saw in vs. 14b, for the scene on the mount of the Transfiguration is described in the Synoptic Gospels in terms evocative of God's appearance to Moses on Sinai, and the building of tents or tabernacles is specifically mentioned (Mark ix 5). Thus, there is much to recommend the suggestion that 14c,d is an echo of the Transfiguration.

However, it remains no more than a possibility that the Johannine writers knew of the Transfiguration scene.

It is worth while to compare Bultmann's exegesis of vs. 14 with that of Käsemann. Stressing the kenotic aspect of 14a, Bultmann, p. 40, speaks of the scandal implicit in the realization that the revealer is none other than a man. As for the "we have seen his glory," this is not an unrestricted vision. If we were to see transparently, the flesh would be meaningless; were we not to see at all, there would be no revelation. Käsemann, writing against Bultmann, insists on the glorious character of the Word-become-flesh. The flesh is not simply an incognito through which men must see; rather the glory of the Word keeps breaking through the flesh in the miraculous works which can be seen. Käsemann would thus draw together the miracles of the Johannine Jesus and his revelatory discourses (and to some extent destroy the dichotomy of sources that Bultmann has posited—see Introduction, Part II:B[2]). The miraculous in John is not the dross left from the sign-source but is an essential part of the presentation of the incarnate Word. In "the Word became flesh," Käsemann sees not so much that the revealer is only a man, but that God is present in the human sphere.

The theme of enduring covenant love (*hesed* and *'emet*—see NOTE) that appears in vs. 14e and is taken up in 16 fits in well with the Tabernacle and glory references that we have discussed. The great exhibition of the enduring covenant love of God in the OT took place at Sinai, the same setting where the Tabernacle became the dwelling for God's glory. So now the supreme exhibition of God's love is the incarnate Word, Jesus Christ, the new Tabernacle of divine glory. If our interpretation of "love in place of love" is correct, the hymn comes to an end with the triumphant proclamation of a new covenant replacing the Sinai covenant.

Parenthesis: *John the Baptist Testifies to the Pre-existence of Jesus* (vs. 15)

Verse 14 has stated that the pre-existent heavenly Word became flesh. Apparently the redactor who added vss. 6–9 has also added 15, intending to confirm vs. 14 with John the Baptist's testimony that Jesus is pre-existent. There is obvious polemic against any suggestion that John the Baptist might be greater than Jesus because he began his ministry first. See COMMENT on i 30. J. A. T. Robinson's suggestion that, like vss. 6–7, vs. 15 was part of the original opening of the Gospel is difficult, especially since then there would be no apparent reason for the same statement in vs. 30. We suggest that the final redactor, seeing that it might be useful here to emphasize the theme of pre-existence, copied into the Prologue the sentence from vs. 30.

Verses 17–18. As we have explained in the NOTE, vs. 17 merely spells out what has been said in 16 by naming the two occasions of God's demonstration of covenant love, namely, in the gift of the Law to Moses on Sinai, and in Jesus Christ. Verse 17 suggests more clearly than the hymn the superiority of the enduring love expressed in Jesus Christ, and vs. 18 spells out that superiority. Naturally it is the failure of Moses to have seen God that the author wishes to contrast with the intimate contact between Son and Father. In Exod xxxiii 18 Moses asks to see God's glory, but the Lord says, "You cannot see my face and live." Isaiah (vi 5) exclaims in terror, "Woe! I am lost . . . for my eyes have seen the King, the Lord of Hosts," where it is not even a question of seeing God's face. Against this OT background that not even the greatest representatives of Israel have seen God, John holds up the example of the only Son who has not only seen the Father but is ever at His side. We may well suspect that this theme was part of the Johannine polemic against the Synagogue, for it is repeated in v 37 and vi 46. However, the theme that only the Son had seen the Father would also impress the Hellenistic world which knew of the invisible God whose substance could not be grasped by men.

The editorial expansion of the hymn in vs. 18 is not lacking in adroitness; the editor has managed to incorporate in it several inclusions with vs. 1. Just as in vs. 1 the Word was God, so here the only Son is called God. Just as in vs. 1 the Word was in God's presence, so in 18 the only Son is ever at the Father's side. It is the unique relation of the Son to the Father, so unique that John can speak of "God the only Son," that makes his revelation the supreme revelation.

BIBLIOGRAPHY

Aucoin, Sister M. A., "Augustine and John Chrysostom: Commentators on St. John's Prologue," ScEccl 15 (1963), 123–31.

Barclay, W., "John i 1–14," ET 70 (1958–59), 78–82, 114–17.

Boismard, M.-E., *St. John's Prologue* (Westminster: Newman, 1957).

——"Dans le sein du Père," RB 59 (1952), 23–39.

Braun, F.-M., "Messie, Logos, et Fils de l'Homme," *La Venue du Messie* (Recherches Bibliques, VI; Louvain: Desclée de Brouwer, 1962), pp. 133–47. Also JeanThéol, II, pp. 137–50.

——"Qui ex Deo natus est," *Aux sources de la tradition chrétienne* (Mélanges Goguel; Paris: Delachaux, 1950), pp. 16–31.

de Ausejo, Serafin, "¿Es un himno a Cristo el prólogo de San Juan?" EstBíb 15 (1956), 223–77, 381–427.

de la Potterie, I., "De interpunctione et interpretatione versuum Joh. i, 3.4," VD 33 (1955), 193–208.

Dodd, C. H., "The Prologue to the Fourth Gospel and Christian Worship," SFG, pp. 9–22.

Dyer, J. A., "The Unappreciated Light," JBL 79 (1960), 170–71.

Eltester, W., "Der Logos und sein Prophet," *Apophoreta* (Haenchen Festschrift; Berlin: Töpelmann, 1964), pp. 109–34.

Gaechter, P., "Strophen im Johannesevangelium," ZKT 60 (1936), especially pp. 99–111.

Green, H. C., "The Composition of St. John's Prologue," ET 66 (1954–55), 291–94.

Haenchen, E., "Probleme des johanneischen 'Prologs,'" ZTK 60 (1963), 305–34.

Jeremias, J., "The Revealing Word," in *The Central Message of the New Testament* (London: SCM, 1965), pp. 71–90.

Jervell, J., " 'Er kam in sein Eigentum.' Zum Joh. 1, 11," *Studia Theologica* 10 (1956), 14–27.

Kačur, P., "De textu Joh. 1, 14c," VD 29 (1951), 20–27.

Käsemann, E., "Aufbau und Anliegen des johanneischen Prologs," *Libertas Christiana* (Delekat Festschrift; München: Kaiser, 1957), pp. 75–99.

Kuyper, L. J., "Grace and Truth: an Old Testament Description of God and Its Use in the Johannine Gospel," Interp 18 (1964), 3–19.

Lacan, M.-F., "L'œuvre du Verbe Incarné, le don de la vie (Jo. i, 4)," RSR 45 (1957), 61–78.

Lund, N. W., "The Influence of Chiasmus upon the Structure of the Gospels," ATR 13 (1931), especially pp. 41–46.

Mehlmann, J., "De mente S. Hieronymi circa divisionem versuum Joh i 3s.," VD 33 (1955), 86–94.

——"A Note on John i 3," ET 67 (1955–56), 340–41.

Nagel, W., " 'Die Finsternis hat's nicht begriffen' (Joh i 5)," ZNW 50 (1959), 132–37.

Pollard, T. E., "Cosmology and the Prologue of the Fourth Gospel," VigChr 12 (1958), 147–53.

Robinson, J. A. T., "The Relation of the Prologue to the Gospel of St. John," NTS 9 (1962–63), 120–29.

Sahlin, H., "Zwei Abschnitte aus Joh i rekonstruiert," ZNW 51 (1960), especially pp. 64–67.

Schmid, J., "Joh 1, 13," BZ 1 (1957), 118–25.

Schnackenburg, R., "Logos-Hymnus und johanneischer Prolog," BZ 1 (1957), 69–109.

Spicq, C., "Le Siriacide et la structure littéraire du Prologue de saint Jean," *Mémorial Lagrange* (Paris: Gabalda, 1940), pp. 183–95.

Vawter, B., "What Came to Be in Him Was Life (Jn 1, 3b–4a)," CBQ 25 (1963), 401–6.

II. THE BOOK OF SIGNS

The public ministry of Jesus where in sign and word he shows himself to his own people as the revelation of his Father, only to be rejected.

"To his own he came
yet his own people did not accept him."

Part One: The Opening Days of the Revelation of Jesus

OUTLINE

PART ONE: THE OPENING DAYS OF THE REVELATION OF JESUS
(i 19–51, followed by ii 1–11)

A.   i 19–34: THE TESTIMONY OF JOHN THE BAPTIST

(19–28) *Division 1*—Testimony concerning his role in relation to the one to come. (§ 2)

(a) 19–23: First interrogation of John the Baptist:
19–21: John the Baptist disclaims traditional roles.
22–23: John the Baptist claims the role of the Isaian voice.

(b) 24–28: Second interrogation of John the Baptist: He describes his own baptism as preliminary and exalts the one to come.

(29–34) *Division 2*—Testimony concerning Jesus. (§ 3)

(a) 29–31: Jesus is:
29: the Lamb of God;
30–31: the pre-existent one.

(b) 32–34: Jesus is:
32–33: The one on whom the Spirit descends and rests;
34: the chosen one.

B.   i 35–51: THE BAPTIST'S DISCIPLES COME TO JESUS AS HE MANIFESTS HIMSELF

(35–42) *Division 1*—The first two disciples and Simon Peter. (§ 4)

(a) 35–39: Two disciples—Jesus acknowledged as rabbi.

(b) 40–42: Simon Peter—Jesus as Messiah

(43–51) *Division 2*—Philip and Nathanael. (§ 5)

(a) 43–44: Philip—(Jesus as fulfillment of Law and prophets [vs. 45]).

(b) 45–50: Nathanael—Jesus as Son of God and King of Israel.

51: A once-independent saying about the Son of Man.

This Part has its conclusion in ii 1–11, the scene at Cana where Jesus manifests his glory and his disciples believe in him. This Cana scene also serves as the opening scene of Part Two and will be discussed there.

2. THE TESTIMONY OF JOHN THE BAPTIST:
—CONCERNING HIS ROLE
(i 19–28)

I 19 Now this is the testimony John gave when the Jews sent priests and Levites from Jerusalem to ask him who he was.
20 He declared without any qualification, avowing, "I am not the Messiah."
21 They questioned him further, "Well, who are you? Elijah?" "I am not," he answered.
"Are you the prophet?" "No!" he replied.
22 Then they said to him, "Just who are you?—so that we can give some answer to those who sent us. What have you to say for yourself?"
23 He said, quoting the prophet Isaiah, "I am—

> 'a voice in the desert crying out,
> "Make the Lord's road straight!"'"

24 But the emissaries of the Pharisees 25 questioned him further, "If you are not the Messiah, nor Elijah, nor the Prophet, then what are you doing baptizing?" 26 John answered them, "I am only baptizing with water; but there is one among you whom you do not recognize— 27 the one who is to come after me, and I am not even worthy to unfasten the straps of his sandal." 28 It was in Bethany that this happened, across the Jordan where John used to baptize.

21: *answered.* In the historical present tense.

NOTES

i 19. *Now.* A *kai* begins this section, as it also begins many of the books of LXX (II Samuel, I and II Kings). Before the Prologue was prefixed, this verse may have opened the Gospel, although a more likely possibility is that vss. 6–7(8?) preceded vs. 19 and constituted the original opening.

this is the testimony. In vss. 6–7 we heard that John the Baptist was sent to testify to the light, and now here is his testimony. We expect a testimony to Jesus, but that comes only in vss. 29–34 on the next day. The original sequence has probably been disturbed by editing; see pp. 67–71 below.

the Jews. For the Johannine use of this term as a reference to the religious authorities hostile to Jesus, particularly those in Jerusalem, see Introduction, Part V:B.

sent. Many good witnesses add "to him"; but this is missing in both Bodmer papyri and is probably a scribal clarification.

priests and Levites. To ask about his baptizing they send the specialists in ritual purification. Such a confrontation of John the Baptist and the priests is interesting in view of the Lucan tradition that John the Baptist was a priest's son (Luke i 5). Normally "Levites" refers to an inferior priestly class but sometimes in the rabbinic documents to temple police. They are rare on the NT scene (only in Luke x 32; Acts iv 36).

Jerusalem. In John's Greek this is always the Hellenized *Hierosolyma;* in Revelation, always the more primitive *Hierousalēm*—certainly an indication of different scribes.

20. *declared without any qualification, avowing.* Literally "He avowed and did not deny, and avowed"—tautological even for John. This may be a sign of editing, for there is no other example in John of such a triple combination of positive, negative, positive.

I am not the Messiah. Some suggest that the "I" is emphatic: I am not but another is. There is not much evidence, however, that John the Baptist identified the one to come after him as the Messiah in the strict sense, i.e., anointed Davidic king. John iii 28 is the only specific reference to John the Baptist's preparing the way for the Messiah; it may be implied in Luke iii 15–16.

21. *Well. Oun* is John's favorite connecting particle (195 times); it never occurs in I John—again an interesting indication of different scribes in the Johannine works.

who are you? Elijah? Other divisions of these words are attested, but this is supported by the Bodmer papyri.

23. The common NT form of citing Isa xl 3 comes substantially from LXX, where "in the desert" modifies the "voice," rather than from MT, where "in the desert" is part of what is said, thus:

> A voice crying out,
> "Prepare the road of the Lord in the desert;
> make straight a highway for our God in the wilderness."

The fact that John the Baptist was in a desert region when he raised his prophetic voice made the LXX form more suitable for NT purposes. The symbolism of preparing a road for Yahweh is probably drawn from the preparations for processions in honor of the statues of gods or in honor of visiting potentates. Garofalo, *art. cit.,* points out a good parallel in a 3rd-century B.C. Ptolemaic papyrus which describes preparations being made for the visit of the captain of the royal guard. The instructions are "to make a road" for his approach (Grenfell Hunt, *Greek Papyri,* Series II [1897], p. 28, xivB).

a voice. Augustine (*Sermons* 293:3; PL 38:1328) remarks poetically that John the Baptist was a voice for a while (John v 35), but Christ is the eternal Word in the beginning.

24. *the emissaries of the Pharisees.* This is a somewhat ambiguous translation to cover the possibilities offered by the two different Greek readings of this verse and the various scholarly interpretations of them: (a) "And the ones sent were from the Pharisees"—an article before the participle. This has the weaker attestation. Presumably "the ones sent" would be a reference to the priests and Levites mentioned in vs. 19, although Bernard sees in this reading an attempt to

introduce a new group. The basic difficulty is that priests and Levites would normally belong to the Sadducee persuasion. Lagrange, p. 37, gives evidence to show that some priests sided with the Pharisees, but this is scarcely a satisfactory explanation of the present passage. Others use this as a proof that the evangelist knew nothing of Palestine. The evangelist, however, never goes into detail about the various groups in Palestine (even the tax collectors and the Herodians have disappeared in John) because, by the time this Gospel was written, these groups were no longer so meaningful. The Judaism that survived the destruction of the Temple was of strongly Pharisaic persuasion, and for a Gospel written with this situation in mind "Pharisees" and "Jews" would be the most meaningful titles for the Jewish authorities. Thus we may have here a simplification. We shall also see the possibility that the mention of the Pharisees is the product of editing. We may recall Matt iii 7 where Sadducees and Pharisees come to John the Baptist. (b) The Greek reading without the article before the participle, translated either as, "And some Pharisees had been sent" (Dodd, *Tradition*, pp. 263–64) or as, "And they had been sent from the Pharisees" (Bernard). This reading is attested by both Bodmer papyri. Dodd's translation avoids the difficulty by introducing a new delegation; the second, more difficult translation has the best chance of being correct.

25. *questioned him further*. Same expression as in vs. 21; perhaps a sign of editorial duplication.

27. *the one who is to come*. Either as a participle (*ho erchomenos*) or as a finite verb (*erchetai*), this phrase marks John the Baptist's expectations both in the Gospels and Acts. In view of the discussion in the COMMENT that perhaps John the Baptist expected Elijah to come, we note that Mal iii 1, a passage frequently associated with Elijah, says, "Behold, he is coming [*erchetai*]," and Matt xi 14 speaks of "Elijah who is to come." Thus, "the one to come" may have been a title for Elijah.

worthy. *Axios*; strangely both Bodmer papyri read "fit" (*hikanos*), a reading that is a harmonization with the Synoptics—see COMMENT.

unfasten the straps. A slave's task. Bernard, I, p. 41, cites a rabbinic axiom that a disciple might offer to do any service for his teacher which a slave did for his master, except that of unfastening his sandals.

28. *Bethany*. This is not the town near Jerusalem (xi 18), but a site in the Transjordan of which no trace remains. Parker, *art. cit.*, has attempted to solve the problem of the disappearance of this second Bethany by a translation which would eliminate it altogether: This happened in Bethany, across from the point on the Jordan where John had been baptizing. Thus, he places the whole incident in Bethany near Jerusalem, offering an explanation of why the Jewish authorities are at hand. Another solution was offered by Origen (*Comm.* VI 40; GCS 10:149) who said that although *almost all* the manuscripts read Bethany, he could find no such town in the Transjordan (ca. A.D. 200). Therefore he preferred another reading, "Bethabara," a town whose existence is also attested in the Talmud. ("Bethabara" is read in the OS of John.) If Bethabara, "the place of crossing over," is the correct reading (and a critic like Boismard follows Origen in this), then John may be calling attention to the Joshua-Jesus parallelism. Just as Joshua led the people *across* the Jordan into the promised land, so Jesus is to *cross over* into the promised land at the head of a new people. Pilgrim tradition identifies the same site on the Jordan for both Joshua's crossing and Jesus' baptism. Perhaps, however, this very plausible symbolism makes the poorly attested name Bethabara all the more suspect. Even the name Bethany is open to symbolic

interpretation; Krieger, *art. cit.*, suggests that it derives from *bet-aniyyah*, "house of response/witness/testimony," a derivation which would make the name appropriate for the place where John the Baptist gave testimony to Jesus. On this basis Krieger and others deny the geographical reality of the site; but where there is symbolism in John, it generally stems from an ingenious interpretation of fact rather than from purely imaginative creation. Scholars have become more cautious now that some Johannine place names, once accounted to be purely symbolic (e.g., Bethesda in v 2), have been shown to be factual.

COMMENT: GENERAL

The Gospel proper begins with the testimony of John the Baptist given on three days (i 29, 35), days which have symbolic rather than strictly chronological import. On the first day John the Baptist's testimony about his own role is largely negative; on the second John the Baptist testifies positively to what Jesus is; on the third John the Baptist sends his own disciples to follow Jesus. As Dodd, *Tradition*, p. 248, has pointed out, this threefold progression is simply spelling out the pattern defined in advance in i 6–8: first, John the Baptist himself was not the light; second, he was to testify to the light (=Jesus); third, through him all men might believe.

In the Synoptics we have one great trial of Jesus before the Sanhedrin on the night preceding his death. One of John's techniques is to show that themes occurring in one place in the Synoptics had a reality throughout the whole of Jesus' ministry, and this is particularly true of the theme of Jesus on trial. The Word of God has now been spoken to men, and throughout Jesus' ministry men will seek to put the truth of this Word on trial by seeking witnesses for it. Legal vocabulary like confession, interrogation, testimony, is found throughout John; and in v 31–40, in a climactic moment, Jesus brings forward a whole series of witnesses to the truth of God's word: God Himself, the Scriptures, Moses, and John the Baptist. Thus, it fits John's purpose that even before Jesus appears, the Gospel opens with a trial and John the Baptist under interrogation.

As we know from the Synoptics and from Josephus (*Ant.* XVIII.v.2; ✗118), John the Baptist attracted great crowds by his ministry in the Jordan valley. He had come down from the desert of Judea, those barren hills to the west of the Dead Sea, and with apocalyptic zeal was proclaiming the day of judgment. He administered a baptism of water to those who accepted his message and acknowledged their own sinfulness. Little of this appears in John; for the evangelist is not interested in John the Baptist as a baptizer or as a prophet, but only in his being a herald of Jesus and the first witness in the great trial of the Word. John i 26 simply presupposes that the reader knows that John the Baptist was a baptizer.

Can John's account of John the Baptist, which seemingly has little in common with the Synoptic tradition, be reconciled with the other Gospels? Does John give us reliable, independent information about John the Baptist? These are questions that shall occupy our discussion below.

COMMENT: DETAILED

There are two interrogations on the first day: vss. 19–23 and 24–27. In the first, John the Baptist disclaims any of the traditional eschatological roles for himself with progressively more abrupt negatives: "I am not the Messiah . . . I am not . . . No!" He claims for himself only a herald's role, thus focusing all the attention on the one to come. In the second interrogation, he justifies his baptizing also in terms of preparation for the one to come.

First Interrogation, Phase One: John the Baptist disclaims traditional roles (i 19–21)

At this time there was no uniform Jewish expectation of a single eschatological figure. A majority of the Jews expected the Messiah. Yet some of the apocryphal books describe God's intervention without ever mentioning the anointed Davidic king; and in parts of Enoch the figure of the Son of Man, and not the Messiah, embodies the expectations of the author. The Qumran Essenes seem to have expected three eschatological figures: a prophet, a priestly messiah, and a royal messiah. Passages like John i 21; Mark vi 15; Matt xvi 14, give witness to the variety in popular eschatological anticipation. Although John is our only witness for this interrogation of John the Baptist as to which of the more popular eschatological figures he identified himself with, there is nothing implausible about it. In baptizing, John the Baptist was performing an eschatological action; his message was one of divine intervention; crowds were beginning to follow him; he was operating in an area not far from the Essene center on the Dead Sea (and the Jerusalem authorities were suspicious of the Essenes). The authorities may well have wondered who he thought he was. Matt iii 7–10 mentions that Pharisees and Sadducees came to hear John the Baptist and describes his hostility toward them; Mark xi 30–32 and Matt xi 18, xxi 32, show that the authorities did not believe in John the Baptist.

(1) **John the Baptist was not the Messiah.** It is difficult to be certain if there is any hierarchy in the three roles proposed for John the Baptist, but the expectation of the Messiah seems to have been the closest to a national expectation. It is noteworthy that, although Jesus did not claim the title of Messiah for himself and accepted the designation only with reluctance and reservations, the early Christians seized on "Messiah" as his title par excellence and in its Greek form "Christ" became part of his proper name.

Is John's stress that John the Baptist was not the Messiah more than a historical reminiscence? Is this part of John's apologetic against the claims of the Baptist sectarians? We cannot be certain that in the 1st century his followers proclaimed John the Baptist to be the Messiah; but they seem to have done so later on, if we can depend on the evidence of the Pseudo-Clementine *Recognitions* (see Introduction, Part V:A, and Schnackenburg, "Die Johannesjünger," pp. 24–25). In the Latin of *Recognitions* I 54 (PG 1:1238) and I 60 (PG 1:1240) we find Baptist sectarians stressing that their master, not Jesus, was the Messiah. That John is refuting an early form of this claim is possible, especially in view of the evidence in Luke iii 15 that people thought that John the Baptist might be the Messiah.

(2) **John the Baptist was not Elijah.** According to a popular tradition (II Kings ii 11), Elijah had been taken up to heaven in a chariot; and the idea that he was still alive and active was fostered by the strange appearance of a letter from him some time after he had been taken away (II Chron xxi 12). In post-exilic expectations Elijah was to return before the day of the Lord (not necessarily before the Messiah). In Mal iii 1 (ca. 450 B.C.) there is a reference to the angel who would prepare the way of the Lord, and a (slightly later?) addition to the book (iv 5 [iii 23H]) identifies this messenger as Elijah. In the 2nd century B.C. or earlier, En xc 31 and lxxxix 52 in its elaborate animal allegory of history pictures Elijah's return before the judgment and before the appearance of the great apocalyptic lamb. The latter reference is interesting when we remember that John the Baptist was proclaiming the Lamb of God. Still another 2nd-century reference is found in Sir xlviii 10: "You are destined, it is written, in time to come to put an end to wrath before the day of the Lord." The expectation of Elijah was evidently widespread in Palestine at the time of Jesus (Mark viii 28, ix 11) and continued into the Judaism of the post-Christian era. By the 2nd century A.D. it was maintained that Elijah would anoint the Messiah—see J. Klausner, *The Messianic Idea in Israel* (London: Allen and Unwin, 1956), pp. 451–56; G. Molin, "Elijahu der Prophet und sein Weiterleben in den Hoffnungen der Judentums und Christenheit," *Judaica* 8 (1952), 65–94.

The interrogators would have had good reason to ask John the Baptist if he claimed to be Elijah. He wore garments like those of Elijah (compare Mark i 6 with II Kings i 8, although the hairy mantle may have been standard prophetic garb, as Zech xiii 4 indicates). All the Gospels connect John the Baptist with Isa xl 3, the voice in the desert. Molin, p. 80, gives evidence that Isa xl 3 was later combined with Mal iv 5 and reinterpreted to refer to Elijah (see Mark i 2, combining Isaiah and Malachi).

Once again, is John's stress that John the Baptist was not Elijah part of the polemic against the Baptist sectarians? Richter, *art. cit.*, thinks that the sectarians identified John the Baptist with Elijah inasmuch as Elijah was a messianic figure (messianic in a sense broader than a reference to the Davidic king). Later on Elijah was thought of as a priestly messiah alongside the Davidic Messiah; for example, see N. Wieder, "The Doctrine of Two Messiahs among the Karaites," JJS 6 (1955), 14–25. But, as we shall see below, there is not sufficient evidence for a messianic view of Elijah at the time John was written, although Elijah as a forerunner of the

Lord may have replaced the Davidic Messiah in certain eschatological expectations. The real objection to Richter's theory is that there is no clear evidence that the sectarians thought of John the Baptist as Elijah. Yet in the Syriac form of the Pseudo-Clementine *Recognitions* I 54, the sectarians picture John the Baptist as being hidden in concealment, presumably to return; this is not unlike a description of Elijah. Also, *if* the material in the Lucan infancy narrative about John the Baptist came from Baptist sectarians, Luke i 17 describes John the Baptist as Elijah. The question of anti-sectarian polemics remains uncertain, and the question about Elijah put to John the Baptist may be simply a historical reminiscence.

John the Baptist's repudiation of the role of Elijah in John does present a different picture from that of Mark and Matthew. Mark i 2 applies Mal iii 1 to John the Baptist, thus identifying him as Elijah. Matt xi 14 reports these words of Jesus concerning John the Baptist: "If you are willing to accept it, he is Elijah who is to come." Finally, both Mark ix 13 and Matt xvii 12 show Jesus maintaining that Elijah had already come, presumably in John the Baptist. Luke seems to hold a middle position, for outside of the reference in the infancy narrative, the Gospel of Luke proper never identifies John the Baptist as Elijah. In fact, Luke seems deliberately to omit passages in Mark which would abet such identification. Jesus is the Elijah-like figure for Luke (cf. iv 24–26, vii 11–17 with I Kings xvii 18–24; the "going up" of ix 51 with II Kings ii 11; xii 49 with I Kings xviii 38).

How do we solve such diverse views about the relationship of John the Baptist to the Elijah expectation? Sahlin, *art. cit.*, seeks to remove the difficulty in John by a reconstruction that makes John the Baptist affirm that he is Elijah. There is absolutely no evidence for his rearrangement of verses, and his solution would not bring the Lucan evidence into consideration. A more conservative explanation seeking to harmonize the Gospels dates back to patristic days: in person John the Baptist was not Elijah (John), but he exercised toward Jesus the function of Elijah by preparing his way (Mark, Matthew)—thus, Gregory the Great PL 76:1100. However, this solution avoids the real difficulty, for the question put to John the Baptist concerns precisely the function that he is exercising; and he denies that he is exercising the function of Elijah.

A far more likely solution has been proposed by J. A. T. Robinson, *art. cit.*, who thinks that John is preserving a historically correct reminiscence that John the Baptist did not think of himself as playing the role of Elijah. There are clear passages in the Synoptics (Mark vi 14–15, viii 28) indicating that the people and Herod distinguished between John the Baptist and Elijah; and in Matt xvii 10–13 the disciples of Jesus, among whom there were former disciples of John the Baptist (Peter?), betray that they have never thought of John the Baptist as Elijah. As for those passages cited above which identify John the Baptist and Elijah, this is not the view of John the Baptist himself but the view of early Christian theology which saw in the role of Elijah the best way to interpret the relation of John the

Baptist to Jesus, namely John the Baptist was to the coming of Jesus what Elijah was to have been to the coming of the Lord.

(3) **John the Baptist was not the Prophet**—an echo of Deut xviii 15–18. The Deuteronomic legislation was concerned with various functionaries in the government and society of Israel: judges (xvi 18), king (xvii 14), priests (xviii 1), and prophets. However, the general legislation concerning the prophet, because of its phrasing ("A prophet like me [Moses] will the Lord, your God, raise up") came to be interpreted as the prediction of the coming of a particular figure who would be the Prophet-like-Moses. See H. M. Teeple, *The Mosaic Eschatological Prophet* (JBL Monograph, x, 1957). We find in I Macc iv 41–50, xiv 41, the expectation of the coming of a prophet who could solve legal problems on the pattern of Moses. At Qumran the Essenes are told to cling to the Torah and the ancient laws of the community until a prophet comes—presumably the Prophet-like-Moses (L. H. Silberman, VT 5 [1955], 79–81; R. E. Brown, CBQ 19 [1957], 59–61). The biblical reference to this Prophet is given a prominent place in a Qumran collection of passages dealing with eschatological triumph over enemies (4Q *Testimonia*, ca. 100 B.C.—wrongly called a messianic anthology; see P. Skehan, CBQ 25 [1963], 121–22). Acts iii 22 identifies Jesus as the Prophet-like-Moses. The expectations of the people concerning the coming of this Prophet are seen in John vi 14 and vii 40 in contexts where Moses is in mind (see also vii 52). For detail consult R. Schnackenburg, "Die Erwartung des Prophetens nach dem Neuen Testament und den Qumran-Texten," StEv, I, pp. 622–39.

It is interesting that in their questions to John the Baptist the priests collocate Elijah and the Prophet-like-Moses. Another Johannine writing, Rev xi, describes two eschatological witnesses in terms evocative of Moses and Elijah. These two figures appear together in the Synoptic scene of the Transfiguration (Mark ix 4). The fact that Elijah, like Moses, was associated with Mount Sinai or Horeb (I Kings xix 8) probably joined them in popular thought, and this desert background may have suggested that they had something in common with John the Baptist. See Glasson, *Moses*, pp. 27–32. Once again Richter, *art. cit.*, thinks that John's emphasis that John the Baptist was not the Prophet-like-Moses is rooted in Johannine apologetics against the Baptist sectarians. There is no evidence that the sectarians considered John the Baptist to be this prophet, although Mark xi 32 reports that all the people regarded John the Baptist as *a* prophet, and Jesus himself said that John the Baptist was more than a prophet (Matt xi 9).

Recently A. S. van der Woude in *La secte de Qumran* (Recherches Bibliques, IV; Louvain: 1959), pp. 121–34, has suggested that the three eschatological roles proposed by the priests for John the Baptist are to be associated with the three figures expected by the Qumran sectarians. There are many links, geographical and ideological, that connect John the Baptist to these Essenes; and without necessarily having been an Essene, John the Baptist may well have been influenced by contact with them. If Van der

Woude is right, the priests were positing such a connection in their selections from the gallery of eschatological possibilities. In 1QS ix 11 we have the phrase, ". . . until the coming of a prophet and the messiahs of Aaron and Israel." For the evidence that identifies these three figures as the Prophet-like-Moses, a priestly messiah and the royal messiah see our article in CBQ 19 (1957), 53–82. Two of the figures expected by Qumran were the same as two of the possibilities suggested to John the Baptist: the Messiah and the Prophet. The real difficulty is whether Elijah was the priestly messiah, as Van der Woude maintains. There was a tradition that Elijah was a priest, and Jeremias, TWNTE, II, p. 932, suggests that this tradition may go back to pre-Christian times. However, the Qumran Essenes insisted on a priesthood of pure Zadokite lineage (i.e., descended from Zadok, priest in Jerusalem in David's time), and there is no evidence that Elijah was a Zadokite priest. For further arguments against identifying Elijah and the priestly messiah see J. Giblet in *L'attente du Messie* (Recherches Bibliques, I; Louvain: Desclée de Brouwer, 1954), pp. 112 ff. In our opinion Van der Woude's suggestion is possible but not proved. For other, less happy attempts by Brownlee and Stauffer to interpret the questions in John i 20–21 against the background of the Dead Sea Scrolls, see H. Braun, ThR 28 (1962), 198–99.

First Interrogation, Phase Two: John the Baptist claims the role of the Isaian voice (i 22–23)

Having disclaimed the traditional eschatological roles, John the Baptist now identifies himself in the same humble terms by which the Synoptics identify him, namely, as the preparatory voice of Isa xl 3. The Isaian passage originally referred to the role of the angels in preparing a way through the desert by which Israel might return from the Babylonian captivity to the land of Palestine. Like a modern bulldozer the angels were to level hills and fill in the valleys, and thus prepare a superhighway. But John the Baptist is to prepare a road, not for God's people to return to the promised land, but for God to come to His people. His baptizing and preaching in the desert was opening up the hearts of men, leveling their pride, filling their emptiness, and thus preparing them for God's intervention.

John's reference to Isa xl 3 differs in two respects from that of the Synoptic Gospels. *First,* the Synoptic evangelists themselves apply the text to John the Baptist, while in John it is John the Baptist who applies it to himself. This has generally been interpreted as John's method of having John the Baptist give testimony. Now, however, we know that it is perfectly plausible that John the Baptist did use the text of himself. The Qumran Essenes used precisely this text to explain why they chose to live in the desert: they were preparing the way for the Lord by studying and observing the Law (1QS viii 13–16). The use of the Isaian text may be another point of contact between John the Baptist and Qumran. *Second,* John reports the citation in a slightly different form from that of the Synoptics. While both follow the general tradition of LXX (see NOTE), the Synoptics vary from LXX in but one phrase:

A voice in the desert crying out,
"Prepare the Lord's road;
make straight his [LXX: God's] path."

John, on the other hand, has only one line of message, "Make straight the Lord's road"; and this contains elements from both lines of the Synoptic-LXX message. One might suggest that John has simply abridged the traditional form; but as Dodd, *Tradition*, p. 252, insists, John is highly independent in citing Scripture.

Second Interrogation: John the Baptist describes his own baptism as preliminary and exalts the one to come (i 24–28)

The emissaries have had an answer to their questions concerning John the Baptist's role; now they want a justification for his baptizing. Those scholars who believe that there are two groups of emissaries involved in i 19 and 24 (see NOTE) think that the second question is more theoretical and worthy of the theologically minded Pharisees. However, the further questioning by the emissaries *may* simply be the result of literary reduplication; see pp. 67–71 below. The question in vs. 25 is not noticeably a progression over the question in vs. 19, since even the earlier question was undoubtedly provoked by John's baptizing.

The objection posed by the Pharisees has its logic: if John the Baptist does not claim any recognizable eschatological role, why is he performing an eschatological action like baptizing? There are some interesting features in John the Baptist's answer. He professes to be baptizing only with water; and in i 33 we shall hear that Jesus is to baptize with a holy Spirit. This distinction of two types of baptism is common to all four Gospels and seems to be a Christian contribution, for in Hebrew thought baptism or cleansing with water and with a holy spirit come together. In Ezek xxxvi 25–26 God promises, "I will sprinkle clean *water* upon you, and you will be clean from all your impurities. . . . A new heart will I give you, and a *new spirit* will I put within you." Zech xiii 1–3 proclaims, "On that day there will be opened for the house of David and for the inhabitants of Jerusalem a *fountain to purify* them from sin and from uncleanness . . . I will *remove* from the land the *unclean spirit.*" In their rule of life the Qumran Essenes maintained (1QS iv 20–21): "God will . . . cleanse man through a holy spirit, and will sprinkle upon him *a spirit of truth as purifying water.*" Christian thought has divided these two aspects of baptism or cleansing, and thus succeeded in explaining the relation of John the Baptist's baptism to Christian Baptism. This note still persists in Acts xix 1–6, where the disciples baptized with John's baptism are distinctive because they have not received the Spirit.

We may compare John i 26–27 and 33 with what the Synoptics have to say about the two baptisms and the one to come after John the Baptist:

Mark i 7–8: There is coming after me (*opisō mou*) one who is mightier
             than I;
             I am not even fit (*hikanos*) to stoop and unfasten the straps
             of his sandals.
             I have baptized you with water (*hydati*),
             but he will baptize you with a holy Spirit.
Luke iii 16: I baptize you with water (*hydati*);
             but there is coming one who is mightier than I
             for whom I am not even fit to unfasten the straps of his
             sandals.
             He will baptize you with a holy Spirit and fire.
Matt iii 11: I baptize you with water (*en hydati*) for repentance;
             but the one who is coming after me (*opisō mou*) is mightier
             than I,
             for whom I am not even fit to carry his sandals.
             He will baptize you with a holy Spirit and fire.
Acts xiii 25: But behold, there is coming after me (*met' eme*) one
             for whom I am not worthy (*axios*) to unfasten the sandal of
             his feet.

Because this portion of John's treatment of John the Baptist has Synoptic
parallels, some have suggested that we have an editorial addition borrowed from the Synoptic tradition. We have maintained in the Introduction
(Part III:B) that most of Johannine tradition is independent of the Synoptic
tradition. Let us test this here by seeing if John's account can be explained
as a borrowing from any Synoptic Gospel.

First, John has features in common with Acts as opposed to the other
Gospels, namely, the use of "sandal" in the singular, the use of "worthy"
(*axios*) instead of "fit" (*hikanos*), a failure to describe the one to come as
"mightier than I." Yet, in using *opisō mou* for "after me," John agrees
with Mark and Matthew against Acts with its *met' eme*. In speaking of
unfastening the straps of the sandal, John is closest to Luke, for all the
others have variations (Mark: "stoop"; Matt: "carry sandals"; Acts: "unfasten sandal"). In not mentioning a baptism with fire, John is closest to
Mark, against Matthew and Luke. In using the phrase *en hydati*, John is
closest to Matthew, against Mark and Luke (*hydati*). Mark puts the two
types of baptism in immediately antithetic or contrasting parallelism,
whereas Matthew and Luke separate the two baptisms by intermediary
lines; John goes even further in separating them by a number of verses.
From this evidence it should be quite clear how difficult and complicated
it is to seek to explain John's form of the saying as a borrowing from the
Synoptic Gospels. As Dodd, *Tradition*, p. 256, remarks, "The simplest, and
surely the most probable, hypothesis is that this part of the Baptist's preaching, which was evidently regarded in the early Church as of crucial importance, was preserved in several branches of the tradition, and that
variations arose in the process of oral transmission."

In place of "one who is mightier than I," John the Baptist according to

John speaks of "the one among you whom you do not recognize." This description is not meant as a reproach to the audience for its blindness, for John the Baptist freely admits (vs. 33) that he himself could not recognize Jesus without help from God. Rather, in this description we may have an echo of a popular theory about the Messiah, that is, the theory of the hidden Messiah. According to the "normal" messianic expectations the Messiah would be known because he would make his appearance at Bethlehem (John vii 42; Matt ii 5). But there seems also to have been an apocalyptic strain of messianic expectation where the Messiah's presence on earth would be hidden until suddenly he would be shown to his people. We have an echo of this in John vii 27 (which see). The theology of the hidden Messiah is enunciated by the Jew Trypho in his 2nd-century argument with Justin: "Messiah, even if he be born and actually exist somewhere, is an unknown" (*Dialogue* VIII 4, CX 1). Trypho maintains that the Messiah must wait until Elijah comes to anoint him and make him known. (It is interesting that just as Elijah is to point out the Messiah, John the Baptist points out Jesus.) This type of messianism is much closer to the hidden-Son-of-Man expectations of Enoch than to the standard Davidic expectations associated with Mic v 2, and may really represent a conflation of the two strains. In the Synoptics, if we find the standard Davidic expectations in the infancy narratives, the theme of the hidden Messiah seems to come to the fore in the Petrine confession (Mark viii 27–30 and par.) where Peter recognizes as Messiah a Jesus whose true identity has been hidden from men and known only to God. For a fuller discussion of the hidden Messiah see S. Mowinckel, *He that Cometh* (Nashville: Abingdon, 1954), pp. 304–8; E. Stauffer, "Agnostos Christos," BNTE, pp. 281–99.

John alone tells us that John the Baptist shared in these apocalyptic expectations of a hidden one to come, and this is perfectly plausible. Is this reference also part of the apologetic against the Baptist sectarians? In the Syriac form of the Pseudo-Clementine *Recognitions* I 54, the sectarians maintained that after his death John the Baptist was really in concealment and was presumably to return. Is this possibly an indication that the sectarians looked on John the Baptist as the hidden Messiah? Stauffer, p. 292, and others think so. In this case, polemic against the claims of the sectarians guided John in recording the reminiscence that for John the Baptist it was the one to come after him who would be the Unknown One.

There is one other point that should be mentioned before we leave i 26–27. Cullmann, ECW, pp. 60 ff., is one of those who see a strong reference to the Christian sacrament of Baptism in these verses. In i 26 Cullmann believes that John is contrasting John the Baptist's baptism with water and the person of Jesus himself. He states that the contrast in John is not, as it is in the Synoptics,

I am baptizing with water   *vs.*   He will baptize with a holy Spirit;
but I am baptizing with water   *vs.*   There is one among you whom you
                                                              do not recognize.

However, as we have pointed out, it is only Mark who makes an *im-*

mediate contrast between the two types of baptism. Moreover, the real contrast in John is not between baptism with water and the person of Jesus, but between John the Baptist and the Unknown One to come. In TS 23 (1962), 197–99, we have discussed the proposed references to Christian Baptism in this passage and found that they were not very convincing. Of course, the baptism of Jesus by John the Baptist had an important influence on the theory and practice of Christian Baptism—Thomas Aquinas regarded it as the occasion of the institution of Christian Baptism (see F.-M. Braun, "Le baptême d'après le quatrième évangile," RThom 48 [1948], 358–62). But the question at hand is whether John's account of this has any *special* sacramental import, and we find no such evidence.

This first day closes with a reference to the site where John the Baptist gave witness. Closing a section with a geographical reference is common in John (vi 59, viii 20, xi 54). This site across the Jordan will be mentioned again by way of inclusion in x 40, which in an earlier stage of the Gospel may have marked the end of the public ministry. John has other geographical information about John the Baptist not found in the Synoptics, for example, concerning John the Baptist's ministry at Aenon near Salim (iii 23). As Dodd, *Tradition,* pp. 249–50, insists, these geographical details lend color to the theory that the Fourth Gospel preserves independent tradition about John the Baptist.

[The Bibliography for this section is included in the Bibliography at the end of § 3.]

3. THE TESTIMONY OF JOHN THE BAPTIST:
—CONCERNING JESUS
(i 29–34)

I ²⁹ The next day, when he caught sight of Jesus coming toward him, he exclaimed,

> "Look! Here is the Lamb of God
> who takes away the world's sin.

³⁰ "It is he about whom I said,

> 'After me is to come a man
> who ranks ahead of me,
> for he existed before me.'

³¹ "I myself never recognized him, though the very reason why I came and baptized with water was that he might be revealed to Israel."

³² John gave this testimony also,

> "I have seen the Spirit descend
> like a dove from the sky,
> and it came to rest upon him.

³³ "And I myself never recognized him; but the One who sent me to baptize with water told me, 'When you see the Spirit descend and rest on someone, he is the one who is to baptize with a holy Spirit.' ³⁴ Now I myself have seen and have testified, 'This is God's chosen one.'"

29: *caught sight, exclaimed.* In the historical present tense.

NOTES

i 29. *next day.* Seemingly (from vs. 32) the Johannine scene takes place after the baptism of Jesus, not mentioned by John. Among the Synoptics only Matt iii 14 implies a knowledge of Jesus by John the Baptist before the Baptism. Luke does not, even though according to the Lucan infancy narrative John the Baptist and Jesus are related.

the lamb of God. The meaning of the genitive will depend on the interpretation of "the Lamb" (see COMMENT). If the Lamb is the Servant, then John's phrase is patterned after the Servant *of Yahweh.* If the Lamb is the paschal lamb, then the genitive may have the sense of "supplied by God."

takes away . . . sin. The present here may have future force (ZGB, § 283):

"will take away." This verb *airein* occurs in LXX of I Sam xv 25, xxv 28, in the sense of pardoning sin or removing guilt. I John iii 5 has "take away sins [plural]." The plural refers to sinful acts, while the singular refers to a sinful condition. Since the clause "who takes away the world's sin" is found only in John i 29, and not with the other mention of the Lamb in i 36, some regard it as the evangelist's addition to a more original tradition wherein John the Baptist said simply, "Here is the Lamb of God."

30. *about whom.* The reading *peri,* which clearly means "about," must now, with the additional evidence of P[66,75], yield to *hyper,* which offers two possible meanings. Bernard, I, p. 47, opts for "in whose behalf"; but BDF, § 231[1], and ZGB, § 96, suggest that *hyper=peri* in this case.

I said. Verse 30 is almost identical with vs. 15; the "I said" may be an editorial attempt to make allowance for the introduction of vs. 15 into the Prologue hymn. Actually John the Baptist has *not* said this on a previous occasion in the Gospel. We find a similar instance of self-quotation without an exact antecedent in iii 28.

After me is to come a man. Verse 15 speaks of "the one to come [*ho erchomenos*] after me"; here we have *erchetai*—see NOTE on vs. 27. Dodd, *Tradition,* pp. 273–74, suggests that this need not be a note of time but may refer to following as a disciple; so also Boismard, "Les traditions," pp. 28–29. However, the Synoptic parallels we saw in the COMMENT on vs. 27 refer to time, and that is probably what is meant in John.

he existed before me. Literally "he was [*einai*] before me"; when the existence of Jesus is involved, John prefers the verb "to be," rather than the verb "to become" (*ginesthai*—same contrast in viii 58). Seemingly the word for "before," the adjective *prōtos* ("first") used as a comparative, has temporal significance. It is possible to render this clause as "he was my superior [*prōtos* as a substantive]"; but such a translation ruins the contrast:

$$\begin{array}{lll} \text{is to come } [erchesthai] & \text{after} \quad [opis\bar{o}] & =\text{time} \\ \text{has come to be } [ginesthai] & \text{ahead of } [emprosthen] & =\text{rank} \\ \text{was } [einai] & \text{before} \quad [pr\bar{o}tos] & =\text{time} \end{array}$$

The real reason that commentators avoid the temporal reference in the third clause is that it places the theme of the pre-existence of Jesus on the lips of John the Baptist (see COMMENT). Dodd's attempt to circumvent this is elaborate (*Tradition,* p. 274): "There is a man in my following who has taken precedence of me, because he is and always has been essentially my superior." Others attribute only the first two lines to John the Baptist, and the last to the evangelist. This would leave John the Baptist with a contrast between following in time and preceding in rank; the last line which concerns precedence in time seems essential.

31. *and baptized.* Literally "baptizing"; see ZGB, § 283–84, for the possible future sense: "I came to baptize."

with water. On slim patristic evidence, Boismard, "Les traditions," p. 10, omits this as a gloss.

revealed. Phaneroun is frequent in John (9 times as contrasted with once in the Synoptics, Mark iv 22), particularly for Jesus' coming out of obscurity and being seen by men.

Israel. In general, this term in Johannine usage has a good connotation (as opposed to "the Jews"), and refers to God's people.

32. *have seen.* The perfect tense indicates that the action, which took place presumably at Jesus' baptism, is still having its effect, namely, the Spirit is still with Jesus. For the verb *theasthai* see App. I:3; in the parallel reference in vs. 33 to seeing the Spirit, *horan* (*eidein*) is used.

like a dove. This phrase is omitted in OSˢⁱⁿ; and there is minor hesitation on its sequence in the Greek mss. For some this is evidence that it has been interpolated from the Synoptics. Perhaps, however, the confusion was caused by the absence of the phrase in vs. 33; the hesitancy about the sequence may reflect the influence of different Synoptic sequences on ms. copyists. Why a dove should be the symbol of the Spirit is not totally clear. Perhaps the hovering of the spirit over the primeval waters in Gen i 2 may have suggested the hovering of a bird (as in Deut xxxii 11); this observation appears in Jewish tradition (Bernard, I, p. 49). A. Feuillet, RSR 46 (1958), 524–44, gives a full treatment of the question and suggests that the symbol of the dove is an allusion to the people of the New Israel as the fruit of the Spirit.

it came to rest upon him. This phrase is also found in the description of the baptism in the *Gospel according to the Hebrews* (Jerome *In Isaia* xi 2; PL 24:145). Is *GHeb* drawing from Johannine tradition? We know of relatively few parallels between the two works, and it is more likely that both John and *GHeb* are drawing on non-Synoptic tradition.

33. *the one who sent me.* See NOTE on i 6.

with water. Boismard treats as a gloss; see NOTE on vs. 31.

told me. John the Baptist is one to whom the word of God has come (Luke iii 2).

who is to baptize with a holy Spirit. Boismard treats this too as a gloss. However, the suggestion that it was interpolated from the Synoptics has to meet the objection that the Johannine form is not the same as any one of the Synoptic forms of the clause. In particular, Matthew and Luke mention baptism "with a holy Spirit *and fire.*" These are really alternatives, for baptism with a holy Spirit is a beneficial cleansing, while baptism with fire is a destructive purgation (Isa iv 4)—P. van Imschoot, "Baptême d'eau et baptême d'esprit saint," ETL 13 (1936), 653–66. The "and fire" may have been part of the original logion, for the Christian omission of the phrase is easier to account for than the addition.

34. *have seen . . . have testified.* Perfect tenses; the action continues.

God's chosen one. This reading is found in the original hand of Codex Sinaiticus, OL, OS, and some Fathers, and may have support in Oxyrhynchus Papyrus 208 (3rd century). The vast majority of the Greek witnesses read "the Son of God," as do commentators like Bernard, Braun, Bultmann, etc. On the basis of theological tendency, however, it is difficult to imagine that Christian scribes would change "the Son of God" to "God's chosen one," while a change in the opposite direction would be quite plausible. Harmonization with the Synoptic accounts of the baptism ("You are [This is] my beloved *Son*") would also explain the introduction of "the Son of God" into John; the same phenomenon occurs in vi 69. Despite the weaker textual evidence, therefore, it seems best—with Lagrange, Barrett, Boismard, and others—to accept "God's chosen one" as original. For an interesting parallel to the two readings contrast Luke xxiii 35 with Matt xxvii 40. In an Aramaic text from Qumran, a figure who seems to have a special role in God's providential plan (the Messiah?) is called "God's chosen one" (*bḥyr 'lh'*). See J. Starcky, "Un texte messianique araméen de la grotte 4 de Qumran," *Mémorial du cinquantenaire de l'Ecole des langues orientales de l'Institut Catholique de Paris* (Paris: Bloud et Gay, 1964), pp. 51–66. Starcky is probably too confident of the identification as Messiah, as pointed out by J. Fitzmyer, CBQ 27 (1965), 348–72.

COMMENT

John the Baptist, who has been so taciturn about his own role, now becomes voluble in giving testimony to Jesus—an indication that John puts all the stress on John the Baptist as a witness to Jesus. In a series of profound testimonials John the Baptist identifies Jesus as the Lamb of God (vs. 29), as the pre-existent one (30), and as the vehicle of the Spirit (32–34). Thus, John unfolds for us here on the lips of John the Baptist a whole christology. Those familiar with the portrait of John the Baptist found in the Synoptic tradition will have difficulty in imagining that John the Baptist knew of the pre-existence of Jesus or of his suffering and death. For some critics this is no problem since for them John the Baptist has simply become the spokesman of the evangelist's theology, and the words attributed to John the Baptist are theological invention rather than historical reminiscence. Perhaps, however, the solution is not so simple. We shall see below that the statements attributed to John the Baptist may have had for him a sense quite harmonious with his OT eschatological outlook. In this case the evangelist's work was not to create the testimonies of i 29–34, but to take traditional material about John the Baptist and to make it the vehicle of a deeper Christian insight into the mystery of Jesus. We have expounded this view at length in an article cited in the Bibliography.

As with the previous section, this section may be divided into two parts: 29–31: Jesus as *the Lamb of God* and *the pre-existent one;* and 32–34: Jesus as *"vehicle" of the Spirit* and *God's chosen one.* Each part mentions that John the Baptist was baptizing with water, that he saw Jesus, that he testified to him, and that he did not previously recognize him.

Jesus as the Lamb of God (i 29)

In this verse we encounter for the first time a formula of revelation that John uses on several occasions. M. de Goedt, NTS 8 (1961–62), 142–50, has analyzed the formula thus: a messenger of God *sees* a person and *says,* "*Look!*" This is followed by a description wherein the seer reveals the mystery of the person's mission. Other instances of the pattern are found in i 35–37, 47–51, xix 24–27. This formula has its roots in the OT, for instance in I Sam ix 17: "When Samuel *saw* Saul, the Lord *said* to him, 'Look! Here is the man . . . who shall rule over my people.'" However, its use in the NT is peculiarly Johannine, so that we know that whatever traditional material may be found in i 29 has been recast in a Johannine mold.

Let us now turn to the symbol of "the Lamb [*amnos*] of God," a symbol about whose meaning there is a great deal of discussion. A convenient summary of the literature between 1950–60 can be found in Virgulin, *art. cit.* Without pretending to be exhaustive, we shall discuss three principal suggestions.

(1) The Lamb as the apocalyptic lamb. Dodd, *Interpretation,* pp. 230–38, accepts this as the meaning intended by the evangelist. However, along with Barrett, *art. cit.*, we believe that this interpretation of the Lamb can be better understood as the meaning intended by John the Baptist.

In the context of final judgment there appears in Jewish apocalyptic the figure of a conquering lamb who will destroy evil in the world. The Testament of Joseph xix 8 speaks of a lamb (*amnos*) who overcomes the evil beasts and crushes them underfoot. There are Christian interpolations in this passage from the Testaments of the Twelve Patriarchs, but Charles, APCh, II, p. 353, maintains that the principal figure is not an interpolation. (The value of this passage will depend to some extent on one's theory of the composition of the Testament of the Twelve Patriarchs, i.e., whether it is basically a Jewish or Christian work.) In En xc 38, which is part of the great animal allegory of history, there comes at the end a horned bull who turns into a lamb with black horns. (Unfortunately, the Ethiopic reads "word" instead of "lamb," so that our reading represents a conjecture, but probably a correct one.) In the context of the last judgment we are told that the Lord of the sheep rejoiced over the lamb. In the NT the figure of the conquering lamb appears in Revelation: in vii 17 the Lamb is the leader of peoples; in xvii 14 the Lamb crushes the evil powers of the earth.

The picture of the apocalyptic, destroying lamb fits in very well with what we know of John the Baptist's eschatological preaching. John the Baptist warned of the coming wrath (Luke iii 7), that the ax was already laid to the root of the tree, and that God was ready to cut down and throw into the fire every tree not bearing good fruit (Luke iii 9). Both Matt iii 12 and Luke iii 17 reflect the graphic ferocity of John the Baptist's expectation of judgment by the one to come: "His winnowing fork is in his hand to clean out his threshing floor. He will gather the wheat into his barn, but the chaff he will burn up with unquenchable fire." It is not at all implausible that John the Baptist could have described such a one to come as the apocalyptic lamb of God.

There are two objections to this interpretation of "the Lamb of God." First, there is a vocabulary difference in these references to "lamb": in John i 29 the word is *amnos,* while in Revelation the apocalyptic lamb is *arnion.* However, while John and Revelation are works of the Johannine school, they frequently reflect differences of vocabulary—a sign that they were written by different hands. Moreover, the vocabulary of apocalyptic writing tends to be formalized, and Revelation may simply be using a standard apocalyptic term for "lamb." Enoch, in what is preserved of it in Greek, seems to use *arēn,* of which *arnion* is a diminutive. Finally, the Testament of Joseph uses *amnos* for the conquering lamb. John's own choice of *amnos* may be determined by the interesting theological possibilities of the word, as seen below.

A second objection is based on the clause that describes the Lamb of God: he takes away the world's sin. Understood against the background of the salvific actions of Jesus, such a description scarcely seems to fit the Synoptic picture of John the Baptist's preaching where the one to come is to destroy the evildoer. However, perhaps on the lips of John the Baptist the phrase can be interpreted as a reference to the destruction of the world's sin. It is interesting to study the parallelism between *airein* ("take away") and *luein* ("destroy") in I John:

iii 5: "The reason he revealed himself was to *take away sins.*"

iii 8: "The Son of God revealed himself to *destroy the devil's works.*"

Thus we suggest that John the Baptist hailed Jesus as the lamb of Jewish apocalyptic expectation who was to be raised up by God to destroy evil in the world, a picture not too far from that of Rev xvii 14.

Dodd, *Interpretation,* p. 236, insists on the messianic aspect of this apocalyptic lamb. However, as we shall see below, it is not certain that John the Baptist expected a royal Davidic Messiah.

(2) The Lamb as the Suffering Servant. The Servant of Yahweh is the subject of four songs in Deutero-Isaiah: xlii 1–4 (or 7, or 9), xlix 1–6 (or 9, or 13), l 4–9 (or 11), lii 13–liii. There is a great deal of dispute whether this Servant is an individual (Jeremiah, Moses), or a collectivity (Israel), or a corporate personality. Of course, the NT authors would not have thought of these songs as an isolated body of literature as we do, but they may have seen that a common theme of the Servant of God is to be found in Isaiah. Indeed, it is quite probable that they connected the striking portrayal of the suffering of this Servant in Isa liii with other pictures of suffering innocents in the OT, for example, Ps xxii. Morna Hooker, *Jesus and the Servant* (London: SPCK, 1959), has criticized, too broadly perhaps, the abuse of the Servant theme by NT exegetes who seem to think that the evangelists anticipated Duhm's isolation of the Servant songs in 1892. Be this as it may, we are simply asking here whether the use of "Lamb of God" in John i 29 was colored by the use of lamb to refer to the Suffering Servant of Yahweh in Isa liii.

This really involves two questions: first, could John the Baptist have had such an understanding of the Lamb of God; second, could the evangelist? J. Jeremias, Cullmann, and Boismard answer in the affirmative to the first question; and the arguments for this view find a good exposition in De la Potterie, *art. cit.* We look in vain, however, in the Synoptics for any indication that John the Baptist thought that the one to come after him would suffer and die. Indeed, there is no clear evidence that before Christian times the Suffering Servant had been isolated and had entered the gallery of expected eschatological figures, or that the Messiah had been identified with the Suffering Servant. Despite the allegations of Dupont-Sommer and Allegro, there is simply no proof that the Qumran Essenes had a theology of a suffering Messiah; see J. Carmignac, *Christ and the Teacher of Righteousness* (Baltimore: Helicon, 1962), pp. 48–56. There are Qumran references to the Servant passages of Isaiah; but rather than applying these texts to a messianic or eschatological figure, the Essenes seem to have looked on their community as suffering righteously for others (so H. Ringgren, *The Faith of Qumran* [Philadelphia: Fortress, 1963], pp. 196–98). Thus, while we cannot deny that it is possible that John the Baptist thought of Jesus as the Suffering Servant, there is no real proof he did.

That the evangelist interpreted the Lamb of God against the background of the description of the Servant in Isaiah can be supported by several arguments. (a) Isa liii 7 describes the Servant thus: "He opened not his mouth, like a sheep that is led to the slaughter and like a lamb [amnos] before its shearers." This text is applied to Jesus in Acts viii 32, and so the comparison was known to Christians (also Matt viii 17=Isa liii 4; Heb ix 28=Isa liii 12). At the end of the 1st century, Clement of Rome (i 16) applied Isa liii in full to Jesus. (b) All the songs that refer to the Servant are found in the second part of Isaiah (xl–lv). The NT associates this part of Isaiah with John the Baptist, for "the voice crying out in the desert" is from the opening lines (Isa xl 3). (c) There are two items in John the Baptist's description of Jesus in i 32–34 that can be related to the Servant theme. In vs. 32 John the Baptist says he saw the Spirit descend upon Jesus and remain on him; in 34 John the Baptist identifies Jesus as God's chosen one. In Isa xlii 1 (a passage which the Synoptics also connect with John the Baptist's baptism of Jesus) we hear: "Look! Here is my servant whom I uphold; my chosen one in whom my soul is pleased [see Mark i 11]. I have put my spirit upon him." See also Isa lxi 1, "The spirit of the Lord God is upon me." This argument assumes that the evangelist made a connection between the Servant in Isa xlii and the Servant in Isa liii. (d) Jesus is described in terms of the Suffering Servant elsewhere in John (xii 38=Isa liii 1). These arguments are but a summary of the evidence (see Stanks, op. cit.).

There are two special points that should be considered. The Lamb of God is said to take away (airein) the world's sin. This is not the same imagery found in Isa liii 4, 12, where the Servant is said to take on or bear (pherein/anapherein) the sins of many. This difference, however, is not of major importance, for the early Christians would scarcely draw a sharp distinction as to whether in his death Jesus took away sin or took it on himself. LXX uses both airein and pherein to translate Heb. naśāʾ. Nevertheless, the reference to taking on sins in Isa liii 12 cannot be used to prove that the Lamb is the Suffering Servant, as is sometimes done. A second point is the suggestion that "lamb" in John is a mistranslation of the Aram. ṭalyâ which can mean both "servant" and "lamb"; and thus what John the Baptist actually said was, "Look! Here is the Servant of God" (so Ball, Burney, Jeremias, Cullmann, Boismard, De la Potterie). Dodd's refutation of this in Interpretation, pp. 235–36, seems to us conclusive. The Servant of Isaiah is known in Hebrew as the ʿebed YHWH (Aram. ʿabdâ); there is absolutely no evidence of ṭalyâ (Heb. ṭāleh) being used for the Servant. Nor, it may be added, is ṭāleh ever rendered by amnos in LXX. Yet, even without these two dubious points, there seem to be enough indications in the Gospel to connect the Lamb of God and the Suffering Servant.

(3) The Lamb as the paschal lamb. Many of the Western Fathers favored this interpretation (while the Eastern Fathers favored the Suffering Servant), and it has found an eloquent spokesman in Barrett. There are several supporting arguments. (a) The paschal lamb is a real lamb,

while in the Suffering Servant interpretation "lamb" is only an isolated and incidental element in the description of the Servant's death. (*b*) Passover symbolism is popular in the Fourth Gospel, especially in relation to the death of Jesus; and this is important because in Christian thought the Lamb takes away the sin of the world by his death. John xix 14 says that Jesus was condemned to death at noon on the day before Passover, and this was the very time when the priests began to slay the paschal lambs in the Temple. While Jesus was on the cross, a sponge full of wine was raised up to him on hyssop (xix 29); and it was hyssop that was smeared with the blood of the paschal lamb to be applied to the doorposts of the Israelites (Exod xii 22). John xix 36 sees a fulfillment of the Scripture in the fact that none of Jesus' bones was broken, and this seems to refer to Exod xii 46 which states that no bone of the paschal lamb should be broken. (See also John xix 31.) (*c*) Jesus is described as the Lamb in another Johannine work, Revelation; and the Passover motif appears there. The Lamb of Rev v 6 is a slain lamb. In Rev xv 3 the Song of Moses is the song of the Lamb. In Rev vii 17 and xxii 1 the Lamb is seen as the source of living water, and this may be another connection with Moses who brought forth water from the rock. Rev v 9 mentions the ransoming blood of the Lamb, a reference particularly appropriate in the paschal motif where the mark of the lamb's blood spared the houses of the Israelites.

One objection brought against interpreting the Lamb of God as the paschal lamb is that in Jewish thought the paschal lamb was not a sacrifice. This is true, although by Jesus' time the sacrificial aspect had begun to infiltrate the concept of the paschal lamb because the priests had arrogated to themselves the slaying of the lambs. In any case, the difference between the lamb's blood smeared on the doorpost as a sign of deliverance and the lamb's blood offered in sacrifice for deliverance is not very great. Once Christians began to compare Jesus to the paschal lamb, they did not hesitate to use sacrificial language: "Christ our Passover has been *sacrificed*" (I Cor v 7). In such a Christian deepening of the concept of the paschal lamb, the function of taking away the world's sin could easily be fitted.

A more important objection is that the Greek Pentateuch normally speaks of the paschal lamb as *probaton,* not as *amnos.* That the two words are not greatly different is seen, curiously enough, in Isa liii 7, the Suffering Servant passage, where *probaton* ("sheep") and *amnos* are in parallelism. But there also may be evidence that *amnos* was used by Christians for the paschal lamb. I Pet i 18–19 assures Christians that they have been emancipated with precious blood, as of an unblemished and spotless lamb (*amnos*), namely, the blood of Christ. Although we cannot give arguments here, we point to the possibility that I Peter should be interpreted against the background of a Christian *paschal* baptismal ceremony. The description of the *amnos* as unblemished recalls Exod xii 5 where a lamb without imperfection is specified for Passover. Thus, the vocabulary difference is not decisive.

With such good arguments for the views that the evangelist intended the Lamb of God to refer to the Suffering Servant and to the paschal lamb, we see no serious difficulty in maintaining that John intended both references. Both fit into John's christology and are well attested in 1st-century Christianity. Indeed, a similar twofold reference can probably be found in I Peter where, although the paschal theme is prominent, the Suffering Servant theme also appears (ii 22–25=Isa liii 5–12). The late 2nd-century paschal homily of Melito of Sardis weaves the two themes together; for while Melito says that Jesus came in place of the paschal lamb, he describes Jesus' death in terms of Isa liii 7: ". . . led forth as a lamb, sacrificed as a sheep, buried as a man." That besides these two themes John may also have brought over some echoes of John the Baptist's original reference to the apocalyptic lamb is not impossible, but there is no other reference to the apocalyptic lamb in the Gospel (only in Revelation).

We have given the more important suggestions for the meaning of "the Lamb of God." Other scholars call to mind Jer xi 19, "I was a gentle lamb [arnion] led away to be slaughtered." Since Jeremiah may have been the pattern on which Deutero-Isaiah fashioned the image of the Suffering Servant, this suggestion can be incorporated into the interpretation of the Lamb as the Servant. Another theory is that the Lamb of God is a reference to the lamb (amnos: Exod xxix 38–46) offered twice a day in the Temple, or to the lamb (probaton: Lev iv 32) offered as a sin offering. While the latter is attractive because it would explain the idea of the Lamb's taking away the world's sin, it must be noted that the bull and the goat were more common sin offerings. In any case there is no other evidence that such sacrifices formed the background for Johannine christology. Glasson, Moses, p. 96, reminds us that in the Jerusalem Targum on Exod i 15 Moses is compared to a lamb, and that in the Isaac story (Gen xxii 8) we hear the phrase, "God will provide the lamb [probaton]." Both the Jesus/Moses symbolism (passim) and the Jesus/Isaac symbolism (perhaps John iii 16=Gen xxii 2; John xix 17=Gen xxii 6) are known in the Fourth Gospel.

Jesus as the Pre-existent (i 30–31)

The theme of the pre-existence of Jesus is found in the Prologue, viii 58, and xvii 5; therefore, as indicated in the NOTE, we find unacceptable the attempts to avoid an implication of pre-existence here. The real problem, of course, concerns the likelihood of such a testimony to pre-existence on the lips of John the Baptist. It should be noted that vs. 30, with its variant in vs. 15, matches to some extent vs. 27 (just as 31 matches 26 in the theme of not recognizing Jesus):

FIRST CLAUSE

vs. 15: The one who comes after me
vs. 30: After me is to come a man
vs. 27: the one who is to come after me

SECOND CLAUSE

vss. 15, 30: ranks ahead of me
vs. 27:   I am not even worthy to unfasten the straps of his sandal

Now we saw in the COMMENT on vs. 27 that both the ideas and wording of that verse have parallels in the Synoptic tradition of John the Baptist's words. Therefore, there is nothing in the first two clauses of vs. 30 that does not fit the general Gospel picture of John the Baptist; our problem centers on the third clause, ". . . for he existed before me."

The stress on Jesus' pre-existence may be looked on as part of the polemic against the Baptist sectarians, as Cullmann, *art. cit.,* has pointed out. The sectarians claimed superiority for John the Baptist over Jesus because their master came first, and priority in time involved priority in dignity. Notice how Gen xlviii 20 stresses that Jacob put Ephraim before (*emprosthen*) Manasseh. One answer to the argument of the sectarians (an answer that helps to establish that there was such a sectarian argument) is found in the Pseudo-Clementines, where it is maintained that priority does not mean superiority but inferiority, for evil comes before good, Cain came before Abel, etc. (*Homilies* II 16, 23; PG 2:86, 91). John presents a different answer: priority *does* indicate superiority, but despite appearances Jesus was really prior to John the Baptist because Jesus pre-existed.

While giving this statement an apologetic turn, the evangelist may still have been drawing on a traditional saying of John the Baptist. J. A. T. Robinson, *art. cit.,* has made a very convincing case for the thesis that John the Baptist thought he was preparing the way for Elijah. We have mentioned in the NOTE on i 27 that "the one to come" may have been a title for Elijah based on Mal iii 1. John the Baptist anticipated that the one to come would purify with fire (Matt iii 12); Elijah's work is compared to a refining fire in Mal iii 2, iv 1; Sir xlviii 1. If John the Baptist did expect Elijah to come, then it becomes clear why the disciples expected Jesus to act like Elijah (Luke ix 52–56), and why Luke presents Jesus as Elijah (see above, p. 48). Perhaps Robinson's thesis may be used to explain how John i 30 could represent John the Baptist's words. If John the Baptist thought of the one to come as pre-existing him, it was not in any Christian sense of the pre-existence of God's Son, nor in the Johannine sense of the pre-existence of the Word, but in terms of pre-existence as Elijah. Elijah had existed nine hundred years before John the Baptist, and yet he was expected to return as a messenger before God's final judgment. Of him John the Baptist could say: "He ranks ahead of me because he existed before me."

In this light it is important to note that J. Jeremias, *The Servant of God* (SBT No. 20), p. 57, thinks that possibly Elijah was thought of as the Servant of God. Sir xlviii 10 speaks of Elijah's re-establishing the tribes of Israel, seemingly a reference to the Servant passage in Isa xlix 6. Both Mark ix 13 and Rev xi 3 ff. seem to picture Elijah as suffering. If this tenuous evidence should be verified, then we can combine the reference to Elijah as the pre-existent one with the reference to the Lamb of God=the Suffering Servant=Elijah.

In vs. 31 the theme of the unknown one or hidden Messiah reappears from vs. 26. The apocalyptic character of this expectation discussed there might fit in with the expectation of Elijah's coming. By the 2nd century it is Elijah who is to unveil the hidden Messiah; but in the period before the destruction of the Temple when eschatological expectations were more varied, Elijah himself may have been thought of as the hidden Messiah.

Verse 31 also has a role in the polemic against the Baptist sectarians. Christians did not find it easy to explain why Jesus allowed himself to be baptized with John the Baptist's baptism of repentance. In the *Gospel according to the Hebrews* (Jerome *Against Pelagius* III 2; PL 23:570–71) this difficulty is answered by having Jesus protest, "In what have I sinned that I should go and be baptized by him [John the Baptist]?" Another echo of this difficulty is heard in Matt iii 14–15 where John the Baptist protests to Jesus that their roles should be reversed. We suggest that the same problem is reflected in John i 31. For John there is no problem of Jesus' receiving a baptism of repentance, for the whole purpose of John the Baptist's baptism consisted in revealing to Israel the one to come. The re-mission of sins is not associated with John the Baptist and his preaching a baptism of repentance as in Mark i 4, but rather with the Lamb of God who takes away the world's sin. Thus John has removed from his account of the incident any aspects of the baptism that the sectarians might glory in.

The statement that until the baptism John the Baptist did not recognize Jesus as the one to come implies that John the Baptist was not too familiar with Jesus, although some would claim that he knew Jesus, but not as the pre-existent one (Bernard, I, p. 48). It is not clear if this can be reconciled with the relationship between the two posited in the Lucan infancy narra-tive. However, Luke i 80 does suggest that John the Baptist grew up as a solitary in the desert of Judea, apart from any family contacts.

Jesus as the one upon whom the Spirit descends and rests (i 32–33)

The fact that John refers to the baptism of Jesus only obliquely as the mo-ment when the Spirit descended upon him may also reflect the evangelist's desire to give the sectarians no succor. We may compare John's account of the descent of the Spirit with that of the Synoptics:

Mark i 10:	The Spirit	like a dove descending	on [*eis*] him
Matt iii 16:	God's Spirit	descending like a dove, coming	on [*epi*] him
Luke iii 22:	The Holy Spirit	descends in bodily form like a dove	on [*epi*] him
John i 32:	The Spirit	descending like a dove from the sky	on [*epi*] him

In using "the Spirit" without a modifier John is closest to Mark, but in describing the descent John is closest to Matthew. John differs from all the Synoptics in two elements: John does not describe the baptism itself, and in describing the descent of the Spirit John has the phrase "from the sky [*ex ouranou*]." The Synoptics mention *the voice from the sky* (Luke: *ex ouranou;* Mark-Matthew: *ek tōn ouranōn*), and in the Greek of the phrase

Luke is the same as John. The eclecticism of the similarities is again an argument against Johannine borrowing; nor, on the presumption of borrowing, is there any discernible motif in what John omits (the opening of the skies, the voice and its message).

If, therefore, the Johannine description of the descent of the Spirit seems to represent an independent tradition, slightly variant from the Synoptic tradition(s), it has in its present form become the vehicle of Johannine theology. John says that the Spirit came to rest (*menein*—a favorite Johannine word; see Appendix I:8) on Jesus; and since Jesus permanently possesses the Spirit, he will dispense this Spirit to others in Baptism. The theme of the dispensation of the Spirit after the death and resurrection of Jesus will recur throughout the Gospel (iii 5, 34, vii 38–39; the Paraclete passages in xiv–xvi, xx 22).

Another detail that harmonizes with Johannine theology is that God's testimony to Jesus is not spoken directly but through John the Baptist (vs. 33). In ch. v we are told that God's testimony to Jesus comes through several channels, of which the first mentioned is John the Baptist (v 33–35).

Nevertheless, the Synoptic accounts of the theophany at the baptism have also undergone considerable theologizing; and from the standpoint of comparative primitiveness, John's account does not fare badly. In Mark-Matthew it is Jesus who sees the Spirit descend, while Luke seems to presuppose a wider audience in stating that Spirit descended in *a bodily form.* John's claim that John the Baptist alone saw the Spirit is relatively modest. Mark and Luke have a heavenly voice addressed to Jesus, and this time it is Matthew that seems to presuppose a wider audience by casting the message of the voice in the third person ("This is my beloved Son"). Although John has no aversion to direct divine testimony from the sky (xii 28), the narrative here claims only that God had previously spoken to John the Baptist.

Even without the external testimony described in the Synoptic accounts, John clearly understands the impact of the Spirit's descent on Jesus much in the same manner as the other Gospels, namely, that it marks him out as God's unique instrument, and in particular as the Messiah and the Servant of the Lord. In Isa xi 2 we are told that the spirit of Yahweh shall rest (LXX *anapauein*, not *menein*) on the shoot from the stump of Jesse who is the Davidic king. In the Testaments of the Twelve Patriarchs the spirit comes both upon the Davidic Messiah (The Testament of Judah xxiv 1–3) and upon the priestly messiah (The Testament of Levi xviii 7—where it rested: *katapauein*). And we have mentioned that Isa xlii 1 says that Yahweh has put his spirit on the Servant.

Jesus as the chosen one (i 34)

If this reading is correct (see NOTE), then the theme of the Servant is continued in this title which echoes Isa xlii 1. Braun, JeanThéol, II, pp. 71–72, objects that God *chose* many figures in the OT and that the "chosen one" is not necessarily a reference to the Isaian Servant. But this fails to explain the fact that Isa xlii 1 is also a part of the Synoptic account of the baptism ("This is my beloved Son *in whom I am well pleased*"), and so is the most natural place to look for the reference to the "chosen one." Above, we mentioned other echoes of the Servant theme in this section.

Verse 34 ends this two-part scene of the testimony of John the Baptist in vss. 19–28 and 29–34. As often, John signifies this by an inclusion: vs. 19 began, "This is the testimony John gave . . . ," and vs. 34 ends when John the Baptist says, "I have testified. . . ." When we look back on the wealth and depth of the material contained in the intervening verses, we appreciate John's genius at incorporating a whole christology into one brief scene.

■ ■ ■

Literary Criticism

In our commentary we discussed i 19–34 as it is now found in the Gospel on the general principle that, no matter what its literary prehistory may have been, the section in its present form made sense at least to the final editor of the Gospel. In our Introduction, Part II, we discussed the theories of the composition of the Gospel, especially the theories of sources and of various editions. While it will not be possible to show how these theories are applied by the various commentators to the whole Gospel, we shall take this one scene and show how the theories are applied here. From this illustration we hope to demonstrate the ingenuity, the contributions, and the shortcomings of the literary reconstructions of the Fourth Gospel.

There are certain indications in i 19–34 that betray a reworking of the material. (*a*) There are passages with clear Synoptic parallels (vss. 23, 26 ["I am baptizing with water"], 27, 32, 33 ["baptize with a holy Spirit"]), and other passages that have no Synoptic parallels—an effect that *might* be explained by the combination of two traditions. (*b*) There is a certain lack of sequence in the narrative. Verse 19 begins with an announcement of the testimony of John the Baptist; but the testimony to Jesus does not begin immediately, and the whole scene is spread over two days. Verse 21 would be more logically followed by 25 than by 22. Verses 26 and 31 seem as if they should be in direct sequence. (*c*) There are a whole series of doublets: two sets of emissaries (19, 24); "They questioned him further" occurs twice (21, 25); "Look! Here is the Lamb of God" occurs twice (29, 36); "I myself never recognized him" occurs twice (32, 33); the descent of the Spirit is described twice (32, 33). And we may add that vs. 30 repeats 15.

Let us now see how these difficulties can be solved, first, by a theory of sources as illustrated in Bultmann's reconstruction, and then, by a theory of various editions as illustrated in Boismard's reconstruction.

According to his general hypothesis (see p. xxx above) Bultmann maintains that a basically simple narrative composed by the evangelist has been retouched by the Ecclesiastical Redactor who introduced parallels to the

Synoptic tradition and thus caused both the lack of sequence and doublets. Undoing the work of the Ecclesiastical Redactor, Bultmann, p. 58, gives his reconstruction of the original account of the evangelist. We present this below, adapted to the English of our translation; the reader will note how its smooth sequence avoids most of the difficulties mentioned above. (The sign /// indicates where Bultmann omits the additions of the Redactor; notice too the rearrangement of verses at the end.)

19 Now this is the testimony John gave when the Jews sent to him priests and Levites from Jerusalem to ask him who he was. 20 He declared without any qualification, avowing, "I am not the Messiah." 21 They questioned him further, "Well, who are you? Elijah?" "I am not," he answered. "Are you the Prophet?" "No!" he replied. /// 25 But they questioned him further, "If you are not the Messiah, nor Elijah, nor the Prophet, then what are you doing baptizing?" 26 John answered them, "/// There is one among you whom you do not recognize. /// 31 I myself never recognized him, though the very reason why I came and baptized was that he might be revealed to Israel. /// 33 But the one who sent me to baptize told me, 'When you see the Spirit descend and rest on someone, he is the one///.' 34 Now I myself have seen and have testified, 'This is God's Son.'" 28 It was in Bethany that this happened, across the Jordan where John used to baptize.

Then follows 29–30, 35 ff.

Van Iersel, a Catholic scholar, has accepted Bultmann's basic reconstruction and carried it even further. He makes more use of John's connectives than Bultmann does, for instance vss. 22a, 24. He avoids the doublet involving the Lamb of God (29, 36) that Bultmann keeps by omitting most of 29.

The theory of various editions takes another approach to i 19–34, as illustrated in Boismard, "Les traditions." Following Wellhausen, Boismard thinks in terms of rewritten parallel narratives. The steps in his reconstruction of the Johannine account may be listed as follows: (a) The Gospel proper originally began with the material now found in John iii 22–30, namely that Jesus came into Judea while John the Baptist was baptizing, and John the Baptist testified that Jesus must increase while he himself would decrease. (References to past encounters between John the Baptist and Jesus in iii 24, 26 are editorial.) Boismard substantiates this by pointing out the parallels between John iii 22–30 and Mark i 4–5. He thinks that originally the material on John the Baptist was followed by the Cana incident, so that the bridegroom/marriage motif ran through both passages. (b) Later on the evangelist himself replaced this narrative of the relations of John the Baptist and Jesus (iii 22–30) with another, entirely different narrative of these relations. (Here Boismard differs from Wellhausen who thought simply of a variant account of the same scene.) The theme of the new narrative was the baptism of Jesus by John the Baptist as the manifestation of the hitherto hidden Messiah. John the Baptist gives his testimony before the Pharisees who inexcusably refuse to believe. This narrative of the baptism, which thus reflects a certain polemic against the Jews, Boismard calls Version X. (c) Still later, the evangelist himself retouched Version X to make it clearer and closer to the Synoptic tradition. He made the OT allusions more specific and emphasized the theme of pre-existence. This time the polemic thrust of the passage was directed against semi-Christians who denied the divinity of Jesus, and perhaps also against the Baptist sectarians. This narrative is Version Y.

There remains a fourth step, but let us interrupt for a moment to see how Boismard sets up Versions X and Y along with the introduction that they share in common. (The translation of John has been adapted to our English translation.)

| VERSION X | VERSION Y |

6 Now there was sent by God a man named John 7 who came as a witness to testify to the light so that through him all men might believe. 8 But only to testify to the light, for he himself was not the light.

19 Now this is the testimony given when the Pharisees [Jews in Text Y] sent priests and Levites from Jerusalem to ask him who he was: 20 he declared without any qualification, avowing, "I am not the Messiah." 21 They questioned him further "Well, who are you? Elijah?" "I am not," he answered. "Are you the prophet?" "No!" he replied.

VERSION X	VERSION Y
25 They questioned him further, "If you are not the Messiah, nor Elijah, nor the prophet, then what are you doing baptizing?"	22 Then they said to him, "Just who are you—so that we can give some answer to those who sent us. What do you have to say for yourself?"
26a John answered them	23 He said, quoting the prophet Isaiah, "I am 'a voice in the desert crying out, Make the Lord's way straight!'
26c "There is one among you whom you do not recognize;	30b After me is to come a man who ranks ahead of me for he existed before me.
31 I myself never recognized him, though the very reason why I came and baptized was that he might be revealed to Israel."	33 And I myself never recognized him, but the One who sent me to baptize told me,
32 John gave this testimony also: "I have beheld the Spirit descend like a dove from the sky, and it came to rest on him."	'When you see the Spirit descend and rest on someone, he is the one.' /// 34 Now I myself have seen and have testified, 'This is God's chosen one.' "

28 It was in Bethany that this happened, across the Jordan where John used to baptize.

VERSION X	VERSION Y
35 The next day John was there with two disciples, 36 and watching Jesus walk by, he said, "Look! Here is the Lamb of God	29 The next day when he caught sight of Jesus coming toward him, he said, "Look! Here is the Lamb of God

who takes away the world's sin."

(d) A redactor, different from the evangelist (for Boismard the redactor is Luke), decided that all these onetime introductions should be incorporated into the final Gospel. He took (a) and put it after the Nicodemus story, thus giving a geographical pattern in chs. iii–iv of Jerusalem, Judea, Samaria, and Galilee (of the Gentiles—see the Lucan order in Acts i 8). The redactor took X and Y and combined them into one narrative which was left at the beginning of the Gospel.

Let us now compare the two theories represented by Bultmann and Boismard. Are they really different? Bultmann's is much simpler, and many will find implausible Boismard's theory that the evangelist composed three different openings for his Gospel. Actually Bultmann's reconstruction is not too different from Boismard's Version X, since each has been isolated by removal of material that has Synoptic parallels. A major difference is that for Bultmann the material with Synoptic parallels was added by the Ecclesiastical Redactor, while Boismard thinks of this material as belonging to Version Y, the work of the evangelist himself.

The crucial factor, then, seems to be the material with Synoptic parallels; and if Bultmann is right, we should be able to detect in this material an element which would either correct the original account or make it more orthodox, for such were the motives that guided the hand of the Ecclesiastical Redactor. Yet, if one wanted to correct the original as Bultmann posits it, the first thing one would do is to remedy its most glaring omission, namely, the account of the baptism of Jesus. The added material does not mention the baptism of Jesus, nor even the heavenly voice. Van Iersel, p. 266, is perfectly correct in affirming that in this instance, if there was a redaction, it was for the sake of supplementing rather than correcting.

Moreover, any suggestion that the additional material was taken from the Synoptics runs up against the discrepancies mentioned in our commentary. Recently, Dodd (*Tradition*), Buse, and Van Iersel have painstakingly studied this section and concluded that there are formidable difficulties against a theory of direct borrowing. In the Johannine material in i 19–34 that has parallels with the Synoptic tradition, there are thirty-eight *words* that John and Mark share, forty that John and Matthew share, and thirty-seven that John and Luke share—obviously there is no clear dependence on one Synoptic more than on the others. As for *phrasing*, there are two expressions that only John and Mark use, three that only John and Matthew use, one that only John and Luke use. Independent, parallel accounts of the same material seem to be indicated by such statistics.

Another observation must be made in estimating the capability of the one who gave the present form to i 19–34. The delicate balance between the two days of testimony betrays considerable literary artistry: they contain about the same amount of material; each has its theme; each is neatly subdivided into two parts; an inclusion holds the whole together. Despite the slight traces of unevenness in the final product, does not one have to admit that the result is considerably richer than Bultmann's hypothetical original?

Boismard's theory, complicated and unwieldy as it is, explains better the doublets and the fact that all the material of the section has a harmonious tone. (We abstract, as always, from his identification of the final redactor as Luke, an identification which, in our opinion, is pushed far beyond the evidence.) His first step is too theoretical and defies proof, but steps two and three make the evangelist himself responsible for all the material contained in i 19–34. That at some time in the history of the composition of the Gospel two Johannine accounts of John the Baptist's testimony to Jesus were put together into what we now have is perfectly plausible, although we cannot be certain that such joining was the work of the final redactor. Personally, we are more inclined to see the hand of the final redactor in the addition of the Prologue and the consequent dislocation of i 6–7(8?), and to attribute the joining of the accounts to one of the several stages of formation of the body of the Gospel (see above, pp. XXXV–XXXVI—Stages 3 and 4).

BIBLIOGRAPHY

Barrett, C. K., "The Lamb of God," NTS 1 (1954–55), 210–18.

Barrosse, T., "The Seven Days of the New Creation in St. John's Gospel," CBQ 21 (1959), 507–16.

Boismard, M.-E., *Du Baptême à Cana (Jean 1.19–2.11)* (Paris: Cerf, 1956).

———"Les traditions johanniques concernant le Baptiste," RB 70 (1963), 5–42. English summary in TD 13 (1965), 39–44.

Brown, R. E., "Three Quotations from John the Baptist in the Gospel of John," CBQ 22 (1960), 292–98. Also in NTE, Ch. VIII.

Buse, I., "St. John and 'The First Synoptic Pericope,'" NovT 3 (1959), 57–61.

Cullmann, O., *"Ho opisō mou erchomenos,"* *Coniectanea Neotestamentica* 11 (1947: Fridrichsen Festschrift), 26–32. Also in *The Early Church* (London: SCM, 1956), pp. 177–84.

de la Potterie, I., "Ecco l'Agnello di Dio," BibOr 1 (1959), 161–69.

Garofalo, S., "Preparare la strada al Signore," RivBib 6 (1958), 131–34.

Giblet, J., "Jean 1.29–34: Pour rendre témoignage à la lumière," BVC 16 (1956–57), 80–86.

Krieger, N., "Fiktive Orte der Johannestaufe," ZNW 45 (1954), 121–23.

Leal, J., "Exegesis catholica de Agno Dei in ultimis viginti et quinque annis," VD 28 (1950), 98–109.

Parker, P., "Bethany beyond Jordan," JBL 74 (1955), 257–61.

Richter, G., "Bist du Elias? (Joh 1, 21)," BZ 6 (1962), 79–92, 238–56; 7 (1963), 63–80.

Robinson, J. A. T., "Elijah, John, and Jesus: an Essay in Detection," NTS 4 (1957–58), 263–81. Also in TNTS, pp. 28–52.

Sahlin, H., "Zwei Abschnitte aus Joh i rekonstruiert," ZNW 51 (1960), especially pp. 67–69.

Schnackenburg, R., "Das vierte Evangelium und die Johannesjünger," *Historisches Jahrbuch* 77 (1958), 21–38.

Stanks, Thomas, *The Servant of God in John I 29, 36* (Louvain Dissertation, 1963).

van Iersel, B. M. F., "Tradition und Redaktion in Joh. i 19–36," NovT 5 (1962), 245–67.
Virgulin, S., "Recent Discussion of the Title, 'Lamb of God,'" *Scripture* 13 (1961), 74–80.

4. THE BAPTIST'S DISCIPLES COME TO JESUS:
—THE FIRST TWO DISCIPLES AND SIMON PETER
(i 35–42)

I 35 The next day John was there again with two disciples; 36 and watching Jesus walk by, he exclaimed, "Look! Here is the Lamb of God." 37 The two disciples heard what he said and followed Jesus. 38 When Jesus turned around and noticed them following him, he asked them, "What are you looking for?" They said to him, "Rabbi, where are you staying?" ("Rabbi," translated, means "Teacher.") 39 "Come and see," he answered. So they went to see where he was staying and stayed on with him that day (it was about four in the afternoon).

40 One of the two who had followed him, after hearing John, was Andrew, Simon Peter's brother. 41 The first thing he did was to find his brother Simon and tell him, "We have found the Messiah!" ("Messiah," translated, is "Anointed.") 42 He brought him to Jesus who looked at him and said, "You are Simon, son of John; your name shall be Cephas" (which is rendered as "Peter").

36: *exclaimed;* 38: *asked;* 39: *answered;* 41: *did was to find and tell.* In the historical present tense.

NOTES

i 35. *was there.* Literally "was standing"; Bernard, I, p. 53, takes it in the sense that John the Baptist was standing, awaiting Jesus. More likely the verb simply implies that he was present; see BAG, p. 383 (II 2ᵇ).

two disciples. One was Andrew (vs. 40); the other is not named. Is he to be identified with the "other disciple"="the disciple whom Jesus loved" (traditionally identified as John, son of Zebedee; see above, p. xcⅢ)? The scribe who was responsible for ch. xxi may have thought so, for he describes the Beloved Disciple in a situation closely resembling what we have here (xxi 20). All the lists of the Twelve name Simon, Andrew, James, and John as the first four; the Synoptics mention these same four (Luke omits Andrew) as the first disciples called while fishing on the Sea of Galilee (Mark i 16–20 and par.). *A priori,* then, there might be a certain likelihood that the unnamed disciple would be one of the four, especially since the Fourth Gospel names Andrew and Peter as two of the first three called. Thus, there is some basis for identification of the unnamed disciple of this passage as John.

Boismard, *Du Baptême,* pp. 72–73, argues that Philip is the unnamed disciple, stressing that Philip and Andrew go together in this Gospel (vi 5–9, xii 21–22) and come from the same village (i 44). It may also be pointed out that Andrew and Philip are joined in the list of the Twelve in Mark iii 18 (the two names are adjacent in Acts i 13, but not joined by a conjunction as a pair). However, the lists in Matthew and Luke separate their names. The real difficulty for Boismard is that i 43 seems to introduce Philip for the first time and makes it difficult to believe that he has already been mentioned. Some have suggested that this scene in John is an adaptation of the Synoptic scene where John the Baptist sends his disciples to question Jesus (Matt xi 2; Luke vii 19). There are very few similarities between the two scenes.

disciples. All the Gospels agree that John the Baptist had disciples. Seemingly they were a group set apart by his baptism, with their own rules of fasting (Mark ii 18 and par.; Luke vii 29–33) and even their own prayers (Luke v 33, xi 1). John iii 25 and iv 1 suggest a certain rivalry between John the Baptist's disciples and those of Jesus. Mark vi 29 and perhaps Acts xix 3 mention these disciples after John the Baptist's death.

36. *watching.* The verb *emblepein* (twice in John; here and vs. 42) means to fix one's gaze on someone, and thus to look with penetration and insight. Such a meaning is more appropriate for vs. 42 than here.

37. *The two disciples.* The Greek mss. read "his two disciples"; but the position of "his" varies so much that it is probably to be considered a later scribal clarification.

38. *noticed.* For *theasthai* see App. I:3. Here the verb has no special meaning; the closely parallel description in xxi 20 uses the simple *blepein*.

looking for. In his efforts to establish the Aramaic substratum of John, Boismard, *Du Baptême,* p. 73, makes the point that the Aramaic verb *be'â* means both "to seek or search for" and "to want," and that both meanings are involved here. He sees a surface meaning of "What do you want?" and a deeper meaning of "What are you searching for?" However, both of these shades of meaning can be found in the Gr. *zētein* without recourse to Aramaic. The variant reading, *"Whom* are you looking for?", reflects an understanding of the scene as giving a theology of discipleship. See also xx 15.

"Rabbi." Literally "my great one [=lord, master]"; John's translation as "teacher" is not literal but is true to usage. (It is implied in Matt xxiii 8.) The question has been raised as to whether the appearance of "rabbi" as a form of address in the Gospels is anachronistic. There is no Jewish evidence for the prefixing of "rabbi" to the name of any of the sages in the period before 70. The Epistle of Sherira Gaon (10th century A.D.) says that the first person to bear the title "rabban" was Gamaliel (*ca.* mid-1st century), a datum which agrees with the evidence that only with the school at Jamnia did "rabbi" come into any regular use as a title for "ordained" scholars. However, E. L. Sukenik, *Jüdische Gräber Jerusalems um Christi Geburt* (Jerusalem: 1931) discovered an ossuary on the Mount of Olives where *didaskalos,* the word used in John for "teacher," is used as a title (Pl. 3 in *Tarbiz* 1 [1930]; Frey, *Corpus Inscriptionum Judicarum,* 1266). Sukenik dates this ossuary several generations before the destruction of the Temple. If *didaskalos* represents rabbi (it also represented *mōreh* at this time), the ossuary may indicate that the NT usage of rabbi is not anachronistic after all. See H. Shanks, JQR 53 (1963), 337–45 (with a caution that his hypothesis that Gamaliel the Elder lived beyond seventy is unusual).

Payne
vic-CRRS?   BV 800 P38 1970

Proverbs
    PN 6414 S24 1145
    PN 6416 A5 Roban

Cic pro Milone 30.53   res ipsa

                                        like from like

Tilley L 282
        PN 6420 T5 Large

                                Eric Morse?

Petr. Sat. 45
Ezek 16.44

Only John makes frequent use of the term "rabbi." Luke does not use it; in Matthew Judas alone addresses Jesus thus. In John the frequency of the terms "rabbi" and "teacher," used by the disciples in addressing Jesus, seems to follow a deliberate plan: these terms appear almost exclusively in the Book of Signs, while in the Book of Glory the disciples address Jesus as *"kyrios* [lord]." In these forms of address John may be attempting to capture the growth of understanding on the disciples' part.

staying. For the verb *menein,* which occurs three times in vss. 38–39, see App. I:8. On the level of normal conversation *menein* can mean "to lodge" (Mark vi 10; Luke xix 5), but here the term has theological overtones—see COMMENT. The topic of where Jesus lives is raised in Matt viii 18–22 (Luke ix 57–60): a scribe says, *"Teacher,* I will *follow* you wherever you go"; but Jesus says that the Son of Man has nowhere to lay his head. This is followed by another incident where Jesus says to a disciple, "Follow me." Note the parallels in these Synoptic scenes to John's account.

39. *four in the afternoon.* Literally "the tenth hour"; presumably John is reckoning the hours from daylight at 6 A.M. N. Walker, "The Reckoning of Hours in the Fourth Gospel," NovT 4 (1960), 69–73, has revived the suggestion of Belser and Westcott that, unlike the Synoptic Gospels, John reckons hours from midnight, as was the custom of the Roman priests, the Egyptians, etc. He claims that 10 A.M. would make better sense in the present context. Nevertheless, it is quite clear in the Johannine account of Jesus' death that the next day, the Passover, would begin in early evening, and not at midnight; this detail favors a reckoning of the night hours from 6 P.M., and the daylight hours from 6 A.M. Is the time indication of any significance? Sometimes Johannine notes on time do seem to have special import, e.g., "noon" in xix 14; other times they do not, e.g., "noon" in iv 6. The fact that ten is a significant number in the OT and a perfect number for the Pythagoreans and Philo makes Bultmann, p. 70, suggest that John mentions the tenth hour as the hour of fulfillment. A more impressive suggestion is that the day was a Friday, hence Sabbath eve; thus, the disciples had to stay on with Jesus from 4 P.M. on Friday until Saturday evening when Sabbath was over, for they could not move any distance once Sabbath had begun on Friday evening. See NOTE on ii 1.

40. *Simon Peter's brother.* Peter is presumed to be better known to the reader. John shows a marked preference for the combined name, Simon Peter. Like the rest of the NT, except II Pet i 1 (and perhaps Acts xv 14), John uses "Simon" not "Symeon" for Peter. ("Simon" was a genuine Greek name; "Symeon" would be a better transliteration for the Hebrew name *Šim'ōn.*) Matt x 2 and Luke vi 14 agree that Andrew and Peter were brothers.

41. *The first thing he did was.* There are several possible readings and translations: **(a)** *prōton.* The adverbial use of the neuter of the adjective (=Andrew *first* found his brother before he did anything else) is the best attested reading, supported by P[66,75]; it is adopted here. Abbott, JG, § 1901[b], interprets *prōton* as accusative modifying Simon and indicating that Peter has first place; so also Cullmann, *Peter* (2 ed., 1962), p. 30. **(b)** *prōtos.* The nominative masculine adjective modifying "Andrew" is found in Sinaiticus and the later Greek mss. This reading (Andrew was the first to find his brother Simon Peter) has been taken by many to imply that subsequently the other, unnamed disciple (John?) went to find his brother (James). Some see this implication also in the reading *prōton,* e.g., Abbott, JG, 1985. **(c)** *prōi.* This adverb, meaning "early the next morning," has OL, and OS[sin] support; it is adopted by Bernard and Boismard because it favors

the seven day hypothesis (p. 106 below). However, another day seems to be implied by i 39 even without this translation, although the reading *prōi* by stressing the morning hour runs contrary to the Sabbath hypothesis mentioned in relation to vs. 39. The adverb is an "easy reading" and may be a scribal attempt to clarify the obscure *prōton*. (d) The word is omitted altogether by Tatian, OS^{cur}, and some Fathers.

his brother. The Greek has *idios* which might be translated "his *own* brother" in favor of the theory of two set of brothers mentioned under (*b*) above. BDF, § 286[1], however, insists that it is not emphatic.

Messiah. The Greek transliteration of the Aram. *mešīḥâ* (=Heb. *māšīaḥ*) occurs in the NT only here and in iv 25.

"Anointed." Literally *Christos;* on the analogy of i 38 this should not be transliterated as English "Christ," but translated as to meaning.

42. *looked at.* See NOTE on "watching" in vs. 36.

son of John. The later textual witnesses read "son of Jonah," by assimilation to Bar Jonah in Matt xvi 17. It is not clear whether "Jonah" and "John" represent two Greek forms of the same Hebrew name, or are two different names for Simon's father. In I Chron xxvi 3, LXX renders the Hebrew for "John" with the Greek equivalent of "Jonah," but this may represent confusion.

Cephas. Only John among the Gospels gives the Greek transliteration of Peter's Aramaic name *Kēphâ*, or, perhaps, in Galilean Aramaic *Qēphâ*, since Greek kappa usually renders Semitic qoph (BDF, § 39[2]); an interchange of qoph and kaph is attested for Galilean Aramaic. Matt xvi 18 supposes the Aramaic substratum but does not express it (the play on "Peter" and "rock" is not good in Greek where the former is *Petros* and the latter is *petra;* it is perfect in Aramaic where both are *kēphâ*). Neither *Petros* in Greek nor *Kēphâ* in Aramaic is a normal proper name; rather it is a nickname (like American "Rocky") which would have to be explained by something in Simon's character or career.

COMMENT: GENERAL

Chapter i 35–50 is joined to the testimony of John the Baptist in i 19–34 by the simple expedient of repeating John the Baptist's testimony to Jesus as the Lamb. The reiterated testimony in i 36, however, no longer has revelatory value in itself; its purpose is to initiate a chain reaction which will bring John the Baptist's disciples to Jesus and make them Jesus' own disciples. As i 7 promised, through John the Baptist men have begun to believe.

The same plan of division that we found in vss. 19–34 is found here. The material is spread across a span of two days, mentioned specifically in 35 and 43 (another day may well be implied in 39, but the evangelist does not capitalize on it). Within each day there is a pattern of subdivision, as may be seen clearly in the Outline (p. 41).

In vss. 35–50 John mentions five disciples: Andrew, an unnamed disciple, Peter, Philip, and Nathanael; elsewhere this Gospel mentions Judas Iscariot, another Judas, and Thomas (the "sons of Zebedee" in xxi 2 may be a gloss). Although John mentions "the Twelve" (vi 67, xx 24), there is no Johannine list of the Twelve.

The Johannine account of the call of the first disciples is quite different from the Synoptic account, even though at least two of the same characters (Peter, Andrew) are involved. According to John the call seems to have taken place at Bethany in the Transjordan, and the first disciples were former disciples of John the Baptist. According to the Synoptics the call took place on the shore of the Sea of Galilee where Peter, Andrew, James, and John were fishing. The standard harmonization is that Jesus first called the disciples as John narrates but that they subsequently returned to their normal life in Galilee until Jesus came there to recall them to service, as the Synoptics narrate. There may be some basic truth in this reconstruction, but it goes considerably beyond the evidence of the Gospels themselves. In John, once the disciples are called, they remain Jesus' disciples without the slightest suggestion of their returning to normal livelihood. Nor in the Synoptic account of the call in Galilee is there any indication that these men have seen Jesus before. In fact, Luke seems embarrassed as to why these men should follow Jesus on first contact, and he changes the Marcan order of the material in order to make the scene more reasonable. (In iv 38–v 11 Luke puts the healing of Peter's mother-in-law before the call of Peter to provide the motive of a miracle to explain why Peter follows Jesus.) Such a procedure would scarcely have been necessary if it were presupposed that Peter and Andrew already knew Jesus and had heard the testimony of John the Baptist.

Nevertheless, John's information is quite plausible, as the very awkwardness of the Synoptic account might indicate. There is an echo in Acts ii 21–22 that the first disciples actually had joined Jesus at the time of his baptism; for Peter insists that the one to take Judas' place must be one of the men "who have accompanied us during all the time that the Lord Jesus went in and out among us, *beginning from the baptism of John.*" Since this observation does not match Luke's own account in the Gospel, there is every reason to take it seriously.

However, even if historical information underlies John's account, it has been reorganized under theological orientation. In i 35–51 and ii 1–11 John presents a conspectus of Christian vocation. On each day there is a gradual deepening of insight and a profounder realization of who it is that the disciples are following. This reaches a climax in ii 11 where Jesus has revealed his glory and the disciples believe in him. Also, just as the evangelist used John the Baptist's testimony to present the reader with a rich christology, so in i 35–51 he draws from the disciples a testimony to Jesus that constitutes an even richer christology. In the Synoptics and Acts we find that before and after the resurrection the disciples applied to Jesus titles drawn from the OT through which they gave expression to their insight into his mission. Indeed some of the modern approaches to NT christology consists of a study of such titles. What John has done is to gather these titles together into the scene of the calling of the first disciples. In vss. 35–42 Jesus is referred to as rabbi (teacher) and Messiah; in 43–50, as the one described in the Mosaic Law and the prophets, as Son of God and King of Israel; finally in 51 Jesus refers to himself as Son of Man.

That the disciples did not attain such an insight in two or three days at the very beginning of the ministry is quite obvious from the evidence of the Synoptics. For instance, only halfway through Mark's account (viii 29) does Peter proclaim Jesus as Messiah, and this is presented as a climax. Such a scene would be absolutely unintelligible if, as narrated in John, Peter knew that Jesus was the Messiah before he ever met him. The Fourth Gospel itself subsequently insists on the gradual evolving of the disciples' faith (vi 66–71, xiv 9); and indeed, John is the most insistent of all the Gospels that full understanding of Jesus' role came only after the resurrection (ii 22, xii 16, xiii 7). Thus, we cannot treat John i 35–51 simply as a historical narrative. John may well be correct in preserving the memory, lost in the Synoptics, that the first disciples had been disciples of John the Baptist and were called in the Jordan valley just after Jesus' baptism. But John has placed on their lips at this moment a synopsis of the gradual increase of understanding that took place throughout the ministry of Jesus and after the resurrection. John has used the occasion of the call of the disciples to summarize discipleship in its whole development.

COMMENT: DETAILED

Two Disciples follow Jesus as Rabbi (i 35–39)

This time John the Baptist's proclamation of Jesus as the Lamb of God finds an audience as two disciples *follow* Jesus. The theme of "following" Jesus appears in vss. 37, 38, 40, 43. This means more than walking in the same direction, for "follow" is the term par excellence for the dedication of discipleship. We hear of following as a disciple in viii 12, x 4, 27, xii 26, xiii 36, xxi 19, 22; and in Mark i 18 and par. (the disciples by the Sea of Galilee). The imperative "Follow me" appears in the Synoptic accounts of the call of disciples (Mark ii 14: call of Levi; Matt viii 22: call of an unnamed disciple; Matt xix 21: call of the rich young man). Thus, from the very first words John hints that the disciples of John the Baptist are about to become disciples of Jesus. Because of this, John the Baptist can now disappear from the scene and allow his disciples to take up the task of bearing witness to Jesus. "He [Jesus] must increase while I must decrease" (iii 30).

Notice that in the beginning of the process of discipleship it is Jesus who takes the initiative by turning and speaking. As John xv 16 will enunciate, "It is not you who chose me. No, I chose you." Jesus' first words in the Fourth Gospel are a question that he addresses to every one who would follow him, "What are you looking for?" By this John implies more than a banal request about their reason for walking after him. This question touches on the basic need of man that causes him to turn to God, and the answer of the disciples must be interpreted on the same theological level.

Man wishes to stay (*menein:* "dwell, abide") with God; he is constantly seeking to escape temporality, change, and death, seeking to find something that is lasting. Jesus answers with the all-embracing challenge to faith: "Come and see." Throughout John the theme of "coming" to Jesus will be used to describe faith (iii 21, v 40, vi 35, 37, 45, vii 37, etc.). Similarly, "seeing" Jesus with perception is another Johannine description of faith. It is interesting that in v 40, vi 40, 47, eternal life is promised respectively to those who come to Jesus, to those who look on him and to those who believe in him—three different ways of describing the same action. If the training of the disciples begins when they *go* to Jesus to *see* where he is staying and *stay* on with him, it will be completed when they *see* his glory and *believe* in him (ii 11). This scene is the anticipation of what we shall hear in xii 26: "If anyone would serve me, let him follow me; and where I am, my servant will also be."

We should note that some of the language of this passage stems from the motif of Jesus as divine Wisdom (see Introduction, Part VIII:D), as Boismard points out in *Du Baptême,* pp. 78–80. From Wis vi, for instance, one may draw these parallels:

vi 12: Wisdom is easily *seen* by those who love her and *found* by those who *look for* her.

vi 13: "She anticipates those who desire her by first making herself known to them," just as Jesus takes the initiative.

vi 16: "She makes her rounds seeking those worthy of her and graciously appears to them as they are on their way"—see John i 43.

In Prov i 20–28 Wisdom cries aloud in the streets inviting people to come to her; those who refuse this call look for her and do not find her. He who finds Wisdom finds life (viii 35). So too in the subsequent verses of John the disciples will go forth triumphantly to announce to others what they have found (i 41, 45).

Andrew finds Simon and brings him to Jesus the Messiah (i 40–42)

Even though this may have taken place on another day (see NOTE on vs. 39), John does not mention another day lest the connection with the preceding scene be lost. The disciples must begin to act like apostles and bring others to Jesus.

By the time Andrew finds Peter, Andrew knows that Jesus is the Messiah. Dodd, *Tradition,* p. 290, relates this identification to John the Baptist's proclamation of Jesus as the Lamb of God (a title equivalent for Dodd to Messiah). However, after Andrew and his companion had heard this proclamation of the Lamb, they addressed Jesus merely as rabbi. It is their stay with Jesus that, according to Johannine theology, has given them a deeper insight into who he is.

While in the Fourth Gospel Andrew confesses Jesus as Messiah, that privilege in the Synoptic tradition falls to Simon (Mark viii 29 and par.). It is interesting that John connects the messianic confession with the call of Simon and, like Matt xvi 16–18, with the change of Simon's name to Peter. All the evangelists know that Simon bore the sobriquet of Peter, but only Matthew and John mention the occasion on which he received it (Mark iii 16 simply mentions the fact of the change without necessarily implying that it had already taken place when Jesus called the Twelve). In John the change of name takes place in the beginning of the ministry; in Matthew it takes place more than halfway through the ministry. As is known from the OT, the giving of a new name has a direct relation to the role the man so designated will play in salvation history (Gen xvii 5, xxxii 28). On this point Matthew's account is more polished than John's, for Matthew explains the relation of the new name ("rock") to Peter's role as the foundation stone of the Church. John stresses only that the name came from Jesus' insight into Simon ("Jesus looked at him"). John's use of the Aramaic form of the name is another factor in support of the antiquity of the Johannine form of the tradition.

Bultmann, p. 71[2], tries to harmonize John and Matthew by insisting on the future tense in John i 42: "Your name *shall* be called Cephas." He thinks that John's account is to be treated as a prophecy of a future scene like Matt xvi 18, which John did not narrate because it was too well known. However, Bultmann's interpretation of the future tense is certainly dubious, for the future tense is part of the literary style of name changing, even when the name is changed on the spot. The future is used in LXX of Gen xvii 5 and 15 even though the author consistently uses the new name from that moment on. Seemingly, then, John's account means that Simon's name was changed to Peter at his first encounter with Jesus. For more on the interrelation of the Petrine scenes in John and Matthew see COMMENT on vi 69.

Origen (*Catena Frag.* XXII; GCS 10:502) gives us the first instance of an important interpretation of John i 42. He sees here a hint that Simon will take Jesus' place since Jesus *who is the rock* calls Simon "rock," even as Jesus who is the shepherd (x 11, 14) makes Simon a shepherd (xxi 15–17). It is true that John hints at the imagery of Jesus as the rock struck by Moses in the desert (vii 38), but this Gospel never specifically calls Jesus the rock (as does I Cor x 4) nor speaks of Jesus as the cornerstone (Acts iv 11; Rom ix 33; Matt xxi 42). Consequently, Origen's interpretation seems to be more a case of theologizing from general NT evidence than an exegesis of John. See below, p. 91.

[The Bibliography for this section is included in the Bibliography at the end of § 5.]

5. THE BAPTIST'S DISCIPLES COME TO JESUS: —PHILIP AND NATHANAEL
(i 43–51)

I 43 The next day he wanted to set out for Galilee, so he found Philip. "Follow me," Jesus said to him. 44 Now Philip was from Bethsaida, the same town as Andrew and Peter. 45 Philip found Nathanael and told him, "We have found the very one described in the Mosaic Law and the prophets—Jesus, son of Joseph, from Nazareth." 46 But Nathanael retorted, "Nazareth! Can anything good come from there?" So Philip told him, "Come and see for yourself." 47 When Jesus saw Nathanael coming toward him, he exclaimed, "Look! Here is a genuine Israelite; there is no guile in him." 48 "How do you know me?" Nathanael asked. "Before Philip called you," Jesus answered, "I saw you under the fig tree." 49 Nathanael replied, "Rabbi, you are the Son of God; you are the King of Israel." 50 Jesus answered, "You believe, do you, just because I told you that I saw you under the fig tree? You will see far greater things than that."

51 And he told him, "Truly, I assure all of you, you will see the sky opened and the angels of God ascending and descending upon the Son of Man."

43: *found, said;* 45: *found, told;* 46: *told;* 47: *exclaimed;* 48: *asked;* 51: *told.* In the historical present tense.

NOTES

i 43. *he wanted . . . he found.* The identity of the subject is not clear. Peter was last mentioned and so grammatically would be the best choice for subject. However, while John might tell us that Peter found Philip, he would scarcely stop to tell us that Peter wanted to go to Galilee. In the present sequence Jesus is probably meant to be the subject, although in an earlier stage of the narrative Andrew may have been the subject (see COMMENT).

to set out. Seemingly Jesus is still in the region of Bethany at two days' distance from Galilee (ii 1).

found. Those who think that Philip was one of the two disciples mentioned in i 35 ff. interpret this to mean "found again." They point to the use of "find" in v 14 and ix 35 where Jesus searches out a man who had been with him a short time before. However, in those instances the peculiar connotation of "find again" is clarified by the context. Verse 43 seems to be no different from 41, where "find" is used to introduce a character.

Philip. He is the third disciple to be named in John, after Andrew and Simon Peter; the same order is found in Papias' list of the elders whom he consulted (above, pp. XC–XCI). Although Philip is named in all the lists of the Twelve, only John gives him any role in the Gospel narrative (vi 5–7, xii 21–22, xiv 8–9). Philip's memory was honored at Hierapolis, the see of Papias, and the presence there of Philip's daughters is mentioned (Eusebius *Hist.* III 31:3; GCS 9¹:264). The latter detail probably points to a confusion with Philip, one of the seven leaders of the Hellenists (Acts vi 5), who lived at Caesarea with four daughters (xxi 8–9).

44. *Now.* Or perhaps, "for," if the fact that Philip was from Galilee was the reason why Jesus called him before setting out for Galilee.

Bethsaida. John thinks of Bethsaida as in Galilee (explicitly in xii 21); actually it was in Gaulanitis, Philip's territory across the border from Herod's Galilee. John's localization may reflect popular usage: it appears also in Ptolemy's *Geography* (v 16:4); Josephus, *Ant.* XVIII.i.1;⚹4, speaks of Judas the revolutionary as from Gaulanitis, but in i.6;⚹23 calls him a Galilean. Or else John's information may reflect the political divisions of a later period (Bernard, II, p. 431, suggests that by A.D. 80 the extension of Galilee included Bethsaida).

the same town as Andrew and Peter. Philip's territory was heavily Gentile, a fact that may explain that Jews like Andrew and Philip bear Greek names (see also NOTE on Simon/Symeon, i 40). That the home of Andrew and Peter was at Bethsaida does not agree with Mark i 21, 29 which seems to locate their home at Capernaum. Following Origen, Boismard, *Du Baptême*, p. 90, suggests that Bethsaida has been introduced into John's account because it means "place of hunting [fishing]," and thus we have a symbolic reference to the theme of Matt iv 19: "Follow me and I will make you *fishers* of men." Abbott, JG, § 2289, harmonizes on the basis of a distinction between the prepositions *ek* and *apo;* he suggests that Philip (and also Peter and Andrew) was from Bethsaida in the sense that he had been born there, but his actual home was at Capernaum. The grammatical basis is weak; but if harmonization is necessary, this is a possible solution.

45. *Nathanael.* This disciple, known only to John, does not appear in any list of the Twelve. Since he is from Cana, Greek tradition identifies him with Simon the Cananean (Mark iii 18; Matt x 4)—a wrong etymology. In the 9th century Ish'odad of Merv identified him with Bartholomew because, just as Nathanael comes after Philip in John, so Bartholomew's name follows Philip's in all the lists of the Twelve except that of Acts i 13. The name Nathanael means "God has given," and this has led some to identify him with Matthew, whose name means "gift of Yahweh." All of these identifications are farfetched and imply that the disciple bore two Hebrew names. It is better to accept the early patristic suggestions that he was not one of the Twelve; see the carefully documented discussion by U. Holzmeister, Bib 21 (1940), 28–39. Although John means Nathanael to serve as a symbol of Israel coming to God, there is no evidence that Nathanael is a purely symbolic figure.

Jesus, son of Joseph. This is the normal way of distinguishing this particular Jesus from others of the same name at Nazareth (also vi 42; Luke iv 22). Another designation, "son of Mary" (Mark vi 3), is strange and may be an insinuation of illegitimacy—see E. Stauffer, *Jesus and His Story* (London: SCM, 1960), pp. 23–25.

46. *"Nazareth! Can anything good come from there?"* The saying may be a local proverb reflecting jealousy between Nathanael's town of Cana and nearby Nazareth. Boismard, *Du Baptême*, p. 93, points to the doubt expressed in vii 52 that the Messiah could come from Galilee; however, Philip has not specifically told Nathanael that Jesus was the Messiah. Another suggestion by Boismard that Nathanael is invoking the theory of the hidden Messiah (see above, p. 53) seems to go beyond the evidence. If Galilee, rather than Nazareth, is the real focus of the objection, then it may be noted that Galilean "prophets" had already caused trouble, e.g., Judas the Galilean of Acts v 37 (Josephus *Ant.* XX.v.2; ⌗102).

47. *a genuine Israelite.* Literally "truly an Israelite"; the adverb *alēthōs* in such position may serve as the equivalent of an adjective (*alēthinos*). See App. I:2. Bultmann, p. 73[6], says that it means "one worthy of the name of Israel."

there is no guile in him. It is not clear what there is about Nathanael to provoke this observation. Is it perhaps his readiness to believe when shown?

48. *How do you know me?* Literally "Where do you know me from?"; Jesus will answer as to *where* he has seen him. For Semitic and classic parallels for the crossing of interrogative words like "whence" and "how" see Barrett, p. 154.

under the fig tree. John underlines Jesus' ability to know things beyond the normal human range. The impression that Jesus' statement makes on Nathanael, however, has led commentators to speculate about what Nathanael was doing under the tree. Sometimes rabbis taught or studied under a fig tree (Midrash Rabbah on Eccles v 11) and even compared the Law to the fig tree (TalBab *Erubin* 54a); thus there arose a tradition that Nathanael was a scribe or rabbi. The mention of the Law in vs. 45 has been used to support this; and it is on the basis that Nathanael was learned that Augustine excludes him from the Twelve! Jeremias, *art. cit.*, thinks of the symbolism of the tree of knowledge in Paradise. He suggests that perhaps Nathanael was confessing his sins to God under the tree and that Jesus is assuring him that his sins have been forgiven by God (see Ps xxxii 5). C. F. D. Moule, *art. cit.*, recalls the Susanna story (deuterocanonical Dan xiii) where the witnesses are tested by questions concerning the tree under which the adultery took place. He cites Talmudic evidence for the formula, "Under which tree?", as an examination of evidence; and he thinks that it is possible that Jesus is showing that he has accurate knowledge about Nathanael. Because of the reference to Nathanael as an Israelite (Israel= Jacob) still others suggest that he was reading the stories of Jacob from Genesis. Others remind us that in Mic iv 4 and Zech iii 10 "sitting under the fig tree" is a symbol for messianic peace and plenty. We are far from exhausting the suggestions, all of which are pure speculation.

49. *Rabbi.* The disciples continue to call Jesus "Teacher," even though they give much more significant titles. This is an element of historical reminiscence within the theological theme of increased insight.

50. Compare this verse to xi 40: "Didn't I assure you that if you believed, you would see the glory of God?" The promise of *seeing* in i 50 is fulfilled in ii 11 with the manifestation of Jesus' *glory* at Cana where the disciples *believe*.

51. *Truly, I assure all of you.* We shall use this expression and variants like: "Let me firmly assure you"; "I solemnly assure you" to translate "Amen, amen."

The Synoptics use either "I say to you" or "Amen, I say to you"; the single "amen" occurs 31 times in Matthew, 13 times in Mark, 6 times in Luke. Only John uses the double "amen" (see Matt v 37 for "yes, yes"), and this occurs 25 times. The Jews used "amen" (doubled in Num v 22) in corroboration and response, particularly to prayer, somewhat the way congregations respond to evangelical preachers. Jesus' use of "amen" as a preface to a statement is peculiar and undoubtedly an authentic reminiscence. (See D. Daube, JTS 45 [1944], 27–31 for two Jewish examples which he thinks akin to Jesus' usage. J. Naveh, IEJ 10 [1960], 129–39, has published a Hebrew letter from the 7th century B.C. in which 'mn is used as an affirmation that a statement or oath is true.) Jesus has heard from the Father all that he says (viii 26, 28), and the "amen" with which he introduces what he says assures us that God guarantees the truth of his statements. He is the Word of God; he is the Amen (Rev iii 14; II Cor i 19). The Hebrew root involved ('mn) means "to confirm, make sure, support"; in the passive "to be supported" means "to be true." We have tried to capture these connotations in our translation.

you will see. The added "from now on," appearing in late manuscripts, is a scribal gloss from Matt xxvi 64: "From now on you will see the Son of Man seated at the right hand of the Power, and coming on the clouds of heaven."

Son of Man. This title has its roots in Ezekiel, Dan vii 13 (=human symbol of God's victorious people), and Enoch (=pre-existent saviour). All the Gospels agree that Jesus used this as a self-designation, and seemingly more often than any of the other titles associated with him. In the Synoptics there are three groups of Son of Man sayings: (1) those that refer to the earthly activity of the Son of Man (eating, dwelling, saving the lost); (2) those that refer to the suffering of the Son of Man; (3) those that refer to the future glory and parousia of the Son of Man in judgment. There are twelve Son of Man passages in John, all in the Book of Signs except xiii 31. Although Jesus speaks often of his return in the Last Discourse (xiii–xvii), he does not use "the Son of Man" in such references. Three of the Son of Man passages concern his being "lifted up" (iii 14, viii 28, xii 34), an expression that refers both to the crucifixion and to the return to the Father's presence in heaven—thus passages that touch on Synoptic groups 2 and 3. The majority of the Johannine Son of Man passages concern future glory; the final judgment is mentioned in v 27. Synoptic group 1 is not represented in the Johannine Son of Man passages. See R. Schnackenburg, "Der Menschensohn im Johannes-evangelium," NTS 11 (1964–65), 123–37.

COMMENT: GENERAL

The two divisions of the narrative that describes the coming of the first disciples to Jesus (i 35–42 and 43–50) have an even closer balance of parts than the two divisions of the narrative of John the Baptist's testimony (i 19–28 and 29–34). Notice the following parallels:

§ 4 (35–42)	§ 5 (43–50)
35–39	*43–44*
Jesus encounters two disciples	Jesus (?) finds Philip
They follow him	"Follow me"
"Come and see"	

40–42	45–50
One of the two, Andrew, finds Simon	Philip finds Nathanael
Andrew: "We have found the Messiah"	Philip: "We have found the one described . . ."
	"Come and see"
Jesus looks at Simon	Jesus sees Nathanael coming
Jesus greets Simon as Cephas	Jesus greets Nathanael as a genuine Israelite

The balance is not perfect. In § 4 the long dialogue is in the first part; in § 5 it is in the second part. The same may be said of "Come and see." The division between the two parts of § 4, as indicated by the time notation of vs. 39, is sharper since it may be inferred that the second part takes place on another day. There is no such break in §5, the translation of which we have printed as one paragraph. (Boismard, *Du Baptême*, p. 95, divides § 5 between vss. 46–47 and, without the slightest justification in the text, supposes that the last part of the scene took place on another day. His division neglects the obvious similarity between 45 and 40–41, a parallelism which indicates that the division should come before 45 just as it comes before 40.)

We saw (pp. 70–71) that the delicate division and balancing of parts in "The Testimony of John the Baptist" (i 19–28 and 29–34, § 2 and § 3) was the result of editing and combining accounts. The imperfections which betray the editing process may also be visible here, especially in the obscurity found in the opening of § 5 (vs. 43—Note). Bultmann, p. 68, makes a telling point when he says that the passage would make more sense if Andrew was the one to find Philip. Not only are Andrew and Philip close friends in the Gospel, but also this would explain the enigmatic vs. 41: Andrew *first* found his brother Simon; then he found Philip. But in the process of editing, the introduction of the theme of Jesus' going to Galilee has now made Jesus the subject who finds Philip, and thus a balance has been created with the opening of § 4 where Jesus takes the initiative. Such a change is, of course, of little real import.

COMMENT: DETAILED

Philip follows Jesus (i 43–44)

Accepting the present state of the narrative where Jesus is the one who finds Philip, we find a suggestion that Jesus' decision to leave the Jordan valley for Galilee is related to Philip's call. Perhaps, before he left the region, Jesus is thought of as wanting to finish the call of all of the disciples of John the Baptist who would follow him. Some suggest that Jesus particularly wanted Philip because, being from Bethsaida in Galilee, he could act as a guide for the journey. This would make sense if Jesus were going immediately from the Jordan valley to the Sea of Galilee (as

in the Synoptics: Mark i 14–16; Matt iv 12–13), the region familiar to
Philip. But in John Jesus will return to his own region, the highlands of
Nazareth and Cana. Perhaps the fact that Philip would call Nathanael who
was from Cana, the site of the next story, is the key to the evangelist's
reasoning.

We have been presuming that the call of Philip took place in the Jordan
valley. Others interpret vs. 43 to mean that Jesus had actually set out for
Galilee and met Philip on the way, perhaps near the Sea of Galilee. Then,
they would maintain, Philip found Nathanael in Galilee. The indication in
ii 1, however, is that the journey took place after the call of Philip and
Nathanael.

Nathanael comes to Jesus, the Son of God and King of Israel (i 45–50)

The call of Philip has not involved the granting of any new title to Jesus
and has, seemingly, not developed the theme of growing insight. However,
as Philip's words to Nathanael show, there have been both new titles and
insight. The identification of Jesus as "the very one described in the Mosaic
Law and the prophets" is probably a general statement that Jesus is the fulfillment of the whole OT. Luke xxiv 27 indicates that after the resurrection the disciples did come to such an understanding of Jesus, for Jesus
explained to the two disciples on the road to Emmaus how all things in
the Scriptures concerned himself, "beginning with Moses and all the
prophets." (Tradition has connected the Johannine and Lucan scenes by
identifying Nathanael as one of the two: Epiphanius *Adv. Haer.* xxiii 6;
PG 41:305.) In John v 39 we are told that the Scriptures testify on Jesus'
behalf; in v 46, that Moses wrote about him; in vi 45, that what is written
in the prophets is acted out in his ministry.

Is anything more specific intended in Philip's description? The "one described in the Mosaic Law" could well identify Jesus as the Prophet-like-
Moses of Deut xviii 15–18. The "one described by the prophets" is harder
to identify: it could be the Messiah, the Son of Man (Daniel), or even
Elijah (Malachi). The last possibility is tempting, for then Philip would be
identifying Jesus as the Prophet-like-Moses and Elijah—the two great
representatives of the Law and the prophets. Adding this to the identification of Jesus as the Messiah in vs. 41, we would then have the disciples of
John the Baptist recognizing Jesus under the same three titles that John
the Baptist had disclaimed—but perhaps this is too neat.

Nathanael reacts to Philip's news about Jesus with disparaging doubt,
a reaction that Jesus will encounter all too often among those who believe
in the Law and the prophets (e.g., vii 15, 27, 41). But when Philip persists,
Nathanael is willing to come and see; he is not, then, like "the Jews" of
ch. ix who claim to accept Moses (ix 29), but reject Jesus' challenge to see
and thus sink into blindness (ix 41). Because of Nathanael's willingness to
come to the light, Jesus hails him as one truly representative of Israel. Here
John may be close to the distinction that Paul makes in Rom ix 6: "Not

all who are descended from Israel [Jacob] belong to Israel"; the true
Israelite believes in Jesus.

The proclamation of Nathanael as a genuine Israelite without guile is another example of the revelatory formula isolated by De Goedt (see p. 58
above). What is the exact point of this designation of Nathanael? A comparison with Jacob seems to be implied; for, although Jacob was the first to bear
the name of Israel (Gen xxxii 28–30), his dealings with Laban and with
Esau marked him as a man of guile (Gen xxvii 35). Other scholars bring
into the picture the theme of the Suffering Servant "in whose mouth there
was no guile" (Isa liii 9). Boismard, *Du Baptême,* pp. 96–97, thinks of the
Servant theme especially as it is found in Isa xliv. In Isa xliv 3–5, God assures his servant Jacob that He will *pour forth His spirit* on Jacob's descendants who shall bear symbolic names, including the name *"Israel."* Verses
6–7 stress that only the Lord, *the King of Israel,* is God. Thus, in the messianic days the true bearer of the name of Israel will be one who is faithful
to Yahweh and serves no other gods. In this interpretation, "guile" would
have the meaning that it sometimes has in the OT of religious infidelity to
Yahweh (Zeph iii 13). The tenuous nature of these parallels to the Servant
theme should be obvious.

Boismard, *ibid.,* pp. 98–103, has popularized still another interpretation of
"a genuine Israelite": this one flows from the ancient popular (erroneous)
etymologies of the name "Israel" in terms of "seeing God." Nathanael
would be worthy of the name of "Israel" because he would see God, just as
Jacob saw God face to face at the time his name was changed to Israel
(Gen xxxii 27–30). This could be tied in with Jesus' promise to Nathanael
in vs. 50, "You will *see* far greater things," and perhaps help to explain the
vision promised in i 51. A final suggestion worth noting is that Nathanael
is the last of the disciples to be called, and in him is fulfilled the purpose for
which John the Baptist had come: "The very reason why I came and
baptized with water was that he [Jesus] might be revealed *to Israel*" (i 31).

In the NOTE on vs. 48 we have already mentioned how difficult it is to
explain why the fact that Jesus had seen Nathanael under the fig tree produces such an impression. Certainly it seems to go beyond amazement at
supernatural knowledge, but no explanation is totally satisfactory. Nathanael,
brought to deep insight by Jesus' knowledge of him, proclaims Jesus as Son
of God and King of Israel. The second of these titles is a reference to the
messianic king, but this confession is on a higher plane than that of the
Messiah in vs. 41. At the end of the public ministry, as Jesus enters
Jerusalem, he will be acclaimed as a king (xii 12–19), but he will show that
he is not a king in a nationalistic sense. His kingdom does not belong to
this world (xviii 36); and his subjects are not Jews but believers. It is
Nathanael, the genuine Israelite, who hails him; and therefore "the King of
Israel" must be understood as the king of those like Nathanael who believe. In this sense, this title is climactic in the series of titles that we have
seen.

The former of the two titles, "the Son of God," was probably a messianic title, although Mowinckel, *He that Cometh,* pp. 293–94, and others question this. In the coronation formulae of the OT the Davidic king, the messiah, was called "son" by Yahweh (II Sam vii 14; Ps lxxxix 27); in particular, Ps ii 6–7 would be excellent background for joining the titles "Son of God" and "King of Israel." It may well be, however, that John intends to give "Son of God" a more profound meaning. In the theological progression indicated by the titles of ch. i which capsulizes the disciples' gradual growth in insight throughout the whole ministry of Jesus, John may well have wished to include in "Son of God" a confession of the divinity of Jesus. The Gospel itself will conclude in xx 28 with a disciple's confession of Jesus as Lord and God; and we remember too that one explanation of the designation of Nathanael as an Israelite was that he would see God. Certainly, the readers of the Gospel in the late 1st century would have become accustomed to a more profound meaning for "Son of God." In any case, this chapter dealing with John the Baptist and his disciples comes to a climax on the same note on which the baptismal scene ends in the Synoptic tradition: the proclamation of Jesus as God's Son (Mark i 11 from Ps ii 7).

Though John has sketched the development of the disciples' understanding, this sketch is not complete when they believe because Jesus has spoken; they must also see his works, that is, the signs that manifest his glory. And so in vs. 50 Jesus tells Nathanael that he will yet see far greater things, thus preparing the stage for the Cana miracle, the first of Jesus' signs which will lead the disciples to see his glory and believe in him (ii 11). Once again John is capsulizing a longer process: the disciples will see Jesus' glory to the full only when they have seen the final "great thing," the supreme work of the death, resurrection and ascension, and it is only then that they will fully believe. (See v 20–21 and xiv 12, which tie in the resurrection-ascension with the theme of "greater things.")

A Detached Saying about the Son of Man (i 51)

At the very end of this part on the call of the disciples in the Jordan valley, there comes a verse that has caused as much trouble for commentators as any other single verse in the Fourth Gospel. Our first question must be whether i 51 has always been associated with the context in which it is now found. There are certain indications to the contrary. *First,* Jesus has been talking to Nathanael in i 50; if i 51 merely continues the conversation, why do we get a new rubric, "And he [Jesus] told him [Nathanael]"? A glance at xi 11 shows that John usually manages to indicate more smoothly a later continuation of conversation. *Second,* although the saying is addressed to Nathanael, the "you" in 51 is plural, as we have tried to indicate by translating it as "all of you." Was 51 once addressed to a group, or in its present context are we to think of it as addressed to all the disciples called in ch. i or, at least, to Philip and Nathanael? *Third,* we have indicated that the Cana story would be a good sequel to 50, illustrating the "greater things" that Nathanael would see. Verse 51 does not seem to make the sequence any better; to a certain extent it is repetitive in its promise of seeing. *Fourth,* there is nothing in what follows 51 to indicate that its promise was ever fulfilled, if the vision promised is to be taken literally. *Fifth,* as we pointed out in the NOTE, even the early scribes saw the similarity between the saying in 51 and what Jesus says in his trial before Caiaphas in Matt xxvi 64. If the Johannine saying has something to do with Jesus' exaltation, the setting of the similar saying in Matthew just before Jesus' death, resurrection, and ascension is more appropriate. Another interesting Synoptic saying is that of Matt xvi 27–28: *"The Son of Man* will come in the glory of his Father *with* his *angels . . . I assure you* that some of those standing here shall in no way taste death until *they see the Son of Man* coming in his kingdom." Matthew places this saying shortly after Simon's confession of Jesus as Messiah and the changing of Simon's name, even as John i 51 follows shortly after i 41–42. Thus, parallels in Matthew provide us with an objective basis for suspecting that a primitive saying concerning a future vision of the Son of Man, preserved in vs. 51 in its Johannine form, was once found in another sequence than that in which it now stands.

We may also suspect that the original meaning of the saying was a reference to the resurrection or to the parousia, where the presence of the angels about the glorified Son of Man would be appropriate. There are no angelophanies in the Johannine account of the public ministry; but angels are associated in all the Gospel accounts with the empty tomb and often with the final judgment. Windisch, in his second article, makes a special point of the account of the resurrection in the *Gospel of Peter,* 36–40, and also in the Codex Bobiensis of Mark xvi 4 where it is narrated that angels *descended* from heaven and *ascended* with Jesus. That the Johannine saying was a reference to this particular account is, however, very dubious, especially since vs. 51 mentions ascending before descending.

No matter how plausible a reconstruction can be made of what the saying originally meant, we are faced with the problem of what it means in its present sequence; for whether it was placed in its present sequence in the editing or the final redaction of the Gospel, it made sense to someone where it now stands. Even if the saying originally referred to the resurrection or parousia, there is no reason to think that it does so where it now stands, for the vision of vs. 51 is no more remote a promise than the vision mentioned in 50. To give meaning to 51 in its present sequence we must look for a figurative meaning which can be fulfilled in the immediate future of the ministry, even as 50 is fulfilled at Cana.

Since the time of Augustine (but not before—Bernard, I, pp. 70–71), exegetes have seen a connection between vs. 51 and Gen xxviii 12, where in a dream Jacob sees a ladder stretching from earth to heaven, ". . . and the angels of God were ascending and descending on it." Michaelis has called into question this connection between John and Genesis, but it seems con-

vincing on the basis of the clear mention of angels ascending and descending, especially if we recall the previous reference to Jacob-Israel in the
Nathanael scene. Yet, even if Genesis supplies the imagery for the Johannine saying about the Son of Man, what is the interpretation of the saying?
Are the disciples who will help to form the new Israel, and of whom
Nathanael is an example, promised a spiritual insight comparable to Jacob's
vision? When scholars try to be more precise, their different answers are
ingenious. We must sample a few of the more important.

It will be noted that in vs. 51 the angels are ascending and descending on
the Son of Man, while Genesis mentions ascending and descending "on it,"
presumably the ladder (so LXX). However, a few rabbis read "on him,"
that is, on Jacob (Midrash Rabbah LXIX 3 on Gen xxviii 13). Some scholars think that the latter reading lies behind John's form of the saying. This
would make the Son of Man (a collective figure in Dan vii) a replacement
for Jacob (=Israel, and to some extent a collective figure). The whole theory
is dubious. It is possible but not certain that the Son of Man in John is a collective figure; xii 32–34 distinguishes between the Son of Man and all those
who believe in him. Secondly, it is Nathanael in John who is the equivalent
of Israel, not Jesus, the Son of Man.

Another variant on the Jacob story is also brought into the discussion.
In the Midrash Rabbah LXVIII 12 on Gen xxviii 12, we find that Jacob's
true appearance is in heaven while his body lies on the earth, and the
angels are traveling back and forth between them. Applying this to John,
some suggest that Jesus is really with the Father as Son of Man, and yet he
is on earth at the same time; the angels constitute the communication
between the heavenly and earthly Jesus. A more plausible variation would
be that Jesus himself is the connection between heavenly reality and the
earth. With variations, a theory like this is proposed by Odeberg, Bultmann,
Lightfoot and others. It should be pointed out that the rabbinic source for
the theory is no earlier than the 3rd century A.D., although the interpretation
of Genesis may be earlier.

In still another variation, the Targums (Onkelos and Jerusalem) have
God's *shekinah* (see p. 33 above) on the ladder. Justin *Trypho* LXXXVI 2
(PG 6:680) reflects the early Christian belief that Christ was on the lad-
der. Thus in having the angels ascending and descending on the Son of
Man instead of on the ladder, John may be continuing the theme of the
Prologue that Jesus is the localization of the *shekinah*. (See COMMENT on
John xii 41.) Quispel, *art. cit.*, carries this suggestion further by associating vs. 51 with the *merkabah* mystique in Judaism, based on speculation
about the divine chariot seen by Ezekiel (i 4 ff.). Quispel thinks of angels
ascending to the Son of Man in heaven above and descending to Nathanael
below (even though John says descending *upon the Son of Man*). Another
variation concentrates on the place where Jacob had his vision, namely,
Bethel, the "house of God . . . gate of heaven." The idea is that, since the
angels ascend and descend upon the Son of Man, Jesus is taking the place of
Bethel as the house of God—an instance of the Prologue's theme of Jesus

as the Tabernacle and the Gospel's theme of Jesus as the Temple. This interpretation is defended in detail by Fritsch, *art. cit.* Jeremias stresses the rock at Bethel on which Jacob slept and which became a ceremonial pillar there (Gen xxviii 18). In Jewish literature, which Jeremias cites, a mystique grew up about this rock as the first stone created by God and the one which He spread out to form the world. The application to John would be that in vs. 51 Jesus has replaced the rock of Bethel, and this would be an instance of the theme of Jesus the rock who makes Simon the rock (i 41–42).

No one of these variations is particularly convincing. However, in the theme that they have in common they are probably correct; whether it is as the ladder, the *shekinah*, the *merkabah*, Bethel, or the rock, the vision means that Jesus as Son of Man has become the locus of divine glory, the point of contact between heaven and earth. The disciples are promised figuratively that they will come to see this; and indeed, at Cana they do see his glory.

We should call attention to a few specific details. Verse 51 promises, "You will see *the sky opened.*" Thus, although John omitted the reference to the opening of the sky in describing the descent of the Spirit upon Jesus at the baptism, the reference appears here, just as vs. 49 had the equivalent of the baptismal proclamation of Jesus as God's Son. John's expression in 51 is closest to Luke iii 21: both have the singular of *ouranos* ("sky"—Mark and Matt have the plural) and both use *anoigein* ("to open"—Mark uses another verb). If vs. 51 was once in another sequence, the possible relation of the opening of the sky to the baptismal theme may have been a factor, along with the Jacob reference, in attracting it to its present situation. Michaelis, *art. cit.*, would also connect the mention of the angels with the presence of angels in the scene of the temptations of Jesus (Matt iv 11), which in the Synoptic tradition follows immediately after the baptism.

We have spoken of the sequence of titles in ch. i. Verse 51 introduces "the Son of Man" (which is not found in the Genesis background of Jacob's dream). This is the only title in the chapter that Jesus uses of himself, a fact that may reflect a historical reminiscence that Jesus did use this title, as distinct from the titles given to him by the disciples after the resurrection, e.g., Son of God. If, in its present sequence, vs. 51 means that the disciples shall see the glory of the Son of Man during his ministry, it is the only example of this type of Son of Man passage in John (see NOTE). Nathanael has hailed Jesus as the King of Israel (seemingly equaling "Messiah"); Jesus answers him by promising a vision of himself as the Son of Man. In Matt xxvi 64—the passage we pointed out as a startling parallel to John i 51—when the high priest asks him if he is the Messiah, Jesus answers him by promising a vision of the Son of Man.

BIBLIOGRAPHY

See Barrosse and Boismard in Bibliography on § 3.

Encisco Viana, J., "La vocación de Natanael y el Salmo 24," EstBib 19 (1960), 229–36.

Fritsch, I., "'. . . videbitis . . . angelos Dei ascendentes et descendentes super Filium hominis' (Io. 1, 51)," VD 37 (1959), 3–11.

Jeremias, J., "Die Berufung des Nathanael," *Angelos* 3 (1928), 2–5.

Michaelis, W., "Joh 1, 51, Gen 28, 12 und das Menschensohn-Problem," TLZ 85 (1960), 561–78.

Moule, C. F. D., "A Note on 'under the fig tree' in John i 48, 50," JTS N.S. 5 (1954), 210–11.

Quispel, G., "Nathanael und der Menschensohn (Joh 1, 51)," ZNW 47 (1956), 281–83.

Schulz, S., *Menschensohn*, pp. 97–103 on i 51.

Windisch, H., "Angelophanien um den Menschensohn auf Erden," ZNW 30 (1931), 215–33.

————"Joh i 51 und die Auferstehung Jesu," ZNW 31 (1932), 199–204.

THE BOOK OF SIGNS

Part Two: From Cana to Cana

OUTLINE

Part Two: From Cana to Cana
(Various responses to Jesus' ministry
in the different sections of Palestine)
(chs. ii–iv)

A.   ii 1–11: The First Sign at Cana in Galilee (§ 6)
Jesus changes water to wine and his disciples come to believe in him.

      ii 12: Transition—Jesus goes to Capernaum. (§ 7)

B.   ii 13–22: The Cleansing of the Temple in Jerusalem (§ 8)
Jesus is challenged by the Jewish authorities.

      (13–17) The cleansing of the temple precincts.
      (18–22) The saying about the destruction of the Temple.

      ii 23–25: Transition—Reaction to Jesus in Jerusalem. (§ 9)

C.   iii 1–21: Discourse with Nicodemus in Jerusalem (§ 10)
Jesus speaks of begetting from on high, and is not understood.

      (2–8) *Division 1*—Begetting from on high through the Spirit.
      (9–21) *Division 2*—This is made possible through faith when the Son has ascended.
      (a) 11–15: The Son must ascend to the Father.
      (b) 16–21: Belief in Jesus is necessary to profit from this gift.

      iii 22–30: The Baptist's Final Witness to Jesus (§ 11)

      iii 31–36: Discourse Completing the Two Previous Scenes of This Chapter (§ 12)

      iv 1–3: Transition—Jesus leaves Judea. (§ 13)

D.   iv 4–42: DISCOURSE WITH THE SAMARITAN WOMAN AT JACOB'S
                WELL (§ 14)
                Jesus offers the gift of living water and is hailed by the
                Samaritans as Saviour of the world.

                (4–6)   Introduction and setting.
                (6–26) *Scene 1:* Discourse with the Samaritan woman:
                (a) 6–15:   Dialogue about living water.
                (b) 16–26: Dialogue about true worship.
                (27–38) *Scene 2:* Discourse with the disciples:
                        27–30: Connective between the two scenes.
                (a) 31–34: Dialogue about Jesus' food.
                (b) 35–38: Parabolic proverbs of the harvest:
                            35–36: Negation of the proverb about an
                                    interval between sowing and har-
                                    vest.
                            37–38: Affirmation of the proverb about
                                    one sowing and another reaping.
                (39–42) Conclusion: conversion of the townspeople.

      iv 43–45: TRANSITION—Jesus enters Galilee. (§ 15)

E.   iv 46–54: THE SECOND SIGN AT CANA IN GALILEE (§ 16)
                Jesus heals the royal official's son and the official's house-
                hold become believers.

6. THE FIRST SIGN AT CANA IN GALILEE—
CHANGING OF WATER TO WINE
(ii 1–11)

II 1 Now on the third day there was a wedding at Cana in Galilee. The mother of Jesus was there, 2 and Jesus himself and his disciples had also been invited to the celebration. 3 When the wine ran short, Jesus' mother told him, "They have no wine." 4 But Jesus answered her, "Woman, what has this concern of yours to do with me? My hour has not yet come." 5 His mother instructed the waiters, "Do whatever he tells you." 6 As prescribed for Jewish purifications, there were at hand six stone water jars, each one holding fifteen to twenty-five gallons. 7 "Fill those jars with water," Jesus ordered, and they filled them to the brim. 8 "Now," he said to them, "draw some out and take it to the headwaiter." And they did so. 9 But as soon as the headwaiter tasted the water made wine (actually he had no idea where it came from; only the waiters knew since they had drawn the water), the headwaiter called the bridegroom, 10 and pointed out to him, "Everyone serves choice wine first; then, when the guests have been drinking awhile, the inferior wine. But you have kept the choice wine until now." 11 What Jesus did at Cana in Galilee marked the beginning of his signs; thus he revealed his glory and his disciples believed in him.

3: *told;* 4: *answered;* 5: *instructed;* 7: *ordered;* 8: *said;* 9: *called;* 10: *pointed out.* In the historical present tense.

NOTES

ii 1. *on the third day.* Theodore of Mopsuestia (*In Joanne* [Syr.]—CSCO 116:39) counts this as the third day after baptismal scene of i 29–34, with the first day mentioned in i 35, and the second in i 43. Although this is certainly a possible exegesis, most exegetes now count from the day of Philip's and Nathanael's call, suggesting that that day and the next (or perhaps two intervening days) were spent in the journey from the Jordan valley to Galilee. Since the second Cana miracle also occurs "after two days" (iv 43), some suggest a purely symbolic reference to the resurrection.

a wedding. The usual festivities consisted of a procession in which the bridegroom's friends brought the bride to the groom's house, and then a wedding supper; seemingly the festivities lasted seven days (Judg xiv 12; Tob xi 19). The Mishnah (*Kethuboth* 1) ordained that the wedding of a virgin should take place on Wednesday. This would agree with the guess that i 39 immediately preceded the Sabbath; the action of i 40–42 would have taken place on Saturday evening–Sunday; that of i 43–50 on Sunday evening–Monday; Monday evening–Tuesday would have been the second day of the journey; and Jesus would have arrived at Cana on Tuesday evening or Wednesday morning.

Cana. In the NT this town is mentioned only by John (also xxi 2); Josephus mentions it in his *Life* 16 (※86). The site pointed out to pilgrims since the Middle Ages, Kefr Kenna, 3½ miles northeast of Nazareth, is probably wrong (etymologically from the Greek we would expect the Semitic name to be preserved as Qana, not Kenna). Khirbet Qânâ, 9 miles north of Nazareth, is better etymologically and seems to fit Josephus' localization. Only John and Luke (iv 14–16) know of activity by Jesus in the Galilean hill country near Nazareth immediately after the baptism; Mark-Matthew begin the ministry at the Sea of Galilee.

The mother of Jesus. Among Arabs today the "mother of X" is an honorable title for a woman who has been fortunate enough to bear a son. John never calls her Mary.

was there. There is an apocryphal tradition that Mary was the aunt of the bridegroom, whom an early 3rd-century Latin Preface identifies as John son of Zebedee. This is to be associated with the tradition that Salome, wife of Zebedee and mother of John, was Mary's sister, a relationship which makes John the cousin of Jesus (see NOTE on xix 25 in The Anchor Bible, vol. 29A). The presence of Jesus makes it not implausible that a relative was involved in the wedding, unless the invitation came through Nathanael, who was from Cana.

2. *his disciples.* Presumably, those who were called in ch. i have now become the regular followers of Jesus. They have abandoned the ascetic ways of John the Baptist for the less abstemious practices of Jesus (Luke vii 33–34). In consistently referring to these men during the ministry as "disciples," and in avoiding the title of "apostle," John shows a historical sense, for "apostle" is a term that belongs to the post-resurrectional period—see J. Dupont, "Le nom d'Apôtres, a-t-il été donné aux Douze par Jésus?" *L'Orient Syrien* 1 (1956), 267–90, 425–44.

3. *When the wine ran short.* Many commentators (Lagrange, Braun, Bultmann, Boismard) prefer the longer reading of the original hand of Sinaiticus and of the OL: "Now they had no wine for the wine provided for the feast had been used up." However, both Bodmer papyri support the shorter reading.

Jesus' mother told him. Why is Mary especially concerned and why does she turn to Jesus? Many have thought that she was asking for a miracle. However, there is no evidence of any previous miracles performed by Jesus, and there is nothing in the OT picture of the Messiah which would have led the Jews to expect him to work miracles on behalf of individuals (yet see vii 31). An expectation of miracles is more understandable if Jesus is thought of as the Prophet-like-Moses or as Elijah come back to life, for the OT attributed miracles to both Moses and Elijah. Most commentators, including Catholics like Gaechter, Braun, Van den Bussche, Boismard, Charlier, see no evidence in Mary's request of the expectation of a miracle. Van den Bussche, I, pp. 38–39 (also Zahn, Boismard), does not think that Mary is even asking Jesus to do anything but is simply reporting the desperate situation. Jesus' answer, however, wherein he refuses to become involved, does seem to indicate that something was being asked of him.

"They have no wine." In the multiplication of the loaves for 4000, Mark viii 2 (Matt xv 32) reads: "They have nothing to eat."

4. *Woman.* This is not a rebuke, nor an impolite term, nor an indication of a lack of affection (in xix 26 the dying Jesus uses it for Mary). It was Jesus' normal, polite way of addressing women (Matt xv 28; Luke xiii 12; John iv 21, viii 10, xx 13); and as such it is attested in Greek writing also. What is peculiar is the use of "Woman" alone (without an accompanying title or a qualifying adjective) by a *son* in addressing his *mother*—there is no precedent for this in Hebrew nor, to the best of our knowledge, in Greek. Certainly it is not an attempt to reject or devalue the mother-son relationship, for Mary is called the "mother of Jesus" four times in vss. 1–12 (twice after Jesus has addressed her as "Woman"). All of this leads us to suspect that there is symbolic import in the title, "Woman." To translate it as "Mother" would both obscure this possibility and cloak the peculiarity of the address. See below, NOTE on iv 21.

what has this concern of yours to do with me? Literally "What to me and to you?"—a Semitism. (Semitisms in John appear more frequently in conversation than in third person narrative; see Bonsirven, "Les aramaïsmes de saint Jean l'Evangéliste?" Bib 30 [1949], 432.) In the OT the Hebrew expression has two shades of meaning: (a) when one party is unjustly bothering another, the injured party may say, "What to me and to you?" i.e., What have I done to you that you should do this to me? What subject of discord is there between us? (Judg xi 12; II Chron xxxv 21; I Kings xvii 18); (b) when someone is asked to get involved in a matter which he feels is no business of his, he may say to the petitioner, "What to me and to you?" i.e., That is your business; how am I involved? (II Kings iii 13; Hos xiv 8). Thus, there is always some refusal of an inopportune involvement, and a divergence between the views of the two persons concerned; yet (*a*) implies hostility while (*b*) implies simple disengagement. Both shades of meaning appear in NT usage: (*a*) appears when the demons reply to Jesus (Mark i 24, v 7); seemingly (*b*) appears here. It is interesting, however, that some of the Greek Fathers interpret John ii 4 in sense (*a*) and think of a rebuke to Mary. For patristic exegesis see Reuss and Bresolin; for a complete study of the phrase see Michaud, pp. 247–53. We may mention that there has been an attempt to introduce a variant of (*b*) into the interpretation of John. In II Sam xvi 10, "What to me and to you?" seems to mean, "This is not *our* concern"; therefore, some suggest that Jesus is telling Mary that it is neither his concern *nor hers.* However, the fact that he speaks of "my hour" would seem to indicate that he is denying only his own involvement.

My hour has not yet come. The ancient translation of this as an affirmative interrogative ("Has my hour not now come?"), supported by Gregory of Nyssa and Theodore of Mopsuestia, has been revived by Boismard, *Du Baptême,* pp. 156 ff. and Michl, *art. cit.* This is certainly a possible Greek construction when the word *oupō* begins a clause, e.g., Mark viii 17. Yet the word *oupō* occurs twelve times in John, and all the other uses are negative. The comparison with the very similar constructions in vii 30 and viii 20 should serve to convince that the phrase is negative here, corresponding with the negation implicit in "What has this concern of yours to do with me?"

hour. For this technical Johannine term referring to the period of the passion, death, resurrection and ascension, see App. I:11. The attempt to understand "hour" in this verse as the moment of the opening of the ministry or of Jesus' initial glorification by his first miracle is understandable in view of the context; yet it runs against the rest of the Johannine use of the term and is refuted by the reiteration in vii 6, 8, 30, viii 20, that Jesus' time or hour has not yet come. Especially, the suggestion must be rejected that the hour of miracles was advanced by Jesus at Mary's request, for in Johannine thought the hour is not in Jesus' control but in that of the Father (xii 27; also Mark xiv 35—for Jesus' limitations in this regard see Haible, *art. cit.*). Bresolin shows that the understanding of the "hour" as the hour of the passion antedates Augustine; the Greek Fathers, according to Reuss, think more of the hour of the first miracle.

5. *"Do whatever he tells you."* Mary's instructions echo those of Pharaoh in Gen xli 55, "Go to Joseph, and do whatever he tells you." P. Gächter, *Maria im Erdenleben* (Innsbruck: 1953), p. 192, maintains that we should understand this to mean: "If he should tell you anything, whatever it may be, do it." This is attractive but not really justified by the Greek. Mary seems to have no doubt that Jesus will intervene and is uncertain only about the manner of intervention.

6. *six stone water jars.* In the search for symbolism, attention has been called to the number six (one less than seven—a symbol of Jewish imperfection) and to the mention of *stone* jars (Exod vii 19 where Moses changes to blood the water in the Egyptians' stone jars—a sign according to vii 9). Both attempts at symbolism are farfetched. The use of stone jars was probably the offshoot of the levitical laws of ritual impurity (Lev xi 29–38): whereas earthen jars could become ritually contaminated and have to be broken, stone jars could not become impure (see Mishnah *Betsah* 2:3). For Jewish purifications consult Mark vii 3–4.

fifteen to twenty-five gallons. The jars hold two or three measures; a measure is about eight gallons.

8. *draw some out.* This verb is used normally in reference to a well, and Westcott suggests that a well, and not the jars, is the source of the water. This suggestion seems to run against the obvious context; for it is unlikely that having made the servants fill the jars with some 120 gallons of water, Jesus now makes them draw more water from the well. The problem is that many feel uneasy with the implication that Jesus changed 120 gallons of water into wine. Another attempt to avoid this is Dacquino's suggestion (VD 39 [1961], 92–96) that only the water drawn from the jars was turned to wine. This is possible, but it is not the obvious meaning of the account.

headwaiter. The word *architriklinos* has as its primary reference (BAG, p. 112) the slave who was responsible for managing a banquet, hence, "headwaiter, butler." Actually Jewish literature offers us no exact parallel for the functionary envisaged in John; and it may well be that in the telling of the story, the functionary has taken on some of the aspects of the *arbiter bibendi*, well known in the Gentile world. Some see a parallel in the one who presides at the dinner in Sir xxxii 1; in this instance the one who presides is not a servant, nor the best man, but a guest chosen to run the affair because he is on familiar terms with the bridegroom.

10. *Everyone serves choice wine first.* We have no attestation for this custom in the contemporary literature, but it is the type of shrewd practice that is common to human nature. The suggestion that the custom is an *ad hoc* creation is overcritical.

11. *he revealed his glory.* Compare xii 23, xvii 24; for John the true glory

of Jesus is revealed only in "the hour." Since vii 39 states clearly that during the ministry Jesus had not yet been glorified, we are to think of vs. 11 either as referring to a partial manifestation of glory, or as being part of the capsulizing of the training of the disciples where their whole career, including their sight of the glory of the resurrected Jesus, is foreshadowed.

COMMENT

Reconstructing the Basic Story

Theological themes and innuendo so dominate the Cana narrative that it is very difficult to reconstruct a convincing picture of what is thought to have happened and the motivation of the dramatis personae. Some commentators would relieve us of this burden by denying that there is any basic traditional story of Jesus behind the account and by regarding the whole as a purely theological creation. Of course, for those who deny the possibility of the miraculous, all the miracle stories concerning Jesus are suspect. But why is the Cana story more suspect than others?

Of the seven miraculous signs narrated by John (see App. III), three are variant accounts of incidents narrated in the Synoptics, and three are miracles of a type found in the Synoptics. Only the Cana miracle has no parallel in the Synoptic tradition. Thus, Bultmann and others suggest strong pagan influence in the formation of the story, especially the influence of the cult of Dionysus, the god of vintage. The Dionysus feast was celebrated on January 6th, while the Cana reading became part of the Epiphany liturgy celebrated on the same date. During the feast the fountains of the pagan temples on Andros spouted wine instead of water.

While this evidence is interesting, it is scarcely conclusive for the origins of the Johannine narrative. We must remember that both the dates and motifs of Christian feasts were often deliberately selected to replace pagan feasts. Moreover, it may be legitimately asked if the evangelist, who has shown himself to be working within the general framework of the traditional miracles of Jesus in six of his seven narratives, would be likely to introduce a seventh narrative from an extraneous tradition? As for the uniqueness of the miracle, is changing water into wine so different from the multiplication of loaves? Both have echoes in the Elijah-Elisha tradition which supplies the OT background for Jesus' miracles, probably because only in this cycle of stories does the OT narrate numerous miracles done on behalf of individuals. The multiplication of the loaves is anticipated in II Kings iv 42–44, and perhaps the changing of water to wine to supply the wedding party may be compared with Elijah's miraculous furnishing of meal and oil in I Kings xvii 1–16 and Elisha's supplying of oil in II Kings iv 1–7. All of these are miracles which answer an unexpected physical need that in the particular circumstances cannot be satisfied by natural means. Another obstacle to the thesis that the Cana story was borrowed from Hellenistic miracle legends is the modest and discreet way in which the miraculous is introduced into the narrative—so untypical of the atmosphere of the Hellenistic wonders. John does not tell us how or when the water became wine but reveals the miracle almost in an aside. P.-H. Menoud, RHPR 28–29 (1948–49), 182, stresses how much Cana differs from a pagan metamorphosis.

Thus, it seems that we cannot so easily escape the problem of attempting to reconstruct a basic narrative underlying the theological themes. We may begin with the shortage of wine which some suggest was caused by the unexpected presence of Jesus and his disciples (although we need not discuss the ridiculous interpretations centered on the heavy drinking of Jesus and Mary's attempts to get him to go home). Derrett, who is an expert in Oriental law, has made a careful study of Jewish wedding customs, and found that the wine supply was dependent to some extent on the gifts of the guests. He thinks that Jesus and his disciples, because of their poverty, had failed in this duty and had thus caused the shortage.

The conversation between Mary and her son and its aftermath are more difficult to understand. Evidently Mary called Jesus' attention to the desperate situation (see NOTE). In other Johannine scenes (v 5–7, vi 5, 9, xi 21) there are similar presentations of insoluble human situations without any expectation of or request for intervention by Jesus. However, Mary does seem to expect some answer or action on Jesus' part. The exact nature of the expectation is not clear from the narrative, and none of the many guesses by the commentators is convincing. If Derrett's thesis is correct, Mary may have been reminding Jesus of the results of his failure to observe the custom of a wedding gift. Jesus' negative answer to Mary is in harmony with the Synoptic passages that treat of Mary in relation to Jesus' mission (Luke ii 49; Mark iii 33–35; Luke xi 27–28): Jesus always insists that human kinship, whether it be Mary's or that of his disbelieving relatives (John vii 1–10), cannot affect the pattern of his ministry, for he has his Father's work to do. As Schnackenburg, p. 30, states, the mystery of Jesus is such that, although truly flesh, he cannot be bound by the attachments of flesh and blood. He is the first of those whose true begetting is not by blood, nor by carnal desire, nor by man's desire, but by God (i 13). The refusal is polite; there is no indication that Mary is being rebuked for being out of order, any more than in Luke ii 49. Nor, as we stated in the NOTE, is there a rejection of her as mother—what is being denied is a role, not a person. Jesus is placing himself beyond natural family relationships even as he demanded of his disciples (Matt xix 29).

Mary's persistence in face of refusal is a difficulty, not to be explained away by supposing that through signs or through the gentleness of his manner Jesus indicated to Mary that he was not really refusing. The difficulty can at least be illuminated by the examples of similar persistence in the face of Jesus' refusal exhibited by characters in Matt xv 25–27 (also viii 6–8 if vs. 7 is read as a negative question) and in John iv 47–50 (the other Cana miracle). Such persistence always seems to win Jesus over to acting. And so it is that despite Jesus' refusal Mary's intervention becomes the occasion of the first of Jesus' signs. Writers on Mariology have made a great deal of this fact, and yet it must be honestly noted that the evangelist does nothing to stress the power of Mary's intercession at Cana. If the miracle is a response to her persistent faith, this motif is not made explicit, as it is in the Synoptic examples. Even Mary's final words, "Do whatever he tells you," stress the sovereignty of Jesus and not Mary's impetration; and indeed, it seems to be precisely the willingness to rely on Jesus' sovereignty that prepares the way for the miracle. Schnackenburg (pp. 37–38), a Catholic, thinks that Jesus' decision to perform the miracle is, in the mind of the evangelist, to be related not so much to his mother's request as to an unmentioned directive from the Father—an observation which may be true, but which goes beyond the evidence.

This sequence of the events at Cana is obviously incomplete: what seems to be a purely natural request on Mary's part is met by a refusal on Jesus' part, as if the request somehow affected the substance of his ministry. We shall see below that this conversation makes sense on the level of Johannine theology, but what it could have meant on the level of historical tradition is not clear. Some recent Catholic authors are so impressed by the seeming inconsistencies of the narrative that, while they accept the basic action at Cana as historical, they characterize the dialogue between Jesus and Mary as the evangelist's creation inserted for theological purposes (so M. Bourke, CBQ 24 [1962], 212–13, and his pupil, R. Dillon, pp. 288–90). Other exegetes will prefer the suggestion that the dialogue was also part of the primitive tradition, but that the evangelist has given us only those snatches of dialogue that served his theological purpose, thus leaving us with an incomplete and inadequate account when we try to pry beneath the theological level.

Theological Motifs in the Narrative

Here our problem is not a poverty of detail but an embarrassment of riches. As we shall often discover in the Johannine use of symbols, the evangelist shows many different facets of his theology through one narrative. Fortunately, the main import of the story is spelled out for us in vs. 11. There we are told that Cana was the beginning of Jesus' signs. Thus, despite all the scholarly attempts to emphasize the uniqueness of this miracle and its affinity to Dionysiac mysteries, John specifically relates it to the other miracles of Jesus and to a concrete place in the ministry of Jesus. Then John tells us what the sign accomplished: through it Jesus revealed his glory and his disciples believed in him. Thus, the first sign had the same purpose that all the subsequent signs will have, namely, *revelation about the person of Jesus*. Scholarly interpretations to the contrary, John does not put *primary* emphasis on the replacing of the water for Jewish purifications, nor on the action of changing water to wine (which is not described in detail), nor even on the resultant wine. John does not put primary emphasis on Mary or her intercession, nor on why she pursued her request, nor on the reaction of the headwaiter or of the groom. The primary focus is, as in all Johannine stories, on Jesus as the one sent by the Father to bring salvation to the world. What shines through is *his glory,* and the only reaction that is emphasized is the *belief* of the disciples.

More than most commentators, Schnackenburg has brought out clearly the centrality of christology in the Cana narrative, according to the clear directions of the evangelist. But we must ask further questions. In what way did the changing of water to wine make Jesus' glory shine forth to his disciples? And for the readers of the Gospel to whom the evangelist gives this story in a fixed sequence, how is the Cana narrative related to what precedes and what follows? Let us turn to answering these points one by one.

(1) *How did Cana reveal the glory of Jesus?*—Messianic replacement and abundance. We may answer this question first in relation to the reader of the Gospel who has the whole sequence of the ministry before him, and then we may turn to the meaning of the Cana story for the disciples who saw the miracle. John tells the reader that this was the beginning of the signs and thereby clearly indicates that Cana is to be connected with what follows in the Book of Signs. As we have pointed out in discussing the outline of the Book (p. CXL), one of the themes of Part II (chs. ii–iv) is the replacement of Jewish institutions and religious views; and Part III (chs. v–x) is dominated by Jesus' actions and discourses on the occasion of Jewish feasts, often again by way of replacing the motif of the feasts. Jesus is the real Temple; the Spirit he gives will replace the necessity of worshiping at Jerusalem; his doctrine and his flesh and blood will give life in a way that the manna associated with the exodus from Egypt did not; at Tabernacles, not the rain-making ceremony but Jesus himself supplies the living water; not the illumination in the temple court but Jesus himself is the real light; on the feast of Dedication, not the temple altar but Jesus himself is consecrated by God. In view of this consistent theme of replacement, it seems obvious that, in introducing Cana as the first in a series of signs to follow, the evangelist intends to call attention to the replacement of the water prescribed for Jewish purification by the choicest of wines. This replacement is a sign of who Jesus is, namely, the one sent by the Father who is now the only way to the Father. All previous religious institutions, customs and feasts lose meaning in his presence.

Turning now from the vantage point of the Gospel reader to that of the disciples whom John presents as witnesses of the miracle, and *trying to work with the historical setting envisaged by the evangelist,* we see that the disciples are thought to have seen Jesus' glory in the Cana scene itself without the advantage of foreseeing the theme of replacement worked out in the whole ministry. How? We may introduce our answer by noting that some of the symbols at Cana are familiar and meaningful scriptural symbols that would have been known to the disciples. The dramatic action is set in the context of a wedding; in the OT (Isa liv 4–8, lxii 4–5) this is used to symbolize the messianic days, and both the wedding and the banquet are symbols on which Jesus drew (Matt viii 11, xxii 1–14; Luke xxii 16–18). The wedding appears as a symbol of messianic fulfillment in another Johannine work, Rev xix 9. Another symbol at Cana is the replacement of water with choice wine, better than the wine the guests had been drinking. In the Synoptic tradition, seemingly in the context of a wedding feast (Mark ii 19), we find Jesus using the symbolism of new wine in old wineskins in order to compare his new teaching with the customs of the Pharisees. (Note that this incident occurs at the beginning of the Synoptic account of the ministry just as Cana is at the beginning of the Johannine account.) Thus the headwaiter's statement at the end of the scene, "You have kept the choice wine until now," can be understood as the proclamation of the coming of the messianic days. In the light of this theme Mary's statement, "They have no wine," becomes a poignant reflection on the barrenness of Jewish purifications, much in the vein of Mark vii 1–24.

The abundance of wine (120 gallons—see NOTE on vs. 8) now becomes intelligible. One of the consistent OT figures for the joy of the final days is an abundance of wine (Amos ix 13–14; Hos xiv 7; Jer xxxi 12). Enoch x 19 predicts that the vine shall yield wine in abundance; and in II Bar xxix 5 (a Jewish apocryphon almost contemporary with the Fourth Gospel) we find an exuberantly fantastic description of this abundance: the earth shall yield its fruit ten thousandfold; each vine shall have 1000 branches; each branch 1000 clusters; each cluster 1000 grapes; and each grape about 120 gallons of wine. (Irenaeus *Adv. Haer.* v 33:3–4; PG 7:1213–14, attributes this passage to Papias of Hierapolis who is intimately associated with the early traditions about John.)

Through such symbolism the Cana miracle could have been understood by the disciples as a sign of the messianic times and the new dispensation, much in the same manner that they would have understood Jesus' statement about the new wine in the Synoptic tradition. The reference in vs. 11 to Jesus' revealing his glory fits into this theme, for the revelation of divine glory was to be a mark of the last times. In Ps Sol xvii 32 we hear that the Messiah shall make the glory of the Lord to be seen by all on earth. En xlix 2 speaks of the glory of the Chosen One (John i 34), the Son of Man; and Ps cii 16 promises that the Lord will appear in His glory (also Ps xcvii 6; Isa lx 1–2, etc.).

(2) *How did Cana complete the call of the disciples?* The evangelist not only indicates that the Cana miracle is to be connected to the signs that follow; he also (vs. 1) relates it to what precedes by dating it in reference to the call of the disciples. By emphasizing the reaction of belief on the part of the disciples, the evangelist shows that he has not forgotten the theme of evolving discipleship that was elaborated in ch. i. Belief is the culmination of the following that began in i 37; what they see at Cana fulfills the promise of i 50 (and 51). See NOTE on vs. 11.

Some scholars posit an even more elaborate connection of Cana to ch. i. Bernard, Boismard, Strathmann and others believe that in its frequent mention of days in i and ii 1, the Fourth Gospel wishes to portray a week of seven days to open the ministry—a week beginning the new creation just as

Gen i–ii 3 frames the work of the first creation within a week of seven days. One schematization of this is as follows:

Wednesday	Day 1: i 19–28 —	John the Baptist's testimony concerning his own role
Thursday	Day 2: i 29–34 —	John the Baptist's testimony concerning Jesus
Friday	Day 3: i 35–39 —	The first two disciples follow Jesus
Saturday night–Sunday	Day 4: i 40–42 —	Simon Peter comes to Jesus
Monday	Day 5: i 43–50 —	Philip and Nathanael; beginning of journey to Galilee
Tuesday	Day 6:	one of the two days implied in ii 1 for the journey to Galilee
Tuesday night–Wednesday	Day 7: ii 1–11 —	Jesus at the wedding feast of Cana

We must distinguish in evaluating this schema. If we leave aside the identification of the weekdays (Wed. to Wed.), the simple differentiation of days has in its favor the fact that every day it supposes is indicated in John— only Day 4 is somewhat speculative. We prefer this calculation to that of Boismard who without evidence introduces a day between i 46 and 47 (see above, p. 85). However, the schema becomes quite speculative if we identify the weekdays—see NOTES on i 39 and ii 1 for the rationale. Yet, the fact that the week, thus reconstructed, begins on Wednesday is important, as pointed out by P. Skehan, CBQ 20 (1958), 197–98; for in the ancient solar calendar (followed in Jubilees and at Qumran) the week always began on Wednesday. As Skehan remarks, Cana marks both the end of the first week of the ministry (seventh day), and, as a Wednesday, the beginning of the next week (eighth day). The mystique of the eighth day, the ogdoad, is well attested in early 2nd-century Christianity (*Barnabas* xv 8–9; Justin *Trypho* XLI 4; PG 6:565). For application to Cana see M. Balagué, *Cultura Bíblica* 19 (※187, 1962), 365 ff. This very speculative reconstruction would confirm our view that Cana both completes the sequence in ch. i and introduces the sequence in ii–iv.

The application of the theory of *seven* days to John i 19–ii 11 is very attractive, but how can we possibly be sure that we are not reading into the Gospel something that was never even thought of by the evangelist or the redactor? There is a real danger that we have here one more instance of the passion for finding sevens in the Fourth Gospel (see above, p. CXLII). The Gospel itself counts Cana as occurring on the *third* day, and the day that covers i 40–42 is only obliquely indicated. That the reference to seven days fits well with clear parallels to Genesis in the Prologue (and with the theme of the "woman" at Cana, as seen below) is true, but this does no more than at most to make the theory of seven days a *possible* interpretation.

Another theme that binds Cana to ch. i is the presence of the Wisdom motif that we saw in the call of the disciples (see above, p. 79). This has been well developed in Dillon, *art. cit.* Prov ix 5 describes how Wisdom prepares a banquet for men, inviting them to eat of her bread and *drink of her wine*. In Isa lv 1–3 and Sir xv 3 and xxiv 19, 21, we have men given the food and drink of wisdom. The act of dining at Wisdom's table and drinking her wine is a symbol for accepting her message. The Wisdom motif will be clear in ch. vi where Jesus is the bread of life who feeds men with doctrine —a scene set in Galilee just before Passover (vi 4). Here, at Cana in Galilee just before Passover (ii 13), we have Jesus giving men wine in abundance to drink, and this leads his disciples to believe in him. It seems, on a comparative basis, that the Wisdom motif is intended at Cana. This may also tie in with the replacement motif, for in Sirach Wisdom is in many ways equivalent to the Law. It is not the bread and wine of the Law that feeds men, but Jesus himself, the incarnation of divine Wisdom.

Is the Wisdom motif echoed in vs. 9 where we are told that the head-waiter does not know where the wine is from? Man's ignorance of where Wisdom is from is poetically voiced in Job xxviii 12–20. Bar iii 14–15 challenges man to learn where Wisdom is in its various aspects. When we encounter in John the question of where Jesus is from, we shall associate this with the theme of where Wisdom is from; Schnackenburg, pp. 28–29, applies this approach to the wine at Cana. The allusion may be too subtle.

(3) *The symbolism of the Mother of Jesus, the "woman," at Cana.* If Cana is primarily concerned with the christological theme of the manifestation of Jesus' glory, it also has, as do many of the Johannine stories, subordinate theological motifs. The present discussion centers around the symbolic import of the conversation between Jesus and his mother. Perhaps nowhere in John is the difference of theological predisposition between Catholic and Protestant more painfully evident that in the exegesis of ii 4. There is an enormous amount of Catholic literature on this verse, much of it not rising above the level of pious eisegesis; yet most Protestant commentators pass over the verse as if it were unthinkable that Mary played a role in Johannine theology. That we are seeing the dawn of better days is witnessed in the more sober approach to the Mariology of the scene found in Schnackenburg, Braun, and others, and by passing references in Protestant circles to Mary's importance in the Johannine scene, for example, Bultmann, p. 81, who thinks the story may have come from circles favorable to Mary. Thurian's treatment is not only the best Protestant evaluation of the Mariological question, but far better than many Catholic treatments.

We must begin the treatment of the symbolism of Mary at Cana by drawing on Rev xii; this once again presumes that Revelation may be used as a witness to some of the thought patterns and interests of the Johannine school. (To substantiate what follows see A. Feuillet, "Le Messie et sa Mère d'après le chapitre xii de l'Apocalypse," RB 66 [1959], 55–86; now in English in JohSt, pp. 257–92.) In Rev xii there is a mysterious, symbolic figure of "a woman" who is a key figure in the drama of salvation. There can be no doubt that Revelation is giving the Christian enactment of the drama foreshadowed in Gen iii 15 where enmity is placed between the serpent and *the woman*, between the serpent's seed and her seed, and the seed of the woman enters into conflict with the serpent. In Revelation the woman in birth pangs brings forth a male child who is the Messiah (xii 5 ‖ Ps ii 9) and is taken up to heaven. The great dragon, specifically identified as the ancient serpent of Genesis by Rev xii 9, frustrated by the child's ascension, turns against the woman and her other offspring (xii 17).

It is generally agreed that the woman of Revelation is a symbol of the people of God. Israel is frequently portrayed as a woman in the OT and her anguish as birth pangs (Isa xxvi 17–18, lxvi 7). As for the NT, Revelation (xix 7) itself describes the Church as a bride. The drama of the woman, the people of God, spans the two Testaments: as Israel she brings forth the Messiah who cannot be defeated by the serpent; as the Church, she continues on earth after the Ascension, persecuted but protecting her children.

However, often in the Bible collective figures are based on historical ones. Thus, the fact that the woman represents the people of God would not at all preclude a reference to an individual woman who is the basis of the symbolism. Since the woman is described as the mother of the Messiah, many commentators suggest that Mary is meant. The figure of Eve in Gen iii 15 is the background for the description of the woman in Rev xii; and it is important that from the earliest days of Christianity Mary was seen as both a symbol of the Church and the New Eve (Justin *Trypho* c 5; PG 6:712; and Irenaeus *Adv. Haer.* III 22:4; PG 7:959). For a complete list of references see H. de Lubac, *The Splendour of the Church* (New York: Sheed and Ward, 1956), Ch. IX; for an exhaustive treatment of the woman of Rev xii as both the people of God and Mary, see B. LeFrois, *The Woman Clothed with the Sun* (Rome: "Orbis Catholicus," 1954).

Turning to John, we find that the mother of Jesus appears at Cana and in one other incident, namely, when she stands at the foot of the cross and receives the Beloved Disciple as her son (xix 25–27—see COMMENT in The Anchor Bible, vol. 29A). A number of important parallels are shared by Rev xii and these scenes in John. (a) The figure in Rev xii is described as "a woman"; in both Johannine scenes Jesus addresses his mother as "Woman," which, as we saw in the NOTE, is a peculiar form of address that needs an explanation. The term would be intelligible in all these cases if Johannine thought is presenting Mary as Eve, the "woman" of Gen iii 15. (b) Rev xii is unquestionably set against the background of Gen iii; we have seen how many echoes there are of the early chapters of Genesis in John i–ii. A background in Genesis for John xix 25–27 is more difficult to discern, but certainly the death of Jesus is in the framework of the great struggle with Satan foretold in Gen iii, at least as that passage was interpreted by Christian theology (see John xiii 1, 3, xiv 30). The birth pangs mentioned in Gen iii 16 and Rev xii 2 may be associated with the death of Jesus, as we point out in the COMMENT on John xvi 21–22 (The Anchor Bible, vol. 29A). (c) Rev xii 17 mentions the woman's other offspring against whom the dragon makes war; thus, the seed of the woman (Gen iii 15) is not only the Messiah, but includes a wider group, the Christians. In both of her appearances in John, Mary is associated with Jesus' disciples. At Cana her action is in the context of the completion of the call of the disciples. (Some exegetes have drawn the parallel between her request as the occasion of Jesus' first manifestation of glory to his disciples and Eve's request as the occasion of man's first sin. This probably puts more emphasis on the causality of Mary's request than the evangelist intends.) At the foot of the cross Mary is made the mother of the Beloved Disciple, the model Christian, and so she is given offspring to protect.

Having seen the relationship of the three scenes in the Johannine corpus in which the woman (Mary, the mother of the Messiah, as a symbol of the Church) appears, we may now interpret the conversation at Cana. On a theological level it can be seen that Mary's request, whether by her intention or not, would lead to Jesus' performing a sign. Before he does perform this sign, Jesus must make clear his refusal of Mary's intervention; she cannot have any role in his ministry; his signs must reflect his Father's sovereignty, and not any human, or family agency. But if Mary is to have no role during the ministry, she is to receive a role when *the hour* of his glorification comes, the hour of passion, death, resurrection, and ascension. John thinks of Mary against the background of Gen iii: she is the mother of the Messiah; her role is in the struggle against the satanic serpent, and that struggle comes to its climax in Jesus' hour. Then she will appear at the foot of the cross to be entrusted with offspring whom she must protect in the continuing struggle between Satan and the followers of the Messiah. Mary is the New Eve, the symbol of the Church; the Church has no role during the ministry of Jesus but only after the hour of his resurrection and ascension.

The plausibility of these suggestions about the Johannine symbolism that surrounds Mary has been advocated by Protestants like Hoskyns (p. 530) and Thurian and by Catholics like Braun and Feuillet. It will be noted that this interpretation must be kept clearly distinct from a later Mariology which will attach importance to the person of Mary herself; we believe that the Johannine stress is on Mary as a symbol of the Church. Both in Luke and in John Mariology is incipient and is expressed in terms of collective personality.

(4) *The choice wine at Cana and the Eucharist.* Possibly, another subordinate theological motif in the Johannine scene is sacramental; our general cautions about Johannine sacramentality (see Introduction, Part VIII:B) would lead us to insist, however, that if there is eucharistic symbolism, it is incidental and should not be exaggerated. As for other sacramentalism, in TS 23 (1962), 199–200, we argued against the attempt by some Catholic writers (Vawter, Stanley, J.-P. Charlier, Galot) to see in the Cana narrative a reference to Matrimony as a sacrament. To suggest that the wedding feast of Cana is a foreshadowing of the nuptials of the Lamb (Rev xix 9) in the sense that Mary symbolizes the Church as the spouse of Christ is not only to confuse symbolism (Mary and Jesus are not being married at Cana), but also to give major stress to an incidental background. Likewise,

we reject the attempt (e.g., Niewalda, p. 166) to see baptismal symbolism at Cana. Though the water for Jewish purifications is replaced, it is not replaced by the waters of Christian Baptism but by wine.

The suggestion (Clement of Alexandria, Cyril of Jerusalem, Cyprian) that the "choice wine" of the Cana story may have been intended to remind the readers of the Gospel of eucharistic wine deserves more serious consideration. Such symbolism would be secondary, for the primary meaning of the wine is clearly Jesus' gift of salvation, for which light, water, and food are other Johannine symbols. What are the external and internal criteria used to establish the possibility of this interpretation? *Externally,* a 2nd- or 3rd-century fresco in an Alexandrian catacomb joins Cana and the multiplication of the loaves, thus bread and wine (Niewalda, p. 137); and in John the multiplication of the loaves has undeniable eucharistic overtones. Irenaeus (*Adv. Haer.* III 16:7), speaking of Cana, mentions that Mary wanted beforetime to partake of "the cup of recapitulation"; and this seems to be a reference to the eucharistic cup (Sagnard, SC 34: 295–97). *Internally,* the Gospel itself does draw a connection between the Cana scene and the hour which is to begin formally at the Last Supper (xiii 1). Also, the dating of the Cana scene (ii 13), of the multiplication of the loaves (vi 4), and of the Last Supper to the period before Passover does seem to bind the three scenes together and to aid in associating the wine of Cana with the bread of the multiplication as a symbolic anticipation of the eucharistic bread and wine. Others associate Mary's presence at Cana and her presence at the foot of the cross when *blood* flowed from the side of Christ (Kilmartin, *art. cit.*). The fact that wine is the blood of the grape (Gen xlix 11; Deut xxxii 14; Sir l 15) has also been invoked. And it is true that "choice wine" in place of the waters for Jewish purification could stand for the true cleansing agent of the Christian dispensation—"the blood of Jesus, His Son, cleanses us from all sin" (I John i 7). However, many of these internal indications of sacramental intent are at most poetic allusions which do no more than make a eucharistic interpretation *possible.*

BIBLIOGRAPHY

Boismard, M.-E., *Du Baptême à Cana* (Paris: Cerf, 1956), especially pp. 133–59.
Braun, F.-M., *La Mère des fidèles* (2 ed.; Paris: Casterman, 1954). Johannine Mariology.
Bresolin, A., "L'esegesi di Giov. 2,4 nei Padri Latini," *Revue des Etudes Augustiniennes* 8 (1962), 243–73.
Charlier, J.-P., *Le Signe de Cana* (Bruxelles: Pensée Catholique, 1959).
Derrett, J. D. M., "Water into Wine," BZ 7 (1963), 80–97.
Dillon, R. J., "Wisdom Tradition and Sacramental Retrospect in the Cana Account (Jn 2, 1–11)," CBQ 24 (1962), 268–96.
Feuillet, A., "L'heure de Jésus et le signe de Cana," ETL 36 (1960), 5–22. (In Eng. in *JohSt*, pp. 17–37.)

Gächter, P., "Maria in Kana," ZKT 55 (1931), 351–402.

Haible, E., "Das Gottesbild der Hochzeit von Kana," *Münchener Theologische Zeitschrift* 10 (1959), 189–99.

Kilmartin, E. J., "The Mother of Jesus Was There," ScEccl 15 (1963), 213–26.

Michaud, J.-P., "Le signe de Cana dans son contexte johannique," *Laval Théologique et Philosophique* 18 (1962), 239–85; 19 (1963), 257–83.

Michl, J., "Bemerkungen zu Joh. 2,4," Bib 36 (1955), 492–509.

Reuss, J., "Joh 2,3–4 in Johannes-Kommentaren der griechischen Kirche," NTAuf, pp. 207–13.

Schnackenburg, R., *Das erste Wunder Jesu* (Freiburg: Herder, 1951).

Thurian, M., *Mary, Mother of All Christians* (N.Y.: Herder and Herder, 1964), especially pp. 117 ff.

7. JESUS GOES TO CAPERNAUM
(ii 12)

A Transitional Passage

II 12 After this he went down to Capernaum, along with his mother and brothers [and his disciples], and they stayed there only a few days.

NOTES

ii 12. *After this.* This is not the vague *meta tauta*, but *meta touto*. Bernard, I, p. 83, and Lagrange, p. 63, take the latter to mean real chronological sequence; Bultmann, p. 85[6], and Barrett, p. 162, maintain that there is no difference between the two phrases, and that each is vague.

went down. Cana is in the hill country; Capernaum is on the Sea of Galilee, below sea level.

brothers. The later manuscripts have "his brothers"; the Bodmer papyri favor omission of the possessive. The Synoptic tradition gives names (James, Joseph, or Joses, Simon, Judas—Matt xiii 55; Mark vi 3) to a group of the "brothers" of Jesus, but John gives no names. Are these *adelphoi* blood-brothers of Jesus? Greek *adelphos* normally refers to a real brother. Hebrew *'aḥ* covers masculine relatives of varying degrees (brother, half-brother, cousin, brother-in-law), and LXX uses *adelphos* to render all these shades of meaning—see BAG, p. 15; J. J. Collins, TS 5 (1944), 484–94. Christians who accept the early tradition that Mary remained a virgin consider these *adelphoi* to have been putative half-brothers (sons of Joseph by a previous marriage—theory of Epiphanius) or cousins (sons of Joseph's brother—or of Mary's sister: theory of Jerome). The Anglican Bernard, I, p. 85, comments: "It is difficult to understand how the doctrine of the Virginity of Mary could have grown up early in the second century if her four acknowledged sons were prominent Christians, and one of them bishop of Jerusalem." See NOTE on xix 25, in The Anchor Bible, vol. 29A.

[and his disciples]. This phrase is omitted in Codex Sinaiticus and the early versions. Some have suggested that the "brothers" originally referred to the disciples (as in xx 17), and that some copyist, misunderstanding it to refer to the relatives of Jesus, added the disciples as a third party. In support of this, it is curious to find the "brothers" of Jesus following him along with his mother and his disciples who believed in him. The "brothers" appear as unbelievers (vii 5) in the Gospel tradition of the ministry.

they stayed. Some ancient evidence reads "he stayed." Perhaps the original "they" seemed to a scribe to imply that afterwards all these followers went to Jerusalem, and so he changed it to "he" to adapt the sentence to what follows in ii 13 where *Jesus* goes up to Jerusalem.

a few days. Bultmann, p. 85[5], treats this as a harmonization with ii 13.

COMMENT

The number of textual variants in this verse indicates its awkwardness. For a full discussion see our remarks in CBQ 24 (1962), 11–13, or NTE, pp. 156–58. Within the Johannine tradition there is no prolonged activity of Jesus at the Sea of Galilee (only ch. vi), while for the Synoptics Capernaum is Jesus' headquarters and home during the early ministry. It is difficult to treat this verse as a real connective between Cana and the next scene at Jerusalem, for a journey to Capernaum is a long detour from the road to Jerusalem.

This verse has echoes in the Synoptic tradition. Luke iv 31 mentions Jesus' descent to Capernaum after his initial failure at Nazareth (see also Matt iv 13). All the Synoptics (Mark iii 31 and par.) know that Jesus' mother and his brothers came down (from Nazareth) to see what he was doing at Capernaum, perhaps because of hostile reports about his activities (Mark iii 21). It has been suggested that the redactor of John borrowed the notice in vs. 12 from a melange of such Synoptic information in order to harmonize John with the Synoptics. However, the vocabulary in vs. 12 is not the same as in the various Synoptic parallels. And so, while the verse may well be the addition of the redactor, it is possible that he has fashioned the verse from independent tradition, perhaps even from early Johannine tradition that had hitherto not been incorporated into the narrative (see Dodd, *Tradition*, pp. 355–56).

In any case, if the verse was an attempt to harmonize Johannine and Synoptic chronologies, it has not been successful. All that happens at Capernaum in the Synoptics occurs *after* John the Baptist's arrest and imprisonment (Mark i 14; Matt iv 12). In John this verse precedes the arrest of John the Baptist, who is still active in iii 23, iv 1.

8. THE CLEANSING OF THE TEMPLE IN JERUSALEM
(ii 13–22)

II 13 Since the Jewish Passover was near, Jesus went up to Jerusalem. 14 In the temple precincts he came upon people engaged in selling oxen, sheep, and doves, and others seated, changing coins. 15 So he made a [kind of] whip out of cords and drove the whole pack of them out of the temple area with their sheep and oxen, and he knocked over the money-changers' tables, spilling their coins. 16 He told those who were selling doves, "Get them out of here! Stop turning my Father's house into a market place!" 17 His disciples recalled the words of Scripture: "Zeal for your house will consume me."

18 At this the Jews responded, "What sign can you show us, authorizing you to do these things?" 19 "Destroy this Temple," was Jesus' answer, "and in three days I will raise it up." 20 Then the Jews retorted, "The building of this Temple has taken forty-six years, and you are going to raise it up in three days?" 21 Actually he was talking about the temple of his body. 22 Now after his resurrection from the dead his disciples recalled that he had said this, and so they believed the Scripture and the word he had spoken.

NOTES

ii 13. *Jewish.* Literally "of the Jews"; this phrase modifies Passover in vi 4 and xi 55, and Tabernacles in vii 2. It may indicate a hostility to these feasts which are to be replaced by Jesus. For the possibility of a Christian Passover see ch. vi.

Passover. This is the first of three Passovers mentioned in John (vi 4, xi 55). Some scholars consider them to have merely symbolic value; others accept them as time indications and posit that Jesus had a ministry lasting at least two years. Should the Synoptic localization of this scene before the last Passover of Jesus' life be correct and should the present position of the scene in John be the result of editorial transplantation, it is still possible that the Johannine tradition preserved the memory of a journey of Jesus to Jerusalem at a Passover early in his ministry, and that originally this was the setting for ch. iii.

Jesus. The personal name appears in different sequence in the various witnesses. Perhaps, before vs. 12 was added, the original subject was simply "he," a subject that would not be ambiguous after vs. 11. The insertion of vs. 12 may have led scribes to insert the name for clarity's sake.

went up. This is the normal verb for a journey to the holy city situated on a mountain.

14. *temple precincts*. The *hieron* means the outer court of the Temple, the Court of the Gentiles. The Temple proper, the building or sanctuary (*naos*), is mentioned in vss. 19–21.

oxen, sheep, and doves. The animals were sold to be sacrificed; the doves or pigeons were the sacrifices of the poor (Lev v 7), and this may explain the milder treatment of the dovesellers. Only John mentions the larger animals.

changing coins. Because of the imperial or pagan portraits that they bore, Roman denarii and Attic drachmas were not permitted to be used in paying the temple tax of a half-shekel (Matt xvii 27; a half-shekel equaled two denarii or a didrachma). The money changers exchanged these coins for legal Tyrian coinage and made a small profit in the transaction.

15. [*kind of*]. The Bodmer papyri now support the early versional evidence for this reading.

whip out of cords. No sticks or weapons were allowed in the temple precincts. Jesus may have fashioned his whip from the rushes used as bedding for the animals. Only John mentions this.

drove the whole pack of them out. Seemingly Jesus used the whip on the merchants.

with their sheep and oxen. Bultmann, p. 86[10], regards this phrase as a secondary addition; he suggests that the rest of this verse as well as the beginning of 16 was borrowed from Mark xi 15 or Matt xxi 12. The connective *te*, unusual for John, occurs in this phrase.

knocked over. The textual witnesses vary between several Greek verbs, probably reflecting scribal harmonization with the Synoptics.

16. *my Father's house*. The Temple is frequently described in the OT as "the house of God"; so also Mark ii 26. In Luke ii 49 we have the same idea as in John.

market place. Literally "a *house* of market"; note the play on "house."

17. *recalled*. At this moment, or after the resurrection as in vs. 22? Haenchen, *art. cit.*, thinks of this verse as an editorial addition.

will consume. The future is the correct reading, although some manuscripts and the early versions conform it to the "has consumed" of the MT and LXX (?) of Ps lxix 9.

18. *the Jews*. This is a good example of Johannine use, for the Synoptic parallel (Mark xi 27 and par.) speaks of chief priests, scribes, and the elders of the people.

sign. For the usual Johannine use of "sign" see App. III; here, however, it means a miraculous apologetic proof for unbelievers, as in the Synoptic requests for signs made by the scribes, Pharisees, Sadducees, and Herod (Matt xii 38–39, xvi 1–4; Luke xxiii 8). This usage probably stems from the occasional OT use of "sign" as a divine mark of credence. Jesus never obliges such a request.

authorizing you to do these things. Compare Mark xi 28 and par. (after the cleansing of the Temple): "By what authority do you do these things?"

19. *Destroy*. Dodd, *Interpretation*, p. 302[1], notes that the use of an imperative for a condition (=If you destroy) is a Semitism which may mean that John's form of this saying is quite old. But, as Bultmann, p. 88, insists, this imperative is more than a simple condition; it is the ironical imperative found in the prophets (Amos iv 4; Isa viii 9); it means: "Go ahead and do this and see what happens."

Temple. Naos; see NOTE on vs. 14.

20. *forty-six years*. Josephus, *Ant.* XV.xi.1;※380, says that the Temple re-

construction was begun in the 18th year of Herod the Great (20/19 B.C.—this date is more reliable than the 15th year of Herod given in *War* I.xxi.1;⨳401). Reckoning from this we reach a date of A.D. 27/28, or more exactly, the Passover of 28. The hazards of establishing an exact chronology for the ministry of Jesus are well known, but this date agrees with that of Luke iii 1, which fixes the ministry of John the Baptist in the 15th year of Tiberius (October 27 to 28, according to the Syrian calendar with antedating). The number in John obviously refers to the Temple; however, because John says that the temple is Jesus' body and because of viii 57 ("You're not even fifty years old"), Loisy and others accept 46 as the age of Jesus, suggesting that he died at the Jubilee age of 50. The fact that the Greek letters in the name of Adam have the value of 46 was the basis of the interpretation of many Fathers, especially Augustine, who saw this number as a reference to Jesus' human nature; see Vogels. While we do not regard "forty-six years" as a reference to Jesus' age, we by no means exclude the possibility that Jesus was considerably older than Luke's approximation of "about thirty years of age" (iii 23) might indicate.

has taken. Literally aorist, "took." The Temple was not completed until A.D. 63 under the Procurator Albinus (Josephus *Ant.* XX.ix.7;⨳219). Some would see here an egregious error of the evangelist in portraying the building as complete in A.D. 28. We have taken the aorist as complexive, summing up the whole process of building which is not yet completed. A perfect parallel is found in LXX of Ezra v 16: ". . . from that time until now [the Temple] has been in building [aorist; same verb] and is not yet finished." See also John iv 3 (NOTE), 20 ("worshiped").

21. *was talking.* The imperfect may be modal: "wished to refer."

the temple of his. There is some patristic evidence for the omission of these words, thus giving the reading: "He was talking about the body" (so Tatian, Irenaeus, Tertullian, Origen).

22. *after his resurrection.* Literally "when he had been raised [i.e., by the Father]" or "when he had risen." *Egerthē* is passive in form but may be either passive or intransitive in meaning (ZGB, § 231; C. F. D. Moule, *Idiom Book of New Testament Greek* [2 ed.; Cambridge, 1963], p. 26). In the earlier Gospels the passive is probably to be preferred, in line with the nineteen times that the NT says that God the Father raised Jesus from the dead. But in the Fourth Gospel it has become clear that the Father's power is also Jesus' power (see COMMENT on x 30), and John insists that Jesus rose by his own power (x 17–18).

the Scripture. It is not clear if this is a reference to the OT in general or to a particular passage, e.g., Ps xvi 10, or perhaps to Ps lxix 9 cited in vs. 17. In preaching, the apostles quickly found OT testimonies to the resurrection (I Cor xv 4: ". . . he was raised on the third day in accordance with the Scriptures").

COMMENT

Comparison of the Johannine and Synoptic Accounts

The scene that John narrates has parallels in three separate Synoptic narratives. (1) The Synoptics describe a similar cleansing of the temple precincts during Jesus' only ministry in Jerusalem just before he died. In Matt xxi 10–17 and Luke xix 45–46 Jesus does this on the day on which he enters Jerusalem in triumph; in Mark xi 15–19 he does this on the day after he entered Jerusalem in triumph. (2) On the occasion of the cleansing Jesus' action is not challenged; but some time later the chief priests, scribes, and elders ask, "By what authority do you do these things?" (Mark xi 27–28 and par.). Jesus refuses to answer unless they commit themselves about John the Baptist. (3) At the trial of Jesus before the Sanhedrin false witnesses report that Jesus threatened to destroy the Temple and rebuild it in three days (Mark xiv 58; Matt xxvi 61). We hear other echoes of this threat attributed to Jesus by the passers-by at the foot of the cross (Mark xv 29; Matt xxvii 40). It reappears in the trial of Stephen in Acts vi 14 (the only Lucan reference).

The Synoptic accounts, although not perfectly harmonious among themselves, present some marked differences from John. We may discuss these differences under the headings of chronology and of the likelihood of John's containing independent and reliable tradition.

Chronology: at the beginning or at the end of the ministry? Later on we shall discuss the question of whether the action attributed to Jesus is a historical likelihood. Assuming for the moment that it is, which chronological localization is the more plausible? That we cannot harmonize John and the Synoptics by positing two cleansings of the temple precincts seems obvious. Not only do the two traditions describe basically the same actions, but also it is not likely that such a serious public affront to the Temple would be permitted twice. Let us look at the arguments that favor John's dating and those that favor the Synoptic dating.

Many scholars (J. Weiss, Lagrange, McNeile, Brooke, J. A. T. Robinson, V. Taylor) think that the Johannine dating is the more plausible. They point out that in the Synoptic tradition there is only one journey to Jerusalem, the journey that precedes Jesus' death; and since the Temple is in Jerusalem, the first three evangelists had no option about where to place the scene. The Johannine outline, which has several journeys to Jerusalem, was freer to locate the scene at the point in time where it really happened. It is also argued that the Synoptics themselves betray some traces of a much earlier setting for the scene. For instance, we saw that in answering the challenge about his right to do these things, Jesus raises the question of John the Baptist. Does this not indicate that John the Baptist's ministry is a recent memory, an indication that fits John's localization better? Again, at the trial of Jesus his statement about the Temple is recalled with difficulty by the witnesses as if it had been uttered long before; in John's chronology it would have been uttered at least two years before.

Other scholars (Bernard, Hoskyns, Dodd, Barrett, Lightfoot) argue for the Synoptic chronology. They say that such a serious affront to Temple worship would have forced the priests to take quick action against Jesus. In the Synoptic chronology they quickly put him to death; but in John he is allowed to function for at least two years after the event and to visit the Temple on several subsequent occasions. It is also argued that to be in a position to cleanse the temple precincts Jesus had to have public status as a prophet and a numerous following. Such a status and following fit the Synoptic sequence, where Jesus has entered Jerusalem in triumph at the end of his ministry, rather than John's sequence where Jesus is just beginning to act in public.

Perhaps a solution can be offered that answers the most telling arguments of each view. If John offers parallels to several Synoptic scenes, is it not possible that John is giving us the correct sequence of one of these scenes, but not of the other(s)? The best arguments for the Johannine sequence concern the statement about the destruction of the Temple; the best arguments for the Synoptic sequence concern the actual cleansing of the temple precincts. We suggest as a plausible hypothesis that on his first journey to Jerusalem and to the Temple at the beginning of his ministry Jesus uttered a prophetic warning about the destruction of the sanctuary. The Synoptics give evidence that later on this warning was recalled and used against Jesus, although they never tell us at what precise moment the warning had originally been given. On the other hand, it seems likely that Jesus' action of cleansing the temple precincts took place in the last days of his life.

Why does the cleansing appear at the beginning of John's account? We suggest that the editing of the Gospel led to the transposition of the scene from the original sequence which related it to the last days before Jesus' arrest. We shall see that the story of Lazarus, which is probably a late addition to John's sequence, has become in John the chief motive for Jesus' arrest, displacing all the other factors that contributed to the tragedy. If the insertion of the Lazarus narrative caused a displacement of the cleansing scene, what more natural than to join it to an anti-Temple statement that was found in the beginning of the Johannine narrative? The fact that Jesus' first journey to Jerusalem occurred at Passover may have been another factor prompting the new localization of a scene that had originally been associated with the last Passover of Jesus' life. The new sequence even had a theological attractiveness. John the Baptist, prominent in the first chapter of John, fulfilled the first clause of Mal iii 1, "I send my messenger to prepare the way before me." The second clause is: "The Lord whom you seek will suddenly come to his Temple," a clause that finds fulfillment in the present sequence in John. All of this is hypothetical, but it does make sense.

Independence and Reliability of the Johannine Account. As we pointed out, the Synoptic accounts of the various scenes differ among themselves in details. Which is the most reliable? Braun thinks Matthew is; Haenchen thinks Mark is; Mendner thinks Luke is. We face a similar disagreement when we ask if John's account is an adaptation of one or the other Synoptic account (so Mendner), or an independent tradition similar to the Synoptic account (Haenchen, Dodd), or drawn from a pre-canonical account used by the Synoptics as well (Buse). We must examine this in detail.

(1) The cleansing of the temple precincts (ii 13–17). There are several features peculiar to John: the presence of the oxen and sheep, the making

of the whip, the words attributed to Jesus. Mendner, p. 104, thinks that the presence of oxen and sheep in the temple precincts is not historical since the Jewish sources do not mention such a practice. Mishnah Tractate *Shekalim* 7:2 is not really clear on where the stalls of the cattle dealers were; but Epstein, *art. cit.*, points out that the presence of any animals in the temple precincts was extraordinary because if they got loose, they might find their way into the sanctuary and violate it. He suggests that the normal place for the animal markets was in the Kidron valley or on the slopes of the Mount of Olives (the *Ḥanûth* or market place). He points out that in the year 30 the Sanhedrin moved its meeting place from the temple area to the market place. Epstein suggests that this was a reflection of a struggle between the high priest Caiaphas and the Sanhedrin, and that to avenge himself on the merchants of the *Ḥanûth* for offering hospitality to his enemies, Caiaphas allowed rival merchants to set up animal stalls in the temple confines. Such a theory removes the objection to John's accuracy.

For the whip see NOTE on vs. 15. As for the citation in vs. 17 of Ps lxix 9, this Psalm is one of those most frequently drawn upon for testimonies to Jesus, and the reference may very well have been supplied by John as an interpretation of the scene. The statement in vs. 16 is, as we shall see, an implicit allusion to Zech xiv 21, just as Jesus' words in the Synoptics are an even clearer allusion to Isa lvi 7 and Jer vii 11. All that can be demonstrated from this is that the two traditions draw on a different combination of testimonies, a fact that argues for independent formation (so Dodd, *Tradition*, p. 160).

On the other hand, the features that John shares with the Synoptic accounts are many: *temple precincts; driving out the sellers of doves; overturning the tables of the money-changers; reference to the Temple as a house.* There are too many of the same Greek words to posit accidental similarity of the two traditions. If we find that the details peculiar to John may be authentic, then the logical solution is that the accounts draw on a common source which has been adapted and expanded with additional information in each tradition.

(2) The challenge of the Jewish authorities (ii 18). The above suggestion is bolstered when we turn to vs. 18 in John. As we pointed out, the challenge to Jesus in the Synoptics (Mark xi 27–28) is separated from the cleansing (Mark xi 15–17); yet the challenge does seem to refer to the cleansing of the temple area. As Buse and Dodd suggest, it is quite possible that the intervening material in Mark has split up what was originally one scene. If this is true, John's present sequence is quite like the supposed pre-Marcan sequence.

(3) The prediction of the destruction of the Temple (ii 19). We are handicapped in comparing this saying as it occurs in John and in the Synoptics because in the latter it is always on the lips of Jesus' enemies, and at least in one instance these are *false* witnesses. Some of the differences from John's form of the saying could be attributable to falsification. Let us see the various forms of the saying:

False witnesses at the trial:
Mark xiv 58: "I will destroy this Temple that is made with hands
and in three days I will build another not made with hands."
Matt xxvi 61: "I am able to destroy the Temple of God and to rebuild
in three days."
Passers-by at the crucifixion (Mark xv 29; Matt xxvii 40):
"You who would destroy the Temple and rebuild in three days."
False witnesses attribute the following to Stephen (Acts vi 14):
"This Jesus of Nazareth will destroy this place."
Jesus himself (John ii 19):
"Destroy this Temple and in three days I will raise it up."
For "destroy" all the non-Johannine references use *katalyein* while John
uses *lyein*. For "in three days" the trial scene uses *dia triōn hēmerōn;*
the crucifixion scene and John use *en trisin hēmerais,* a less elegant expres-
sion. (Neither expression is overly influenced by the accounts of the resurrection, for the expression usually connected with the resurrection is "on the
third day" or "after three days.")

One important difference in the forms of the saying is that John uses
egeirein, "to raise up," while the Synoptics use *oikodomein*, "to rebuild."
The latter is applicable only to a building; the former is a proper word for
construction, but may also refer to the resurrection of a body. John's
choice of word fits the evangelist's theological interpretation of the saying.
Another difference is John's use of the imperative, "Destroy," which puts
the burden of the destruction of the Temple on the Jewish authorities.
All the other accounts have Jesus himself destroying the Temple, and this
was undoubtedly the way that Jesus' enemies understood his words.

All the evangelists have to face the difficulty that Jesus did not literally
fulfill the promise involved in this saying. In relation to the non-Johannine
forms of the saying, Jesus did not destroy the Temple; in relation to all forms
of the saying, Jesus did not rebuild the Temple. Perhaps this is why Luke
omits the saying altogether. Matthew's solution is found in the nuanced
verb, "I am able . . ." Mark and John seek a figurative meaning in the
promise. Mark introduces a distinction between a Temple built with hands
and another not built with hands; John reinterprets the statement to apply
to Jesus' death and resurrection. Thus while Mark speaks of two different
Temples, John seems to imply that the same Temple is meant in both
clauses. Dodd, *Tradition,* pp. 90–91, is correct when he says that there
is no real evidence that John's form of the saying is dependent on the
Synoptic form.

The general import of these observations is that the material in John
ii 13–22 is not taken from the Synoptic Gospels, but represents an independent tradition running parallel to the Synoptic tradition. Each tradition
has its own theological developments; and some of the close similarities
between the two can be best explained if they are both dependent on an
earlier form of the story.

Johannine Interpretation of the Scene

The evangelist has been kind enough to warn us in vs. 22 (and perhaps 17) that his theological understanding of the scene far exceeds what was understood when the scene took place. Thus we must investigate what the scene meant to those who saw it and what the scene meant in later NT theology.

The Original Import of the Scene. Jesus' action in cleansing the temple precincts seems to mean roughly the same thing to the Synoptics and to John, namely, a protest like that of the prophets of old against the profanation of God's house and a sign that the messianic purification of the Temple was at hand. In John this fits in with motifs already seen at Cana: replacement of Jewish institutions, and an abundance of wine heralding the messianic times. In the Synoptics the cleansing is set amid a group of scenes that warn of the rejection of Israel; for instance, Luke xix 41–44, which immediately precedes the cleansing, predicts Jerusalem's destruction; in Matt xxi 18–22 the cleansing is followed by the curse on the fig tree and the Parable of the Wicked Tenants (xxi 33–41).

Could those who saw the cleansing have understood this meaning? If Jesus' action was seen as the removal of an abuse, they would have had the example of the OT prophets against which to interpret what Jesus was doing. But was there abuse involved? We have mentioned Epstein's thesis that the presence of the animals in the temple precincts was an innovation by Caiaphas. It is not so easy to see the changing of coins as an abuse, unless those engaged in the practice were charging an unjust commission or bribing the priests. The corruption of the priestly house of Annas was notorious, but any suggestion of bribery goes beyond the Gospel accounts. The evangelists seem to take for granted that Jesus' action was called for without explaining just what motivated it.

If the tradition is correct, then Jesus' action had precedents in the OT. A prophet like Jeremiah, whom Jesus resembled in many ways (Matt xvi 14), had warned the priests of his time that the Temple had become a den of thieves (Jer vii 11—the very text that Mark and Matthew record to explain Jesus' action). He prophesied that God would destroy the Jerusalem sanctuary even as He had destroyed the one at Shiloh. The second part of Zechariah (xiv 21), written against the background of the postexilic Temple, had promised that on the ideal day of the Lord all would be holy in Jerusalem and *no merchant* would be found in the Temple, and this seems to be the OT text implied in John's account (ii 16). In Mal iii 1, which, as we saw, may also enter into John's account, the Lord's intervention in the Temple follows a strong castigation of the abuses in levitical worship. Isaiah lvi 7, cited in Mark and Matthew, held up the prophetic ideal that the Temple would become a perfect house of prayer on the holy mountain attracting all the nations of the world. Thus, an action by Jesus of purifying the temple area by correcting abuses would have been perfectly understandable in the light of the claim that he was a prophet and even the Messiah. (For other texts see Hag ii 7–9; Mic iii 12; Sir xxxvi 13–14.) Some years later (A.D. 62) another Jesus, Jesus bar Ananias, would publicly attack the Temple and warn of its destruction (Josephus *War* VI.v.3;✗300 ff.). There is a rabbinic tradition (TalBab *Gittin,* 56a; Midrash Rabbah on Lam i 5, ✗31) that Rabbi Zadok began fasting about A.D. 30 to forestall the destruction of Jerusalem; this would mean that in Jesus' time there was apprehension about the destruction of the Temple.

Some have suggested that John's account of the cleansing with its sweeping violence shows even more fundamental opposition to the Temple on Jesus' part, an opposition tending toward doing away with the Temple rather than reforming it. For instance, in driving the animals out is Jesus only protesting against their presence in a sacred place, or is he rejecting animal sacrifice altogether? There are passages in Matthew (ix 13, xii 7) that have implications of the latter attitude; however this is probably later Christian insight, since the early Christians saw no difficulty about offering sacrifice at the Temple. That John may have deepened the opposition to the Temple in reporting the cleansing is perfectly possible, for John belongs to that branch of NT writing (also Hebrews; Stephen's sermon in Acts vii 47–48) that was strongly anti-Temple. Cullmann, *art. cit.,* relates this to the Hellenist movement (Acts vi) and points to similar sentiments among other groups in Israel like the Qumran Essenes and the Samaritans. In wondering whether we can trace any of this fundamental opposition to the Temple back to Jesus, we might note that he was called a Samaritan (John viii 48).

The second part of John's scene concerns Jesus' statement about destroying and raising up the Temple (vss. 18–22); this could have been understood by the audience in terms of the messianic *rebuilding* of the Temple. We have suggested that the saying about the rebuilding of the Temple and the action of cleansing the temple precincts were once separate; therefore, historically there may have been no real juxtaposition of the theme of purifying the Temple and that of completely rebuilding it. Yet, even without this literary criticism, the Johannine scene is not self-contradictory. Jesus' cleansing of the temple area is only a step in the right direction, and the priests must do more if they are to avert God's wrath. As we saw in the NOTE on vs. 19, Jesus is insisting that they are destroying the Temple, even as the disobedience of their ancestors provoked the destruction of the Tabernacle at Shiloh and of Solomon's Temple. If they do destroy the Temple, Jesus claims that he will replace it shortly with the messianic Temple of unspecified nature. Just as the OT offered background for the purification of the Temple, so it also speaks of rebuilding the Temple. Ezek xl–xlvi describes in detail the rebuilt Temple; Tob xiii 10(12) and xiv 5(7) speak of a rebuilt Tabernacle or house of God; the Qumran community had copies of an Aramaic Description of the New Jerusalem (5Q15), based on Ezekiel, which describes an ideal Temple. As Simon, *art. cit.,* points out, the hope of a new Temple survived the destruction of the Herodian Temple, for the fourteenth of the *Eighteen Benedictions* (see p. LXXIV) unites the expectation of the rebuilding of the Temple and the coming of the Messiah.

In our view, then, vs. 19 was originally an eschatological proclamation referring to the Jerusalem Temple and would have been understandable as such to those who knew the OT background. The insight that it referred to the body of Jesus was a post-resurrectional amplification. Some scholars, taking vs. 21 literally ("he was talking about the temple of his body"), have thought that Jesus was not referring to the Jerusalem Temple but his body and that he indicated this, perhaps by pointing to himself when he said "this Temple." Dubarle, *art. cit.*, thinks that the first half of vs. 19 referred to the Jerusalem Temple, and the second half to Jesus' body. Léon-Dufour, *art. cit.*, is perfectly correct when he insists that the key to the problem lies not in the two halves of the statement but in two levels of meaning. Those who would bring the resurrection of Jesus' body into the basic meaning of the saying have insisted on the mention of "three days." What would that phrase have meant if Jesus were talking about the Temple? The most facile solution is to regard the "three days" as a phrase added by the evangelist to facilitate the post-resurrectional interpretation of the passage. However, we should not forget that it appears in the various Synoptic forms of the saying where there is no clear attempt to interpret Jesus' words as a reference to the resurrection. Perhaps the best solution lies in recognizing that "three days" was an expression that meant a short, but indefinite time. It is thus used in Exod xix 11; Hos vi 2; Luke xiii 32—see Black, pp. 151–52. By promising that the messianic Temple would be rebuilt in such a short time Jesus may have been hinting at its miraculous nature.

That "the Jews" understood Jesus to be referring to the Jerusalem Temple is clear in John from their retort. That they understood his claims to rebuild the Temple as a reference to a messianic rebuilding seems to be evident in the Synoptic account of the trial. When the false witnesses had recalled Jesus' statement about rebuilding the Temple, the high priest asked him, "Are you the Messiah?" (Mark xiv 61).

Thus, as we have interpreted it, the cleansing of the temple precincts and the statement about the destruction and rebuilding of the Temple that John joins to the cleansing are intelligible on the historical level of understanding prevalent during the ministry of Jesus. Let us now see how the theme became a vehicle of Johannine theology.

Johannine Theology of the Scene. In vs. 17 John uses the words of Scripture to interpret the cleansing of the Temple; he probably means that the disciples came to understand the cleansing in terms of Ps lxix 9 after the resurrection. The interpretation of Jesus' actions in terms of OT fulfillment probably began with Jesus himself; but the NT works agree that it was only after the resurrection that the disciples saw in the OT the key to understanding Jesus (Luke xxiv 27). It is important to cite both vss. 8 and 9 of the Psalm:

8 I have become a stranger to my brothers,
   an alien to my mother's sons.
9 For zeal for your house has consumed me,
   and the insults of those who blaspheme you fall upon me.

John cites only 9a, but the Psalm was known to early Christians and the context of the verse may have been intended as well. The separation from the brothers in 8 may be significant in relation to John ii 12; Jesus left his brothers to come to Jerusalem, and they would be separated from him through unbelief during the ministry. Verse 9b of the Psalm is also appropriate since in John the cleansing of the Temple is met with the challenge of "the Jews."

In citing vs. 9a John adapts it to Jesus' action by rendering it as a future (see NOTE on vs. 17) and thus making it a prophecy. No longer is "consume" a simple reference to the burning intensity of the zeal; John interprets the Psalm to mean that zeal for the Temple will destroy Jesus and bring his death. Thus, even though John does not place the cleansing of the temple precincts immediately before Jesus' death as do the Synoptics, his account still preserves the memory that the action led to his death. In the present sequence the interpretation of the cleansing in reference to the death of Jesus prepares for the interpretation of the saying about the Temple in reference to his resurrection.

Turning now to vs. 21, we find that John has taken a slightly different interpretation of Jesus' saying about rebuilding the Temple than that found in Mark xiv 58. In seeking to explain what Jesus meant by a rebuilt Temple, Mark adds "not made with hands" (certainly later Christian theological vocabulary, as in Heb ix 11)—an indication that the Temple is a spiritual Temple. In the NT, in addition to the Johannine interpretation of the Temple as Jesus' body, we find at least three different strains of Christian thought about the spiritual Temple: (a) the Christian Temple or house of God is the *Church*—Eph ii 19–21; I Pet ii 5, iv 17. (b) the Temple is the *individual Christian*—I Cor iii 16, vi 19; see Ignatius *Phila* vii 2; *II Clem* ix 3. A passage like II Cor vi 16 hovers between (a) and (b). (c) the Temple is *in heaven*—this is the tradition of the apocalyptic works (II Bar iv 5), where the earthly Temple and Jerusalem are only copies of the heavenly. Rev xi 19 and Heb ix 11–12 have this interpretation. Hebrew ix 11–12 is important for interpreting Mark: "Through the greater and more perfect Tabernacle (not made with hands, that is, not made of this creation) he entered once and for all into the Holy Place." If the Tabernacle is the humanity of Christ (Augustine, Calvin, Westcott), then the same phrase that is used in Mark to describe the new Temple is used in Hebrews to describe the body of Christ. Notice, however, that for Hebrews Jesus is not the Holy Place, for that is in heaven.

Which of these views of the spiritual Temple Mark held is not clear; but, after all, they are only slightly different aspects of the same reality. The emphasis on the resurrected Jesus as the Temple is clearest in the Johannine works; to the present passage we may add Rev xxi 22 (and also

John i 14 where Jesus is the Tabernacle). Yet, if Mark understood the Temple to be the Church, and John understands it to be the body of Jesus, even these views are not far apart once we realize that the same Ephesian community that is thought to have been John's audience had heard that the Church is the body of Christ (Eph i 23; Col i 18). As an indication that John's interpretation of Jesus as the new Temple is not strange in the framework of Gospel theology, we may recall the saying attributed to Jesus in Matt xii 6: "A greater than the Temple is here."

Further theological emphasis has been suggested for John ii 13–22. Van den Bussche, *art. cit.*, has underlined the contrast between the Cana scene where the disciples react with belief and the Jerusalem scene where "the Jews" react to Jesus with incomprehension and hostility. Dubarle and Cullmann, ECW, p. 74, suggest a eucharistic, sacramental symbolism in the "body" of Jesus after the reference to the wine (=blood) of Jesus at Cana. However, the eucharistic combination in John is flesh/blood (vi 51 ff.), not body/blood; and we see nothing whatsoever in the Johannine account of the temple scene to support a eucharistic reference. Dubarle would also connect ii 21, where Jesus' body is the Temple, with i 51, where Jesus replaces Bethel, the "house of God." This suggestion hinges on the much-disputed interpretation of i 51. Finally, John ii 18–22 offers an interesting parallel to Matt xii 38–40. In both instances the Jewish authorities ask for a sign; in Matthew Jesus answers them by referring to Jonah; in John he answers in terms of the destruction and rebuilding of the Temple. Each evangelist interprets Jesus' answer in terms of the resurrection on the third day (cf. Matt xii 40 with xvi 4 and Luke xi 29–30).

BIBLIOGRAPHY

Braun, F.-M., "L'expulsion des vendeurs du Temple," RB 38 (1929), 178–200.
———"In Spiritu et Veritate, I," RThom 52 (1952), especially pp. 249–54.
Buse, I., "The Cleansing of the Temple in the Synoptics and in John," ET 70 (1958–59), 22–24.
Cullmann, O., "L'opposition contre le Temple de Jerusalem," NTS 5 (1958–59), 157–73. Eng. tr. in ET 71 (1959–60), 8–12, 39–43.
Dubarle, A. M., "Le signe du Temple," RB 48 (1939), 21–44.
Epstein, V., "The Historicity of the Gospel Account of the Cleansing of the Temple," ZNW 55 (1964), 42–58.
Haenchen, E., "Johanneische Probleme," ZTK 56 (1959), especially pp. 34–46.
Léon-Dufour, X., "Le signe du Temple selon saint Jean," RSR 39 (1951), 155–75.
Mendner, S., "Die Tempelreinigung," ZNW 47 (1956), 93–112.
Simon, M., "Retour du Christ et reconstruction du Temple dans la pensée chrétienne primitive," *Aux Sources de la Tradition Chrétienne* (Goguel Festschrift; Paris: Delachaux, 1950), pp. 247–57.
van den Bussche, H., "Le signe du Temple," BVC 20 (1957), 92–100.
Vogels, H., "Die Tempelreinigung und Golgotha (Joh 2:19–22)," BZ 6 (1962), 102–7.

9. REACTION TO JESUS IN JERUSALEM
(ii 23–25)

Transition and Introduction to the Nicodemus Scene

II 23 While he was in Jerusalem during the Passover festival, many believed in his name, for they could see the signs he was performing. 24 For his part, Jesus would not trust himself to them because he knew them all. 25 He needed no one to testify about human nature, for he was aware of what was in man's heart.

NOTES

ii 23. *during the Passover festival.* Literally "in the Passover in the festival." Barrett, p. 168, interprets the latter phrase to refer to the festival crowd, citing vii 14, which he interprets in the same way. Historically, the pilgrimage feast had been that of the Unleavened Bread, but Passover was amalgamated to it to form one feast. John does not speak of the Feast of the Unleavened Bread as do the Synoptics; Luke xxii 1 makes the two names equivalent.

believed in his name. This expression in i 12 describes a faith that is adequate; here seemingly it does not.

see. Theōrein (see App. I:3); the translation "notice," suggested by Bernard, I, p. 99, seems too casual.

signs. We are never told what these consisted in, but obviously they were miraculous. In iv 45 we shall hear again of all that Jesus had done in Jerusalem at the feast; yet iv 54 seems to ignore these signs when it counts the healing of the royal official's son as the second sign Jesus had done.

24. *trust.* This is the same verb, *pisteuein* (App. I:9), that meant "believed" in the previous verse; to their *pisteuein* Jesus does not respond with *pisteuein*.

25. *about human nature . . . in man's heart.* Literally "about man . . . in man."

COMMENT

These verses prepare the way for the discourse with Nicodemus, who will be presented as one of the many at Jerusalem who had come to believe in Jesus. Dodd, *Tradition*, p. 235, says that this passage is not transitional in the sense that ii 12, for instance, is transitional; for this passage seems to be largely of the evangelist's own fashioning rather than drawn from traditional material. What is clear is that the passage contains much Johannine vocabulary, a fact that still leaves open the possibility that the core of what is narrated was traditional.

Verses 24–25 show us that the faith produced by Jesus' signs in vs. 23 is not satisfactory. As we shall see in App. III, the reaction described here is intermediary. It is better than the hostile blindness of "the Jews" in the temple scene, but it is not equal to the faith of the disciples at Cana in ii 11 who are brought through the sign to see Jesus' glory. Here at Jerusalem there is a willingness to see the sign and be convinced by it, but all that is seen through the sign is that Jesus is a wonder-worker.

The reason that John advances for Jesus' refusal to accept such faith is that "he knew them all" and that "he was aware of what was in man's heart." Bernard, I, p. 99, is not sure that John means us to understand Jesus' special knowledge as being different from that of other great men. Bultmann, p. 71[4], thinks of the extraordinary knowledge claimed by the "divine men" of the Hellenistic world, for example, Apollonius of Tyana, who knew people's thought. Occasionally rabbis possessed this power and it was attributed to God's holy spirit working within them. While these parallels are interesting, it cannot really be doubted that for John the reason Jesus possessed this power was not because it had been given to him, but because of who he is. He has come from God; he remains united to God; and therefore he has God's power of knowing man's inmost thoughts (Jer xvii 10).

The exact connotation of Jesus' not trusting himself to the inhabitants of Jerusalem who believed in him is more difficult. Chrysostom suggested that Jesus did not entrust to them the secret of his person or doctrine, but John gives little emphasis to secret revelations by Jesus during the ministry. For John failure to believe fully is to be traced to the unwillingness of the hearers, not to any secrets on Jesus' part. A more general reference to having no confidence in their enthusiasm may be all that is meant. However, E. Stauffer would press vs. 24 further; for in *"Agnostos Christos,* Joh. ii 24 und die Eschatologie des vierten Evangeliums," BNTE, p. 292, he sees here an echo of the theme of the hidden Messiah. This Messiah, even after he has worked signs and attracted followers, remains an *incognitus* —an aspect that will persist to the end of the ministry (xiv 9, xvi 12 ff.).

10. DISCOURSE WITH NICODEMUS IN JERUSALEM
(iii 1–21)

III 1 Now there was a Pharisee named Nicodemus, a member of the Jewish Sanhedrin, 2 who came to him at night. "Rabbi," he said to Jesus, "we know you are a teacher who has come from God; for, unless God is with him, no one can perform the signs that you perform." 3 Jesus gave him this answer:

"I solemnly assure you,
no one can see the kingdom of God
without being begotten from above."

4 "How can a man be born again once he is old?" retorted Nicodemus. "Can he re-enter his mother's womb and be born all over again?" 5 Jesus replied:

"I solemnly assure you,
no one can enter the kingdom of God
without being begotten of water and Spirit.
6 Flesh begets flesh,
and Spirit begets spirit.
7 Do not be surprised that I told you:
you must all be begotten from above.
8 The wind blows about at will;
you hear the sound it makes
but do not know where it comes from or where it goes.
So it is with everyone begotten of the Spirit."

9 Nicodemus replied, "How can things like this happen?" 10 Jesus answered, "You hold the office of teacher of Israel, and still you don't understand these things?

11 I solemnly assure you,
we are talking about what we know,
and we are testifying to what we have seen;
but you people do not accept our testimony.
12 If you do not believe
when I tell you about earthly things,

4: *retorted.* In the historical present tense.

how are you going to believe
when I tell you about heavenly things?

13 Now, no one has gone up into heaven
except the one who came down from heaven—
the Son of Man [who is in heaven].

14 And just as Moses lifted up the serpent in the desert,
so must the Son of Man be lifted up,

15 that everyone who believes
may have eternal life in him.

16 Yes, God loved the world so much
that He gave the only Son,
that everyone who believes in him may not perish
but may have eternal life.

17 For God did not send the Son into the world
to condemn the world,
but that the world might be saved through him.

18 Whoever believes in him is not condemned,
but whoever does not believe has already been condemned
for refusing to believe in the name of God's only Son.

19 Now the judgment is this:
the light has come into the world,
but men have preferred darkness to light
because their deeds were evil.

20 For everyone who practices wickedness
hates the light,
and does not come near the light
for fear his deeds will be exposed.

21 But he who acts in truth
comes into the light,
so that it may be shown
that his deeds are done in God."

NOTES

iii 1. *Now*. This seems to tie the beginning of ch. iii to ii 23–25.

a Pharisee. Literally "a man of the Pharisees"; perhaps this use of "man" is designed to recall the end of the last verse (ii 25) where we heard that Jesus was aware of what was in *man's* heart. Notice here how Jesus knows what is in Nicodemus' heart.

Nicodemus. Mentioned only in John (also vii 50, xix 39), he represents a group among the Jewish leaders who hesitantly came to believe in Jesus (see xii 42). There is no reason to regard him as purely symbolic. "Nicodemus" was a Greek name that was not unusual among the Jews as "Naqdimon." TalBab

Taanith 20a knows of Naqdimon ben Gurion (or Bunai) who was a wealthy and generous man in Jerusalem in the years before 70; he is probably not the Nicodemus of John.

member of the Jewish Sanhedrin. Literally "a ruler." Nicodemus almost certainly belonged to the highest governing body of the Jewish people composed of priests (Sadducees), scribes (Pharisees), and lay elders of the aristocracy. Its seventy members were presided over by the high priest.

2. *at night.* John consistently recalls this detail (xix 39) because of its symbolic import. Darkness and night symbolize the realm of evil, untruth, and ignorance (see ix 4, xi 10). In xiii 30 Judas leaves the light to go out into the night of Satan; Nicodemus, on the other hand, comes out of the darkness into the light (vss. 19–21). On a purely natural level, the nighttime visit may have been a stealthy expedient "for fear of the Jews" (xix 38); or it may reflect the rabbinic custom of staying up at night to study the Law (StB, II, p. 420).

we know. There are other examples of the use of the plural in collective speech by the Pharisees (ix 24; Mark xii 14). Dodd, *Tradition*, p. 329, points out that the opening of the Nicodemus dialogue has some traditional characteristics; he suggests that we may have here a meager remnant of a dialogue of Synoptic form taken over in John to introduce the body of the discourse which consists of Johannine material. However, if one recognizes a historical substratum in the body of the Nicodemus discourse, then such a traditional introduction may have always been part of the narrative.

3. *no one can.* Jesus picks up Nicodemus' expression from vs. 2; the verb *dynasthai,* "can," appears six times in vss. 2–10.

see. This means "to experience, encounter, participate in," as, e.g., in "see death" (viii 51), "see life" (iii 36). Notice the synonymous, parallel expression "enter" in vs. 5; perhaps "see" brings out more clearly the relationship of the kingdom to the revelation brought by Jesus, revelation that has to be seen, accepted, believed.

the kingdom of God. This expression, so frequent in the Synoptics, appears in John only here in vss. 3, 5 (a sign that there is traditional material in the Nicodemus discourse?). See pp. 135–36.

begotten. The passive of the verb *gennan* can mean either "to be born," as of a feminine principle, or "to be begotten," as of a masculine principle; the same two meanings are possible for the Hebrew root *yld.* The early versions took *gennan* here in the sense "to be born," and, more precisely, in the OL, "to be reborn" (*renasci=anagennan*—there are traces of this interpretation also in OS^sin, Vulg., Greek Fathers). Despite the fact that the Spirit, mentioned in vs. 5 as the agent of this birth or begetting, is feminine in Hebrew (neuter in Greek), the primary meaning seems to be "begotten." In the Gospels there is no attribution of feminine characteristics to the Spirit; and there are Johannine parallels that clearly refer to being begotten rather than being born (i 12; I John iii 9). It is not impossible that the meaning "to be [re]born" is intended by John on a secondary, sacramental level—see COMMENT.

from above. The Gr. *anōthen* means both "again" and "from above," and the double meaning is used here as part of the technique of misunderstanding. Although in vs. 4 Nicodemus takes Jesus to have meant "again," Jesus' primary meaning in vs. 3 was "from above." This is indicated from the parallel in iii 31, as well as from the two other Johannine uses of *anōthen* (xix 11, 23). Such a misunderstanding is possible only in Greek; we know of no Hebrew or Aramaic word of similar meaning which would have this spatial and temporal ambiguity.

Once again, it is not impossible that the meaning "again" is intended by John on a secondary, sacramental level—see COMMENT.

5. *kingdom of God.* Codex Bezae and some other Western witnesses read "kingdom of heaven," and Lagrange accepts this on the grounds that "God" is a harmonization with vs. 3. Bultmann, p. 98[1], however, suggests that "heaven" was introduced on the model of Matt xviii 3, "Unless you change and become like children, you shall not enter the kingdom of heaven."

of water and Spirit. The two nouns are anarthrous and are governed by one preposition. For a parallel to being begotten of Spirit we have Matt i 20, spoken of Jesus: "What is begotten in her [Mary] is of a holy Spirit."

6. *Flesh begets flesh.* Literally "What is begotten of flesh is flesh." The OL and OS add explanatory clauses: "What is begotten of flesh is flesh because it is begotten of flesh." For John "flesh" emphasizes the weakness and mortality of the creature (not the sinfulness as in Paul); Spirit, as opposed to flesh, is the principle of divine power and life operating in the human sphere.

7. *Do not be surprised.* This is a characteristic rabbinic usage (Bultmann, p. 101[2]).

you. The pronoun in "I told you" is singular; that in "you must all be begotten" is plural. Nicodemus came speaking as "we"; so through him Jesus addresses a wider audience.

8. *wind.* The Gr. *pneuma*, as well as its Hebrew counterpart *rûaḥ*, means both "wind" and "spirit"; and there is a clever play on both meanings here, a play that cannot be reproduced in English. "Wind" seems to be the primary meaning in the comparison, although the Latin versions translate as "Spirit."

sound. Literally "voice"; this is part of the play on the double meaning: the sound of the wind; the voice of the Spirit.

do not know. To the ancients with no profound knowledge of scientific meteorology, the invisible movement of the wind had a divine and mysterious quality. In primitive thought the wind was described as God's breath. In the late Jewish apocalyptic, among the mysteries revealed to the seer in his guided tour of the heavens was the dwelling place of the winds (En xli 3, lx 12; II Bar xlviii 3–4). Ignatius *Phila* vii 1 seems to recall this verse of John: "The Spirit [personal or impersonal?] is not deceived; being from God, it knows where it comes from and where it goes."

begotten of the Spirit. Notice the article missing in vs. 5. Sinaiticus, the OL and OS insert "of water and" in imitation of 5.

9. *Nicodemus.* This is the last we hear of him in the scene.

10. *You hold the office.* Lagrange and others suggest an implicit contrast: You are supposed to be the teacher, not I. This is uncertain, but there does seem to be a reference back to the title "teacher" in vs. 2.

still you don't understand. Evidently a knowledge of the OT should have enabled Nicodemus to understand. Bultmann, p. 103, rejects this interpretation in favor of a general emphasis on the inability of rabbinic scholarship to give the real answer. Verse 12, however, distinguishes between what should have been understood and what is too profound.

11. *I solemnly assure you.* This "you" is singular; in vss. 11d and 12 it is plural.

talking. This is the first time the verb *lalein* appears on Jesus' lips in John. It is the Koinē Greek word "to speak"; in classical Greek it has the meaning of "chatter" but is infrequent; however, it was used in LXX for the transmission of the revealed word by the prophets. In Acts it is very frequent for the transmission of the gospel, while in John it is the verb *par excellence* for Jesus' revelation of the truth from God.

we are talking about what we know. For the same idea expressed in the first person singular, see viii 38, xii 50. There are many attempts to explain Jesus' use of the plural here: a plural of majesty; an association of the Father's witness with the Son's; a reference to Jesus and his disciples [Are they present?]. However, any suggestion that Jesus is joining others in speaking founders on the emphasis on Jesus' uniqueness in vs. 13. Some have thought that in vs. 11 John is slipping into a dialogue between the Church ("we") and the Synagogue ("you," plural). Certainly some of John's thought is addressed apologetically to the Synagogue; however, one must remember that the evangelist returns to "I" in vs. 12, even though he keeps the "you" plural; and thus if the Church is speaking, it does so only for one verse. Perhaps the most satisfactory answer is to see vs. 11 as the continuation of the rebuttal of Nicodemus in his own words begun in 10. Just as in vs. 10 Jesus picks up the theme of "teacher" from Nicodemus' words in vs. 2, so in vs. 11 Jesus picks up the "we know" from vs. 2 and turns it against Nicodemus. Thus, the use of "we" is a parody of Nicodemus' hint of arrogance.

12. *earthly things . . . heavenly things.* Johannine dualism tends to be spatial in its imagery; see D. Mollat, "Remarques sur le vocabulaire spatial du quatrième évangile," StEv, I, pp. 510–15. It is difficult to determine what these two terms refer to. The simplest explanation is that what Jesus has already said comes under "earthly" and what he is going to say comes under "heavenly." In this case the dualism is not like flesh/Spirit, for what Jesus has already said includes such a lofty subject as begetting from above by the Spirit; and therefore "earthly" is not derogatory. Rather, the contrast is between two types of divine action, one more heavenly and mysterious than the other. Why are the things spoken of in vss. 3–8 designated as "earthly"? Perhaps it is because they were illustrated by earthly analogies like birth and wind; perhaps it is because they take place on earth, while what is to follow concerns going up to heaven or being lifted up. The other NT examples of the earthly/heavenly contrast (I Cor xv 40; II Cor v 1; Philip ii 10, iii 19–20; James iii 15) are of little use here. An interesting parallel to John is found in a statement of Rabbi Gamaliel to the Emperor (TalBab *Sanhedrin* 39a): "You do not know that which is on earth; should you know what is in heaven?" Thüsing, pp. 255 ff., argues strongly for an interpretation quite different from that just given: the "earthly things" cover Jesus' whole ministry on earth; the "heavenly things" do not refer to the content of vss. 13–15 but to the post-ascensional words of Jesus spoken through the Paraclete. There is little in the present passage to support his view.

13. *has gone up.* The use of the perfect tense is a difficulty, for it seems to imply that the Son of Man has already ascended into heaven. For those scholars who believe that the evangelist is speaking here and not Jesus, the evangelist is simply reflecting back on Jesus' ascension. Others like Lagrange and Bernard think that the past tense is meant only to deny that up to that time anyone had ever gone up to heaven to know heavenly things, and that what especially refers to the Son of Man is the descent, not the ascent. It is possible that this was the original meaning but that in the course of post-resurrectional preaching the clause came to be understood as a reference to the ascension. In the Johannine references to Jesus there is a strange timelessness or indifference to normal time sequence that must be reckoned with (iv 38).

Son of Man. E. M. Sidebottom, "The Ascent and Descent of the Son of Man in the Gospel of St. John," ATR 39 (1957), 115–22, points out that only in John is the Son of Man portrayed as descending. Enoch (e.g., xlviii 2–6) portrays the Son of Man as pre-existent in heaven (and this seems to be implied in John), but does not speak of his descent. Sidebottom finds the proposed Hellenistic and Gnostic parallels wanting. Ephesians iv 9 refers to the descent and ascent of Jesus, but seemingly in reference to his descent into the lower regions after death. The whole purpose of vs. 13 in John is to stress the heavenly origin of the Son of Man.

[*who is in heaven*]. This phrase is found in a few Greek mss., the Latin and some Syriac versions. The textual evidence is not strong, but the phrase is so difficult that it may well have been omitted in the majority of manuscripts to avoid a difficulty. Lagrange, Boismard, and Wikenhauser are among those who accept it. The Son in John remains close to the Father even when he is on earth (i 18).

14. *Moses lifted up the serpent.* In both MT and LXX of Num xxi 9 ff. we hear that Moses *placed* the serpent on a standard-bearing pole; but the Targums (Neof. I; Ps Jon) have that he "placed the serpent on an elevated place" or that he "suspended" it. Boismard, RB 66 (1959), 378, points out that Jesus may be citing the Targum (see also vii 38). The word in both MT and LXX for "standard-bearing pole" is literally the word for "sign." (Could this be one of the factors that led to the Johannine use of "sign" for the miracles of Jesus?) Matt xxiv 30 mentions the *sign of the Son of Man* as the parousia. In Wis xvi 6–7 we have a midrash (i.e., a popular enlivening for didactic purposes) of the serpent story: "They had a symbol of salvation to remind them of the precept of your Law. For he who turned toward it was saved, not by what he saw, but by you, the Saviour of all." This fits the Johannine thought that Jesus lifted up becomes the source of salvation to all (xii 32) and whoever sees Jesus sees the Father (xiv 9). The Targum, too, interprets the meaning of looking on the serpent: it means turning one's heart toward the *memra* of God (see App. II). Targum Ps Jon mentions *the name* of the *memra,* just as John iii 18 mentions *the name* of God's only Son. The *Epistle of Barnabas* xii 5–6 uses the typology of the serpent, perhaps in dependence on John—see Braun, JeanThéol, I, pp. 83–85; also Glasson, pp. 33–39.

15. *who believes/may have eternal life.* Compare Num xxi 8: "that he who looks on it [the serpent] shall live."

eternal life. This is the first use of the phrase in John; see App. I:6.

in him. This phrase can be put with "believe"; however, the best reading is *en autō* (P[75]; Vaticanus), not *eis auton* which is usual in the phrase "believe in him." For the idea of having life in Jesus, see xx 31, xvi 33.

16. *loved.* The aorist implies a supreme *act* of love. Cf. I John iv 9: "In this way was God's love revealed in our midst: God has sent His only Son into the world that we may have life through him." Notice that in I John the love is oriented toward Christians ("we") while in John iii 16 God loves the world. In all other examples in John, God's love is directed to the disciples, for in its dualism John does not mention God's love for the unjust as does Matt v 45. See Barrosse, *art. cit.* The verb here is *agapan;* and if Spicq is right (see App. I:1), we have a perfect example of *agapan* expressing itself in action, for vs. 16 refers to God's love expressing itself in the Incarnation and the death of the Son.

so much/that. The following result clause is in the indicative—the only time in John. The classical use of this construction is for the purpose of stressing the reality of the result: "that he *actually* gave the only Son."

gave. The verb *didonai* here refers not only to the Incarnation (God sent the Son into the world; vs. 17), but also to the crucifixion (gave up to death— the idea found in being "lifted up" in vss 14–15). It is similar to the use of *paradidonai* in Rom viii 32; Gal ii 20; and *didonai* in Gal i 4. The background may be that of the Suffering Servant of Isa liii 12 (LXX): "He was given up [*paradidonai*] for their sins."

the only Son. This is the best attested reading, although later scribes, provoked by the awkwardness of the phrase, changed it to "His only Son." See NOTE on "only Son" in i 14; also Moody, *art. cit.*

perish. The alternatives are either to perish or to have eternal life; the same contrast is in x 28 (see xvii 12). *Apollynai* is a characteristic Johannine term, occurring ten times; intransitively, it has two meanings: (*a*) to be lost; (*b*) to perish, be destroyed. We find Jesus also speaking about not *losing* any of those whom the Father has given him (vi 39, xviii 9).

17. *send.* This is parallel to "gave" in vs. 16; we find the same pair, "send" and "give," used of the Paraclete in xiv 16 and 26. "Send" with reference to the mission of Jesus is expressed in John by two verbs without any apparent distinction of meaning: *pempein* (26 times) and *apostellein* (18 times). The Synoptics use *apostellein* for the mission of Jesus (except Luke xx 13); Paul uses *pempein*. For John Jesus is sent to the world; for the Synoptics Jesus is sent to Israel (Matt xv 24; Luke iv 43).

the Son. The absolute use of "the Son," as contrasted to "the Father," appears in only two Synoptic sayings (in Mark xiii 32, and in the "Johannine logion" of Matt xi 27 and Luke x 22). The absolute use is frequent in John, almost paralleling the use of "Son of Man" in the Synoptic tradition. John has probably capitalized on an ancient, but occasional, usage attributed to Jesus.

condemn. The Greek root involved in *krinein* and *krisis* means both "to judge" and "to condemn"; we shall have to shift back and forth between these two meanings according to the context. In the COMMENT on viii 15 we shall give a study of Jesus' relationship to judgment according to John.

that the world might be saved. A comparison with vs. 16 shows that "to be saved" means to receive eternal life. Cf. I John iv 14: "The Father has sent the Son as Saviour of the world"; also John xii 47 (see COMMENT). Some manuscripts of Luke ix 56 read: "The Son of Man did not come to destroy the souls of men but to save them."

18. *but.* Although this is omitted in important witnesses, the readings of the Bodmer papyri add to the evidence favoring it.

for refusing to believe. Literally "because he has not believed"; the perfect indicates a continuing disbelief.

19. *the judgment is this.* This is not a reference to the sentence but to what the judicial action consists in.

preferred. Literally "loved more than"; Hebrew has no word to express the shade of meaning in "prefer," and so "love" and "hate" are often contrasted to convey the idea. See NOTE on xii 25; also Matt vi 24; Luke xiv 26.

20. *practices wickedness.* The use of a verb "to do, practice" with "good" or "truth" or "evil" (here *phaula prassein;* in vs. 21 "acts in truth" is literally "to do the truth"—*tēn alētheian poiein*) is a Semitism. The usage in the NT is peculiar to John (see v 29); Rev xxii 15 has "to do falsehood"—*poiein pseudos.* See below for Qumran parallels.

exposed. The Gr. *elenkein* means "to expose, convict, reprimand" and thus is very hard to capture in one English expression. Its positive counterpart in vs. 21 is *phaneroun,* "shown." We hear similar language in the Dead Sea Scrolls, for CDC xx 2–4 speaks of the deeds of the wicked man being exposed and his being reprimanded.

21. *acts in truth.* Literally "does the truth"; see NOTE on vs. 20. In the OT "to do truth" (*'aśāh 'emet*) means "to keep faith." In the Dead Sea Scrolls, however, the sectarians are urged to do truth; and this has a connotation much like John's usage, namely, one of commitment of life (1QS i 5, v 3, viii 9). We must note, though, that the Greek phrase occurs in LXX in this way too (Isa xxvi 10; Tob iv 6, xiii 6). See Zerwick, *art. cit.;* also App. I:2 on "truth."

COMMENT: GENERAL

The Nicodemus scene is our first introduction to the Johannine discourse. It is the first oral exposition in John of the revelation brought by Jesus, and in capsule form it gives the principal themes of that revelation.

Historicity

When we try to think of this scene occurring in the ministry of Jesus, there are many problems that must be faced, not the least of which is setting. The opening statement of Nicodemus in vs. 2 implies that Jesus has worked many miracles in Jerusalem, and this is also the burden of ii 23 and iv 45. Yet, the fact that no miracle done in Jerusalem has been narrated by John has led many to suggest that the Nicodemus story should come later in the Gospel after miracles in Jerusalem have been described. Mendner, *art. cit.,* suggests that the authentic setting for the Nicodemus story is in vii 51. Mendner supposes that, after Nicodemus had spoken on Jesus' behalf, he went to investigate him. In his *Diatessaron* (Codex Fuldensis), a 2nd-century harmony of the Gospels, Tatian placed the Nicodemus scene in Holy Week, an arrangement Lagrange finds tempting. A prediction of death, such as found in vs. 14, would be more in harmony in Holy Week. Gourbillon, *art. cit.,* would relocate iii 14–21 between xii 31 and 32, thus giving part of the Nicodemus scene a setting toward the end of Jesus' life. Such exercises of ingenuity are always interesting, but in the end one is discouraged by the lack of proof.

John obviously intends Nicodemus to illustrate a partial faith in Jesus on the basis of signs and has prepared the way for this with ii 23–25. Such an illustration comes logically after examples of more satisfactory faith (the disciples at Cana) and of complete lack of faith ("the Jews" at the Temple). Thus, the sequence is at least logical. To seek perfect chronological sequence in John is a vain endeavor, for the evangelist himself has warned us that such was not his interest (xx 30).

The question of historical value affects not only the setting but also the contents of the discourse. In the NOTES we have pointed out the numerous difficulties: in vss. 3–4 a play on words possible only in Greek; in vs. 11

Jesus speaks in the plural as if the Church were speaking; in vs. 13 it seems as if the Son of Man has already ascended. These problems lead some to regard the whole discourse as a Johannine creation, or else to regard only the introduction as showing signs of origin in earlier tradition (see NOTE on vs. 2). Many scholars suggest that at least some part of vss. 12–21 is a homily by the evangelist himself rather than the words of Jesus. The reference to Baptism in vs. 5 has led even so conservative a scholar as Lagrange, p. 72, to remark that this whole exposé would appear more natural on the lips of a Christian catechist long after the Church's foundation than on Jesus' lips as his opening words of the ministry.

As we remarked in the Introduction, the relation of the Johannine dialogues to the primitive tradition about Jesus of Nazareth and his sayings is not a question open to facile solution. Certainly there has been a reworking of material by the evangelist in vss. 1–21, a changing of perspective, a development of later themes. But there are Synoptic parallels to many of the isolated statements attributed to Jesus in these verses, and it seems probable that a solid nucleus of traditional material has been elaborated in homiletic fashion into the present form of the discourse. The attempt to attribute a certain number of verses to Jesus and a certain number to the evangelist is, in our opinion, impossible. There are no stylistic differences in vss. 12–21 to tell us where such a division should be marked. Rather, throughout the whole the threads of tradition and homiletic development are too interwoven ever to allow precise separation.

Plan of the Discourse

How are vss. 1–21 to be subdivided? On the basis of form, we note that Nicodemus makes three statements in 2, 4, and 9; the last two are explicit questions, the first is treated as an implicit question. To all three Jesus gives an answer that begins, "I solemnly assure you" (3, 5, 11—the last is preceded by an *ad hominem* remark). The three answers of Jesus are progressively longer in their development. Thus, from the standpoint of form alone, the section is not so haphazard as some of the attempts at rearrangement might indicate.

There is also a development in thought. Roustang points out a reference to the three divine agents that may, at least, form a secondary motif: the words of Jesus in vss. 3–8 concern the role of *the Spirit;* those in 11–15 concern *the Son of Man;* those in 16–21 concern God *the Father.* Perhaps a combination of form and thought pattern gives us the best division (see Roustang, p. 341; De la Potterie, pp. 430–31). After the introductory first verse which follows ii 23–25 and sets the scene more precisely, we have:

1. Vss. 2–8. Begetting from on high through the Spirit is necessary for entrance into the kingdom of God; natural birth is insufficient.

    (a) 2–3: First question and answer: the fact of begetting from on high.

    (b) 4–8: Second question and answer: the how of the begetting— through the Spirit.

2. Vss. 9–21. All of this is made possible only when the Son has ascended to the Father, and it is offered only to those who believe in
Jesus.

>   9–10: Third question and answer introduces this whole section.

>   (a) 11–15: The Son must ascend to the Father (in order to give the
>   Spirit).

>   (b) 16–21: Belief in Jesus is necessary to profit from this gift.

We believe that the evangelist has left some signs that this was roughly the
plan he followed in organizing the discourse. Division 1 begins with Nicodemus' assurance, "We know that you are a teacher"; this is balanced
at the beginning of Division 2 by Jesus' statement, "You hold the office of
teacher of Israel . . . we are talking about what *we know*." Besides the
similar pattern in the two divisions, the whole discourse seems to be held
together by an inclusion. The discourse begins with Nicodemus coming
to Jesus at night; it ends on the theme that men have to leave the darkness
and come to the light. Nicodemus opens the conversation by hailing Jesus
as a *teacher* who has *come from God;* the last part of the discourse shows
that Jesus is God's only Son (vs. 16) whom God has sent into the world
(17) as the light for the world (19). If we consider ii 23–25 as the
introduction to the Nicodemus scene, there is still another inclusion. In
ii 23 we heard of those who "believed in his name," but their belief was
unsatisfactory because they did not come to see who he was; in iii 18 we
find an insistence that salvation can come only to those who "believe in the
name of God's only Son."

COMMENT: DETAILED

Division 1. The Basic Meaning of iii 2–8

Our first interest will be the basic meaning of the interchange that the
evangelist reports as having taken place between Jesus and Nicodemus,
that is, the meaning that Nicodemus should have been able to understand
in the scene *as it is portrayed*. Then, in a separate discussion we shall
discuss the baptismal orientation of the scene as it may have been secondarily
reinterpreted in the Johannine liturgical preaching.

Nicodemus is one of those mentioned in ii 23–25 who believe in Jesus
because of the signs they have seen; his "we" might almost make him their
spokesman. In ii 24–25 Jesus reacted unfavorably toward their faith, and
this same reaction greets Nicodemus. All that the signs have taught Nicodemus is that Jesus is a distinguished rabbi, one of the many rabbis to whom
miracles are attributed in Jewish writings. Some scholars would interpret
"a teacher who has come from God" as a reference to the Prophet-like-
Moses of Deut xviii 18. However, it would be difficult to explain Jesus'
unfavorable reaction if Nicodemus' faith were that profound; moreover,
the indefinite article before "teacher" seems to rule out such a precise
reference.

In our interpretation, then, Nicodemus' approach to Jesus is well-intentioned but theologically inadequate. As an aside we may note that in ancient times Nicodemus' visit was looked on as part of the Pharisees' scheme to entrap Jesus. We shall discuss Papyrus Egerton 2 below (p. 229); this work combines John iii 2 (plus x 25) with the trick question about tribute to Caesar (Matt xxii 15–22):

> Coming to him, they tempted him with a tricky question, saying, "Teacher Jesus, we know that you have come from God, for what you are doing gives testimony above all the prophets. So tell us, is it lawful to render to kings what belongs to their rule or not?"

Jesus' answer in iii 3 seems to treat Nicodemus' greeting as an implicit request about entrance into the kingdom of God. One is reminded of another member of the Sanhedrin (Luke xviii 18) who came and addressed Jesus as "Teacher" and asked him what must be done to inherit eternal life. At the end of the conversation Jesus remarked on how hard it was for such rich men to "enter into the kingdom of God" (see John iii 5). There is no particular reason for identifying the Lucan and Johannine scenes, but the parallel is useful in showing that John's scene is not so unique as might first seem. In both cases the approach to Jesus in faith is looked upon as a desire to enter the kingdom that Jesus was proclaiming.

Jesus' answer is meant to show Nicodemus that Jesus has not come from God in the sense that Nicodemus thought (a man approved by God), but in the unique sense of having descended from God's presence to raise men to God. Commentators have noted that Jesus does not answer Nicodemus' question directly. However, the tactic of the Johannine discourse is always for the answer to transpose the topic to a higher level; the questioner is on the level of the sensible, but he must be raised to the level of the spiritual. An appreciation of the radical difference between the flesh and the Spirit is the true answer to Nicodemus.

In the NOTES we have pointed out that there are several misunderstandings involved in Nicodemus' reaction to Jesus' words. These misunderstandings —a frequent device in the Johannine discourse—lead Jesus to explain more fully. In interpreting what Jesus says to Nicodemus, we shall be mistaken if we fail to recognize the basic simplicity of the ideas involved. A man takes on flesh and enters the kingdom of the world because his father begets him; a man can enter the kingdom of God only when he is begotten by a heavenly Father. Life can come to a man only from his father; eternal life comes from the heavenly Father through the Son whom he has empowered to give life (v 21). The crude realism of the begetting of eternal life is even more brutal in I John iii 9 where it is said that one begotten by God has God's *seed* abiding in him. The imagery of begetting, regeneration, and divine seed is shared by the Johannine works, I Pet i 23, and Titus iii 5. Another imagery used by the early Christians to explain how they were sons of God was that of adoption by God found in the main Pauline works (Gal iv 5; Rom viii 23).

Nicodemus misunderstands what Jesus has said about begetting from above and thinks of coming forth from the womb again. Was there anything in Jewish thought that would have prepared him for understanding Jesus' theme of becoming God's sons through begetting by the Father? In the early stages of OT theology the whole people of Israel was treated as God's first-born child (Exod iv 22; Deut xxxii 6; Hos xi 1). However, we cannot say that sonship is a major theme in the relationship between Israel and Yahweh; moreover, where sonship is mentioned, it is the result of covenant choice—there is no clear idea of begetting by God. With the establishment of the Davidic monarchy, the anointed king (messiah) of God's people was hailed as the son of God (II Sam vii 14; Pss ii 7, lxxxix 27). Although the imagery may have had its roots in pagan (Egyptian) parallels where it was thought that a god sexually begot the king of a human mother, the specific Israelite concept associated sonship with the anointing which made a man a king. It is important that the term "begetting" appears in Ps ii to describe the anointing. (Compare I John ii 20, 27, which speak of the Christian being anointed by God and being begotten by God's seed.)

Only in the postexilic stage of Israelite thought do we find pious individual Israelites designated as sons of God. In certain passages this is clearly looked on as a future reward, that is, in the last times the just man will be accounted a son of God (Wis v 5; Ps Sol xvii 30). Other passages regard the pious man in his present life as a son of the Most High who is addressed as a Father (Sir iv 10, xxiii 1, 4; Wis ii 13, 16, 18). The same phenomenon of aspirations to present and to future sonship, flourishing side by side, is found in the NT. The Synoptics seem to regard sonship as a promise to be realized only after death (Luke xx 36; and vi 35 compared with Matt v 44–45). For John sonship is realized on this earth once the resurrected Jesus gives the Spirit (see COMMENT on xx 17, 22, in The Anchor Bible, vol. 29A). Christian theology has reconciled these viewpoints by recognizing that future life in the presence of God is different in manner and intensity from the life we possess now, but not different in kind. We are sons of God now, though after death we shall be sons in a more perfect manner. Another difference between the Synoptic outlook and that of John should be noticed: for the Synoptics good acts make one like God and thus a member of His family; John speaks of begetting by God.

Thus there was, at least, a limited OT background that should have enabled Nicodemus to understand that Jesus was proclaiming the arrival of the eschatological times when men would be God's children. This concept was known to Judaism even if the theme of divine begetting had not hitherto received much emphasis. It is precisely on the theme of begetting that Nicodemus stumbles; and his misunderstanding causes Jesus in vss. 5 ff. to explain further. We have seen that I John uses the metaphor of God's seed to explain how God begets sons; John rather resorts to the concept of the Spirit. There is a good account of the Hebrew notion of spirit or breath of life (the words are interchangeable) in articles by P. van Imschoot, RB 44 (1935), 481–501, and J. Goitia, EstBib 15 (1956), 147–85, 341–80;

16 (1957), 115–59. Today, one of the simplest tests of life is to see whether a person is still breathing; so also for the ancient Hebrew the breath or spirit was the principle of life. Man is both flesh and spirit, but his spirit is perishable; and it is the catalytic agency of God's spirit that keeps man alive. God had given life to man when He breathed into him the breath of life at creation (Gen ii 7); death occurs when God takes back His spirit or breath (Gen vi 3; Job xxxiv 14; Eccles xii 7).

If natural life is attributable to God's giving spirit to men, so eternal life begins when God gives His Holy Spirit to men. The begetting through Spirit of which vs. 5 speaks seems to be a reference to the outpouring of the Spirit through Jesus when he has been lifted up in crucifixion and resurrection (see COMMENT on vii 39, xix 30, 34–35). The resurrected Jesus speaks of the disciples as his brothers and tells them that his Father is now their Father because he breathes on them and they are recreated by the Holy Spirit they receive (see COMMENT on xx 17, 22, in The Anchor Bible, vol. 29A).

The gift of the Spirit from God seems to be the principal idea in vs. 5; however, there is an ancient patristic interpretation of "begetting of spirit" in terms of accepting Jesus' revelation in faith and living out the spiritual life—thus, not so much the Spirit of God, but a new spirit within the individual. De la Potterie, pp. 420–22, cites the *Shepherd of Hermas,* Justin, Irenaeus, and Augustine for this view, and suggests that this is the primary reference in vs. 5. We do not accept this reference as primary, but there is nothing in this view of 5 that need contradict our view. To the giving of God's Spirit there must correspond on the part of the believer an acceptance in faith and a new way of life. But the gift of the Spirit of God is primary, for it is that Spirit, the Spirit of truth, that enables men to know and believe in Jesus' revelation (xiv 26, xvi 14–15).

Could Nicodemus have understood this begetting of Spirit? The pouring forth of God's spirit was an important feature in the OT picture of the last days. For Isa xxxii 15 the coming of those times is described as when "the spirit is poured on us from on high." In Joel ii 28–29 we hear the promise that in those days, "I will pour out my spirit upon all flesh." In several passages the themes of water and spirit are joined as they are in John iii 5; for example, in Ezek xxxvi 25–26 Yahweh had said: "I will sprinkle clean water upon you . . . a new heart will I give you and a new spirit will I put within you . . . I will put my spirit within you" (also Isa xliv 3). The connection between the gift of the spirit and becoming children of God is found in the 2nd century B.C. in Jub i 23–25: "I will create in them a holy spirit and I will cleanse them . . . I will be their Father and they shall be my children." In Nicodemus' own time, all who entered the Qumran Essene community heard this description of the day of divine visitation when God would root out the spirit of falsehood from man: "He will cleanse him of all wicked deeds by means of a holy spirit; like purifying waters He will sprinkle upon him the spirit of truth" (1QS iv 19–21). Thus, while Nicodemus could not have been expected to understand the particular aspect of the Spirit that is proper to Jesus' teaching, at least Jesus' words should have meant for him that the eschatological outpouring of the Spirit was at hand, preparing man for entrance into God's kingdom.

As we continue in John, vs. 6 gives another aspect of Johannine dualism: flesh and Spirit are contrasted, just as begetting in an earthly sense was contrasted with begetting from above. The contrast between flesh and Spirit has nothing to do with the contrast between body and soul that flows from Greek anthropological dualism; nor has it anything to do with a contrast between material and spiritual, for in John there is no Gnostic distrust of the material as such. "Flesh" refers to man as he is born into this world; and in this state he has something both of the material and of the spiritual, as Gen ii 7 insists. The contrast between flesh and Spirit is that between mortal man (in the Hebrew expression, "a son of man") and a son of God, between man as he is and man as Jesus can make him by giving him a holy Spirit.

Verses 7–8 admit that there is something mysterious about this begetting from above through the Spirit. One need not be surprised at this, for all that comes from God has an element of mystery. A simile is given, not to explain the precise character of the mystery, but to show that the fact of mystery does not in any way take away from the reality of the Spirit's action. It is not surprising that being begotten through *pneuma* (Spirit) is mysterious; for, although we can see the effects of *pneuma* (wind—see NOTE on vs. 8) all about us, no one can actually see the *pneuma* (wind) that causes these effects. So too one can see those who are begotten from above through *pneuma* (Spirit), those who have accepted Jesus, without seeing just when or how this *pneuma* (Spirit) begets them, and without knowing why one man accepts Jesus and another does not. We may add that the inability of men to know where the *pneuma* comes from or where it goes is not unlike the ignorance of men about where Jesus comes from or where he is going (e.g., vii 35). The Spirit is the Spirit of Jesus; both the Spirit and Jesus are from above, and therefore they are mysterious to men from below.

The simile of the wind is not original with John. We find something similar in Eccles xi 5: "As you do not know how the spirit comes to the bones in the womb [or: As you do not know the way of the wind, or how the bones grow in the womb], so you do not know the work of God who does all things." The confusion as to whether Ecclesiastes means "spirit" or "wind" is not unlike the ambiguity of John iii 8. Dodd, *Tradition*, pp. 364–65, compares the simile in vs. 8 with a line in the little parable of Mark iv 26–29: "the seed sprouts and grows without the man who planted it knowing how." Both are parabolic sayings based on the recognition of the spontaneity and inscrutability of the natural process. This is another indication that the discourse with Nicodemus has verses that seem to reflect early tradition.

Addendum to Division 1. The Baptismal Interpretation of vs. 5

Thus far we have interpreted Jesus' discourse to Nicodemus on a level that Nicodemus himself could have understood against a background of OT ideas about sonship, spirit, etc. However, there can be little doubt that the Christian readers of John would have interpreted vs. 5, "being begotten of water and Spirit," as a reference to Christian Baptism; and so we have a secondary level of sacramental reference. Needless to say, if we think of John iii as based on a historical scene, Nicodemus could have understood nothing of Christian Baptism or of the theology of rebirth associated with it. At most, if it were well known that Jesus was a baptizer like John the Baptist (iii 26), Nicodemus could have understood the reference to water in terms of this type of baptism. Or else Jewish proselyte baptism could have come to his mind, a custom wherein the baptized proselyte was compared to a new-born child (the custom of proselyte baptism seems to have taken hold in Judaism some time in the 1st century A.D.). Neither of these baptisms is the same as Christian Baptism, so we must investigate a level of understanding that goes beyond the historical scene envisaged in the narrative.

Since the allusion to Baptism hinges on the phrase "of water" in vs. 5, the question comes up as to whether we are to consider this phrase as belonging to the earliest tradition of the scene or as a later addition. Some ask whether it was spoken by Jesus or added by the evangelist. Others (often those who take it for granted that the whole discourse is purely Johannine composition and that none of it was spoken by Jesus of Nazareth) ask whether the phrase was part of the evangelist's work or was added by the redactor. For Bultmann, for instance, the phrase is the contribution of the Ecclesiastical Redactor who was attempting to introduce sacramentalism into the Gospel. Among those who regard it as a later addition in one form or another are K. Lake, Wellhausen, Lohse, and an increasing number of Catholics, for example: Braun, Léon-Dufour, Van den Bussche, Feuillet, Leal, De la Potterie, who propose the theory of addition with varying shades of probability.

Since there is no textual evidence whatsoever against the genuineness of the phrase "of water," what makes scholars think that it is a later addition to the Johannine tradition? *First,* the phrase does not seem to fit in with the ideas and words in the context. This is the only reference to water in the whole discourse. If we omit the phrase, vs. 5 then reads "without being begotten of Spirit"; and this is a better parallel in length and form to vs. 3, "without being begotten from above," than the present reading of 5. The ideas of 5 are developed in 6–8, but in those verses there is mention only of Spirit, and not of water. Indeed, 8 almost repeats 5 when it speaks of "everyone begotten of the Spirit," and it does not mention water. These observations carry weight.

A *second* argument used against the originality of the phrase "of water" is theological. The objection that Nicodemus could not have understood the phrase and that therefore it was not part of the original tradition is weak. We have shown above that many of the OT passages which mention the outpouring of the spirit also mention water; thus water and spirit do go together. Moreover, several other passages in the Johannine works join water and Spirit (vii 38–39; I John v 8), and so vs. 5 is not an isolated instance. If the phrase "of water" were part of the original form of the discourse, then it would have been understood by Nicodemus against the OT background rather than in terms of Christian Baptism.

The *third* argument is based on the presupposed anti-sacramentalism of the evangelist; this means that all references to the sacraments have to be attributed to the Ecclesiastical Redactor. We have rejected this view in the Introduction, and we find it particularly unconvincing here. The phrase "of water" is not the only reference to Baptism in this scene, and so its presence cannot be explained as an isolated act of censorship. The Nicodemus discourse is followed immediately by a story in which it is emphasized that both John the Baptist and Jesus were *baptizing*. We shall see that this story is not in real chronological sequence to the Nicodemus discourse, and one of the most plausible reasons for its having been placed where it now stands is precisely because its baptismal motif matched that of the Nicodemus scene. Another suggestion of a reference to Baptism is found in the verb "to be begotten" in vss. 3 and 5; as we saw in the NOTE, this verb could also have been understood by the early Christians in the sense "to be born." (Bultmann, p. 96, even suggests that this was the meaning intended by the evangelist.) The theme of "being born [again]" is a baptismal theme in I Pet i 23 (cf. "rebirth" in Titus iii 5). The fact that the early versions translated John iii 3 and 5 in terms of being born again means that from the earliest days this passage was thought of in a baptismal context. For the early baptismal use of iii 5 in catacomb art and inscriptions see F.-M. Braun, RThom 56 (1956), 647–48.

When all these arguments are weighed, we find no certainty. The baptismal motif that is woven into the text of the whole scene is secondary; the phrase "of water" in which the baptismal motif expresses itself most clearly may have been always part of the scene, although originally not having a specific reference to Christian Baptism; or the phrase may have been added to the tradition later in order to bring out the baptismal motif.

In favor of the former alternative we may add the example of a Synoptic saying of Jesus which seems to have been reinterpreted as a reference to Baptism. We speak of Matt xviii 3 (Mark x 15; Luke xviii 17): "Unless you turn and become like children, you will never enter the kingdom of heaven." This verse is so close to what we have in John iii 3, 5 (becoming children= being begotten; in both verses this is the requirement for entering the kingdom of heaven) that Bernard and J. Jeremias think they are variants of the same saying of Jesus. Dodd, *Tradition*, pp. 358–59, is inclined to agree; and he thinks that John's form of the saying comes from an earlier, independent form of the tradition, rather than from any adaptation of Matthew. J. Dupont, *Les Béatitudes* (Louvain: Nauwelaerts, 1954), pp. 150–58, argues that the original meaning of the Matthean saying was a demand to become one of the *anawim,* that is, those humble who are dependent on God, the remnant who had prepared themselves for God's messianic intervention and who are represented in the NT by the poor, the outcast, the sick, and little children. The disposition of dependence on God, symbolized by becoming little children, predisposed one to accept Jesus and thus enter the kingdom. However, the Matthean saying was reinterpreted in terms of Baptism, so that to "become like little children" meant to be baptized; for proofs see J. Jeremias, *Infant Baptism in the First Four Centuries* (London: SCM, 1960), pp. 48–52. It is interesting to note that Justin *Apology* I 61 (PG 6:420) seems to cite a combined form of the Matthean and Johannine sayings: "Unless you are reborn, you shall not enter the kingdom of heaven." The 4th-century *Apostolic Constitutions* adapts John freely, "Unless a man is baptized of water and Spirit, he shall not enter the kingdom of heaven" (VI 3:15).

One more problem must be discussed. On the level of baptismal interpretation what relationship does John iii 5 envisage between water and Spirit? Is the begetting of Spirit accomplished through the begetting of water? Or are the two the same action (the Greek has but one preposition)? Or are there two separate and equal begettings? In short, there are several possibilities: identification, subordination, co-ordination. For a complete history of the interpretation see De la Potterie, pp. 418–25. An added complication has entered the discussion from the use of this text in Protestant-Catholic disputes about the necessity for salvation of Baptism by water. For example, Calvin maintained that real water was not necessarily involved, but that "water" indicates the purifying action of the Spirit. This view, attacked by the Anglican Westcott in his commentary (p. 49), was condemned by Session VII of the Council of Trent (DB, § 858).

Fortunately for our purposes here, such theological disputes about the universal necessity of Baptism by water, and the corresponding existence of limbo for unbaptized infants, go beyond the direct scope of the text, which is what interests the exegete. Accepting "water" at its face value, we do not think there is enough evidence in the Gospel itself to determine the relation between begetting of water and begetting of Spirit on the level of sacramental interpretation. Begetting of Spirit, while it includes accepting Jesus by faith, is primarily the communication of the Holy Spirit. If we take iii 5 as a reference to Baptism and faith, then begetting of water and Spirit are two co-ordinate exigencies for entering the kingdom of God. If we take vs. 5 as a reference to Baptism and the giving of the Spirit (note that John mentions Spirit after water), then John may be thinking of the communication of the Spirit through Baptism.

Division 2a. The Son must ascend to the Father (iii 9–15)

Thus far Nicodemus has heard that entrance into God's kingdom requires the eschatological outpouring of the Spirit and is something that man cannot accomplish on his own. In vs. 9 he asks another question; this time his question does not concern man's role as did vs. 4, but the action of God from above and through the Spirit. That there is an element of incredulity in the question may explain the hint of sarcasm in Jesus' answer in vs. 10 (see NOTES). With this question, Nicodemus' role in the scene has been played; like so many of the characters in the Johannine discourses he has served as a foil whose misunderstanding or failure to understand causes Jesus to expound his revelation in detail. As Jesus launches into the long explanation of vss. 11–21, Nicodemus fades off into the darkness whence he came. The dialogue becomes a monologue; and Jesus alone holds the stage, his light shining out into the darkness and attracting men to come to him and become sons of God (vss. 19–21).

In the mention of testimony in vs. 11 the legal element of which we spoke above (p. 45) reappears. Nicodemus' incredulity is spoken of as an instance of a wider failure to accept Jesus' testimony. Jesus has spoken of begetting from above; well he is in a position to know of this, for he has come from above. Despite Nicodemus' failure to understand what must happen to man in order to enable him to enter the kingdom of God ("earthly things"; see NOTE on vs. 12), Jesus will answer Nicodemus' question about how such things happen by speaking of the heavenly origins of this begetting through the Spirit. And Jesus insists that he is the only one who can do so since no one else has ever gone up into heaven.

As we pointed out in the NOTE, there are various interpretations of vs. 13, but it means at least that Jesus is the only one who has ever been in heaven because he came down from heaven. What about the legends concerning the various apocalyptic seers who were supposed to have been taken in vision up to heaven (Daniel, Enoch, Baruch)? We may remember also that Moses was thought to have seen heavenly things on Mount Sinai and to have been admitted into heaven after his death. Evidently Jesus refuses to be put on a plane with these heavenly pilgrims; his association with heaven is much more profound than what had been given by a vision. Some OT texts are interesting in this regard. In Prov xxx 3–4 the author denies that he possesses divine knowledge: "Who has ascended to heaven and comes down? Who has gathered the wind in his fists?" (Note the collocation of the secret of the wind and ascension into heaven.) Wisdom ix 16–18 has a similar idea: "We can hardly fathom the things upon the earth . . . but when things are in heaven, who can search them out . . . except you give wisdom and send your holy spirit from on high?" Baruch iii 29 asks, "Who has gone up to heaven and got her [Wisdom] and brought her down from the clouds?" (Also Deut xxx 12.) Thus it is quite clear that the privilege that Jesus is claiming in vs. 13 goes beyond the lot of men; this verse is another way of stating what is found elsewhere in John, namely, that only Jesus has seen God (i 18, v 37, vi 46, xiv 7–9). See vi 62 where Jesus answers another objection to the mysteriousness of his teaching by speaking of the Son of Man's ascension to heaven.

In vss. 14–15 Jesus proceeds to the actual answer to Nicodemus' question, "How can things like this happen?" Begetting through the Spirit can come about only as a result of Jesus' crucifixion, resurrection, and ascension. Verse 14 is the first of three statements in John referring to Jesus' being "lifted up" (viii 28, xii 32–34). The phrase "to be lifted up" refers to Jesus' death on the cross. This is clear not only from the comparison with the serpent on the pole in vs. 14, but also from the explanation in xii 33. Bernard, I, p. 114, argues that this is the only meaning of the phrase.

However, the verb *hypsoun*, "to be lifted up," is used in Acts (ii 33, v 31) for references to the ascension of Jesus. In Hebrew there is a twofold use of *nasāh* ("to lift up") which can cover both meanings of death and glorification, as in Gen xl 13 and 19; Aram. *zᵉqap* means both "to crucify, hang" and "to raise up." Thus, in John "being lifted up" refers to one continuous action of ascent: Jesus begins his return to his Father as he approaches death (xiii 1) and completes it only with his ascension (xx 17). It is the upward swing of the great pendulum of the Incarnation corresponding to the descent of the Word which became flesh. The first step in the ascent is when Jesus is lifted up on the cross; the second step is when he is raised up from death; the final step is when he is lifted up to heaven. This wider understanding of "being lifted up" explains a statement like viii 28: "When you lift up the Son of Man, you will realize that I AM." The justice of Jesus' claim to the divine name "I AM" (see App. IV) was scarcely evident at the crucifixion; it was recognized only after the resurrection and ascension (xx 28). Nor was the claim in xii 32 verified in the crucifixion alone: "When I am lifted up from the earth, I shall draw all men to myself."

We have mentioned that there are three statements concerning the "lifting up" of the Son of Man in John. There has been a strong tendency among scholars to write off these statements with their peculiarly Johannine phrasing as the creations of the evangelist. However, these statements are the Johannine equivalents of the three predictions of the passion, death, and resurrection found in all the Synoptics (Mark viii 31, ix 31, x 33–34, and par.). The mention of the Son of Man is common to both groups of sayings. If we compare Mark viii 31 and John iii 14, we find in both the "must" that implies the divine will: "So *must* the Son of Man be lifted up"; "The Son of Man *must* suffer many things, . . . be killed, and after three days rise again." The similarity of these groups of sayings is another reason for insisting that "to be lifted up" in John includes more than the crucifixion. There is no reason to think that the fourth evangelist is dependent on the Synoptics for his form of the sayings; indeed, on a comparative basis the Johannine sayings are far less detailed and could be more ancient. The chief influence on the Johannine sayings seems to be the theme of the Suffering Servant (Isa lii 13): "Behold my servant shall prosper: he shall be lifted up [*hypsoun*] and glorified exceedingly." The statement that the Son of Man *must* be lifted up reflects the theme that his being lifted up was predicted in Scripture (especially Isa lii–liii) and thus was part of God's will.

Verse 15 shows why Jesus introduced into the discourse the imagery of being lifted up, namely, that his being lifted up will lead to the gift of eternal life to all who believe in Jesus. This eternal life is the life of the sons of God, the life begotten from above, the life begotten of the Spirit. When Jesus will be lifted up in crucifixion and ascension, his communication of the Spirit will constitute a flowing source of life for those who believe in him (vii 37–39).

Division 2b. The Necessity of Belief in Jesus, or of Coming to the Light (iii 16–21)

Verse 16 marks a subdivision in the second part of the discourse; and, as Roustang points out, the role of God the Father now becomes prominent. However, we should not exaggerate the change. The theme of Jesus' death, introduced in 14–15, appears again in 16 (see NOTE). Just as that death was portrayed under the OT symbol of the serpent in 14–15, so is there seemingly an implicit reference to the OT in the language of 16. Abraham was commanded to take his *"only"* son Isaac whom he *loved* to offer to the Lord (Gen xxii 2, 12); many scholars (Westcott, Bernard, Barrett, Glasson) think this lies behind: "God *loved* the world so much that He gave the *only* Son." Even the mention of "the world" fits in with this background, for Abraham's generosity in sacrificing his only son was to be beneficial to all the nations of the world (Gen xxii 18; Sir xliv 21; Jub xviii 15). See xix 17 for the possibility of more Isaac typology.

But vs. 16 not only parallels 14–15; it also leads forward to 17. If 16 assures us that the purpose of the Father's giving the Son in Incarnation and death was eternal life for the believer, 17 paraphrases this in terms of salvation for the world. Beginning with 17 we enter into the Johannine theological domain of realized eschatology (see Introduction, Part VIII:C). The very presence of Jesus in the world is a judgment in the sense that it provokes men to judge themselves by deciding either for Jesus or against him.

Boismard, "L'évolution," has made a very interesting comparison of the eschatological theme as it is found in iii 16–19 and xii 46–48. As we shall propose in discussing xii 44–50, that passage is an independent, displaced fragment of Johannine discourse material that for reasons of convenience has been inserted (see above, p. xxxvii) in its present location at the end of the public ministry. At least in part it seems to be a variant form of what we have in chapter iii.

xii	iii
46. As light have I come into the world	19. The light has come into the world
that everyone who believes in me	15. that everyone who believes may have eternal life in him.
	16. that everyone who believes in him may not perish
may not remain in darkness.	
47. I did not come to condemn the world	17. God did not send the Son to condemn the world but that the world might be saved through him.
but to save the world.	
48. Whoever rejects me and does not accept my words already has his judge (*krinein*).	18. Whoever does not believe has already been condemned (*krinein*).

There are noticeable stylistic differences (xii is in the first person); and Boismard thinks that iii is closer to the style of I John (see NOTE on vs 16). Thus, the same basic tradition of Jesus' words may have been preserved by different disciples in the Johannine school. But the important difference is theological. In part, at least, the eschatology in xii is *final* eschatology; xii 48 says of the man who rejects Jesus: "The word that I have spoken—that is what will condemn him *on the last day*." And so, in two Johannine reports of the words of Jesus, the one in iii brings out the realized aspect of his eschatology; the one in xii, the final aspect. We shall find the same phenomenon in v 19–25 and 26–30.

We may study iii 18 along the same lines: "Whoever believes in him is not condemned, but whoever does not believe has already been condemned." Dodd, *Tradition*, pp. 357–58, points out that it is a variant form of the saying that we have in the longer ending of Mark (xvi 16): "Whoever has believed (and been baptized) will be saved; whoever has not believed will be condemned." In Mark it is a post-resurrectional statement referring to future judgment; in John it is in the context of realized eschatology. Again we have a traditional saying of Jesus interpreted in two ways. (We may add that I John v 10, which resembles John iii 18 in several details, seems also to be based on this saying.) It is interesting that the theme of Baptism appears in the Marcan form of the saying, while, as we have insisted, a baptismal motif permeates ch. iii of John.

It should be noted that the dualistic vocabulary of vss. 19–21 (light/darkness; practicing wickedness/doing truth) has remarkable resemblances in the Dead Sea Scrolls, especially in 1QS iii–iv. We have compared Johannine and Qumranian dualism in CBQ 17 (1955), 405–18, 559–61 (now NTE, pp. 105–23), and must refer the reader there for detail. Here we cite only the well-known Qumran division between the sons of light and the sons of darkness, and also the text of 1QS iv 24: "According as man's inheritance is in truth and righteousness, so he hates evil; but insofar as his heritage is in the portion of perversity, so he abominates truth." In comparing this to the very similar thought in John iii 20–21, it is noteworthy that this Qumran passage occurs only a few lines after the passage on the role of water and spirit that we cited above (p. 140) in reference to John iii 5.

If there is a twofold reaction to Jesus in John, we must emphasize that the reaction is very much dependent on man's own choice, a choice that is influenced by his way of life, by whether his deeds are wicked or are done in God (vss. 20–21). There is a consistency in the two sides of the dualism: evildoers are disbelievers, while good works and faith go together. Thus, there is no determinism in John as there seems to be in some passages of the Qumran scrolls. Bultmann, p. 114, points out that the purpose clauses which end vss. 20 and 21 are not to be understood as giving the subjective reason why men come or do not come to the light, that is, a man does not really come to Jesus to have it confirmed that his deeds are good. Rather, the idea is that Jesus brings out what a man really is and the real nature of his life. Jesus is a penetrating light that provokes judgment by making it apparent what a man is. The one who turns away is not an occasional sinner but one who *"practices* wickedness"; it is not that he cannot see the light, but that he hates the light. As S. Lyonnet insists in his article on sin in John (VD 35 [1957], 271–78), it is a question of radical evil.

Addendum to Division 2. The identity of the Speaker.

We have mentioned the view of many scholars that only some verses of this division of chapter iii belong to Jesus' discourse with Nicodemus and the rest are an added commentary by the evangelist. Here we would give in detail our reasons for rejecting such a view. The two principal places suggested within these verses for the change of speaker are vs. 13 (Tillmann, Belser, Schnackenburg) and vs. 16 (Westcott, Lagrange, Bernard, Van den Bussche, Braun, Lightfoot).

Schnackenburg argues strongly that vs. 12 is the last verse of the real discourse. It has the last "you" in this section; 13 treats the ascension as past (see NOTE). However, this view faces many difficulties. Verse 13 begins with a connective (*kai*) as if it were related to what has preceded; there is not the slightest indication of a change of speaker. If one argues from the tense in 13 that the ascension has already taken place, what about the obviously future reference to death, resurrection, and ascension in 14? Verse 14 is one of three Johannine statements about the lifting up of the Son of Man; are we to attribute this one to the evangelist and the next two to Jesus? It is true that in vss. 13 ff. there is a shift into the third person, but this is not unusual in John; in the other places where it occurs there is not the slightest evidence that Jesus has stopped speaking. In the OT, students of Deuteronomy are finally giving up change of person and number as a criterion for change of editor; similar caution should be observed by exegetes of John.

We do not find the arguments for a change of speaker at vs. 16 any more impressive than those advanced for the change at vs. 13. The past tense of "gave" is a difficulty if it refers to the crucifixion; but perhaps on Jesus' lips it was meant to refer only to the Incarnation, and it is the evangelist who has included the whole career of Jesus (see NOTE). We saw that vs. 16 is not to be completely dissociated from 14–15 in theme; and once again 16 starts with a connective (*gar*) that works against any theory of a new speaker. The last clauses of 15 and 16 are the same, and it does seem arbitrary to attribute them to different speakers.

These detailed arguments support our general observations (pp. 136–37) of homogeneity of style and of inclusions that hold the whole passage together. Of course the evangelist has been at work in this discourse, but his work is not of the type that begins at a particular verse. All Jesus' words come to us through the channels of the evangelist's understanding and rethinking, but the Gospel presents Jesus as speaking and not the evangelist.

[The Bibliography for this section is included in the Bibliography at the end of § 12.]

11. THE BAPTIST'S FINAL WITNESS
(iii 22–30)

III 22 Later on Jesus and his disciples came into Judean territory, and he spent some time there with them, baptizing. 23 Now John too was baptizing, at Aenon near Salim where water was plentiful; and people kept coming to be baptized. (24 John, of course, had not yet been thrown into prison.) 25 This led to a controversy about purification between John's disciples and a certain Jew. 26 So they came to John saying, "Rabbi, the man who was with you across the Jordan—the one about whom you have been testifying—well, now he is baptizing, and everybody is flocking to him." 27 John answered,

> "No one can take anything
> unless heaven gives it to him.

28 You yourselves are my witnesses that I said, 'I am not the Messiah, but am sent before him.'

> 29 It is the bridegroom who gets the bride.
> The bridegroom's best man,
> who waits there listening for him,
> is overjoyed just to hear the bridegroom's voice.
> That is my joy, and it is complete.
> 30 He must increase
> while I must decrease."

NOTES

iii 22. *Later on.* A vague connective with no real chronological precision. This whole verse is an itinerary fragment like those that Mark uses to frame a narrative. Dodd, *Tradition*, p. 279, suggests that it is based on precanonical tradition.

Judean territory. Jesus has been in Judea, at Jerusalem. Bultmann, p. 123[8], argues that the real inference is that Jesus went out from the city into the country districts of Judea; and we believe that this could be the adapted meaning in the present context. However, *gē* probably originally meant "territory," not "country district," translating Heb. *'ereṣ;* in iv 3, which can only refer to Judea as a territory, the Western tradition has added *gē*. The site is not given, but many think of the Jordan valley.

spent some time. This is not the usual Johannine *menein*, but *diatribein*. That this is the only occurrence of the verb in John may support Dodd's precanonical theory.

baptizing. The verbs are imperfect, a fact indicating repeated action. Although this verse says that Jesus baptized, iv 2 adds by way of modification that he himself did not baptize. The usual attempt at harmonization maintains that Jesus is said to have baptized in the sense that the disciples baptized in his name. John, of course, gives no hint of this. This baptism is probably not to be thought of as Christian Baptism which in NT thought receives its efficacy from the crucifixion and resurrection; it is baptism like that of John the Baptist.

23. *Aenon.* The name is from the Aramaic plural of the word for "spring," while "Salim" reflects the Semitic root for "peace." There are three important traditions for localizing these sites. (*a*) In Perea, the Transjordan. We know that John the Baptist was active in this region (i 28), and the reference to Judea in vs. 22 may imply that he was close by (Perea is just across the river). The 6th-century mosaic Madeba map (BA 21 [1958, No. 3]) has an Aenon just northeast of the Dead Sea, opposite Bethabara (see NOTE on i 28); there are contemporary pilgrim indications to the same effect. (*b*) In the northern Jordan valley, on the west bank some eight miles south of Scythopolis (Bethshan). In the 4th century Eusebius (*Onomasticon*, in GCS 11[1], p. 40:1–4; p. 153:6–7) has this tradition, as has the pilgrim Aetheria. The Madeba map has another Aenon in this vicinity. Eusebius speaks of Salim in reference to Salumias, and there is a modern Arabic name of Tell Sheikh Salim in the area. There is no remnant of the name Aenon in the area. One objection to both these sites in the Jordan valley is that, with the river Jordan nearby, John's mention of the availability of water seems superfluous. (*c*) In Samaria. Four miles east-southeast of Shechem there is a town of Sâlim known from early times; eight miles northeast of Sâlim lies modern 'Ainûn (1:100,000 map: 187190). In the general vicinity there are many springs, although modern 'Ainûn has no water. W. F. Albright defends this localization in HTR 17 (1924), 193–94. It would agree very well with the strong traditional ties that connect John the Baptist with Samaria.

The usual attempt to dismiss the peculiarly Johannine geographical information as pure symbolism is made here. Krieger, ZNW 45 (1953–54), 122, speaks of fictional springs (Aenon) near salvation (Salim). One may well ask why John would have associated the baptism of John the Baptist and not that of Jesus with the symbolic site of salvation. If we are told that John the Baptist was *near* salvation, that is, near Jesus, then we may ask why Jesus is not placed at Salim, instead of in Judea? Bultmann, p. 124[5], believes that the names are real but that possibly they have a symbolic meaning for the evangelist.

25. *controversy about purification.* The relation of the controversy to what follows in vs. 26 is not clear. Are we to think it was about the relative value of the baptisms of John the Baptist and of Jesus? Or, since the word "purification" reminds us of the water "prescribed for Jewish purifications" in ii 6, are we perhaps to think of a dispute about the relative value of John the Baptist's baptism and of standard Jewish purificatory washings? Was this Jew posing questions about John the Baptist's baptism like those put by the Pharisees in

i 25? Or was there a general controversy about the value of all the types of purification by water (the various baptisms; the washings of the Pharisees; Essene lustrations)?

a certain Jew. There is good evidence, including P66, for the reading "the Jews"; but the best witnesses, including P75, read the singular which is the more difficult reading. The plural may be on the analogy of Mark ii 18 and par. which associate the *Pharisees* and the disciples of John the Baptist on the legal question of fasting. (Boismard, however, accepts the plural, suggesting that the singular *Ioudaiou* is by analogy with *Iōanou*.) If we read the singular, the connection of the verse with what follows is not totally clear. Loisy, p. 171, along with others (Bauer, Goguel), thinks that the text originally read "Jesus," but that pious reasons caused scribes to expunge a reference to a dispute between the disciples of John the Baptist and Jesus. There is no textual support, but the reading would give excellent sense.

26. *Rabbi.* John reflects the memory that John the Baptist was looked on as a teacher, as well as a prophet (Luke xi 1).

about whom. Here and in vs. 28 *martyrein* takes the dative of person, a syntax found in Luke; nineteen other times in John the verb takes *peri.* We shall point out in the COMMENT that these clauses in vss. 26 and 28 are editorial.

everybody is flocking. The Synoptics give us a picture of this success during the Galilean ministry (Mark i 45, iii 7). The universality of Jesus' appeal is found elsewhere in John, e.g., xi 48: "everybody will believe."

27. *unless heaven gives it to him.* Compare with the words to Pilate in xix 11: "You would have no power over me at all unless it were given to you from above."

28. *but am sent before him.* This is not an exact citation of what John the Baptist had said. In i 20 he said, "I am not the Messiah"; but he has not said, "I am sent [*apostellein*] before him [the Messiah]." In i 6 we heard, "There was sent [*apostellein*] by God a man named John" and in i 33 we heard that God sent (*pempein*) John the Baptist to baptize. As for the phrase "before him," John the Baptist has said, "The *one who comes after me* ranks ahead of me." Thus, while the second clause in the quotation of vs. 28 is in the spirit of John the Baptist, it is really only a composite of what he has said. It identifies the one to come after John the Baptist as the Messiah, something that John the Baptist never does elsewhere. Dodd, *Tradition,* p. 271, suggests that "I am sent before him" echoes Mal iii 1: "I send my angel before my face" (see Matt xi 10; Luke vii 27). If this should be true, it was originally simply a designation of John the Baptist's own role, without really implying much about the nature of the one to follow him.

29. *best man.* Literally "the friend of the groom"; see Van Selms, *art. cit.* This is the *shoshben* of Jewish custom, the groom's closest friend who takes care of arranging the wedding. Paul claims this role in II Cor xi 2; and Moses was given this role by the rabbis in the marriage between God and Israel. Because of this special trust any impropriety between the best man and the bride was regarded as particularly heinous (whence Samson's anger at the injustice in Judg xiv 20). Thus John the Baptist, as the best man, could never marry the bride; his only function was to prepare her for Jesus.

hear the bridegroom's voice. The exact picture is not clear. Some think of the best man as at the bride's house, standing guard and waiting to hear the noise of the groom's procession as it comes to fetch the bride. Others picture the best man as at the groom's house after the bride has been brought there; he rejoices to hear the groom speaking with the bride.

In this little parable and the aphorism that follows it, Black, p. 109, has found traces of a number of Aramaic plays on words that indicate a Semitic original, e.g., "bride" is *kalleṭâ;* "voice" is *qâlâ;* "to be complete" is *kelal;* "to decrease" is *qelal.*

30. *must.* The same divine imperative theme that we saw in iii 14.

increase . . . decrease. This verse has played a significant role in the tradition concerning John the Baptist. Just as the birthday of Jesus was fixed at December 25, the time of the winter solstice after which the days *grow longer* (the light has come into the world; he must increase), so John the Baptist's birthday was fixed at June 24, the time of the summer solstice after which the days *grow shorter* (he was not the light; he must decrease). The two Greek verbs in vs. 30 are also used for the waxing and the waning of the light of heavenly bodies.

decrease. The Greek verb *elattoun* is related to *elassōn,* the adjective "inferior" used to describe the ordinary wine at Cana (ii 10). Thus, there are three parallels between iii 22–30 and the Cana scene: (*a*) "purification" in 25; (*b*) the marriage theme; and (*c*) this vocabulary similarity. It seems adventurous, however, to regard these rather incidental parallels as theologically significant. They are interesting, however, in view of the possibility (to be mentioned in the COMMENT) that the material in iii 22–30 once immediately preceded the Cana scene.

COMMENT: GENERAL

This scene is a difficult one because, externally, its sequence is poor and, internally, the logic of the story is not clear (see NOTE on vs. 25). Let us consider here the problems of sequence caused by the context. Jesus has been in Jerusalem of Judea according to ch. ii; yet now he comes into Judea. Verse 24 mentions that John the Baptist has not yet been arrested; the verse is a parenthetical addition of the redactor inserted to avoid objections based on a chronology like that of the Synoptics. According to Mark i 14 (Matt iv 12), Jesus went to Galilee to begin his ministry only after John the Baptist had been arrested; but in John, Jesus has already been to Galilee and to Jerusalem and still John the Baptist has not been arrested. It is true that the Synoptics do not tell us exactly when John the Baptist was arrested, so that all that John has narrated might have occurred before the official opening of the Galilean ministry (John does not fully describe a Galilean ministry). Nevertheless, the impression gained from the Synoptics is that the Galilean ministry opened immediately after the baptism of Jesus and that the arrest of John the Baptist also was closely associated with the baptism (especially Luke iii 19–20). An even greater sequential difficulty is raised by vs. 26. The disciples of John the Baptist have heard their master testify eloquently to Jesus in ch. i: Jesus is the Lamb of God; John the Baptist's whole purpose in baptizing was that Jesus might be revealed to Israel. Yet now they cannot understand why people are coming to Jesus and they resent it. Notice that this cannot be explained away by saying that these are other disciples than those of ch. i, for vs. 28 specifically identifies them as disciples who had heard John the Baptist's message about Jesus.

Some scholars like Wellhausen and Goguel have thought that iii 22–30 is a doublet of the scene in ch. i where John the Baptist identified Jesus as the one to come after him. Certainly the themes are much the same.

(a) i 19–21: John the Baptist is not the Messiah, Elijah or the prophet

    iii 28: John the Baptist is not the Messiah

(b) i 30: John the Baptist is preparing for the one to come after him

    iii 28: John the Baptist is sent before him

(c) i 30: The one to come after John the Baptist ranks ahead of John the Baptist

    iii 30: He must increase while John the Baptist must decrease

(d) i 31: John the Baptist has been given the role of revealing him to Israel

    iii 29: John the Baptist is the best man arranging the marriage of the bride and groom

Nevertheless, while the themes are the same, the actual conversation is quite different. Rather than variants of the same scene, we seem to have here fragments of a larger Johannine tradition about John the Baptist, a tradition that has been split up into the scenes in chs. i and iii. Boismard, "Les traditions," thinks that this scene in iii was the original beginning of the Gospel before it was replaced by the present opening (see above, pp. 68–70). This theory is more precise than the evidence warrants; but Boismard seems to be on the right track in maintaining that iii 22–30 belongs to the *opening* relations between John the Baptist and Jesus, rather than in the sequence in which the scene now appears.

Let us see how placing iii 22–30 in the same setting as ch. i solves the difficulties of sequence that we have mentioned. (In this theory the clause set off by dashes in vs. 26 and the whole of vs. 28 must be thought of as additions made by the redactor to adapt the scene to the final setting in which he placed it—see NOTES.) Jesus comes into Judean territory (vs. 22), not after having been at Jerusalem with Nicodemus, but toward the beginning of the Gospel narrative. We hear similar statements in the Synoptic tradition in relation to the time of Jesus' baptism: "Jesus came from Galilee to the Jordan" (Matt iii 13); "There went out to him [John the Baptist] all the country of Judea" (Mark i 5). The puzzled hostility of the disciples of John the Baptist toward Jesus can be understood if Jesus is just appearing on the scene and John the Baptist has not yet given to all his disciples the testimony to Jesus of which we hear in ch. i. Verses 27, 29–30 belong to the same general type of initial testimony to Jesus that appears in i 29–34.

If we are pressed to reconstruct even further the relations between i 19–34 and iii 22–30, we may suggest that the scene in iii 22–30 originally followed shortly after that of i 19–34. John the Baptist is no longer at Bethany across the Jordan but at Aenon near Salim. Jesus, who was baptized by John the Baptist, is now in the Jordan valley conducting his own ministry of baptism and followed by the disciples (iii 22) whom John the Baptist had sent to him. In iii 22–30 we have John the Baptist's testimony at Aenon to another group of his disciples. This all takes place before Jesus' ministry in

Galilee, where he will abandon the baptizing ministry and begin to concentrate on teaching. It is precisely that change in the way Jesus was conducting himself (a change that took place after John the Baptist was imprisoned) which led John the Baptist to send from prison to inquire if, after all, Jesus was really the one to come (Luke vii 20). Thus, we believe that iii 22–30, if understood properly, gives us very reliable information about the early days of Jesus, material not preserved in the Synoptics but which Dodd, *Tradition*, pp. 279–87, correctly classifies as very ancient. There is no plausible theological reason why anyone would have invented the tradition that Jesus and his disciples once baptized. The practice of Christian Baptism certainly did not need such support; and, as a matter of fact, the information that Jesus once imitated John the Baptist in baptizing would be a dangerous weapon in the hands of the sectarians of John the Baptist (whence probably the modification in iv 2).

Why has this scene been transposed from the beginning of the Gospel to its present site and adapted (in vss. 26 and 28) to make it fit? Perhaps the editing of ch. i to work out the theological pattern of the training of the disciples on a series of days resulted in the displacement of what we now have in iii 22–30. But also the present location probably reflects a desire to bring out the baptismal motif of the Nicodemus story. We shall find another example in vi 51–59 of how the desire to underline the sacramental motif of a scene (already, but only subtly, present) led to the localizing of a displaced fragment of Johannine tradition.

COMMENT: DETAILED

The basic message of the scene is found in what John the Baptist says of Jesus in vss. 27, 29–30 (which should be read as a unit without vs. 28). Verse 27 is a rather cryptic aphorism justifying Jesus' greater success. Our first question concerning vs. 27 is whether the people are represented as coming to John the Baptist or to Jesus. Does vs. 27 mean that if only a few people come to John the Baptist, that is all that God has given him? Or does it mean that if many people come to Jesus, it is because God has ordained it thus? The difference is not very significant, but the latter does seem more probable. Yet even if vs. 27 does refer in general to the coming of people to Jesus, there are still two variations, as Boismard, "L'ami," p. 290, points out: **(a)** the "him" of 27 is the believer; the "it" is the privilege of coming to Jesus. No one can come to Jesus unless God directs him. Faith or coming to Jesus is God's gift to the believer. This resembles vi 65: "No one can come to me unless it be granted to him by the Father." **(b)** The "him" of 27 is Jesus; the "it" is the believer. No one can come to Jesus unless God gives him to Jesus. The believer is God's gift to Jesus. This resembles vi 37: "Whatever the Father gives to me will come to me" (note: the neuter refers to believers). The theme that the Father has given believers to Jesus is frequent in John (iii 35, vi 39, x 29, xvii 2, 9, 11, 24).

Since vs. 27 is meant to contrast the different roles of John the Baptist and of Jesus, a direct reference to Jesus (*b*) seems more plausible, as Boismard maintains.

The fact that God has given all these followers to Jesus causes John the Baptist to assess his own role in vs. 29 by means of a parabolic saying (Dodd, *Tradition*, pp. 282–83). The use of figurative language is attributed to John the Baptist in the Synoptics too (Matt iii 10, 12) and indeed would be expected of a prophetic figure. We find this same parabolic theme of the bridegroom on Jesus' own lips early in the Synoptic tradition (as well as in the parables of Matt xxii 1, xxv 1). When he is asked why John the Baptist's disciples fast while his own do not, Jesus answers, "Can the wedding guests fast while the bridegroom is with them?" (Mark ii 18–19 and par.). Both of these parabolic references to the bridegroom may have been traditional wisdom sayings before they were used in the context of the Gospels (see NOTE on vs. 29 for Aramaisms). Both parables as they appear in the Gospels compare the situation of Jesus and that of the bridegroom; and both seem to reflect the well-known OT theme of the marriage between God and Israel (Hos i–ii; Jer ii 2; Isa lxi 10; Song of Solomon). As Taylor, p. 210, recognizes in discussing Mark, Jesus is the messianic bridegroom of Israel. This theme becomes explicit in another work of the Johannine school (Rev xix 7, xxi 2) under the imagery of the marriage of the Lamb, but it is already anticipated in John iii 29. Now that John the Baptist has prepared the bride for Jesus' coming (i 31), he has only to fade into the background.

That John the Baptist's work is over and his destiny is to decrease is a note that we did not find in ch. i, but in iii 30 (and already in the parenthetical vs. 24) it is very clear. The last line of vs. 29 tells us that John the Baptist accepted his role and destiny with joy, the same joy that Rev xix 7 associates with the marriage of the Lamb. The words of vs. 30, as the last words spoken by John the Baptist in this Gospel, are very appropriate. It is not unlikely that their preservation was by way of answer to the sectarians of John the Baptist. Verse 30 with its contrast between increase and decrease is not too far removed from the Synoptic report of Jesus' estimation of the relative merit of John the Baptist (Matt xi 11; Luke vii 28): "Among those born of women none is greater than John; yet he who is least in the kingdom of heaven is greater than John."

It is Augustine with his epigrammatic flair (*In Jo.* XIII 12; PL 35:1498) who has best captured the Johannine contrast between John the Baptist and Jesus:

I listen; he is the one who speaks; (iii 29)
I am enlightened; he is the light; (i 6–9)
I am the ear; he is the Word. (iii 29)

[The Bibliography for this section is included in the Bibliography at the end of § 12.]

12. THE DISCOURSE CONCLUDED
(iii 31–36)

III 31 "The one who comes from above is above all;
the one who is of the earth is earthly,
and he speaks on an earthly plane.

The one who comes from heaven [(who) is above all]
32 testifies to what he has seen and heard,
but no one accepts his testimony.
33 Whoever does accept his testimony
has certified that God is truthful.

34 For the one whom God has sent
speaks the words of God;
truly boundless is his gift of the Spirit.
35 The Father loves the Son
and has handed over all things to him.

36 Whoever believes in the Son
has eternal life.
Whoever disobeys the Son
will not see life,
but must endure God's wrath."

NOTES

iii 31. *The one who comes.* John the Baptist uses this as a title for the one whom he is expecting; see NOTE on i 30. Also Matt xi 3; Luke vii 19: "Are you the one to come?"

from above. Here *anōthen* (see NOTE on iii 3) clearly means "from above," since it is in parallelism with "from heaven" in the same verse.

is above all. Rom ix 5 speaks of "Christ [who is?] God *over all*, blessed for ever." It is difficult to decide whether the "all" in John is masculine (above all teachers) or neuter (above all things). John probably means above the whole realm of man.

of the earth. "Earth" in John does not usually have the implication of hostility that "world" has (see App. I:7). It refers to the natural level of man's existence (God created man of the dust *of the earth*—LXX of Gen ii 7) as contrasted with the supernatural or heavenly. The "world" has the cloak of Satanic hostility about it (I John v 19). To illustrate the difference (which is not always preserved) we may contrast "one who is *of the earth*" in our present passage with the false prophets and antichrists of I John iv 5 who are "of the world and speak on a worldly plane." As a parallel for John iii 31 we may cite IV Ezra iv 21: "Those who dwell on earth can understand only what is on earth, while those who are above the heavens can understand what is above the heavenly heights."

on an earthly plane. Literally "of earth."

[(*who*) *is above all*]. There are two possible readings for the end of vs. 31 and beginning of vs. 32: (a) "The one who comes from heaven is above all; what he has seen and heard, this is what he testifies to." (b) "The one who comes from heaven testifies to what he has seen and heard." The witnesses for the two readings are about evenly divided, as are the Bodmer papyri (with P[75], curiously enough, on the side of the Western witnesses). There are good logical arguments for both readings.

32. *seen and heard.* "Seen" is perfect in tense, while "heard" is aorist; BDF, § 342[2], says that such a combination of tenses puts the emphasis on "seeing." We have an interesting parallel in I John i 3, "What we have seen and heard we proclaim in turn to you," where both tenses are perfect. In I John human witnesses are involved, and "seeing" and "hearing" are on an even plane.

33. *certified.* Literally "sealed"; the metaphor is one of setting a seal indicating approval on a legal document. See vi 27 where "setting a seal" means to accredit. This use of "seal" may be more Semitic (*ḥātam*) than Greek.

34. *boundless.* Literally "not by measure"; although *ek metrou* is not found elsewhere in Greek writings, the equivalent expression, "by measure," is not uncommon in rabbinic literature. In the Midrash Rabbah on Lev xv 2, Rabbi Aḥa says, "The Holy Spirit rested on the prophets by measure." If a similar idea is behind the statement in John, then Jesus is being contrasted with the prophets (as in Heb i 1). However, the statement may simply mean that with Jesus we have the definitive eschatological outpouring of the Spirit.

his gift. Literally "not by measure *does he give* [present tense]." Some later manuscripts identify the subject of the giving: "does *God* give"; but this is probably a scribal attempt at clarification. In the COMMENT we shall discuss the problem of whether the "he" represents the Father or the Son. We may note, however, that gifts from the Father to the Son are normally expressed in John by the perfect (17 times) or the aorist (8 times), and only once by the present tense (vi 37). Thus, the use of the present tense here suggests that the Son is the giver. For a study of the verb "to give" (*didonai*) in John see C.-J. Pinto de Oliviera, RSPT 49 (1965), 81–104.

of the Spirit. This phrase is omitted in the original of Codex Vaticanus and OS[sin]; Bultmann, p. 119[1], thinks the omission may be original.

35. *loves.* The verb is *agapan*, while in v 20 it is *philein*.

handed over all things to him. Literally "given into his hand"; also in xiii 3 with the plural, "hands."

36. *disobeys.* The Latin tradition reads "disbelieves" on the analogy of iii 18 and because this gives a better contrast to "believes" in the first line of vs. 36. "Disobeys," the more difficult reading, occurs only here in John; its introduction by scribes is not easily explained, and so it is probably original.

see life. In iii 3 we heard of "seeing" the kingdom of God; eternal life and the kingdom of God are closely allied concepts for John.

must endure God's wrath. Literally "God's wrath remains on him"; the present tense indicates that punishment has begun and will last. The Synoptics use the phrase "the wrath to come" in John the Baptist's prediction of what will happen when the one for whom he is preparing comes. For John this eschatological theme is realized here and now.

COMMENT: GENERAL

The most prominent problem in these verses concerns the speaker. Since John the Baptist was the last speaker (vss. 27–30) and no change of speaker has been indicated, some scholars (Bauer, Barrett) believe that he is still speaking. In this interpretation John the Baptist is contrasting himself to Jesus in vs. 31; and the reference to the "gift of the Spirit" in 34 probably describes Jesus' baptizing of which we heard in 22 (see also the contrast between John the Baptist's baptism and Jesus' baptism implied in i 26 and 33). Black, p. 109, points out that there are Aramaic features in 31 ff., just as there were in 29–30 (see NOTE on vs. 29); this might imply a continuity between the two passages. However, the Aramaisms he finds in 31 ff. are not impressive and are dependent on emending the Greek (see Barrett, p. 188).

An even stronger case can be made for Jesus as the speaker (Schnackenburg, *art. cit.*). Some of those who do accept Jesus as the speaker transpose iii 31–36 so that it becomes part of the Nicodemus discourse and comes before iii 22–30 (so Bernard and Bultmann). However, as Dodd, *Interpretation*, p. 309, points out, even if vss. 31–36 are placed after 1–21, the connection between 21 and 31 remains awkward; the theme of 31–36 is closer to that of 11–15 than to that of 21. Gourbillon, *art. cit.*, thinks 31–36 originally followed iii 13, and that it was displaced when 14–21 was brought in and added to 13.

Lagrange, p. 96, thinks of the evangelist as the speaker in 31–36; he thinks that just as 16–21 was the evangelist's commentary on the Nicodemus scene, so 31–36 is the evangelist's commentary on the scene concerning John the Baptist (22–30).

Amid all these theories it should be clearly observed that the discourse in vss. 31–36 resembles closely the style of speech attributed to Jesus in the Gospel, and in particular it has close parallels in Jesus' words to Nicodemus:

- "from above" in vss. 3, 7, and 31.
- "the one who comes [came] down from heaven" in 13 and 31.
- dualistic contrasts like flesh/Spirit in 6 (earthly/heavenly in 12), and "from above"/"of earth" in 31.
- testifying to what has been seen in 11 and 32.
- failure to accept this testimony in 11 and 32.
- "the one [Son] whom God has sent" in 17 and 34.
- the theme of the Spirit in 5–8 and 34.
- "Whoever believes in the Son has eternal life" in 15, 16, and 36.

■ dualism between "whoever believes" and "whoever disbelieves [disobeys]" in 18 and 36.

No such close parallels can be advanced between vss. 31–36 and the words of John the Baptist. We suggest that in 31–36 we may well have still a third variant of the discourse of Jesus found in 11–21 and also in xii 44–50 (see above, p. 147).

If vss. 31–36 do represent a discourse of Jesus, why would an editor have inserted it where it is now found, namely, after words by John the Baptist and without an introduction? That a discourse of Jesus can be added without an extensive introduction we can clearly see in the instance of xii 44–50; however, there Jesus is at least identified as the speaker. Some have suggested that an editor saw the close relationship of 31–36 to the Nicodemus scene and wanted to place it nearby; however, this does not explain why it was added after iii 30 instead of after iii 21. The best solution seems to be Dodd's, namely, that the editor wanted to use 31–36 to recapitulate the whole of iii 1–30 and to summarize both the Nicodemus and the John the Baptist scenes. If the editor regarded the words as pertaining to the John the Baptist scene as well, then his failure to indicate a break between vss. 30 and 31 may be somewhat more intelligible.

Thus, we believe that what was once an isolated discourse of Jesus (treating much the same themes as in iii 11–21 and xii 44–50) has been attached to the scenes of ch. iii as an interpretation of those scenes. Many problems about the interpretation of individual verses in 31–36 can be solved if we recognize two levels of meaning corresponding to the two stages in the history of this discourse.

COMMENT: DETAILED

The real parallel for the dualism of vs. 31 is the contrast between flesh and spirit in vs. 6, for vs. 31 is another reference to the radical inability of the natural to raise itself. The only help is from the one who comes from above, that is, Jesus. However, if vs. 31 was originally a general contrast between earthly and heavenly, has it taken on an additional and more precise meaning in its present context? There is an ancient dispute as to whether "the one who comes from above" and "the one who is of the earth" were meant to contrast Jesus and John the Baptist. Origen says (*In Jo. Frag.* xlix; GCS 10:523–24) that the heretics thought that John the Baptist was "the one who is of the earth"; yet John Chrysostom did not hesitate to make the identification (*In Jo. Hom.* xxx; PG 59:171). Schnackenburg doubts that in Johannine thought John the Baptist would be designated as "of the earth," since he was a man sent by God (i 6). However, as we pointed out in the NOTE, there is nothing hostile about "of the earth." This comparison would be no more unfavorable to John the Baptist than some of the others we have seen (*forerunner to the one to come; not worthy to unfasten his sandal straps; baptizing with water as contrasted with baptizing with a holy Spirit; best man to the bridegroom; destined to decrease while he increases).*

It would be quite consistent both with John's conception of John the Baptist and with the polemic against the sectarians of John the Baptist to insist that John the Baptist and his baptism were radically impotent to give eternal life. That is why I John v 6 insists that Jesus did not come in water only; the power to beget from above can come only through water *and Spirit* (John iii 5), and the Spirit is the gift of the one from above. John the Baptist may, like the prophets of old, have been sent by God; but he is not "from above," for that term applies to Jesus alone (iii 13). Thus, there is no real objection to the suggestion that in placing vss. 31–36 where they now stand, the editor intended to contrast Jesus and John the Baptist and their respective baptisms.

The theme of vs. 32 is the same as that of 11: the failure of Jesus' audience to accept his testimony even though he has come from above and knows whereof he speaks. The "no one" is not categorical, as the next verse (33) shows. Verse 33 takes on added significance against the background of 26, which reported that everyone was flocking to Jesus to be baptized. If the Nicodemus scene justified the pessimism of 32, then the success reported in the John the Baptist scene justifies the affirmative character of 33. Verse 33 also points out the relationship that borders on identity between Jesus' testimony and the Father's truth. I John v 9–10 will state that God Himself has given testimony about His Son, and whoever does not believe has made *God* a liar. This is why Jesus can say in xiv 6, "I am the truth," and can insist that it is through him that the Father is known by men (xiv 9). This theme flows over into vs. 34.

The last part of vs. 34 introduces the theme of the Spirit. This must be understood both against the background of begetting through the Spirit in vs. 5 and Jesus' baptizing in 22. (Once again we stress that such a reference relating Jesus' baptism to the giving of the Spirit stems from the context in which vss. 31–36 have been placed; it does not imply at all that in Johannine thought Jesus' early ministry of baptizing actually communicated the Spirit—see vii 39.) The present position of the pericope, by referring to the Spirit, enables the editor to underline once more against the sectarians of John the Baptist the unique distinction between Christian Baptism and the baptism of their master (Acts xix 2–6).

Whose gift of the Spirit is boundless in vs. 34? Many modern commentators (Bernard, Bultmann, Cullmann, Barrett) agree with the ancient scribes (see NOTE) that God is the one who gives the Spirit; others like Lagrange and Thüsing think that "the one whom God has sent," that is, Jesus, is the subject. On the one hand, if 34c is thought of as parallel to 35, then the Father's gift of the Spirit to the Son is part of handing over all things to him. On the other hand, as Thüsing, pp. 154–55, points out, vi 63 ("The words that I have spoken to you are both Spirit and life") is a good parallel to vs. 34, and there it is Jesus who speaks the words and thus gives the Spirit. One wonders if it is crucial to decide whether John means that the Father or Jesus gives the Spirit; the two ideas are found in John (xiv 26, xv 26). In the present context, the Spirit that begets and the Spirit that is communicated in Baptism comes from above or from the Father, but only through Jesus.

The theme of vs. 35—that the Father has handed over all things to the Son—is a favorite one in John. Among the things that John mentions as having been given by Father to Son are: judgment (v 22, 27), to have life in himself (v 26), power over all flesh (xvii 2), followers (vi 37, xvii 6), what to say (xii 49, xvii 8), the divine name (xvii 11, 12), and glory (xvii 22). The closest Synoptic parallel to vs. 34 is in the so-called Johannine passage (Matt xi 27; Luke x 22): "All things have been given over to me by my Father." Such statements ultimately led Christian theologians to recognize that the Son does what the Father does, and hence that they act with the same power and have one nature.

The discourse closes in vs. 36 on the theme of dualistic reaction to Jesus, the same theme that closed the Nicodemus discourse in vss. 18–21. Notice the present tenses, "believes," "disobeys"; John is not thinking of a single act but of a pattern of life. Notice too that the contrast to believing is disobeying; we saw in 18–21 the strong connection between the way a man lives, acts, and keeps the commandments and his belief in Jesus. Evil deeds and disobedience to God's commands express themselves in refusal to believe in Jesus; and since God's commandment means eternal life (xii 50—the last verse of the other variant of this discourse), "whoever disobeys the Son will *not see life*." Disobedience is greeted here and now with God's enduring wrath, just as vs. 18 stressed that the man who refuses belief is *already condemned*. The positive side of this realized eschatology is seen in the affirmation that whoever believes in the Son *has* eternal life.

BIBLIOGRAPHY

Barrosse, T., "The Relationship of Love to Faith in St. John," TS 18 (1957), especially pp. 543–47 on iii 14–21.

Boismard, M.-E., "L'évolution du thème eschatologique dans les traditions johanniques," RB 68 (1961), especially pp. 507–14 on iii 16–19.

———"Les traditions johanniques concernant le Baptiste," RB 70 (1963), especially pp. 25–30 on iii 22–30.

———"L'ami de l'époux (Jo. iii 29)," *A la rencontre de Dieu* (Gelin vol.; Le Puy: Mappus, 1961), pp. 289–95.

Braun, F.-M., "La vie d'en haut (Jn iii, 1–15)," RSPT 40 (1956), 3–24.

de la Potterie, I., "Naître de l'eau et naître de l'Esprit," ScEccl 14 (1962), 351–74—excellent bibliography.

Gourbillon, J.-G., "La parabole du serpent d'airain," RB 51 (1942), 213–26.

Mendner, S., "Nikodemus," JBL 77 (1958), 293–323.

Moody, D., "'God's Only Son': the Translation of John iii 16 in the RSV," JBL 72 (1953), 213–19.

Roustang, F., "L'entretien avec Nicodème," NRT 78 (1956), 337–58.

Schnackenburg, R., "Die 'situationgelösten' Redestücke in Joh 3," ZNW 49 (1958), 88-99.

Spicq, C., "Notes d'exégèse johannique," RB 65 (1958), especially pp. 358-60 on iii 14.

van den Bussche, H., "Les paroles de Dieu. Jean 3, 22-36," BVC 55 (1964), 23-28.

van Selms, A., "The Best Man and the Bride—from Sumer to St. John," JNES 9 (1950), 65-75.

Zerwick, M., "Veritatem facere (Joh. 3, 21; I Joh. 1, 6)," VD 18 (1938), 338-42, 373-77.

13. JESUS LEAVES JUDEA
(iv 1–3)

A Transitional Passage

IV 1 Now when Jesus learned that the Pharisees had heard that he was winning and baptizing more disciples than John (2 in fact, however, it was not Jesus himself who baptized, but his disciples), 3 he left Judea and once more started back to Galilee.

NOTES

iv 1. *Jesus.* Important witnesses from Egypt read, "When *the Lord* learned that the Pharisees had heard that *Jesus* was . . ."; important Western witnesses read, "When *Jesus* learned that the Pharisees had heard that *Jesus* was . . ." The original was probably "When *he* learned"; and the above readings represent scribal attempts to clarify the pronominal subject. We have transferred the subject "Jesus" from the subordinate clause to the main clause for smoother reading.

2. *not Jesus himself.* This is clearly an attempt to modify iii 22, where it is said that Jesus did baptize, and serves as almost indisputable evidence of the presence of several hands in the composition of John. Perhaps the final redactor was afraid that the sectarians of John the Baptist would use Jesus' baptizing as an argument that he was only an imitator of John the Baptist. The unusual word for "however" (*kaitoi ge*) may be another indication of a different hand.

3. *Judea.* There is some evidence for reading "Judean territory," the same expression found in iii 22 (see NOTE).

started back to. Literally "went back into"; a complexive aorist for a whole action not yet completed, as in ii 20 (see NOTE). Some suggest on the strength of this tense that iv 43–45 was once joined to 1–3 and that the Samaria incident was later interpolated into the outline.

COMMENT

The awkwardness of these transitional lines pointed out in the NOTES makes it likely that a morsel of Johannine itinerary material has been used to make a framework for the Samaria incident. This does not necessarily mean that the incident in Samaria did not take place on the way from

Judea to Galilee, just as John describes it, but simply that the description of the journey now found in 1–3 was not always part of the Samaria narrative.

As the story now stands, the reason for Jesus' sudden departure from Judea is not clear. There were Pharisees in Galilee too, and so his shift of activities to Galilee would not end their opposition. Does the fact that the Pharisees have turned their attention from John the Baptist (i 24) to Jesus mean that John the Baptist has been arrested by Herod (iii 24—see p. 153)? If that is the case and Jesus wishes to avoid being arrested, his movements are still not explained, for Galilee was as much Herod's territory as was Perea (the Transjordan) where John the Baptist had been first baptizing (i 28). Perhaps the centering of attention on Jesus is to be explained simply by the fact that John the Baptist had already been forced out of Judea to Aenon, and now the Pharisees were trying to make Jesus depart as well. In any case, Jesus' departure from Judea seems to mean the end of his ministry of baptizing; henceforth his ministry will be one of word and sign.

[The Bibliography for this section is included in the Bibliography at the end of § 15.]

14. DISCOURSE WITH THE SAMARITAN WOMAN
AT JACOB'S WELL
(iv 4–42)

Introduction

IV 4 He had to pass through Samaria; 5 and his travels brought him
to a Samaritan town called Shechem, near the plot of land which
Jacob had given to his son Joseph. 6 This was the site of Jacob's well;
and so Jesus, tired from the journey, sat down at the well.

Scene 1

It was about noon; 7 and when a Samaritan woman came to draw
water, Jesus said to her, "Give me a drink." (8 His disciples had gone
off into town to buy supplies.) 9 But the Samaritan woman said to
him, "You are a Jew—how can you ask me, a Samaritan woman, for a
drink?" (Jews, remember, use nothing in common with Samaritans.)
10 Jesus replied:

> "If only you recognized God's gift
> and who it is that is asking you for a drink,
> you would have asked him instead,
> and he would have given you living water."

11 "Sir," she addressed him, "you haven't even a bucket, and this
well is deep. Where, then, are you going to get this flowing water?
12 Surely, you don't pretend to be greater than our ancestor Jacob
who gave us this well and drank from it with his sons and flocks?"
13 Jesus replied:

> "Everyone who drinks this water
> will be thirsty again.
> 14 But whoever drinks the water I shall give him
> shall never be thirsty.
> Rather, the water I shall give him
> will become within him a fountain of water
> leaping up unto eternal life."

5: *brought;* 7: *came, said;* 9: *said;* 11: *addressed.* In the historical present tense.

15 The woman said to him, "Give me this water, sir, so that I won't get thirsty and have to keep coming here to draw water."

16 He told her, "Go, call your husband and come back here." 17 "I have no husband," the woman replied. Jesus exclaimed, "Right you are in claiming to have no husband. 18 In fact, you have had five husbands, and the man you have now is not your husband. There you've told the truth!"

19 "Lord," the woman answered, "I can see that you are a prophet. 20 Our ancestors worshiped on this mountain, but you people claim that the place where men ought to worship God is in Jerusalem." 21 Jesus told her:

> "Believe me, woman,
>   an hour is coming
>   when you will worship the Father
>   neither on this mountain
>   nor in Jerusalem.
> 22 You people worship what you do not understand,
>   while we understand what we worship;
>   after all, salvation is from the Jews.
> 23 Yet an hour is coming and is now here
>   when the real worshipers
>   will worship the Father in Spirit and truth.
>   And indeed, it is just such worshipers
>   that the Father seeks.
> 24 God is Spirit,
>   and those who worship Him
>   must worship in Spirit and truth."

25 The woman said to him, "I know there is a Messiah coming. Whenever he comes, he will announce all things to us." (This term "Messiah" means "Anointed.") 26 Jesus declared to her, "I who speak to you —I am he."

Scene 2

27 Now just then his disciples came along. They were shocked that he was holding a conversation with a woman; however, no one asked, "What do you want?" or "Why are you talking to her?" 28 Then, leaving her water jar, the woman went off into the town. She said to the people, 29 "Come and see someone who has told me everything that

15: *said;* 16: *told;* 17: *exclaimed;* 19: *answered;* 21: *told;* 25: *said;* 26: *declared;* 28: *said.* In the historical present tense.

I have ever done! Could this possibly be the Messiah?" 30 [So] they set out from the town to meet him.

31 Meanwhile the disciples were urging him, "Rabbi, eat something." 32 But he told them,

> "I have food to eat
> that you know nothing about."

33 At this the disciples said to one another, "You don't suppose that someone has brought him something to eat?" 34 Jesus explained to them:

> "Doing the will of Him who sent me
> and bringing His work to completion—
> that is my food.
> 35 Do you not have a saying:
> 'Four [more] months
> and the harvest will be here'?
> Why, I tell you,
> open your eyes
> and look at the fields;
> they are ripe for the harvest!
> 36 The reaper is already collecting his wages
> and gathering fruit for eternal life,
> so that both sower and reaper can rejoice together.
> 37 For here we have the saying verified:
> 'One man sows; another reaps.'
> 38 What I sent you to reap
> was not something you worked for.
> Others have done the hard work,
> and you have come in for the fruit of their work."

Conclusion

39 Now many Samaritans from that town believed in him on the strength of the woman's word. "He told me everything that I have ever done," she testified. 40 Consequently, when these Samaritans came to him, they begged him to stay with them. So he stayed there two days, 41 and through his own word many more came to faith. 42 As they told the woman, "No longer is our faith dependent on your story. For we have heard for ourselves, and we know that this is really the Saviour of the world."

34: *explained.* In the historical present tense.

NOTES

iv 4. *had to pass.* This is not geographical necessity; for, although the main route from Judea to Galilee was through Samaria (Josephus *Ant.* XX.vi.1;⅍118), if Jesus was in the Jordan valley (iii 22) he could easily have gone north through the valley and then up into Galilee through the Bethshan gap, avoiding Samaria. Elsewhere in the Gospel (iii 14) the expression of necessity means that God's will or plan is involved.

5. *Shechem.* Almost all the manuscripts read "Sychar"; a Syriac witness reads Shechem, and Jerome identified Sychar with Shechem. A mistake which may have corrupted Gr. *Sychem* (=Shechem) into *Sychar* is plausible, perhaps under the influence of the *ar* sound in Sam*ar*ia. The reading "Sychar" creates a problem; for, although there are some traces in ancient reports of the existence of a Sychar, no traces of such a town have been found in the pertinent area of Samaria. The identification of Sychar with modern 'Askar, about one mile northeast of Jacob's well, is probably wrong on several counts: (*a*) the site is a medieval settlement; (*b*) the dubious similarity of name is useless since the Arabic name 'Askar does not reflect an ancient designation of the site but simply that the place has served as a military campsite; (*c*) 'Askar has a good well of its own, a fact which makes the woman's long journey to Jacob's well inexplicable. On the other hand, if the real reading is Shechem, everything fits, for Jacob's well is only 250 ft. from Shechem. Probably Shechem was only a very small settlement at the time.

Jacob. For the references to Jacob and Shechem see Gen xxxiii 18, xlviii 22; Josh xxiv 32.

6. *Jacob's well.* A well about 100 feet deep is first mentioned in this area in Christian pilgrim sources of the 4th century; Jacob's well is not mentioned in the OT. The site presently identified as Jacob's well at the foot of Mount Gerizim can be accepted with confidence. The descriptions of ch. iv show a good knowledge of the local Palestinian scene.

sat down. In the better Greek mss. the verb is followed by the adverb *houtōs,* "thus, so," which we have not translated explicitly. It probably modifies the verb, e.g., "he sat *right* down" or "he sat down without more ado." But it could modify the adjective "tired," e.g., "tired as he was."

at the well. Literally "on the well"; the well was a vertical shaft covered by a stone. P⁶⁶ reads "on the ground," a reading which Boismard, RB 64 (1957), 397, thinks may be original.

noon. Literally "the sixth hour." The woman's choice of time for coming to the well is unusual; such a chore was done in the morning and evening. There is little likelihood in the suggestion (Lightfoot, p. 122) that the scene is deliberately being related to the crucifixion, where noon is also the hour (xix 14) and Jesus is again driven to express his thirst (xix 28). However, the great medieval hymn the *Dies Irae* seems to have made this connection: "Quaerens me sedisti lassus; redemisti crucem passus." The suggestion that hours should be reckoned from midnight rather than from 6:00 A.M. (see NOTE on i 39) would change the time notation in this verse to 6:00 A.M. Such an hour would fit the scene at the well, but would not fit "the sixth hour" of xix 14.

7. *came to draw water.* For similar scenes at wells in the OT see Gen xxiv 11, xxix 2; Exod ii 15.

9. *Jews . . . Samaritans.* The Samaritans are the descendants of two groups: (*a*) the remnant of the native Israelites who were not deported at the fall of the Northern Kingdom in 722 B.C.; (*b*) foreign colonists brought in from Babylonia and Media by the Assyrian conquerors of Samaria (II Kings xvii 24 ff. gives an anti-Samaritan account of this). There was theological opposition between these northerners and the Jews of the South because of the Samaritan refusal to worship at Jerusalem. This was aggravated by the fact that after the Babylonian exile the Samaritans had put obstacles in the way of the Jewish restoration of Jerusalem, and that in the 2nd century B.C. the Samaritans had helped the Syrian monarchs in their wars against the Jews. In 128 B.C. the Jewish high priest burned the Samaritan temple on Gerizim.

use nothing in common. D. Daube, JBL 69 (1950), 137–47, points to this meaning and suggests that the background is the general assumption that the Samaritans were ritually impure. A Jewish regulation of A.D. 65–66 warned that one could never count on the ritual purity of Samaritan women since they were menstruants from their cradle!—see Lev xv 19. Probably this regulation was simply canonizing an earlier attitude toward Samaritan women. There is respectable Western evidence for the omission of this whole parenthetical clause in vs. 9, a view shared by BDF, § 193[5].

10. *God's gift.* Some commentators (Osty, Van den Bussche) understand the gift to be Jesus himself (iii 16); others more plausibly think of something that Jesus will give men (his revelation, the Spirit—see COMMENT).

asking you for a drink. Literally "saying to you, 'Give me a drink.'"

10–11. *living water . . . flowing water.* This same Greek expression is a perfect example of Johannine misunderstanding. Jesus is speaking of the water of life; the woman is thinking of flowing water, so much more desirable than the flat water of cisterns. The word for "well" in 11–12 is *phrear*, whereas in the earlier verses it was *pēgē.* In LXX usage there is little difference between the two terms; but *phrear* (Heb. *be'ēr*) is closer to "cistern," while *pēgē* (Heb. *'ayin*) is closer to "fountain." The idea may be that in the earlier conversation which concerns natural water Jacob's well is a fountain (*pēgē*) with fresh, flowing water; but when the conversation shifts to the theme of Jesus' living water, Jesus is now the fountain (*pēgē* in vs. 14), and Jacob's well becomes a mere cistern (*phrear*).

11. *Sir.* The Greek *kyrie* means both "Sir" and "Lord"; most likely there is a progression from one to the other meaning as the woman uses it with increasing respect in vss. 11, 15, and 19.

she addressed. Most witnesses have "the woman" as the subject of the verb. We follow P[75], Vaticanus, Coptic, OS[sin].

12. *greater than . . . Jacob.* This is a perfect example of Johannine irony (see Introduction, p. CXXXVI), for the woman is unconsciously stating a truth.

ancestor. Literally "father."

who gave us this well. Although there is no OT reference for this event, perhaps we have here an echo of the story of Jacob and the well of Haran. J. Ramón Díaz, "Palestinian Targum and the New Testament," NovT 6 (1963), 76–77, cites the Palestinian Targum of Gen xxviii 10 concerning the well of Haran: "After *our ancestor Jacob* had lifted the stone from the mouth of the well, the

well rose to its surface and overflowed, and was *overflowing* twenty years."
Notice that in John Jesus supplies living (flowing) water that is eternal.

14. *leaping up.* The verb *hallesthai* is used of quick movement by living beings,
like jumping; this is the only instance of its being applied to the action of water,
although its Latin counterpart *salire* has both uses. *Hallesthai* is used in LXX for
the "spirit of God" as it falls on Samson, Saul, and David, which is background
for the thesis that in John the "living water" is the Spirit. Ignatius *Romans* vii 2
seems to recall this verse in John: ". . . water living and speaking in me, and
saying to me from within, 'Come to the Father.'"; also Justin *Trypho* LXIX 6
(PG 6:637): "As a fountain of living water from God . . . has this our Christ
gushed forth."

16. *call your husband.* It is useless to ask what would have happened if she
had returned with her paramour.

18. *five husbands.* Jews were allowed only three marriages (StB, II, p. 437);
if the same standard was applicable among the Samaritans, then the woman's life
had been markedly immoral. There is no particular reason why the conversation
between Jesus and the woman about her life need have more than the obvious
import. However, since earliest times many have seen a symbolism in the husbands. Origen (*In Jo.* XIII 8; GCS 10:232) saw a reference to the fact that the
Samaritans held as canonical only the five books of Moses. Others today think of
II Kings xvii 24 ff., where the foreign colonists brought in by the Assyrian conquerors are said to have come from five cities and to have brought their pagan
cults with them. (Actually xvii 30–31 mentions seven gods that they worshiped,
but Josephus *Ant.* IX.XIV.3; ⁂288 implies a simplication to five gods.) Since the
Hebrew word for "husband" (*ba'al,* "master, lord") was also used as a name for
a pagan deity, the passage in John is interpreted as a play on words: the woman
representing Samaria has had five *be'ālīm* (the five gods previously worshiped)
and the *ba'al* (Yahweh) that she now has is not really her *ba'al* (because the
Yahwism of the Samaritans was impure—vs. 22). Such an allegorical intent is
possible; but John gives no evidence that it was intended, and we are not certain
that such an allegory was a well-known jibe of the time which would have been
recognized without explanation. Bligh, pp. 335–36, has a curious interpretation.
He thinks that in claiming to have no husband the woman was lying to Jesus
because she had matrimonial designs on him; he points out that in the parallel
OT scenes of men and women at the well (see NOTE on vs. 7) there is a
matrimonial situation, and that Jesus has been described as a bridegroom in iii
29.

19. *Lord.* See NOTE on "Sir" in vs. 11.

prophet. This identification of Jesus stems from the special knowledge that he
has exhibited, but may also refer to his obvious wish to reform her life. The
Samaritans did not accept the prophetical books of the OT, so the image of the
prophet probably stems from Deut xviii 15–18 (see above, p. 49), a passage
which in the Samaritan Pentateuch, as well as in some Qumran material, comes
after Exod xx 21b. This Prophet-like-Moses would have been expected to settle
legal questions, whence the logic of the implicit question in vs. 20. Also Bowman,
"Eschatology," p. 63, says that the Samaritans expected the Taheb (see NOTE on
vs. 25) to restore proper worship.

20. *this mountain.* In the Samaritan Pentateuch we read in Deut xxvii 4 the
instruction to Joshua to set up a shrine on Gerizim, the sacred mountain of the
Samaritans. This reading is probably correct, for the reading "Ebal" in MT may

well be an anti-Samaritan correction. The Samaritans also made the obligation to worship on Gerizim part of the Decalogue; contrast II Chron vi 6.

the place. Codex Sinaiticus omits this. It refers to the Temple (xi 48).

21. *woman.* Jesus normally uses this form of address (see NOTE on ii 4). "Woman" is not an entirely happy translation and is somewhat archaic. However, modern English is deficient in a courteous title of address for a woman who is no longer a "Miss." Both "Lady" and "Madam" have taken on an unpleasant tone when used as an address without an accompanying proper name.

an hour. Without the article or a possessive, "hour" in John is not necessarily the hour of glory (see App. I:11); yet it may well be so here.

22. *do not understand.* The antithesis in this verse is expressed in typically strong Semitic fashion with no mean between ignorance and knowledge.

we understand. Bultmann, p. 139[6], takes the "we" to be the Christians as opposed to both Samaritans and Jews; such an exegesis, of course, does not take seriously the historical setting given to the episode.

after all. Literally "because."

salvation is from the Jews. Cf. Ps lxxvi 1: "In Judah God is known." Bultmann would reduce this to a gloss since it does not fit in with Johannine hostility to "the Jews." However, the Jews against whom Jesus elsewhere speaks harshly really refers to that section of the Jewish people that is hostile to Jesus, and especially to their rulers. Here, speaking to a foreigner, Jesus gives to the Jews a different significance, and the term refers to the whole Jewish people. This line is a clear indication that the Johannine attitude to the Jews cloaks neither an anti-Semitism of the modern variety nor a view that rejects the spiritual heritage of Judaism.

23. *is coming and is now here.* When we contrast this with vs. 21, we find in John the same eschatological tension that is apparent in the Synoptic references to the kingdom—it is future, and yet it is at hand. The idea seems to be that the one is present who, at the hour of glorification, will render possible adoration in Spirit by his gift of the Spirit.

in Spirit and truth. Both nouns are anarthrous, and there is one preposition.

24. *God is Spirit.* This is not an essential definition of God, but a description of God's dealing with men; it means that God is Spirit toward men because He gives the Spirit (xiv 16) which begets them anew. There are two other such descriptions in the Johannine writings: "God is light" (I John i 5), and "God is love" (I John iv 8). These too refer to the God who acts; God gives the world His Son, the *light* of the world (iii 19, viii 12, ix 5) as a sign of His *love* (iii 16).

25. *a Messiah.* See NOTE on i 41. The Samaritans did not expect a Messiah in the sense of an anointed king of the Davidic house. They expected a Taheb (*Ta'eb*=Hebrew verb *šûb*=the one who returns), seemingly the Prophet-like-Moses. This belief was the fifth article in the Samaritan creed. Bowman, "Studies," p. 299, shows that the conversation in John iv 19–25 fits the Samaritan concept of the Taheb as a teacher of the Law (see NOTE on "prophet" in vs. 19), even though the more familiar Jewish designation of Messiah is placed on the woman's lips.

will announce. OS[sin] and Tatian read "give." Black, p. 183, and Boismard, EvJean, p. 46, suggest the possibility of an Aramaic original with confusion between the roots *tn'*, "announce," and *ntn*, "give."

26. *I am he.* For *egō eimi* see App. IV; it is not impossible that this use is intended in the style of divinity. It is interesting that Jesus, who does not give

unqualified acceptance to the title of Messiah when it is offered to him by Jews, accepts it from a Samaritan. Perhaps the answer lies in the royal nationalistic connotations the term had in Judaism, while the Samaritan Taheb (although not devoid of nationalistic overtones) had more the aspect of a teacher and lawgiver. J. Macdonald, *The Theology of the Samaritans* (London: SCM, 1964), p. 362, says that the Samaritans did not expect the Taheb to be a king.

27. *were shocked.* Imperfect tense, indicating more than momentary surprise. Sir ix 1–9 describes the care to be taken lest one be ensnared by a woman; and rabbinic documents (*Pirqe Aboth* i 5; TalBab *'Erubin* 53b) warn against speaking to women in public.

no one asked. For a similar hesitation to question Jesus see xvi 5.

What do you want? Was this addressed to the woman (so Bernard, I, p. 152)? Some ancient witnesses took it this way, as variants indicate, e.g., "What does *she* want?" However, these variants may stem from Tatian who, as an Encratite, might like to make it appear that Jesus did not take the initiative with a woman. Almost certainly, as hinted in vs. 34, the question concerns Jesus, with the implication that perhaps he had asked her for food after they had gone to get some. It is curious, as Bultmann points out, that they were more shocked because he was talking with a woman than because he was talking with a Samaritan.

28. *leaving her water jar.* We are not to seek a practical reason for this (e.g., that she left it for Jesus to drink; that she was in a hurry to get back to the town). This detail seems to be John's way of emphasizing that such a jar would be useless for the type of living water that Jesus has interested her in.

people. Literally "men"; however, any leering suggestion that the *men* were interested in finding out the woman's past is out of place.

29. *Could this possibly be the Messiah?* Literally "the Anointed," as in vs. 25. The Greek question with *mēti* implies an unlikelihood (BDF, § 427²); therefore the woman's faith does not seem to be complete. However, she does express a shade of hope. Bultmann, p. 142, suggests that the viewpoint of the question is that of the townspeople.

30. *[So].* This has good attestation, including P⁶⁶; and Bernard, I, p. 153, shows how it could have been lost in scribal transmission. Others prefer the better attested, more abrupt opening without a connective, on the principle that the more difficult reading is usually the more original.

32. *food.* Apparently there is little distinction between the *brōsis* of vs. 32 and the *brōma* of 34, although Spicq, *Dieu et l'homme*, p. 97³, claims that the latter has a special connotation of nourishment. It is possible that the use of *brōma* in vs. 34 is to be accounted for simply by a desire for assonance with *thelēma*, "will," in the same verse. *Brōma* is never used again in John, while *brōsis* appears in vi 27, 55.

34. *Doing the will of Him who sent me.* Both this (cf. v 30, vi 38) and "bringing His work to completion" (cf. v 36, ix 4, xvii 4) are Johannine descriptions of the nature of Jesus' ministry. In the Synoptics "to do the will of God" has a more general connotation (Mark iii 35; Matt vii 21). The theme of 34 is not far from that of Deut viii 3: "Man does not live by bread alone but by every word of God"—a citation attributed to Jesus in Matt iv 4.

35. *Do you not have a saying.* Literally, "Do you not say"; for an example of such an expression used to introduce a proverb see Matt xvi 2. It has been observed that the proverb in John is in iambic trimeter (for scanning see Dodd, *Tradition*, p. 394), and thus some have thought that Jesus was citing a Greek

proverb. This is not impossible, but we would more likely attribute a Greek proverb to the evangelist. However, most commentators believe that the iambic meter is accidental; for, as Bligh, p. 343, points out, iambic meter is close to ordinary speech patterns. One can discover a series of accidental, rough iambic trimeters in the NT (Mark iv 24; Acts xxiii 5).

Four [more] months and the harvest will be here. We have considered the saying in John as a proverb, and its brevity and construction favor this view. In such an interpretation the four months is simply a traditional period. The Gezer calendar of the 10th century B.C. puts exactly four months between sowing and harvest; and there are early rabbinic reckonings to the same effect (Barrett, p. 202). Nevertheless, some scholars have taken vs. 35 not as a proverb, but as an actual observation made by the disciples; in this case we would have a chronological reference dating the scene at Samaria as taking place four months before harvest. Harvest in the plain of Maḥneh, east of Shechem, would run from mid-May (barley) to mid-June (wheat), and consequently the scene at the well would be dated in January or early February. With such a reckoning, the unnamed feast in the next chapter (v 1) would probably be Passover, occurring in late March or early April. Bernard, I, p. 155, objects on the grounds that January and February are in the rainy season, when Jesus could have found water along the way rather than waiting to come to the well.

[more]. This is omitted by the Western mss., OS^{cur}, and P^{75}—a strong combination. Yet the omission could have been by homoioteleuton, i.e., the failure to write *eti* ("more") after *hoti*.

open your eyes. Literally "lift up your eyes"; it suggests deliberate gaze.

look at. Theasthai; see App. I:3.

fields . . . ripe for the harvest. This may be purely a symbolic harvest as in Matt ix 37. However, if there is any real time indication in the Samaritan scene, this would be a far more likely one than the four months mentioned above. The harvest refers primarily to the townspeople who are coming out to Jesus, but the metaphor may have been suggested by the sight of the ripe grainfields near Shechem. The time would then be May or June. If the sequence of the narratives in John is chronological, then the Samaritan interlude was not too long after the Passover (March or April) mentioned in ch. ii; certainly iv 43–45 tries to create that effect.

36. *already.* Some place this word with the last clause of vs. 35: "They are already ripe for harvest." Compare I John iv 3.

collecting his wages. The Gr. *misthos* means both "wage" and "reward."

gathering fruit for eternal life. Tosephta *Peah* 4:18, cited by Dodd, *Interpretation,* p. 146, is an interesting parallel: "My fathers gathered treasures in this age; I have gathered treasures in the age to come."

sower and reaper. Thüsing, p. 54, connecting this back to vs. 34, suggests that the Father is the sower and Jesus is the reaper. This would mean, however, that the identifications of the sower and reaper in vs. 36 are different from those in 37–38, for in 38 the reapers are clearly the disciples.

38. *I sent.* The "I" is expressed and perhaps emphatic: "It was I who sent."

you. In the early tradition of the gospel parables there is often an application of the parable to a particular audience and situation.

the fruit of their work. Literally "their work"; but the context makes clear that the product of the work is intended.

39. *woman's word.* There is a contrast between this belief on the basis of the

woman's word and belief on the basis of Jesus' word (vs. 41)—is this an adumbration of the *logos* concept of the Prologue?

40. *stay. Menein;* App. I:8.

42. *story.* The Greek word here is *lalia,* not the *logos* of vss. 39, 41.

Saviour. In the OT (Ps xxiv 5; Isa xii 2; also Luke i 47) Yahweh is the salvation of Israel and of the individual Israelite. The Messiah king is not called a saviour (but see Zech ix 9 where LXX has "saving" for "victorious"). En xlviii 7 speaks of the Son of Man as saving men. What would be the meaning of the title on the lips of the Samaritans? Perhaps for Hellenized Samaria we should seek the meaning of the term in the Greek world where it was applied to gods, emperors (Hadrian was called "Saviour of the world"), and heroes. The term "Saviour" was a common post-resurrectional title for Jesus, particularly in the Lucan and Pauline works, but this is the only instance in the Gospels of its being applied to Jesus during the public ministry.

COMMENT: GENERAL

We may begin with the question of the historical plausibility of the scene. A ministry of Jesus in Samaria is mentioned only in John. The missionary discourse in Matt x 5 forbids the disciples to enter a Samaritan city. Of the Synoptics Luke shows the greatest interest in the Samaritans: in x 29–37 we have the Parable of the Good Samaritan; in xvii 11–19 the one leper to give thanks is a Samaritan. Yet even Luke in ix 52–53 reflects a certain hostility between the Samaritans and Jesus because Jesus insists on going to Jerusalem. After the ministry of Jesus, Acts viii 1–25 reports that when the Hellenist Christians were scattered from Jerusalem after Stephen's death, Philip, one of the seven Hellenist leaders, proclaimed Christ to a city of Samaria, where he encountered Simon Magus. The ministry of Philip led to the baptism of many Samaritans, and Peter and *John* came down from Jerusalem to lay hands on the new converts so that they would receive the Holy Spirit.

The story of Christianity's spread to Samaria some years after the ministry of Jesus will help us to explain some details in John's account; yet we should note that Acts gives no hint that Jesus already had followers in Samaria before Philip came, as the Fourth Gospel would indicate. The difficulty may be explained away by insisting that John iv 39–42 means simply that a small village came to believe in Jesus. Nevertheless, the Johannine story has to stand without support or corroboration from the rest of the NT.

Its intrinsic claim to plausibility has merit. The *mise en scène* is one of the most detailed in John, and the evangelist betrays a knowledge of local color and Samaritan beliefs that is impressive. We may mention: the well at the foot of Gerizim; the question of legal purity in vs. 9; the spirited defense of the patriarchal well in vs. 12; the Samaritan belief in Gerizim and the Prophet-like-Moses. And if we analyze the repartee at the well, we find quite true-to-life the characterization of the woman as mincing and coy, with a certain light grace (Lagrange, p. 101). Though characters like

Nicodemus, this woman, the paralytic of ch. v, and the blind man of ch. x are—to a certain extent—foils used by the evangelist to permit Jesus to unfold his revelation, still each has his or her own personal characteristics and fitting lines of dialogue. Either we are dealing with a master of fiction, or else the stories have a basis in fact. Bligh, p. 332, tends in the latter direction, at least for part of the story. He suggests that vss. 1–8 may have been a pre-Johannine pronouncement story (a story remembered because it was the setting of a solemn pronouncement by Jesus). The pronouncement may have been one assuring the universal character of God's plan of salvation, including Samaritan and Jew, a theme not unlike that of vss. 19–26.

The solemn discourse of Jesus seems to be the main obstacle to historical plausibility. Granting that this discourse has been shaped by the Johannine technique of misunderstanding, plays on words, etc., we may still wonder if a Samaritan woman would have been expected to understand even the most basic ideas of the discourse. The answer to this question is impeded by our limited knowledge of Samaritan thought in the 1st century A.D. In Judaism, two of the expressions used by Jesus, "the gift of God," and "living water," were used to describe the Torah. If Samaritan usage was the same, the woman could have understood that Jesus was presenting himself and his doctrine as the replacement of the Torah in which the Samaritans believed. As we pointed out in the NOTES on vss. 19 and 25 the woman seems to understand Jesus' claims against the background of the Samaritan expectation of the Taheb. Therefore, it is not at all impossible that even in the conversation we have echoes of a historical tradition of an incident in Jesus' ministry. We shall see that the dialogue with the disciples has Synoptic parallels.

If, as we suspect, there is a substratum of traditional material, the evangelist has taken it and with his masterful sense of drama and the various techniques of stage setting, has formed it into a superb theological scenario. Misunderstanding (vs. 11), irony (12), the quick changing of an embarrassing subject (19), the front and back stage (29), the Greek chorus effect of the villagers (39–42)—all these dramatic touches have been skillfully applied to make this one of the most vivid scenes in the Gospel and to give the magnificent doctrine of living water a perfect setting. Much more than in the Nicodemus scene, Jesus' discourse is worked into a dialogue and a background that gives it meaning.

COMMENT: DETAILED

Scene One: The Dialogue with the Samaritan Woman (iv 4–26)

It is very important to understand the literary analysis of the two subdivisions of the scene, for such an analysis highlights the main ideas and their development. Here we follow Roustang very closely.

Scene 1a: The Living Water (vss. 6–15). This consists of two short dialogues, each with three exchanges:

First, vss. 7–10:
- vs. 7. *Jesus* asks the Samaritan for water, violating the social customs of the time.
-      9. *Woman* mocks Jesus for being so in need that he does not observe the proprieties.
-     10. *Jesus* shows that the real reason for his action is not his inferiority or need, but his superior status.
      He issues a TWO-PART CHALLENGE:
      i. If she recognizes who is speaking to her,
      ii. she will ask him for living water.

In summary, then, the exchanges in this first dialogue introduce the topic of living water and Jesus' claim.

Second, vss. 11–15:
- vss. 11–12. *Woman* misunderstands the water on a material, earthly level; hence she misunderstands Jesus as less than Jacob.
-     13–14. *Jesus* clarifies that he is speaking of the heavenly water of eternal life.
-        15. *Woman*, intrigued, ASKS FOR WATER, thus fulfilling one part of Jesus' challenge mentioned in vs. 10.

However, another part of the challenge remains to be answered, for the woman has not yet recognized who Jesus is. She understands that he is speaking of an unusual type of water, but her aspirations are still on the level of earth.

Scene 1b: True Worship of the Father (vss. 16–26). This also consists of two short dialogues, each with three exchanges:

First, vss. 16–18:
- vs. 16. *Jesus* takes the initiative in leading the woman to recognize who he is by referring to her personal life.
-     17. *Woman* gives an ambiguous and even deceptive answer in instinctive reaction against moral probing.
-     18. *Jesus* uses the answer to uncover her evil deeds.

We heard in iii 19–21 that those whose deeds are evil do not come near the light lest their deeds be exposed. The dialogue in 16–18 constitutes the crucial moment of judgment: will she turn her back on the light?

Second, vss. 19–26:
- vss. 19–20. *Woman* looks to the light, although she would divert the rays away from her life to something less personal. In broaching the topic of worship, she is beginning hesitantly to think on a spiritual or heavenly level, although there is still much of the earthly in her concepts.
-     21–24. *Jesus* explains that true worship can come only from those begotten by the Spirit of truth. Only through the Spirit does the Father beget true worshipers.
-     25–26. *Woman* finally RECOGNIZES WHO JESUS IS (as far as she is able) and Jesus affirms it.

The other part of the challenge made in vs. 10 has now been answered. The second part of Scene 1a led the woman to ask for water; the second part of Scene 1b led the woman to recognize who he is who asked her for a drink—namely, *egō eimi* (see NOTE on vs. 26).

In this scene John has given us the drama of a soul struggling to rise from the things of this world to belief in Jesus. Not only the Samaritan woman but every man must come to recognize who it is that speaks when Jesus speaks, and must ask Jesus for living water.

Passing from the literary analysis of the development of the scene to its contents, we find two topics that must be discussed: in Scene 1a the topic of living water, and in Scene 1b the topic of worship in Spirit and truth.

a. "Living water" (iv 10–14). What was Jesus referring to when he spoke of giving "living water" to the woman? Clearly the living water is not Jesus himself but something spiritual that he offers to the believer who can recognize God's gift. The living water is not eternal life but leads to it (vs. 14). The very use of the symbol of water shows how realistically John thought of eternal life: water is to natural life as living water is to eternal life.

McCool, *art. cit.*, draws attention to the many suggestions that exegetes have made by way of interpreting "living water." For instance, from medieval times it has been popular among systematic theologians to treat "living water" as a symbol for sanctifying grace. Within the scope of Johannine theology there are really two possibilities: living water means the revelation which Jesus gives to men, or it means the Spirit which Jesus gives to men. As Wiles, pp. 46–47, points out, both these interpretations go back to the 2nd century; and we shall find convincing arguments for both.

(1) "Living water" is Jesus' revelation or teaching. The OT uses the symbolism of water for God's wisdom that grants life. Prov xiii 14 says, "The teaching of the wise is a fountain of life that a man may avoid the snares of death"; also xviii 4, "The words from a man's mouth are deep water; the fountain of wisdom is a flowing brook." In Isa lv 1, in a context where Yahweh invites men to hear so that their souls may live (vs. 3), Yahweh says, "All you who are thirsty come to the water." The best OT parallel for John iv 14 (and vi 35) seems to be Sir xxiv 21 where Wisdom sings her own praises: "He who eats of me will hunger still; he who drinks of me will thirst for more." In John, Jesus says, "He who drinks the water I shall give him shall never be thirsty."

Since in the circle of the scribes Wisdom was identified with the Torah, it is no surprise that Sir xxiv 23–29 tells us that the Torah fills men with wisdom like rivers overflowing their banks. The rabbis made frequent allegorical use of water to refer to the Law, although only rarely did they allegorize *"living* water." However, now we have clear Qumran evidence for the use of "living water" to describe the Law (CDC xix 34; also see iii 16, vi 4–11). We may also mention that the expression "gift of God" that appears in John iv 10 was used in rabbinic Judaism to describe the Law (Barrett, p. 195).

For Jesus to refer to his own revelation as "living water" with this background in mind is perfectly plausible, for in John Jesus is presented as divine wisdom and as the replacement of the Law. The glimmer of understanding that the woman receives of this living water seems to lie in this direction, for she hails him as the Prophet-like-Moses who will announce all things (see NOTES on vss. 19 and 25). The use of "living water" for Jesus' revelation would be paralleled elsewhere in John by the use of the symbols of light and the bread of life for Jesus' revelation.

(2) "Living water" is the Spirit communicated by Jesus. As we saw in discussing iii 5 (pp. 140–41), the connection between water and spirit is frequent in the OT. Especially here we may recall 1QS iv 21: "Like purifying waters He will sprinkle upon him the spirit of truth." Moreover, for the identification of "living water" as the Spirit we have the specific evidence of John vii 37–39. There are many supporting indications in iv 10–14 for this interpretation. If the water leaps up to eternal life (14), we hear elsewhere (vi 63) that it is the Spirit that gives life. Also see NOTE on "leaping up" in vs. 14. The expression "gift (of God)" in vs. 10 was an early Christian term for the Holy Spirit, not only in Acts (ii 38, viii 20, x 45, xi 17), but also in Hebrews (vi 4), a work that has many affinities with John. The second part of the scene with the Samaritan woman explicitly introduces the theme of the Spirit (vss. 23–24). The gift of the Spirit was a mark of the messianic days, and the dialogue with Jesus leads the Samaritan woman to speak of the Messiah (vs. 25). We may add, finally, that it is the understanding of "living water" as the Spirit that led medieval theologians to think of it as grace; the remark of Aquinas in his commentary on John is worth citing: "The grace of the Holy Spirit is given to man inasmuch as the very font of grace is given, that is, the Holy Spirit."

We see no reason for having to choose between these two interpretations of "living water," and McCool, *art. cit.*, argues ably that both meanings are intended. Johannine symbolism is often ambivalent, especially where two such closely related concepts as revelation and Spirit are involved. After all, the Spirit of truth is the agent who interprets Jesus' revelation or teaching to men (xiv 26, xvi 13). We shall encounter a similar difficulty of being sure whether the Spirit or the word of God is involved in I John ii 27, so there is good reason to believe that the evangelist intended no sharp cleavage between them. It is interesting that in the passage of Aquinas cited, he also insists that Jesus' doctrine is the living water.

Is there a secondary sacramental reference to Baptism in this passage, much as there was in the mention of water and Spirit in iii 5 (also i 33)? Here the symbolism is different: not a birth through water, but the *drinking* of living water. Nevertheless, once we eliminate any direct equivalence (living water *is* the water of Baptism), we have the wider question of whether or not the author intended the passage to remind his Christian readers of Baptism and to teach them that one of the effects of Baptism was the giving of the Spirit. We note that this discourse and the Nicodemus discourse are set almost in tandem, separated by the baptizing incident of iii 22–30. Again, the transition to the Samaritan incident in iv 1–3 brings up a reference to Jesus' baptizing. These indications would strongly favor an affirmative answer to the question proposed. The fact that the water is to be drunk is not a major obstacle if we recall I Cor xii 13: "For by one Spirit we were all baptized into one body, . . . and all were made *to drink* of one Spirit." One of the early Christian symbols associated with Baptism is the hart drinking the flowing (living) water (Ps xlii); and indeed, the scene with the Samaritan at the well appears in early catacomb art as a symbol for Baptism (Niewalda, p. 126). Thus, there is a good *possibility* that a baptismal motif was intended in this discourse.

b. **Worship "in Spirit and truth"** (iv 23–24). In vs. 23 the particular point in question shifts from the place of worship (20–21) to the manner of worship. Today most exegetes agree that in proclaiming worship in Spirit and truth, Jesus is not contrasting external worship with internal worship. His statement has nothing to do with worshiping God in the inner recesses of one's own spirit; for the Spirit is the Spirit of God, not the spirit of man, as vs. 24 makes clear. In fact, one could almost regard "Spirit and truth" as a hendiadys (see NOTE on vs. 23) equivalent to "Spirit of truth." An ideal of purely internal worship ill fits the NT scene with its eucharistic gatherings, hymn singing, baptism in water, etc. (unless one assumes that John's theology is markedly different from that of the Church at large).

The contrast between worship in Jerusalem or on Gerizim and worship in Spirit and truth is part of the familiar Johannine dualism between earthly and heavenly, "from below" and "from above," flesh and Spirit. Jesus is speaking of the eschatological replacement of temporal institutions like the Temple, resuming the theme of ii 13–22. In ii 21 it was Jesus himself who was to take the place of the Temple, and here it is the Spirit given by Jesus that is to animate the worship that replaces worship at the Temple. Notice that it is a question of worshiping *the Father* in Spirit. God can be worshiped as Father only by those who possess the Spirit that makes them God's children (see Rom viii 15–16), the Spirit by which God begets them from above (John iii 5). This Spirit raises men above the earthly level, the level of flesh, and enables them to worship God properly.

Verse 24 couples Spirit and truth. In xvii 17–19 we shall hear that the truth is an agent of consecration and sanctification, and thus truth also enables man to worship God properly. The Johannine themes are closely intertwined: Jesus is the truth (xiv 6) in the sense that he reveals God's truth to men (viii 45, xviii 37); the Spirit is the Spirit of Jesus and is the Spirit of truth (xiv 17, xv 26) who is to guide men in the truth. Thus, it would be foolish to ask what the Spirit contributes to worship as distinct from what truth contributes. "Spirit and truth" merely spell out what we saw already in discussing "living water" as revelation and Spirit. Not only on the literary level but also in its theological themes, the dialogue with the Samaritan woman is a closely knit whole.

Schnackenburg, "Anbetung," has shown how the close connection between spirit and truth in the Qumran writings offers some interesting parallels to John's thought. At Qumran in an eschatological context God pours forth His spirit on the sectarians and thus purifies them for His service. This spirit is the spirit of truth in the sense that it instructs the sectarians in divine knowledge, that is, the observance of the Law insisted on at Qumran (1QS iv 19–22). The purity thus obtained turns the community into the temple of God, "a house of holiness for Israel, and assembly of the Holy of Holies for Aaron" (viii 5–6, ix 3–5). We may well have here the background making intelligible Jesus' remarks about worship in Spirit and truth replacing worship at the Temple. However, worship in the Johannine sense does not involve ritual purity, and truth is not concerned with an interpretation of the Law; and so there remain obvious differences between John and Qumran.

Before we close the treatment of the dialogue with the Samaritan woman it should be emphasized that in this scene John has revived and expanded themes treated earlier in the Gospel (Temple of ii 13–22; water and Spirit of Nicodemus discourse). This method of resuming themes after an interval will be encountered again in John.

Scene Two: The Dialogue with the Disciples (iv 27–38)

This scene too is carefully constructed. Scene 1 told us how Jesus came to the woman and led her to faith; but the short introduction to Scene 2 in vss. 27–30, played out backstage in the village, indicates that this scene will concern the coming of men to Jesus. And so, while Jesus opened the dialogue in Scene 1, the disciples open the dialogue in Scene 2.

The misunderstanding about food in the first lines (vss. 31–33) of the exchange resembles the misunderstanding about water in vss. 7–11. In each instance Jesus is speaking on a spiritual level while the other party is speaking on the material level. (Bligh, p. 334, suggests that just as the water theme in Scene 1 looks back to the Nicodemus and John the Baptist episodes in ch. iii, so the food theme of Scene 2 points forward to the bread/food symbolism of ch. vi.) In each instance, the misunderstanding leads Jesus to clarify what he means. The explanation that Jesus' food is his mission (vs. 34) leads rather naturally into the extension of the metaphor in terms of harvest (vs. 35), that is, the fruit of his mission is represented by the Samaritans who are coming to him.

The harvest imagery expounded in vss. 35–38 has definite parallels in the Synoptic tradition of agricultural parables, especially in vocabulary like "sowing," "harvesting," "fruit," "labor," "wages." Dodd points out that the theological vocabulary that is the hallmark of the Fourth Gospel is not very frequent in these verses (only "eternal life" in vs. 36; "verified" in 37); he surmises (*Tradition*, pp. 391–99) that the backbone of this short discourse is a group of independent traditional sayings of Jesus that have been sewn together. As they now stand, these verses embody the theme of realized eschatology. If in the harvest parables of Matt xiii the imagery depicts a harvesting of men at the end of time, in John the harvest is already going on in the ministry of Jesus (and of the Church).

The substance of vss. 35–38 consists of two proverbial sayings, the first of which Jesus denies, the second of which he affirms. That Jesus cited popular proverbs we see in the Synoptic tradition. In Luke iv 23 Jesus contradicts a proverb even as he does in our first instance in John. The proverb in Matt xvi 2–3 is based on the processes of nature, again like John iv 35. Let us consider in detail the two proverbs in John and Jesus' exposition of them:

(i) *The first proverb* and its commentary are found in vss. 35–36; it concerns the interval that nature has established between sowing and harvest. Jesus announces that in the eschatological order which he has introduced the proverbial principle is no longer valid, for there is no longer any such interval. The OT had prepared for this. Lev xxvi 5 had promised, by way of ideal reward to those who would keep the commandments: "Your threshing shall last till the time of vintage, and the vintage till the time of sowing"—in other words, the abundance of crops shall be so great that the idle intervals between the agricultural seasons will disappear. Amos' dreams of the messianic days pictured the plowman overtaking the reaper (ix 13). So now in Jesus' preaching the harvest is ripe on the same day on which the seed has been sown, for already the Samaritans are pouring out of the village and coming to Jesus.

The best Synoptic parallel for the second part of vs. 35 is found in Matt ix 37–38 (Luke x 1–2) where, when Jesus sees the crowds coming toward him, he says: "The harvest is plentiful, but the laborers are few; therefore pray to the Lord of the harvest that he send out laborers into the harvest."

Verse 36 comments on the harvest theme of vs. 35 and advances the imagery: not only is the harvest ripe, but the reaper is already at work. (It may be that vs. 36 was an independent saying before it was incorporated into the present context.) The theme shifts from the speed with which the harvest has come to the joy of reaping the harvest. One is reminded of Ps cxxvi 5–6: "May those who sow in tears reap with shouts of joy." There is also the parable of the kingdom in Mark iv 26–29 where the seed has to be allowed to grow by itself and then, when the grain is ripe, the farmer puts in the sickle "because the harvest has come." For John the reaper is already collecting his wages.

(ii) *The second proverb* and its commentary are found in vss. 37–38. The distinction between the sower and reaper has many antecedents in the OT (Deut xx 6, xxviii 30; Job xxxi 8); but the reference there is a pessimistic one, namely, that a catastrophe intervenes to prevent a man from reaping what he has sown. Mic vi 15 is a good example: "You shall sow, but not reap." Therefore, it is quite likely that the proverb that Jesus cites, "One man sows; another reaps," was originally a pessimistic reflection on the inequity of life. (Barrett, p. 203, cites Greek parallels which in his estimation are very close to the Johannine form of the proverb; however, such an aphorism was probably the common reflection of many ancient peoples.) It is interesting to note that a contrast between sowing and reaping appears in Matt xxv 24: "You are a hard man; you reap where you did not sow."

In vs. 38 Jesus applies the proverb in an optimistic fashion. That the disciples are sent to reap where they did not sow is another reflection of eschatological abundance. There are several difficulties in this verse. Jesus says to the disciples, "I *sent* [aorist] you to reap"; when did he do this? Bligh's suggestion that this is a reference to their having been sent into the town for food is rather banal. Not only does the text say that they were sent *to reap*, but also there is nothing in the description of their going into the town (vs. 8) that says they were *sent*. Rather the mission spoken of in vs. 38 seems to be religious in character.

There are two likely possibilities. *First,* some suggest that we must place ourselves in the post-resurrectional outlook of the evangelist. The sending is the great post-resurrectional mission of xx 21 which made the disciples apostles, that is, ones sent (see NOTE on ii 2). It seems that by anticipation this mission is referred to in xvii 18, also in the past: "I sent them into the world." *Second,* there is the possibility that iv 38 is a reference to a mission of the disciples during the ministry of Jesus, a mission that has not been narrated. The Synoptic tradition reports such missions of the disciples into surrounding towns to preach and to heal (Luke ix 2, x 1). It is always risky, of course, to explain John by something from the Synoptic tradition; however, the fact that vs. 38 may have once been an independent saying at least makes this interpretation possible. Above we cited a Lucan parallel (Luke x 1–2) to John iv 35 about plentiful harvest and a paucity of laborers; we should note that the next verse in Luke has these words: "Behold I send you out . . ." Does John, perhaps, give us a similar saying transposed into the past? Dodd, *Tradition,* p. 398, cites a group of Synoptic sayings that are similar in format to John iv 38.

The last part of vs. 38 is very difficult. Who are the "others" who have done the hard work? In the actual setting of the story we may think of Jesus as having sowed the seed of faith in the Samaritan woman and thus having done the work; the disciples are now being asked to help him reap the fruit of that seed as represented by the townspeople. But then why a plural ("others")? Is it merely a generalization? Or is Jesus associating the Father with himself in the work (vs. 34)? Another suggestion is that the "others" does not refer to Jesus but to those who prepared the Samaritans for receiving Jesus' message. Figures from the OT have been mentioned, but this interpretation is limited by the fact that the Samaritans accepted only the Pentateuch. J. A. T. Robinson, *art. cit.,* has proposed that the "others" is a reference to John the Baptist and his disciples who had preached in Samaria at Aenon near Salim (see NOTE on iii 23). However, would the disciples of John the Baptist be presented by John as having prepared the way for Jesus? Perhaps the combined work of John the Baptist and of Jesus would be a better variant of this theory.

Whatever meaning the "others" may have had in the context in which the story is placed, the whole passage takes on new meaning when we think of its being narrated in Johannine circles familiar with the story of the conversion of Samaria as told in Acts viii. Cullmann, *art. cit.*, has pointed out that there was a distinction between sowers and reapers in the christianizing of Samaria: the sower of the Christian faith was Philip, a Hellenist like Stephen and presumably an opponent of worship at the Jerusalem Temple; but the reapers were Peter and *John* who came down to confer the Spirit. This difference of function may even have led to some jealousy, as it did at Corinth—see I Cor iii 6 where Paul resorts to an agricultural symbol: "I planted; Apollos watered; but God gave the growth." What more natural than to comment on such a situation by recalling a saying of Jesus which gave assurance that such a difference between sower and reaper was envisaged in the eschatological harvest.

In fact such a theory throws additional light on the whole of ch. iv. The statement about the ultimate desuetude of worship at Jerusalem may have been preserved as an argument against those in the Jerusalem church who disapproved of the attitude of the Hellenists against the Temple and who may have wanted even the Samaritan converts to shift their allegiance to Jerusalem as part of Christian practice (see Acts ii 46 for daily Christian worship at the Temple). Verse 21 would show that such an attitude and such a dispute had no place in the new age that Jesus had begun. The rich harvest of vs. 35 would reflect the success of the mission of Philip in Samaria, and the "I sent" of 38 would refer to a particular facet of the post-resurrectional commission, namely, that in guiding the destiny of the Church Jesus had used persecution to send his disciples on the Samaritan mission. The emphasis on the importance of the Spirit (in vss. 23–24 and under the imagery of "living water" in 10–14) would take on new meaning in light of the coming of Peter and John to give the Spirit to Samaria and the dispute with Simon Magus, who wanted power to give the Spirit. If the context of the conversion of Samaria explains much of the scene that we have been studying in John iv, one would not do justice to the elements of authenticity that we have seen to suggest that the whole story is a purely imaginative and fictional *ad hoc* composition. The only adequate solution seems to be that traditional material with a historical basis has been rethought and formulated into a dramatic synthesis for a theological purpose.

Conclusion: The Conversion of the Townspeople (vss. 39–42)

John is too good a dramatist to leave the story without a conclusion that would bring together the themes of the two scenes. The woman who was so important in Scene 1 is recalled because it is on her word that the townspeople believe. But the completion of the Father's work (vs. 34), the harvest of the Samaritans, is to have greater durability; for the townspeople come to believe on Jesus' own word that he is the Saviour of the world. If our story in ch. iv, particularly in Scene 1, has portrayed the steps by which a soul comes to believe in Jesus, it also portrays the history of the apostolate, for the harvest comes outside of Judea among foreigners. We can scarcely believe that the evangelist did not mean for us to contrast the unsatisfactory faith of the Jews in ii 23–25 based on a superficial admiration of miracles with the deeper faith of the Samaritans based on the word of Jesus. Nicodemus, the rabbi of Jerusalem, could not understand Jesus' message that God had sent the Son into the world so that the world might be saved through him (iii 17); yet the peasants of Samaria readily come to know that Jesus is really the Saviour of the world.

[The Bibliography for this section is included in the Bibliography found at the end of § 15.]

15. JESUS ENTERS GALILEE
(iv 43–45)

A Transitional Passage

IV 43 When the two days were up, he departed from there for Galilee. (44 For Jesus himself had testified that it is in his own country that a prophet has no honor.) 45 And when he arrived in Galilee, the Galileans welcomed him because, having gone to the feast themselves, they had seen all that he had done in Jerusalem on that occasion.

NOTES

iv 43. *departed.* The construction in Greek is somewhat stiff, and some witnesses have added another verb to soften the construction: "he departed and set out from there for Galilee."

44. *had testified.* The pluperfect indicates the parenthetical character of the remark.

45. *welcomed.* The verb *dechesthai* occurs only here in the Johannine works.

all that he had done in Jerusalem. Presumably this refers to the signs mentioned in ii 23.

COMMENT

These three verses constitute a notorious crux in the Fourth Gospel. In the early 3rd century Origen (*In Jo.* XIII 53; GCS 10:283) said of vs. 44, "This saying seems completely to defy sequence." In the early 20th century Lagrange, p. 124, confessed that there was no apparent means of explaining this passage according to the rules of strict logic.

As vs. 43 now stands, it makes perfect sense as a transition from the Samaritan interlude. However, it resembles iv 3b closely ("He once more started back for Galilee"), and we have mentioned the theory that what was once a continuous journey from Judea to Galilee has been broken up by the insertion of the Samaritan incident. However, whether vs. 43 continues 40 or 1–3, it is still related to what has preceded.

Verse 45, on the other hand, introduces what follows. Dodd, *Tradition*, p. 238, makes the remark that it leads to nothing, but this does not seem to be true. The mention of the welcome accorded to Jesus by those who had seen what he did in Jerusalem suggests why the royal official (vss. 46 ff.) comes to him expecting a miracle.

The problem centers on vs. 44, an interruption that seems to contradict 45. In 44 Jesus compares his situation to that of a prophet who has no honor in his own country; yet in 45 his native Galilee gives him an enthusiastic welcome. To solve this some have suggested that "his own country" in vs. 44 is an allusion, not to Galilee, but to Judea. This is a view that goes back at least to Origen (*In Jo.* xiii 54; GCS 10:284). The idea, then, is that having received no honor in Judea, as exemplified by his rejection at the Temple, Jesus comes into Galilee, where he is welcomed. Such an interpretation must relate iv 43–45 to 1–3; for as the verses now stand, Jesus is leaving Samaria, not Judea. However, even if we regard the whole Samaritan incident as an insertion, the suggestion that Jesus' own country is Judea faces objections. John constantly stresses Jesus' Galilean origins (i 46, ii 1, vii 42, 52, xix 19); this Gospel does not even tell us that Jesus was born in Judea. It is true that in John Jesus spends much time in Judea, but this scarcely makes Judea his own country. Moreover, there is an implication in this explanation that Jesus was disappointed with the reception he had received in Judea and had come back to Galilee to be accorded the honor denied him in Judea. Such a search for human praise is abhorrent to the ideals of the Fourth Gospel (ii 24–25, v 41–44).

A better solution for the problem created by vs. 44 is to regard it as an addition by the redactor, exactly on the same pattern as ii 12. From a tradition akin to that of the Synoptic Gospels, the redactor had a saying to the effect that Jesus was not properly appreciated in Galilee. He added this saying to the Gospel just before a story that will illustrate the unsatisfactory faith of the Galileans, a faith based on a crude dependence on signs and wonders (vs. 48). In his estimation the welcome given to Jesus in Galilee (vs. 45) is just as shallow as the reaction that greeted Jesus in Jerusalem (ii 23–25). Therefore, the insertion of vs. 44 does not contradict 45 once we understand that a superficial welcome based on enthusiasm for miracles is no real *honor*.

As with ii 12 the parallels with the Synoptic tradition are very close. First, we may note that the whole Synoptic scene (Mark vi 1–6; Matt xiii 53–58; Luke iv 22 ff.) which enshrines the statement parallel to John iv 44 has echoes in John. Mark and John offer the most interesting points of comparison:

Mark vi 2: *many are astonished at the knowledge Jesus possesses,* John vii 15

3: *Jesus is a local figure whose relatives are known,* John vi 42
6: *Jesus is annoyed by the lack of belief,* John iv 48

Now let us compare the different forms of the saying about the prophet:

Mark vi 4: A prophet is not without honor except in his own country.
Luke iv 24: No prophet is welcomed in his own country.
John iv 44: A prophet has no honor in his own country.

John resembles Luke in the negative cast of the sentence but is closer to Mark in vocabulary (although the Lucan "welcomed" appears in the next verse in John—see NOTE). It seems best to classify John's saying as a variant form of a traditional statement, rather than as a selective borrowing from Mark and Luke. The redactor has not adapted the saying to the Johannine style of the rest of the Gospel. The word "honor" (*timē*) is employed rather than the more usual "glory" (*doxa*). Also the article is omitted before the proper name "Jesus"—according to Bernard, I, pp. 42–43, such an omission is not characteristic of John, but R. C. Nevius, NTS 12 (1965–66), 81–85, argues that the anarthrous usage, as witnessed in the Codex Vaticanus of John, is the true Johannine style.

The Synoptic scene in which we have found these parallels is that of the rejection of Jesus at Nazareth, a scene that Luke puts at the beginning of the Galilean ministry and Mark-Matthew at the end of the ministry in Galilee proper. Do the resemblances found in John iv 44–45 to this scene help us set up a chronological synchronization between the Johannine and Synoptic accounts? In particular is John's second entrance of Jesus into Galilee to be compared with Luke iv 16 ff., where Jesus was rejected at Nazareth when he came back to Galilee after his baptism by John the Baptist and the arrest of John the Baptist (Luke iii 19–20)? We discussed above the difficulties encountered in any synchronization based on the time of Jesus' entrance into Galilee (see p. 153), and in this instance the differences within the Synoptic tradition about the time of the rejection are an added hazard. We may note that while in John the statement about the prophet's having no honor in his own country is followed immediately by the story of the healing of the boy at Capernaum, both Matthew and Luke have this healing separated by several chapters from the statement about the prophet.

We have seen that in their estimation of enthusiasm based on miracles, iv 44–45 and ii 23–25 have much in common. These two passages also have a similar function in the outline of John. After the description in ii 23–25 of those in Jerusalem who believed in Jesus because of his signs, one of these "believers," Nicodemus, came to Jesus with his inadequate understanding of Jesus' powers. Jesus had to explain to Nicodemus that he was really one who had come from above to give eternal life. So also, after the description in iv 44–45 of the Galileans who welcomed Jesus because of his works, a royal official from Galilee comes to Jesus with an inadequate understanding of Jesus' power. Jesus will lead the man to a deeper understanding of his function as the giver of life.

BIBLIOGRAPHY

Bligh, J., "Jesus in Samaria," *Heythrop Journal* 3 (1962), 329–46.
Bowman, J., "Early Samaritan Eschatology," JJS 6 (1955), 63–72.
———"Samaritan Studies," BJRL 40 (1957–58), 298–329.
Brown, R. E., "The Problem of Historicity in John," CBQ 24 (1962), especially pp. 13–14 on iv 43–45. Also in NTE, pp. 158–60.

Cullmann, O., "Samaria and the Origins of the Christian Mission," *The Early Church* (London: SCM, 1956), pp. 185–92.

McCool, F. J., "Living Water in John," BCCT, pp. 226–33.

Robinson, John A. T., "The 'Others' of John 4.38," StEv, I, pp. 510–15. Also in TNTS, pp. 61–66.

Roustang, F., "Les moments de l'acte de foi et ses conditions de possibilité. Essai d'interprétation du dialogue avec la Samaritaine," RSR 46 (1958), 344–78.

Schnackenburg, R., "Die 'Anbetung in Geist und Wahrheit' (Joh 4, 23) im Lichte von Qumran-Texten," BZ 3 (1959), 88–94.

Willemse, J., "La Patrie de Jésus selon saint Jean iv. 44," NTS 11 (1964–65), 349–64.

16. THE SECOND SIGN AT CANA IN GALILEE— HEALING THE OFFICIAL'S SON
(iv 46–54)

IV 46 And so he arrived again at Cana in Galilee where he had made the water wine. Now at Capernaum there was a royal official whose son was ill. 47 When he heard that Jesus had come back from Judea to Galilee, he went to him and begged him to come down and restore health to his son who was near death. 48 Jesus replied, "Unless you people can see signs and wonders, you never believe." 49 "Sir," the royal official pleaded with him, "come down before my little boy dies." 50 Jesus told him, "Return home; your son is going to live." The man put his trust in the word Jesus had spoken to him and started for home.

51 And as he was on his way down, his servants met him with the news that his boy was going to live. 52 When he asked [them] at what time he had shown improvement, they told him, "The fever left him yesterday afternoon about one." 53 Now it was at that very hour, the father realized, that Jesus had told him, "Your son is going to live." And he and his whole household became believers. 54 This was the second sign that Jesus performed on returning again from Judea to Galilee.

49: *pleaded;* 50: *told.* In the historical present tense.

NOTES

iv 46. *Now at Capernaum.* Boismard thinks that this was the original opening of the story, as in iii 1; he regards the first sentence of vs. 46 as the work of a redactor, a view shared by many other scholars.

royal official. The word *basilikos* may designate a person of royal blood (Codex Bezae and the Latin tradition take him to be a petty king) or a servant to the king. The latter is meant here; the king whom he serves is Herod, the tetrarch of Galilee whom the NT regularly calls a king (Mark vi 14, 22; Matt xiv 9). It is not impossible that he was a soldier (the Synoptics speak of a [Roman] centurion), for Josephus uses *basilikos* in reference to Herodian troops (*Life* 72;⚹400). However, Capernaum was a border town, and there were probably many types of royal administrative officials there.

48. *you people*. The official is looked upon as representing the Galileans of vss. 44–45. In the Synoptic account (Mark vii 27) of the healing of the Syrophoenician's daughter, a story in many ways parallel to John's narrative here (see COMMENT), Jesus, in rebuffing the woman, treats her as a representative of a national group.

signs and wonders. This is the only use of "wonders" in John; it is obviously unfavorable, for in Johannine thought an overemphasis on the wondrous blinds the eye to the miracle's ability to reveal who Jesus is (see App. III). An interesting parallel to this verse is Exod vii 3–4 where God says to Moses, "Though I multiply my signs and wonders in the land of Egypt, Pharaoh will not listen to you."

49. *Sir*. *Kyrios* means both "sir" and "lord"; perhaps the latter is meant here. In the Syrophoenician story (Mark vii 28) the woman's response to Jesus' rebuke also employs *kyrios*.

little boy. *Paidion*, a diminutive of *pais* (see vs. 51); elsewhere John uses *huios*, "son."

50. *live*. Semitic has no exact word for "recover"; "to live" covers both recovery from illness (II Kings viii 9: "Shall I live from this disease") and return to life from death (I Kings xvii 23: "Your son lives" to a mother whose son was dead). The twofold meaning is convenient for John's theological purposes.

put his trust in. *Pisteuein* with the dative; this is not so firm a religious commitment as *pisteuein eis* (see App. I:9).

the word. In the Synoptic story of the centurion: "Say but the *word* and my boy shall be restored to health."

51. *on his way down*. This description agrees implicitly with vs. 46a. In going to Capernaum from Cana one must go east across the Galilean hills and then *descend* to the Sea of Galilee. The twenty-mile journey was not accomplished in one day, so it is the next day when the servants meet the official who had already begun the descent. These indications suggest that the author knew Palestine well.

servants. Or "slaves" (*douloi*); these also appear in the Synoptic story of the centurion, for he has *douloi* to order around (Matt viii 9).

that his boy was going to live. Some good texts, including P[66], give direct discourse.

boy. See NOTE on vs. 49. This is the only occurrence of *pais* in John, and even here some important texts read *huios*. Kilpatrick, *art. cit.*, accepts *huios* on the grounds that *pais* is a scribal harmonization with the Synoptics. However, the insertion of *huios* in place of *pais* may be explained as a scribal attempt to make the usage in the story uniform.

52. *asked*. The verb *pynthanesthai* occurs only here in John. It is most frequently Lucan in the NT, and Boismard uses it as an indication that Luke redacted this scene in John.

[them]. The word is omitted in Vaticanus and P[75]; the many texts that have it vary as to its position; it may well be a scribal clarification.

time. Literally "hour" as in vs. 53.

The fever left him. For the same expression see Mark i 31; Matt viii 15.

yesterday afternoon about one. Literally "yesterday at the seventh hour." Some object that if the official left Cana at 1:00 P.M., by the next day he should have been home and not still on his way. But there are many unknown factors. Did he set out immediately? How is the next day reckoned? According to one form of Jewish reckoning, the next day began that evening, and so he may have been traveling only a few hours. See NOTE on i 39.

53. *became believers.* Literally "believed"=*pisteuein* used absolutely.

54. *second . . . again.* Literally, "Again this second sign Jesus performed on coming from Judea to Galilee." Even when we have moved "again" close to the verb, John's expression is pleonastic. It is found also in xxi 16; but, *pace* Ruckstuhl, *Die literarische Einheit,* p. 201, it is scarcely an indicator of Johannine style, for a similar expression is used in Matt xxvi 42; Acts x 15. Such a pleonasm is attested in secular Greek (BAG, p. 611).

COMMENT

Relation to the Synoptics

To the story of the healing of the centurion's boy. Since the time of Irenaeus (*Adv. Haer.* ii 22:3; PG 7:783), scholars have suggested that John's account of the official's son is a third variant of the story of the centurion's boy or servant of which forms with minor variants appear in Matt viii 5–13 and Luke vii 1–10. Let us compare the details: (a) The name Capernaum appears in all three. In John Jesus is at Cana, and the royal official from Capernaum comes to Cana. In Matthew the centurion meets Jesus at the entrance to Capernaum. In Luke the centurion stays at his home in Capernaum and sends two delegations to Jesus. Many scholars believe that originally the Johannine story was localized at Capernaum, and it was the desire to draw attention to the parallelism between this healing and the (first) Cana miracle that led to a transfer of scene (see NOTE on vs. 46). Schnackenburg, pp. 63–64, shows himself favorable to the oft-made suggestion that this miracle was originally the sequel to ii 12 wherein Jesus goes to Capernaum. However, as he notes, the theory that the healing has been moved from a Capernaum setting must postulate the secondary character of all the indications of locality in vss. 47, 51 ("way down"), 52 ("yesterday"), and 54—not merely 46. (b) A person of rank asks a favor of Jesus. In both John and Luke (vii 3) this person has *heard* of Jesus; both use the verb *erōtan,* "to ask." In Matthew and Luke the person is a centurion, definitely a Gentile, and probably a Roman. In John he is in Herod's service, and nothing is said to indicate that he is not a Jew. Here the Synoptic tradition is the most theologically developed, for the story is connected to a saying about faith outside of Israel. Matthew has developed the point even further than Luke by adding vss. 11–12 about the salvation of many from the east and west (=Luke xiii 28–30). However, even though John's story has nothing specific to do with the salvation of the Gentiles, we shall see that this theme may be represented by subtle allusions. (c) The favor asked pertains to a boy in this man's household. In Matthew it is the *pais* of the centurion, a word that means "boy," both in the sense of "son" and in the sense of "servant boy, slave." Luke too speaks of a *pais* (vii 7), but more often of a *doulos* (vii 2, 3, 10), which clearly means "servant boy." John speaks of the official's *huios* which means "son," although *paidion* appears in vs. 49, and perhaps *pais* in 51 (see NOTES). It has been suggested that an original *pais* was understood in one way in John (as "son") and in another way in Luke ("servant boy"). Such a suggestion presupposes Johannine dependence on a Greek form of the Synoptic tradition. More likely the original story had "son," which in the form of the story used by Matthew was rendered in Greek as *pais,* and in the form of the story used by John as *huios.* It was Luke or a Lucan forerunner who, in the Greek stage of the tradition, understood *pais* as servant boy and began to speak of a *doulos.* That Luke's use of *doulos* is secondary is suggested by the fact that it appears in those verses (2, 3, 10) where the Lucan story differs from that of Matthew. (d) The boy is sick. In Matthew the *pais* is lying paralyzed in terrible distress. In Luke the *doulos* is sick and at the point of death. In John the *huios* is ill and near death with fever. John's account is perfectly plausible here since fever would explain the crisis more easily than Matthew's paralysis. As Schnackenburg, p. 74, points out, Matthew has a tendency to specify illnesses. (e) The response of Jesus. In Luke Jesus says nothing but goes with the delegation. In John Jesus is displeased with the general desire for the miraculous and seemingly refuses the request. In Matthew the meaning of viii 7 is uncertain: the response of Jesus may be affirmative, "I shall come and heal him"; or it may be a sarcastic question, "Am I supposed to come and heal him?" If it is the latter, Matthew is not too far from John in thought pattern. (f) The reply to Jesus. In John the official repeats his plea more earnestly, asking Jesus to come down to his home. In Matthew he repeats his plea, but feels he is unworthy to have Jesus come under his roof. In Luke he sends a second delegation telling Jesus of this unworthiness. See NOTE on "word" in vs. 50. (g) The boy is healed at a distance. This is absolutely clear in John where the official hears of the healing from his servants (see NOTE on vs. 51) while he is on the way home. In Matthew, though there is no mention of the centurion's returning home, the boy is healed while the centurion is speaking to Jesus. In Luke the delegation finds the slave well when they return to the centurion's house. (h) Both John and Matthew mention that the boy was healed "at that very hour."

When we analyze these points, we find both differences and similarities. However, most of the differences are susceptible of logical explanation, either in terms of the vagaries of independent traditions, or as a reflection of the peculiarities of the individual evangelists. The similarities seem to indicate that the same incident lies behind all three accounts. In details (*a, c, h*) and perhaps (*e*) John is closer to Matthew than to Luke; in (*b*) and (*d*) John is closer to Luke; in still other details John is close to neither. This would lead us to agree with Haenchen and Dodd (*Tradition,* pp. 194–95) that John's account is independent of the two Synoptic stories. Where the various accounts differ, it is not always possible to determine which is the oldest tradition.

To the story of the healing of the Syrophoenician woman's daughter. Dodd has pointed out that there are many parallels between John's account and the story found in Mark vii 24–30 and Matt xv 21–28 (the parallels to the latter form are less notable). These parallels affect particularly the elements in John's account that were not matched in the story of the centurion's son. We may point out the following relevant details in the Syrophoenician story (see also NOTES on vss. 48, 49):

- The woman hears of Jesus as he comes into her territory and comes to him.
- Her daughter is lying in bed at home (possessed by a demon).
- Her request for help is met by a disparaging response from Jesus, but she persists.
- Jesus tells her, "Go on your way; the demon has left your daughter."
- She returns home and finds that the demon has left the child.

The parallels are not close enough to make us believe that John borrowed the added details in the account of the royal official's son from the Synoptic story of the Syrophoenician woman; but they are close enough to make us think twice about the assumption that the fourth evangelist invented the added details.

Before we close this discussion of parallels, we should mention the story in TalBab *Berakoth* 34b, recording how Gamaliel sent to Rabbi Ḥanina ben Dosa to ask for help for Gamaliel's son who was ill with fever. Rabbi Ḥanina told the envoys, "Go, the fever has left him"; and the boy was healed at that very hour.

Similarity to the First Cana Miracle

Some of the peculiarities in John's account of the healing of the royal official's son may stem from the fact that this miracle story is closely patterned on the story in ii 1–11. The evangelist calls the similarity to our attention by reminding us twice of the first Cana miracle (vss. 46, 54), at both the beginning and the end of this second Cana story. The general pattern of the two miracles is the same: Jesus has just come back into Galilee; someone comes with a request; indirectly Jesus seems to refuse the request; the questioner persists; Jesus grants the request; this leads another group of people (the disciples; the household) to believe in him. In neither story are we told exactly how the miracle was accomplished. There are even similarities in context; for, as Temple, p. 170, points out, the two Cana miracles are the only two Johannine signs that do not lead immediately into a discourse. After each Cana miracle Jesus goes up to Jerusalem and the Temple.

Such similarities have caused scholars to suggest that the two Cana stories stem from a unique tradition. Support for this is given by iv 54, which characterizes the healing of the official's son as the second sign that Jesus performed. Perhaps all this statement means is that this is the second sign performed under the peculiar condition of coming from Judea into Galilee. But if the statement is taken absolutely, it seems to ignore the signs worked at Jerusalem and mentioned in ii 23 and iv 45. (Knowledge only of Galilee miracles seems to be implied also in vii 3; see also vi 2.)

This observation is the backbone of the theory of a collection of signs as one of the sources for John (see Introduction, p. xxix). In such a source the second Cana miracle would have immediately followed the first, whether or not ii 12 intervened and Capernaum was the original locus of the healing. Spitta, Bultmann, Schweizer, Wilkens, Boismard, Temple, and Schnackenburg are just a few who accept such a solution.

Such a theory is certainly possible. We have not accepted a source theory of the composition of John, at least in the Bultmannian sense. However, it is reasonable to suppose that there were collections of miracles in the corpus of Johannine material that was edited to give us the Gospel. In one of the stages of editing two closely related miracles may have been split up to form the beginning and the end of Part Two of the Book of Signs, "From Cana to Cana," in the Gospel (see Outline, p. cxl). Such a process would have been motivated also by theological reasons; for the first Cana miracle has a great deal of meaning in its present position as the culmination of the training of the disciples, and we shall see below that the second Cana miracle has added significance from its present position following Jesus' activities in Judea and Samaria. The present arrangement of these two miracles may be related to the history of iii 22–30. If, as we have suggested, this final scene pertaining to John the Baptist was once closely associated with the material in ch. i, then it probably lost that association when the first Cana scene was introduced to complete the call of the disciples and to introduce Part Two. All of this is hypothesis, of course, and it should not deflect us from seeking meaning in the present sequence of the Gospel.

The Editing of iv 46–54

Verses 48–49 offer difficulty on several counts. They are not found in the Synoptic story of the centurion's son (although see Matt viii 7 in *e*, and the story of the Syrophoenician woman). Jesus' reaction to the request for help seems unduly harsh and not in accord with his treatment of other instances of sickness; indeed in v 6 and ix 6 Jesus takes the initiative in working a sign. Moreover, it is not very clear why Jesus went ahead and worked the miracle after this seeming refusal. One explanation is that Jesus wanted to raise the man from a faith based on seeing signs to a faith based on Jesus' word, and the latter part of vs. 50 is cited in support of this. However, the official did not come to complete faith on the strength of Jesus' word, but only after he found out that the sign had actually been performed (vs. 53). Therefore, to be precise, the pedagogy was not to lead the official away from a faith based on signs; rather, it was to lead him to a faith that would not be based on the wondrous aspect of the sign but on what the sign would tell him about Jesus. The man was led through the sign to faith in Jesus as the life-giver (see below). This fits in with the whole Johannine theology of signs (App. III).

Thus, vss. 48–49 have a place in the Johannine theology of the scene and agree with 44–45 in expressing a low estimate of a faith based on the superficiality of the miraculous. However, precisely because these verses do echo Johannine theology, the question has been asked whether or not they belong to the original content of the scene. Schweizer, Haenchen, and Schnackenburg agree in evaluating vss. 48–49 as an addition by the evangelist to the more original story, which without these verses would be quite similar to the Synoptic story of the centurion's boy. Certainly, if 50 followed 47, the narrative would flow very smoothly, and we would never miss 48–49. However, the fact that we do have a parallel to the rejection of a request (48) in the Synoptic narrative of the Syrophoenician cautions us to go slowly.

Boismard has another approach to these verses. He believes that vss. 48–49 and 51–53 represent the Lucan redaction of the original Johannine story. This is another instance of his theory that Luke was the final redactor of John, a theory that we have not found convincing as applied elsewhere. One of his arguments is that 48 is the only instance in John of the combination "signs and wonders," while it occurs nine times in Acts. The argument backfires, however, because all the instances in Acts employ the combination favorably, while John employs it unfavorably. Boismard also uses the argument that in John Jesus rarely calls his miracles "signs" as he does in vs. 48 (Jesus himself speaks of "works"). However, both here and in vi 26 Jesus' words reflect, not his own ideas, but the mentality of his audience. In reference to vss. 51–53 Boismard finds the act of faith (53) tautological since the official has already come to believe in vs. 50; but, as we have explained above, this is not true, for the faith in vs. 53 is an advance—now the official has come through the sign to believe in Jesus as the life-giver. Moreover, to attribute 51–53 to Luke is to neglect the fact that in 53 ("at that very hour") John agrees with the Matthean rather than with the Lucan form of the story of the centurion.

One point that Boismard makes (also Dodd, *Tradition,* p. 193) is worth considering, namely, that the confession of faith in vs. 53 would be more at home in a later stage of Christianity than in the context envisaged in the Gospel narrative. One could almost translate it: "He and his whole household were converted to Christianity." The best parallels are found in Acts where we have a series of individuals who became believers along with their (whole) households (x 2, xi 14, xvi 15, 31, 34, especially xviii 8). All of these individuals are Gentiles, and we shall discuss the theological importance of this below. Nevertheless, this is scarcely enough to prove that Luke redacted the scene in John; in fact, there is a small but significant difference between John and Acts even here, for John uses *oikia* for "household" while Acts uses *oikos*. Boismard says that in using *oikia* Luke is adapting his redaction to Johannine style, but this explanation is not valid since both *oikos* and *oikia* appear in John and with about the same frequency.

The Theological Import of the Scene

The second miracle at Cana has a twofold significance: first, it stresses faith, and thus is a culmination of the preceding scenes in Part Two of the Book of Signs; second, it stresses Jesus' power to give life and thus introduces one of the major themes of Part Three.

The Theme of *Faith*. We pointed out on p. CXLIII that a major theme in chs. ii–iv was the reaction of individuals to Jesus in terms of faith. A glance at the outline we gave there shows the different types of faith exhibited by the main characters of these stories. In discussing the conversion of the Samaritans we saw that while Jesus encountered disbelief or inadequate faith in Jerusalem, when he comes to Samaria, the Samaritans believe on the strength of his word. In Galilee, in both the first and the second Cana stories, an understanding of Jesus' signs leads the disciples and the official's household to faith. A linear progression in the perfection of faith is difficult to trace through these chapters. We have already expressed doubts that John intended a progression in faith from the Jews of ii–iii through the Samaritans (half-Jews) to the Gentiles at Cana.

Boismard, with his Lucan interests, sees in these chapters a geographical progression, a capsulizing of the spread of Christianity outlined in Acts i 8 ("You shall be my witnesses in Jerusalem and in all Judea and Samaria and to the end of the earth"). We saw that the Samaritan scene in John did have echoes of the conversion of the Samaritans in Acts viii; and it is not impossible that the phrase "He and his whole household became believers" is an allusion to Christianity's triumphs in later days, especially among the Gentiles. If John capsulized the development of the disciples in Part One of the Book of Signs, there is no *a priori* objection to the symbolic capsulization of the history of the Christian mission in Part Two. Yet one must admit that the allusions on which this interpretation is based are subtle and uncertain.

The Theme of *Life*. In Part Two there are also references which may be a preparation for the theme of life found in the second Cana miracle. In the discourse with Nicodemus Jesus said that God gave the only Son that everyone who believes in him might have eternal life (iii 16, 36); in the dialogue with the Samaritan woman Jesus speaks of the water that gives life. Finally, in the present scene Jesus performs a sign that gives life. The evangelist emphasizes this by his stress on the word "live" in vss. 50, 51, and 53. Of course, in Johannine thought the life (i.e., restoration to health —see NOTE on vs. 50) given to the boy remains on the level of a sign of the eternal life that Jesus will give after his resurrection. Some think that this is hinted at in the narrative by the time indication in iv 43, "after two days." The first Cana miracle was dated "on the third day," a date which some rather imaginatively take as an allusion to the resurrection on the third day; with a little more justification it is pointed out that in the second Cana miracle "life" is restored on the third day. We suspect, however, that this is an instance where the interpreter is more ingenious than the evangelist; for, to be precise, "after two days" is given by the evangelist as the date of the departure from Samaria, and not primarily as the date of the healing of the boy.

If in Part Two there has been some preparation for the life theme of the second Cana miracle, the main thrust of that theme is not as a culmination of what has preceded, but as a foretaste of what is to come. Feuillet, *art. cit.*, has advanced strong arguments for seeing iv 46–54 as the introduction to Part Three in the Book. He points out that Part Two opened in ch. ii with two actions, one at Cana, the second at Jerusalem, which formed the subject and offered the motifs for the discourses that followed in chs. iii–iv 42. So, at the beginning of Part Three, Feuillet would join the second Cana miracle to the healing of the paralytic at Jerusalem to get another Cana-Jerusalem pair that forms the subject of the discourse in the rest of ch. v. He notes that the theme of living in iv 50, 51, 53, is picked up in the discourse in v 21 ff. Moreover, each Cana miracle which reaches a climax in faith (ii 11, iv 53) offers a dramatic contrast to the subsequent Jerusalem action which leads to disbelief and opposition on the part of the Jews (ii 18, v 16).

The positive part of Feuillet's argumentation is convincing. Good pedagogue that he is, the evangelist has introduced in this second Cana miracle the theme of life, not only because it will be the subject of ch. v, but also because it will appear in subsequent chapters of Part Three (*the bread of life* in vi, *the living water* in vii 37–39, *the light of life* in viii 12, also viii 51, x 10, 28). Yet, we believe that structurally the evangelist wished iv 46–54 to serve primarily as the conclusion of Part Two (chs. ii–iv) and only secondarily as the introduction to Part Three. The strong emphasis that this is the second Cana miracle and the similarities that it has with the first Cana miracle make it an obvious inclusion with ii 1–11, and inclusion is the Johannine way of marking off parts. We have already explained how the same scene can serve as the conclusion of one part and the introduction to the next (see p. CXLIII).

BIBLIOGRAPHY

Boismard, M.-E., "Saint Luc et la rédaction du quatrième évangile (Jn. iv, 46–54)," RB 69 (1962), 185–211.

Feuillet, A., "La signification théologique du second miracle de Cana (Jo. IV, 46–54)," RSR 48 (1960), 62–75. Now in English in JohSt, pp. 39–51.

Haenchen, E., "Johanneische Probleme," ZTK 56 (1959), especially pp. 23–31.

Kilpatrick, G. D., "John iv. 51 PAIS OR YIOS?" JTS 14 (1963), 393.

Schnackenburg, R., "Zur Traditionsgeschichte von Joh 4, 46–54," BZ 8 (1964), 58–88.

Schweizer, E., "Die Heilung des Königlichen, Joh. 4, 46–54," EvTh 11 (1951–52), 64–71. Also in *Neotestamentica* (Zurich: Zwingli, 1963), pp. 407–15.

Temple, S., "The Two Signs in the Fourth Gospel," JBL 81 (1962), 169–74.

THE BOOK OF SIGNS

Part Three: Jesus and the Principal Feasts of the Jews

OUTLINE

PART THREE: JESUS AND THE PRINCIPAL FEASTS OF THE JEWS
(chs. v–x, introduced by iv 46–54)

(iv 46–54: Jesus gives *life* to the official's son at Cana)

A.   v: JESUS ON THE SABBATH
Jesus performs works that only God can do on the Sabbath.

(1–15) The gift of *life* [healing] to the man at the pool
of Bethesda. (§ 17)
(16–47) Discourse explaining the two preceding signs
which gave life:

16–18: Introduction—Jesus' right to work on
the Sabbath. (§ 18)
19–25: *Division 1*—The twofold Sabbath work
of Jesus, namely, giving life and judging
—realized eschatology. (§ 18)
26–30: Duplicate of Division 1—final
eschatology. (§ 18)
31–47: *Division 2*—Jesus defends his claim before the Jews (§ 19):
(a) 31–40: List of witnesses for Jesus'
claim.
(b) 41–47: Attack on the root of Jewish disbelief and appeal to
Moses.

B.   vi: JESUS AT PASSOVER
Jesus gives bread replacing the manna of the Exodus.

(1–15) The multiplication of the loaves. (§ 20)
(16–21) Walking on the Sea of Galilee. (§ 21)
(22–24) Transition to the Bread of Life Discourse—crowd
comes to Jesus. (§ 22)
(25–71) Discourse on the Bread of Life, explaining the
multiplication:

25–34: Preface—Request for bread/manna. (§ 23)

35–50: Body of the Discourse—The Bread of Life is primarily Jesus' revelation; secondary eucharistic undertones. (§ 24)

51–58: Duplicate of the Discourse—The Bread of Life is the Eucharist. (§ 25)

59: Geographical note on the setting of the Discourse. (§ 25)

60–71: Epilogue—Reactions to the Discourse. (§ 26)

C.   vii–viii: JESUS AT TABERNACLES
Jesus figuratively replaces the water and light ceremonies of the feast;
collection of arguments between Jesus and the Jews.

vii (1–13) Introduction—Will Jesus go up to the feast? (§ 27)

(14–36) *Scene 1*—Discourse delivered in the middle of the feast (§ 28):
14–24: Jesus' right to teach:
resumption of the Sabbath question.
25–36: Origins of Jesus;
his return to the Father.

(37–52) *Scene 2*—Jesus on the last day of the feast (§ 29):
37–39: Jesus proclaims himself to be the source of *water*.
40–52: Reactions of the crowd and of the Sanhedrin.

[vii 53–viii 11: The Adulteress—a non-Johannine interpolation. (§ 30)]

viii (12–59) *Scene 3*—Miscellaneous discourses:
(a) 12–20: A discourse at the temple treasury: Jesus the *light* of the world and his witness to himself. (§ 31)
(b) 21–30: An attack on the unbelieving Jews and the question of who Jesus is. (§ 32)
(c) 31–59: Jesus and Abraham (§ 33):
31–41a: Abraham and the Jews.
41b–47: The real father of the Jews.
48–59: The claims of Jesus; comparison with Abraham.

ix–x 21: AFTERMATH OF TABERNACLES

ix (1–41) As a sign that he is the *light,* Jesus gives sight to
a man born blind. (§ 34)

    1–5: Setting.
    6–7: Miraculous healing.
    8–34: Interrogations of the blind man:
        8–12: Questioning by neighbors and ac-
        quaintances.
        13–17: Preliminary interrogation by Phari-
        sees.
        18–23: Man's parents questioned by the
        Jews.
        24–34: Second interrogation of the man by
        the Jews.
    35–41: Jesus leads the blind man to that spiritual
    sight which is faith;
    the Pharisees are hardened in blindness.

x (1–21) Jesus as the sheepgate and the shepherd—a figurative attack on the Pharisees. (§ 35)

    1–5: Parables drawn from pastoral life:
        1–3a: Parable of the correct approach to
        the sheep.
        3b–5: Parable of the intimacy of shep-
        herd and sheep.
    6: Reaction to the parables.
    7–18: Explanation of the parables:
        (a) 7–10: Jesus is the gate:
        7–8: the gate whereby the shepherd ap-
        proaches the sheep.
        9–10: the gate whereby the sheep go to
        pasture.
        (b) 11–18: Jesus is the model shepherd:
        11–13: the shepherd who lays down his
        life for the sheep.
        14–16: the shepherd who knows his sheep
        intimately.
        17–18: the theme of laying down his life.
    19–21: Reaction to the explanations.

D.   x 22–39: JESUS AT DEDICATION (§ 36)
                   Jesus as Messiah and Son of God;
                   Jesus is consecrated in place of the temple altar.

    (22–31) Jesus as the Messiah:

               22–24: Setting; the question, "Is Jesus the Messiah?"
               25–30: Jesus' response.
                    31: Reaction—attempt to stone Jesus.

    (32–39) Jesus as the Son of God:

               32–33: Transition; the question of whether Jesus is making himself God.
               34–38: Jesus' response.
                    39: Reaction—attempt to arrest Jesus.

APPARENT CONCLUSION TO THE PUBLIC MINISTRY (§ 37)

           x 40–42: Jesus withdraws across the Jordan to where his ministry began.

17. JESUS ON THE SABBATH:
—THE HEALING AT BETHESDA
(v 1–15)

The gift of life [healing] to the man at the pool

V 1 Later, on the occasion of a Jewish feast, Jesus went up to Jerusalem. 2 Now in Jerusalem, by the Sheep Pool, there is a place with the Hebrew name Bethesda. Its five porticoes 3 were crowded with sick people who were lying there, blind, lame, and disabled [, waiting for the movement of the waters].   [4]   5 In fact, one man there had been sick thirty-eight years. 6 Jesus knew that he had been sick a long time; so when he saw him lying there, he said to him, "Do you want to be cured?" 7 "Sir," the sick man answered, "I haven't anybody to plunge me into the pool once the water has been stirred up. By the time I get there, someone else has gone in ahead of me." 8 Jesus said to him, "Stand up; pick up your mat, and walk around." 9 The man was immediately cured, and he picked up his mat and began to walk.

Now that day was a Sabbath. 10 Therefore, the Jews kept telling the man who had been healed, "It's the Sabbath, and you are not allowed to be carrying that mat around." 11 He explained, "It was the man who cured me who told me, 'Pick up your mat and walk.'" 12 "This person who told you to pick it up and walk," they asked, "who is he?" 13 But the man who had been restored to health had no idea who it was, for, thanks to the crowd in that place, Jesus had slipped away.

14 Later on Jesus found him in the temple precincts and said to him, "Remember now, you have been cured. Sin no more, for fear that something worse will happen to you." 15 The man went off and informed the Jews that Jesus was the one who had cured him.

6, 8: *said;* 14: *found.* In the historical present tense.

NOTES

v 1. *a Jewish feast*. Codex Sinaiticus reads *"the* feast," which would probably be a reference either to Tabernacles (Bernard) or to Passover (Lagrange); but the evidence for the omission of the article is overwhelming. An early tradition in the Greek church identifies this unnamed feast as Pentecost, a view accepted by some modern scholars (see F.-M. Braun, RThom 52 [1952], 263–65). It would explain the references to Moses in the discourse (v 46–47); for, in that process which connected originally agricultural feasts to events in Israel's history, the Feast of Weeks (Pentecost) was identified with the celebration of Moses' receiving the Law on Mount Sinai. We are not certain how old this identification is; for a complete discussion favoring an early date see B. Noack, "The Day of Pentecost in Jubilees, Qumran, and Acts," *Annual of the Swedish Theological Institute* 1 (1962), 72–95. However, the only identification given in John is that the feast was a Sabbath (v 9); other identifications have no more than secondary interest.

to Jerusalem. Jews were obliged to go to Jerusalem at the three major feasts of Passover, Pentecost, and Tabernacles, whence the suggestions above. Jesus was last in Jerusalem for Passover (ii 13); and *if* he went back to Galilee through Samaria in May (see NOTE on iv 35: "fields . . . ripe"), identifying this feast as Pentecost would imply a very short stay in Galilee. It is an open question, of course, how much chronological sequence has been preserved in these narratives.

2. *by the Sheep Pool*. The manuscript evidence is quite confused; the best manuscripts have these words, but with two possible interpretations: **(a)** In Jerusalem, by the Sheep _____, there is a pool with the Hebrew name, etc. **(b)** In Jerusalem, by the Sheep Pool, there is a _____ with the Hebrew name, etc. Each reading seems to demand that we supply a word that has been left understood. We have opted for the second, supplying the general noun "place." Those who opt for the first interpretation customarily supply "gate," for we know of a Sheep Gate near the Temple. It would do less violence to the Greek in either interpretation to supply "pool," thus indicating two pools: the Sheep Pool and the Pool of Bethesda. In any case, John is speaking of the area northeast of the Temple where the sheep were brought into Jerusalem for sacrifice; and the name of this region and/or its pool was Bethesda.

Hebrew name. The Johannine writings frequently mention the Semitic names of places (even in Revelation ix 11, xvi 16). "Hebrew" is used loosely, often for names that are Aramaic.

Bethesda. In the witnesses to the text the name appears in various forms: **(a)** "Bethsaida" has the strongest attestation, but this may be a scribal confusion with the town of Bethsaida on the Sea of Galilee. **(b)** "Be(t)zatha" is found in Codices Sinaiticus and Bezae. Josephus (*War* II.xv.5;※328) speaks of a quarter of the city called Bezetha, near the northeast corner of the temple area. Also Eusebius *Onomasticon* (GCS 11¹, p. 58:21–26—"Bezatha"). **(c)** "Bethesda," found in Codex Alexandrinus, has the weakest attestation. The fact that it can have the symbolic meaning of "house of mercy" has made it suspect as a scribal guess. We now have added evidence from the copper scroll found at Qumran (3Q15 xi 12–13;※57) and published by J. T. Milik in *Discoveries in the Judean Desert*, III (1962), p. 271. According to Milik's translation, in the general area of the Temple, on the eastern hill of Jerusalem, an (imaginary) treasure was buried "in Bet 'Ešdatayin, in the pool at the entrance to its smaller basin." The name of the region or pool seems then to have been "Bet 'Ešdâ" ("house of the flowing"—root *'šd*); it appears in the dual in the scroll because there were two basins. "Bethesda" seems to be an accurate Greek rendition of the singular form of the name, while Milik suggests that "Bezatha" is a rendition of the Aramaic emphatic plural of the name ("Bet 'Ešdātâ"). All of this is plausible, but unfortunately the reading is not entirely certain (see CBQ 26 [1964], 254).

In this century the pool described in John has been discovered and excavated in Jerusalem on the property of the White Fathers near St. Anne's Church (see Jeremias, Bagatti). The pool was trapezoidal in form, 165–220 feet wide by 315 feet long, divided by a central partition. There were colonnades on the four sides and on the partition—thus, John's "five porticoes." Stairways in the corners permitted descent into the pools. In this hilly area the water may have come from underground drainage; some of it, perhaps, from intermittent springs.

3. *disabled*. That is, with atrophied limbs. The fact that the people are lying outside in the porticoes indicates that this is not a winter scene.

[*waiting . . . waters*]. This clause is found in the Western tradition (Bezae, Koridethi, OS, Vulg.), and it may be original. Bernard suggests that its addition was prompted by vs. 7, but this seems unlikely.

[4]. Codex Alexandrinus and the later Greek mss. have a verse omitted by all the early witnesses, including those that have the additional clause in vs. 3. It reads: "For [from time to time] an angel of the Lord used to come down in the pool, and the water was stirred up. Accordingly, the first one to enter [after the stirring of the water] was cured of whatever sickness he had had." In the West, Tertullian (ca. A.D. 200) gives evidence of having known this verse; Chrysostom (ca. 400) is the first of the Greek writers to do so. That it is a gloss is indicated not only by the poor textual attestation, but also by the presence of seven non-Johannine words in one sentence. This ancient gloss, however, may well reflect with accuracy a popular tradition about the pool. The bubbling of water (vs. 7), caused perhaps by an intermittent spring, was thought to have healing power; and this may well have been attributed in the popular imagination to supernatural powers. The Mohammedans of Palestine in modern times have traditions about the jinni of a particular spring.

5. *sick thirty-eight years*. It is *not* said that he was at the pool all this time. The suggestion that the number is symbolic, e.g., the 38 years of wandering in Deut ii 14, is unnecessary. That an ailment was not temporary is often indicated in NT miracles: the woman of Luke xiii 11 was sick 18 years (also Acts iv 22, ix 33); it was one of the ways of underlining the hopelessness of the case.

6. *Jesus knew*. Jesus' extraordinary knowledge of men is a Johannine theme (ii 25).

he saw him. The Synoptics also use the description of Jesus' seeing someone (and explicitly or implicitly taking pity on him) as a means of introducing a miracle (Luke vii 13, xiii 12).

7. *stirred up*. Perhaps by the flowing of an intermittent spring.

8. *Stand up . . . walk around*. The command of Jesus is the same as that given to the paralytic let down through the roof in Mark ii 11.

mat. Both John and Mark (in the paralytic scene) use *krabbatos*, the vulgar *koine* word for the pallet or mattress used by the poor as bedding; in the same Synoptic scene Matthew and Luke use *klinē* or *klinidion*.

9. *immediately.* Stress on the immediate effect of Jesus' power is not unusual in the Synoptic tradition; it is explicit in Luke xiii 13, implicit in Luke vii 15.

10. *the Jews.* An obvious instance where this term (see Introduction, p. LXXI) does not mean the Jewish people, since the former paralytic was certainly a Jew himself.

carrying that mat. Carrying things from one domain to another is the last of 39 works forbidden in Mishnaic tractate *Sabbath* 7:2; carrying empty beds is implicitly forbidden in 10:5.

12. *told you to pick it up.* The wonderful healing has been lost sight of; only the Sabbath violation is important to the authorities.

13. *Jesus had slipped away.* In Mark especially it is characteristic of Jesus to avoid drawing public attention to his miracles (vii 33, viii 23).

14. *temple precincts.* The pool lay just north-northeast of the temple area—another indication of the evangelist's knowledge of Jerusalem in the days before the Roman destruction.

Sin no more. Elsewhere Jesus does not accept the thesis that because a man was sick or suffering, it was a sign that he had committed sin (John ix 3; Luke xiii 1–5). Nevertheless, on a more general scale he does indicate a connection between sin and suffering. (Later theology would say that suffering is a consequence of original sin and that some sufferings are the penalties of actual or personal sin.) Jesus' healing miracles in the Synoptic Gospels were part of his attack on the sinful realm of Satan (see our article, "The Gospel Miracles," BCCT, pp. 184–201). In the Synoptic story of the paralytic lowered through the roof, the power to forgive sins is the major point of the narrative.

COMMENT

See p. 201 for the division of ch. v. Although sign and discourse here have the unifying theme of the Sabbath, the unity is not so close as to guarantee that sign and discourse were always one.

Evaluation of the Tradition

Exegetically, the question of the possibility of the miraculous does not concern us here. We ask only whether or not the Johannine story is a variant of a Synoptic narrative; and if it is not, whether it has the mark of primitive tradition.

As we have pointed out in the NOTES on vss. 8 and 14, the Johannine story has some verbal parallels with the Synoptic account of the healing of the paralytic at Capernaum, especially as it is found in Mark ii 1–12. However, outside of the basic fact that the sick person is a man who cannot walk and that Jesus tells him to stand up, pick up his mat and walk (a not unexpected directive to a healed paralytic), the two stories are quite diverse:
▪ in setting: Capernaum vs. Jerusalem;

■ in local details: a man brought to a house by his friends and lowered through the roof vs. a man lying at the side of a pool;

■ in emphasis: a miracle illustrative of Jesus' power to heal sin vs. a healing with only a passing reference to sin (14).

It is true that in Matthew the cure of the paralytic (ix 1–8) follows shortly after the healing of the centurion's boy (viii 5–13), just as the Bethesda healing in John follows the incident of the royal official's son; but this is not really significant since Mark and Luke have an order for these two stories quite different from that of Matthew. Therefore, Haenchen's close study of the problem is probably right in maintaining that the Johannine story does not refer to the same incident as the Synoptic story.

Is John's account of the healing plausible as primitive tradition about Jesus? The setting in vss. 1–3 is a bit more elaborate than usual for stories of healing; yet the Synoptics, as in Mark ii 1–2, do not hesitate to give more elaborate introductions when it is necessary for the development of the narrative. Actually, the Johannine introduction is of importance for the plot, as we see in the reference to the pool in vs. 7. The factual details found in the introduction, as we have pointed out in the NOTES, are very accurate. They betray a knowledge of Jerusalem that militates against a late or non-Palestinian origin of the story.

The account of the healing in vss. 5–9 resembles the ordinary Synoptic healing narrative (for detail see Dodd, *Tradition*, p. 175—our NOTES on vss. 5, 6, 9); and there are also Synoptic parallels in vss. 13 and 14. We shall discuss below the problem posed by 9b–13; but in general there is nothing to persuade us that the basic narrative underlying vss. 1–15 is a creation of the evangelist. The story of the healing seems to stem from primitive tradition about Jesus.

It is true that the crippled or paralytic man stands forth as a person more strongly than is customary in the Synoptic narratives. Yet, one can scarcely speak of a Johannine stereotype; in his obtuseness this man is, for instance, very different from the clever blind man whom Jesus heals in ch. ix. The personality traits that he betrays serve no particular theological purpose and are so true-to-life that they too may have been part of the primitive tradition. If the paralytic's malady were not so tragic, one could almost be amused by the man's unimaginative approach to the curative waters. His crotchety grumbling about the "whippersnappers" who outrace him to the water betrays a chronic inability to seize opportunity, a trait reflected again in his oblique response to Jesus' offer of a cure. The fact that he had let his benefactor slip away without even asking his name is another instance of real dullness. In vs. 14 it is Jesus who takes the initiative in finding the man, and not vice versa. Finally, he repays his benefactor by reporting him to "the Jews." This is less an example of treachery (as Theodore of Mopsuestia urged: *In Jo.* [Syriac]; CSCO 116:73) than of persistent naïveté. A character such as this could have been invented, but one would expect to see clearer motivation for such a creation.

The Question of the Sabbath Motif

That the violation of the Sabbath is the main theme of the miracle as it is now reported is clear both from the discourse that follows and from the place of ch. v in Part Three of the Book of Signs, a part which deals with Jewish feasts. We must ask if this Sabbath motif belonged to the original healing narrative, or if it was supplied later to make the healing narrative a suitable introduction to the discourse.

The question does not lend itself to an easy answer. That Jesus violated the rules of the scribes for the observance of the Sabbath is one of the most certain of all the historical facts about his ministry. From the Synoptic evidence it would seem that he deliberately worked miracles on the Sabbath as test cases providing an opportunity for him to proclaim his relationship to the Law. Therefore, there is no *a priori* difficulty about the presence of the Sabbath motif in the original form of John's healing narrative. But there is a difficulty in the way in which John's story is told. Verses 1–9a contain the whole account of the miracle; then, at the end of vs. 9, the Sabbath theme is introduced almost as an afterthought. (In Synoptic Sabbath miracles the fact that it is Sabbath is mentioned at the beginning of the story—Mark iii 2; Luke xiii 10, xiv 1.) Perhaps, this is an instance of peculiar Johannine technique, for the same procedure is followed in ix 14 where we are told that it is Sabbath only late in the story.

Nevertheless, Haenchen contends that the whole paragraph from vss. 9b–13 constitutes a secondary addition to the healing narrative. It is true that the first part of vs. 9 connects smoothly with vs. 14, and the story would be quite complete without vss. 9b–13. However, what meaning would this healing narrative have without vss. 9b–13, and why would the passage be preserved in the tradition? Similar Synoptic narratives that have no Sabbath theme generally illustrate the faith of the sick man or of the bystanders, a faith which calls forth Jesus' miraculous power. But there is no such faith displayed in John's story. It could serve only as a manifestation of Jesus' pity, resembling perhaps the raising of the widow's son in Luke vii 11–17; but usually in this type of story Jesus' compassion is more explicitly expressed. One almost needs the Sabbath motif to give this story significance.

The close analogy of the Johannine story with the Lucan narrative of the healing of the crippled woman (Luke xiii 10–17) also suggests that the Sabbath motif was part of the original story. In Luke Jesus heals a woman who had been sick for eighteen years without any expression of faith on her part. After the healing, the ruler of the synagogue becomes indignant because Jesus has violated the Sabbath. This leads to a statement of Jesus about the Sabbath, just as John's story leads into a discourse on the Sabbath. Nevertheless, even if these reasons lead us to believe in the original character of the Sabbath motif, Haenchen is perhaps partly correct in that vss. 9b–13 may be a later *expansion* of the Sabbath motif.

The Possibility of a Baptismal Reference

From patristic days (Tertullian, Chrysostom) a baptismal motif has been suggested for this story: this man whom the waters of Judaism could not heal has been cured by Christ. Along with the story of Nicodemus in chapter iii and the blind man in ix, this was one of the three great Johannine readings used in preparing catechumens for Baptism in the early Church. Modern scholars like Cullmann and Niewalda propose a similar interpretation. Bligh, p. 122, suggests that the pool (stirred by an angel) is a symbol of the Law given by an angel; some see in its five porticoes a symbol of the Pentateuch. "Bethesda" has become a real "house of mercy," a real "house of grace." Balagué, p. 108, sees in the question asked by Jesus in vs. 6, "Do you want to be cured?", an example of the question and answer technique of primitive Baptism.

Certainly, some of this symbolism is possible; however, it is extremely difficult to determine that it was intended by the evangelist and is not simply eisegesis. The main argument against the baptismal interpretation is the lack of internal indication (see our criteria, p. cxiii). The theme of water is incidental to the story; it has nothing to do with the healing; the primary emphasis is more on the Sabbath setting than on the healing as such. Tertullian's attempt (*De Bap.* v 5–6; SC 35:74) to find baptismal significance in the fact that the angel stirred the waters and thus gave them healing power is extraneous to the interpretation of John. Not only do the waters not heal the man, but also vs. 4 was probably not part of the text of John. Thus, as we have stated in more detail in TS 23 (1962), 195–97, the basis for a baptismal interpretation of v 1–15 seems too fragile to warrant confidence.

[The Bibliography for this section is included in the Bibliography for ch. v, at the end of § 19.]

18. JESUS ON THE SABBATH:
—DISCOURSE ON HIS SABBATH WORK
(v 16–30)

Introduction and Division One

Introduction

V 16 And so, because he did this sort of thing on the Sabbath, the Jews began to persecute Jesus. 17 But he had an answer for them:

"My Father is at work even till now,
and so I am at work too."

18 For this reason the Jews sought all the more to kill him—not only was he breaking the Sabbath; worse still, he was speaking of God as his own Father, thus making himself God's equal.

Division One: Twofold Sabbath Work

19 This was Jesus' answer:

"I solemnly assure you,
the Son cannot do a thing by himself—
only what he sees the Father doing.
For whatever He does,
the Son does likewise.
20 For the Father loves the Son,
and everything that He does, He shows him.
Yes, much to your surprise,
He will show him even greater works than these.
21 Indeed, just as the Father raises the dead and grants life,
so also the Son grants life to those whom he wishes.
22 In fact, it is not the Father who judges anyone;
no, He has turned all judgment over to the Son,
23 so that all men may honor the Son
just as they honor the Father.
He who refuses to honor the Son,
refuses to honor the Father who sent him.

24 I solemnly assure you,
the man who hears my word
and has faith in Him who sent me
possesses eternal life.
He does not come under condemnation;
no, he has passed from death to life.
25 I solemnly assure you,
an hour is coming and is now here
when the dead shall hear the voice of God's Son,
and those who have listened shall live.

26 Indeed, just as the Father possesses life in Himself,
so has He granted that the Son also possess life in himself.
27 And He has turned over to him power to pass judgment
because he is Son of Man—
28 no need for you to be surprised at this—
for an hour is coming
in which all those in the tombs will hear his voice
29 and will come forth.
Those who have done what is right will rise to live;
those who have practiced what is wicked will rise to be damned.
30 I cannot do anything by myself.
I judge as I hear;
and my judgment is honest
because I am not seeking my own will
but the will of Him who sent me."

NOTES

v 16–18. We treat these verses as an Introduction to the discourse since there
is a lapidary saying in vs. 17 which supplies the subject for what follows.
Others would connect these verses to what precedes.

this sort of thing. Evidently we are to think of other Sabbath healings of
which we have not been told (see xx 30); yet vii 21 speaks of Jesus' having
performed just one work. The healing in chapter ix will also take place on the
Sabbath.

persecute. This is the first active hostility against Jesus reported in John;
in iv 1 it is only implied.

17. *answer.* Here and vs. 19 are the only times in John that this Greek
verb appears in the middle voice, as compared to some 50 uses of the passive.
Abbott, JG, § 2537, suggests that the middle voice implies a more formal answer.

18. *making himself God's equal.* "The Jews" are charging Jesus with rebellion
and pride similar to Adam's sinful attempt to be like God (Gen iii 5–6). Perhaps,
as Bligh, p. 125, suggests, their charge was not based simply on his calling God

"My Father," but also on his doing so in a context wherein he claims to be above the Sabbath law. What does the evangelist wish his reader to think about the charge—that Jesus is equal to God and the Jews refuse to admit it, or that the charge is a misunderstanding of Jesus? Would the evangelist present Jesus as God's equal? Christians who accept the 5th-century "Athanasian" creed believe that the Son "is equal to the Father according to divinity, less than the Father according to humanity." However, the NT view of the relationship is primarily from the viewpoint of the humanity of the Son (see above, pp. 24–25). Paul says (Philip ii 6) that Jesus did not consider "being equal to God" a thing to be clung to. John xiv 28 reports the words: "The Father is greater than I."

19. *the Son . . . the Father*. If this was originally a parabolic saying (see COMMENT), the articles reflect the generic references found in parabolic style, e.g., *"the* sower" in Mark iv 3. Yet see NOTE on iii 17, "the Son."

the Son cannot do a thing by himself. This verse is not unlike Num xvi 28: "The Lord has sent me to do all these works, and it has not been of myself." Is Jesus hurling Moses' words back at the legalists? Ignatius *Magnesians* vii 1 seems to betray knowledge of this passage in John: "As then the Lord was united to the Father and did nothing without Him . . ." (see Braun, JeanThéol, I, p. 275.

sees the Father doing. There is reference to a (pre-existent?) vision of the Father in vi 46, viii 38. Jesus is the only one who has ever seen the Father.

20. *loves. Philein;* although the two verbs "to love," *agapan* and *philein*, are almost interchangeable in John (see App. I:1), this is the only time in John that *philein* is used for the love between Father and Son. (*Agapan* is used six times for this.) Gächter, *art. cit.*, points to this unusual use as a proof for a pre-Johannine parable.

much to your surprise. Literally "in order that you may be surprised"; the "you" is emphatic and perhaps derogatory ("people like you"). This is recalled in vii 21: "I have performed just one work, and all of you are surprised."

greater works. The physical healing ("life") is merely a sign of the power to give eternal life.

21. *just as*. John uses *hōsper* only here and in vs. 26; the verses are clearly parallels.

22. *all judgment over to the Son*. See COMMENT on viii 15 for the complete picture of Jesus and judgment in John. If the unnamed feast of v 1 is Pentecost, then the theme of judgment is reminiscent of the relation of that feast to the giving of the Law on Sinai.

23. *so that all men may honor the Son*. Bligh, p. 128, insists that both vs. 20 and vs. 21 form the basis of this clause: the honor flows both from the power to give life and the power of judgment. This is true, but we believe that his criticism of the NEB translation is unjustified. "Judgment" in vs. 22 is salvific judgment which includes the power to give life; and so grammatically the final clause under discussion can be left in dependence on 22 alone and still reflect the two ideas.

He who refuses. This sentence is a variant of the saying found in Luke x 16 (cf. Matt x 40): "He who rejects me rejects the one who sent me." In John xv 23 we have, "He who hates me hates my Father also"; see I John ii 23. Perhaps these Johannine sayings are part of an apologetic against some Christians of the evangelist's time who refuse to give proper honor to the Son.

24. *I solemnly assure you*. That both vs. 24 and vs. 25 begin thus is a sign that isolated sayings have been woven together. There is an inclusion with vs. 19.

who hears . . . and has faith . . . possesses eternal life. The same promise is given to everyone who believes in the Son, in iii 16, 36.

does not come under condemnation. The theme of escaping condemnation is found in iii 18. This is not purely Johannine, for Rom viii 1 says, "There is now no condemnation for those who are in Christ Jesus."

passed from death to life. I John iii 14: "We know that we have passed from death to life."

25. *an hour is coming and is now here.* See NOTE on iv 23; also App. I:11.

dead. The reference is primarily to the spiritually dead (Eph ii 1: "He made you alive when you were dead through trespasses and sins."). However, vss. 26–30 show that the physically dead are not forgotten.

hear . . . listened. The same Greek verb with two connotations, as also in Matt xiii 13.

26. *possess life.* The common possession of life by Father and Son was used in patristic times as an anti-Arian argument. However, "life" here does not refer primarily to the internal life of the Trinity, but to a creative life-giving power exercised toward men. Ps xxxvi 9: "With you is the fountain of life; in your light do we see light." As for the Son's possessing life, Rev i 18 calls Jesus Christ "the living one."

27. *because he is Son of Man.* The expression "Son of Man" is anarthrous; it is the only time in the Gospels that there is no article before either noun. Some suggest that the expression here means simply "man," thus: ". . . to pass judgment on what [*ho ti* for *hoti*] man is." In our opinion the context renders this unlikely. There is no article in the Greek of Dan vii 13 (see COMMENT). In the Synoptic picture of the final judgment and the separation of the good from the evil, the Son of Man has an important role (Mark xiii 26; Matt xiii 41; xxv 31; Luke xxi 36).

28. *no need for you to be surprised at this.* This could be a negative question: "You are not surprised at this, are you?" (BDF, § 427[2]), but the imperative fits well.

at this. Chrysostom (*In Jo.* XXXIX 3; PG 59:223) understood the surprise to refer to what precedes (he is Son of Man); most scholars today take it to refer to what follows (his role in the resurrection of the dead). By enclosing the clause in dashes we attempt to preserve the ambiguity, for the evangelist may have meant the surprise to refer to the whole complex of ideas.

for. The word could be translated "that," and the whole clause thus turned into an appositional explanation of "this" in the preceding line.

29. *to live . . . to be damned.* That men will be rewarded or punished according to their deeds is common to John, Paul (Rom ii 6–8), and the Synoptics (Matt xxv 31–46); this is complementary to reward or punishment according to faith (Mark xvi 16).

practiced what is wicked. See p. 149, and NOTE on iii 20.

30. *as I hear.* Namely, from the Father, on the analogy of vs. 19 (seeing what the Father does).

honest. Dikaios; cf. viii 16: "Even if I do judge, my judgment is valid (*alēthēs*)."

I am not seeking my own will. Also vi 38: ". . . not to do my own will but the will of Him who sent me." If we compare this with the saying in Mark xiv 36; Matt xxvi 39; Luke xxii 42, it is closer to Luke's form: "Not my will but yours be done."

COMMENT

The discourse that follows the healing is one of the most exalted in John. Truly here Jesus is portrayed as making claims unlike those of any mortal man, claims tantamount to divinity. The critical tendency is to evaluate such a discourse as the product of late 1st-century Christian theology, with little or no foundation in the primitive tradition of Jesus' words. Nevertheless, the discourse evinces a knowledge of the theology and the rules of the scribes concerning the Sabbath, as well as of the laws of testimony and the Mosaic writings. These themes are so interwoven in the discourse that it is very difficult for one to understand it without such rabbinic background. Moreover, embedded in the discourse are sayings that have every reason to be considered genuine traditional sayings of Jesus. Therefore, it is not at all impossible that parts of this discourse have solid foundations in the controversies with the Pharisees that were part of Jesus' ministry, even if the evangelist has given to the final product an organization and theological depth that reflects a later and more mature insight. See Bligh, p. 131.

Division One of the discourse comments on themes that have been highlighted in the last two miracles (just as the discourses in chs. iii–iv commented on the first two scenes of Part Two). In the second Cana miracle there was stress on the theme of life (iv 50, 51, 53) and there was an instance of belief in Jesus' word (iv 49); this discourse stresses Jesus' power to grant life (v 21, 26) and the importance of hearing his word and believing (24, 28). The Sabbath motif was dominant in the healing at Jerusalem; and in the discourse it comes to the fore, not only explicitly in vs. 17 but implicitly in the reference to the power to give life and to judge in vss. 19–25.

Introduction. Jesus defends his Sabbath work (v 16–18)

When Jesus is accused of violating the Sabbath, the Synoptic tradition records two ways in which he defends himself: (a) on humanitarian grounds. Jesus argues that on a Sabbath a man may water an animal or pull it out of a hole; therefore why may he not do the greater good of healing a man (Luke xiii 15, xiv 5)? Something approaching this argument may be found in John vii 23: if a man may be circumcised on the Sabbath, why may not the whole man be made well on the Sabbath? (b) on theological grounds. In the Synoptic tradition Jesus argues that in the OT the priests of the Temple were allowed to do work on the Sabbath; yet now something greater than the Temple is present (Matt xii 5–6). "The Son of Man is Lord of the Sabbath" (xii 8). This type of argument leads to a majestic claim by Jesus, and our present passage in John is quite similar.

Verse 17 must be set against the background of the relation of God to the Sabbath rest. In the commandment concerning the Sabbath (Exod xx 11, but contrast Deut v 15) we have this explanatory clause: "In six days the Lord made the heavens and the earth . . . but on the seventh He rested. That is why the Lord has blessed the Sabbath and made it holy." However, the theologians of Israel realized that God did not really cease to work on the Sabbath. There are a whole series of rabbinic statements (Bernard, I, p. 236; Barrett, p. 213; Dodd, *Interpretation,* pp. 321–22) to the effect that Divine Providence remained active on the Sabbath, for otherwise, the rabbis reasoned, all nature and life would cease to exist.

In particular, as regards men, divine activity was visible in two ways: men were born and men died on the Sabbath. Since only God could give life (II Kings v 7; II Macc vii 22–23) and only God could deal with the fate of the dead in judgment, this meant God was active on the Sabbath. As Rabbi Joḥanan (TalBab *Taanith* 2a) put it, God has kept in His hand three keys that He entrusts to no agent: the key of the rain, the key of birth (Gen xxx 22), and the key of the resurrection of the dead (Ezek xxxvii 13). And it was obvious to the rabbis that God used these keys even on the Sabbath.

In v 17 Jesus justifies his work of healing on the Sabbath by calling the attention of "the Jews" to the fact that they admitted that God worked on the Sabbath. That the implications of this argument were immediately apparent is witnessed by the violence of the reaction. For the Jews the Sabbath privilege was peculiar to God, and no one was equal to God (Exod xv 11; Isa xlvi 5; Ps lxxxix 8). In claiming the right to work even as his Father worked, Jesus was claiming a divine prerogative.

Before we turn to Jesus' reply to "the Jews" in vs. 19, we may point out another facet of the theology of Jesus' statement in vs. 17. In the statement that the Father is still at work, Cullmann, *art. cit.,* sees a reflection of a thought that appears frequently among the Church Fathers: God did not rest after creation but only after Jesus' death. Jesus worked during the ministry (ix 4), but after his death came the Sabbath rest promised to the people of God (Heb iv 9–10). This theory now receives interesting support in the 2nd-century Gnostic treatise, the *Gospel of Truth.* There (xxxii 18 ff.) we hear that even on the Sabbath Jesus *worked,* for he *kept alive* the sheep that had fallen into the pit. As Ménard, *L'Evangile de Vérité* (Paris: Letouzey, 1962), has recognized, the *Gospel of Truth* here combines the Matthean theme of the sheep that falls into a pit (xii 11) with John v. The idea that Jesus worked is taken from v 17 (the same Coptic word found in all the Coptic versions of this verse is used in the *Gospel of Truth*); the idea that Jesus kept the sheep alive is taken from vs. 21, where it is said that Jesus can grant life (again the Coptic of the *Gospel of Truth* and of the Gospel of John is the same). In the light of this it is interesting to read what follows in the *Gospel of Truth:* Jesus did this "that you may understand . . . what the Sabbath is, namely, that in which it is not fitting that salvation be idle." Thus, salvation must be worked out even on the Sabbath. Finally, the *Gospel of Truth* speaks of that perfect day on high which has no night, with the implication that this is the true Sabbath of eternity.

Division 1. The twofold Sabbath work of Jesus, namely, to give life and to judge—realized eschatology (v 19–25)

In vs. 19 Jesus tells the Jewish authorities that there is nothing arrogant in what he has said. He is not a rebellious son setting himself up as a rival to the Father; rather, he is completely dependent on the Father and claims nothing on his own. That Jesus does none of his works on his own reflects a favorite theme in John (also, ix 4). John also tells us that none of what Jesus *says* is his own (iii 34, viii 26, xii 49), and that the Son did not come of his own accord (vii 28, viii 42). All of this is summed up in x 30: "The Father and I are one." As Giblet, "Trinité," points out, a Johannine passage like vs. 19 ultimately led Christian theologians to an understanding that the Father and the Son possess one nature, one principle of operation.

Certainly, then, vss. 19–20a bear all the marks of Johannine theological insight; yet one must not be tempted to evaluate these verses as pure formulations of the evangelist. Independently, Dodd and Gächter have made the plausible suggestion that these verses were once a parable in the following format:

Negation: A son cannot do anything by himself—only what he sees his father doing.

Affirmation: Whatever the father does, the son does likewise.

Explanation: For the father [loves his son and] shows his son everything he is doing.

Dodd, *art. cit.*, points out that this same format is found in a parable like Matt v 15. The parable that Dodd finds in John could be set in an apprentice shop where a youth is learning a trade. He cites a series of references from the Oxyrhynchus papyri (from Egypt of NT times), where it is insisted that the apprentice must do what the master does; and whatever he does, the apprentice does likewise. In a simple society like that of Palestine, a trade would be taught within a family, and the *son* would have to imitate the *father's* work. Jesus was known as a carpenter's son (Matt xiii 55) and as a carpenter (Mark vi 3). Even the love of the father for the son mentioned in vs. 20a would fit into such a parable, for Sir xxx 1 has a phrase to this effect in a passage dealing with the training of children.

Thus, it may well be that Jesus calls on a proverb to explain the relation of his work to that of the heavenly Father. Then in the rest of vs. 20 he begins to expound the nature of the works that he has seen the Father do and which he is imitating. They are the same works that according to Jewish theology it was proper for the Father to do on the Sabbath. In vs. 21 the *first* of these works is mentioned: Jesus grants life. Now we understand that the life that Jesus granted to the royal official's son was only a sign of the life from above that he can truly give because the Father has empowered him to do so. The connection between the healing of the cripple at Bethesda and the order to stop sinning (vs. 14) becomes clearer. To those who are in the realm of that death which is sin the Son has the power to grant life, and the only threat to the life that he grants is further sin.

In vss. 22–23 the *second* of the works is mentioned: Jesus is the judge, for the Father has turned over the power of judgment to the Son. This "judgment" is to be taken in the common OT sense of vindicating the good (Deut xxxii 36; Ps xliii 1) and this is complementary to giving life. This salvific judgment which in the OT is the prerogative of Yahweh causes men to honor the Son and to recognize his relation to the Father. Yet, as in iii 19–21, the judgment on behalf of those who believe has its negative side as well; it is at the same time a condemnation of those who refuse the Son sent by the Father. Once again the realized eschatology of this Gospel comes to the fore: judgment, condemnation, passing from death to life (vs. 24) are part of that hour which is now here. Just as the royal official listened to Jesus' word and believed in it, thus receiving the life of his son (iv 50), so also those who stand before Jesus and hear his words in the discourse of ch. v have the opportunity to receive life. These words are the source of life for those who are spiritually dead (vs. 25).

Duplicate of Division 1. The same themes in terms of final eschatology (v 26–30)

According to the theory proposed in the Introduction (p. xxxvii), we have in vss. 26–30 another version of the speech reported in 19–25, coming from a different stage of the Johannine tradition. Let us list the similarities of word and thought between the two forms of the discourse:

vss. 26–30		*vss. 19–25*
26	*The power of life shared by the Father and the Son* (see Note on *hōsper* in vs. 21)	21
27	*The power of judgment shared by the Father and the Son*	22
28	*The reaction of surprise*	20
28	*An hour is coming (and is now here) when the dead hear the voice of the Son*	25
29	*Those who have done right (have listened) shall live*	25
30	*The Son does nothing by himself*	19
	The Son sees or hears what he must do	

It will be noticed that the sequence of the main ideas is roughly the same in both forms of the discourse, the one exception being the parallelism between 30 and 19. This exception can be explained as an editorial attempt to produce an inclusion binding the whole passage together. Léon-Dufour, *art. cit.*, sees a slightly different pattern from the one we have suggested. He makes 24 the middle verse in a chiasm (see above, p. cxxxv); however, his parallels are not impressive, and he runs into the difficulty of having vss. 25 and 28 on the same side of the division.

If the words and thoughts of the two forms of the discourse are remarkably the same, the theological emphasis differs markedly. In vss. 26–30, except for vs. 26, we do not find the peculiar Son-Father terminology that is so characteristic of John. Rather we find the "Son of Man," a title well known in the Synoptic tradition but not so frequent in John (see NOTE on i 51). As the title appears in vs. 27, it seems to echo the *locus classicus* of the OT, Dan vii 13, where the figure of "a son of man" appears in the context of final divine judgment. And *final* judgment seems to be what is in mind in John v 26–30. We hear in vs. 28 that "an hour is coming," but the "and is now here" of 25 is missing. Again, in 28 when we hear of resurrection, it is not a question of the spiritually dead as in 25, but of those already in the tomb. This is the resurrection of the physically dead, and their coming forth from the tomb at the voice of Jesus is an apocalyptic scene not unworthy of Ezekiel's vision of the revivifying of the dead bones (xxxvii 4: "O dry bones, hear the word of the Lord"). The results of the judgment in vs. 29 is a clear echo of Dan xii 2, the first passage in the OT to proclaim clearly a resurrection into the afterlife: "Many of those who sleep in the dust of the earth shall awake: some to eternal life; others to eternal shame and disgrace." We shall point out in our commentary on ch. xi that the Lazarus story, where a dead man actually comes forth from the tomb at the word of Jesus, echoes many of the words and the ideas of vss. 26–30.

The contrast, then, between the final eschatology of vss. 26–30 and the realized eschatology of 19–25 is quite marked. For Bultmann, the Ecclesiastical Redactor has been busy in 26–30, specifically in 28–29, trying to conform John's realized eschatology to the official eschatology of the Church. However, as we have insisted (pp. cxviii ff.), such a dichotomy between the two eschatologies is unwarranted; and Boismard, *art. cit.,* makes a good case for considering vss. 26–30 to be the earlier form of the discourse wherein the eschatological outlook resembles that of the majority of Synoptic passages. If this is so, 19–25 would represent a rethinking of the same sayings of Jesus at a later date when realized eschatology had come to the fore as an answer to the delay in the second coming. Boismard points out the parallels between 19–25 and I John (see NOTES on vss. 23, 24) as a sign of lateness, and he stresses that the relations between the Father and the Son are more developed in 19–25 than in 26–30.

All of this has been an analysis of vss. 19–30 as they now stand. Gächter has pointed out, however, that the pre-history of the passage is probably even more complicated. We may well have here a collection of what were once isolated sayings (see NOTE on vs. 24). It is interesting to note the use of personal pronouns. Outside of the introductory "*I* solemnly assure *you*" statements (19, 24, 25) and the reference to "*your* surprise/*you* to be surprised" (20, 28), virtually the whole discourse is in the third person. (There is a "me" in 24; 30 is in the first person.) Gächter makes this distinction of persons too absolute a criterion of the original layers of the discourse; after all, the third person is frequently associated with the Son of Man in the Synoptic tradition as well (compare Luke xii 8 with Matt x 32). Nevertheless, the change of persons may indicate to some extent different provenance of sayings.

Gächter thinks that 19 and 30 were the original verses of the passage. Verse 19(–20a) was a parable, as we have explained; and 30, which immediately followed 19, was the application of the parable. Certainly, 30 is closely related to 19, as we saw in our analysis of the parallels above; and if 30 was the personal explanation of a parable, the appearance of the first person in 30 would be justified. We would then posit that other independent sayings were attached to the parable by way of further application (much the way Luke xvi 9–13 grew), a process that gave rise to a small discourse. Actually the Johannine tradition preserved two forms of the discourse in 21–25 and 26–29. The final phase in the history of the passage would be when an editor joined the duplicate forms of the discourse, and then broke up the original unit of vss. 19(–20a) and 30 by inserting the combined discourse in between. Moving 30 to the end not only gave an inclusion, but also allowed vs. 30 to act as a summary of the various themes of the discourse. The editor thus achieved a complete exposition of the work that the Father had given Jesus to do both in his ministry and in the future, work that outranked the importance of the Sabbath rest.

[The Bibliography for this section is included in the Bibliography for ch. v, at the end of § 19.]

19. JESUS ON THE SABBATH:
—DISCOURSE ON HIS SABBATH WORK (*continued*)
(v 31–47)

Division Two

a. Witnesses for Jesus

V 31 "If I am my own witness,
  my testimony cannot be verified.
 32 But there is Another who is testifying on my behalf,
  and the testimony that He gives for me
  I know can be verified.

 33 You have sent to John,
  and he has testified to the truth.
(34 Not that I myself accept such human testimony—
  I simply mention these things for your salvation.)
 35 He was the lamp, set aflame and burning bright,
  and for a while you yourselves willingly exulted in his light.

 36 Yet I have testimony even greater than John's,
  namely, the works the Father has given me to complete.
  These very works that I am doing
  testify on my behalf
  that the Father has sent me.

 37 And the Father who sent me
  has Himself given testimony on my behalf.
  His voice you have never heard;
  nor have you seen what He looks like;
 38 and His word you do not have abiding in your hearts,
  because you do not believe
  the one He sent.

39 You search the Scriptures
   in which you think you have eternal life—
   they also testify on my behalf.
40 Yet you are not willing to come to me
   to have that life.

b. Attack on Jewish Disbelief

41 Not that I accept human praise—
42 it is simply that I know you people
   and in your hearts you do not possess the love of God.
43 I have come in my Father's name;
   yet you do not accept me.
   But let someone else come in his own name,
   and you will accept him.
44 How can people like you believe,
   when you accept praise from one another,
   but do not seek that glory which is from the One [God]?
45 Do not think that I shall be your accuser before the Father;
   the one to accuse you is Moses
   on whom you have set your hopes.
46 For if you believed Moses,
   you would believe me,
   since it is about me that he wrote.
47 But if you do not believe what he wrote,
   how can you believe what I say?"

NOTES

31. *my own witness.* The same maxim is found in viii 17, where it is said
to be found in the Law. The legal principle stems from Deut xix 15, where
it is stated that a man cannot be convicted of a crime on the testimony of one
witness. Deut xvii 6 and Num xxxv 30 demand several witnesses for a conviction in the case of capital crime. Probably because Jesus invoked the principle,
it was widely cited in the primitive Church. Matt xviii 16 specifies that there
shall be several witnesses to confirm a warning given to a recalcitrant Christian
before he is expelled from the Church (see also II Cor xiii 1; I Tim v 19;
Heb x 28). Nevertheless, all these other examples in the OT and the NT are
different from John's use of the principle, as has been observed by J.-P.
Charlier, "L'exégèse johannique d'un précepte légal: Jean viii 17," RB 67 (1960),
503–15. John is not dealing with witnesses necessary to condemn a man, but
with witnesses to confirm someone's testimony. We find a similar broadening of
the legal principle in the rabbinic documents; in the Mishnaic tractate *Kethuboth*
2:9 it is cited as a principle that no man may bear witness on his own behalf.
   cannot be verified. There is a formal contradiction of this verse in viii 14:

"Even if I am my own witness, my testimony *can* be verified." As we shall see, there is no real contradiction; but one may doubt if the same editor wrote both lines.

32. *Another.* As recognized from the time of Cyprian (*Epist.* LXVI[II] 2; CSEL 3²:727), this is the Father. Chrysostom (*In Jo.* XL 1; PG 59:230) thought it meant John the Baptist; but this seems to be ruled out by the contrast between vs. 32, where apparently Jesus accepts this testimony given by Another, and vs. 34, where he does not accept human testimony. That the Father is involved is confirmed by viii 17–18.

33. *sent to John.* A reference to the mission of i 19.

he has testified. The perfect tense appears here as in i 32–34, iii 26; the testimony still has value.

to the truth. Because of the possible relationship of John the Baptist to the Qumran Essenes, it is worth noting that in 1QS viii 6 the Essenes qualify themselves as "witnesses to the truth at the judgment."

34. *Not . . . accept such human testimony.* I John v 9: "If we accept human testimony, the testimony of God is far better."

35. *the lamp, set aflame.* This may be an echo of the description of Elijah in Sir xlviii 1 where it is said that his word was "a flame like a torch." In speaking of the two *lamp*stands, Rev xi clearly uses imagery drawn from Elijah's career. Thus, this may represent the Johannine form of Jesus' testimony to John the Baptist as Elijah (see Matt xvii 12–13, compared to Mark ix 13). In the Synoptic scene Jesus stresses that the people did not really understand John the Baptist and what he was. F. Neugebauer, ZNW 52 (1961), 130, traces the designation of John the Baptist to Ps cxxxii 17, "I have prepared a lamp for my anointed," in the sense that he was a lamp before the Messiah (which was not the original meaning of the Psalm).

exulted in his light. Josephus (*Ant.* XVIII.v.2;⌗118) says that men were highly elated at listening to John the Baptist, and it is to such passing enthusiasm that our verse refers. Boismard, EvJean, pp. 56–57, sees in the Johannine expression the reflection of an Aramaic original. Instead of "exult, rejoice," the Syriac tradition reads "boast, took glory"; and the one Aramaic verb (root *bhr*) in its different conjugations has the two meanings. He thinks that the "in" of "in his light" reflects the Semitic preposition *be*, meaning "at, by."

36. *greater than John's.* Presumably, this means "greater than the testimony John *gave*," rather than "greater than the testimony John *had*," even though the latter is better syntactically. There is another well-attested reading (Vaticanus, P⁶⁶) whereby "greater" is in the nominative: "I who am greater than John have testimony." This antithesis does not fit the sequence of ideas.

works the Father has given me to complete. There is another way in which this could be translated: "works the Father has enabled me to complete." Vanhoye, *art. cit.*, has given exhaustive proof favoring the translation we have chosen, but see the companion verse xvii 4. As we shall insist in App. III, Jesus' own designation for his miracles is "works," not "signs." In iv 34 Jesus speaks of bringing the Father's *work* (singular) to completion. The works (miracles) are part of that work which is the economy of salvation entrusted by the Father to Jesus.

works that . . . testify on my behalf. Repeated in x 25: "The works that I am doing in my Father's name give testimony for me"; also xiv 10–11.

37. *The Father who sent me/has Himself given testimony.* Repeated in viii 18 in the present tense: "The Father who sent me *gives* testimony for me."

His voice you have never heard. All of this may be an implicit reference to the scene at the foot of Sinai where (Exod xix 9) God told Moses, "I am coming to you in a thick cloud that the people may hear when I speak to you." The people heard the thunders (literally "the voices") as God came upon the mountain.

nor have you seen what He looks like. Once again the background may be Sinai. Exod xix 11 promised: "On the third day the Lord will come down upon Mount Sinai in the *sight* of all the people"; and the Midrash Mekilta comments on this: "It teaches that at that moment they saw what Isaiah and Ezekiel never saw." Thus, there seems to have been a popular tradition about hearing and seeing God at Mount Sinai, and John presents Jesus as arguing against this. (John's presentation seems more in harmony with Deut iv 12, 15, where it is stated that the people did not see God, although they heard His voice; the latter privilege is surrendered in Deut v 23–27.) The argument would be particularly fitting if the unnamed feast of v 1 was Pentecost, when the giving of the Law at Sinai was being celebrated. For the theme that no one (except Jesus) has ever really seen God see i 18, vi 46; I John iv 12.

38. *and His word you do not have abiding in your hearts.* It is possible that the last two lines of vs. 37 are a parenthesis, and that this first line of vs. 38 should begin with a "yet" and continue line two of vs. 37: "The Father . . . has Himself given testimony on my behalf; yet His word you do not have abiding in your hearts." The implication in this verse is that the *believer* does have the word of God abiding in his heart; the same is said of the word of Jesus in xv 7.

39. *You.* This is addressed to "the Jews" (vs. 18). In Papyrus Egerton 2 (see below, p. 230) it is addressed to "the rulers of the people"—an interesting confirmation of what John means by the Jews.

You search. Origen, Tertullian, Irenaeus, and Vulg. take the verb as an imperative, challenging the Jews to search the Scriptures. The indicative, however, suits the line of argument better, and most modern commentators prefer it. M.-E. Boismard devoted an article to this verse in RB 55 (1948), 5–34, tracing two textual traditions, both stemming from the same putative Aramaic original: (*a*) "You search the Scriptures because you think to have eternal life"; (*b*) "Search the Scriptures in which you think to have life." In his opinion the present text is conflate. The verb "search" represents the technical Hebrew verb *dāraš* used for Scripture study.

Scriptures/in which you think you have eternal life. In Hebrew thought, the Law was par excellence the source of life. *Pirqe Aboth* ii 8 says: "He who has acquired the words of the Law has acquired for himself the life of the world to come"; vi 7: "Great is the Law for it gives to those who practice it life in this world and the world to come." Paul argues against such a view in Gal iii 21; Rom vii 10. Once again, this verse of John would have special meaning if the feast on which the discourse is uttered is thought of as Pentecost, the feast of the Law.

eternal. This is omitted in some versions (OL, OS, Armenian) and Papyrus Egerton 2.

40. *not willing.* The refusal is deliberate. Compare Matt xxiii 37, where judgment is rendered on disbelieving Jerusalem: "I would have gathered your children together; yet you were not willing."

41. *praise.* The same Greek word, *doxa,* covers "praise" from men and

"glory" from God; see the contrast in vs. 44. Distrust in human praise and self-glory is restated in vii 18, viii 50, xii 43. Barrosse describes this love in TS 18 (1957), 549, thus: "Love for the glory of men is a man's love for a (false) greatness, a greatness enjoyed apart from God. . . . This love of something possessed independently of God prevents acceptance of God's offer of himself in Christ."

42. *I know you people/and in your hearts you* . . . This has been translated somewhat literally to preserve the Greek word balance of the two lines. The syntax reflects a frequent Aramaic construction whereby the subject of the subordinate clause is attracted into the main clause as an object: "I know that you people in your hearts do not possess the love of God."

love of God. The genitive may be possessive, meaning God's love for men (Wikenhauser, SB), or objective, meaning man's love for God (Lagrange, Bernard, Lightfoot, Barrett, Bultmann). The former meaning is the one found in the rest of the Gospel; it seems more probable on the analogy of vs. 38, i.e., God's love like God's word must permeate one if he is to recognize and accept Jesus. Yet, a case may also be made for the latter meaning on the analogy of iii 19, i.e., man's failure to love God is part of his preferring the darkness. Some would suggest that the evangelist left the phrase ambiguous to cover both meanings. The love of God was the essence of the Law (Luke x 27); when Jesus tells "the Jews" that they do not possess it, he is leading up to the theme that they have betrayed Moses (vss. 45–47; also vii 19).

43. *let someone else come in his own name.* This is probably a general observation similar to the Synoptic predictions of "false messiahs" who are to come in the *name* of Jesus (Mark xiii 6, 22). P. W. Schmiedel in *Encyclopedia Biblica* (1902), 2551, took this as a specific historical reference to Simon Bar-Kochba (Ben Kosiba), the leader of the Second Jewish Revolt (A.D. 132–135), and thus used this verse to date the Gospel in the mid-second century. The Church Fathers often took the verse as a specific reference to the anti-Christ.

44. *when you accept praise from one another.* The same reason is advanced for the disbelief of the Sanhedrin in xii 43. It is characteristic of the rabbinic literature to give the greatest deference to famous rabbis.

do not seek that glory . . . Perhaps here also Jesus is implicitly holding up the example of Moses to them, for Moses sought the glory of God and received glory from God (Exod xxxiv 29).

[God]. This is omitted by very important witnesses including Vaticanus and both Bodmer papyri. Bernard, I, p. 256, however, shows how it could easily have been lost by scribal omission.

45. *the one to accuse you.* Literally a present participle: "the one accusing you." It is not impossible that the evangelist thinks of Moses as having already begun his accusation; however, BDF, § 339²ᵇ, points out that such a participle has the same future force as the previous verb: "I shall be your accuser."

Moses. At the end of Deuteronomy (xxxi 19, 22) Moses is said to have written a song which would serve as a witness against the Israelites if they violated the covenant; and indeed the whole Mosaic Book of the Law was to serve as a witness (xxxi 26).

46. *about me that he wrote.* This may be a reference to a specific passage like Deut xviii 18; or it may be a more general reference to Jesus' fulfilling the whole Law.

COMMENT

Division 2a. Jesus lists the witnesses who support his claim (v 31–40)

After Jesus makes his claim to work on the Sabbath and explains this twofold work, we may suppose a tacit objection on the part of "the Jews," an objection such as that which becomes vocal in viii 13: "You are your own witness, and your testimony cannot be verified." Who can bear witness to Jesus' claim that his work of giving life and of judging are only what he has seen the Father doing? Jesus meets this legal difficulty with an argument that recognizes the prescriptions of the Law (see NOTE on vs. 31). He has the testimony of several witnesses as demanded by the Law, and he lists these witnesses in four "strophes" discussed below. It is important to stress that the four witnesses are, in Jesus' mind, only four different aspects of the witness of "Another," that is, the Father, on his behalf.

(1) Verses 33–35. The first to come to the witness stand is John the Baptist, who reflects the Father's witness because he is "a man sent by God" (i 6). That Jesus used John the Baptist in his arguments with the Jerusalem authorities is seen in Mark xi 27–33 and par. For the content of John the Baptist's testimony the reader need but reflect on his rich doctrine about the one to come in i 19–34 and iii 27–30.

(2) Verse 36. Next, Jesus' miracles are brought forward as testimony. These, too, represent the witness of the Father, for they were given to the Son by the Father. The appeal to Jesus' works also has a parallel in the Synoptic tradition, and, interestingly enough, in connection with John the Baptist. John the Baptist in prison has heard of *the works* of Jesus (Matt xi 2), and so he sends his disciples to inquire if Jesus is the one to come. Jesus answers him by appealing to the miracles that he has been doing (xi 5).

(3) Verses 37–38. Thirdly, Jesus mentions that the Father Himself has given testimony. It is not certain if Jesus is thinking of a particular occasion. Some have suggested the baptismal scene; but we remember that in John, unlike the Synoptics, no voice spoke from heaven. If a theophany is meant, it is more likely an OT scene (see xii 41); indeed, as indicated in the NOTE, much of what is said in vs. 37 fits the Sinai scene. The idea may be that at Sinai God gave witness to Jesus in the sense that He gave the Law, and this Mosaic Law testifies to Jesus (see vs. 46). But the Law is no longer alive in the hearts of "the Jews" and so they do not believe. All of these remarks are predicated on the possibility that a particular occasion of the Father's testimony is meant, an external theophany. But it is even more probable that we have here a more general reference to the Father's internal testimony within the hearts of men (vs. 38). The testimony of God would then consist in the self-authenticating quality of His truth, a

truth immediately recognizable to those called to believe. This is certainly the idea in I John v 9–10: "This is the testimony that God has given about His Son. He who believes in the Son of God has this testimony within himself" (see also I John ii 14). Most modern commentators (Bernard, Barrett, Dodd) incline toward such an interpretation. Bligh, p. 132, joins our third and fourth witnesses as one, putting the first part of vs. 37 with 36, and the last part of vs. 37 plus 38 with 39.

(4) Verse 39. The fourth witness is the Scriptures (in particular, probably the Law) which clearly come from God and are thus another aspect of the Father's witness. That Jesus used the Scriptures to challenge the authorities and to prove his claim is certainly clear in the Synoptic tradition (Mark xii 10, 35–37). The early Church soon gathered a collection of testimonies, or OT passages fulfilled by Jesus, as a reflection of the Christian outlook that the OT Scriptures have the gift of life because they point to Jesus.

These are the witnesses who come forward for Jesus, and yet the sad outcome of the trial (vs. 40) is that "the Jews" are not ready to believe in Jesus. We have pointed out above that the witnesses evoked in John have parallels in the arguments that Jesus advances against the Jewish authorities in the Synoptic tradition. Therefore, it is plausible that the roots of this Johannine discourse may be found in the primitive tradition of Jesus' words. But it is obvious that nowhere in the Synoptic Gospels do we find such a logical and completely developed apologetic for Jesus' claims. We may well surmise, then, that what we have in John is the product of the apologetic of the Christian Church against the Jewish objections to Christ, an apologetic grounded in Jesus' own arguments, but now systematized. The whole of ch. v fits in very well with the purpose of the Gospel to persuade Jewish Christians to leave the Synagogue and openly to profess their faith in Jesus.

Division 2b. Jesus directly attacks the disbelief of "the Jews" (v 41–47)

Disbelief in face of these witnesses must be motivated by pride; it is a deliberate disbelief. Jesus is now portrayed as attacking the roots of this disbelief with vigor. If it were an intellectual problem, it could be met by explanation; but it is really a problem of the moral orientation of life and of the love of God, and so it is met by prophetic accusation. What "the Jews" are rejecting is not one sent from God—they willingly accept self-proclaimed messiahs (vs. 43). They are actually rejecting the giving or dedicating of one's life to God ("love of God" in 42; seeking the glory of God in 44) which is the implicit demand of Jesus' message. The failure to accept Jesus is really the preference of self.

If Jesus is angry with "the Jews" for not coming to him, it is because he sees this as a rejection of God, not because he is interested in their praise (vs. 41). Jesus is not interested in any personal glory that is not the same as the glory of the Father (44). Thus, by inclusion, the end of the discourse picks up the theme with which it began. In vs. 18 the Jews had protested that Jesus was arrogant in making himself equal to God; but Jesus' only claim to glory is a reflection of the Father's glory. His glory is the glory of the Father's only Son (i 14); it is the Father (xvii 1, 5) who glorifies the Son. Verse 43 puts this same idea in another way: Jesus has not come in his own name but in his Father's name, the name that Father has given him (xvii 11, 12) and which he manifests to men (xvii 6, 26).

The last verses of the discourse (45–47) attack "the Jews" on their most sensitive point. They justify their refusal to believe in Jesus in the name of their loyalty to Moses (ix 29), and yet Moses will condemn them for this failure to believe. In Jewish thought (StB, II, p. 561) Moses was to intercede before God for Jews; now he will become their prosecutor.

The attack of Jesus on "the Jews" is a strong one, but no stronger than the attacks of Jesus on the Pharisees in the Synoptic tradition. If the discourse in John is a condemnation of the traditionalism of the scribes and the honor paid to the great Jewish teachers (see NOTE on vs 44—the rabbinic situation is later than Jesus' time, but it is an heir to the thought of the scribes and Pharisees), we find similar condemnations of sterile tradition and the seeking of praise in Matt xxiii. It is no accident that the strongest condemnation of the Jewish authorities appears in the two Gospels, John and Matthew, most closely associated with the Jewish-Christian question. The hostility to Christians that became public synagogue policy after the destruction of the Temple has caused these two evangelists to emphasize this strain in Jesus' words and to apply it to their own times.

Bultmann, p. 204, points out, however, that this passage in John is capable of a wider application. The quest for human praise is a universal motive, for gaining the estimation of one's fellow man is a means of self-assurance. But the challenge presented by Jesus always shakes this assurance. Only when the self-assurance of a man is shaken is he ready to make an act of faith expressive of his dependence on God. The rebellion of "the Jews" against this is a rebellion common to the world.

We wish to note that for reasons that we shall discuss in treating chapter vii, many scholars would join a portion of the dialogue in vii to v 47. Bernard, Bultmann, Schnackenburg would join vii 15–24 here; Bligh would join vii 19–24.

Addendum: Papyrus Egerton 2

In 1935 two British scholars, H. I. Bell and T. C. Skeat, published some *Fragments of an Unknown Gospel* from a British Museum papyrus which is dated to mid-2nd century A.D. Braun, JeanThéol, I, pp. 404–6, gives the Greek text, and, on pp. 87–94, a thorough discussion of the relation of this "unknown gospel" to John. Three possibilities have been considered: (a) The gospel in this Egerton papyrus is one of the sources of John. One should remember that the date assigned above is for the papyrus copy, not for the original composition of the work. (b) Both this gospel and John draw on a common source. (c) This gospel draws on verses of John which it combines with verses from the Synoptics and other material. It is the last view that has the largest following today (Lagrange, Jeremias, Dodd, Braun). It might be debated whether the author of the unknown gospel was citing John by memory rather than from a written copy; yet Boismard uses Egerton 2 as an important early witness to the text of John. Here is an excerpt from Fragment 1, verso, lines 5–19:

And turning to the rulers of the people, he spoke this word: "Search the Scriptures

John v 39   in which you think you have life— they testify on my behalf.

Do not think that I have come to be your accuser before

John v 45   the one to accuse you is Moses |my Father; on whom you have set your hopes."

John ix 29   But then they said, "Well, we know that God spoke to Moses, but we don't even know where you come from." Jesus answered them:

"Now your unbelief accuses you . . ."

It will be noted that there are only minor differences from John with the exception of the last line, which may be a summary of v 46–47. We gave another portion of Papyrus Egerton 2 above on p. 138 in relation to iii 2.

BIBLIOGRAPHY

Bagatti, B., "Il lento disseppellimento della piscina probatica a Gerusalemme," BibOr 1 (1959), 12–14.

Balagué, M., "El Bautismo como resurrección del pecado," Cultura Bíblica 18 (1961), 103–10 on v 1–18.

Bligh, J., "Jesus in Jerusalem," Heythrop Journal 4 (1963), 115–34.

Boismard, M.-E., "L'évolution du thème eschatologique dans les traditions johanniques," RB 68 (1961), especially pp. 514–18 on v 19–29.

Cullmann, O., "Sabbat und Sonntag nach dem Johannesevangelium (Joh. 5. 17)," IMEL, pp. 127–31.

Dodd, C. H., "A Hidden Parable in the Fourth Gospel," More New Testament Studies (Grand Rapids: Eerdmans, 1968), pp. 30–40.

Gächter, P., "Zur Form von Joh 5, 19–30," NTAuf, pp. 65–68.

Giblet, J., "Le témoignage du Père (Jn. 5, 31–47)," BVC 12 (1955), 49–59.

——"La Sainte Trinité selon l'Evangile de saint Jean," LumVie 29 (1956), especially pp. 98–106 on v 17–30.

Haenchen, E., "Johanneische Probleme," ZTK 56 (1959), especially pp. 46–50 on v 1–15.

Jeremias, J., The Rediscovery of Bethesda (Louisville: Southern Baptist Seminary, 1966).

Léon-Dufour, X., "Trois chiasmes johanniques," NTS 7 (1960–61), especially pp. 253–55 on v 19–30.

Vanhoye, A., "L'œuvre du Christ, don du Père (Jn 5, 36 et 17, 4)," RSR 48 (1960), 377–419.

20. JESUS AT PASSOVER:
—THE MULTIPLICATION OF THE LOAVES
(vi 1–15)

VI 1 Later on Jesus crossed the Sea of Galilee [to the shore] of Tiberias, 2 but a large crowd kept following him because they saw the signs he was performing on the sick. 3 So Jesus went up the mountain and sat down there with his disciples. 4 The Jewish feast of Passover was near.

5 When Jesus looked up, he caught sight of a large crowd coming toward him; so he said to Philip, "Where shall we ever buy bread for these people to eat?" (6 Actually, of course, he was perfectly aware of what he was going to do, but he asked this to test Philip's reaction.) 7 He replied, "Not even with two hundred days' wages could we buy enough loaves to give each of them a mouthful."

8 One of Jesus' disciples, Andrew, Simon Peter's brother, remarked to him, 9 "There is a lad here who has five barley loaves and a couple of dried fish, but what good is that for so many?" 10 Jesus said, "Get the people to sit down." Now the men numbered about five thousand, but there was plenty of grass there for them to find a seat. 11 Jesus then took the loaves of bread, gave thanks, and passed them around to those sitting there; and he did the same with the dried fish—just as much as they wanted. 12 When they had enough, he told his disciples, "Gather up the fragments that are left over so that nothing will perish." 13 And so they gathered twelve baskets full of fragments left over by those who had been fed with the five barley loaves.

14 Now when the people saw the sign[s] he had performed, they began to say, "This is undoubtedly the Prophet who is to come into the world." 15 With that Jesus realized that they would come and carry him off to make him king, so he fled back to the mountain alone.

5: *said;* 8: *remarked;* 12: *told.* In the historical present tense.

NOTES

vi 1. *Later on.* A vague sequential reference (*meta tauta*—see NOTE on ii 12). How Jesus got back to Galilee is not explained.

[*to the shore*]. This phrase, found in Codices Bezae and Koridethi, Chrysostom, and Eth, may be original (see Boismard, RB 64 [1957], 369). The problem of where the multiplication took place will be discussed below on vs. 23. If the Johannine account originally located the multiplication near Tiberias on the southwest shore of the lake, the omission of the phrase indicating this location may represent a scribal attempt to conform John with Luke ix 10, which places the location at Bethsaida on the northeast shore. Mark does not share Luke's tradition, for in Mark vi 45 only after the multiplication do the disciples cross the lake to Bethsaida. The invention of a second Bethsaida to harmonize Mark and Luke, so that the multiplication could happen at one Bethsaida and the disciples could subsequently row to the other, is documented in C. McCown, JPOS 10 (1930), 32–58. Ancient pilgrim sources, beginning with Aetheria, associate the multiplication with Heptapegon ("Seven Fountains") or modern Et-Tabgha on the northwest shore (see H. Senès, *Estudios Eclesiásticos* 34 [1960], 873–81).

of Tiberias. Without the bracketed phrase we have two genitives in a row, both giving the name of the lake. Mark and Matthew speak of "the Sea of Galilee"; Luke v 1 speaks of "the Lake of Gennesaret" (from the Hebrew name Chinnereth; Josephus and I Macabbees speak of "the Lake [or water] of Gennesar"); in the NT only John (also xxi 1) gives it the name of Tiberias. Since Herod had just completed the building of the town of Tiberias in the 20s, it was probably only after Jesus' time that the name "Tiberias" became common for the lake. The name is encountered in 1st-century Jewish literature (Josephus; Sibylline Oracles).

2. *saw the signs.* The imperfect of the verb *theōrein* seems to be the best reading; this verb was used in ii 23 where the sight of Jesus' miracles produced an enthusiasm that did not win Jesus' approval. Actually only one sign performed on the sick has been reported as taking place in Galilee (iv 46–54). Those scholars who favor a Sign Source for John would regard this verse as coming from that source and indicating a larger collection of signs from which the evangelist has only excerpted.

3. *the mountain.* This "mountain" in Galilee, always with the definite article, appears frequently in the Synoptic tradition and is associated with important theological events (Sermon on the Mount, Matt v 1; call of the Twelve, Mark iii 13; post-resurrectional appearance, Matt xxviii 16). There is no way of localizing it, although tradition associates it with the northwest shore of the lake and a hill called "the Mount of the Beatitudes." The Gospels may have simplified several localities into one which, as "the mountain," was thought of as a Christian Sinai. John vi has the same theme as Matthew's Sermon on the Mount, namely, a contrast between Jesus and Moses.

sat down there. Jesus, like the rabbis, usually sat down to teach (Mark iv 1, ix 35; Matt v 1; Luke iv 20). In this scene, however, John does not mention teaching, as does Mark vi 34.

with his disciples. These were last heard of in Samaria in iv 33. In the Synoptic account of the multiplication for 5000 the Twelve are involved (Mark vi 30—"the apostles" who are the Twelve of vi 7). Are the "disciples" of John the Twelve? See NOTE on vs. 60 below.

4. *Passover*. In the present sequence considerable time seems to have elapsed since the feast of v 1, whether that be Pentecost, Tabernacles, or the preceding Passover. This is the second Passover mentioned in John (see ✗5 in the chart in COMMENT).

5. *looked up . . . caught sight*. Same verbs as iv 35.

a large crowd. The lack of an article is strange, especially if this is the same crowd mentioned in vs. 2. In ✗2 of the chart (see COMMENT) we see that the Synoptic tradition is not harmonious in either multiplication, for there are references both to a crowd that is following him or with him and to a crowd that comes to him. These are not likely to have been crowds of Passover pilgrims since the lake was not on the pilgrim route from Galilee to Jerusalem; moreover, pilgrims would be carrying food.

coming toward him. In vss. 2–3 the crowd seems to be already with him. This may be a reflection of the theological theme of coming to Jesus (see p. 79).

Philip. See NOTE on i 43. He is closely associated here (vs. 8) with Andrew as also in xii 21–22. If the scene takes place in Bethsaida, as in Luke, a question to Philip is logical since he was from Bethsaida.

Where shall we ever buy bread for these people to eat? A similar question is found in the Matthean account of the multiplication for 4000 (Chart, ✗7a). It is reminiscent of Num xi 13 and the question asked by Moses of Yahweh (Matthew is closer): "Where am I to get meat to give all these people?" Other parallels between John vi and Num xi include:

Num xi 1: people grumbling (John vi 41, 43);

Num xi 7–9: description of the manna (John vi 31);

Num xi 13: "Give us flesh that we may eat" (John vi 51 ff.—but LXX of Numbers does not use *sarx* as John does);

Num xi 22: "Shall all the fish [*opsos*] of the sea be gathered [*synagein*] to suffice them?" (John vi 9 uses *opsarion;* 12 uses *synagein*).

6. *test Philip's reaction*. Elsewhere in the Gospels this verb *peirazein* has a pejorative sense of temptation, trial, trickery. This parenthetical verse is an editorial attempt to forestall any implication of ignorance on Jesus' part.

7. *two hundred days' wages*. Literally "200 denarii"; a denarius is a day's wage in Matt xx 2.

9. *lad*. *Paidarion* is a double diminutive of *pais* of which *paidion* is the normal diminutive (iv 49). In II Kings *paidarion* is used to designate Gehazi the servant of Elisha (iv 12, 14, 25, v 20).

barley loaves. Wheat bread was more common; barley loaves were cheaper and served for the poor. Luke xi 5 seems to indicate that three loaves were looked on as a meal for one person. "Loaves" is literally "breads."

dried fish. *Opsarion* is a double diminutive of *opson* (cooked food eaten with bread); the meaning became more specifically "fish," especially "dried or preserved fish." See the use of *opsos* cited under vs. 5 above.

10. *sit down*. Literally "lie down, recline."

men. In all the accounts of the multiplications (see Chart, ✗9) just the men are numbered, as Matthew makes specific.

11. For the minor variants in this verse see Boismard, RB 64 (1957), 367–69.

gave thanks. In both classical and secular *Koine* Gr. *eucharistein* has this meaning; it is distinguished from *eulogein*, "to bless" (the verb of the Synoptic multiplication for 5000: see Chart, ※11c). The relation to the thought that the Eucharist is an act of thanksgiving is obvious. However, J.-P. Audet, RB 65 (1958), 371–99, points out that the use of *eucharistein-eucharistia* in the NT reflects the Jewish use of *bārak-berākāh*, "bless, blessing." He maintains that it was only in the 2nd century A.D. that the "thanksgiving" motif began to dominate in Christian circles as the ancient roots of the service were forgotten. Therefore, although for convenience we have translated *eucharistein* and *eulogein* differently, we do not stress a difference in meaning as far as Jesus' action in the multiplication is concerned. We can see the interchangeability in Mark viii 6–7. Dodd's treatment of *eucharistein* in *Tradition*, p. 205, is marred by overlooking Audet's contribution. In general, John prefers *eucharistein* even where there are no sacramental overtones, e.g., xi 41. Jesus may have spoken in giving thanks or blessing; a typical Jewish blessing over bread was: "Blessed are you, O Lord, king of the universe, who bring forth bread from the earth."

passed them around. Jesus himself distributes the loaves even as he will at the Last Supper (Chart, ※11e); the number of the crowd, however, suggests that this is a simplification and that the Synoptics are correct in involving the disciples in the action.

12. *had enough.* This is the only use of *empimplasthai* in John (see Dodd, *Tradition*, p. 204[2]). Both it and the Synoptic word *chortazesthai* ("to be satisfied, filled"—Chart, ※12) are used in LXX to translate Heb. *śbʿ*. The Synoptic term is more redolent of the divine promises of abundance in the OT (Pss xxxvii 19, lxxxi 16, cxxxii 15). *Chortazesthai* appears pejoratively in John vi 26: "You are looking for me . . . because you have eaten your fill of the loaves."

Gather up. Synagein, which in the multiplication accounts is used only in John (Chart, ※13), appears in the OT account of gathering the manna (Exod xvi 16 ff.). A word of the same root, *synaxis,* served as the name of the first part of the Christian eucharistic gathering.

fragments. The Greek word *klasma* is used in the *Didache* (ix 3, 4) for the eucharistic bread.

left over. Léon-Dufour, p. 492[29], warns against confusing this with "the remnant" of OT thought, for the Greek root *periss/* never translates the Hebrew root *śʿr* which is used for "remnant." Here we have a question not of remnant but of surplus.

13. *twelve.* Some suggest that there was one basket for each of the Twelve, but this would be the first time that the disciples in John would be identified with the Twelve. See NOTE on vs. 67, § 26.

fed with the five barley loaves. John pays little attention to the fish, unlike Mark (Chart, ※13), because only the bread will be the subject of the discourse. The verb "feed with, upon" (*bibrōskein*) is used to prepare the way for the discussion of "food" (*brōsis*) in vi 27, 55.

14. *sign[s].* There is strong evidence, including Vaticanus and P[75], for reading a plural. One can see how a plural might have been changed to a singular to make the reference to the multiplication clear; the opposite process is difficult to explain. However, the plural could be an echo of vs. 2.

the Prophet who is to come into the world. Most likely this is a reference to the expectation of the Prophet-like-Moses (see p. 49), for in vs. 31 these people draw a connection between the food supplied by Jesus and the manna given by Moses. However, if vss. 14–15 were once independent of the multiplication narrative, a more general reference to a prophet is possible. Miracles are associated with a prophet in ix 17; also Luke vii 16, xxiv 19. Still another possibility is suggested by the qualification "who is to come into the world." As we have pointed out (NOTE on i 27), the "one who is to come" is a description of the prophet Elijah; here Jesus has multiplied barley bread as did Elijah's follower Elisha (II Kings iv 42–44). In I Kings xix a definite parallel was drawn between Elijah and Moses, and the popular expectation in this verse of John may represent an amalgamation of the two figures.

15. *would come.* This may reflect the pleonastic Semitic use of "come"; see ZGB, § 363.

carry . . . off. This is a violent word with connotations of force.

make him king. In certain strains of Judaism it was expected that the Messiah or anointed Davidic king would come at Passover. The seeming identification of the Prophet and the (messianic) king is difficult, for i 21 and vii 40–41 distinguish between the Prophet(-like-Moses) and the Messiah. At Qumran the coming of a prophet preceded that of the Messiahs (see p. 49). Lagrange, p. 166, and Glasson, p. 29, point out that the passages that distinguish Prophet and Messiah are set in Judea and against the background of the learning of the Pharisees, who would be more precise than the ignorant Galileans. Glasson, p. 31, mentions that Philo (*Life of Moses* I 158) refers to Moses as a king.

fled back. The majority of witnesses read "went back up," perhaps in a scribal attempt to soften an embarrassing flight by Jesus. "Fled" is attested by Sinaiticus, the Latin, and the Latin Fathers. Bligh, p. 16, sees in Jesus' "ascending" the mountain a prefiguration of his exaltation, but the verb used gives no evident support to this.

to the mountain. Had he been off the mountain mentioned in vs. 3? Or are we to think of his going farther up the mountain, while his disciples went down? See the suggestion in the COMMENT that vss. 14–15 were once not attached to the multiplication scene.

COMMENT

The Order of the Chapters

Nowhere has the theory of rearrangements in John (see Introduction, p. XXVI) had more following than in the reversal of chapters v and vi. Not only those who practice rearrangement on a large scale (Bernard, Bultmann), but even those who make little of rearrangement in general (Wikenhauser, Schnackenburg) reverse these chapters. The reasons for rearrangement are patent. In chapter v Jesus has been in Jerusalem; but at the beginning of vi he is in Galilee and we are never told how he got there. If we reverse v and vi, however, we have a better geographical sequence:

  end of iv: Jesus is at Cana in Galilee
       vi: Jesus is on the shore of the Sea of Galilee
        v: Jesus goes up to Jerusalem
      vii: Jesus can no longer travel in Judea so he goes
           about Galilee

The sequence is not perfect, however, even with the rearrangement. There is no transition between the scene at Cana and the scene at the Sea of Galilee, such as we saw in ii 12.

Other arguments are advanced for rearrangement. The reference of the "signs" in vi 2 is not clear (see NOTE). Some maintain that such a reference would make better sense if it followed a healing in Galilee, namely the one at Cana in chapter iv; however, we remember that that healing was worked at a distance and not seen by a crowd. The reference in vi 2 is probably to be explained as a general remark like the description of the enthusiasm of the Galileans in iv 45. Another argument advanced for putting vi before v is that Passover, which is near in vi 4, could then be the unnamed feast which prompts Jesus' journey to Jerusalem in v 1. Yet this does not fit well with the chronology of iv (see NOTES on iv 35) which seemingly took place a short time *after* Passover; if iv is followed by vi, then nearly a year has gone by and there cannot be much sequence between the healing in iv and the enthusiasm in vi.

Others argue for the reversal of chapters on the basis of closeness between v and vii. Chapter v deals with a Sabbath healing in Jerusalem, and in the Jerusalem scene of vii 21 Jesus refers to this as if it were something recent. Again, v 18 refers to the wish of the Jews to kill Jesus, and this theme begins vii. However, on the other hand, one could argue that vii 3 implies that in the recent past Jesus has not been in Jerusalem working miracles, and this implication is strange if vii follows immediately after v.

The projected rearrangement is attractive in some ways but not compelling. There is no manuscript evidence for it, and we must not forget that there are other indications that favor the present order. For instance, in our COMMENT on vii 37–39 we shall point out that the sequence of the manna in vi and the water theme in vii seems to be a deliberate reference to OT passages with the same sequence. No rearrangement can solve all the geographical and chronological problems in John, and to rearrange on the basis of geography and chronology is to give undue emphasis to something that does not seem to have been of major importance to the evangelist.

Relation to the Synoptics

The multiplication of the loaves is the only miracle from the public ministry of Jesus that is narrated in all four Gospels. The accounts are markedly alike, and we are faced once again with the problem of whether or not John's account is dependent on the Synoptic accounts. Some like Mendner proclaim with insistence that dependence is obvious; others like Dodd and E. D. Johnston deny dependence. Haenchen thinks that John's independent tradition is quite late and came to the evangelist in a form that had evolved considerably and which he retouched slightly; Bultmann sees the evangelist's hand only in vss. 4, 6, 14, 15; Wilkens insists that the work of the evangelist can be seen in almost every verse and that it is impossible to separate a complete original tradition from the evangelist's reworking. Wilkens thinks that the viewpoint of the evangelist is entirely kerygmatic and non-historical. The question is important enough to warrant a full treatment, for truly the problem of the dependence and the value of John's tradition comes to a head here.

In comparing John and the Synoptics, one principle of judgment seems sound, namely: if the fourth evangelist copied from one or from several of the Synoptic accounts, for the most part what he reports should be found in the words of the Synoptic accounts. If there are differences in John, then on the theory of copying, there should be some motive, theological or literary, that can explain why a change has been introduced. It is true that we can never be certain that in copying the evangelist did not make changes on pure whim and without any visible reason; but to accept this possibility as an explanatory principle is to reduce analysis to irrationality. If we find a considerable number of differences in wording, sequence, and detail and these differences have no apparent explanation, the most logical assumption is that John's account was not copied from the Synoptics but represents independent tradition. In that eventuality we shall have to weigh the value and antiquity of the Johannine tradition against that of the Synoptic tradition.

The comparison between John and the Synoptics is complicated by the fact that Mark and Matthew have two accounts of multiplications of loaves and fish, one for five thousand men and a second for four thousand men, while Luke has only one account. It has long been argued whether the second multiplication is really a separate incident or simply a variant form of the same incident. In the latter case we would have in Mark and Matthew a phenomenon similar to what is encountered in the Pentateuch, where several accounts of the same event are recorded, often side by side. There are several arguments for considering the two accounts in Mark and Matthew as variant reports of the same multiplication. (a) The first account is found in Mark vi 30–44; the second in viii 1–9. In general Luke follows Mark rather closely, but Luke has nothing corresponding to that section of Mark that runs from vi 45 to viii 26. In other words, Luke breaks off from Mark after the first multiplication account and rejoins the Marcan outline shortly after the second multiplication. Did Luke deliberately omit this section because he thought the second multiplication account repetitious? Or did Luke use an early form of Mark which did not have this material? (b) In the second multiplication account there is not the slightest suggestion that the disciples were seeing something that they had seen before. Their puzzlement about where the crowd will get food is rather hard to explain if they had already witnessed a multiplication. (c) Mark vi 30–vii 37 constitutes a passage very much like viii 1–26. Not only do both begin with a multiplication, but also the succeeding incidents are very much the same in their themes (see Taylor, *Mark,* pp. 628–32). We may have here two preaching complexes of material, each based on the multiplication of the loaves, and now both preserved in Mark and Matthew.

We cannot pretend to settle this complicated problem, but let us work with what seems the more probable hypothesis, namely, that Mark and Matthew give us two accounts of the same multiplication. We must then ask which is older, the first account (Mark-Matthew-Luke) or the second account (Mark-Matthew)? Both Haenchen and Dodd incline to the hypothesis that the second is older; one point in their argument is that a smaller number of people is involved in the second account. However, one might argue that the use of *eucharistein* in the second account indicates a greater conformity to the eucharistic liturgy and therefore a later stage of tradition than the *eulogein* of the first account (see Chart below, ✗11c). If we are dealing with variant traditions, it seems probable that neither account can be designated *in toto* as older than the other; the individual details of each will have to be evaluated, and sometimes details that seem to be older will be found in one account, sometimes in the other.

We must compare John with all the Synoptic accounts and not merely with Mark, even though Mark is often taken as the source of the other Synoptic accounts. Yet, for instance, in the first multiplication account Matthew and Luke agree on many details against Mark, especially by way of omission; and L. Cerfaux argues that there are two forms of the first multiplication, Matthew-Luke and Mark, not dependent on one another but both dependent on a common source ("La section des pains," *Synoptische Studien* [Wikenhauser Festschrift; Munich: 1954], pp. 64–77; also RecLC, I, pp. 471–85). In the second multiplication account he thinks that Matthew is more original than Mark in many details.

Sequence in John compared with that of Mark

We shall begin our comparison with the general sequence of the events that follow the multiplication. As we have mentioned, Luke omits much that is in Mark; here Matthew is roughly the same as Mark; therefore it will suffice to compare John and Mark. Many years ago J. Weiss noted some interesting parallels in sequence between Mark and John; and these have been expanded by Gärtner, pp. 6–8. Developing this still further, we may set up this comparison:

Multiplication for 5000	John vi	1–15	Mark vi 30–44
Walking on the sea		16–24	45–54

(Then skipping to the end of Mark's second multiplication account which is found in Mark viii 1–10)

Request for a sign		25–34	viii 11–13
Remarks on bread		35–59	14–21
Faith of Peter		60–69	27–30
Passion theme; betrayal		70–71	31–33

Now, obviously, this table of parallels cloaks important differences. For instance, the remarks on bread in John constitute a whole discourse, and this is not true in Mark. But granting that each tradition has developed differently the content of parts of the outline, we do think that the general similarity of sequence can scarcely be fortuitous. The order in John resembles very closely Taylor's (*Mark*, p. 631) reconstruction of the pre-Marcan order of the material now scattered through chapters vi–viii of Mark. It is possible that in copying from the Synoptic tradition, the fourth evangelist recognized the similarity of the first and second multiplication accounts in Mark-Matthew and by a process of elimination happened upon the sequence that modern scholars consider more original. But it would be far less taxing to assume that the fourth evangelist had available to him this more primitive sequence (so Gärtner, p. 12). Was he perhaps copying from a precanonical form of Mark that had only one multiplication? Such a suggestion was made above to explain Luke's order; but if both Luke and John were dependent on a precanonical Mark, it must be noted that Luke and John do *not* have the same sequence of events. Perhaps a more fruitful possibility is that the fourth evangelist drew on an independent tradition which had the same general sequence as precanonical Mark.

So much for what the over-all sequence of events can tell us. Let us now compare the details of the actual multiplication accounts. We do this in an accompanying chart that we must ask the reader to study carefully before continuing with our remarks.

John's account of the multiplication and Synoptic accounts I and II

In ⌖1, 5(?), 7b, 8, 9, 10 (*grass*), and 13, as well as in being followed by the story of the walking on the sea, John's account seems closer to Synoptic account I. On the other hand, in ⌖3, 4, 6, 7a, 10 (*sit down*), and 11c, John's account seems closer to Synoptic account II. Thus, it is difficult to defend the theory that John represents straight copying from either of the Synoptic accounts. Even if it is proposed that the evangelist blended details from I and II, one must admit that there is no recognizable scheme or pattern to the borrowing. One of the few items that could be explained as mixed borrowing is ⌖10. What is especially important is that John has a number of details not found in either Synoptic account, as seen in ⌖1, 5, 7, 8, 11e, 12, 13. Although some of these details can be explained as theologically motivated, not all can. Moreover, it is extremely hard, if we presume copying, to account for John's omission of Synoptic details that could have helped Johannine theological themes. The omission of "desert place" in ⌖1 is curious since it would have prepared the way for the manna theme in John vi 31. Again, since the Johannine account has eucharistic overtones, why did the evangelist omit the breaking of the bread in ⌖11d? The suggestion that the evangelist was thinking of the paschal lamb whose bones were not broken (Exod xii 46; Num ix 12; John xix 36) is not convincing. John also omits the looking up to heaven in ⌖11b, and this action too may have been part of the ancient eucharistic rite. There is one logical explanation for all of these features, omissions, additions, and parallels, namely, that the evangelist did not copy from the Synoptics but had an independent tradition of the multiplication which was like, but not the same as, the Synoptic traditions.

The relative age of John's tradition when compared with Synoptic I and

CHART COMPARING THE MULTIPLICATION IN JOHN AND THE SYNOPTICS

	I FIRST SYNOPTIC ACCOUNT: Mk vi 31-44 Mt xiv 13-21 Lk ix 10-17	II SECOND SYNOPTIC ACCOUNT: Mk viii 1-19 Mt xv 29-38	JOHANNINE ACCOUNT vi 1-15
Setting			
#1	Mk-Mt: goes in a boat to a *desert* place. Lk: withdraws to Bethsaida (contrast with Mark vi 45).	Mk: no localization; but vii 31 mentions Decapolis region near the Sea of Galilee. Mt: passing along the Sea of Galilee.	Crosses the Sea of Galilee (to Tiberias?); see vi 22-24. It is somewhere across the Sea from Capernaum (vi 17). For *desert* theme see vi 31.
#2	Mk-Mt: sees a large crowd as he lands. Lk: the crowds follow him.	Mk: a large crowd is with him. Mt: a large crowd came to him (30). BOTH: crowd(s) have been there 3 days.	Vs. 2: a large crowd keeps following. Vs. 5: sees a large crowd coming toward him.
#3	Mk: no healings mentioned; he teaches. Mt-Lk: he heals the sick in the crowds.	Mk: new story seemingly unconnected with previous healing of deaf mute. Mt (30-31): crowds had brought afflicted whom he healed; they had seen and wondered.	The crowd had seen the signs he was performing on the sick.
#4	Mk-Mt: only after the multiplication does Jesus go off to/climb up (*anabainein*) the mountain to pray (Mk vi 46; Mt xiv 23). ALL: the twelve disciples/apostles are with him.	Mt (29): Jesus climbs up (*anabainein*) the mountain and sits down there. BOTH: the disciples are with him.	Jesus goes up (*anerchesthai*) the mountain and sits down there. with his disciples.
#5	Mk-Mt: In #10 both mention grass; Mk says "green grass," implying springtime.		Near Passover; thus springtime.

Dialogue	SYNOPTIC I	SYNOPTIC II	JOHN
#6	ALL: The disciples take initiative. MK–MT: worried about the late hour. ALL: They urge Jesus to send the people away to buy food for themselves.	ALL: Jesus takes initiative, worried about feeding the crowd that has been with him 3 days and will faint if he sends them away.	Jesus takes initiative, worried about feeding the crowd.
#7a	ALL: Jesus answers by telling the disciples themselves to feed them.	The disciples answer by asking: "Where are we to get bread in the desert to satisfy such a crowd?" (MT).	Jesus asks Philip: "Where shall we ever buy bread for these people to eat?"
7b	MK: They say, "Shall we go and buy 200 denarii worth of bread and give it to them to eat?" LK (13): "... unless we are to go and buy food for all these people."		Philip replies, "Not even with 200 denarii could we buy loaves enough to give each of them a mouthful."
#8	MK: Jesus asks them, "How many loaves have you? Go and see." They find out. ALL: "We have five loaves and two fish [ichthys]." MT: Jesus says, "Bring them here to me."	BOTH: Jesus asks them, "How many loaves have you?" They say, "Seven—" MT: and a few small fish [ichthydion, but ichthys in 36]." MK: (later in 7). They have a few small fish (ichthydion).	Andrew tells Jesus, "There is a lad here who has five barley loaves and a couple of dried fish [opsarion] but what good is that for so many?"
#9	ALL: There are about 5000 men MT: besides women and children. (Only LK, like JN, mentions the number at this point; MK–MT mention it at the end of the account.)	MK: There are about 4000. MT: There are about 4000 men besides women and children. (Both mention the number at the end of the account.)	The men number about 5000.

	SYNOPTIC I	SYNOPTIC II	JOHN
Multiplication	MT: He orders the crowds to take a place (*anaklinein*) on the grass. MK: He commands them all to take places (*anaklinein*) by companies on the green grass. So they sit down in groups by 100s and 50s.	He directs the crowd to sit down (*anapiptein*).	Jesus says, "Get the people to sit down [*anapiptein*]."
✣10	LK: He says to his disciples, "Get them to take places [*kataklinein*] in groups of about fifty each." And they do so and make all take their places.		There is plenty of grass there; so they sit down.
✣11	See special chart below for Jesus' action over the loaves and the fish.		
✣12	And they all eat and are satisfied.	And they all eat and are satisfied.	—just as much as they want. When they have enough,
✣13	ALL: And they take up (*airein*) 12 baskets (*kophinos*) of the fragments. MT-LK: of what is left over. MK: and of the fish. MK-MT: And those who have eaten (MK: the loaves) are about 5000 men =✣9.	And they take up (*airein*) 7 hampers (*spyris*) of the fragments that are left over. There are about 4000 (MT: who have eaten)=✣9.	he tells his disciples, "Gather up [*synagein*] the fragments that are left over so that nothing will perish." And so they gather 12 baskets (*kophinos*) full of fragments left over by those who have been fed with the 5 barley loaves.

SPECIAL SUBDIVISION OF THE CHART: Comparison of Jesus' actions over the loaves in the multiplication accounts with the eucharistic action over the bread at the Last Supper (Mk xiv 22; Mt xxvi 26; Lk xxii 19; I Cor xi 23–24)

	SYNOPTIC MULTIPLICATION I	SYNOPTIC MULTIPLICATION II	JOHANNINE MULTIPLICATION	LAST SUPPER
※11a	And taking the five loaves and the two fish (*ichthys*),	Mt: He takes the seven loaves and the fish (*ichthys*); Mk: And taking the seven loaves,	Jesus then takes the loaves;	Mk-Mt-Lk: And taking bread, Paul: He takes bread;
11b	and looking up to heaven,			
11c	he blesses (*eulogein*)	and giving thanks (*eucharistein*),	and giving thanks (*eucharistein*),	Mk-Mt (over bread): and blessing (*eulogein*), Lk-Paul (over bread) and ALL over wine: and giving thanks (*eucharistein*),
11d	and breaks (the loaves)			he breaks
11e	and gives (the loaves) to the disciples/ disciples (*didonai*)	and gives to the disciples (*didonai*)	he gives them around (*diadidonai*)	Mk-Mt-Lk: and gives to them/ the disciples (*didonai*).
11f	to set them out before the crowd(s).	Mk: to set them out. And they set them out before the crowd. Mt: and the disciples give them to the crowds.	to those sitting there;	
11g	Mk (only): And he divides the two fish (*ichthys*) among them all.	Mt: see ※11a Mk: And they have a few small fish (*ichthydion*); and blessing (*eulogein*) them, he tells them to set them out.	and the same with the dried fish (*opsarion*).	Action over the wine.

II is difficult to fix. In some details, like that of the money in ✕7b, John's account seems to be later than Synoptic ✕1 (for Mark 200 denarii suffice; for John the sum is inadequate—however, this may be more a question of spontaneous exaggeration than of real development). Yet, in another detail like ✕7a John's account seems to have greater antiquity; for it is hard to believe that a late tradition would report a statement that might seem to attribute ignorance to Jesus. (Either the editor or the final redactor of John betrays that he is uncomfortable with this seeming ignorance on Jesus' part, and inserts the parenthetical vs. 6 to explain the difficulty away.) The solution, then, is probably the same one we reached in evaluating the relative ages of Synoptic I and II: in each of the three traditons there are very ancient details, and in each there are details that have been elaborated in the course of transmission. Nor is John's tradition itself entirely homogeneous, as a study of ✕2 shows. Therefore, each detail would have to be evaluated on its own merits.

John's account and the multiplication in the individual Synoptic Gospels

We observed that in speaking of Synoptic accounts I and II we may be oversimplifying; for instance, some scholars find two traditions in I, namely, that of Mark and that of Matthew-Luke. Let us therefore compare John and each Synoptic Gospel in order to settle the question even more thoroughly.

In some details John is indisputably close to Mark I, for example, the figure of 200 denarii in ✕7b. John resembles Mark I and II in ✕11g in mentioning the distribution of the fish. Yet even in these instances there is no identity: the vocabulary is different in ✕11g, and the ability of the sum to suffice differs in ✕7b. In passages where Mark has material that Matthew-Luke do not have, for example, ✕3, 10, John shows no affinity to Mark.

In ✕4, 7a, John has peculiar features that are close to Matthew II, although again with vocabulary differences. There is nothing in John to match the features of Matthew II in ✕8, 9 ("besides women and children"). John differs from Matthew I even more than from Mark I.

Luke and John are alike in that they both have only one multiplication account, but they do not share much similarity of detail (see ✕2, 9). The notable features that John shares with Mark I are not found in Luke.

Thus, our comparison of John and the individual Synoptics confirms the conclusion reached in the more general discussions in the Introduction, namely, that the Johannine account was not copied from any one Synoptic Gospel nor pieced together from several Gospels. It is not impossible that the final redactor added to the basically independent Johannine account details from Mark, for example, 200 denarii. However, it is just as possible that such details were part of the Johannine tradition from its earliest traceable stage.

Evaluation of Details Peculiar to John

In John's account of the multiplication there is a theological orientation just as there is in the Synoptic accounts. Some scholars, especially those who think that John's account was copied from the Synoptic tradition, would use this theological orientation to explain all the details proper to John, details which they regard as creative additions rather than an echo of early tradition. This is a delicate question. All that we can do is to study the details peculiar to John and point out theological motivation where it exists. We do not think that all the peculiar details have theological motivation; but even where they do, we cannot *a priori* conclude that, therefore, they were invented by the evangelist to suit his theology. It must be emphasized that it is perfectly logical to think that primitive Christian theology was built up on what was actually contained in the tradition, and that that is why the details fit the theology. The following important details are peculiar to John.

(1) *The Passover setting in* ⚡5. Synoptic account I seems implicitly to fix the time of the multiplication in the spring when there would be green grass on the ground. Indeed, in the sequence that follows Synoptic account II, there may be an implicit reference to Passover in the passage where Jesus warns against the leaven of the Pharisees (Mark viii 14–21). Such an allusion would be most appropriate at Passover, when unleavened bread was required. However, John's explicit introduction of the Passover theme may be designed to prepare for the discourse that will follow in ch. vi. Bultmann, p. 156[6], thinks that the Passover reference was added by the Redactor who added vss. 51–59 to the chapter. It may be said in favor of his theory that, as we saw in the NOTES, there are several peculiar features in the introduction to the multiplication (Tiberias in vs. 1; signs in vs. 2; crowd in vss. 2 and 5) that suggest a complicated history for vss. 1–4. However, the Passover motif fits not only vss. 51–59, but also the mention of the manna in vs. 31, for manna is prominently mentioned in the liturgy of the Passover meal. This liturgy also mentions the crossing of the Reed Sea which *may* be associated with the walking on the water in vi 16–21 (see discussion below).

If Aileen Guilding's observations about the synagogue readings are correct (see p. 278 below), then woven into the very fabric of Jesus' discourse are many of the motifs that were being read in the synagogues at Passover time. She would maintain that the evangelist artificially made up the discourse on the basis of such themes taken from the synagogue readings; but, at least in principle, if there is some historical basis to the scene in ch. vi, then Jesus would be simply referring in his discourse to OT ideas that he knew were fresh in the mind of people at this season of the year. For further possible reflections of the Jewish Passover ritual see vi 28 ff., as discussed below (pp. 266–67). Thus, the mention of Passover certainly fits the whole theological outlook of the chapter. Its presence is not an isolated act of editorship; and there is nothing to contradict the possibility that the scene was originally connected with Passover.

(2) *The identification of Philip and Andrew in* ※7, *8.* Scholars repeat monotonously that the introduction of personal names into a narrative is often the sign of a later imitator trying to give his work an air of authenticity. If this is applied to John, one must admit, however, that the evangelist has chosen strangely, for Philip and Andrew are among the more obscure members of the Twelve. The fact that both of these disciples were honored in Asia Minor, the traditional locus of John's Gospel (see NOTE on i 43), is worth considering. It may persuade some that the names were introduced to make the Gospel more acceptable in Asia Minor; it may persuade others that these disciples were originally involved in the narrative and the memory of this was preserved only in the tradition of a community which had a devotion to them.

(3) *The special details of* ※8. John specifies that a *lad* (*paidarion*) had five *barley* loaves and *dried fish* (*opsarion*). There is nothing implausible about any of these details, but the "lad" and the "barley loaves" recall the Elisha story in II Kings iv 42. We remember that the NT establishes a parallelism between Jesus and the closely connected figures of Elijah and Elisha. Bultmann, p. 157[3], questions the connections of John's account to the story in II Kings, but the parallels are startling. A man comes to Elisha with twenty *barley loaves* (one of the four uses of "barley" as an adjective in LXX). Elisha says, "Give to the men that they may eat." There is a servant present (designated as *leitourgos* here, but as *paidarion* five verses before, and the latter is his normal designation—see NOTE on vs. 9). The servant asks, "How am I to set this before a hundred men?"—a question similar to vs. 9 in John. Elisha repeats the order to give the food to the men, and they eat and have some left.

Another background for John's mention of barley bread has been proposed by Daube, p. 42, and Gärtner, p. 21. In Ruth ii 14, Boaz gives Ruth some parched grain to eat; she ate and was filled and had some left over. Although the grain is usually taken as wheat, the action is at the time of the barley harvest; and these scholars suggest that it was barley bread that was involved. The theological import would lie in the rabbinic interpretation of the Ruth scene as an anticipation of the messianic banquet. In our judgment, this association with Ruth is too tenuous.

A third item that John mentions is "dried fish." Here the *ichthys* of the Synoptic traditions might be considered the more theological term since in early Christianity (2nd century, but with earlier roots?) its letters became an acrostic for Christ. As we pointed out in the NOTES on vss. 9 and 5, John's *opsarion* might echo Num xi; but this seems farfetched. Mendner argues that this word is not important in John, for it was added by the same editor who added ch. xxi, where it appears in vss. 9, 10, and 13. However, the argument should be the reverse: whoever was responsible for xxi was not responsible for the use of *opsarion* in vi; for in xxi the word is used for freshly caught fish, while in vi it has the more classical sense of preserved food.

(4) *The eucharistic features in* ※11, 12, 13. Seemingly, in all the accounts

of the multiplication there is a strong eucharistic motif. This miracle does not fit the normal pattern of Jesus' miracles in the Synoptic tradition (see our study, "The Gospel Miracles," BCCT, pp. 184–201), where even the nature miracles are treated as acts of power establishing the kingdom of God against Satan's dominion. According to the evangelists, why does Jesus work this miracle? The motive of compassion does not seem to be the main explanation; for the Gospels stress that the disciples did not understand the import of the multiplication (Mark vi 52, viii 14–21), and they should have had no difficulty understanding compassion. Thus, even in the Synoptic tradition, this miracle seems to border on the concept of a miracle as a sign, as something designed to teach those who saw it about Jesus. Seemingly, the Synoptic evangelists saw it as a messianic sign fulfilling the OT promises that in the days to come God would feed His people with plenty (see NOTE on vs. 12). For instance, in promising the exiles in Babylon a new exodus, Deutero-Isaiah (xlix 9 ff.) echoes the words of the Lord: "They shall be fed along the ways; on the heights shall be their pasture. They shall not hunger, nor shall they thirst."

Now, as the account of the multiplication was handed down in the teaching tradition of the Christian community, its connection with the special food of God's people, the Eucharist, was recognized. A glance at the chart for ⌘11 shows the close parallels in gesture and wording between Synoptic accounts I and II and the descriptions of the Last Supper. The most plausible explanation is that the wording of the multiplication accounts was colored by the eucharistic liturgies familiar to the various communities. G. Boobyer (JTS 3 [1952], 161–71) has argued against eucharistic influence on the Synoptic accounts of the multiplication, but we doubt if the parallels in our chart can be explained otherwise. E. Goodenough (JBL 64 [1945], 156 ff.), on the other hand, goes too far when he maintains that account I of the multiplication was the original eucharistic narrative. As a final instance of eucharistic flavoring, we may mention that the multiplication was used in 2nd-century catacomb art to symbolize the Eucharist, and the late 2nd-century epitaph of Abercius at Hieropolis mentions the fish (*ichthys*), symbolizing Christ, and the bread and wine of the Eucharist all together.

It is not surprising, then, that John's account of the multiplication also shows adaptation to the scene of the institution of the Eucharist. Even though John reports no institution scene (see vi 51), we see no reason to suspect that the churches of Asia Minor, presumably the audience of the Fourth Gospel, were unfamiliar with a primitive eucharistic liturgy such as that preserved in Paul-Luke and Mark-Matthew. The eucharistic adaptations in the Johannine account of the multiplication are different from the adaptations in the Synoptic accounts (⌘11d), as we might expect if John's tradition of the multiplication was independent. An exception is ⌘11c, where both John and Synoptic account II use *eucharistein*. A peculiar Johannine feature is found in ⌘11e where Jesus himself distributes the loaves over which he has given thanks, just as he did at the Last Supper (see NOTE on vs. 11). Perhaps also John's phrase, "When they had enough . . ." (⚹12), echoes the eucharistic liturgy since it also appears in the account of the eucharistic meal in the *Didache*. There, after ch. ix records the eucharistic prayer over the cup and the bread, x 1 begins: "After you have had enough . . ."

Even more clearly there is a eucharistic echo in the Johannine details in ⚹13 where Jesus tells his disciples, "Gather up [*synagein*] the fragments [*klasma*] that are left over so that nothing will perish." As C. F. D. Moule, "A Note on Didache ix 4," JTS 6 (1955), 240–43, has pointed out, John is very close here to the eucharistic prayer of the *Didache* over the bread: "Concerning the fragmented bread [*klasma*], 'We give thanks [*eucharistein*] to you, Our Father. . . . As this fragmented bread was scattered *on the mountains,* but was gathered up [*synagein*] and became one, so let the Church be gathered up from the four corners of the earth into your kingdom.'" Besides the obvious parallels with John's account in the use of *klasma, eucharistein, synagein* (the last of which is peculiar to John's multiplication account), we should note that only John emphasizes that the multiplication took place on a mountain, and only John mentions the theme of Jesus as king (vs. 15). The verse of the *Didache* just cited also has parallels in John xi 52.

Continuing our discussion of the Johannine eucharistic details in ⚹13, we note that some scholars also see a eucharistic echo in the phrase ". . . so that nothing will perish." They think of the care taken of the eucharistic fragments in the early Church. However, the phrase may simply be a preparation for vs. 27, where Jesus says that the people have misunderstood the miracle of the loaves: they are to work for the food that lasts for eternal life, and not for *the food that perishes.* John may be stressing that even the miraculously multiplied loaves can perish. Barrett, p. 231, sees another possible meaning, namely, that this is a poetic reference to the gathering of the disciples that they may not perish. This theme comes up in xvii 12; and the *Didache,* as cited above, uses the gathering of the eucharistic fragments as a symbol of the gathering of the Church. The twelve baskets as a symbol of the Twelve Apostles, each gathering in for Christ, has also been proposed. One more *possible* eucharistic reference may be mentioned, namely, that in the early Church *barley* bread was used for the Eucharist (see J. McHugh, VD 39 [1961], 222–39).

Thus, even if we cannot be sure of every detail, the eucharistic coloring of the Johannine account of the multiplication seems beyond doubt. One may be hesitant, however, about claiming that John's account is more eucharistic than the Synoptic accounts. The eucharistic elements in the various multiplication accounts are about the same in number, even though different in detail. That all the traditions would have eucharistic coloring means that the insight into the relationship of the multiplication and the action at the Last Supper must have been gained early in the preaching tradition. Indeed, it is far from impossible that Jesus himself connected the feeding of the crowd with loaves and the institution of the Eucharist (both in a Passover context) by a deliberate sameness in the pattern of his actions.

We shall see the importance of these observations when we deal with Bultmann's claim that it was only the addition of vss. 51–59 that brought a eucharistic motif into ch. vi of John. Rather, the addition of those verses highlighted a eucharistic motif that was already there.

(5) *The conclusion of the scene in vss. 14–15.* After Synoptic account I, Jesus compels his disciples to depart by boat for the other side of the sea; then he dismisses the crowd and goes up the mountain to pray. (The sequence after account II is of less importance, since in John's next scene—the walking on the sea—John is close to account I.) No reason is given for the abrupt sending away of the disciples and the dismissal of the crowd.

John's account provides a reason for this puzzling behavior, namely, the danger of a political manifestation on the part of the crowd. Yet there are difficulties about this information in vss. 14–15. In vss. 25 ff. Jesus meets the same crowd the next day. Not only is there no reference to making him king, but the crowd has doubts about him. We may claim that this is an example of the fickleness of crowds, but the sequence is difficult. Moreover, if the plural, "signs," is read in vs. 14, then 14–15 are only loosely attached to the multiplication of the loaves and refer to all the miracles of the Galilean ministry.

Even though the Synoptics do not narrate the incident found in vss. 14–15 of John, they do have information that is helpful in evaluating those verses. Chapter vi of Mark, which contains multiplication account I, marks one of the major divisions of the Gospel. At the beginning of this chapter Jesus is rejected at Nazareth. This is coupled with the story of the death of John the Baptist at the command of Herod. These two stories, the latter of which seems to constitute a threat to Jesus, cause him to end his Galilean ministry and to withdraw from Herodian territory. The reason for the Herodian threat to Jesus is made apparent by Josephus *Ant.* XVIII.v.2;※118: "Herod feared that the great influence John [the Baptist] had over the people might put it into his power and inclination to raise a rebellion." If Jesus continued to attract great crowds in Galilee, he could easily have become the next target of Herod's wrath. This, then, is the setting that Mark gives to his first account of the multiplication; and such a setting warns us that John is quite plausible in attributing a political reaction to the crowds in vs. 14 and a deep distrust and fear of that reaction to Jesus in vs. 15.

We have pointed out in the NOTES that the relationship in vss. 14–15 between the working of signs and the acclamation of Jesus as "the Prophet" and king is not clear and is susceptible of several explanations. Dodd, *Tradition,* p. 214, points out that in almost all the narratives of Josephus concerning 1st-century political uprisings by would-be liberators (e.g., Theudas; the Egyptian; etc.) the themes of the prophet and the working of signs appear. This is more confirmation for John's attribution of political tone to the people's action.

Thus, whether or not vss. 14–15 were always part of the multiplication scene, we believe that in these verses John has given us an item of correct historical information. The ministry of miracles in Galilee culminating in the multiplication (which in John, as in Mark, is the last miracle of the Galilee ministry) aroused a popular fervor that created a danger of an up-rising which would give authorities, lay and religious, a chance to arrest Jesus legally. The age of this Johannine information may be judged by the contrary tendency to remove from the Gospels anything that might give substance to the Jewish charge that Jesus was a dangerous political figure. If John was written toward the end of the century when Roman persecution of Christians under Domitian was all too real, then the invention of the information in vss. 14–15 seems out of the question.

Finally, we may note that vss. 14–15 play an important role within the scheme of ch. vi. The crassness of the Galilean reaction to signs prepares the way for the deep misunderstanding of the multiplication and indeed of the whole bread of life discourse that we shall see in vss. 26 ff.

We have now treated all the details peculiar to John's account of the multiplication. As we have seen, some of them can be explained as possibly stemming from the evangelist's theological perspective. In general, however, when these details are properly understood, there is nothing that is really implausible or that would weigh against the independent value of the Jo-hannine tradition.

[The Bibliography for this section is included in the Bibliography for ch. vi, at the end of § 26.]

21. JESUS AT PASSOVER:
—WALKING ON THE SEA OF GALILEE
(vi 16–21)

VI 16 As evening drew on, his disciples came down to the sea. 17 Having embarked, they were trying to cross the sea to Capernaum. By this time it was dark, and still Jesus had not joined them; 18 moreover, with a strong wind blowing, the sea was becoming rough. 19 When they had rowed about three or four miles, they sighted Jesus walking upon the sea, approaching the boat. They were frightened, 20 but he told them, "It is I; do not be afraid." 21 So they wanted to take him into the boat, and suddenly the boat reached the shore toward which they had been going.

19: *sighted;* 20: *told.* In the historical present tense.

Notes

vi 16. *evening.* Perhaps the time is late afternoon, for vs. 17 would indicate that it did not become dark until they were out at sea.

to the sea. Or "to the seashore." The same Greek phrase is used in xxi 1: "Jesus appeared to the disciples *at the Sea* of Tiberias." There he stands on the seashore.

17. *embarked.* Literally "got into *a* boat." Since Mark and Matthew mentioned a boat at the beginning of Synoptic account I, here they speak of *the* boat; the later Greek witnesses put the article in John also.

trying to cross. Literally "were going"; the imperfect is probably conative (BDF, § 326).

still Jesus had not joined them. The sequence of the action indicates that they are already out at sea. How, then, was Jesus to join them? Perhaps they were sailing close to land expecting to meet Jesus on the shore. Bultmann, p. 159, sees this line as the work of the Redactor, for the disciples had no reason to expect Jesus once they were out at sea. Wikenhauser, p. 121, thinks of the clause as expressing the reason why they had embarked, and thus the last half of vs. 17 becomes a parenthesis explaining the first half.

18. *moreover.* The Gr. *te* is a strong connective, infrequent in John.

19. *three or four miles.* Literally "25 or 30 stadia"; a stadium was about 607 feet, roughly a furlong. Josephus, *War* III.x.7;✗506, gives the measurements of the "Lake of Gennesar" as 40 stadia wide by 140 long; actually, at its greatest extent it is 61 stadia (7 miles) wide and 109 stadia (12 miles) long. Mark vi 47

mentions the boat's being "in the midst of the sea." Were this to be taken literally, it would mean that the boat was 20–30 stadia offshore, a distance that would agree with John's information. But Mark's designation simply means "at sea," for in Mark vi 47 it is also said that Jesus can see them from the land.

sighted. Is the historical present a reflection of eyewitness tradition?

upon the sea. This is the same Greek phrase as "to the sea" in vs. 16 (there *epi* with the accusative; here with the genitive). Bernard, I, p. 186, suggests that this means "by the seashore" and that the Johannine narrative was not originally the story of a miracle. Then, however, the story seems pointless. In vi 25, moreover, it is implied that Jesus crossed the sea in an unexpected way. Mark vi 49 uses the same vague expression as John; but Matthew's use of the preposition with the accusative in xiv 25 shows clearly that the first evangelist thought of Jesus as walking upon the water.

20. *It is I.* For *egō eimi* see App. IV. This is a borderline case where one cannot be certain if a divine formula is meant.

do not be afraid. OS^cur omits this, and it could be a scribal addition from the Synoptic tradition.

21. *they wanted.* As this verb is used in vii 44 and xvi 19, it refers to an unrealized wish; as it is used in i 43 and v 35, it refers to a realized wish. John does not make it clear whether or not Jesus got into the boat. Torrey suggested that the root Aramaic consonants *b'w* were misinterpreted by the one who translated John into Greek and that the original meaning was: "they rejoiced greatly"; but this is a rather desperate solution.

suddenly the boat reached the shore. Miraculously?

toward which they had been going. Omitted in Chrysostom and Nonnos.

COMMENT

Relation to the Synoptic Account

In both Mark-Matthew and in John (but inexplicably, not in Luke) the multiplication of the loaves for the five thousand is followed by the walking on the sea. In the Synoptic account this story is intimately bound to what goes before and constitutes the conclusion of the multiplication scene; what follows the walking on the sea is simply a group of incidents with no apparent connection. In John vss. 14–15 constitute the conclusion of the multiplication scene, and thus the walking on the sea has more independence as a narrative. It serves as a transition between the multiplication and the scene that takes place the next day, when the crowd comes to Jesus and hears the Discourse on the Bread of Life. Since it would have been simpler for the fourth evangelist, if he were simply a creative artist, to have placed the discourse on bread immediately after the multiplication, his inclusion of the walking on the sea indicates that he was controlled by an earlier tradition in which the multiplication and the walking on the sea were already joined.

In comparing the Synoptic and Johannine accounts, one notes immediately that there are many more similarities of vocabulary here than there were in the multiplication accounts, for instance: *evening drawing on, embarking, boat, crossing, sea, wind, rowing, stadia, walking upon the sea, "It is I; do not be afraid."* Of course, most of these similarities are in the nautical terms, and one cannot tell a story about an incident at sea without a certain basic nautical vocabulary.

There are also differences—so impressive, as a matter of fact, that Chrysostom (*In Jo.* XLIII 1; PG 59:246) thought the Synoptics and John were describing different events! In general, John's account is by far the shorter. It is told more from the viewpoint of the disciples who are waiting for Jesus, while the Synoptic account is from the viewpoint of Jesus who is alone on the land and sees the disciples distressed, etc. The element of the wonderful is more prominent in the Synoptic account, especially in Matthew (see NOTE on vs. 19) where Jesus walks across the sea to a boat that is many stadia distant from the land. Also in the Synoptic account Jesus, to the utter amazement of the disciples, stills the storm.

Turning to a more detailed comparison, we may distinguish:

Setting:

    Syn.: Jesus makes the disciples embark while he dismisses the crowd and stays to pray on the mountain.

    John: Jesus has fled back to the mountain from the crowd. The disciples come down to the shore and embark on their own initiative.

Time:

    Syn.: By the time that evening draws on they are out to sea—even though Matt xiv 15 has fixed the hour for the multiplication at the time when evening was drawing on (Mark vi 35: when the hour was already advanced)! Both Gospels have Jesus come to the disciples about the fourth watch of the night (3 A.M.).

    John: As evening draws on they come down to the shore. It becomes dark probably after they have embarked (see NOTE on vs. 17); Jesus comes to them only after they have rowed a distance.

Weather:

    Syn.: The wind is against them. Matthew adds that they are being beaten by the waves; Mark adds that they are distressed in rowing.

    John: A strong wind is blowing; the sea is becoming rough.

Position:

    Syn.: Mark says that they are out at sea but Jesus can see them from the land. Matthew says that they are many stadia distant from land.

    John: They have rowed twenty-five or thirty stadia, but the distance from land is not specified.

Jesus comes:

    Syn.: He walks on the sea; Mark adds that he intends to pass them by.

    John: Not clear whether they see him walking on the sea or on the shore.

Reaction:
   Syn.: They think it is a ghost and are terrified. Jesus reassures them,
   "It is I; do not be afraid."
   John: They are frightened, but Jesus reassures them, "It is I; do not
   be afraid."

Ending:
   Matt alone: The story of Peter's walking to meet Jesus.
   Syn.: Jesus gets into the boat and the wind is calmed. Matthew adds that
   the disciples worship Jesus, hailing him as God's Son.
   John: It is not clear if Jesus gets into the boat; the boat comes to shore
   suddenly and perhaps miraculously.

In evaluating these individual details, we find the situation somewhat
unusual. John's account patently has a claim to be considered as the more
primitive form of the story. John's brevity and lack of emphasis on the
miraculous are almost impossible to explain in terms of a deliberate
alteration of the Marcan narrative. Rather, it would seem that into the
Marcan form of the story there have been introduced elements from
other stories, for example, the calming of the storm (Mark iv 35–41). This
process of amalgamation seems still more developed in the Matthean form
of the story where there is a profession of faith like the one elsewhere
attributed to Peter (Matt xvi 16), and where there is an incident of Peter's
getting out of the boat to come across the water to Jesus. We may compare
the latter to the post-resurrectional story of Peter in John xxi 7; for, as
Dodd has pointed out, there are elements appropriate to the literary form
of the post-resurrectional narrative in the story of the walking on the
water—"The Appearances of the Risen Christ," *Studies in the Gospel*,
ed. D. E. Nineham (Lightfoot vol.; Oxford: Blackwell, 1957), pp. 23–24.
Thus, John's account of the walking on the water seems to represent a
relatively undeveloped form of the story.

The Meaning of the Scene

In the Marcan-Matthean version where Jesus calms the sea and gets
into the boat, this miracle story takes on the aspect of a nature miracle
in which the disciples are rescued. However, in John, where such elements
are missing, the substance of the miracle is significantly different. (We take
for granted that the evangelist does intend to portray a miracle; see NOTE
on vs. 19.) The most plausible explanation is that John treats the scene as a
divine epiphany centered on the expression *egō eimi* in vs. 20. Since this
expression occurs in both the Synoptic and Johannine forms of the story,
it may be considered as belonging to the primitive form of the tradition.
But the fourth evangelist has taken the expression, neutral in itself (see
App. IV), and made it a leitmotiv of the Gospel as that form of the divine
name which the Father has given to Jesus and by which he identifies himself.
Probably, in the primitive form of the story, this was a miracle that gave

expression to the majesty of Jesus, not unlike the Transfiguration. In John the special emphasis on *egō eimi* in the rest of the Gospel does seem to orient this story more precisely, that is, the majesty of Jesus is that he can bear the *divine* name. Matthew's form of the story seems to have taken a similar direction independently, as witnessed in the worship rendered to Jesus by the disciples and their confession of him as God's Son.

What role does this miracle play in relation to the multiplication and to the rest of the chapter? To a certain extent the evangelist uses it as a corrective of the inadequate reaction of the crowd to the multiplication. Impressed by the marvelous character of that sign, they were willing to acclaim him as a political messiah. But he is much more than can be captured by the traditional titles of "the Prophet" and king; the walking on the water is a sign that he interprets himself, a sign that what he is can be fully expressed only by the divine name "I am."

Is there also a Passover symbolism in the walking on the sea by way of a reference to the crossing of the Reed Sea at the time of the Exodus? (This would fit the miracle into the general context of ch. vi.) The Passover *Haggadah,* the liturgical narrative recited at the Passover meal, as it is preserved for us from a slightly later period, closely associates the crossing of the sea and the gift of the manna. Since the latter theme appears in vi 31, John may be making the same association. It will be seen below that John vi 31 seems to recall Ps lxxviii 24. This same psalm mentions in vs. 13 how the Israelites passed through the sea. Thinking of the Johannine scene as a divine epiphany, we note that the Midrash Mekilta on Exodus (cited by Gärtner, p. 17) mentions that God made a way for Himself through the sea when man could not. Gärtner, p. 28, connects the *egō eimi* formula with the divine action in delivering Israel from Egypt; the formula *"I am* the Lord" of Exod xii 12 is dwelt upon in the Passover *Haggadah.*

In Ps lxxvii 19, in a poetic description of the Exodus crossing, it is said of God, "Your way was *on* [or *in*] *the sea;* your path was on the many waters; yet your footsteps were not seen." This echoes a more general description of Yahweh whom Ps xxix 3 describes as "the Lord upon many waters." Aileen Guilding (see p. 278 below) points out that one of the synagogue readings (a *haphtarah*) for the Passover cycle was Isa li 6–16 in which there are references to how the redeemed pass over the depths of the sea (vs. 10) and the Lord God stirs up the sea so that its waves roar (15); moreover, vs. 12 is one of the most important *egō eimi* passages in the OT. Perhaps the most complete assemblage of OT parallels to the themes of John vi can be found in Ps cvii: in 4–5 we hear of the people wandering hungry in desert wastes; in 9 we are told that the Lord fills [John's *empimplasthai*] these hungry people with good things; in 23 some go down to the sea in ships; in 25 the Lord raises a stormy wind that lifts up the waves of the sea; in 27–28 they are troubled and cry out to the Lord; in 28–30 He delivers them, calming the sea and bringing them to their haven.

Thus, there are OT passages, particularly among those dealing with the Exodus, that help to explain why the episode of Jesus' walking on the sea may have fitted in with the general Passover motif of ch. vi of John and thus have stayed in close association with the multiplication. Of course, it is difficult to prove that the evangelist had any one of these passages in mind, but they are numerous enough to make it plausible that he meant the miracle to reflect the general symbolism of the crossing of the sea at the time of the Exodus and the prerogative of Yahweh to make a path on or in the waters.

[The Bibliography for this section is included in the Bibliography for ch. vi, at the end of § 26.]

22. JESUS AT PASSOVER:—THE CROWD COMES TO JESUS
(vi 22–24)*

Transition to the Bread of Life Discourse

VI 22 The next day the crowd which had remained on the other side of the sea observed that there had only been one boat there and that Jesus had not gone along with his disciples in that boat, for his disciples had departed alone. 23 Then some boats came out from Tiberias near the place where they had eaten the bread [after the Lord had given thanks]. 24 So, once the crowd saw that neither Jesus nor his disciples were there, they too embarked and went to Capernaum looking for Jesus.

* NOTE: There are a great number of textual variants in these few verses. Codex Sinaiticus (original hand) has a remarkably aberrant form of the text, and there are still more variants in the *Diatessaron,* Chrysostom, and the early versions. For a complete study see Boismard, RB 60 (1953), 359–70.

NOTES

vi 22. *The next day.* This need not be a real chronological indication; but, like the "days" of ch. i, it may have been used simply to give the chapter a unified literary structure.

observed. As phrased, this statement is illogical. What is meant is that on the next day they remembered that *on the day before* they had observed only one boat there.

boat. Ploiarion, literally "a little boat," is a diminutive of *ploion;* but it is dubious whether such a diminutive designates a different type of boat, as Bernard, I, p. 188, thinks. In vss. 17, 19, 21, John has used *ploion* for the disciples' boat. If *ploiarion* describes the same boat, does the change of term indicate a different Johannine hand in 22–24? The textual witnesses for 22 vary between *ploiarion* and *ploion,* the latter reading betraying a desire of the scribes to harmonize. After "boat," some of the Western textual witnesses and Sinaiticus add for clarification: "the one in which the disciples of Jesus had embarked."

23. *Tiberias near the place.* We have deliberately left the English obscure. While the best witnesses to the text seem to imply that the boats had come from Tiberias *to* near the place of multiplication (a rather awkward description), other witnesses read: "Tiberias which was near the place." The latter reading fixes Tiberias as the vicinity of the multiplication (see NOTE on vs. 1).

[*after the Lord had given thanks*]. This clause is not found in Bezae, OL, and OS. The absolute use of *eucharistein* here is almost liturgical, and the use of "the Lord" is not Johannine. Some of the Vulgate witnesses have the crowd giving thanks instead of Jesus.

24. *embarked*. Literally "got into the boats" (which had come from Tiberias).

COMMENT

The textual variants in these verses suggest a very complicated history. Boismard proposes that the form of the text that we have translated is an amalgamation of two different textual traditions. In one of these there is a crowd which had been with Jesus at the time of the multiplication; in the other the crowd consists of people who were near the spot where the disciples landed after crossing the lake during the storm. (To support the latter interpretation of the crowd, it may be mentioned that in some Coptic and Ethiopic mss. the disciples and the crowd go together to Capernaum.) Boismard points out that in the verses that follow, this same confusion about the crowd seems to persist. In vss. 26–27 Jesus addresses a crowd that has eaten with him the day before; in 30–31 the crowd asks for a sign as if they have never seen one (compare with vs. 14!) and wants him to imitate the miracle of the manna by supplying them with bread.

If we grant that there is some confusion in the text of vss. 22–24, what value has the passage as historical tradition? There is no real parallel in the Synoptic tradition. In Synoptic account I, when Jesus and his disciples land, they are at Gennesaret (Mark vi 53; Matt xiv 34). The people of this region recognize him and bring their sick to be cured. After account II, Jesus and his disciples go by boat to Dalmanutha/Magadan (Mark viii 10; Matt xv 39–a geographical puzzle, unless it is a garbled form of Magdala, near Gennesaret); and seemingly when he lands, the Pharisees come to ask him for a sign. But in neither instance does the crowd that witnessed the multiplication follow Jesus. If in John's account there is a hint of the presence of a new crowd at the place where Jesus lands, this may be by parallelism with Synoptic account I.

The details that John narrates are difficult. Are we to think that five thousand men were transported across the sea to catch up with Jesus? If the multiplication took place near Tiberias (see NOTES on vss. 23 and 1), the presence of boats from Tiberias is not hard to explain; but if it took place at Bethsaida or on the Transjordanian side of the sea, there is a difficulty. Bultmann, p. 160, thinks that in the story the crowd was originally at Capernaum, but that the evangelist confused this crowd with the crowd that had witnessed the multiplication and so had to invent a means of transporting the latter crowd to Capernaum. Yet, if the evangelist is really giving fictional information, why does he introduce Tiberias? The introduction of boats from Capernaum would have been the obvious solution. Thus, there seems no facile solution for the difficulties involved. One may harmonize with a certain plausibility: the multiplication took place near Tiberias; the next day boats from Tiberias picked up a few of those who had seen the multiplication and brought them to Capernaum and it was this group that Jesus addressed in vss. 26–27; but also there were people from Capernaum who had gathered to see Jesus and it was this other part of the mixed crowd that spoke to Jesus in vss. 30–31. Or perhaps one may theorize that two scenes have been woven together: one that was the aftermath of the multiplication and concerned people who had seen that sign; the other that was an introduction to the Bread of Life Discourse and concerned people in the synagogue at Capernaum: the awkwardness in vss. 22 ff. would reflect that attempt to bridge these two scenes.

We may note that in vss. 22–24 there is a deepening of the theological motifs that we found in the multiplication scene. If the bracketed clause in 23 is original, then the fact that the Lord had given thanks (*eucharistein*) has become very important, an emphasis reflecting the eucharistic interpretation of the scene. No longer is it a question of the loaves (plural) but of the *bread,* again a seeming concession to the eucharistic language of the NT.

[The Bibliography for this section is included in the Bibliography for ch. vi, at the end of § 26.]

23. JESUS AT PASSOVER:—PREFACE TO THE
DISCOURSE ON THE BREAD OF LIFE
(vi 25–34)

VI 25 And when they found him on the other side of the sea, they
said to him, "Rabbi, when did you come here?" 26 Jesus answered,

> "Truly, I assure you,
> you are not looking for me because you have seen signs,
> but because you have eaten your fill of the loaves.
> 27 You should not be working for perishable food
> but for food that lasts for eternal life,
> food which the Son of Man will give you;
> for it is on him that God the Father has set His seal."

28 At this they said to him, "What must we do, then, to 'work' the
works of God?"
29 Jesus replied,

> "This is the work of God:
> have faith in him whom He sent."

30 "So that we can put faith in you," they asked him, "what sign are you
going to perform for us to see? What is the 'work' you do? 31 Our ancestors had manna to eat in the desert; according to Scripture, 'He gave
them bread from heaven to eat.'" 32 Jesus said to them:

> "Truly, I assure you,
> it is not Moses who gave you the bread from heaven,
> but it is my Father who gives you the real bread from heaven.
> 33 For God's bread comes down from heaven
> and gives life to the world."

34 "Sir," they begged, "give us this bread all the time."

NOTES

vi 25. *on the other side of the sea.* Literally "across the sea." The place where they found him was Capernaum (vss. 24, 59), on the north shore of the lake, slightly west. The description in this verse seems to favor localizing the multiplication on the east shore, rather than at Tiberias on the west shore; however, it is not impossible that "across the sea" could cover a journey from Tiberias to Capernaum.

Rabbi. Nicodemus addressed Jesus by this title in iii 2 when he came as the spokesman of those in Jerusalem who had been impressed by Jesus' signs (ii 23); the situation, following the incident in vs. 14, is quite similar here. The title reflects a *general* attitude toward Jesus as a teacher, for in John's account Jesus had not taught in connection with the multiplication as he had done in Mark's account (Chart in § 20 above, ✳3), but see NOTE on vs. 3, "sat down."

when did you come here? Literally "When have you been here?"—a question that is a cross between "When did you get here?" and "How long have you been here?" We have translated the perfect of the verb *ginesthai* (here almost with the sense of *paraginesthai*, "to arrive") as an aorist.

26. *looking for me.* This theme is taken from vs. 24.

eaten your fill. Chortazesthai; see NOTE on vs. 12, "had enough."

27. *working for.* Not in the sense that any eternal gift can be gained by sheer human endeavor; rather the sense of striving after or working toward. BAG, under *ergazesthai,* 2e (p. 307), suggests the possible meaning of "digest, assimilate;" but all the plays on "work" in the next few verses make that doubtful.

perishable food. This may be an echo of vs. 12, where the fragments were collected so that nothing would *perish.* Ignatius may reflect the *idea* of vs. 27 in *Romans* vii 3: "I have no pleasure in corruptible nourishment . . . I desire the 'bread of God,' which is the flesh of Jesus Christ . . . and for drink I desire his blood, which is incorruptible love." The second part of the citation is reminiscent of John vi 53 ff.

food that lasts. This is the favorite Johannine verb *menein* (see App. I:8). The idea is not that the food lasts forever, but that the food is imperishable because it gives eternal life. Compare iv 14: "The water I shall give him will become within him a fountain of water leaping up unto eternal life."

the Son of Man will give. In iv 14: "I shall give." Would the crowds understand this term? The Jerusalem crowd does not in xii 34.

will give. A present tense is well attested, but P[75] tips the scales decisively in favor of the future. Those who reject the future think it is a theological adaptation to the theme of the Eucharist which *will* be given later; however, the present is probably a scribal assimilation to vs. 32.

set His seal. In iii 33 we heard that by accepting Jesus' testimony the believer has certified (set his seal of approval) that God is truthful. Here God sets His seal on the Son, not so much by way of approval, but more by way of consecration (x 36). The verb is in the aorist so that commentators think of a particular action, like the Incarnation (Spicq) or the baptism (Bernard). Westcott suggests that this is a consecration to sacrifice. Others think of the Son as bearing the seal-image of the Father (Col i 15), even as he bears the divine name. It has also been proposed that this sealing of Jesus by the Father is contrasted to the crowd's attempt in vs. 15 to make Jesus king.

28. *to 'work' the works.* This translation preserves the Greek play on words, but "work" here does not mean "to work for" as in vs. 27, but "to perform." Bultmann, p. 162[8], does not think that this half-understanding of Jesus' words befits the crowd, for in vs. 34 they seem to show no understanding at all that he is speaking of the work of God.

the works of God. The works that God desires of men.

29. *the work of God.* Here the expression can have the same meaning, but it also may mean the work that God accomplishes in men.

have faith. This is a present subjunctive with a durative import.

30. *are you going to perform.* The "you" is emphatic: *you* who are telling others to work.

31. *ancestors.* Literally "fathers."

manna. The providing of manna was regarded as the greatest of Moses' miracles; the basic narratives are Exod xvi and Num xi. Josephus, *Ant.* III.i.6;⌗30, speaks of it as a "divine and miraculous" food.

Scripture. The citation in John is not an exact rendering of any one OT passage. We may note the following:

Exod xvi 4:   I shall rain loaves *from heaven* on you.
Exod xvi 15: This is *the bread which the Lord has given* you *to eat.*
Ps lxxviii 24: He rained on them manna *to eat*
              and *gave them the bread* of *heaven.*
Wis xvi 20:   You fed your people with the nourishment of angels,
              and you sent them *from heaven bread* that took no labor.

32. *it is not Moses.* Borgen, "Observations," pp. 233–34, has shown that this is a good example of typical Jewish exegesis. The crowd has cited Scripture: "He gave them bread from heaven to eat." In the pattern of Jewish exegesis the interpreter says, "Do not read _____, but _____." So Jesus says, "Do not interpret the 'he' as Moses and do not read the past tense 'gave'; but interpret the 'he' as the Father and read 'gives.'" The tense correction is based on a different Hebrew vocalization wherein the consonants *ntn* are read as *nōtēn* rather than as *nātan.* By these changes Jesus indicates that the OT is being fulfilled now in his own work. The manna given by Moses was not the real bread from heaven of which the OT speaks; it is Jesus' teaching. If we recall that in rabbinic thought bread was a symbol of the Torah (StB, II, p. 483), we may have a contrast here between Moses and Jesus, between the Law and Jesus' teaching, as in i 17.

gave. The textual evidence is divided between reading an aorist or a perfect ("has given"). Some suggest that the aorist comes from the use of that tense in vs. 31. Notice the contrast between the past (aorist or perfect) tense and the present tense in the final line in vs. 32: the Father's giving has begun and will continue. Torrey's attempt to read this clause as a question ("Did not Moses give you the bread from heaven?") is unnecessary. See COMMENT.

the real bread. The position of "real" is emphatic. This statement may have added meaning if the later rabbinic argument was already current on whether or not manna was truly the heavenly nourishment of the angels (StB, II, p. 482).

33. *God's bread comes down.* Literally "the bread of God is *that which* [or *he who*] comes down." Scholars are divided on whether the predicate is personal or impersonal. Perhaps both are meant, for Johannine ambiguity is often

intentional. The people take it impersonally in vs. 34, but the personal connotation prepares for the ideas of vss. 35 ff. The phrase "which [or who] comes
down from heaven" occurs seven times in this discourse. It was taken over in
the Nicene creed to refer to Jesus: "For us men and our salvation he came
down from heaven."

COMMENT

The problem of the division of the great Discourse on the Bread of
Life is difficult, and almost every commentator has his own division. We
think that it would be more profitable to discuss this problem in an addendum
(see § 25, p. 293) after the commentary on the whole discourse.

Verses 25–34 serve as a preface or introduction to the Bread of Life
Discourse, and thus the arrangement resembles that of ch. v, where vss.
16–18 set the theme for the long discourse that followed. Verses 25–34
not only serve this purpose in ch. vi, but they also serve (somewhat
artificially) to tie the discourse to what has preceded (again like v 16–18).
We refer the reader to the brief table of sequence parallels between John
and Mark on p. 238. Mark vi 34 says that Jesus taught on the occasion
of the multiplication (account I); in John Jesus teaches the next day. In Mark
viii 14–21, after multiplication account II, there is a request for a sign and
some brief remarks of Jesus about bread indicating the failure of the
disciples to understand the multiplications. All of these themes appear in
John vi 25–34, but in much tighter chronological and geographical relation
to the multiplication. See also the figurative use of bread in Mark vii 24–30
in the preaching sequence that follows multiplication account I. These
parallels lead us to suspect that while the Bread of Life Discourse, as it
now stands, reflects the organizing genius of the fourth evangelist (much
as the Sermon on the Mount reflects the genius of the first evangelist),
nevertheless it is composed of elements of traditional material.

Verses 25–27

As we have pointed out in our remarks on vss. 14–15 and on 22–24,
there are many difficulties about the identification of the crowd to whom
the Bread of Life Discourse is directed with the crowd who witnessed the
multiplication. No longer in vs. 25 is Jesus thought of as "the Prophet" and
king (14–15); he is addressed with the modest title of "Rabbi." The awkward
question in 25, "When did you come here?" (see NOTE), may have a deeper
theological meaning if the evangelist is thinking here of the question of Jesus'
origins, which is a favorite theme (vii 28, etc.). In terms of such a theme the
mention of the Son of Man and the bread *from heaven* would constitute a
theological answer to how Jesus had come here: he is the Son of Man who
has come down from heaven (iii 13). On the factual level, however, the
question seems to remain unanswered.

Again on the factual level vs. 26 is difficult. How can Jesus tell the crowd that they are not looking for him because they have seen signs, when in vss. 14–15 we were told that the people wanted to come and carry Jesus off precisely because they had seen the signs he had performed? While such a difficulty reflects the complex history of the editing of this scene, it offers no difficulty on the theological level of the evangelist's understanding of signs. The enthusiasm of 14–15 was based on the physical seeing of the marvelous aspect of the sign, but there was no real sight of what the sign taught about Jesus—their concept of him as a Davidic king was political. It is the deeper insight into the sign of which vs. 26 speaks, contrasting it with the eating of the miraculous loaves. It will require the long discourse by Jesus to explain that the multiplication was a sign of his power to give life through the bread of his teaching and of his flesh, a power that he has because he has come down from heaven. The same misunderstanding of bread (and leaven) on a purely natural level is found in Mark viii 14–21; Matt xvi 5–12; and especially in Matt xvi 12 it is clear that Jesus has been talking of teaching.

In vs. 27 Jesus presses the lesson home in terms of the familiar Johannine dualism: perishable food and the food that lasts for eternal life. In ch. iv the contrast was between water that could quench thirst temporarily and the water for eternal life that would satisfy thirst forever. Although the expression is Johannine, such symbols are frequent in the Bible. Isa lv 1 invites everyone who is thirsty to come to the waters and everyone who has no money to buy and eat. This drink and food is not anything that money can buy; it is the word of God to which they must listen. Parallel to John's "You should not be working for perishable food," we hear in Luke xii 29: "Do not seek what you are to eat or what you are to drink. . . . Instead seek His kingdom."

In vs. 27 Jesus identifies the food that lasts for eternal life as the gift of the *Son of Man*. This is often an eschatological title (see NOTE on i 51), and the use here probably reflects Johannine realized eschatology. Whether we read "will give" or "gives," the food that lasts for eternal life is in part a present gift, just as eternal life itself is a present gift. These heavenly realities are realized in the ministry of Jesus.

Verses 28–31

In vss. 28 ff. there is a play on the theme of "work" which has been introduced in 27, and this theme seems almost to constitute a separate motif in the larger discussion of food and bread. Bultmann, p. 164, thinks of it as belonging to a lost dialogue in reference to works, some of which is preserved in viii 39–41. Yet, if the Discourse on the Bread of Life concerns Jesus' revelation, then since faith is the essential response to Jesus' revelation, 28–29 have a place in the preface to the discourse in the sense that they give the traditional contrast between faith and works. The crowd has been led by Jesus to penetrate beyond the superficial, material level of food, but their response (28) is in terms of works that they can do. Jesus, in turn (29), puts the emphasis on faith. Paul and James are the NT names we associate with the problem of faith and works, but here we have the Johannine solution. Obtaining eternal life is not a question of works, as if faith did not matter; nor is it a question of faith without works. Rather, having faith is a work; indeed, it is the all important work of God. Yet, as Bultmann has remarked, this believing is not so much a work done by man as it is submission to God's work in Jesus. Acts xvi 30–31 shows a scene in early Church life that illustrates for us the life-situation in which vss. 28–29 of John vi would have had meaning and would have been preserved.

The mention of faith makes the crowd unfriendly and they begin to question Jesus' claims (vs. 30). They put to him a demand for a sign similar to that which we heard from the temple authorities in ii 18; and as we have mentioned, there is a Synoptic parallel after the second multiplication account in Mark viii 11. Verse 31 would indicate that the sign that the crowd wants is a supply of bread; see above (p. 258) for the difficulty of reconciling this with the indication that this is the same crowd that saw the multiplication the day before. What is important is the crowd's introduction of the theme of manna as a pattern for the sign. The challenge to Jesus to produce manna or its equivalent as a sign is quite understandable if they thought of him as the Prophet-like-Moses (see NOTE on vs. 14).

We have evidence in later Jewish documents of a popular expectation that in the final days God would again provide manna—an expectation connected with the hopes of a second Exodus. The 2nd-century A.D. apocryphon II Bar xxix 8 says: "The treasury of manna shall again descend from on high, and they will eat of it in those years." The Midrash Mekilta on Exod xvi 25 says: "You will not find it [manna] in this age, but you shall find it in the age that is coming." The Midrash Rabbah on Eccles i 9 says: "As the first redeemer caused manna to descend, as it is stated, 'Because I shall cause to rain bread from heaven for you (Exod xvi 4),' so will the latter redeemer cause manna to descend." The homiletic Midrash Tanḥuma (*Beshallaḥ* 21:66) is of particular interest when it speaks of the manna in a sapiential way: "It has been prepared for the righteous in the age to come. Everyone *who believes* is worthy and eats of it" (cited by Hoskyns, pp. 293–94). We shall see how the theme of believing is worked into Jesus' Discourse on the Bread of Life. Besides the general eschatological expectation of the manna, it seems that manna was particularly associated with Passover time, and thus the reference to manna in vs. 31 fits well with John's setting for the multiplication scene. Midrash Mekilta on Exod xvi 1 says that manna fell for the first time on the 15th day of the second month, a date associated with the celebration of Passover by those who missed the regular date (Num ix 11). Josh v 10–12 says that manna fell for the last time on Passover eve. The expectation grew that the Messiah would come on Passover, and that the manna would begin to fall again on Passover (Gärtner, p. 19). Although all these texts illumine the passage in John, we must stress that the rabbinic references come from a later period, and we cannot be certain how important the manna theme was in Jesus' time. However, Dodd, *Interpretation,* p. 335, cites a fragment of a Sibylline oracle which may be pre-Christian: "Those who fear God will inherit true eternal life . . . feasting upon the sweet bread from the starry heaven."

Verses 32–34

Jesus now tells the crowd that their eschatological expectations have been fulfilled. They have cited the manna given by Moses, but this is only a foreshadowing of the real bread from heaven which is Jesus' own teaching. Such a contrast between manna as physical nourishment and the power of God to grant spiritual nourishment is not new. There is background for it in Deut viii 3 where Moses tells the people: God "fed you with manna which you did not understand, nor did your ancestors understand, that He might make you realize that man does not live by bread alone, but that man lives by everything [or every word] that proceeds from the mouth of the Lord." This interpretation of the manna is echoed in Wis xvi 20 (see NOTE on vs. 31) which speaks of manna and xvi 26 which says: "That your sons whom you loved might learn, O Lord, that it is not the various kinds of fruit that nourish man, but it is your word that preserves those who believe in you." Perhaps the same emphasis is achieved in the balance of clauses in Neh ix 20: "You gave your good spirit to instruct them, and did not withhold your manna from their mouth, and gave them water for their thirst." Philo allegorized manna to refer to wisdom. Thus, there was a certain preparation for the symbolism that Jesus was about to use in applying the manna or bread from heaven to his revelation. (Of course, Jesus goes beyond all the OT background in speaking of himself as the bread from heaven and thus identifying himself as incarnate revelation.) But, as vs. 34 shows, the crowd fails completely to understand the symbolism and retreats to a purely materialistic understanding of the bread. This misunderstanding causes Jesus to begin the great Bread of Life Discourse.

Recently scholars such as Gärtner and Kilmartin have seen an added Passover motif in vss. 25–34, for they think that they have found within the question and answer pattern of these and succeeding verses an echo of the Jewish Passover *Haggadah.* During the liturgy of the Passover meal four children ask questions about what is being enacted; and Gärtner finds parallels to these four questions in vss. 28, 32, 42, 52. (We may note that the analysis of the questions from the *Haggadah* by Daube, pp. 158–69, is slightly different from that of Gärtner.) For instance, in the first question at the meal the wise child asks about the ordinances of God; so in vs. 28 the crowd asks about working the works of God. A child too young to ask questions is taught about a passage in Scripture; so in vs. 32 Jesus interprets the Scripture passage concerning the manna. The mocking ques-

tion in vs. 42 is equated with the question posed at the meal by the wicked
child. A fourth question at the meal is supposed to be a practical question
about living to be asked by a sincere child; by a stretch of the imagination
this is found in vs. 52. All of this correlation seems quite artificial and
strained, and we doubt that the backbone of John's account was supplied
by the ritual questions of the Passover meal (although Passover themes
are present throughout the chapter). Need we point out that the above theory
has to overlook questions (cf. remarks on vss. 25, 34) to make the pattern
fit?

As far as we can see, the question and answer format of vss. 25–34 is part
of the technique of Johannine misunderstanding. It has a perfect parallel
in ch. iv, where there is no question of the influence of the Passover ritual:

John vi	*John iv*
Q: 25 "Rabbi, when did you come here?"	Q: 9 "How can you, a Jew, ask me, a Samaritan, for a drink?"
A: 27 "You should not be working for perishable food."	A: 13 "Everyone who drinks this water will be thirsty again."
Q: 30–1 "What sign are you going to perform for us to see? Our ancestors had manna to eat in the desert."	Q: 11–2 "Where are you going to get this flowing water? Surely you don't pretend to be greater than our ancestor Jacob who gave us this well?"
A: 32–3 "My Father gives you the real bread from heaven. For God's bread comes down from heaven and gives life to the world."	A: 14 "The water that I shall give him will become within him a fountain of water leaping up unto eternal life."
REACTION: 34 "Sir, give us this bread all the time."	REACTION: 15 "Sir, give me this water so that I won't get thirsty."

[The Bibliography for this section is included in the Bibliography for ch.
vi, at the end of § 26.]

24. JESUS AT PASSOVER:
—DISCOURSE ON THE BREAD OF LIFE
(vi 35–50)

VI 35 Jesus explained to them:

"I myself am the bread of life.
No one who comes to me shall ever be hungry,
and no one who believes in me shall ever again be thirsty.
36 But, as I have told you,
though you have seen [me], still you do not believe.
37 Whatever the Father gives me will come to me;
and anyone who comes to me I will never drive out,
38 because it is not to do my own will
that I have come down from heaven,
but to do the will of Him who sent me.
39 And it is the will of Him who sent me
that I should lose nothing of what He has given me;
rather, I should raise it up on the last day.
40 Indeed, this is the will of my Father,
that everyone who looks upon the Son
and believes in him
should have eternal life.
And I shall raise him up on the last day."

41 At this the Jews started to murmur in protest because he claimed: "I am the bread that came down from heaven." 42 And they kept saying, "Isn't this Jesus, the son of Joseph? Don't we know his father and mother? How can he claim to have come down from heaven?" 43 "Stop your murmuring," Jesus told them.

44 "No one can come to me
unless the Father who sent me draws him.
And I shall raise him up on the last day.
45 It is written in the prophets:
'And they shall all be taught by God.'
Everyone who has heard the Father
and learned from Him
comes to me.

46 Not that anyone has seen the Father—
   only the one who is from God
   has seen the Father.
47 Let me firmly assure you,
   the believer possesses eternal life.
48 I am the bread of life.
49 Your ancestors ate manna in the desert, but they died.
50 This is the bread that comes down from heaven,
   that a man may eat it and never die."

NOTES

vi 35. *I myself am.* Although we have translated the "I" emphatically as the context demands, this is a frequent type of *egō eimi* clause in John (see App. IV). The *egō eimi* with a predicate does not reveal Jesus' essence but reflects his dealings with men; in this instance, his presence nourishes men. Borgen, "Observations," p. 238, points out that Jesus' words here are illustrative of Jewish exegesis (see NOTE on vs. 32). Jesus is identifying himself as the bread mentioned in the Scripture citation from Exodus quoted in vs. 31, just as John the Baptist identified himself as the voice mentioned in Isa xl 3 (John i 23). Borgen gives impressive Jewish parallels.

the bread of life. This means the bread that gives life. Compare vi 51, "the living bread."

comes to me . . . believes in me. These are in parallelism, as also in vii 37–38; they mean the same (see above, p. 79). These two lines of vs. 35 echo Sir xxiv 21: "He who eats of me [Wisdom] will hunger still; he who drinks of me will thirst for more." Although at first reading the words of Jesus seem to negate Sirach, the meaning of both is the same. Sirach means that men will never have too much Wisdom and will always desire more; Jesus' words mean that men will never hunger or thirst for anything other than Jesus' own revelation. John also may echo Isa xlix 10 ("They shall not hunger, nor shall they thirst"), a passage cited above (p. 247) as OT background for the multiplication.

36. *as I have told you.* Abbott, JG, § 2189–90, stresses that the *hoti* introducing discourse is often used in John when Jesus is citing his own words; often it is not clear whether it is introducing direct or indirect discourse. Actually, the words that Jesus is supposed to have said are not found as such in what has preceded. In vs. 26 we heard, "You are not looking for *me* because *you have seen signs*"; but that is still quite far from what is said in vs. 36. Bultmann, p. 163, puts 36–40 after 41–46, thus obtaining a better sequence. Another possibility is to put 36 after 40. However, in neither of these suggested transpositions are the words of vs. 36 found in what Jesus has said. Borgen, "Observations," p. 239, suggests another translation for 36: "But I have said, '*You*,' because [*hoti* causative, not recitative], though you have seen, still you do not believe." He thinks of vs. 36 as part of the exegesis technique already discussed in the NOTE on vs. 32. Jesus means that when in 32 he gave the exegesis of the Scripture cited by the Galileans in 31, he said "you" instead of "them" (vs. 31—Scripture cited: "He gave *them* bread from heaven to eat"; vs. 32—Jesus: "It is not Moses who gave *you* the

bread from heaven"). The reason why he applied the Scripture to his hearers was their lack of belief.

though . . . still. For this translation of *kai . . . kai,* see Abbott, JG, § 2169; BDF, § 444[3].

[*me*]. The two Bodmer papyri increase the evidence for this reading; the omission may represent a scribal desire to leave vs. 36 more vague so that its antecedent might be found in vs. 26.

37. *Whatever.* In both John (also vs. 39, xvii 2, 24) and I John (v 4) we find the neuter singular where we would expect the masculine plural. BDF, § 138[1], offers a plausible explanation: "The neuter is sometimes used with reference to persons if it is not the individuals but a general quality that is to be emphasized." Zerwick (*Analysis Philologica*) suggests Semitic influence; for *kol d[e]*, "all that which," does not distinguish gender or number. However, it may be wondered if the evangelist (who knows perfectly well how to say "everyone who" in vs. 40) may not want to give a greater collective force here. Bernard, I, p. 200, cites the example of the usage in xvii 21: "that they all may be one [neuter]."

gives me. Contrast the perfect, "has given," in vs. 39; God's action is not bound by the categories of time. That believers are given to Jesus by the Father is mentioned in x 29, xvii *passim*, xviii 9.

38. *my own will . . . the will of Him who sent me.* This same contrast is found in the Synoptic description of the agony in the garden (Mark xiv 36; especially Luke xxii 42). For the relation of John to the agony scene, see below, pp. 470–71.

come down. This is one of the few echoes of the bread from heaven theme (vs. 33) that are found in vss. 36–40.

39. *last day.* Here, as in xi 24 and xii 48, a reference to the day of judgment. This verse speaks of the resurrection of the just; compare the double resurrection of bad and good in v 28–29.

40. *looks upon. Theōrein* (see App. I:3)—not only physically, but with spiritual insight.

the Son . . . him. In these two lines Jesus suddenly switches to speaking of himself in the third person, while the rest of vss. 36–40 is in the first person. Perhaps we have a joining of sayings from different strata of the Johannine tradition, although difference of person is not necessarily an absolute criterion.

And I. The last line of vs. 40 seems to be an independent sentence, unlike the similar clause in the last line of 39 which is explanatory of the will of God. In 40 the switch of person back to the first person is abrupt and the "I" is emphatic.

41. *the Jews.* This is the first time in John that the people of Galilee have been referred to as "the Jews," a term which generally refers to those hostile to Jesus at Jerusalem. It cannot be said that these are visiting leaders from Jerusalem (as in Mark vii 1) because they know the local details of Nazareth village life. It may be that this objection has been introduced here from another scene.

murmur. The same word appears in LXX account of the murmuring of the Israelites during the Exodus (Exod xvi, 2, 7, 8); I Cor x 10 also uses it to describe this situation. The image is one of critical complaint rather than of open hostility.

because he claimed. Borgen, "Observations," pp. 235–37, points out that this type of objection has parallels in contemporary Jewish exegesis. Thinking of the objection from Exod xvi that they posed in vs. 31, they are objecting to the radical exegesis proposed by Jesus in vss. 32, 35.

42. *this.* There is an element of disparagement in this pronoun: "this fellow."

Jesus, the son of Joseph. The parallel in the Synoptics is found in the rejection of Jesus at Nazareth:

- Mark vi 3: "Isn't this the carpenter, the son of Mary and the brother of James, Joses, Jude, and Simon? And aren't his sisters here among us?"
- Matt xiii 55: "Isn't this the son of the carpenter? Isn't his mother called Mary, and aren't his brothers James, . . . ?"
- Luke iv 22: "Isn't this the son of Joseph?"

Obviously John is closer to Luke, although John mentions the mother, as do Mark and Matthew. We have seen other Johannine parallels to this Synoptic scene at Nazareth in the COMMENT on iv 43–45 (in § 15).

and mother. This is omitted by some witnesses associated with the Western group and by the OS.

How. Some witnesses have "So how [*oun*]"; others have "How now [*nyn*]." It seems more probable that particles have been added to a briefer original. Borgen, "Observations," p. 235, points to the use of *kêṣad*, "How [then]," in introducing rabbinic objections against an interpretation of Scripture. Compare too the objection of Nicodemus beginning with "How" in iii 4.

44. *draws.* The rabbinic sources use the expression "to bring nigh [to the Torah]" to describe conversion. *Pirqe Aboth* i 12, says: "The natural desire of one who feels thus [has love] toward his fellow men is to 'bring them nigh to the Torah,' for this means to make them sharers in the fuller knowledge of God." For John, what makes men sharers in the knowledge of God is to be drawn nearer to Jesus. The theme of drawing will reappear in xii 32: "And when I am lifted up from the earth, I shall draw all men to myself." Bernard, I, p. 204, suggests that a background for this may be found in LXX of Jer xxxviii (MT, xxxi) 3 where God says of Israel: "I have *drawn* you with kindness." Some deny that LXX gives the correct translation of the Hebrew of this verse, but see A. Feuillet, VT 12 (1962), 122–24. Note that a parallel to vs. 44 in John is found in vs. 65, where instead of "unless the Father draws him," we hear "unless it is granted to him by the Father."

45. *in the prophets.* This plural is perhaps a generalization, although some have thought of a collection of prophetical testimonies used by the early Church. Still another possibility is unfolded by the homiletic pattern discovered by Borgen; this may represent the notation that the subordinate citation from the prophets is being introduced (see COMMENT).

'And they shall all be taught by God.' This is a free citation of Isa liv 13:
        MT: "All your sons shall be taught by the Lord."
        LXX: "And I shall make all your sons to be taught by God."

heard the Father/and learned from Him. Literally "heard from the Father and learned."

46. *Not that anyone has seen the Father.* This is the same theme as i 18; and the contrast with Moses suggested there (p. 36) is probably in mind here as well, in view of vs. 32. See also NOTE on v 37.

49. *Your ancestors.* Literally "fathers." This is one of the instances of "your" indicating the deep cleavage that exists between Church and Synagogue at the time when the evangelist is writing; see "your Law" in viii 17, and "your father Abraham" in viii 56.

died. In vs. 49 physical death is meant; in vs. 50, spiritual death. Compare xi 25–27.

50. *This is the bread.* The wording is close to Exod xvi 15; see NOTE on vs. 31.

COMMENT: GENERAL

The meaning of "The Bread of Life"

Before commenting on the discourse proper, we must raise the question of what Jesus means when he speaks of bread. We have mentioned above (pp. 265–66) that manna was interpreted in some Jewish circles as signifying divine word or instruction; thus there was preparation for understanding "the bread from heaven" or "the bread of life" of which Jesus spoke as *divine revelation* given to men by and in Jesus. However, in vss. 51–58 "the bread of life" is identified with the flesh of Jesus, and there it seems that Jesus is speaking of *eucharistic bread*. (In what follows we shall discuss not only vss. 35–50, but also 51–58.)

Even in antiquity there was no agreement. Some of the early Church Fathers, like Clement of Alexandria, Origen, and Eusebius, understood the whole discourse (vss. 35–58) spiritually: for them the flesh and blood of 53 ff. meant no more than did the bread from heaven—a reference to Christ, but not in a eucharistic way. For Augustine the flesh referred to Christ's immolation for the salvation of men. In the heart of the patristic period, Chrysostom, Gregory of Nyssa, the Cyrils of Jerusalem and of Alexandria gave a preponderance to the eucharistic theory. Skipping to the Reformation, we find that many of the reformers did not accept the eucharistic interpretation, but then neither did the Catholic champion Cajetan. The Council of Trent, after much discussion, took no position, largely lest it give ammunition to the Hussites, who used John vi 53 to demand communion under both species.

In modern times we may distinguish the following theories: (a) The whole discourse (vss. 35–58) refers to the revelation by and in Jesus or his teaching. This "sapiential" interpretation of 35–58 is championed by Godet, B. Weiss, Bornhäuser, Odeberg, Schlatter, Strathmann. (b) Only the first part of the discourse (35–50 or 35–51) has this sapiential theme, but in 51–58 the bread refers to the eucharistic flesh of Jesus. This half-and-half view has attracted Lagrange, E. Schweizer, Menoud, Mollat, Mussner, Bultmann. (The views of Dodd and Barrett also seem to imply two successive themes in the discourse.) Many of these would regard 51–59 as a later addition. (c) The whole discourse (35–58) refers to eucharistic bread. Different shades of this view are supported by Loisy, Tobac, Buzy, Cullmann, Van den Bussche. (d) The bread refers to *both* revelation and the eucharistic flesh of Jesus. Léon-Dufour sees these themes running throughout the discourse (35–58). Our view, which is also that of Feuillet, sees the two themes in the first part of the discourse (35–50) which refers primarily to revelation but secondarily to the Eucharist; the second part (51–58) refers only to the Eucharist.

THE SAPIENTIAL THEME IN vi 35–50. Let us begin by justifying the claim

that the sapiential theme is primary in the discourse proper (vss. 35–50).
The fundamental reaction to Jesus' presentation of himself as bread in 35–50
is that of belief (35, 36, 40, 47) or of coming to him, which is a synonym
for belief (35, 37, 44, 45). Only once (50) in this section is it said that anyone must eat the bread of life; it is in 51–58 that "eating" appears over and
over again. The citation that Jesus uses (45) to illustrate what is happening
to the people who hear him and come to him is: "And they shall all be
taught by God"—a clear reference to the sapiential symbolism of the bread.
The nearest parallel for the bread of life is the theme of living water in ch.
iv, and that water is also a symbol for revelation (see p. 178 above).

We have found that most of Jesus' sayings in John have some OT or
Jewish background that makes them partially intelligible to the audience
portrayed in the scene. This is true in ch. vi as well, for the divine word and
wisdom are often presented under the symbolism of food or bread in the OT.
In discussing the reference to manna in vs. 31, which introduces the topic
of the bread of life, we have already seen this symbolic background. The
words of Amos viii 11–13 are interesting in light of the hunger of the crowds
and their search for Jesus: "Behold the days are coming when I shall send a
famine on the land, not a famine of bread or a thirst for water, but for hearing the word of the Lord. . . . They shall run back and forth seeking the
word of the Lord, but they shall not find it." The Wisdom Literature of the
OT offers the greatest number of parallels. We have seen in the NOTE on vs.
35 that the opening lines of the Bread of Life Discourse seem to echo Sir
xxiv 21. In this discourse Jesus is like Wisdom who in Prov ix 5 issues an
invitation: "Come, eat of my bread; drink of the wine I have mixed." The
description in Sir xv 3 of what Wisdom will do for the one who fears God
and practices the Law is also apropos: "She will nourish him with the bread
of understanding and give him the water of learning to drink."

More OT background for the Bread of Life Discourse is found in the
descriptions of the messianic banquet, as Feuillet, pp. 814–22, has pointed
out. In Israelite thought the joys of the messianic days were often pictured
under the imagery of an intimate banquet with Yahweh or with His Messiah.
Isa lxv 11–13 warns those who forsake the Lord and His holy mountain
that they will go hungry and thirsty while Yahweh's servants shall eat and
drink. In the Synoptic Gospels this banquet is pictured as taking place in
the afterlife or the second coming (Matt viii 11, xxvi 29), but in John Jesus
announces that this banquet is at hand. Jesus is the bread of life for those
servants of Yahweh who believe in the one that Yahweh has sent. In this
(realized) eschatological context Jesus speaks of himself as the Son of Man
(vs. 27).

The best preparation for the sapiential reorientation of the messianic
banquet is found in Isa lv. In commenting on the command in vs. 27 not to
work for perishable food, we have already cited the water and food of Isa
lv 1 which is not purchasable by money. Verse 3 of the Isaian passage makes
clear that this is Yahweh's invitation to eat as part of his promises to renew
the covenant with David, and therefore a messianic banquet. It is in this

atmosphere that Yahweh says: "Incline your ear and come to me; listen that you may have life"—words quite reminiscent of John vi 35–50. Of particular interest are Isa lv 10–11: "As rain and snow *come down from heaven* . . . making the earth bring forth and sprout, giving seed to the sower and *bread* to the eater, so shall *my word* be that goes forth from my mouth." The fruitfulness of the messianic days is here associated with God's word come down from heaven to give food to men. That Isa lv may have been in mind in the composition of John's Bread of Life Discourse is suggested by the direct citation of the preceding chapter of Isaiah (liv 13) in vi 45.

We may add that since the coming of the Messiah was sometimes associated with Passover, the Passover meal had certain characteristics of an anticipation of the messianic banquet. At the final Passover of his life Jesus will institute the Eucharist as his own anticipation of the messianic banquet. But in ch. vi, in the Galilee setting, he wishes to show that the banquet given to the five thousand just before Passover was messianic in a way that they have not recognized: it was a sign that Wisdom has come to give food to all who seek.

THE SACRAMENTAL THEME IN vi 35–50. If "bread of life" in this part of the discourse refers primarily to revelation in and by Jesus, there are also indications of secondary, eucharistic undertones. Indeed, we would be surprised if there were not, for John relates this discourse to the multiplication of the loaves, which has itself undergone eucharistic adaptation. Moreover, as we pointed out, the transition between the two scenes (vs. 23) highlights the eucharistic impact of the multiplication. In the discourse itself, it is significant that Jesus identifies himself as the bread of life. We remember that in ch. iv Jesus spoke of giving the living water but did not identify himself with the water; yet he *is* the bread of life. While such identification is not impossible in a purely sapiential interpretation of vss. 35–50, it certainly fits the eucharistic motif very well.

The juxtaposition of hunger and thirst in vs. 35 does seem strange in a discourse on bread which never mentions water. Once again, such a juxtaposition is not impossible if the bread refers only to revelation (see Sir xxiv 21, cited in NOTE on vs. 35); but it does make more sense if there is also a reference to the Eucharist, which involves flesh and blood and is both to be eaten and drunk.

The mention of manna which introduces the discourse would have had eucharistic associations for early Christian audiences. In I Cor x 1–4 Paul introduces his warning about the eucharistic cup and bread by recalling the example of all those *ancestors* who ate the supernatural *food* (manna) *in the desert* and drank of the supernatural drink from the rock. We suspect too that the petition in the Lord's prayer, "Give us today our tomorrow's [?] bread," echoes the combined themes of the manna and the Eucharist (see TS 22 [1961], 198). Thus, there is respectable evidence for holding that there is a secondary, eucharistic reference in 35–50, and this reference will become primary in 51–58.

The Value of the Discourse as Historical Tradition

We have seen that the connection that John establishes between the Discourse on the Bread of Life and the multiplication may well represent a literary construction. Likewise we must assume that in the discourse itself the eucharistic undertones are most likely the product of Christian insights. There is nothing, however, that would automatically rule out the possibility that the sapiential sayings attributed to Jesus in this section may not represent early tradition. The collection of these sayings into one discourse probably reflects an editorial process (see NOTES on vss. 36–40); the skeleton of the discourse, however, along with the sequence of ideas, may well have been supplied by the tradition, as the Marcan parallels given on p. 238 suggest. By comparing Mark viii 14 and 16, some interpreters have found a parallel for identifying Jesus as bread (i.e., the one loaf is Jesus himself rather than physical bread; for though they have one loaf, they say they have no bread). In Matt xvi 11–12 Jesus makes clear that he is not talking about natural bread but about teaching. Other Synoptic parallels to individual verses will be pointed out in the commentary below. Thus, the Discourse on the Bread of Life is not cavalierly to be evaluated simply as the creation of the evangelist, even though he has contributed much to its present form.

COMMENT: DETAILED

Verse 35

In the questions that preceded the discourse, Jesus spoke of God's bread come down from heaven to give life to the world. Since the reader has read in iii 13 that the Son of Man is the only one who has come down from the Father, he may well suspect that Jesus is talking of himself as the bread. But the crowd does not understand, and Jesus must specifically identify himself as the bread that gives life. We have seen that this means that he is the revealer of the truth, the divine teacher who has come to nourish men. In claiming to personify divine revelation, Jesus advances beyond the OT preparation in the Wisdom literature. When Jesus says that those who believe in him shall never be hungry or thirsty, he is expressing the same idea that he will proclaim in xi 25–27: "I am the life . . . he who believes in me shall never die at all." Under all these metaphors of bread, water, and life, Jesus is symbolically referring to the same reality, a reality which, when once possessed, makes a man see natural hunger, thirst, and death as insignificant.

Verses 36–40

In the NOTES we pointed out that these verses have no close association with the theme of the bread of life and may have a history of their own. By careful analysis Léon-Dufour has found a chiasm in them:

36: seeing and not believing ↓ ——— ↑ 40: looking and believing
37: not driving out what the ↓ ⇄ ↑ 39: losing nothing of what
Father has given   He has given
38: I have come down from heaven.

While these verses have their own organization, Léon-Dufour thinks that the objection of the Jews in vs. 41 presupposes that 35 has been followed by 36–40. They attribute to Jesus the statement, "I am the bread that came down from heaven"; and Léon-Dufour thinks that this is a composite statement made up of "I am the bread" of 35 and "I have come down from heaven" of 38. However, if 35 was once followed immediately by 41–43, then the coming down from heaven could have echoed 33. Thus, the argument on sequence is not convincing.

These verses spell out the necessity of believing in Jesus and the will of the Father that men should have life through him. The eschatology is interesting. In vs. 37 Jesus speaks of not *driving out* anyone who comes to him. This is the same expression the Synoptics use in the context of final judgment when men will be driven out of the kingdom (Matt viii 12, xxii 13). For John the context is that of realized eschatology. However, in 39, which resembles 37, the context switches to final eschatology ("the last day"). And 40 has both aspects: everyone who believes in the Son has eternal life now, and still he will be raised up on the last day. Naturally, Bultmann resorts to the Ecclesiastical Redactor to account for the final eschatology; but it seems more objective to recognize that both strains of eschatology are at home in the evangelist's work.

The stress in vs. 37 that God destines men to come to Jesus does not in the least attenuate the guilt in vs. 36 of those who do not believe. One might conjecture that the reason that they do not believe is because God has not "given" them to Jesus. Yet, it would be unfair to NT thought-patterns to elaborate this as a psychological explanation of the refusal to believe. The NT often gives its explanation on a simplified level wherein all happenings are attributed to divine causality without any sharp distinction between primary and secondary causality. Nor do these verses resolve the disputes about predestination that have been the subject of theological debate since Reformation times. With all John's insistence on man's choosing between light and darkness, it would be nonsense to ask if the evangelist believed in human responsibility. It would be just as much nonsense to doubt that, like the other biblical authors, he saw God's sovereign choice being worked out in those who came to Jesus.

Verses 41–43

With the "murmuring" in vs. 41 (see NOTE) we return to the atmosphere of the Israelites in the desert and the manna. Although the historical connections between the multiplication and the discourse may not have been as close as now portrayed, the evangelist loses no opportunity to show how the same themes run through them. The familiar question of Jesus' origins betrays the usual misunderstanding that greets Jesus as the revealer. If he is the bread from heaven, if he is the Son of Man (27) who is to come on the clouds, how can he have grown up in a family at Nazareth?

Verses 44–50

Jesus never answers the question about his origins on a human plane; his words in vss. 44–46 are an answer, but on a theological plane. He is sent by God (44) and he is from God (46), and that is how he can claim to have come down from heaven. If the Jews will desist from their murmuring, which is indicative of a refusal to believe, and will leave themselves open to God's movement, He will draw them to Jesus. This is the age spoken of by the prophet Isaiah when they are being taught by God, if only they will listen. This teaching has its external aspect in the sense that it is embodied in Jesus who walks among them, but it is also internal in the sense that God acts in their hearts. It is a fulfillment of what Jer xxxi 33 had promised: "I will put my law within them, and on their hearts will write it" (John Bright, The Anchor Bible, vol. 21). This internal moving of the heart by the Father will enable them to believe in the Son and thus possess eternal life.

Verses 48–50 constitute an inclusion, for they resume the introduction to the discourse and its opening verses. Verse 48 is an inclusion with 35; vss. 49–50 take up themes of 31–33. The crowd had held up to Jesus the example of their ancestors who ate manna in the desert, but Jesus (49) points out that this did not save their forebears from death. And then (50), picking up once more the Scripture citation of vs. 31 ("He gave them bread from heaven to eat"), Jesus says that the bread that truly comes from heaven is a bread that does not permit a man to die.

The Jewish Background behind the Technique and Themes of the Discourse

Homiletic Technique in the Discourse. Peder Borgen has contributed some interesting insights into the composition of this discourse. Borgen actually applies his theory to the whole discourse, including vss. 51–58, but everything that he says is equally, if not more, true of vss. 35–50 alone (see p. 294 below). Borgen has carefully studied homiletic pattern in Philo and the Palestinian midrashim, and from this he has distilled some of the features of Jewish preaching in Jesus' time. We have noted some of his observations about exegetical patterns in NOTES on vss. 32, 36, 42; but here we are interested in the general outline.

The pattern is to begin with a citation of Scripture (usually the Pentateuch) which is sometimes paraphrased. The body of the homily comments on the Scripture text almost word by word, although a careful scrutiny will often show that the comments presuppose not only the main verse that has been cited but also other verses within the context. Usually, the statement that opens the homily is repeated at the end of the homily, perhaps not verbatim but at least by recalling its principal words. In the Palestinian midrashim the Scripture citation is repeated at the end of the homily. Commonly, within the homily there is a subordinate citation (often from the Writings or the Prophets) to which a few lines of commentary are devoted. This subordinate citation helps to develop the main commentary.

John vi is amazingly close to this pattern. The initial citation has been given in vs. 31, and it is from the Pentateuch. Although it is like Exod xvi 4, it also has elements of xvi 15 (see NOTE), in accordance with the practice of employing the whole context. Verses 32–33 constitute the paraphrase of the citation by Jesus: "He gave them bread from heaven to eat" becomes "My Father gives you the real bread from heaven." Then in vss. 35–50 we find the homily on this Scripture citation: first, the theme of "bread" is discussed; then, the theme "from heaven"; and finally in 49–50 the theme of "eating." The subordinate citation from the Prophets appears in 45 (see NOTE) with a short commentary. According to homiletic rules, the statement that opened the homily (35) is repeated exactly at the end (48); and indeed even the Scripture citation and its paraphrase (31–33) are taken up again in 49–50. Thus, it seems that 35–50 represents a homily on the text of Scripture in 31.

What light do these observations throw on the historical value of the discourse? Borgen believes that as it now stands the discourse is a Jewish-Christian construction following the typical homiletic pattern of the day. Since Borgen includes vss. 51–58 in the discourse, we would have to agree; for, as we shall explain below, we regard 51–58 as a later construction. However, if one studies just 35–50 and makes the allowance that in part (perhaps 36–40, 42) it is an amalgamation of sayings that were once independent, is there any *a priori* reason why the simple outline of the main part of this section could not have come from Jesus? He is presented as speaking in a synagogue in Capernaum (59). Would he not have conformed himself to the ordinary homiletic style for synagogue preachers? Might he not have taken a Scripture citation, as he did in Luke iv 17–19, and made it the text of his sermon? At least, it seems to us that the recognition of the homiletic pattern in this Johannine discourse does not resolve in any negative way the question of historicity and indeed gives a certain plausibility to John's presentation of the scene.

The Synagogue Lectionary and the Discourse. We must also bring to bear here the interesting observations of Aileen Guilding on the cycle of Scripture readings used in the synagogues. John vi 4 sets the time of this chapter as near Passover; and even if we regard as artificial the one-day connection between multiplication and discourse, Passover time may still have been the setting of the discourse. If we take the six weeks around Passover as the span of our considerations, according to Miss Guilding's theory, the following passages would have served as synagogical readings (*sedarim*) according to the three-year cycle:

Year I: Gen i–viii, with Gen ii and iii being read on the Sabbaths closest
to the feast.

Year II: Exod xi–xvi, with Exod xvi being read about four weeks after
the feast.

Year III: Num vi–xiv, with Num xi being read on the second Sabbath
after the feast.

Now the discourse we have just discussed is obviously centered around
Exod xvi, the *seder* of Year II. But it also echoes the *sedarim* of the other
two years. In our NOTE on vs. 5 we pointed out a series of parallels between Num xi and John vi. Miss Guilding, p. 62, lists some parallels between Gen iii and John vi, particularly centering on the tree of the
knowledge of good and evil in the Garden of Paradise:

Gen iii 3 repeats God's warning from ii 17: "You shall not eat of the
fruit of this tree . . . lest you die." This may be contrasted with
John vi 50: "This is the bread that comes down from heaven that a
man may eat it and never die."

Gen iii 22 has God's decision to drive man out of the garden ". . . lest
he put forth his hand and take also of the tree of life and eat and
live forever." This may be contrasted with the invitation to eat the
bread of life of which John vi 51 says, "If anyone eats this bread, he
will live forever."

Gen iii 24: "So he drove man out." In John vi 37: "Anyone who comes
to me I will never drive out."

The Church Fathers recognized this contrast between the bread of life and
the forbidden fruit in Genesis; for example, Gregory of Nyssa (*Great
Catechism* XXXVII; PG 45:93) presented the eucharistic bread as an antidote
to the forbidden fruit. And if the bread of life in vss. 35–50 primarily
represents the revelation and knowledge that Jesus brings from above, then
it is not unlike the knowledge of good and evil that the first man hungered
after.

Miss Guilding also contends that a reading from the Prophets (*haphtarah*)
accompanied each Pentateuchal reading. In Year I the *haphtaroth* that
accompanied the Genesis readings seem to have included Isa li 6 ff. as a
haphtarah to Gen ii 4, and Isa liv–lv as a *haphtarah* to Gen vi 9 (Guilding
pp. 67, 63). We found parallels in Isa li to the walking on the sea in John
vi (see p. 255 above), and in Isa liv–lv to the Bread of Life Discourse
(see p. 273–74—Isa liv is cited in John vi 45). In Year II Isa lxiii 11 ff.
served as *haphtarah* to Exod xv 22, and there we have again the theme of
the crossing of the sea.

These parallels are impressive, and it seems legitimate to maintain that
John vi reflects a medley of themes drawn from the synagogue readings
at Passover time. For Miss Guilding the setting in John vi is fictional, and it
is a Christian author who has composed the discourse by blending the
themes. However, once again if Jesus did speak in a synagogue (vs. 59),
how can we be certain *a priori* that he was not the one who drew the

themes of the discourse from the synagogue readings? It may be objected that the discourse reflects readings from all three years; yet, in a liturgical tradition, as a cycle is repeated over and over again, one becomes familiar with all the readings for great feasts. Thus, Jesus may have illustrated his general topic taken from the *seder* of one year (Exod xvi) with pertinent phrases from the Passover *sedarim* and *haphtaroth* of other years. We may note that the exact lining up of corresponding *sedarim* and *haphtaroth* is one of the most uncertain parts of Miss Guilding's thesis. This thesis has been subjected to a sharp criticism by Leon Morris, *The New Testament and the Jewish Lectionaries* (London: Tyndale, 1964), and we are reluctant to make our approach to John vi dependent on anything more than the general implication that the themes in John plausibly reflect themes familiar in the synagogue at Passover time.

The observations of Borgen and Miss Guilding can be used, at least in part, to complement each other. It seems to us that both illumine the *possibility* that behind John vi 35–50 we have a homily preached by Jesus on a text selected from a *seder* read in the Capernaum synagogue at Passover time (although, to be exact, neither of these scholars comes to this conclusion). Need we stress once again that we recognize that the present form of the discourse has been expanded by editorial combinations of other material and has been enlightened by Johannine theological reflections?

[The Bibliography for this section is included in the Bibliography for ch. vi, at the end of § 26.]

25. JESUS AT PASSOVER:
—DISCOURSE ON THE BREAD OF LIFE (*continued*)
(vi 51–59)

*Duplicate of the preceding discourse in which the Bread of Life
is now the Eucharist*

VI   51 "I myself am the living bread
        that came down from heaven.
        If anyone eats this bread,   [52]*
        he will live forever.
        And the bread that I shall give
        is my own flesh for the life of the world."

52[53] At this the Jews started to quarrel among themselves, saying,
"How can he give us [his] flesh to eat?" 53[54] Therefore Jesus told
them,

        "Let me firmly assure you,
        if you do not eat the flesh of the Son of Man
        and drink his blood,
        you have no life in you.
    54 He who feeds on my flesh   [55]
        and drinks my blood
        has eternal life.
        And I shall raise him up on the last day.
    55 For my flesh is real food,   [56]
        and my blood, real drink.
    56 The man who feeds on my flesh   [57]
        and drinks my blood
        remains in me and I in him.
    57 Just as the Father who has life sent me   [58]
        and I have life because of the Father,
        so the man who feeds on me
        will have life because of me.

* Verse numbers in the Vulgate. The enumeration of verses in the Latin Vulgate
differs from that of the Greek in vss. 51 ff.—a difference reflected in Catholic and
Protestant translations of the Bible. All our references are to the Greek enumeration,
but for convenience we have added the Vulgate enumeration in brackets.

58 This is the bread that came down from heaven.   [59]
Unlike those ancestors who ate and yet died,
the man who feeds on this bread will live forever."

59[60] He said this in a synagogue instruction at Capernaum.

NOTES

vi 51. *living bread.* For the alternation between "bread of life" (vss. 35, 48) and "living bread" compare the alternation between "water of life" (Rev xxi 6, xxii 1, 17) and "living water" (John iv 10). However, Jesus never identifies himself with the living water.

came down. The aorist here may be compared with the present "comes down" in vs. 50; we saw the same variation concerning "gives" and "has given" in vss. 37, 39. Probably, we should be wary of putting too much theological emphasis on the use of the aorist, but the "coming down" does include the Incarnation.

eats . . . will live forever. There may be an echo of this in *Barnabas* xi 10. Citing the passage of Ezek xlvii 1–12 where a river flows out of the Temple and beautiful trees grow along it, *Barnabas* interprets these as trees of life and says "Whoever shall eat of them shall live forever." *Barnabas* may be associating John's bread of life and the tree of life, an association which, as we have seen, may have been prompted by the Passover synagogue readings.

give . . . my own flesh. Compare the description of voluntary death in I Cor xiii 3: "If I *give over my body* to be burned. . . ." Thus, the connection between the Eucharist and the death of Jesus may be hinted at in John.

for the life of the world. Codex Sinaiticus places this phrase with the verb "to give," rather than with "flesh." This reading, "give for the life of the world," may be an attempt to conform more closely to a eucharistic formula like that of Luke xxii 19: "my body which is *given for you.*"

52. *quarrel.* The Greek suggests a violent dispute.

he. Literally "this [one]"—probably with a note of contempt, as in vs. 42.

[*his*]. There are good witnesses both for inclusion and for omission.

53. *eat . . . drink.* In vi 26, 50, 51, the verb "to eat" (*esthiein, phagein*) takes *ek* and the genitive before its object; it is used with the direct accusative in vi 23, 31, 49, 53. J. J. O'Rourke, CBQ 25 (1963), 126–28, sees a significant difference in this variation, as he does also between *pinein* ("drink") used with *ek* and the genitive in ch. iv, and with the accusative here. The differentiation seems oversubtle.

flesh . . . blood. The Hebrew idiom "flesh and blood" means the whole man. In Reformation times, vss. 53–55 were the center of a theological dispute about whether it was necessary to receive the Eucharist under both species. All that can be decided from this text is that it is necessary to receive the whole Christ. Feuillet, p. 822, suggests that if manna was the OT background for the bread/flesh theme, the mention of the blood of the covenant at Sinai (Exod xxiv 8) prompted the theme of the blood by way of the eucharistic formula "my blood of the [new] covenant" or "the new covenant in my blood."

the Son of Man. See vs. 27. This is the only verse in this section in which Jesus speaks of himself in the third person; however, this is not unusual in Son of Man passages.

you have no life in you. The universality and absoluteness of this statement have caused some churches to adopt the practice of giving the Eucharist to infants. They put this statement on a par with the absoluteness of the requirement of being begotten of water and Spirit (Baptism) in iii 5.

54. *feeds.* In secular Greek this verb *trōgein* was originally used of animals; but, at least from the time of Herodotus, it was used of human eating as well. It had a crude connotation (see Matt xxiv 38) reflected in translations like "gnaw, munch." Some scholars deny this, maintaining that John simply uses it for the present tense system of *esthiein,* the normal verb "to eat." However, it seems more likely that the use of *trōgein* is part of John's attempt to emphasize the realism of the eucharistic flesh and blood. The only other times it appears in John outside of this section is in xiii 18 where in the context of the Last Supper it is deliberately introduced into an OT citation, probably as a eucharistic remembrance.

And I shall raise him. Wilkens, "Abendmahlzeugnis," pp. 358–59, thinks that the emphasis on the resurrection from the dead may be anti-docetist.

55. *real.* Here the word is not *alēthinos,* but *alēthēs* (although there are important witnesses in the Western tradition that read *alēthōs,* an adverb which probably represents an interpretation, especially in the versions). *Alēthinos* ("the only real") which is used to distinguish the heavenly reality from its natural counterpart, or to distinguish the NT reality from its OT counterpart (see App. I:2), would be out of place here, for Jesus is not contrasting his flesh and blood with any natural or OT counterpart. Rather, Jesus is insisting on the genuine value of his flesh and blood as food and drink. The Western reading of an adverb catches the meaning of this verse. See Ruckstuhl, pp. 235–42.

56. *remains in me.* For *menein* see App. I:8. This statement resembles very closely what shall be said of the true vine in xv 3–7, and the vine is probably a eucharistic symbol too.

in him. Here Codex Bezae and some OL mss. add: "as the Father in me and I in the Father [x 38, xiv 10]. I solemnly assure you, unless you receive the body of the Son of Man as the bread of life, you shall not have life in him." Note the use of "receive," a reading that Bezae also has in place of "eat" in vs. 53. Some scholars (see Lagrange, p. 185) think that this reading may be genuine, omitted in other witnesses by homoioteleuton. More likely it is a homiletic Western addition.

57. *the Father who has life.* Literally "the living Father." This is the only instance of this expression in the NT, although "the living God" occurs in both Testaments. Perhaps the usage is determined by "the living bread" in vs. 51. Compare v 26: "Just as the Father possesses life in Himself, so has He granted that the Son also possess life in himself."

because of the Father. The preposition is *dia* with the accusative. Does it mean "through, by means of" (*source:* BAG, p. 180, B II, 4; BDF, § 222) or "for the sake of" (*finality:* more normal meaning of the accusative)? Lagrange favors final causality, but it really does not fit the context, since Jesus seems to be speaking of the chain of sources of life. For Jesus as the source of our life we have I John iv 9: "God has sent His only Son into the world that we may have life through him [*dia* with genitive which must mean source]." The parallel just cited from John v 26 also suggests that source is meant.

feeds. Drinking is mentioned no more after vs. 56. Just as the last part of vss. 35–50 constituted an inclusion with the opening themes of the discourse, so also in the duplicate of the Bread of Life Discourse in 51–58. Therefore, these last verses concentrate on bread.

58. *This is the bread.* The wording is the same as in vs. 50 except that there is no purpose clause following. Although the antecedent of "this" is not expressed, it is clearly the flesh of Jesus.

those ancestors. Not "your ancestors" as in vs. 49.

died. This almost certainly means physical death as contrasted with spiritual life. Yet there was a late Jewish tradition that the generation in the desert died spiritually as well and would have no place in the world to come.

59. *this.* Literally "these things."

in a synagogue instruction. Literally "teaching in a synagogue." The lack of a definite article before *synagōgē* makes some think more of a public meeting (see James ii 2) than of the synagogue. However, the Capernaum synagogue is known to us from the Synoptic tradition (Luke iv 31, vii 5), and Jesus' habit of teaching in synagogues is well attested (Matt iv 23, ix 35, xii 9, xiii 54).

at Capernaum. Codex Bezae, some OL mss., and Augustine add "on a Sabbath." This may represent an educated and correct guess. The objection that all the movement in boats described in vss. 22–24 could not have taken place on the Sabbath is really only one more argument proving the artificiality of John's next-day connection between multiplication and discourse. If the theory that vss. 51–58 are a later addition proves true, then vs. 59 pertains to the original discourse underlying 35–50.

COMMENT: GENERAL

The Meaning of "the Living Bread" in vss. 51–58

In this section the eucharistic theme which was only secondary in vss. 35–50 comes to the fore and becomes the exclusive theme. No longer are we told that eternal life is the result of believing in Jesus; it comes from feeding on his flesh and drinking his blood (54). The Father's role in bringing men to Jesus or giving them to him is no longer in the limelight; Jesus himself dominates as the agent and source of salvation. Even though the verses in 51–58 are remarkably like those of 35–50, a new vocabulary runs through them: "eat," "feed," "drink," "flesh," "blood."

There are two impressive indications that the Eucharist is in mind. The first indication is the stress on eating (feeding on) Jesus' flesh and drinking his blood. This cannot possibly be a metaphor for accepting his revelation. "To eat someone's flesh" appears in the Bible as a metaphor for hostile action (Ps xxvii 2; Zech xi 9). In fact, in the Aramaic tradition transmitted through Syriac, the "eater of flesh" is the title of the devil, the slanderer and adversary par excellence. The drinking of blood was looked on as an horrendous thing forbidden by God's law (Gen ix 4; Lev iii 17; Deut xii 23; Acts xv 20). Its transferred, symbolical meaning was that of brutal slaughter (Jer xlvi 10). In Ezekiel's vision of apocalyptic carnage (xxxix 17), he invites the scavenging birds to come to the feast: "You shall eat flesh and drink blood." Thus, if Jesus' words in vi 53 are to have a favorable meaning, they must refer to the Eucharist. They simply reproduce the words we hear in the Synoptic account of the institution of the Eucharist (Matt xxvi 26–28): "Take, *eat;* this is *my body;* . . . *drink* . . . this is *my blood.*"

The second indication of the Eucharist is the formula found in vs. 51: "The bread that I shall give is my flesh for the life of the world." If we consider that John does not report the Lord's words over the bread and the cup at the Last Supper, it is possible that we have preserved in vi 51 the Johannine form of the words of institution. In particular, it resembles the Lucan form of institution: "This is my body which is given for you" (see NOTE on vs. 51). The important difference is that John speaks of "flesh" while the Synoptic accounts of the Last Supper speak of "body." However, there is really no Hebrew or Aramaic word for "body," as we understand the term; and many scholars maintain that at the Last Supper what Jesus actually said was the Aramaic equivalent of "This is my flesh." One of the earliest ecclesiastical writers, Ignatius of Antioch (a city where the Semitic tradition of Jesus' words may have been preserved), uses "flesh" in numerous references to the Eucharist (*Rom* vii 3; *Phila* iv 1; *Smyr* vii 1). This is also true of Justin *Apol.* I 66 (PG 6:428). It may be, then, that in this respect John is the closest of the Gospels to the original eucharistic language of Jesus. That John vi 51 resembles a eucharistic formula was noticed in early times, for both the OL and Syr. witnesses read for this verse: "This bread which I shall give is my *body* for the life of the world."

The Relation of vss. 51–58 to the Rest of the Chapter

If we grant that the primary meaning of "the bread of life" changes in vss. 51–58 from the meaning that was seen in 35–50, do the two parts of the discourse really belong together? Let us first discuss this question on the *literary* level: Is 51–58 simply an extraneous block of non-Johannine material or is it an integral part of the chapter? (We shall leave for the moment the *historical* question of whether it was originally part of the discourse.) As the chapter now stands, it must be recognized that there are many features in 51–58 that blend in very well with the context. For instance, 51–58 picks up some themes we saw in the introduction (25–34) that were not found in 35–50, e.g., *giving* the bread (51–52, 31–32); the Son of Man (53, 27). Moreover, as we shall see, 51–58 is remarkably like 35–50 in composition and statement. Ruckstuhl has studied the language of 51–58 very carefully, and he thinks there is enough evidence to characterize the section as genuinely Johannine. His arguments have convinced J. Jeremias; but Eduard Schweizer, another expert in Johannine style, does not think there is enough linguistic evidence to decide. Among the more obvious Johannine features in these verses are: "let me firmly assure you" (53); "eternal life" (54); "to feed" (see xiii 18); "to remain" (56). There are other Johannine peculiarities in the use of minor Greek particles.

These observations, in our opinion, show that vss. 51–58 belong to the general body of Johannine tradition; they do not rule out the possibility that 51–58 was added at a late stage of the editing of ch. vi. Any editor who would add these verses would naturally make an effort to bring them into harmony with their new context. However, the above observations make it difficult to believe Bultmann's theory that an Ecclesiastical Redactor added these verses *to correct* the chapter by introducing a non-Johannine sacramental theme that would make the discourse more acceptable to the Church at large. There is evidence that these verses contain genuine traditional material (e.g., eucharistic formula) and that they represent true Johannine thought and not a correction of it. Moreover, an insuperable objection to Bultmann's theory is the evidence of secondary, eucharistic undertones in the multiplication, the transitional verses (22–24), the introduction to the discourse, and the body of the discourse (35–50). This chapter would be eucharistic if 51–58 were not part of it; and if 51–58 are a later addition, they were added not to introduce a eucharistic theme but to bring out more clearly the eucharistic elements that were already there.

Nevertheless, the very fact that the eucharistic element is primary in vss. 51–58, while it is secondary in the rest of the chapter, does suggest that 51–58 had a different provenance from the rest of the chapter. The Discourse on the Bread of Life in 35–50 is complete in itself, as we saw in our study of homiletic technique; it comes to an end with a very carefully arranged inclusion. It seems illogical for the discourse to start all over again in vs. 51. A far more plausible suggestion is that we have here two different forms of a discourse on the bread of life, both Johannine but stemming from different stages of the Johannine preaching.

Let us now turn to the *historical* question of whether the direct eucharistic theme of vss. 51–58 was originally part of Jesus' words to the crowd. For those who regard the whole setting of the Discourse on the Bread of Life in John vi as fictional, there can be no historical question. However, as we have shown from the parallels of sequence in the Synoptics, it does seem that the pre-Gospel tradition had a scene where Jesus explained the import of the multiplication to his disciples. From an analysis of John vi we saw that it is not implausible that Jesus did speak in the synagogue, giving a discourse on elements suggested by the Passover synagogue readings, and that there was OT background for understanding his remarks in 35–50 where he referred to his revelation under the symbolism of bread. Scientifically speaking, we can do no more than establish the plausibility of all this. Yet this is enough to raise the question whether, *if* Jesus did speak of the bread of life in the Capernaum synagogue, the doctrine about the Eucharist as reported in 51–58 could have been part of that discourse. Léon-Dufour has attempted to solve the problem of how the crowd could have understood these verses by maintaining that simultaneously the sapiential meaning of the bread carries through 51–58 and that this meaning could have been understood. However, is there the slightest evidence that the living bread in 51–58 refers to anything other than the Eucharist?

If we answer in the negative, and it seems that we must, then it seems impossible that the words of 51–58 which refer exclusively to the Eucharist could have been understood by the crowd or even by the disciples. They are really out of place anywhere during the ministry except at the Last Supper. Even such a usually conservative critic as Lagrange has recognized this, and he has been followed by many scholars who otherwise show no facile tendency to dismantle the Johannine discourses. Combining, then, our judgments on the literary and historical questions about 51–58, we suggest that 35–50 and 51–58 are two different forms of the Discourse on the Bread of Life, both Johannine in the sense that they are made up of sayings passed down in the Johannine preaching tradition. The form of the discourse in 35–50, although it has amalgamated to itself some extraneous material, represents a far more primitive, sapiential form of the discourse. Its secondary, eucharistic undertones stem from a Christian rethinking of the topic. The form in 51–58 represents a more radical rethinking of the discourse in which the eucharistic theme has become primary. It was added to 35–50 at a fairly late stage in the editing of the Fourth Gospel, probably in the final redaction.

The Possible Origin of the Material in vss. 51–58

We wish to propose here the hypothesis that the backbone of vss. 51–58 is made up of material from the Johannine narrative of the institution of the Eucharist which originally was located in the Last Supper scene and that this material has been recast into a duplicate of the Bread of Life Discourse. This hypothesis accounts for several facts: (*a*) The absence of an account of the institution in ch. xiii, the Last Supper scene where all the other Gospels place the institution. The displacement of the institutional material has left its marks on xiii, for example, the reference to feeding on bread, with the use of the verb *trōgein* in xiii 18. (*b*) The close similarity of vi 51 to an institutional formula. (*c*) The clear reference to the Eucharist in vss. 51–58 would have been understandable at the Last Supper. By way of support, we may note that we have already encountered one possible instance of a scene originally associated with the last Passover of Jesus' life being transposed to the body of the ministry and an earlier Passover, namely, the cleansing of the Temple.

One important feature in our hypothesis is that the material taken from the Last Supper was recast and remodeled on the pattern of the Bread of Life Discourse when it was brought into ch. vi. This is why it fits so well into ch. vi. Below, we give a diagram setting up vss. 35–50 and 51–58 side by side, so that the reader may see how closely parallel the two sections are. By blending the themes of vi with material from the Last Supper, the final redactor has created a second Bread of Life Discourse. His purpose in all of this seems to have been to spell out the eucharistic undertones already implicit in the chapter. He has given 51–58 the same beginning and the same ending as 35–50; the same type of interruption where the Jews protest; the same promise of eternal life. But where the

If we answer in the negative, and it seems that we must, then it seems improbable that the words of 51–58 which relate exclusively to the Eucharist could have been uttered by the crowd or even by the disciples. They are really out of place anywhere during the ministry except at the Last Supper. Even such a usually conservative critic as Lagrange has recognized this. He has been followed by many scholars who otherwise show no predilection to dismantle the Johannine discourses. Consequently, apart from the literary and historical question about 51–58, we suggest that 35–50 and 51–58 are two different treatments of the theme of 1:14; both "fulfilling" in their sense that men are made up of living, played down in the Johannine positive tradition. Therefore, even though in 35–50, although they are adapted to their situations, is presumably represents a far more basically sacramental form of the discourse; the secondary eucharistic interpretation stem from a Christian reminding of the point. The form in 51–58 represents a more precise reliving of the course in which the words of the discourse become, primarily; it were added in 35–50 are a fairly faithful rendering of the Fourth Gospel, probably in the Palestinian tradition.

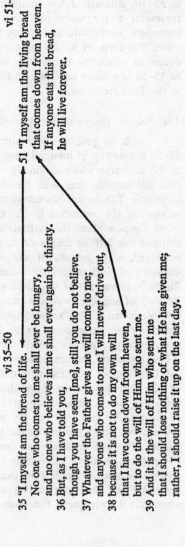

COMPARISON OF THE TWO DISCOURSES

vi 51–58

51 "I myself am the living bread that comes down from heaven. If anyone eats this bread, he will live forever.

vi 35–50

35 "I myself am the bread of life. No one who comes to me shall ever be hungry, and no one who believes in me shall ever again be thirsty.

36 But, as I have told you, though you have seen [me], still you do not believe.

37 Whatever the Father gives me will come to me; and anyone who comes to me I will never drive out,

38 because it is not to do my own will that I have come down from heaven, but to do the will of Him who sent me.

39 And it is the will of Him who sent me that I should lose nothing of what He has given me; rather, I should raise it up on the last day.

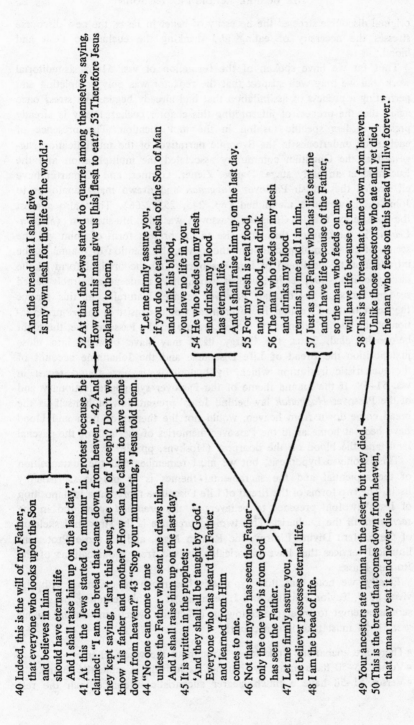

40 Indeed, this is the will of my Father,
that everyone who looks upon the Son
and believes in him
should have eternal life
And I shall raise him up on the last day."

41 At this the Jews started to murmur in protest because he
claimed: "I am the bread that came down from heaven." 42 And
they kept saying, "Isn't this Jesus, the son of Joseph? Don't we
know his father and mother? How can he claim to have come
down from heaven?" 43 "Stop your murmuring," Jesus told them.

44 "No one can come to me
unless the Father who sent me draws him.
And I shall raise him up on the last day.

45 It is written in the prophets:
'And they shall all be taught by God.'
Everyone who has heard the Father
and learned from Him
comes to me.

46 Not that anyone has seen the Father—
only the one who is from God
has seen the Father.

47 Let me firmly assure you,
the believer possesses eternal life.

48 I am the bread of life.

49 Your ancestors ate manna in the desert, but they died.
50 This is the bread that comes down from heaven,
that a man may eat it and never die.

And the bread that I shall give
is my own flesh for the life of the world."

52 At this the Jews started to quarrel among themselves, saying,
"How can this man give us [his] flesh to eat?" 53 Therefore Jesus
explained to them,

"Let me firmly assure you,
if you do not eat the flesh of the Son of Man
and drink his blood,
you have no life in you.

54 He who feeds on my flesh
and drinks my blood
has eternal life.
And I shall raise him up on the last day.

55 For my flesh is real food,
and my blood, real drink.

56 The man who feeds on my flesh
and drinks my blood
remains in me and I in him.

57 Just as the Father who has life sent me
and I have life because of the Father,
so the man who feeds on me
will have life because of me.

58 This is the bread that came down from heaven.
Unlike those ancestors who ate and yet died,
the man who feeds on this bread will live forever."

original discourse stressed the necessity of belief in Jesus, the new discourse stresses the necessity of eating and drinking the eucharistic flesh and blood.

Thus far we have spoken of the formation of vss. 51–58 as editorial work, but we may well suspect that the redactor was only completing and perfecting a process of assimilation that had already begun. We stress once again that the process of interpreting this chapter eucharistically is already present in less specific fashion in the multiplication. The presence of eucharistic undertones in the Synoptic narratives of the multiplication suggests that the Christian community associated the multiplication and the Eucharist at an early stage. Daube, Ziener, Gärtner, and Kilmartin have all studied the Jewish Passover *Haggadah* and drawn many analogies to John vi, as we have mentioned (pp. 245, 255, 266). They also suggest the possibility that a Christian Passover was the life-situation (*Sitz-im-Leben*) in the Church that gave rise to the present form of John vi. The scenes of ch. vi (multiplication of the loaves, the mention of manna in the introduction to the Bread of Life Discourse, and the original form of the discourse in 35–50), set in Passover, would have made an admirably suited reading for such a Christian Passover service. Naturally, at this service the heart of the Christian Passover meal would consist in the *re*-presentation of the eucharistic meal that the Lord ate on the Passover eve, the night before he died. Thus, the liturgy itself may have brought into close juxtaposition the Bread of Life Discourse and the Johannine account of the eucharistic institution which, by hypothesis, is now found recast in vss. 51–58. If the manna theme of the Passover synagogue lectionary and of the Passover *Haggadah* lay behind Jesus' presentation of himself as the bread come down from heaven, would not the themes of flesh and blood have been at home amid the Passover memories of the flesh of the paschal lamb and the blood on the doorpost (Hoskyns, pp. 281 ff.)?

This is only a hypothesis, but we must remember that the juxtaposition of the sapiential and the sacramental themes is as old as Christianity itself. The two forms of the Bread of Life Discourse represent a juxtaposition of Jesus' twofold presence to believers in the *preached word* and in the *sacrament* of the Eucharist. This twofold presence is the structural skeleton of the Eastern Divine Liturgy, the Roman Mass, and all those Protestant liturgical services that have historically evolved from modifications of the Roman Mass.

Finally, we note that this hypothesis has much in common with the views of V. Taylor, Feuillet, and J. Jeremias. It is only tentative, but it is a serious attempt to meet the following difficulties which any theory about vss. 51–58 must take into account:

▪ There are eucharistic undertones throughout the whole chapter.
▪ Verses 35–50 have primarily, but not exclusively, a sapiential theme.
▪ Verses 51–58 have a much clearer eucharistic reference than the rest

of the chapter, a reference scarcely intelligible in the setting in which it now stands.

- Verses 35–50 seem to constitute a well-rounded discourse in themselves, and the shift of emphasis between 35–50 and 51–58 is noticeably abrupt.
- Verses 51–58 have many features in common with the rest of ch. vi, and indeed extremely close parallels in structure to 35–50.
- Verses 60 ff., as we shall see, refer more directly to 35–50 than to 51–58.
- There is no institution of the Eucharist in the Johannine narrative of the Last Supper.
- There may be an influence of the Christian Passover liturgy on John vi.

COMMENT: DETAILED

Verse 51 is a parallel to vs. 35, which is the beginning of the first form of the Bread of Life Discourse, except that in vs. 51 Jesus speaks as "the living bread," instead of as "the bread of life." Although the two are synonymous, "the living bread" is more suitable for the Eucharist. It is interesting that in this verse, where he will speak of the bread as his *flesh*, Jesus stresses that he has come down from heaven. In John i 14 the entrance of the Word into the world was spoken of in terms of becoming flesh; and it is this same flesh that is now to be given to men as the living bread. If vs. 51 echoes the theme of the Incarnation, it also seems to look to the death of Jesus, a theme traditionally associated with the Eucharist; for Jesus is to *give* his flesh for the life of the world (see NOTES on vs. 51 and iii 16 concerning "giving"). In vs. 32 we heard that it is the Father who gives the heavenly bread in the sense that the Son comes from the Father; but when the bread now becomes identified with the flesh of Jesus, he must give it himself. Jesus lays down his life of his own accord (x 18), and that voluntary death makes eucharistic participation in his flesh possible. At the beginning of the Gospel we heard Jesus acclaimed as the Passover Lamb who takes away the world's sin (i 29); now in the context of a discourse set at Passover time we hear that Jesus gives his flesh for the life of the world.

We saw that the use of "flesh" in vs. 51 may echo Jesus' actual words over the bread of the Eucharist. Nevertheless, the term has a certain crudeness and reality; and this connotation, plus the fact that it recalls the Incarnation, may have been employed by the evangelist with anti-docetic intention. John vi does not reach the anti-docetic fervor of I John iv 2 ("Every spirit that acknowledges Jesus Christ come in the flesh is of God"), but it does resist any overspiritualizing of the humanity of Jesus.

In vs. 52 we encounter a misunderstanding that parallels the one in 41–42. Strangely enough, Jesus does not take any pains to explain away the Jewish repugnance at the cannibalistic thought of eating his flesh; rather in 53 he emphasizes the reality of "feeding" (see NOTE) on his flesh and adds the even more repugnant note of drinking his blood. Not only does John vi resist any overspiritualizing of the humanity of Jesus; it also resists any overspiritualizing of the reality of the eucharistic flesh and blood. The objection and answer in vss. 52–53 may reflect a dispute of the evangelist's own time, for the Jewish apologists against Christianity attacked the Eucharist. Origen *Celsus* VI 27 (GCS 3:97) alludes to Jewish charges that Christians ate human flesh. Kilmartin, "Chalice Dispute," suggests that the consistent emphasis on drinking the blood is directed against a Jewish Gnostic circle who opposed the use of the chalice in eucharistic practice because of their deep-rooted fear of blood. However, if the Fourth Gospel makes no concession to Jewish sensibilities and insists stubbornly on the reality of the flesh and blood, it does not go to the other extreme of attributing magical power to the reception of the flesh and blood of Jesus and thus equating the Christian sacrament with a pagan mystery. Verses 53–56 promise the gift of life to the man who feeds on Jesus' flesh and drinks his blood, but this eucharistic promise follows the main body of the Bread of Life Discourse in 35–50 which insisted on the necessity of belief in Jesus. The juxtaposition of the two forms of the discourse teaches that the gift of life comes through a *believing* reception of the sacrament (cf. 54 and 47).

In vs. 54 we again find blended together the two types of eschatology. He who feeds on Jesus' flesh has eternal life here below (realized eschatology); but it is also promised that Jesus will raise him up on the last day (final eschatology). Final eschatology is also implied in the reference to eating the flesh of the Son of Man (53) who is an eschatological figure. We know, of course, that other NT authors intimately associate the Eucharist with final eschatology. I Cor xi 26 describes the Eucharist as a proclamation of the Lord's death *until he comes;* and it is also presented as a pledge of the heavenly banquet in God's kingdom (Mark xiv 25; Luke xxii 18).

A comparison of vss. 54 and 56 shows that to have eternal life is to be in close communion with Jesus; it is a question of the Christian's remaining (*menein*) in Jesus and Jesus' remaining in the Christian. In vs. 27 Jesus spoke of the food that lasts (*menein*) for eternal life, i.e., an imperishable food that is the source of eternal life. In vs. 56 the *menein* is applied not to the food but to the life it produces and nourishes. Communion with Jesus is really a participation in the intimate communion that exists between Father and Son. Verse 57 simply mentions the communion between Father and Son with an assumption that the reader will understand. Dodd, *Interpretation,* p. 340, argues that such an assumption makes sense only if ch. vi follows ch. v (see above, pp. 235–36), for it was in v 17–30 that we heard that Jesus was not an independent source of life but was in an unbroken identity of action with the Father. Be that as it may, in its brevity vs. 57 is a most forceful expression of the tremendous claim that Jesus gives *man a share in God's own life,* an expression far more real than the abstract formulation of II Pet i 4. And so it is that, while the Synoptic Gospels record the institution of the Eucharist, it is John who explains what the

Eucharist does for the Christian. Just as the Eucharist itself echoes the theme of the covenant ("blood of the covenant"—Mark xiv 24), so also the mutual indwelling of God (and Jesus) and the Christian may be a reflection of the covenant theme. Jer xxiv 7 and xxxi 33 take the covenant promise, "You will be my people and I shall be your God," and give it the intimacy of God's working in man's heart. At Qumran (1QS i 16 ff.) the communion of the sectarian with God was looked on as a mark of the new covenant.

Addendum on the division of the Bread of Life Discourse

The reader has seen the division that we have proposed for the Bread of Life Discourse. It is but one of many. Gächter, p. 438, when he wrote in 1935, gave a list of the divisions proposed by Catholic commentators up to that time. Here are examples of more recent proposals:

F. J. Leenhardt proposes three divisions in the discourse, corresponding to the three stages of the action in vss. 1–21:

1–21		26–70
(a) *Multiplication of loaves*	= (a) 26–35:	*The nature of the bread*
(b) *Attempt to make Jesus king*	= (b) 36–47:	*Father must bring men to Jesus*
(c) *Crossing the sea*	= (c) 48–70:	*Necessity for a spiritual understanding* (Jesus comes in another form)

J. Schneider and C. Barrett also propose a threefold division: (a) 27(28)–40, (b) 41–51, (c) 52–58. For Schneider, vs. 51 both closes the second stage and opens the third. One principle behind this division is that a question asked by the crowd comes shortly after the opening statement of each stage. Also each of the three stages has the statement, "I am the bread," as well as a reference to the ancestors in the desert.

S. Temple sees three strands of material that run through the discourse: (a) a core of old tradition: 24–35, 41–43, 45, 47, 60, 66–70; (b) the evangelist's expansion of this core: 36–40, 44, 46, 61–65; (c) a eucharistic homily: 48–59. He sees different literary and theological features in each strand.

P. Borgen, *Bread*, pp. 59–98, proposes a division based on midrashic homiletic pattern: (a) 31–33, the basic Pentateuchal citation, corrected by Jesus; (b) 34–40, systematic exposition of the terms in the citation; (c) 41–48, exegetical debate; (d) 49–58, more exposition of terms in the citation.

J. Bligh proposes two divisions covering 26–65: (a) 26–47, (b) 48–65. In each of these Jesus makes an offer (bread, flesh); the hearers are incredulous and murmur (41–42, 60–61); faith is stressed as a gift of God (43–47, 61–65).

T. Worden finds two basic strands of material in 26–59, which constitute parallel discourses: Discourse A: 26, 30–35, 37–39, 41–44, 48–50, 58–59. Discourse B: 27–29, 36, 40, 45–47, 51–57.

H. Schürmann covers the same material in two divisions: (a) 26–52, (b) 53–58. He believes that 51c refers primarily to the death on Calvary rather than to the Eucharist, and so he begins the eucharistic part of the discourse with 53.

E. Galbiati begins the discourse with 32: (a) 32–50, (b) 48–58. Notice that 48–50 are listed in both stages, closing one and opening the other. Verse 50 forms an inclusion with 32; 48 matches 58.

X. Léon-Dufour and D. Mollat begin the discourse with 35 but place the division after 47: (a) 35–47, (b) 48–58. The support for this division is drawn from the similarity of 35 and 48. The themes of "give" and "eat" mark the second half.

Most scholars who divide, as we do, into 35–50 and 51–58 start the division at the last clause of 51 (51c). We began the division with the beginning of 51.

Obviously we cannot attempt to discuss the arguments for and against each of these divisions. We find Borgen's studies of midrashic technique most persuasive, even though we advocate a somewhat different division. In our opinion, vss. 25–34 give the setting for the discourse, with 31–33 supplying the Pentateuchal passage and paraphrase on which the homily is based. Borgen makes 34 part of the homiletic explanation, but it seems to be transitional. The discourse proper begins in 35. The most persuasive argument for the division into 35–50 and 51–58 can be found in the parallels of structure visible when the two parts are set side by side as in the diagram on pp. 288–89. Note the same beginning, the same ending, the same type of interrupting objection. We pointed out on p. 284 how vss. 48–50 are an inclusion and thus the probable ending for the original Bread of Life Discourse. The internal differences of vocabulary and subject matter that exist between 35–50 and 51–58 add to the case for considering these passages as reflecting two parallel discourses which have been put side by side by an editor.

One may raise the objection that Borgen himself considers 51–58 to be part of the same discourse as 35–50; for, while 34–40 explain the first part of the Scripture citation found in 31, *"He gave them bread from heaven to eat,"* 49–58 explain the last part of the citation, namely, *"to eat."* However, since the theme of eating appears in 49–50, were one to consider 35–50 the whole discourse, one could still find all the parts of the Scripture citation treated. Actually, of course, in the final form of the Gospel where 35–50 and 51–58 have been welded together, there is a certain unity to the whole. But Borgen's argument does not necessarily prove that 51–58 was originally united to 35–50.

[The Bibliography for this section is included in the Bibliography for ch. vi, at the end of § 26.]

26. JESUS AT PASSOVER:—REACTIONS TO THE DISCOURSE ON THE BREAD OF LIFE
(vi 60–71)

VI 60[61]* Now, after hearing this, many of his disciples remarked, "This sort of talk is hard to take. How can anyone pay attention to it?" 61[62] Jesus was quite conscious that his disciples were murmuring in protest at this. "Does it shake your faith?" he said to them.

 62 "If, then, you behold the Son of Man   [63]
   ascending to where he was before . . . ?
 63 It is the Spirit that gives life;   [64]
   the flesh is useless.
   The words that I have spoken to you
   are both Spirit and life.
 64 But among you there are some who do not believe." [65]

(In fact, Jesus knew from the start those who refused to believe, as well as the one who would hand him over.) 65[66] So he went on to say:

  "This is why I have told you
  that no one can come to me
  unless it is granted to him by the Father."

66[67] At this many of his disciples broke away and would not accompany him any more. 67[68] And so Jesus said to the Twelve, "Do you also want to go away?" 68[69] Simon Peter answered, "Lord, to whom shall we go? It is you who have the words of eternal life; 69[70] and we have come to believe and are convinced that you are God's Holy One." 70[71] Jesus replied to them, "Did I not choose the Twelve of you myself? And yet one of you is a devil." (71[72] He was talking about Judas, son of Simon the Iscariot; for, though one of the Twelve, he was going to hand Jesus over.)

* Verse numbers in the Vulgate are indicated by brackets.

NOTES

vi 60. *hearing . . . pay attention.* The same verb, *akouein,* is involved; in the first part of the verse it means to hear without acceptance; at the end of the verse it means to hear with acceptance. The latter connotation, common when *akouein* governs the genitive, resembles that of Heb. *šāmaʻ,* "hear, obey."

his disciples. The previous indications have been that the discourse was addressed to the crowd mentioned in vs. 24 and called "the Jews" in vs. 41. Evidently we are to think that Jesus' disciples were also part of the audience. Are these the disciples who crossed the sea at night (16–21)? Verses 66–67 indicate that the disciples are a larger group than the Twelve. We know of seventy (-two) disciples from Luke x 1.

hard to take. Literally "hard, harsh"; there is a twofold connotation of being fantastic and offensive.

attention to it. Or "to him."

61. *was quite conscious.* Literally "knew in himself"; this is not elegant Greek but reflects Semitic usage. Supernatural knowledge is implied.

shake your faith. Literally "scandalize you."

62. *If, then.* This sentence is elliptic, consisting only of protasis. Scholars have proposed several possible types of apodoses: (a) Those where the apodosis is connected with the scandal mentioned in vs. 61:—"then your scandal will really be great" (Bultmann) [this is an *a fortiori* argument (see i 50, iii 12)];—"then your scandal will be removed" (Bauer) [this suggestion implies that beholding the ascension of the Son of Man will lead them to believe]; (b) those where the apodosis is related to what was said in 48–50:—"then you will understand the bread of life that has come down from heaven" (Thüsing, p. 261); (c) those where the apodosis is related to 51–58:—"then you will judge otherwise of my flesh."

you behold. *Theōrein;* see NOTE on vs. 40. Notice that Jesus does not say definitely that they will see this ascension; it is left hypothetical.

ascending to where he was before. This means to the Father (xvii 5). There is an implication that the Son of Man has descended, a notion which we have seen (see NOTE on iii 13) to be quite unusual. This ascension to the Father is through crucifixion and resurrection.

63. *It is the Spirit.* Bultmann, pp. 341–42, mentions the possibility that the first part of this verse may be a proposition defended by the hearers: "You say, 'It is the Spirit that gives life; the flesh is useless'; but I say, 'The words that I have spoken to you are both Spirit and life.'" However, the whole verse is perfectly intelligible as Jesus' own teaching.

gives life. This verb was used in v 21; it appears seven times in the Pauline writings. The following are of particular interest: II Cor iii 6: "The letter kills, but the Spirit gives life"; I Cor xv 45: "The last Adam became a life-giving Spirit."

flesh. The contrast between the flesh which is useless and the words of Jesus which have the life-giving power of the Spirit is not unlike a contrast found in Isa xl 6–8: "All flesh is grass. . . . The grass withers; the flower fades; but the word of our God will stand forever." This passage of Isaiah was used in early Christian circles (I Pet i 24–25).

words. Some who would connect vss. 60 ff. to 51–58 and to the theme of the Eucharist are puzzled by this reference to "words" as the source of life here and in vs. 68. Jesus seems to be returning to the sapiential theme of 35–50, rather than to the sacramental theme of 51–58. To avoid this difficulty these interpreters would resort to exegeting the Greek in light of Heb. *dābār*, which means both "word" and "thing"; thus, they translate: "The *things* [i.e., the Eucharist—flesh and blood] of which I have spoken." Dodd, *Interpretation*, p. 342³; admits that this is desperate.

I have spoken. The "I" is emphatic. Thinking back to the mention of the manna given by Moses (31–32) and remembering that Deut viii 3 relates the manna to the words of God, some hold that Jesus is stressing the value of his own words as contrasted with those of Moses. Jesus might be challenging the type of Jewish thought we find later exemplified in the Midrash Mekilta on Exod xv 26: "The words of the Law which I have given you are life for you." In this same pattern of contrast, compare John vi 68 which attributes the words of life to Jesus with the statement in Acts vii 38 where it is Moses who received the living words to be given to the people.

are both Spirit and life. Literally "are Spirit and are life." Dodd, *Interpretation*, p. 342, is correct, however, in seeing "Spirit and life" as a virtual hendiadys. See COMMENT.

64. *Jesus knew*. Compare ii 25: "He was aware of what was in man's heart."

from the start. Literally "from the beginning." This is not the beginning mentioned in i 1 where the pre-existence of the Word is involved, but the beginning of the ministry or of the disciples' call (see xvi 4). Once again, as in vi 6, this is an editorial attempt to prevent any misconception which might imply that Jesus had made a mistake. Celsus used the example of the choice of Judas to argue that Jesus did not have divine knowledge (Origen *Celsus* ii 11; GCS 2:138).

would hand him over. A future participle, a grammatical form that is rare in the NT outside the Lucan writings. The Greek verb *paradidonai* means "to deliver up, hand over"; it does not necessarily have a connotation of treachery or betrayal. It is used in the second and third predictions of the passion in Mark ix 31, x 33.

65. *This is why*. Presumably the "this" refers to the lack of faith mentioned in the first part of vs. 64.

I have told you. Once again (see NOTE on vs. 36) what follows is not an exact citation of anything that Jesus has said, although it is almost a composite of what is said in vss. 44 and 37. We may contrast this with the instances in John where Jesus cites his own words quite exactly (viii 24 citing 21; xiii 33 citing viii 21; xv 20 citing xiii 16; xvi 15 citing 14).

66. *At this*. Literally "from this." Is John playing on the notion that the disciples left because the Father had not chosen them, in which case "this" refers to the ending of vs. 65? Or does "this" refer to the whole conversation and the difficulty of Jesus' teaching.

broke away. Literally "went away back"; Bultmann, p. 343⁵, points out the Hebrew idiom *nāsōg 'āḥōr*, "to turn away" (see Isa 1 5).

accompany. Literally "walk with"—another Semitism. Although the immediate aim of this verse concerns the historical situation of Jesus' ministry, John may also be thinking of apostates in the late 1st century (I John ii 19).

67. *the Twelve*. This is the first time they are mentioned in John.

Do you also want? The phrasing of the question implies a negative answer.

68. *words of eternal life*. See NOTE on vs. 63.

69. *we*. The "we" is emphatic: the Twelve contrasted with those disciples whose faith has proved inadequate. In vs. 67 Jesus had addressed the Twelve, and so Peter speaks for them; in 70 Jesus continues to address the Twelve.

believe and are convinced. The latter is literally "know." This is a Johannine combination found in inverse order in xvii 8 and I John iv 16. The two verbs are virtually synonymous; however, it is worth noting that, while Jesus himself is said to *know* God, he is never said to believe in Him.

God's Holy One. Some Greek witnesses, the OS, and the Vulg. have harmonized this with Matt xvi 16, reading "the Messiah, the Son of [the living] God." The phrase "God's holy one" or "the Lord's holy one" is used in the OT to refer to men consecrated to God, e.g., Judg xiii 7 and xvi 17 in reference to Samson (LXX; MT has Nazirite); Ps cvi 16 in reference to Aaron. The closest parallel to this expression elsewhere in John is in x 36 where Jesus speaks of himself as "the one whom the Father consecrated [made holy]"—a reference set against the background of the dedication of the temple altar. Some would even see a reference to the priestly or sacrificial here in vi 69; e.g., Bultmann, p. 345, in view of the subsequent reference to death, sees a possible reference to Jesus as the victim. On the eve of his death Jesus will say of his disciples, "It is for them that I consecrate [make holy] myself" (xvii 19). In the Synoptics the title "Holy One of God" appears on the lips of an unclean spirit (Mark i 24—it is interesting that in John, in response to the use of this title by Peter, Jesus says that one of the Twelve is a *devil*). "Holy" is applied to Jesus in Peter's speeches in Acts iii 14, iv 27, 30.

70. *choose the Twelve*. Such a choice of the Twelve is not recorded in John. See Mark iii 14. "He appointed [made] Twelve to be with him"; Matt x 1, "He called to himself his Twelve disciples"; Luke vi 13, "He called over his disciples and *chose* Twelve from them." That Jesus chose his own followers is repeated in John xiii 18 and xv 16.

a devil. At xiii 2 we hear that "the devil induced Judas" and at xiii 27, "Satan entered his heart." Thus, for John, Judas was definitely the tool of Satan or the devil. J. Jeremias, *The Parables of Jesus* (2 ed.; New York: Scribner's, 1963), p. 81[49], maintains that the designation "the devil" belongs to a later stratum of gospel tradition than does "Satan." Thus, he would maintain that in the scene at Caesarea Philippi which is the Synoptic parallel for this scene in John, "Get behind me, Satan" (Mark viii 33) is older than John's form of the saying.

71. *Judas, son of Simon the Iscariot*. Judas is named eight times in John: (*a*) four times simply as Judas; (*b*) in xii 4 as Judas the Iscariot; (*c*) here and in xiii 26 the best witnesses favor "Judas, son of Simon the Iscariot," a reading where "Iscariot" agrees with Simon; (*d*) in xiii 2 where "Iscariot" agrees with Judas, the reading seems to be, "Judas, son of Simon, the Iscariot." Perhaps the fluctuation in the Greek reflects the original Aramaic idiom where the appellative tends to follow the patronymic, so that in the Aramaic phrase, "X, son of Y, the Iscariot," the adjective "Iscariot" modifies X. But in John, as it now stands, the adjective "Iscariot" seems to be able to modify both Simon and Judas. Only John mentions Simon, the father of Judas; in the Synoptics Judas himself is "the Iscariot" or "Iscarioth." Many suggestions have been given for the meaning of "Iscariot." The best one seems to be that it reflects Heb. *'îš Qᵉriyyōt*, "man of Kerioth [a town in southern Judea]." This is an ancient interpretation, and it is reflected in the reading "from Kerioth" found in some witnesses for this verse in John. It would make Judas a Judean disciple of Jesus (see vii 3), whereas the other members of the Twelve of whom we know were Galileans.

one of the Twelve. The cardinal number is used; however, since sometimes the cardinal number "one" can be used as an ordinal (="first"; BDF, § 247), it has been suggested that John is referring to Judas as "the first of the Twelve." This is implausible; Matt x 2 uses the ordinal for Peter. Judas' position close to Jesus at the Last Supper was not necessarily the result of primacy in rank but of his position as holding the purse.

was going to hand Jesus over. Judas' betrayal has an air of inevitability; this is not a denial of free will but reflects the inevitability of the plan of salvation.

COMMENT

We must begin by asking about the relationship of vss. 60–71 to the Bread of Life Discourse. Does it refer to the whole discourse, including the eucharistic section (51–58), or does it refer only to what we have characterized as the "original" discourse (35–50)? Verse 63 is crucial to this question. Is its exaltation of the Spirit and deprecation of the flesh a reference to the eucharistic flesh spoken of in 51–58? Zwingli thought so and made 63 the keystone of his argument against the real presence, since it seemed to imply that Jesus wanted his presence in the Eucharist to be interpreted in a spiritual manner (see Gollwitzer, *art. cit.*). However, such an interpretation of 63 as a deprecation of the importance of the eucharistic flesh is hard to reconcile with the emphasis in 53–56 on the necessity of eating the eucharistic flesh because it is a source of life.

Today there is greater agreement among scholars that the mention of flesh in vs. 63 does *not* concern the eucharistic flesh of 51–58. In our judgment, Bornkamm, *art. cit.*, has shown conclusively that 60–71 refers not to 51–58 but to 35–50; Schürmann has argued against Bornkamm, but even he admits that in interpreting 60–71, we must consider 53–58 as parenthetical. For the moment, let us suppose that 60 once immediately followed 50 in order to see the excellent sequence. In 50 Jesus claimed to be the bread come down from heaven; in 60 the disciples are indignant about this and murmur even as the crowd murmured about the same claim in 41. The disciples cannot bear *to listen*—notice that all the references in 60–71 concern hearing or believing Jesus' doctrine; there is not a single reference to refusing to eat his flesh or to drink his blood. Since they complain that they cannot listen to his claim to have come down from heaven (*katabainein*), in vs. 62 Jesus asks what they will think if they see him ascending (*anabainein*) to where he was before. He uses the term Son of Man to identify himself with a figure whom both Daniel and Enoch characterize as celestial. (The reader knows that this ascension will only be accomplished through death and resurrection, and it is interesting that the Synoptics use the title "Son of Man" in Jesus' predictions of the passion, death, and resurrection, e.g., Mark viii 31, ix 31, x 33.)

We have somewhat of a parallel to vss. 62–63 in ch. iii. When Nicodemus cannot understand how a man can be begotten from above of water and Spirit, by way of explanation Jesus calls upon the ascension into heaven of the Son of Man (iii 13); for it is the ascended Son of Man who can give the Spirit. So also in vi 63 the Spirit is mentioned immediately after the reference to the ascension of the Son of Man. The contrast between Spirit and flesh in 63 is the same contrast we found in iii 6. Jesus is not speaking of eucharistic flesh but of flesh as he spoke of it in ch. iii, namely, the natural principle in man which cannot give eternal life. The Spirit is the divine principle from above which alone can give life. This contrast between flesh and Spirit appears also in Paul, for example, Rom viii 4: ". . . who walk not according to the flesh but according to the Spirit" (Gal v 16, vi 8). The Synoptic parallel in the Caesarea Philippi scene to "the flesh is useless" is found in Matt xvi 17: "Flesh and blood has not revealed this to you, but my Father who is in heaven."

If "flesh" in 63 has nothing to do with the Eucharist, neither then does the emphasis on Spirit have anything to do with a spiritual interpretation of the presence of Jesus in the Eucharist. The mention of the Spirit, the life-giving principle to be given by the resurrected Christ, follows that of the ascension because, as we shall see in vii 38–39, xx 22, John stresses that the Spirit is given only when Jesus is raised up. The comment on the Spirit is pertinent to the Bread of Life Discourse because vs. 32 characterized the bread from heaven as *real* (*alēthinos*). This meant that the bread belongs to the heavenly, eternal realm, as opposed to the merely natural and passing; and this realm of the real is the realm of the Spirit of truth (*alētheia*).

Thus, in vs. 63 Jesus is once more affirming that man cannot gain life on his own. If Jesus is divine revelation come down from heaven like bread to nourish men, his purpose is to communicate to them the principle of eternal life. The man who accepts the words of Jesus will receive the life-giving Spirit. In ch. iv, when we discussed whether the living water offered by Jesus was his revelation or the Spirit, we saw that the symbolism had to include both. Here too Jesus' words (68) and the Spirit (63) are mentioned side by side as giving life, even as vs. 40 mentions faith and its indispensable connection with eternal life. John does not unravel the interrelationships of these various life-giving factors; that is the work of later theology.

Verse 64 is clearly reminiscent of that part of the Bread of Life Discourse (35–50) where bread refers primarily to Jesus' revelation which must be believed. Jesus repeats to the disciples the charge he made in 36 about not believing. This charge was followed in 37, 40, 44, with references to the working of the Father's will—only those drawn by the Father believe in Jesus. We have exactly the same sequence in 65. Notice that once again in 64 and 65 we have *believing* in Jesus and *coming* to him as parallel expressions; compare 35, 37, 45.

Verse 66 shows that the final reaction of the disciples is one of disbelief. On p. 249, in discussing vi 14–15, we pointed out the parallel between Jesus' flight from messianic coronation and the Synoptic account of the end of the Galilean ministry where Jesus seems to leave Galilee lest Herod involve him in some political snare. We also pointed out parallels between the Synoptic scene of the rejection of Jesus at Nazareth and the rejection of Jesus in John vi 42 (see NOTE). It is not surprising then, since the Synoptic account of the ministry in Galilee ended on a tone of disbelief, to find this same tone in John vi 66. The Twelve believe, but the majority of people do not. After this chapter Jesus will go to Jerusalem to teach, and in xii 37 we shall find that the Jerusalem ministry ends on the same tone: even though there are a few in the Sanhedrin who believe, the majority of the leaders and the people do not.

It is interesting to compare John vi 65–66 with Matt xi 20–28. In Matt xi 20–24 Jesus issues a judgment on the Galilean cities which have refused to believe his mighty deeds; even so in John vi 66 the disciples do not believe in him. In Matt xi 27, which is part of the "Johannine logion" found in Matthew and Luke, we hear: "All things have been given over to me by my Father. No one knows the Son except the Father, and no one knows the Father except the Son and anyone to whom the Son chooses to reveal Him"; this is quite like John vi 65.

The reaction of incredulity and the refusal to come to Jesus fits in well with what we know of the theme of personified Wisdom which colors the Johannine presentation of Jesus and, in particular, supplies background for the sapiential aspect of the Bread of Life Discourse. The invitations of Wisdom to come and eat and drink (e.g., Sir xxiv 19–20) are not accepted by all; there is always the fool who rejects Wisdom and turns away.

Verses 67–71 turn our attention to the different reaction of the Twelve who believe in Jesus. There can be little doubt that this is the Johannine parallel to the Synoptic scene at Caesarea Philippi (Mark viii 27–33 and par.) which is part of the sequence following the second multiplication of loaves (see above, p. 238). John has parallels not only to the shorter Marcan form of the scene, but also to the longer Matthean form:

- Mark viii 27–28 (Matt xvi 13–14): various titles are proposed to identify Jesus, including that of a prophet. John vi 14: This is the prophet.
- Mark viii 29 (Matt xvi 15): Jesus asks the Twelve, "But who do *you* say that I am?" John vi 67: Jesus to the Twelve, "Do *you* also want to go away?"
- Mark viii 29 (Matt xvi 16): (Simon) Peter answers, "You are the Messiah [Matthew: the Son of the living God]." John vi 69: Simon Peter answers, "You are God's Holy One."
- Matt xvi 17: "Flesh and blood has not revealed this to you, but my Father who is in heaven." John vi 63: "The flesh is useless"; vi 65: "No one can come to me unless it be granted to him by the Father."
- Mark viii 31 (Matt xvi 21): First prediction of the passion. John vi 71: the first reference to Judas' betrayal of Jesus.
- Mark viii 33 (Matt xvi 23): Peter expostulates and Jesus rebukes him: "Get behind me Satan." John vi 70: Jesus speaks of Judas: "One of you is a devil." In this instance some suggest that a harsh statement once addressed to Peter has been adapted and reapplied to Judas.

Perhaps one objection to seeing the parallelism between the Synoptic and

Johannine scenes is that of geography. John seems to place Peter's confession at Capernaum, while Mark and Matthew place it at Caesarea Philippi, thirty miles north. (Luke ix 18, following ix 10, would *prima facie* place it at Bethsaida, but Luke's omissions in this scene lessen the value of such geographical conclusions.) We have already seen that chronologically John vi brings together scenes that were once separated; we may have the same phenomenon in geographic matters.

In the list of parallels above we concentrated on those elements of the Caesarea scene found in *John vi*. It is noteworthy that almost every element of the peculiarly Matthean material in the Caesarean scene is found *somewhere* in John:

- Matt xvi 16: Simon says, "You are the Messiah, the Son of the living God." John i 41 associates the designation of Jesus as Messiah with the call of Simon. John xi 27 has this confession on Martha's lips: "You are the Messiah, the Son of God."
- Matt xvi 17: Jesus to Simon, "Flesh and blood . . ."; see fourth parallel above.
- Matt xvi 18: Jesus to Simon son of Jona (so-called in 17): "You are Peter and upon this rock . . ." John i 42: "You are Simon, son of John; your name shall be Cephas" (which is rendered as "Peter").
- Matt xvi 18: Jesus makes Peter the rock on which the Church is to be built. John xxi 15–17: Jesus makes Peter the shepherd of the flock.
- Matt xvi 19: Jesus to Peter (in xviii 18 to the disciples): "Whatever you bind on earth shall be bound in heaven, and whatever you loose on earth shall be loosed in heaven." John xx 23: Jesus to the disciples, "If you absolve men's sins, their sins are absolved; if you hold them, they are held fast."

Because this additional material in Matthew's Caesarea Philippi scene is not present in the Marcan and Lucan scene, and because it is not entirely harmonious with the context, scholars have suggested that Matthew has gathered Petrine material from other contexts and joined it together and added it to the Caesarea Philippi scene. In this eventuality the picture in John where the Petrine material is scattered may be more primitive than the Matthean picture, although we cannot, of course, be certain that John's localization of these individual sayings is always original. For further discussion, see COMMENT on xxi 15–17.

■ ■ ■

We have interpreted 60–71 as if these verses had no reference to 51–58; this agrees with our theory that 51–58 is a later editorial insertion of Johannine material breaking up the unity that once existed between 35–50 and 60–71. But one may ask, even if this theory is correct, does not the final form of the chapter where 60–71 *now* follow 51–58 require that 60–71 have some secondary reference to the Eucharist? We are not convinced that it does; for we believe that the editor or final redactor added 51–58 to bring out the secondary eucharistic motifs in 35–50, but did not make any real attempt to give a new orientation to 60–71 in light of this addition.

Nevertheless, we should at least list some of the suggestions that have been made linking vss. 60–71 to the eucharistic theme. Some see in the theme of the ascension of the Son of Man in 62 an indication to the disciples that only after this ascension will they begin to receive the living bread of the Eucharist. Verse 27 is cited in this connection: ". . . food which *the Son of Man* will give you." The mention of the Spirit in 63 has also received a eucharistic reference, for Wilkens, "Abendmahlzeugnis," p. 363, proposes that the Spirit will waken that faith necessary to see the Eucharist as the flesh and blood of the Son of Man. Others see in 63 the idea that the Eucharist can be received fruitfully only by one who possesses the Spirit, an interpretation that rejects a materialistic approach to the sacrament, or a magical approach akin to that of the mystery religions. Still another suggestion is that 63 means that it is not the dead body or flesh of Jesus which will be of benefit in the Eucharist, but his resurrected body full of the Spirit of life. Craig, JBL 58 (1939), 39[38], thinks of a primitive parallel to the epiklesis or invocation of the Spirit, now associated with the eucharistic rite in the Eastern liturgies.

Boismard maintains that vss. 70–71 belong with 51–58 as part of the displaced eucharistic material from the Last Supper. He points out that the theme of betrayal by Judas would have been perfectly at home in relation to xiii 18–30. He would suggest that it was brought to ch. vi as a replacement for the original rebuke addressed to Peter found in the Synoptic scene at Caesarea Philippi.

These are all ingenious proposals, but more evidence for them would be desirable. Most of them do not really explain how the absolute statement, "The flesh is useless," could ever have been said of the eucharistic flesh of Jesus.

BIBLIOGRAPHY

Bligh, J., "Jesus in Galilee," *Heythrop Journal* 5 (1964), 3–21.
Borgen, P., "The Unity of the Discourse in John 6," ZNW 50 (1959), 277–78.
———"Observations on the Midrashic Character of John 6," ZNW 54 (1963), 232–40.
———*Bread from Heaven* (SNT X, 1965).
Bornkamm, G., "Die eucharistische Rede im Johannes-Evangelium," ZNW 47 (1956), 161–69.
Braun, F.-M., "Quatre 'signes' johanniques de l'unité chrétienne," NTS 9 (1962–63), especially pp. 147–48 on vi 12–13.
Brown, R. E., "The Eucharist and Baptism in St. John," *Catholic College Teachers of Religion Annual* 8 (1962), 14–33. Also in NTE, Ch. v.
Daube, D., *The New Testament and Rabbinic Judaism* (London University, 1956), especially pp. 36–51, 158–69.
Feuillet, A., "Les thèmes bibliques majeurs du discours sur le pain de vie (Jean 6)," NRT 82 (1960), 803–22, 918–39, 1040–62. In English in JohSt, pp. 53–128.
Gächter, P., "Die Form der eucharistischen Rede Jesu," ZKT 59 (1935), 419–41.

Gärtner, B., *John 6 and the Jewish Passover* (*Coniectanea Neotestamentica,* XVII; Lund: Gleerup, 1959).

Galbiati, E., "Il Pane della Vita," BibOr 5 (1963), 101–10.

Gollwitzer, H., "Zur Auslegung von Joh. 6 bei Luther und Zwingli," IMEL, pp. 143–68.

Haenchen, E., "Johanneische Probleme," ZTK 56 (1959), especially pp. 31–34.

Jeremias, J., "Joh. 6, 51ᶜ–58—redaktionell?" ZNW 44 (1952–53), 256–57.

Johnston, E. D., "The Johannine Version of the Feeding of the Five Thousand— an Independent Tradition?" NTS 8 (1961–62), 151–54.

Kilmartin, E. J., "Liturgical Influence on John 6," CBQ 22 (1960), 183–91.

——"A First Century Chalice Dispute," ScEccl 12 (1960), 403–8.

Leenhardt, F. J., "La structure du chapitre 6 de l'Evangile de Jean," RHPR 39 (1959), 1–13.

Léon-Dufour, X., "Le mystère du pain de vie (Jean VI)," RSR 46 (1958), 481–523.

——"Trois chiasmes johanniques," NTS 7 (1960–61), especially pp. 251–53 on vi 36–40.

Macgregor, G. H. C., "The Eucharist in the Fourth Gospel," NTS 9 (1962– 63), 111–19.

Mendner, S., "Zum Problem 'Johannes und die Synoptiker,'" NTS 4 (1957–58), 282–307 on vi 1–30.

Mollat, D., "Le chapitre VI de Saint Jean," LumVie 31 (1957), 107–19. Now in English in *The Eucharist in the New Testament* (Baltimore: Helicon, 1964), pp. 143–56.

Ruckstuhl, E., "Auseinandersetzung mit Joachim Jeremias über die Echtheit von Jh 6, 51ᵇ–58," *Die literarische Einheit des Johannesevangeliums,* pp. 220–72.

Ruland, V., "Sign and Sacrament: John's Bread of Life Discourse," Interp 18 (1964), 450–62.

Schneider, J., "Zur Frage der Komposition von Joh. 6, 27–58 (59)—Die Himmels- brotrede," IMEL, pp. 132–42.

Schürmann, H., "Joh 6, 51ᶜ—ein Schlüssel zur johanneischen Brotrede," BZ 2 (1958), 244–62.

——"Die Eucharistie als Representation und Applikation des Heilsgeschehens nach Joh 6, 53–58," *Trierer Theologische Zeitschrift* 68 (1959), 30–45, 108–18.

Schweizer, Ed., "Das johanneische Zeugnis vom Herrenmahl," EvTh 12 (1952– 53), 341–63. Also in *Neotestamentica* (Zurich: Zwingli, 1963), pp. 371–96.

Temple, S., "A Key to the Composition of the Fourth Gospel," JBL 80 (1961), 220–32 on vi 24–71.

Wilkens, W., "Das Abendmahlzeugnis im vierten Evangelium," EvTh 18 (1958), 354–70.

——"Evangelist und Tradition im Johannesevangelium," TZ 16 (1960), 81–90.

Worden, T. E., "The Holy Eucharist in St. John," *Scripture* 15 (1963), 97–103; 16 (1964), 5–16.

Ziener, G., "Johannesevangelium und urchristliche Passafeier," BZ 2 (1958), 263–74.

27. JESUS AT TABERNACLES:—INTRODUCTION
(vii 1–13)

Will Jesus go up to the feast?

VII 1 [Now,] after this, Jesus moved about within Galilee because, with the Jews looking for a chance to kill him, he decided not to travel in Judea. 2 However, since the Jewish feast of Tabernacles was near, 3 his brothers advised him, "Leave here and go to Judea so that your disciples too may get a look at the works you are performing. 4 For no one keeps his actions hidden and still expects to be in the public eye. If you are going to perform such things, display yourself to the world." (5 In reality, not even his brothers believed in him.) 6 So Jesus answered them:

> "It is not yet time for me,
> but the time is always suitable for you.
> 7 The world cannot possibly hate you,
> but it does hate me
> because of the evidence I bring against it
> that what it does is evil.

8 Go up to the festival yourselves. I am not going up to this festival because the time is not yet ripe for me." 9 After this conversation he stayed on in Galilee. 10 However, once his brothers had gone up to the festival, then he too went up, but [as it were] in secret, not for all to see.

11 Of course, the Jews were looking for him during the festival, asking, "Where is that man?" 12 And among the crowds there was much guarded debate about him. Some maintained, "He is good," while others insisted, "Not at all—he is only deceiving the crowd." 13 However, no one would talk openly about him for fear of the Jews.

6: *answered.* In the historical present tense.

NOTES

vii 1. [*Now*]. An important block of witnesses related to the Western tradition omit the initial *kai*.

after this. Tabernacles is approximately six months after Passover, the feast of the preceding chapter.

the Jews. Here they are thought of as being more active in Judea, and this agrees with the contention that they are the Jerusalem authorities. Yet vi 41 and 52 mentioned "the Jews" in a Galilean setting. Probably the meaning is that only in Judea did they have enough power to execute Jesus.

to kill him. See v 18.

decided not. Or "dared not." A more difficult reading, "was not able," has support in the OL, OS, Augustine, and Chrysostom.

2. *Tabernacles*. The autumnal harvest feast received the name of *Sukkôt* ("huts," but also translated "booths, tents, tabernacles") because people celebrated it outside in the vineyards where they made huts of tree branches. By theological adaptation this was associated with the dwelling of the Israelites in tents during their wanderings in the desert after the Exodus. Lev xxiii 39 fixes the day on which the feast should begin as the 15th of Tishri (September–October). Although Deut xvi 13 mentions a seven-day celebration, Leviticus speaks of an additional, eighth day of solemn rest.

3. *brothers*. See NOTES on "brothers" and "disciples" in ii 12, the last previous mention of these relatives. There they were at Capernaum.

and go. There is some slight evidence for the omission of these words, producing the rough construction, "Leave here for Judea" (see NOTE on iv 43). Boismard, RB 58 (1951), 166, prefers the omission.

disciples. This seems to imply that Jesus' disciples were to be found in Judea; yet ch. vi clearly placed them in Galilee. (If the Twelve are meant, most of them were Galileans.) Had some of those who broke away (vi 66) gone (back) to Judea? Or is this a reference to the believers of ii 23 and iv 1?

the works. Up to this time in the Johannine account the most impressive miracles have been performed in Galilee (*water to wine; healing at a distance; multiplication of loaves; walking on water*).

4. *to the world*. This invitation to the provincial prophet to seek publicity in the metropolis cloaks a more theological challenge to the Light to show himself to the world.

5. *his brothers*. Seemingly the brothers became believers after the resurrection, for they are mentioned in Acts i 14 along with the Twelve. James and Jude became important figures in the Church.

6. *time*. This word, *kairos*, has in general a deeper theological import as a decisive salvific moment than the word *chronos*, which means ordinary, calendar time. "Time" is a Johannine alternate for the "hour" (compare ii 4); we find exactly the same alternation in Matt xxvi 18 and 45. Here, in vs. 6, there are different meanings in the two uses of "time"; the first is a reference to the salvific hour of Jesus' death; the second is more general.

7. *The world*. In vii 1 we heard of the hate of the Judean Jews for Jesus; here it is the world that hates Jesus. Although they are a historical group in the ministry of Jesus, "the Jews" are also the spokesmen of a wider

opposition on the part of the world, an opposition quite evident in the evangelist's time.

8. *not going up to this festival.* The best witnesses add "yet"; it is omitted in Codices Sinaiticus and Bezae, the Latin, and OS. Probably "yet" has been inserted by a scribe to solve the difficulty that, after stating absolutely he was not going up, Jesus later went up. See COMMENT.

ripe. Literally "fulfilled." The theme of eschatological fulfillment of the OT or of the divine plan is common in the NT, especially in regard to the passion (xix 24, 36).

9. *conversation.* Some important witnesses, including P[75], have "with them."

stayed on. A complexive aorist; see NOTE on ii 20 for reflections on its incomplete quality.

10. *[as it were].* Omitted in important witnesses related to the Western tradition, this phrase may have been inserted by a copyist to avoid the impression of deception by Jesus.

11. *that man.* Chrysostom understood this pronoun (*ekeinos*) in a markedly hostile manner ("that fellow," like the hostile use of *houtos*); such an interpretation is based on the fact that the question is being asked by "the Jews."

12. *much guarded debate.* This is the same Greek expression as the "murmuring" of vi 41, 61. There it was hostile to Jesus; here it is more a case of wondering secretly. "Much" is found in different sequences in different manuscripts and may be a copyist's addition. We shall find other such positive-negative debates in John vii 40–41, x 20–21; they have a parallel in later Jewish-Christian debates.

deceiving the crowd. This was a charge advanced by the Jews in their debates with the Christians (Justin *Trypho* LXIX 7; PG 6:640). Luke xxiii 2 makes it a formal charge against Jesus in the trial before Pilate ("perverted the people"), while in Matt xxvii 63 the Pharisees refer to Jesus as a deceiver.

13. *fear of the Jews.* This is a clear indication that "the Jews" are the Jerusalem authorities, for the crowds themselves were certainly Jewish and still they fear the Jews.

COMMENT

Jesus' speeches in the Temple on the occasion of the feast of Tabernacles will meet vicious hostility on the part of "the Jews." John sets the stage for this by showing that before the feast Jesus had been avoiding Judea because he knew of this hostility. He had already been met with murderous intent in his last stay in Jerusalem narrated in ch. v. The fact that ch. vii does recall ch. v has been used by some as an argument for the rearrangement of chapters wherein vii would immediately follow v (see above, pp. 235–36). However, if Jesus had just worked in Jerusalem the miracle narrated in v 1–15, the request in vii 3 that he go to Judea and work some miracles seems odd.

Verse 1 also sets the stage for the conversation between Jesus and his unbelieving relatives. This conversation illustrates the fact that miracles do not in themselves lead to faith. The "brothers" admit that Jesus can perform amazing deeds; yet they do not believe, for they do not see the real meaning behind these signs. We saw in ch. vi that the disbelief of the Galilean Jews had much in common with the Synoptic scene of the rejection of Jesus at Nazareth (see NOTE on vi 42). This is another Johannine parallel to that scene (notice that in Mark vi 3 Jesus' brothers are mentioned).

The brothers want Jesus to show off his miraculous power in Jerusalem. In CBQ 23 (1961), 152–55, we pointed out that three requests made of Jesus in John vi and vii resemble closely the temptations of Jesus in Matt iv 1–11 and Luke iv 1–13:

John	*Temptations*
vi 15: The people would make him king	Satan offers him the kingdoms of the world
vi 31: The people ask for miraculous bread	Satan invites him to turn the stones into bread
vii 3: The brothers want Jesus to go to Jerusalem to show his power	Satan takes Jesus to the Jerusalem Temple and invites him to display his power by jumping from the pinnacle

Thus, it seems that Matthew and Luke are giving in dramatic form the type of temptations that Jesus actually faced in a more prosaic way during his ministry.

The answer that Jesus gives his brothers in vss. 6–10 is a classic instance of the two levels of meaning found in John. On the purely natural level it appears to the brothers that Jesus does not find this an opportune time to go up to the festival at Jerusalem. Jesus' subsequent behavior in going up to the festival shows us, however, that this was not really what he meant. John has prepared the reader to understand Jesus' real meaning by the reference to death at the hand of "the Jews" in vs. 1. When Jesus speaks of his "time," he is speaking on the level of the divine plan. His "time" is his "hour," the hour of passion, death, resurrection, and ascension to the Father; and this time is not to come at this festival of Tabernacles—it is reserved for a subsequent Passover. "The Jews" will try to kill him at Tabernacles (viii 59), as an instance of the world's hate of which Jesus speaks in vs. 7; but they will fail. At this festival he will not *go up* (vs. 8), that is, go up to the Father. John is giving us a play on the verb *anabainein*, which can mean to go up in pilgrimage to Mount Zion and Jerusalem, and can also mean "to ascend." In xx 17 Jesus uses this verb when he speaks of ascending to the Father, and that is the deeper meaning here. In vs. 8 he says his time is not yet ripe (or fulfilled—see NOTE), for the Scriptures and God's plan pertaining to his death and resurrection are not yet ready to be fulfilled. The two levels of meaning were recognized by early commentators. Epiphanius (*Haer.* LI 25; GCS 31:295) says: "He speaks to his brothers spiritually and in a mystery, and they did not understand what he said. For he told them that he would not ascend at that feast, neither into heaven nor on the cross to fulfill the plan of his suffering and the mystery of salvation. . . ."

Is this journey to Jerusalem for Tabernacles to be identified with the only journey to Jerusalem in the Synoptic tradition of the ministry, the one at the end of Jesus' life? In John we never hear of Jesus returning again to Galilee after this journey to Jerusalem. We hear only that he went into the Transjordan (x 40) and that he spent some time at Ephraim in the region near the desert (xi 54). Thus, *if* the Johannine chronology is complete, this is Jesus' last journey to Jerusalem from Galilee. In the Synoptic picture of the journey to Jerusalem, Mark ix 30–33 tells us that Jesus passed through Galilee, stopping at Capernaum (see NOTE on vs. 3, "brothers"); then he went to Judea and the Transjordan (Mark x 1) on the way to Jerusalem (x 32). One interesting parallel is that his journey is marked by secrecy in Mark ix 30, even as it is in John; also, the theme of going up to Jerusalem to die appears in Mark x 33 (*anabainein*). However, the fact that the Synoptic journey to Jerusalem is itself a composite and, especially in Luke, a construction with definite theological purposes makes any historical comparison with John very difficult. We say only that John's picture wherein Jesus remains a long period in the Jerusalem area between Tabernacles and the following Passover may well be more accurate than the crowded Synoptic picture where he seems to arrive in Jerusalem a few days before his death. Much of the material, particularly by way of accusation and trial, that the Synoptics pack into those final days is found in John in the chapters that cover the period from Tabernacles to Passover (see NOTE on vs. 12; also remarks below on x 24, 33, xi 47–53).

[The Bibliography for this section is included in the Bibliography for ch. vii, at the end of § 29.]

28. JESUS AT TABERNACLES:—SCENE ONE
(vii 14–36)

Discourse delivered in the middle of the feast

a. Jesus' right to teach; resumption of Sabbath question

VII 14 The feast was already half over when Jesus went up into the temple precincts and began to teach. 15 The Jews were surprised at this, saying, "How did this fellow get his education when he had no teacher?" 16 So Jesus answered them:

"My doctrine is not my own
but comes from Him who sent me.
17 If anyone chooses to do His will,
he will know about this doctrine—
whether it comes from God,
or whether I am speaking on my own.
18 Whoever speaks on his own
seeks his own glory.
But whoever seeks the glory of the one who sent him—
he is truthful
and there is no dishonesty in his heart.
19 Has not Moses given you the Law?
Yet not one of you keeps the Law.
Why are you looking for a chance to kill me?"

20 "You're demented," the crowd retorted. "Who wants to kill you?"
21 Jesus gave them this answer:

"I have performed just one work,
and all of you are shocked 22 on that account.
Moses has given you circumcision
(really, it did not originate with Moses but with the Patriarchs);
and so even on a Sabbath you circumcise a man.
23 If a man can receive circumcision on a Sabbath
to prevent violation of the Mosaic Law,
are you angry at me
because I cured the whole man on a Sabbath?

24 Do not judge by appearances,
   but give an honest judgment."

b. Origins of Jesus; his return to the Father

25 This led some of the people of Jerusalem to remark, "Isn't this the
man they want to kill? 26 But here he is, speaking in public, and they
don't say a word to him! Have even the authorities recognized that this
is truly the Messiah? 27 Yet we know where this man is from. When the
Messiah comes, no one is to know where he is from." 28 At that, Jesus,
who was teaching in the temple area, cried out,

"So you know me
and you know where I am from?
Yet I have not come on my own.
No, there is truly One who sent me,
and Him you do *not* know.
29 I know Him
because it is from Him that I come
and He sent me."

30 Then they tried to arrest him, but no one laid a finger on him because his hour had not yet come. 31 In fact, many in the crowd came to
believe in him. They kept saying, "When the Messiah comes, can he
be expected to perform more signs than this man has performed? 32 The
Pharisees overheard this debate about him among the crowd, so they
[namely, the chief priests and the Pharisees,] sent temple police to
arrest him. 33 Accordingly, Jesus said,

"I am to be with you only a little while longer;
then I am going away to Him who sent me.
34 You will look for me and not find me,
and where I am, you cannot come."

35 That caused the Jews to exclaim to one another, "Where does this
fellow intend to go that we won't find him? Surely he isn't going off to
the Diaspora among the Greeks to teach the Greeks? 36 What is this he
is talking about: 'You will look for me and not find me,' and 'Where I
am, you cannot come'?"

NOTES

vii 14. *half over*. This is the third or fourth day of the week-long feast. It may
have been a Sabbath, whence the reference in vss. 22 ff.

temple precincts. In the Synoptic account of Jesus' (only) stay in Jerusalem,
he teaches in the temple precincts (Mark xi 27).

15. *How did* . . . A similar reaction is recorded in Mark i 22 at Capernaum and vi 2 at Nazareth (see COMMENT on iv 44).

get his education. Literally "know letters." A knowledge of how to read and write was centered about knowledge of the Scriptures, for this is what the children were trained to read. However, this is more than a question about Jesus' literacy; it is a question about his teaching. Before a man became a rabbi, he normally studied diligently under another rabbi; much of the rabbinical learning consisted in knowing the opinions of famous teachers of the past. Yet Jesus had not undergone any such training. Some would connect this question with v 46 where Jesus showed a knowledge of the Scriptures in claiming that Moses had written of him.

16. *comes from.* Literally "is of"; see vss. 27 ff. and the discussion on where Jesus is from.

18. *glory.* This theme is recalled from v 41–47. Here, perhaps, we have the answer to the challenge hurled at Jesus by his brothers in vii 3–5.

he is truthful. We hear in iii 33 and viii 26 that God is truthful; here it is Jesus who is truthful.

dishonesty. The word *adikia* occurs only here in John (Bultmann treats this last line of vs. 18 as redactionary). Many times in LXX *adikia* translates *šeqer*, "lie"; such a connotation would continue the reflection about being truthful. It is interesting to compare this verse with II Sam xiv 32: "If there is *adikia*, let me be put to death"; Jesus argues that since there is no *adikia* in his heart, they should not be looking to kill him (19).

19. *given you the Law.* Jesus, a Jew, seemingly dissociates himself from the heritage of the Law. In the Synoptic tradition what he dissociated himself from was the Pharisees' interpretation of the Law which, in Jesus' opinion, nullified the Law (Matt xxiii 23). But in John such attacks have been colored by the dispute between the Synagogue and the Church, and the dissociation is more absolute (see "*your* Law" in viii 17, x 34; "*their* Law" in xv 25). In Justin's *Dialogue with Trypho* this same "you" is used by the Christian apologist in addressing the Jews.

not one of you keeps the Law. Literally "does the Law"—a good Semitism. This absolute statement is addressed to "the Jews" (15) in the crowd. See Gal ii 14, where Paul says virtually the same thing to Peter.

20. *You're demented.* Literally "You have a demon"; insanity was looked on as a case of possession. We hear the same charge in Mark iii 22 ("He has Beelzebul"), not long after a scene involving a Sabbath healing (iii 1–6).

21. *one work.* Presumably this is the healing of v 1–15. Bernard, I, p. 263, thinks the objection is not so much based on the healing, but on the labor entailed in that healing (Exod xxxi 15: "Everyone who *does work* on the Sabbath day shall be *put to death*.").

shocked. There was no mention of surprise on the part of those who witnessed the miracle in v 1–15.

22. *on that account.* As the standard versification indicates, a tradition illustrated in the versions and supported by some modern commentators (Westcott, Hoskyns) would connect this phrase to the next line: "On that account Moses has given you circumcision."

Patriarchs. Literally "fathers"; see "ancestor" in iv 12. The ordinance prescribing circumcision is in the Law of Moses (Lev xii 3), but the covenant of circumcision was from Abraham's time (Gen xvii 10, xxi 4). See Rom iv.

even on a Sabbath. Circumcision took place on the eighth day after birth; if birth took place on a Sabbath, so did circumcision. Mishnah *Nedarim* 3:11: "R. Jose says, 'Great is circumcision since it overrides the stringent Sabbath.'"

23. *cured.* This Greek word (*hygiēs*) occurs elsewhere in John only in ch. v (5 times).

whole man. This is an argument *a minori ad maius* (from the lesser to the greater), quite common in rabbinic logic. Circumcision affects only a part of the body; if that is permitted, an action affecting the good of the whole body should be permitted. Actually, the rabbis permitted healing practices on the Sabbath when there was immediate danger to life. But in the case envisaged in ch. v, the man had been sick a long time (v 6), and they would argue that Jesus could have waited until another day to heal him (Luke xiii 14).

24. *judge . . . give . . . judgment.* We have tried to preserve the nuance of the present imperative in the first line, and the aorist imperative in the second. A similar appeal for fair judgment is found in the OT: Isa xi 3 (of the messianic king); Zech vii 9; Deut xvi 18.

25. *the people of Jerusalem.* These seem to be a special group in the larger crowd (vs. 12) which would contain visitors as well. Tabernacles was the most important Jewish feast and well-attended. Notice that John presents these Jerusalemites as quite aware that there is a plot to kill Jesus on the part of the authorities.

26. *they don't say a word to him.* There is a rabbinic expression like this, reflecting tacit approval.

the authorities. Literally "rulers," the word used to describe Nicodemus in iii 1. These are "the Jews," but particularly the Sanhedrin members.

27. *where this man is from.* In a primitive civilization without family names, the place of origin is equivalent to an identifying name, e.g., Joseph of Arimathea, Jesus of Nazareth. This is not only biblical usage (Judg xiii 6; Gen xxix 4), but also current use among the Bedouin who often seek a person's identity by asking, "Where are you from?"

no one is to know where he is from. See p. 53 above for the theory of the hidden Messiah. The Jerusalemites think that the well-known fact that Jesus is from Nazareth militates against his being identified as the hidden Messiah.

28. *truly.* *Alēthinos,* taken adverbially. Codex Sinaiticus and P[66] read: "The One who sent me is true [or truthful—*alēthēs*]"; this reading may be under the influence of viii 26.

One who sent me. Here the verb "to send" is *pempein;* in vs. 29 it is *apostellein,* a sign of the interchangeability of the two verbs.

29. *from Him that I come.* Literally "I am from [*para* with genitive] Him." Sinaiticus reads "with [*para* with dative] Him," a reading supported by the OS, Sah. Boismard, *Prologue,* p. 9[1], prefers this as the more difficult reading.

30. *they tried to arrest him.* The "they" presumably refers to the people of Jerusalem, for this attempt seems to be distinct from that of the authorities in vs. 32.

31. *more signs.* There is no indication in the OT that miracles were expected of the Messiah; passages like Isa xxxv 5–6 ("the eyes of the blind shall be opened") were meant figuratively. Yet the idea of a miracle-working Messiah may have developed by NT times; see Mark xiii 22. Note that in vi 15, after the multiplication, the crowd is ready to crown Jesus as the messianic king. There is another possibility, however: from Matt xii 22–23 it seems that the miracles startled people into realizing that someone extraordinary stood before them, and they began to wonder if this extraordinary person might not be the Messiah. Still another possibility is that the picture of the Messiah has been influenced by the picture of the Prophet-like-Moses and of Elijah, for both Moses and Elijah worked miracles.

32. *debate.* See NOTE on vs. 12.

[*namely* . . .] The bracketed phrase is missing in some of the older versions (OS, OL) and patristic citations (Chrysostom); it appears in the majority of Greek mss. but with different word orders. Perhaps the original subject was "they"; but a copyist, realizing that it was not correct to have the Pharisees in charge of the temple police, introduced "the chief priests" into the text, as well as "the Pharisees." Verse 45 may have guided the insertion. Since the priests and Pharisees are pictured as working together, the author of the bracketed phrase is thinking of the Sanhedrin as responsible (xviii 3; see NOTE on iii 1).

temple police. Blinzler, *Trial,* pp. 62–63, distinguishes two groups: (*a*) the temple Levites, used within the temple precincts and occasionally outside during a crisis; (*b*) the police force of the Sanhedrin used to maintain public order in town and country. He maintains that in the NT the word *hypēretai,* used in this verse of John, always refers to the latter. The distinction is artificial, as a careful study of Blinzler's own evidence will indicate. In this very instance the arrest is ordered by Sadducees and Pharisees (therefore by the Sanhedrin) and is within the temple precincts; therefore it has elements from both of Blinzler's proposed divisions.

33. *a little while.* This is a frequent Johannine theme: xii 35, xiii 33, xiv 19, xvi 16.

34. *will look.* Two minor Greek mss. and Jerome's Vulgate read the present tense. Wordsworth and White remark on this, that Jerome at times followed a type of Greek ms. of which we know but little. See NOTE on x 16.

not find me. This second "me" is omitted in many important Greek witnesses but found in Codex Vaticanus and P75.

where I am. One would expect "where I *go*," as in viii 21; and some have suggested that *eimi* here is from the verb *ienai,* "to go," rather than from the more usual *einai,* "to be." However, more likely this reflects the divine use of *egō eimi*—see App. IV. It is Augustine who captures the atemporality of Jesus' statement, "Christ was ever in that place to which he would return" (*In Jo.* XXXI 9; PL 35:1640). There is a certain similarity in theme to Luke xvii 22: "The days are coming when you will desire to see one of the days of the Son of Man, and you will not see it."

35. *Diaspora.* This term refers to the Jews living outside the Holy Land; the expression "Diaspora of Israel" occurs in LXX in Isa xlix 6; Ps cxlvii 2. For the Christian use of the term (i.e., Christians living in the world and away from their home in heaven) see I Pet i 1.

among the Greeks. Literally "of the Greeks." We understand the term to refer to the pagan Gentiles of the Roman Empire who were influenced by Greek culture, and thus to be broader than Greek nationality. In xii 20 the term is used for proselytes (also Acts xvii 4). Some scholars, like J. A. T. Robinson (p. LXXVII above), have suggested that the genitive is explicative: "the Diaspora which consists of Greeks, i.e., Greek-speaking Jews." However, why would the Jerusalem Jews suggest this possibility, namely, that Jesus would go to seek a better hearing among Jews who spoke another language? A far more likely contrast is that he might have a better hearing among Gentiles. Therefore, with BDF, § 166, we take the genitive as one of direction: they are suggesting that Jesus may go off and become one of the Jews of the Diaspora, living among the Gentiles and teaching them.

COMMENT

As we have indicated in the Outline (p. 202), Scene One of Jesus' Discourse during the feast of Tabernacles, set at a time when the feast was half over, may be divided into two parts, each with its own themes. These themes do have a certain, rambling unity; they will return from time to time in the other scenes of this discourse. (As we shall see, there have been various critical attempts to introduce a better sequence by rearrangement; but following our usual policy, we shall treat the material as we find it in the Gospel.) In many ways the discourse at Tabernacles represents a polemic collection of what Jesus said in replies to attacks by the Jewish authorities on his claims. There are scattered parallels in the Synoptic tradition, particularly in the last days of Jesus' life. Because it is argumentative, this discourse differs in style somewhat from previous discourses, for it is constantly broken up by questions and objections. Nevertheless, the familiar Johannine technique of the double stage appears: while Jesus is arguing with the crowd in the foreground, in the background the authorities are plotting his arrest.

Scene One: (a) Jesus' right to teach; resumption of the Sabbath question
(vii 14–24)

This is the part of the discourse with the closest relation to ch. v; as we mentioned on p. 229, many commentators would transfer it to the end of ch. v. In the present sequence of the Gospel considerable time has elapsed since the miracle reported in v 1–15 (about fifteen months, if that feast was Pentecost); yet that miracle seems to be very much the topic of conversation in vii 21. (See also NOTES on vs. 15, "education," vs. 18, "glory.") However, while John has made the Sabbath healing of ch. v the focus of the discussion in vii 21 ff., we may well suspect that we have here a limitation of the topic for dramatic purposes. The evangelist has carefully selected the few signs he narrates (xx 30–31); and in order to simplify the historical picture, he shows these signs as the direct causes of what happened to Jesus. Acting like a good dramatist, the evangelist never clutters the clean lines of his narrative with too many characters or distracting details. The Synoptic Gospels show us that the charge of violating the Sabbath which was hurled against Jesus was not based on a single Sabbath healing but on a consistent practice. By using one miracle as the specific instance on which the argument was based, John is summing up a much larger ministry. Even though John has put the arguments of chs. vii–viii in a specific historical context, the evaluation of these chapters as a collection of typical polemic warns us against too precise a dependence on the chronological relations between the healing of ch. v and the discussion of ch. vii. We need not worry whether "the Jews" who had seen the miracle a long time before would still be thinking about it; the Christian reader for whom the Gospel was organized (xx 31) would easily see the relation between this discourse and the miracle of which he had read a mere hundred lines before.

The first lines of this scene of the discourse (vs. 15) are centered on the charge that Jesus was an irregular teacher since he had not received his doctrine from a recognized master. Jesus' answer (16) is that he has received his doctrine from a recognized master, namely, his heavenly Father. He has been in the best of all rabbinical schools. The only proof that he offers for his claim (17–18) is the same type of witness he offered in ch. v. There it was a question of having the love or the word of God in one's heart (v 42, 38) and of being intent on seeking God's glory (v 44), for such qualities would enable men to recognize that Jesus had come in the name of the Father (v 43). In vii 17 we are told that anyone who does God's will will recognize that Jesus' doctrine comes from the Father. These requirements are simply variants of the fundamental requirement—being attuned to God's voice in order to recognize one who speaks for God. Doing God's will is more than ethical obedience; it involves the acceptance through faith of the whole divine plan of salvation, including Jesus' work (v 30). We may note that doing God's will is also mentioned in the Synoptic tradition, but there it is a condition for entrance into the kingdom of heaven (Matt vii 21). As we have remarked, the Synoptic picture of the kingdom of heaven shares many features with the Johannine picture of Jesus himself.

The reference to Moses and the Law in vs. 19 is another reason why scholars suggest that this part of the discourse was once connected to the end of ch. v, where Moses is mentioned. However, it is quite possible that the contrast between Jesus' education and the standard training of the Jewish teachers could have led logically to a reference to Moses, for the Law of Moses was the basis of formal education. What is the reason for Jesus' charge that "the Jews" are not keeping the Law? Perhaps this is a general denunciation in the style of Jer v 5, ix 4–6, etc. Some have thought that Jesus is accusing the Jews of breaking the spirit of the Sabbath by not wanting to see a man healed on the Sabbath (see vs. 23). More likely the final line of vs. 19 is the key to the answer. In desiring to kill Jesus (v 18, vii 1) they are violating one of the Commandments. Is John giving us a historical reminiscence in thus picturing a prolonged hostility to Jesus at Jerusalem, even to the point of assassination? The Synoptics, of course, give us no information about the Jerusalem ministry except in the last days, and they concentrate their description of the plot to kill Jesus in that final period. However, Luke iv 29 reports an attempt on Jesus' life in Galilee, a region where we might expect religious feeling to be less acute than in Jerusalem. And we have seen that after the death of John the Baptist, Jesus felt it safer to withdraw from Galilee and the territory ruled by Herod (also Luke xiii 31). Arguing from the Synoptic picture of hostility during the Galilean ministry, we may well suspect that John is giving us reliable tradition in not confining the plot at Jerusalem to kill Jesus to the last days of the ministry.

In vs. 20 the crowd denies any such plot. If this crowd is distinguished from "the Jews" and from "the people of Jerusalem" (25) who knew of the plot, it is quite plausible that there were many, especially pilgrims, who knew nothing about an intent to kill Jesus. But, even if Jesus is speaking primarily to "the Jews," that is, the authorities, the fact remains that in the gospel picture by the end of the Jerusalem ministry *the crowd* will have been swayed by the authorities to ask for Jesus' death (Mark xv 11).

The objection of the crowd causes Jesus to be specific (21) and to recall the past instance of a Sabbath healing for which they had decided to kill him (v 18). The argument that Jesus uses here (22–23) to defend his healing on the Sabbath is less theological than that advanced in v 17, and may be classed with the humanitarian arguments found in the Synoptics (see p. 216). Nevertheless, is it coincidental that the contrast between the *partial* character of the circumcision they permitted on the Sabbath and Jesus' curing of the *whole* man is quite like the contrast between Moses and Jesus found elsewhere in John (i 17)? In general, we believe that John succeeds better than do the Synoptics in unfolding the purpose of healing on the Sabbath. It was not primarily a question of a sentimental liberalizing of a harsh and impractical law. His miracles on the Sabbath were the accomplishment of the redemptive purpose for which the Law was given (Barrett, p. 265).

Scene One: (b) The origins of Jesus; his return to the Father (vii 25–36)

In this part we hear no more of the Sabbath miracle, and the theme shifts to Jesus' person. Perhaps the logic is that in reiterating his Sabbath rights, Jesus has once more betrayed his claims about who he is, even as in v 17–18. The topic of Jesus' person and his claims is a most sensitive one to "the Jews"; hence the hostility mounts dramatically in this scene, and the first attempt to arrest Jesus is recorded. The various confident assertions of the people of Jerusalem and of the Jews concerning Jesus are, in typical Johannine style, shown to betray ignorance, the ignorance of human wisdom when shown up in the penetrating light of incarnate Wisdom.

We see this first in the assertion in vs. 27 that they know where Jesus is from (Nazareth) and that therefore he cannot be the hidden Messiah. Their thought is on the earthly level; they are giving a perfect instance of that judging by appearances against which they were warned in vs. 24. They spoke the truth when they said that no one was to know where the Messiah was from, and actually *they do not know* that Jesus is from heaven and from the Father. Once again in vs. 29 we have an affirmation of Jesus' unique and intimate knowledge of the Father (i 18, vi 46, viii 25, xvii 25). The Synoptic parallel is in the so-called Johannine logion (Matt xi 27; Luke x 22): "No one knows the Father except the Son and any one to whom the Son chooses to reveal Him."

Jesus' claim to divine origins provokes the attempt to arrest him (30), an attempt which betrays Jesus' sovereign power. Even when his hour has come, John will still show that no one can lay a hand on Jesus until he permits it (xviii 6–8). Luke iv 29–30 portrays a similar incapacity of the enemies of Jesus who tried to harm him at Nazareth. The more formal attempt against Jesus by the Sanhedrin authorities in vs. 32 will not be successful either, as we shall see in vii 45 ff.

These attempts on his life lead Jesus in vss. 33–34 to think of his return by death and resurrection to his Father. The verb "to go away," used in vs. 33, will be found in xiii 3 where, in the context of the hour, Jesus says that he is going away to God. The return to the Father will take away from his hearers their opportunity to believe in him. As he stands before them, he is seeking them out; but when he is gone, they will do the seeking, and they will not find. Once more Jesus' remarks are misunderstood to have been spoken on an earthly level, for "the Jews" think that he is speaking of going away on a journey to some other land. This time Jesus does not reply to their confusion because ironically they have spoken the truth. Their sneering suggestion that Jesus might go off to teach the Gentile world had become a reality by the time the Fourth Gospel was written. The Christian Church which the evangelist sees about him in the Roman Empire is largely Gentile, and the Diaspora of the dispersed sons of God gathered by Jesus into one (xi 52) has truly been a Diaspora of the Greeks.

In closing our remarks on this second part of Scene One of the discourse, we should point out that the theme of Jesus as divine Wisdom is very strong here and underlies many of the statements. The question of where Jesus is from in vss. 27 ff. reminds us of Job xxviii 12 ff. which raises the question of where Wisdom can be found; also Bar iii 14–15: "Learn where Wisdom is. . . . Who can find her location?" Just as Jesus has been sent from God (29) to be with men (33), so in the OT man prays to God that Wisdom be sent from heaven to be with him (Wis ix 10; Sir xxiv 8). The theme of looking for and finding (34) is frequent in the OT. In some of the biblical books the theme centers on a search for the Lord, for example, Isa lv 6: "Look for the Lord while He may be found" (also Hos v 6; Deut iv 29). But in the sapiential literature the theme is transferred to Wisdom. In Wis vi 12 we hear that Wisdom "is easily seen by those who love her, and found by those who look for her." Jesus' words in vs. 34 are very much like those of Wisdom in Prov i 28–29: "They may look for me, but they shall not find me because they hated knowledge and have not revered the Lord."

[The Bibliography for this section is included in the Bibliography for ch. vii, at the end of § 29.]

29. JESUS AT TABERNACLES:—SCENE TWO
(vii 37–52)

Jesus on the last day of the feast

VII 37 On the last and greatest day of the festival Jesus stood up and cried out,

"If anyone thirst, let him come [to me];
and let him drink 38 who believes in me.
As the Scripture says,
'From within him shall flow rivers of living water.'"

(39 Here he was referring to the Spirit which those who came to believe in him were to receive. For there was as yet no Spirit, since Jesus had not been glorified.)

40 Some of the crowd who heard [these words] began to say, "This is undoubtedly the Prophet." 41 Others were claiming, "This is the Messiah." But an objection was raised: "Surely the Messiah isn't to come from Galilee? 42 Doesn't Scripture say that the Messiah, being of David's family, is to come from Bethlehem, the village where David lived?" 43 Thus, the crowd was sharply divided because of him. 44 Some of them even wanted to arrest him; yet no one laid hands on him.

45 And so, when the temple police came back, the chief priests and Pharisees asked them, "Why didn't you bring him in?" 46 "Never has a man spoken like this," replied the police. 47 "Don't tell us you have been fooled too!" the Pharisees retorted. 48 "You don't see any of the Sanhedrin believing in him, do you? Or any of the Pharisees? 49 No, it's just this mob which knows nothing of the Law—and they are damned!" 50 One of their own number, Nicodemus (the man who had come to him), spoke up, 51 "Since when does our Law condemn any man without first hearing him and knowing the facts?" 52 "Don't tell us that you are a Galilean too," they taunted him. "Look it up and you won't find the Prophet arising in Galilee."

50: *spoke up.* In the historical present tense.

NOTES

vii 37. *last and greatest day.* Is this the 7th or the 8th day (see NOTE on vii 2)? Since the 8th day was a later addition to the feast, it was more a day of rest than of festival. As we shall see in the COMMENT, Jesus' words on this occasion fit the ceremonies of the 7th day. The designation "the greatest day" also matches the 7th day better. In fact, since "and the greatest" is missing in some minor witnesses, this phrase may even be a later addition to specify that the 7th day was meant.

stood up. We are probably to think that Jesus had been sitting and teaching in the temple precincts. (See NOTE on vi 3.)

cried out. This verb was used of John the Baptist in i 15; in this chapter it is used twice of Jesus (vii 28 and here; again in xii 44) when he makes a solemn proclamation of a truth concerning his person and work.

If anyone thirst . . . water. These four poetic lines of vss. 37–38 have been the occasion of protracted discussion and an immense literature. There are two basic problems of interpretation which must be discussed at length.

First, *who is the source of the rivers of living water, Jesus or the believer?* (*a*) The translation that we have given favors the theory that Jesus is the source (the "christological" interpretation). As H. Rahner has shown (also Boismard, "De son ventre," pp. 523–35), this interpretation goes back to the 2nd century and the time of Justin. We may now have another 2nd-century witness in the *Gospel of Thomas,* 13, where Jesus says: "You have drunk from the bubbling spring which I have measured out." While this reflects a melange of Johannine verses (e.g., iv 14), it does make Jesus the source of water. (See our article in NTS 9 [1962–63], 162.) Other early support for this interpretation, sometimes called the Western interpretation, is found in Hippolytus, Tertullian, Cyprian, Irenaeus, Aphraates, Ephraem. Among the modern commentators who accept it are Boismard, Braun, Bultmann, Dodd, Hoskyns, Jeremias, Macgregor, Mollat, Stanley. The following arguments may be advanced for the christological interpretation: (1) It gives excellent poetic parallelism in the first two lines: the thirsty man in line one comes to Jesus, and the believer in line two drinks from Jesus. That the parallelism is chiastic fits Johannine style (see p. cxxxv). (2) The idea that water will flow from Jesus is supported by xix 34, where it comes from his side. (3) Another Johannine work, Rev xxii 1, shows a river of living water flowing from the throne of God and of the Lamb (i.e., Christ). (4) According to vii 39, the water is the Spirit, and for John it is Jesus who gives the Spirit (xix 30, xx 22).

(*b*) The Greek can be translated in another way which favors making the believer the source of the water:

If anyone thirst, let him come to me and drink.
38 He who believes in me (as the Scripture says),
"From within him shall flow rivers of living water."

This punctuation was supported by Origen and runs through most of the Eastern Fathers. Among the modern commentators who follow it are Barrett, Behm, Bernard, Cortés Quirant, Lightfoot, Michaelis, Rengstorf, Schlatter, Schweizer, Zahn. It is followed by the standard American Catholic (Confraternity) and Protestant (RSV) versions. The best textual argument for it is that this punctuation is found in P[66] (2nd century). One grammatical argument for it is that it makes the participle *ho pisteuōn* ("he who believes") the head of a new construction (a pattern found forty-one times in John), rather than tacking it on to the previous conditional sentence (a practice seemingly not found in John). On the other hand, however, Kilpatrick, *art. cit.*, has shown that making the participle the anticipated subject of the Scripture citation (as must be done in this interpretation) has little support in Johannine style. BDF, § 466⁴, has attempted to defend such an anacoluthon, but the examples offered as parallels are not really apropos for the peculiar instance under discussion. Thus the grammatic arguments really cancel one another out. Is there any parallel in John for the idea of living water flowing from the believer? (There is a parallel in roughly contemporary rabbinic thought; according to Midrash Sifre on Deut xi 22, ⁂48, Rabbi Aqiba said: "The disciple who is beginning is like a well who can give only the water it has received; the more advanced disciple is a spring giving living water.") Many cite John iv 14 (so Cortés Quirant, pp. 293 ff.) where Jesus speaks of a fountain of water within the believer leaping up unto eternal life. However, there is no suggestion in this verse that the believer will be a source for others. Another text cited, xiv 12, seems too general to be probative. When all is said, the best argument for this interpretation is the strong patristic support that it has had. Yet much of this support flows from the initial impetus of the very influential Origen. He saw in vii 37–38 an echo of Philo's doctrine that the perfect Gnostic could become, through his spiritual understanding of the Scriptures, a bubbling source of light and knowledge for others. Such an understanding of John is not very persuasive.

(*c*) There is still a third way to translate the Greek, one that gives no definite indication as to the identity of the source of the water:

> If anyone thirst, let him come to me and drink (i.e.,
>   he who believes in me).
> As the Scripture says, "From within him shall flow rivers
>   of living water."

This translation avoids the objection raised by Kilpatrick against the previous translation: the participle *ho pisteuōn* is no longer the anticipated subject of the Scripture citation, but a clarification of the subject of the verbs "to come" and "to drink." Kilpatrick shows that the participle can serve as subject of both verbs, but his examples of such a participle resuming the indefinite "anyone" are weak. Blenkinsopp, "Crux," defends a translation similar to this, but he insists that "he who believes in me" has no syntactic nexus with the sentence—it is merely a parenthetical explanation drawn from the "those who believe" in vs. 39. There is some versional evidence in the Latin and Syriac for omitting "he who believes in me"; this evidence is not sufficiently strong to make the participle textually doubtful, but it may give support to seeing it as merely parenthetical. Of course, this translation of the Greek loses the almost perfect parallelism that we have posited in our translation. It does nothing to identify the "him" of the Scripture citation; but it seems that once the participle is treated as parenthetical, there is little reason for supposing that the "him" of the citation is the believer.

Second, *what passage of Scripture is cited in vs. 38?* Obviously, the answer to this question will reflect on the first question. The words quoted in John do not reflect exactly any one passage in MT or LXX, and so commentators have had to use a certain ingenuity in tracking down passages that are at least similar.

Those who think of the believer as the source of the water often suggest Prov xviii 4: "The words of a man's mouth are deep waters; the fountain of wisdom is a gushing stream." Isa lviii 11 is worth considering as background; there God promises the Israelite of eschatological times, "You shall be . . . like a spring of water whose waters fail not." Sir xxiv 30–33 (28–31) makes the disciple of Wisdom a channel bringing the waters of Wisdom to others. 1QH viii 16 says, "You, O my God, have put into my mouth, as it were, rain for all [who thirst], and a fount of living waters which shall not fail." One passage that has often been cited is Prov v 15, "Drink water from your own cistern, flowing water from your own well"; but the resemblance to John is only verbal, for the Proverbs text is an injunction against adultery ("cistern/well"=one's wife).

A more plausible direction in which to seek the background of John's Scripture citation is in the various descriptions of the scene that took place during the Exodus when Moses struck the rock and water flowed from it. This rock was seen in the early Church as a type of Christ (I Cor x 4), and therefore this background would favor the christological interpretation of the source in John's citation. Braun, JeanThéol, I, p. 150, mentions that the rock of the desert wanderings was the most frequently painted OT symbol in the catacombs. Frequently it was connected with Baptism through the interpretation of John vii 38. Such symbolism would fit in well with John's predilection for symbols taken from the narratives of the Exodus (i 29: the paschal lamb; iii 14: the brazen serpent; vi 31: the manna; vi 16–21: the crossing of the Reed Sea?). It is perhaps in the poetic commentaries found in the Psalms on the water-from-the-rock theme that we have the best parallels to the wording of John vii. Ps cv 40–41 says: "He gave them their fill of bread from heaven; he cleft the rock and the water flowed forth." This sequence of bread from heaven and water from the rock is exactly the sequence we have in chs. vi and vii of John (a reason, incidentally, for not changing the present sequence of the chapters). Other passages describing the water from the rock are Isa xliii 20, xliv 3, xlviii 21; Deut viii 15; and Aileen Guilding, p. 103, has pointed out that several of these passages were used as synagogue readings in the month when Tabernacles was celebrated. Ps cxiv, whose vs. 8 mentions how God turned the flint rock into a spring of water, was one of the Hallel psalms sung by the pilgrims in the daily processions during Tabernacles.

The passage dealing with the rock of the desert that is perhaps the closest to a verbal parallel to John is Ps lxxviii 15–16: "He cleft the rock in the desert and gave them to drink in copious floods. He led forth streams [LXX, water] from the cliff and brought forth, as it were, *rivers of water.*" (A few verses later in the Psalm, vs. 24, we hear: "He rained manna upon them to eat and gave them the bread of heaven"—see NOTE on vi 31.) Although this standard translation of the Hebrew of the psalm is already like John vii 38, the likeness can be greatly magnified if one accepts the thesis advanced by Boismard that Jesus is really citing a Targum or Aramaic translation of the psalm. According to Boismard the Aramaic may be translated thus: "He led forth streams of water from the rock; and he brought down, as it were, *rivers of flowing water.*" Now, when Jesus was speaking to the people, undoubtedly he often used the Aramaic Scriptures for intelligibility (see NOTE on iii 14), although we might expect this more in Galilee than in Jerusalem. However, not all agree with Boismard's understanding of the Targum (the Targum he cites is quite late). See the controversy with Grelot in the articles cited in the Bibliography.

Another important Scripture passage cited as possible background for John vii 38 comes from the second part of Zechariah (xiv 8). This is an interesting suggestion, for, as we shall point out in the COMMENT, this part of Zechariah builds up a mystique about the feast of Tabernacles. Feuillet has worked out the connection between John and Zechariah by way of Rev xxii 1, 17. He points out that Rev xxii 17 offers the same type of parallelism that we have suggested for John in our translation:

> Let him who is thirsty come;
> let him who wishes take the water of life without price.

If we add this verse to Rev xxii 1, "He showed me the river of life . . . flowing from the throne of God and of the Lamb," we have a very close parallel for the ideas and words of John vii 37–38. Now this chapter in Revelation has its background in Ezekiel and Zechariah (Rev xxii 2=Ezek xlvii 12; Rev xxii 3=Zech xiv 11). In particular, the river described in Revelation as flowing from the throne of God and of the Lamb is a re-use of the symbol of the river in Ezek xlvii; and "the water of life" echoes Zech xiv 8. Feuillet argues that we should attribute this same background, particularly that of Zechariah, to John vii 37–38. This is not out of place in John, for this Gospel draws freely on Zechariah both implicitly (see COMMENT on ii 16) and explicitly (xix 37).

Daniélou, *art. cit.*, argues more strongly than does Feuillet for the dependence of John upon Ezek xlvii 1–11, a passage well known in early Christian literature. In his view Jesus would be the source of the water in the sense that he would be the temple rock from which, in Ezekiel's imagery, the river flows that is the source of life. We have already seen Jesus identified as the Temple in John ii 21; see Daniélou for the patristic tradition identifying Jesus with the temple rock.

In searching for the background of Jesus as the source of living water, must one choose between the rock of the desert and the apocalyptic passages of Zechariah and Ezekiel with their eschatological rivers of living water flowing out of Jerusalem and the Temple? In his 1963 article Grelot shows that in the rabbinic traditions of the Tosephta the texts associated with Tabernacles recalled both motifs. He thinks that this combination of motifs goes back to a period before the destruction of the Temple, and thus John may be reflecting both themes. Citations of two or more passages in combination are not unheard of in John (see xix 36); and we have seen that the background for other Johannine symbolism, like that of the Lamb of God, is also composite (*apocalyptic lamb; suffering servant; paschal lamb*).

38. *From within him.* Literally "from his belly [*koilia*]." Some claim that this is tantamount to "from his heart," since, while for the Hebrews the belly is the seat of man's emotional nature, the heart has the same role in Western symbolism. Behm, TWNT, III, p. 788, shows that in LXX "belly" is often employed in the same sense as "heart"; and even in the NT they are somewhat interchangeable, e.g., Codex Alexandrinus has "heart" in Rev x 9 while other manuscripts read "belly." However, Boismard, "De son ventre," p. 541, shows that this metaphorical use of "belly" is confined with rare exception to passages describing strong emotions. Daniélou, p. 161, in line with the theory proposed above, thinks of a cavity or cave in the temple rock from which the water flows; and he compares this to the cavity in the side of Jesus opened by the centurion's lance in xix 34, a cavity from which water flows. (Most authors agree on the connection between vii 38 and xix 34.) Still another possibility has been suggested by scholars like Torrey, Boismard, Grelot, and Feuillet: they believe that "from his belly" is an overliteral translation from Aramaic. The same Aramaic expression, *min giwwēh*, can mean "from within him" and "from his belly." This

suggestion implies that John is giving the Scripture citation from the Targum. In the same line of thought StB, II, p. 492, followed by Jeremias and Bultmann, associate *koilia* with the Aram. *gûf*, "body, person, self." The normal Greek translation of this word, however, would be *sōma*, not *koilia*.

39. *the Spirit*. The symbolism whereby water stands for spirit seems strange to the Western mind but is well attested in Hebrew, as Audet, *art. cit.*, has pointed out. Verbs applicable to water are used to describe the gift of the spirit, e.g., poured forth (Isa xliv 3). The soul, *nefeš* (which can also be translated as "spirit"), was looked on as the seat of thirst, since *nefeš* seems originally to have meant "throat." Isa xxix 8 says, "A thirsty man dreams he is drinking but wakes up with a dry *nefeš*"; Ps xlii 1–2: "As a hart longs for streams of water . . . my *nefeš* thirsts for you, O God." As OT background for the juxtaposition of ideas in John vii 38–39 (water from the belly=spirit), we may cite Prov xx 27: "The *breath* [another synonym for "spirit"] of man is the lamp of the Lord, searching all the inner parts of his *belly.*" *Nefeš*, besides being the seat of thirst, is also the source of words, e.g., I Sam i 15 says that Hannah has been pouring out her *nefeš* before the Lord in the words of her prayer (notice the water symbolism). This is background for our contention in the COMMENT that the water of vs. 38 stands both for the Spirit and for Jesus' teaching.

who came to believe. We read the aorist participle, supported by both Bodmer papyri, rather than the present. Clearly the parenthetical comment is from a later viewpoint. Interestingly, Bultmann, p. 229[2], attributes vs. 39 to the evangelist and not to the redactor; Bultmann regards the Scripture citation of vs. 38 as the redactional part of the passage.

there was as yet no Spirit. Some manuscripts and versions seek to soften the impact of this, e.g., "the Spirit was not yet *given*" or "not yet *on them*." Probably the scribes saw a theological difficulty, as if John were saying that the Third Person of the Trinity did not exist before Jesus was glorified in passion, death, and resurrection. But a gospel statement such as this is not concerned with the inner life of God; it is concerned with God's relation to us. The Spirit was not a reality as far as man was concerned until the glorified Jesus would communicate the Spirit to men (xx 22). Then the Spirit would operate in a new creation in a way not hitherto possible (see articles by Hooke and Woodhouse).

40. *[these words]*. There are many variants in the witnesses in reporting these words, and they are omitted in the OS[sin]; they are probably a later clarification added by copyists.

the Prophet. See p. 49.

42. *Scripture*. Matthew ii 5–6 is another witness to the popular belief in the 1st century that the Messiah would be born at Bethlehem. The passage cited in Matthew is Mic v 2(1H). In mentioning Bethlehem this passage originally meant no more than a reference to the Davidic origin of the anointed ruler, but in subsequent centuries it seemingly was taken literally as a prediction that the Messiah would actually be born in that town. Strangely, however, Mic v 2 does not make its appearance in rabbinic literature about the Messiah till quite late.

where David lived. There is some minor support in the versions for reading "of David," or "where he lived"; these variants cause SB to omit the phrase.

44. *Some of them*. Presumably, of the crowd; we found the same vagueness in the "they" of vs. 30.

hands. In vs. 30 the singular was used (we translated as "finger"); here the plural is used.

45. *when the temple police came back.* According to the chronology of vs. 37, this is four days after they were sent out. Obviously the arrangement is artificial.

the chief priests and Pharisees. One article governs the two nouns, a detail which gives the impression that they are very much together in this action.

46. *spoken like this.* In Matt vii 29 the Galilean crowds exclaimed that he was teaching them as if he had authority, and not as their scribes.

48. *Sanhedrin . . . Pharisees.* "Sanhedrin" is literally "authorities." There were members of the party of the Pharisees in the Sanhedrin, but here the general party of the Pharisees is meant. Verse 50 points out that, ironically, one of the Sanhedrin did believe in him; see also xii 42.

49. *this mob which knows nothing of the Law.* See StB, II, p. 494, for rabbinic passages attesting the contempt of those educated in the Law for the ordinary, untutored people (*'am hā'āreṣ,* "people of the land") who were often careless about the Law. These "people of the land" were contrasted with the "students of the wise," and *Pirqe Aboth,* ii 6, says that the former could not be saintly. (The poor who were ignorant of the Law were already a problem in Jeremiah's time—see Jer v 4 where Jeremiah seeks to excuse them.) In fact, of course, many of the Pharisees would not have shared this contempt for the ignorant.

and they are damned. Perhaps this curse may be associated with passages like Deut xxvii 26, xxviii 15; Ps cxix 21 which curse those who do not conform to the Law.

50. *One of their own number.* This phrase is in another order in some manuscripts, and is missing in some of the Syriac evidence; it may be a clarifying gloss.

(*the man who had come to him*). An additional indication like "previously," "at night," or "first" appears in many witnesses, but the variance suggests that we are dealing with copyists' clarifications. This parenthesis is an instance of the common Johannine practice of identifying characters already encountered; see xix 39.

51. *without first hearing him.* (There is some slight evidence in the versions for omitting "first.") Exodus xxiii 1 warns against false reports; Deut i 16 has an implicit direction to hear both sides of a case. The rabbinic principle is found in the words of Rabbi Eleazar ben Pedath in Midrash Rabbah on Exod xxi 3: "Unless a mortal hears the pleas that a man can put forward, he is not able to give judgment."

52. *Look it up.* The witnesses of the Western tradition add "in the Scriptures"; this is what is meant, but the phrase is a copyist's clarification.

the Prophet. The vast majority of witnesses read "a Prophet"; but we accept the reading of the two Bodmer papyri (see Smothers, *art. cit.*), for the Johannine concept of *the* Prophet-like-Moses could easily have been misunderstood in the process of copying. The more common reading suggests that no prophet would ever come from Galilee. This had not been true in the past, for Jonah was from Gathhepher, a Galilean town (II Kings xiv 25). It also seems to run against the later idea that Israel had no town or tribe from which a prophet had not come (TalBab *Sukkah* 27b).

COMMENT

Background of the Feast of Tabernacles

To understand what Jesus says in vii 37–38 and later in ch. viii, one must have an intimate knowledge of the celebration of Tabernacles. A convenient treatment is that of G. W. MacRae in CBQ 22 (1960), 251–76. In Jesus' time this was the feast "especially sacred and important to the Hebrews" (Josephus *Ant*. VIII.ıv.1;⁂100). The importance of Tabernacles can be traced into the pre-exilic period; for the dedication of Solomon's Temple took place at Tabernacles (I Kings viii 2), and this gave the feast a special relation to the Temple.

The feast was also associated with the triumphant "day of the Lord." In the setting of Tabernacles Zech ix–xiv describes the triumph of Yahweh: the messianic king comes to Jerusalem, triumphant and riding on an ass (ix 9); Yahweh pours out a spirit of compassion and supplication on Jerusalem (xii 10); He opens up a fountain for the house of David to cleanse Jerusalem (xiii 1); living waters flow out from Jerusalem to the Mediterranean and the Dead Sea (xiv 8); and finally, when all enemies are destroyed, people come up year after year to Jerusalem to keep Tabernacles properly (xiv 16). In this ideal feast of Tabernacles everything in Jerusalem is holy, and there are no more merchants in the Temple (xiv 20–21). The reader will have noticed that the NT picks up many of these themes from Zechariah, and we mentioned in the NOTE that Zech xiv is probably the background not only for John vii 38 but also for Rev xxii. In a recent article C. W. F. Smith has shown the implicit use of the motif of Tabernacles in Mark; and in MD 46 (1956), 114–36, in an extremely important article, Daniélou traces the enduring importance of the feast of Tabernacles among the Jewish Christians. The messianic interest in Tabernacles persisted into the later centuries of Judaism as well. A statement is associated with the 4th-century Rabbi Abba bar Kahana (StB, II, p. 793) that the feast holds within itself the promise of the Messiah. The pseudo-Messiah Bar-Kochba (Ben Kosiba) used symbols from Tabernacles on his coins in the Second Jewish Revolt (A.D. 132–35).

Of particular importance for our purposes are the ceremonies that sprang up in connection with the celebration of Tabernacles at Jerusalem. (See StB, II, pp. 774–812; Jeremias, TWNT, IV, pp. 281–82; and Bornhaüser's commentary on the Mishnaic tractate *Sukkah* in the Töpelmann edition.) The old agricultural background of Tabernacles as the autumnal harvest feast made it adaptable to becoming the occasion of prayers for rain. Tabernacles came at the end of September or early October; and if rain fell during this time, it was looked on as an assurance of abundant early rains, so necessary for fertile crops the following year. Even today, as bitterly as the Jordanian Arabs hate the Israelis, they watch carefully to see if rain falls during the Israeli celebration of Tabernacles as a sign of the weather to come. In line with this belief we find in Zech x 1 instructions to pray for rain, and in xiv 17 a warning that there will be no rain for those who do not come to Jerusalem to celebrate the ideal feast of Tabernacles. The fountain of waters that overflows from Jerusalem, mentioned above as part of Zechariah's vision, can be interpreted against the background of abundant rain sent by God during Tabernacles.

During the feast this was dramatized by a solemn ceremony. On each of the seven mornings a procession went down to the fountain of Gihon on the southeast side of the temple hill, the fountain which supplied the waters to the pool of Siloam. There a priest filled a golden pitcher with water, as the choir repeated Isa xii 3: "With joy you will draw water from the wells of salvation." Then the procession went up to the Temple through the Water Gate. The accompanying crowds carried the symbols of Tabernacles, namely, in the right hand the *lulab*, which was a bunch of myrtle and willow twigs tied with palm (a reminiscence of the branches used to construct the huts—see NOTE on vs. 2), and in the left hand the *ethrog*, which was a lemon or citron serving as a sign of the harvest. They also sang the Hallel psalms (cxiii–cxviii). When they reached the altar of holocausts in front of the Temple, they proceeded around the altar waving the *lulabs* and singing Ps cxviii 25. Then the priest went up the ramp to the altar to pour the water into a silver funnel whence it flowed into the ground. On the seventh day there was a sevenfold circumambulation of the altar.

Jesus, the Source of Living Water (i.e., of Wisdom and of the Spirit):
vii 37–39

It was at this solemn moment in the ceremonies on the seventh day that the teacher from Galilee stood up in the temple court to proclaim solemnly that he was the source of living water (see NOTE for this interpretation). Their prayers for water had been answered in a way they did not expect; the feast that contained within itself the promise of the Messiah had been fulfilled. Zech xiv 8 had predicted that living waters would flow out of Jerusalem, and Ezek xlvii 1 had seen a river flow from the rock underneath the Temple. But now Jesus says that these rivers of living water will flow from his own body, that body which is the new Temple (ii 21). In the desert wanderings which this feast recalled, Moses had satiated the thirst of the Israelites by striking a rock from which he brought forth rivers of living water (Ps lxxviii 16—see NOTE). Now those who thirst need only come to Jesus, and through belief the water of life will be theirs. Just as the manna given to their ancestors in the desert had not been the real bread from heaven (vi 32), so the water from the rock was only a foreshadowing of the true water of life that flows from the Lamb (see Rev vii 17, xxii 1).

What does Jesus mean by "living water"? Verse 39 identifies the water as the Spirit; yet 39 has a parenthetical character which makes us wonder if it represents the primary meaning of 37–38. In our NOTE, where we sought the Scripture background posited in 38, we saw that a number of texts from the Wisdom Literature of the OT could be cited. Abstracting from the fact that these texts are often championed by those who think that the believer is the source of the streams of water, we may nevertheless use these texts to support the suggestion that the water spoken of in 38 is capable of a sapiential interpretation. On pp. 178–79 we saw that the living water of iv 10–14 referred not only to the Spirit but also to Jesus' revelation or teaching, and we cited numerous OT texts to establish this point. These texts are applicable here too and make us think that the water of vii 38 may also refer to Jesus' revelation.

There are a number of details in the immediate context that confirm this. We saw that the looking-finding theme of vii 34 was a wisdom theme (p. 318). It is to be noted that in vs. 37 John says that Jesus stood up and cried out. We may call attention to the passages in Proverbs where Wisdom *sings out* her invitation to men (i 20; and viii 2–3 where she *stands up* and sings out). In Prov ix 3 ff. Wisdom invites the simple, "Come, eat of my food and drink of the wine I have mixed" (also Sir li 23); such invitations resemble that of Jesus in 37–38. We are reminded, too, of the invitation to obtain wisdom in Isa lv 1: "Everyone who thirsts, come to the waters." We have mentioned the use in Qumran and rabbinic circles of (living) water as a symbol of the Law. Old Testament passages like Jer ii 13 left themselves open to reinterpretation in this light: "They have forsaken me, the fountain of living waters, and hewed out cisterns for themselves, broken cisterns that can hold no water." (According to Miss Guilding, p. 105, Jer ii was one of the synagogue *haphtaroth* for Tabernacles, and many have cited it in relation to the Scripture quotation of John vii 38.) The Johannine symbolism where the water flows from Jesus' belly (see NOTE on vs. 38, "from within him") offers no particular difficulty to a sapiential interpretation of the water; for instance, Ps xl 8 says, "Your Law is in my belly." Thus, Jesus' presentation of his revelation as living water may be by way of contrast with Jewish thought about the Law. There are several references to the Law in this same chapter of John (vii 19, 49).

If the water is a symbol of the revelation that Jesus gives to those who believe in him, it is also a symbol of the Spirit that the resurrected Jesus will give, as vs. 39 specifies. At the moment of his death Jesus will hand over the Spirit (xix 30), even as water will come from his side (xix 34). I John v 7 brings together the themes of the Spirit and of the blood and water from the side of Jesus: "There are three witnesses: the Spirit, and water, and blood; and these three are of one accord." On p. 140 we gave a number of OT texts which use the imagery of water for the pouring forth of God's spirit. To these we may add Isa xliv 3, which according to Miss Guilding, p. 105, may have been a synagogal *haphtarah* for the month of Tabernacles: "I shall pour water on the thirsty land, and streams on the dry ground; I shall pour my *spirit* on your descendants." In connection with the water ceremonies at the feast of Tabernacles, the TalJer (*Sukkah* 55a) says that the part of the temple precincts traversed during the procession with the water was called the "Place of Drawing," because from there "they drew *the holy spirit*" (also Midrash Rabbah lxx 8 on Gen xxix 1). There is an interesting historical by-product of the recognition that the water stood for the Holy Spirit. We mentioned in the NOTE that the majority of the Eastern Fathers interpreted vs. 38 to mean that the believer, not Jesus, was the source of the water; one reason for this view was the controversy about the processions in the Trinity in which the Greeks held that the Holy Spirit does not proceed from the Son.

■ ■ ■

If the water of vii 37–39 stands for both Jesus' revelation and the Spirit (as also in ch. iv), is there a baptismal symbolism to be found in these verses? Obviously, if the water refers to the Spirit, we cannot simply identify this water with baptismal water which *communicates* the Spirit. Nevertheless, we are not averse to seeing a broad sacramental symbolism here in the sense that this passage of John would have led the early Christian readers to think of Baptism, much as in ch. iv (see p. 179). As we mentioned, Braun, JeanThéol, I, p. 150, thinks that this text played a role in the early baptismal art of the catacombs. By way of internal indications within the Gospel, there is a close relationship between vii 37–39 and xix 34; and the latter has such strong baptismal significance that Bultmann treats it as a sacramental addition by the Ecclesiastical Redactor. Moreover, it seems that the typology of the rock of the Exodus wanderings lies behind the Scripture citation in vs. 39; and the early Church drew heavily on such Exodus typology to explain Baptism (Pauline epistles; I Peter).

Reactions to Jesus' Statement (vii 40–52)

Jesus' claim to give living water makes some among the crowd think of him as the Prophet-like-Moses. This is quite intelligible if the Scripture reference for vs. 39 is the scene where Moses struck the rock. We saw in vi 14 that the resemblance between Jesus' power to multiply loaves and that of Moses to bring down manna from heaven led the crowd to identify Jesus as the Prophet. The same type of resemblance is at work here. There is a later rabbinic passage in the Midrash Rabbah on Eccles i 9, that is very interesting in this regard: "As the former redeemer [Moses] made a well to rise, so will the latter Redeemer bring up water, as it is stated, 'And a fountain shall come forth from the house of the Lord. . . .'" (Joel iii [ivH] 18).

Others identify Jesus as the Messiah. This expectation fits in with the messianic coloring that Tabernacles had undergone (see NOTE). We remember that the all-important background in Zechariah mentioned a fountain for *the house of David* (xiii 1, also xii 10). The objection that is raised against Jesus' being the Messiah indicates that there was no knowledge in Jerusalem that Jesus had actually been born in Bethlehem, an indication that is hard to reconcile with Matt ii 3 where "all Jerusalem" is upset by the birth of the child. Some commentators would transfer the ignorance of Jesus' birth at Bethlehem from the crowd to the evangelist. They maintain that the silence of John in not giving a rebuttal to the objection in vs. 42 means that the author did not know the tradition of Jesus' birthplace as it is found in Luke and Matthew. Yet, this argument from silence is not convincing. There were two theories about the Messiah (see above, p. 53), and both of them are exemplified in ch. vii. In vs. 27 the objection to Jesus' being the Messiah flows from the theory of the hidden Messiah. The people think that they know where Jesus is from (Galilee), but ironically they are wrong: he is from heaven, and this they do not know. Therefore, Jesus is unknown and can be the hidden Messiah. In vs. 42 the objection to Jesus' being the Messiah flows from the theory of the Davidic descent of the Messiah. The people think that they know that Jesus was born in Nazareth, but ironically they are wrong: he was born at Bethlehem. Therefore, Jesus can be the expected Davidic Messiah. On the basis of the parallelism between 27 and 42, then, we believe that the evangelist knew perfectly well of the tradition that Jesus was born at Bethlehem. Since he expected that this tradition would be known by his readers, the mistake of the Jews in 42 would be apparent to them, even as was the mistake in 27. However, we frankly admit that other interpretations of the evangelist's silence on the question of Jesus' birthplace are also possible, so that no solution can claim certainty.

In vss. 45–52 John gives us a dramatic vignette of the frustration and helplessness of the Sanhedrin authorities when faced with Jesus. Jesus has won a following among the crowds; the temple police are impressed; and even one of the members of the Sanhedrin raises his voice in Jesus' defense. The only refuge of the authorities is in the *argumentum ad hominem* and the sarcasm (52) that closes the scene. In i 46 Nathanael had also scoffed at Jesus' Galilean origins; but he had been honest enough to come and see for himself, and he had found through faith what he was looking for. However, when the Sanhedrin authorities scoff at Jesus' Galilean origins and are invited to hear Jesus speak for himself, they turn a deaf ear. This is the same theme that we shall find in ch. ix: the Pharisees are blind because they refuse to see. It is interesting to note that, while the NT authors are hostile to the Sanhedrin, from time to time they do point out the presence of calm and honest men in this assembly, for example, Nicodemus here, and Gamaliel in Acts v 34.

Before we close ch. vii, we must point out that the second part of Scene One, that is, 25–36, and Scene Two (37–52) share a great number of parallels in the reaction of the crowds and of the authorities to Jesus. Clearly there is some duplication here, and once again we may be dealing with duplicate Johannine accounts of the same scene.

Scene 1b (25–36)		Scene 2 (37–52)
25	Jesus' statements cause *some* of the people or crowd to pass judgment on him.	40
26–27	The question of whether he is the Messiah and an objection.	41–42
30	A poorly defined group wants to arrest him but no one can lay a finger or hand on him.	44
31	His works or his words impress some greatly.	46
32	The beginning and the conclusion of the attempt of the temple police to arrest him.	45–49

BIBLIOGRAPHY

Audet, J.-P., "La soif, l'eau et la parole," RB 66 (1959), 379–86.

Blenkinsopp, J., "John vii 37–39: Another Note on a Notorious Crux," NTS 6 (1959–60), 95–98.

————"The Quenching of Thirst: Reflections on the Utterance in the Temple, John 7:37–9," *Scripture* 12 (1960), 39–48.

Boismard, M.-E., "De son ventre couleront des fleuves d'eau (Jo., vii, 38)," RB 65 (1958), 523–46.

————"Les citations targumiques dans le quatrième évangile," RB 66 (1959), especially pp. 374–76 on vii 37–38.

Cortés Quirant, J., "'Torrentes de agua viva.' Una nueva interpretación de Juan 7, 37–38?" EstBib 16 (1957), 279–306.

Daniélou, J., "Joh. 7, 38 et Ezéch. 47, 1–11," StEv, II, pp. 158–63.

Feuillet, A., "Les fleuves d'eau vive," *Parole de Dieu et sacerdoce* (Weber volume; Tournai: 1962), pp. 107–20.

Grelot, P., "'De son ventre couleront des fleuves d'eau.' La citation scripturaire de Jean, VII, 38," RB 66 (1959), 369–74.

————"A propos de Jean, vii, 38," RB 67 (1960), 224–25.

————"Jean, vii, 38: eau du rocher ou source du Temple," RB 70 (1963), 43–51.

Hooke, S. H., "'The Spirit was not yet,'" NTS 9 (1962–63), 372–80.

Kilpatrick, G. D., "The Punctuation of John vii 37–38," JTS 11 (1960), 340–42.

Kohler, M., "Des fleuves d'eau vive. Exégèse de Jean 7:37–39," *Revue de Théologie et de Philosophie* 10 (1960), 188–201.

Kuhn, K. H., "St. John vii, 37–38," NTS 4 (1957–58), 63–65.

Rahner, Hugo, "Flumina de ventre Christi. Die patristische Auslegung von Joh. 7, 37–38," Bib 22 (1941), 269–302, 367–403.

Smith, C. W. F., "Tabernacles in the Fourth Gospel and Mark," NTS 9 (1962–63), 130–46.

Smothers, E. R., "Two Readings in Papyrus Bodmer II," HTR 51 (1958), 109–11 on vii 52.

Woodhouse, H. F., "Hard Sayings—ix. John 7. 39," *Theology* 67 (1964), 310–12.

30. THE STORY OF THE ADULTERESS
(vii 53, viii 1–11)

A non-Johannine interpolation

[VII 53 Then each went off to his own house, **VIII** 1 while Jesus went out to the Mount of Olives. 2 But at daybreak he again made his appearance in the temple precincts; and when all the people started coming to him, he sat down and began to teach them. 3 Then the scribes and the Pharisees led forward a woman who had been caught in adultery, and made her stand there in front of everybody. 4 "Teacher," they said to him, "this woman has been caught in the very act of adultery. 5 Now, in the Law Moses ordered such women to be stoned. But you—what do you have to say about it?" (6 They were posing this question to trap him so that they could have something to accuse him of.) But Jesus simply bent down and started drawing on the ground with his finger. 7 When they persisted in their questioning, he straightened up and said to them, "The man among you who has no sin—let him be the first to cast a stone at her." 8 And he bent down again and started to write on the ground. 9 But the audience went away one by one, starting with the elders; and he was left alone with the woman still there before him. 10 So Jesus, straightening up, said to her, "Woman, where are they all? Hasn't anyone condemned you?" 11 "No one, sir," she answered. Jesus said, "Nor do I condemn you. You may go. But from now on, avoid this sin."]

3: *led forward;* 4: *said.* In the historical present tense.

NOTES

vii 53. *each went off.* The situation presupposed in this once independent story seems to be one where Jesus has been teaching daily in the temple precincts ("again" in vs. 2). This situation is found in the Synoptic accounts of Jesus' last days in Jerusalem (Luke xx 1, xxi 1, 37, xxii 53).

viii 1. *Mount of Olives.* This name, which occurs three or four times in each Synoptic, is found only here in John. Luke xxi 37 says that during the last days of his life Jesus lodged on the Mount of Olives.

2. *at daybreak. Orthrou* occurs elsewhere in the NT only in Luke and Acts. Luke xxi 38 says that early in the morning all the people came to the temple precincts to hear him.

sat down and began to teach. See NOTE on vi 3.

3. *the scribes.* Mentioned only here in John; the combination "the scribes and Pharisees" is quite common in the Synoptic tradition. We need not distinguish between the two groups as if these were scribes who did not belong to the party of the Pharisees. A few manuscripts read "the chief priests" in place of "the scribes," under the influence of vii 32.

a woman. A married woman, adultery in the Law being concerned with unfaithfulness on the part of the *wife,* and not with affairs between husbands and unmarried women.

caught in adultery. Codex Bezae reads "in sin," an echo of the story of the woman in the *Gospel according to the Hebrews;* see COMMENT. As vs. 4 indicates, the woman was caught in the very act of intercourse. Derrett, pp. 4–5, makes the point that according to Deut xix 15 there must have been at least two witnesses of the action, exclusive of the husband. Nothing is mentioned of her lover, who must have escaped. The deuterocanonical story of Susanna (Vulg.= Dan xiii) offers a good parallel for all of this, e.g., vss. 36–40.

stand there in front of everybody. This is the position for judicial examination in Acts iv 7.

4. *Teacher.* This is a normal address in the Synoptic tradition; in John it is specifically a rendering of "Rabbi" (i 38). Derrett, p. 3, may be correct in saying that, despite the form of address, they are coming to Jesus more as to a prophet than to a rabbi or expert on the Law.

5. *to be stoned.* Lev xx 10 orders the death penalty but leaves the manner unspecified. Deut xxii 21 specifies stoning as the punishment for unchastity on the part of a woman who is betrothed, and this has led some to suggest that the woman in John's story was betrothed, not a married woman sharing her husband's home. However, as Ezek xvi 38–40 shows, stoning was the normal form of the death penalty for all types of adultery; the LXX of the Susanna story (vs. 62) mentions death by mangling on or by rocks. Blinzler, *art. cit.,* has rather conclusively shown that stoning was still in practice in Jesus' time and that only later did the Pharisees adopt strangulation as the punishment for adultery.

6. *They were posing this question to trap him.* This is almost the same as the Greek of John vi 6 (see NOTE there).

so that they could have something to accuse him of. Almost the same Greek is found in Luke vi 7.

drawing. The verb can mean "to write" or "to register"; the simple verb "to write" is found in vs. 8. What did Jesus draw on the ground with his finger? There are many suggestions: (*a*) A tradition that goes back to Jerome and which has found its way into a 10th-century Armenian gospel manuscript is that he wrote the sins of the accusers. This is more appropriate for the writing in vs. 8, unless we are to think that he wrote the same thing both times. (*b*) Manson, *art. cit.,* has called attention to the fact that in Roman legal practice the judge first wrote the sentence and then read it aloud. Thus it may be that in the action described in vs. 6 Jesus wrote the sentence he would deliver in 7; then in 8 he is described as writing what he would say in 11. However, the Pharisees could read; and if he wrote the decision as described in 6, then 7 is hard to explain. S. Daniel, as summarized in NTA 2 (1958), ※553, also thinks that the writing with the finger is to be connected with judgment and cites the parallel of the handwriting on the wall in Dan v 24. (c) Others think that Jesus' action is the acting out of Jer xvii 13: "Those who turn away from you shall be written on the earth, for they have forsaken the Lord, the fountain of living water." (d) Derrett, pp. 16–22, thinks that according to vs. 6 Jesus wrote the words of Exod xxiii 1b: *"You shall not join hands with a wicked man* (to be a malicious witness)." The italicized words fit the number of letters that Jesus could have written in his stooped position without shifting stance, and the text fits the situation that Derrett has conjectured wherein the husband has conspired to have witnesses catch his wife. See below on vs. 8. (e) There remains the much simpler possibility that Jesus was simply tracing lines on the ground while he was thinking, or wished to show imperturbability, or to contain his feelings of disgust for the violent zeal shown by the accusers. Power, Bib 2 (1921), 54–57, gives a number of examples from Arabic literature to illustrate the Semitic custom of doodling on the ground when distraught. For still more views see Derrett, p. 16[4]. There is simply not enough evidence to support conclusively any of these surmises; and one cannot help but feel that if the matter were of major importance, the content of the writing would have been reported.

7. *The man . . . cast a stone at her.* Deut xvii 7 recognizes that the witnesses against the accused have a special responsibility for his death. TalBab *Soṭah* 47b cites the principle that the water test to prove the wife's guilt or innocence will be effective only if the husband himself is free from guilt. This passage in vs. 7 has particular meaning in Derrett's conjecture, (d) above, where the husband has shown greed and jealousy in trapping the wife, and the witnesses have consented to the trap.

8. *write.* Derrett, pp. 23–25, maintains that he wrote again from Exod xxiii; this time it was vs. 7a: *"Keep far away from a false matter* (and slay not the innocent and the just, for I shall not acquit the guilty)." In obtaining Susanna's acquittal, Daniel cites this passage of Exodus (Susanna 53).

9. *audience.* Some less important witnesses add: "convicted by their conscience."
starting with. This may simply mean "including."
elders. There are various attempts in the textual witnesses to finish this phrase: "and continuing to the very last ones"; "so that all went out."

10. *straightening up.* Some of the less important manuscripts add: "and seeing no one but the woman."
where are they all? Surprise? Or gentle sarcasm?
Hasn't anyone condemned you? The witnesses and the accusers have gone; the case falls to pieces. The verb "to condemn" here is the technical verb *katakrinein;* elsewhere John always uses the more ambiguous *krinein* (see NOTE on iii 17).

11. *avoid this sin.* Literally "Sin no more," as in v 14. But while the directive was a general one there (no particular sin had been mentioned), here the adulterous love affair is meant. The "no more" is somewhat tautological after "from now on."

COMMENT

Problems of Authorship and of Canonicity

These problems must be treated as a series of distinct questions. The *first* question is whether the story of the adulteress was part of the original Gospel according to John or whether it was inserted at a later period. The answer to this question is clearly that it was a later insertion. This passage is not found in any of the important early Greek textual witnesses of Eastern provenance (e.g., in neither Bodmer papyrus); nor is it found in the OS or the Coptic. There are no comments on this passage by the Greek writers on John of the 1st Christian millennium, and it is only from ca. 900 that it begins to appear in the standard Greek text. The evidence for the passage as Scripture in the early centuries is confined to the Western Church. It appears in some OL texts of the Gospels. Ambrose and Augustine wanted it read as part of the Gospel, and Jerome included it in the Vulgate. It appears in the 5th-century Greco-Latin Codex Bezae.

However, a good case can be argued that the story had its origins in the East and is truly ancient (see Schilling, *art. cit.*). Eusebius (*Hist.* III 39:17; GCS 9[1]:292) says, "Papias relates another story of a woman who was accused of many sins before the Lord, which is contained in the *Gospel according to the Hebrews.*" If this is the same story as that of the adulteress, the reference would point to early Palestinian origins; but we cannot be certain that our story is the one meant. The 3rd-century *Didascalia Apostolorum* (II 24:6; Funk ed., I, 93) gives a clear reference to the story of the adulteress and uses it as a presumably well-known example of our Lord's gentleness; this work is of Syrian origin, and the reference means that the story was known (but not necessarily as Scripture) in 2nd-century Syria. From the standpoint of internal criticism, the story is quite plausible and quite like some of the other gospel stories of attempts to trap Jesus (Luke xx 20, 27). There is nothing in the story itself or its language that would forbid us to think of it as an early story concerning Jesus. Becker argues strongly for this thesis.

If the story of the adulteress was an ancient story about Jesus, why did it not immediately become part of the accepted Gospels? Riesenfeld has given the most plausible explanation of the delay in the acceptance of this story. The ease with which Jesus forgave the adulteress was hard to reconcile with the stern penitential discipline in vogue in the early Church. It was only when a more liberal penitential practice was firmly established that this story received wide acceptance. (Riesenfeld traces its liturgical acceptance to the 5th century as a reading for the feast of St. Pelagia.)

The *second* question is whether or not the story is of Johannine origin. The fact that the story was added to the Gospel only at a later period does not rule out the possibility that we are dealing with a stray narrative composed in Johannine circles. The Greek text of the story shows a number of variant readings (stemming from the fact that it was not fully accepted at first), but in general the style is not Johannine either in vocabulary or grammar. Stylistically, the story is more Lucan than Johannine.

Nor is the manuscript evidence unanimous in associating the story with John. One important group of witnesses places the story after Luke xxi 38, a localization which would be far more appropriate than the present position of the story in John, where it breaks up the sequence of the discourses at Tabernacles.

If the story was not of Johannine origin and is really out of place, what prompted its localization after John vii 52? (Actually, a few witnesses place it elsewhere in John: after vii 36 or at the end of the Gospel.) There are several views. Miss Guilding, pp. 110–12, 214[1], accounts for the situation of the passage both in John and in Luke on the basis of her lectionary cycle theory. Schilling, p. 97 ff., insisting on the parallels with the Susanna story, draws attention to echoes of Daniel in John, and thus makes the Daniel motif a guiding factor to the introduction of the story of the adulteress into John. A more certain explanation for the localization of the story in the general context of John vii and viii can be found in the fact that it illustrates certain statements of Jesus in those chapters, for example, viii 15, "I pass judgment on no one"; viii 46, "Can any of you convict me of sin?" Derrett, p. 1[3], who thinks that the key to the story lies in the unworthiness of the accusers and the witnesses, points out that the theme of admissibility of evidence comes up in the immediate context of vii 51 and viii 13. Hoskyns, p. 571, hits on a truth when he says that, while the story may be textually out of place, from a theological viewpoint it fits into the theme of judgment in ch. viii.

The *third* question is whether the story is canonical or not. For some this question will have already been answered above, since in their view the fact that the story is a later addition to the Gospel and is not of Johannine origin means that it is not canonical Scripture (even though it may be an ancient and true story). For others canonicity is a question of traditional ecclesiastical acceptance and usage. Thus, in the Roman Catholic Church the criterion of canonicity is acceptance into the Vulgate, for the Church has used the Vulgate as its Bible for centuries. The story of the adulteress was accepted by Jerome, and so Catholics regard it as canonical. It also found its way into the received text of the Byzantine Church, and ultimately into the King James Bible. And so the majority of the non-Roman Christians also accept the story as Scripture.

The Meaning of the Story

No apology is needed for this once independent story which has found its way into the Fourth Gospel and some manuscripts of Luke, for in quality and beauty it is worthy of either localization. Its succinct expression of the mercy of Jesus is as delicate as anything in Luke; its portrayal of Jesus as the serene judge has all the majesty that we would expect of John. The moment when the sinful woman stands confronted with the sinless

Jesus is one of exquisite drama, a drama beautifully captured in Augustine's terse Latin formula: *relicti sunt duo, misera et misericordia* (*In Jo.* XXXIII 5; PL 35:1650). And the delicate balance between the justice of Jesus in not condoning the sin and his mercy in forgiving the sinner is one of the great gospel lessons.

The story prompts several questions. The most difficult concerns the reason why the scribes and Pharisees brought the woman to Jesus. Is she being brought to him for trial or just for sentence? Jeremias, *art. cit.*, suggests that she had already been judged and convicted by the Sanhedrin and that Jesus was only being asked to decide the punishment. However, the question in vs. 10, "Hasn't anyone condemned you?", seems to militate against this explanation. And it does seem unlikely that, after a regular trial by the highest court in the land, the sentence would be left to an itinerant preacher. Or if the sentence had been passed, one can scarcely believe that Jesus would be allowed to countermand it.

Others believe that the woman had not yet been tried because the Sanhedrin had lost its competence in capital cases. As we shall see in discussing xviii 31, there is a tradition that about the year 30 the Romans took away from the Sanhedrin the right of imposing capital punishment. Whether or not this story took place after the Roman action, and whether or not that tradition is correct is difficult to decide. The Fourth Gospel indicates that the Sanhedrin did not have the power of execution, but the other NT writings are not clear on this; and since the adulteress story does not seem to be Johannine in origin, we cannot reconstruct the situation envisaged in the story by arguing from the general attitude of the Fourth Gospel. Nevertheless, *if* the Sanhedrin was not able to try and execute the woman, then the reason for bringing her to Jesus and the nature of the trap involved become clear. If he decides the case in favor of the woman and releases her, he violates the clear prescriptions of the Mosaic Law; if he orders her to be stoned, he will be in trouble with the Romans. This dilemma would be similar to that of the Roman coin in Mark xii 13–17.

Derrett, pp. 10–16, has another suggestion. He believes that, despite the Roman ban, the Pharisees and the mob were going to exercise lynch law and stone the woman. They were fired up with the zeal of Phinehas (Num xxv 6–18), a figure admired in late Judaism (I Macc ii 26). But there was a doubt of law, and for this reason they sought out Jesus. Was it necessary for the woman to have been warned about the punishment her sin would entail? We find a similar instance where a disputed legal problem is brought to Jesus in Matt xix 3. A direct answer by Jesus in the case of the woman would involve him in a legal dispute and put him in trouble with the Romans. According to Derrett (see NOTES on vss. 6, 8), Jesus avoided a direct decision by citing Exod xxiii and thus reminding the over-zealous authorities that their case was not legal. Derrett's interpretation of the scene is highly ingenious but must remain an hypothesis.

An even more practical problem in the story of the adulteress concerns the principle enunciated by Jesus in vs. 7: "The man among you who has no sin—let him be the first to cast a stone at her." Some have used this to paint their portrait of the liberal Christ and have turned it into a maudlin justification for indifference toward sins of the flesh. However, Jesus is not saying that every magistrate must be sinless to judge others, a principle that would nullify the office of judge. He is dealing here with zealots who have taken upon themselves the indignant enforcement of the Law, and he has every right to demand that their case be thoroughly lawful and their motives be honest. He recognizes that, although they are zealous for the word of the Law, they are not interested in the purpose of the Law, for the spiritual state of the woman is not even in question, or whether or not she is penitent. Moreover, Jesus knows that they are using her as a pawn to entrap him. Even further, if Derrett is correct, the husband of the woman may have cynically arranged to have her caught by carefully prearranging that there be witnesses to her sin, instead of seeking to win back her love. The base motives of the judges, the husband, and the witnesses are not according to the Law, and Jesus has every right to challenge their attempt to secure the woman's conviction. Understood in the light of these circumstances, vs. 7 makes sense. But one should beware of attempts to make it a general norm forbidding enactments of capital punishment.

BIBLIOGRAPHY

Becker, U., *Jesus und die Ehebrecherin* (Beihefte zur ZNW, No. 28; Berlin: Töpelmann, 1963).

Blinzler, J., "Die Strafe für Ehebruch in Bibel und Halacha zur Auslegung von Joh. viii 5," NTS 4 (1957–58), 32–47.

Derrett, J. D. M., "Law in the New Testament: The Story of the Woman Taken in Adultery," NTS 10 (1963–64), 1–26. Abbreviated in StEv, II, pp. 170–73.

Jeremias, J., "Zur Geschichtlichkeit der Verhörs Jesu vor dem Hohen Rat," ZNW 43 (1950–51), especially pp. 148–50.

Manson, T. W., "The Pericope *de Adultera* (Joh 7, 53–8, 11)," ZNW 44 (1952–53), 255–56.

Riesenfeld, H., "Die Perikope von der Ehebrecherin in der frühkirchlichen Tradition," *Svensk Exegetisk Arsbok* 17 (1952), 106–11.

Schilling, F. A., "The Story of Jesus and the Adulteress," ATR 37 (1955), 91–106.

31. JESUS AT TABERNACLES:—SCENE THREE
(viii 12–20)

Miscellaneous discourses

a. Jesus as the light of the world; Jesus' witness to himself.
A discourse given at the temple treasury

VIII 12 Then Jesus spoke to them again,

"I am the light of the world.
No follower of mine shall ever walk in darkness;
no, he will possess the light of life."

13 This caused the Pharisees to object, "You are your own witness, and
your testimony cannot be verified." 14 Jesus answered,

"Even if I am my own witness,
my testimony *can* be verified
because I know where I came from and where I am going.
But you know neither where I come from nor where I am going.
15 You pass judgment according to human standards,
but I pass judgment on no one.
16 Yet even if I do judge,
that judgment of mine is valid
because I am not alone—
I have at my side the One who sent me [the Father].
17 Why, in your own Law it is stated
that testimony given by two persons is verified.
18 I am one who gives testimony on my behalf,
and the Father who sent me gives testimony for me."

19 Then they asked him, "Where is this 'father' of yours?" Jesus replied,

"You do not recognize me or my Father.
If you recognized me, you would recognize my Father too."

20 He spoke these words while teaching at the temple treasury. Still, no
one arrested him because his hour had not yet come.

NOTES

viii 12. *them.* This is a vague reference since (if we overlook the intrusive story of the adulteress) Jesus has not spoken since vii 38, where he seems to have been addressing the crowd of pilgrims in the temple precincts. He is now in the temple area again (see vs. 20), and he may be addressing the crowd once more. Strangely enough, however, "the crowd" which was mentioned eight times in ch. vii is not mentioned at all in ch. viii (and indeed not until xi 42). It is also possible that "them" refers to the Pharisees. If viii 12 once followed vii 52, the Pharisees were the last group to be mentioned (vii 47), and they will be mentioned again in the next verse.

light of the world. In Matt v 14 the disciples are told, "You are the light of the world." There is no contradiction here, for the disciples are the light of the world only inasmuch as they reflect Jesus.

walk in darkness . . . the light of life. What is the background of this dualistic contrast between darkness and light? In the OT we hear of "the light of life," i.e., the light that gives life (Ps lvi 13; Job xxxiii 30). Ps xxvii 1 says, "The Lord is my light"; Bar v 9 says, "God will lead Israel with joy, by the light of His glory." Yet, in the OT light and darkness are not opposed as principles of good and evil as they are in John; and for such dualistic opposition the Dead Sea Scrolls offer a far better parallel to Johannine usage. The Qumran Essenes are the sons of light; their hearts have been illumined with the wisdom of life (1QS ii 3); and they can look upon "the light of life" (i.e., the Qumran interpretation of the Law—1QS iii 7). The good spirit that guides their life is called, among other titles, "the prince of lights," while the evil spirit who fights against them is "the angel of darkness" (iii 20–21), and men *walk* according to one or the other of these spirits of light and darkness. See H. Braun, ThR 28 (1962), 218–20, for discussion and bibliography. As a final note we may mention that the present sequence in the manuscripts of John where viii 12 follows the story of the adulteress is interesting when compared to 1QS iii 6–7 which speaks of "the pardon of sins in order to see the light of life."

13. *your testimony cannot be verified.* For this objection and Jesus' answer see the NOTES on v 31. Mishnah *Kethuboth* 2:9 says: "No man can give evidence for himself."

14. *my testimony* can *be verified.* This is a formal contradiction of v 31: "If I am my own witness, my testimony *cannot* be verified." However, the idea in both verses is really the same: his testimony is verifiable because his Father stands behind it (compare v 32 and viii 16, 18).

15. *pass judgment according to human standards.* Literally "according to the flesh"; this is another implicit instance of the dualism between the worlds of flesh and spirit that we saw in iii 6 and vi 63. Paul uses the expression "according to the flesh" as a false standard of judgment in I Cor i 26; II Cor v 16. We recall that in John vii 24 Jesus had warned the crowd not to judge by appearances.

I pass judgment on no one. (This verse may have prompted the insertion of the story of the adulteress into its present position.) Wikenhauser, p. 169, thinks this means: "I judge no one according to the flesh"; however, there are a number of statements where Jesus denies that he is a judge without such qualifications, and it is dubious whether the qualification is meant here. A more plausible solution is the one suggested by Loisy, p. 288, that there are two different types of judgment involved in the two lines of vs. 15. The judgment of the Pharisees is one of evaluation; the judgment of Jesus is the judgment that pertains to salvation and condemnation. See COMMENT.

16. *valid*. This is *alēthinos* (which we often translate as "real"—see App. I:2); in vss. 13 and 14 it was a question of the testimony being "verified" (*alēthēs*, "true"), and that word returns in vs. 17. John does not always keep *alēthēs* and *alēthinos* distinct.

I have at my side the One who sent me. Literally "but I and the One who sent me." Dodd, *Interpretation*, pp. 94–96, points out that the divine statement *egō eimi*, "I am [He]," which plays an important role in John (see App. IV), often appears in post-biblical Hebrew in the form "I and he." In fact, there is evidence that the latter form was used in the Tabernacles ceremony of circling the altar (see p. 327 above). "I and he" seems to underline the quasi-identity of God and His people. Thus, according to Dodd, in saying "I and the One who sent me," Jesus is using a form of the divine name and implying his solidarity with his Father.

[the Father]. This reading (omitted in Sinaiticus*, Bezae, and OS) is supported by impressive witnesses including P[66] and P[75]. Bernard, I, p. 296, however, suggests that it is a scribal borrowing from vs. 18.

17. *your own Law*. For this seeming dissociation of Jesus from the Jewish heritage see NOTE on vii 19. Charlier, p. 506, insists that the real function of the "your" is not to express any hostility or superiority toward the Law, but to say to "the Jews," "It is the Law that you yourselves accept." Jesus wishes to make his argument irrefutable and thus causes the Jews to contradict themselves. Charlier's interpretation has considerable validity for such statements when they are considered in the historical setting of the life of Jesus. But as these statements appear in a late 1st-century Gospel, against a background of Jewish-Christian hostility, the "your Law" has a hostile connotation.

stated. Literally "written"; but the form of the verb (*gegraptai*) is different from the periphrastic construction (*gegrammenon* plus *einai*) that John uses six times in other introductory lemmata to citations of Scripture.

two persons. This usually means two persons besides the one actually concerned; yet in vs. 18 Jesus himself is one of the two witnesses, so that he really has only one additional witness, his Father. (One is surprised that he does not mention John the Baptist, who was sent to testify *to the light*—i 7.) There are some exceptions in rabbinical jurisprudence where the testimony of one additional witness was regarded as sufficient, e.g., it was sufficient if one parent testified that this was his or her child. But it would be strange for Jesus to cite the general law of two or more witnesses, and then to prove his point by an exception. Charlier, p. 514, makes the suggestion that Jesus is presented as really citing two witnesses even when he mentions himself in vs. 18. John presents Jesus, not only as a man, but also as Son of God; therefore, it is not Jesus as a man who is bearing witness to himself, but the Son of God who is bearing witness. The two witnesses are the Son of God and the Father, or, as Loisy (1 ed.), p. 555, put it, the Word-made-flesh and the Father who sent him. This interpretation may be oversubtle, however.

18. *I am*. In line with this interpretation, Charlier, p. 513, treats this as a divine use of *egō eimi*.

one who gives testimony on my behalf. In Rev iii 14 Jesus speaks as "the faithful and genuine [*alēthinos*] witness."

the Father . . . gives testimony. In v 31–39 Jesus listed a series of ways in which the Father *has given* testimony (v 37): John the Baptist; the works of Jesus; the abiding word of God in the hearts of the audience; the Scriptures.

19. *Where is this 'father' of yours?* In vii 27 they were so certain they knew where he was from.

If you recognized me. The same principle concerning the knowledge of the Son and the Father is found in xiv 7 and xvi 3.

20. *at the temple treasury.* Literally "in the temple precincts, in the treasury." As far as we know, the treasury was a storage chamber and hence Jesus would not be inside it. The Greek probably reflects the vague use of prepositions of place in *Koine;* for *en* denoting nearness see BAG, p. 257, I 1c. The temple treasury abutted on the Court of the Women and was also the scene of Jesus' teaching in Mark xii 41.

no one arrested him. See vii 30, 44.

COMMENT: GENERAL

Literary Analysis

An analysis of the structure of ch. viii (12 ff.) is perhaps more difficult than that of any other chapter or long discourse in the first part of the Gospel. The general setting seems still to be the feast of Tabernacles, for the theme of light (viii 12) fits into the Tabernacles motifs. Moreover, there is a certain unity between vii and viii (without the story of the adulteress) since vii begins with the theme of Jesus going up to the feast of Tabernacles in secret (*en kryptō:* vii 10) and viii ends with the theme of Jesus' hiding himself (*kryptein*).

Our breakdown of viii 12–59 into three divisions (see p. 202) follows the indications of the Gospel itself, which seems to indicate a break at 21 and 31. But when we probe into the individual divisions, we find that the sequence within them is far from simple and that often we are dealing with doublets of other discourses. Although commentators like Dodd and Barrett accept the same divisions that we do, Kern, *art. cit.*, has attempted a much more elaborate analysis of the poetic structure of 12–59. He sees five divisions, each with a definite strophic pattern. The theme of the truth of Jesus' judgment runs through the first two divisions (12–19 and 21–30) and is matched by the theme of lying in the last two divisions (41b–47 and 49–58); and the division consisting of 31b–41a serves as an intermediary. There are some interesting possibilities in Kern's analysis, which is basically in the same tradition as Gächter's studies (see p. cxxxiii); however, the poetic structure often seems to be more a *tour de force* of the investigator than the plan of the evangelist.

Turning now to our first division, 12–20, these verses seem to constitute a structural unit, not only because 20 marks a pause in the action and 21 is another heading, but also because there is a minor inclusion between 12 and 20, formed by the repetition of the verb "spoke" in the opening words of these two verses.

Yet, within 12–20 the thought skips and jumps. We may recognize three basic topics: **(a)** *Light*. This is introduced in vs. 12 but is never picked up again until the next chapter, where it is repeated (ix 5) and dramatized as Jesus gives the light of sight to the blind man. **(b)** Jesus' *witness* to himself. This is introduced by the challenge of the Pharisees in vs. 13, and is defended by Jesus in 14a,b and in 17–18, where it overflows into the theme of the Father's witness. (The verses 14c,d, 15–16 really interrupt the sequence between 14b and 17 and will be treated below.) The verses which deal with Jesus' witness have almost word-for-word *parallels in v 31–39*, and it may well be that we are dealing with two different forms of the same discourse. Both viii 14a,b and v 31 treat of the validity of Jesus' witness for himself; both viii 18 and v 37 stress that the Father gives testimony on Jesus' behalf. Of course, v 31–39 is a longer form of the discourse and spells out how the Father gives this testimony. **(c)** Jesus' *judgment* on others. This is found in the intervening verses mentioned above, namely, 14c,d, 15–16, and is to be connected with the knowledge of Jesus' Father in 19–20. These verses have definite *parallels in ch. vii, especially in vss. 25–36* (we have already seen on p. 331 that vii 25–36 has parallels in vii 37–52).

ch. vii		*ch. viii*
27–28	where Jesus came from	14c,d
33–35	where Jesus is going	
24	judgment by appearances, human standards	15
28	knowing Jesus and the One who sent him	19
30	inability to arrest him; hour not yet come	20

There is also *a parallel between viii 16 and v 30* in the one phrase: "my judgment is honest/valid."

Thus the evidence suggests very strongly that viii 12–20 is a composite and must have had a complicated literary history before it took its present form. Attempts to reconstruct that history seem too speculative to warrant detailed consideration.

COMMENT: DETAILED

Jesus the light (viii 12)

Jesus proclaims himself to be the light of the world, even as in vii 37–38 he proclaimed himself to be the source of living water; and both these proclamations seem to have been prompted by the ceremonies of the feast of Tabernacles. As with the water ceremony, there was biblical background for the theme of light at Tabernacles and, indeed, in the same passages in the OT. In the verse before the passage of Zechariah (xiv 8) that describes the living water flowing out from Jerusalem, we hear: "And there shall be continuous day . . . for there shall be light even in the evening." The story of the Exodus wanderings that supplied the imagery of the water from the rock also provided the imagery of a flaming pillar that guided the Israelites through the darkness of the night (Exod xiii 21). That this image could have entered into the background of Jesus' claim to be the light is suggested when we remember that Wis xviii 3–4 gives witness to the tradition that identified this pillar with "the imperishable light of the Law." The other images that Jesus uses for himself are often images that Judaism used for the Law.

In the actual ceremonies of Tabernacles, as they had developed by Jesus' time, on the first night (and perhaps on the other nights as well) there was a ritual of lighting four golden candlesticks in the Court of the Women. Each of these, according to Mishnah *Sukkah* 5:2–4, had four golden bowls on top which were reached by ladders. Floating in these bowls were wicks made from the drawers and girdles of the priests; and when they were lit, it is said that all Jerusalem reflected the light that burned in the House of Water Drawing (that part of the Court of the Women through which the water procession passed—see above, p. 327).

In the Gospel scene Jesus stands in this same Court of the Women and proclaims that he is the light, not only of Jerusalem but of the whole world. Previously we have heard Jesus speak of water that is life-giving and of bread that is life-giving; now he speaks of life-giving light. Since the first two metaphors referred basically to his revelation, we may well suspect that that is what is meant here too. This is confirmed in the dramatic action of ch. ix when, as the light (ix 5), Jesus opens the blind man's eyes to faith (ix 35–38, also xii 46). Just as with the metaphors of water and bread, the Wisdom passages of the OT offer some valuable background for Jesus' use of light as a symbol of his revelation. In Prov viii 22 Wisdom says that she was made at the beginning of the Lord's ways, and in Hebrew tradition the first creation was light (Gen i 3). Wisdom vii 26 tells us that Wisdom is a reflection of everlasting light. Already in the pre-Christian era Wisdom was identified with the Law, and we saw above that the Law was spoken of as imperishable light. We pointed out in the NOTE on vs. 12 that the Johannine thought about light and darkness resembled that of Qumran, and there the light of life is a special interpretation of the Law.

In the Synoptic Gospels too the imagery associated with light is used by Jesus to depict the revelation and teaching he has brought into the world. We think of the parable of the lamp which gives light to the house. In the context of Luke xi 33 this saying is introduced in such a way that the meaning seems to be that Jesus himself is the lamp (even as Jesus is the light in John); but in Mark iv 21 and Luke viii 16 the lamp parable is used to explain why Jesus is *teaching* in parables, namely, to give light to those who would enter.

Elsewhere in the Johannine writings (I John i 5) we shall hear that God is light with no admixture of darkness. In Jesus this light and life has come into the world (John i 4–5, iii 19) to dispel the darkness, for those who come to believe in him do not remain in darkness (xii 46). Shining forth in him as the incarnate revealer, God's light irradiates human existence and gives man knowledge of the purpose and meaning of life.

Jesus the judge (viii 15–16)

In treating ch. v, we discussed the theme of Jesus' bearing witness to himself and of the Father's witness to Jesus. This leaves for discussion here only the theme of judgment. Let us gather together in one place what is said of Jesus and judging (*krinein*) in John.

First, there is a group of statements to the effect that Jesus did not come to judge, that is, to condemn:

iii 17: For God did not send the Son into the world to condemn the world but that the world might be saved through him.

xii 47: I did not come to condemn the world but to save the world.

We believe that the translation of *krinein* as "condemn" in these passages (also in viii 26) is clearly justified by the contrast with "save." Nevertheless, the statement that Jesus did not come to condemn does not exclude the very real judgment that Jesus provokes. In the immediate context of the above statements (in iii 19, xii 48) we are told that he who refuses to believe in Jesus condemns himself, while he who believes escapes condemnation (also v 24). The idea in John, then, seems to be that during his ministry Jesus is no apocalyptic judge like the one expected at the end of time; yet his presence does cause men to judge themselves.

It is in this latter sense that we must understand the *second* group of texts to the effect that Jesus *did* come to judge:

ix 39: I came into this world for judgment.

v 22: The Father has turned over all judgment to the Son.

Although these texts seem to contradict the first group, they simply expand the notion of provoking judgment which is in the context of the first group. The passage we are now considering, viii 15–16, is one example that spans the two groups and has the ideas of both. In 15 Jesus says that he passes judgment on no one; but 16 recalls that judgment is associated with Jesus' presence. When Jesus says, "Even if I do judge [real condition, not contrary to fact], that judgment of mine is valid," he seems to mean that the judgment that he provokes among men is one that the Father will accept. It is a judgment that has eternal consequences and will be ratified in that general judgment when the dead come forth from their tombs. The parallel to "that judgment of mine is valid" is found in v 30: "my judgment is honest." The context in v 26–30 is the context of the judgment at the resurrection from the dead when as the Son of Man, Jesus exercises that judgment which the Father has turned over to him (v 27), a judgment that is the Father's because Jesus judges only as he hears (v 30). So also in viii 16 the reason that Jesus can assert that he provokes a valid judgment among men is the supporting presence of the Father.

[The Bibliography for this section is included in the Bibliography for ch. viii, at the end of § 33.]

32. JESUS AT TABERNACLES:
—SCENE THREE (*continued*)
(viii 21–30)

Miscellaneous discourses

b. Attack on the unbelieving Jews; question of who Jesus is

VIII 21 Then he said to them again,

"I am going away and you will look for me,
but you will die in your sin.
Where I am going, you cannot come."

22 At this the Jews began to say, "Surely he is not going to kill himself,
is he?—because he claims, 'Where I am going, you cannot come.'"
23 But he went on to say,

"You belong to what is below;
I belong to what is above.
You belong to this world—
this world to which I do not belong.
24 That is why I told you that you would die in your sins.
Unless you come to believe that I AM,
you will surely die in your sins."

25 "Well then, who are you?" they asked him. Jesus answered,

"What I have been telling you from the beginning.
26 Many are the things that I could say about you and condemn;
but the only things I say to this world
are what I have heard from Him,
the One who sent me, who is truthful."

27 They did not understand that he was talking to them about the
Father. 28 So Jesus continued,

"When you lift up the Son of Man,
then you will realize that I AM,
and that I do nothing by myself.

> No, I say only those things
> that the Father taught me.
> 29 And the One who sent me is with me.
> He has not left me alone
> since I always do what pleases Him."

30 While he was speaking in this way, many came to believe in him.

NOTES

viii 21. *he said.* The opening rubric of this section is very much like that of the previous section (§ 31). In the previous division we saw an inclusion in the "spoke . . . spoke" of vss. 12 and 20; there is also an inclusion between 21 and 30, but it is not as smooth: "said . . . was speaking."

you will die in your sin. The rest of Jesus' words in vs. 21 are very much like vii 33b–34, except for this line. We have this expression in LXX: Ezek iii 18; Prov xxiv 9.

sin. Here in the singular, but vs. 24, citing this verse, uses the plural.

Where I am going. "Going" appears also in xiii 33; contrast with "where I *am*" in vii 34 and see NOTE there.

23. *You belong . . . I belong.* Literally "to be of." The question may be asked if "I am [*egō eimi*] of what is above" is a special instance of *egō eimi* (see App. IV)? On the one hand, the clear emphasis on *egō eimi* in vss. 24 and 28 gives support to the suggestion; on the other hand, the contrast in 23 with *"You are* of what is below" makes any special emphasis on "I am" less likely.

below . . . above; to this world . . . [not to] *this world.* The same dualism is found in the "from above . . . of the earth" in iii 31. In xvii 16 the disciples are included in the same sphere as Jesus: "They do not belong to the world, any more than I belong to the world." Col iii 1 offers an interesting parallel to this terminology: "If you have been raised with Christ, seek *the things that are above.*"

24. *believe.* Some important witnesses add "me."

surely. This is the only time John uses the indicative in the apodosis of this particular type of negative condition, and we have sought to indicate the special emphasis implied.

25. *What I have been telling you from the beginning.* This verse represents a famous difficulty. Our English translation is smoother than the Greek warrants. The Greek words are not really a sentence, and there have been many attempts to interpret them: **(a)** *As an affirmation:* (1) "Primarily [I am] what I say to you." (2) "First of all [I am] what I say to you." (3) "[I am] from the beginning what I say to you." In comment we must note that the words "I am" are not in the Greek but have to be understood. The Greek simply says "the beginning," and thus the idea expressed by adding "from" is really an interpretation. (There is a grammatical basis for this interpretation [BDF, § 160], but it is more normal for John to use the preposition, e.g., vi 64, viii 44, etc.) Also the Greek verb is literally "I speak," not "I say." **(b)** *As a question:* "How is it that I speak to you at all?" The phrase translated "at all" here and in (c) below does not normally mean "at all" except with a negative. The interrogative

"How is it that" implies the use of a Greek interrogative that is not too frequent (BDF, § 300[2]). **(c)** *As an exclamation:* "That I speak to you at all!" Each of these three types of translations has had its champions, even in antiquity. Nonnus of Panopolis gives a translation like that of (*a*3); Chrysostom and Cyril of Alexandria are in the tradition of (*c*). The Latin translations give prominence to a mistaken reading which cannot be justified by the Greek. They take "the beginning" as a nominative instead of an accusative and render: "[I am] the beginning who also speaks to you" or "[I am] the beginning because I speak to you." In an evaluation of the possible translations, the fact that a question is asked in the first part of vs. 25 may give a slight edge to the likelihood that we have an affirmation by way of response. To obtain an affirmation from what one now finds in the Greek text, one has to supply words; but the many scholars who insist that the Greek as it now stands is corrupt or incomplete may be correct. We now have some textual support for adding words, for P[66] gives a longer text for which there is no other witness: "I told you at the beginning what I am also telling you [now]." This is a tempting reading which makes good sense; both Funk and Smothers champion it, and we have made partial use of it in the translation we have given.

26. *I say . . . what I have heard from Him.* Compare xii 49: "It was not on my own that I spoke."

to this world. Literally "into this world." For this wide use of *eis* see BDF, § 207[1]. We have a somewhat similar idea in xvii 13, "While still in the world, I say all this"; but in the instance at hand, De la Potterie, Bib 43 (1962), 372, is probably correct in insisting that *eis* has an aspect of motion. Jesus has come from the Father to speak to the world.

truthful. Alēthēs; in vs. 17 we heard that the testimony given by two persons is *alēthēs* ("verified"), and the Father who sent Jesus is one of those two witnesses.

27. *the Father.* Some witnesses from the Western tradition add "God," thus giving the reading: "he was telling them that God was [his] Father." This is the import of the verse even without the addition.

28. *lift up.* In crucifixion, leading to resurrection and ascension (see p. 146).

I AM. This is one of the four relatively clear instances of the absolute use of *egō eimi* without a predicate implied (see App. IV). Some have suggested that "Son of Man" is the implied predicate, but it does not fit John's thought that the ultimate insight into the exalted Jesus would be that he is Son of Man. The exalted Jesus is confessed as Lord and God in xx 28, and our reading of the divine use of *egō eimi* here fits in with that estimation.

I do nothing by myself. This complements vs. 26, where Jesus says that he does not *say* anything on his own. This verse may be recalled by Ignatius *Magnesians* vii 1: "as the Lord did nothing without the Father . . ."

29. *He has not left me alone.* This is the same theme as in vs. 16.

I . . . do what pleases Him. In Isa xxxviii 3 Hezekiah prays, "I have done what is pleasing before you." Ignatius *Magn* viii 2 has: "Jesus Christ . . . His Son who in all respects was pleasing to the One who sent him." See Braun, JeanThéol, I, pp. 274–75.

30. *While he was speaking.* A genitive absolute, which is rare in John. Perhaps this sentence is an editor's device for splitting the discourse into divisions.

COMMENT

Literary Analysis

The history of the composition of this division is just as complicated as that of the previous division (§ 31). As we indicated in the NOTE on vs. 21, this unit of vss. 21–30 is marked off by the same type of inclusion that marked off 12–20. Perhaps the various themes of vss. 21–30 flow more smoothly into one another than did the themes of 12–20, but the parallels between individual verses and those of other parts of John are no less noticeable.

On p. 343 we saw that the third theme of 12–20, namely that of judgment, had many cross parallels with vii 25–36. So also the opening verses of this division (viii 21–22) have parallels with that part of vii.

ch. vii		ch. viii
33b	*I am going away*	21a
34a	*You will look for me*	21a
34b	*Where I am (going), you cannot come*	21c
35	*Misunderstanding by the Jews*	22
36	*Jews repeat Jesus' statement*	22

In each of the misunderstandings, "the Jews" ironically speak a truth. The one in vii concerned the possibility of Jesus going off to teach the Greeks, and this came true in the Church. The one here concerns the possibility of his killing himself, and, of course, he will voluntarily lay down his life (x 17–18). Can there be any doubt that John has preserved two different forms of the same scene?

In the subsequent verses of this section there are other parallels. The thought parallels between viii 23 and iii 31, and between viii 28 and iii 14 are interesting, but not close enough to make us think that we have true duplication. In any case, vss. 23–24 are meant to serve as an answer to 22; in vii 33–36 we had no such attempt to answer the Jewish misunderstanding.

In vs. 25 there appears the new theme of who Jesus is. It has been suggested that vss. 25–28 are out of place where they now stand, and that they should be put back into the passage on judgment in the previous section. One order suggested is viii 15, 25–27, 19, 28–29. This is ingenious, but all that is certain are the rather loose parallels between 26 and 17 and between 29 and 16 as we pointed out in the NOTES. Actually, viii 25–28 does not fit too badly right where it stands, explaining as it does vs. 24.

Detailed Comment

Once more Jesus challenges his hearers to a decision before it is too late. He has identified himself as the light (viii 12), and the coming of the light forces men to take the option of seeing or turning away (iii 19–21). But in these Tabernacles discourses there is a note of urgency. Men have but a short time to see Jesus, to look for him and to find him; a unique opportunity is being given to them and it will not be given again. Jesus has offered *living* water (vii 38) and the light *of life* (viii 12). If men refuse this gift of life, they will die in their sin. We note that "sin" is in the singular in vs. 21, for in Johannine thought there is only one radical sin of which man's many sins (plural in vs. 24) are but reflections. This radical sin is to refuse to believe in Jesus and thus to refuse life itself. (See Lyonnet, VD 35 [1957], 271–78.) The Synoptics have the same thought phrased in another way. In Mark iii 29 we hear that whoever blasphemes against the holy Spirit (by attributing the work of the kingdom of God to Satan) is guilty of an eternal sin. The blasphemous refusal of the kingdom of God in the Synoptic tradition is the equivalent of the refusal to see who Jesus is in the Johannine tradition.

Verses 23–24 explain the urgency of Jesus' insisting that, once he goes away, there will be no other possibility for delivering them from sin. He is the one from above who has come into the world to enable men to be begotten from above, and thus to raise them up to God's level from the sphere of what is below. When Jesus himself is lifted up (vs. 28) in crucifixion, resurrection, and ascension, he draws all men to him (xii 32); and in that moment it will be clear to those who have the eyes of faith that he truly bears the divine name ("I AM") and that he has the power of raising men to the Father. But if men refuse to believe, refuse to see, then there is no other way (xiv 6) that leads above to the Father; and men will go to their graves without the gift of life.

In vs. 24, in stressing that men must believe that he comes from above with the power of life from the Father, Jesus says that men must believe that he bears the divine name "I AM." (See App. IV.) With typical Johannine misunderstanding, "the Jews" seek for a predicate and want to know who he is. But how can one explain divinity? All that Jesus can do is to reaffirm his claim in vs. 25. From the beginning, from his very first discourse with Nicodemus, he has claimed to be from above and to be uniquely representative of the Father. Perhaps we should also associate the statement in vs. 25 with the Wisdom tradition (so Feuillet, NRT 82 [1960], 923), for in Prov viii 22 Wisdom says, "The Lord made me the beginning of His ways." In Sir xxiv 9 Wisdom again speaks of the beginning: "Before all ages, from the beginning He created me."

The editorial remark in vs. 27 assures us that we have been interpreting Jesus' words correctly, and that their burden concerns his unique association with divinity, so unique that God is his Father (see NOTE). But once more his words are greeted with a failure to understand. In vs. 28 Jesus insists that only the actual return to the Father will show that God is the one who

sent him, that he bears the divine name, and that God is always with him
(29). But while this return to the Father in crucifixion, resurrection, and
ascension will be the great moment of revelation for those who believe, the
very death of Jesus which is an essential part of this moment will be caused
by those who do not believe. Thus they will judge themselves and reject the
possibility of receiving life. Verse 28 represents the second of the three
Johannine sayings concerning the lifting up of the Son of Man, three sayings
which, as we pointed out (p. 146), have parallels in the three Synoptic
predictions of the Passion. Mark ix 30–31 sets the second of the Synoptic
predictions in the framework of Jesus' journey through Galilee on the way to
Jerusalem. We have already noted parallels between Jesus' journey to
Jerusalem in the Synoptics and his visit at Tabernacles in John vii–viii (see
p. 309).

Verse 30 closes this section on the note of many coming to believe in
Jesus. While vs. 30 makes a convenient inclusion with 21 and thus serves
to break up the long report of Jesus' words into more tractable units, we may
well ask if it does not represent simply a convenient editorial device rather
than an integral part of the discourse. In 22, 25, and 27, we have heard of
consistent misunderstanding and refusal to believe; this will continue in the
following section, e.g., 33, 39. It is rather startling in the midst of this
(30–31) to find some who believe, and to have Jesus addressing his remarks
to believing "Jews" (!—see NOTE below on vs. 31). Previously we have encountered divisions in the crowd, and John has consistently made it clear that
some were inclined to accept Jesus, at least as Messiah. But Jesus has not
addressed his remarks to these as he does in vs. 31. Thus, it seems best to
regard vs. 30 as a summary statement emphasizing an undoubted truth and
inserted for organizational purposes. It was not meant to give the believers
a role in the subsequent discourse as the further insertion of the first line of
vs. 31 has done.

[The Bibliography for this section is included in the Bibliography for
ch. viii, at the end of § 33.]

33. JESUS AT TABERNACLES:
—SCENE THREE (*concluded*)
(viii 31–59)

Miscellaneous discourses

c. Jesus and Abraham

VIII 31 Then Jesus went on to say to those Jews who had believed
him,

"If you abide in my word,
  you are truly my disciples;
32 and you will know the truth,
  and truth will set you free."

33 "We are descendant from Abraham," they retorted, "and never have
we been slaves to anyone. What do you mean by saying, 'You will be
free'?"
34 Jesus answered them,

"Truly, I assure you,
  everyone who acts sinfully
  is a slave [of sin].
(35 While no slave has a permanent place in the family,
  the son has a place there forever.)
36 Consequently, if the Son sets you free,
  you will really be free.
37 I know that you are descendant from Abraham.
  Yet you look for a chance to kill me
  because my word makes no headway among you.
38 I tell what I have seen in the Father's presence;
  therefore, you should do what you heard from the Father."

39 "*Our* father is Abraham," they answered him. Jesus replied,

"If you are really Abraham's children,
  you would be doing works worthy of Abraham.

39: *replied.* In the historical present tense.

40 But actually you are looking to kill me,
     just because I am a man who told you the truth
     which I heard from God.
     Abraham did not do that.
41 You are indeed doing your father's works!"

They protested, "We were not born illegitimate. We have but one
father, God Himself." 42 Jesus told them,

  "If God were your father,
     you would love me,
     for from God I came forth and am here.
     Not on my own have I come,
     but He sent me.
43 Why do you not understand what I say?—
     because you are incapable of hearing my word.
44 The devil is the father you belong to,
     and you willingly carry out your father's wishes.
     He was a murderer from the beginning
     and never based himself on truth,
     for there is no truth in him.
     When he tells a lie,
     he speaks his native language,
     for he is a liar and the father of lying.
45 But since I, for my part, tell the truth,
     you do not believe me.
46 Can any one of you convict me of sin?
     If I am telling the truth,
     why do you not believe me?
47 The man who belongs to God
     hears the words of God.
     The reason why you do not hear
     is that you do not belong to God."

48 The Jews answered, "Aren't we right, after all, in saying that you are
a Samaritan and demented?" 49 Jesus replied,

  "I am not demented,
     but I do honor my Father,
     while you fail to honor me.
50 I do not seek glory for myself;
     there is One who does seek it and He passes judgment.
51 I solemnly assure you,
     if a man keeps my word,
     he shall never see death."

52 "Now we are sure you are demented," the Jews retorted. "Abraham died; so did the prophets. Yet, you claim, 'A man shall never experience death if he keeps my word.' 53 Surely, you don't pretend to be greater than our father Abraham who is dead?—or the prophets who are dead? Just who do you pretend to be?" 54 Jesus answered,

> "If I glorify myself,
> my glory amounts to nothing.
> The One who glorifies me is the Father
> whom you claim as 'our God,'
> 55 even though you do not know Him.
> But I do know Him;
> and if I say I do not know Him,
> I will be just like you—a liar!
> Yes, I do know Him
> and I keep His word.
> 56 Your father Abraham rejoiced
> at the prospect of seeing my day.
> When he saw it, he was glad."

57 This caused the Jews to object, "You're not even fifty years old. How can you have seen Abraham?" 58 Jesus answered,

> "I solemnly assure you,
> before Abraham even came into existence, I AM."

59 Then they picked up rocks to throw at Jesus, but he hid himself and slipped out of the temple precincts.

NOTES

viii 31. *those Jews who had believed him*. That the remarks that follow are directed to believers is very hard to reconcile with the sharp disagreement uttered by these "believers" in vs. 33 and their desire to kill Jesus in vs. 37. Some have pointed out that it is said that these "Jews" believed *him* (dative); it is not said they believed *in him* (*eis* with the accusative, which is a stronger expression). Yet Dodd, *art. cit.*, p. 6, insists that the variation is meaningless here; and even if a partial faith is meant, this can scarcely be reconciled with a desire to kill Jesus a few lines later. Almost certainly the words of Jesus in this section were addressed to the same type of disbelievers that we have been encountering all along. However, when the editorial vs. 30 was inserted to break up the discourse, it was necessary to add a phrase in vs. 31 introducing Jesus' words. Seeing the reference in 30 that there were some who believed in Jesus, the composer of 31 (the final redactor?) thought it reasonable to make them the audience for what would follow and saw no contradiction in describing these believers as "Jews." There was a strain of Johannine material or a stage of Johannine editing in which "the Jews" was used simply to describe the inhabitants of Jerusalem or Judea and did not necessarily refer to the authorities hostile to Jesus (see p. LXXI). We shall see other examples of this usage of the Jews in chs. xi–xii.

abide in my word. In II John 9 we hear, "One who does not abide in the teaching of Christ does not have God." Elsewhere the picture is reversed, and the word of God abides in the believer (John v 38). Bernard, II, p. 305, is correct when he says that it is really the same thing to abide in the word and to have the word abide in oneself.

32. *truth will set you free.* The "truth" meant is the revelation of Jesus, as we see by comparing this with vs. 36 where it is the Son who sets free. The hackneyed use of this phrase in political oratory in appealing for national or personal liberty is a distortion of the purely religious value of both truth and freedom in this passage. Deliverance from sin by truth is not found in the OT. At Qumran it is said (1QS iv 20–21): "And then God will purge by His truth all the deeds of men . . . and will sprinkle on him a spirit of truth like water that cleanses from every lying abomination." It is not said that truth frees from sin but that it destroys sin. In early rabbinic writing (*Pirqe Aboth* iii 6) we find the idea that the study of the Law is a liberating factor, freeing one from worldly care. Thus, we *may* once again have an implicit contrast between the power of Jesus' revelation and that of the Law.

33. *descendant from Abraham.* The word *sperma* in Greek is a collective singular. In the mouth of "the Jews" this phrase may mean, "We are the descendants of Abraham." But it is not impossible that John, like Paul in Gal iii 16, is playing on the singular word to indicate that Jesus is the real descendant of Abraham. We have tried to leave this nuance possible in our translation.

never . . . slaves to anyone. "The Jews" seem to misunderstand Jesus' words about freedom and take them in a political sense. Even on this level, however, their boast is ill founded, for Egypt, Babylonia, and Rome had enslaved them. Perhaps they mean that, being the privileged heirs to the promise to Abraham, they cannot be truly enslaved, although occasionally God has allowed them to be chastised through temporary subjection.

34. *[of sin].* The evidence for omitting this phrase is found in a strong combination of witnesses from the Western family and Clement of Alexandria. In the COMMENT we shall see that there are parallels of thought between these Johannine verses and Paul's argumentation in Galatians and Romans, and so it is possible that a scribe may have added the phrase "of sin" from Rom vi 17, "You were once *slaves of sin*." Outside of John and Romans the picture of men being slaves of sin is found in the NT only in II Pet ii 19, "slaves of corruption."

35. This verse seems to be a parenthetical insertion. The slave here is certainly not the slave of sin in vs. 34. The contrast has changed from that between free and slave in 34 to one of gradation in the household between slave and son. Thus, we probably have a once independent saying from the Johannine tradition that was inserted here because vs. 34 mentions "slave" and 36 mentions "Son." Dodd, *Tradition,* pp. 380–82, makes a good case for interpreting vs. 35 as a short parable of the slave and the son. Definite articles appear before the main nouns as they do in parabolic style. Slave and son are stock characters of the Synoptic parables. As for the moral of the parable, we might think of the Synoptic parable of the vineyard where the tenants are told the vineyard will be taken from them. In John the slave has no permanent place in the household. Also we may think of Matt xvii 25–26 where it is said that earthly kings do not tax their sons for *they are free* (notice the freedom motif in the

Johannine context). John's parable mentions the privileged place of the son. A final parallel that may throw light on the moral of John's parable is in Heb iii 5–6 where Moses is pictured as a household slave while Jesus is the son.

has a permanent place. Literally "abides," the same verb we saw in vs. 31.

the son has a place there forever. This clause is omitted in the Codex Sinaiticus and some minor manuscripts, perhaps because of the difficulty of this verse when read in its present context.

36. *Consequently.* The sequence is from vs. 34: since it is a question of being free from the slavery of sin, only the Son has that power.

37. *a chance to kill me.* This theme last appeared in vii 19, 20, 25. Although these discourses at Tabernacles are loosely connected, some themes run throughout.

makes no headway. Or "has no place." In this latter sense a parallel of thought can be found in v 38: "His word you do not have abiding in your hearts." Also xv 7, addressed to the disciples: "If my words remain a part of you. . . ."

38. *I have seen.* This is a perfect tense, as contrasted with the aorist "heard" in the next line. The tense would seem to imply that Jesus had a pre-existent vision which continues into the present (see v 19). Thüsing, p. 208, prefers this solution to one which would suggest that somehow, even though he was on earth, Jesus remained with the Father in heaven.

you should do what you heard from the Father. This line is somewhat ambiguous, and the manuscripts give evidence of variants that represent scribal attempts to interpret the line. One variant that has support in the Western tradition reads "seen" instead of "heard"; this parallels the "seen" in the first line of the verse. However, if the original reading was "seen" in the second line, then it is very hard to explain how "heard" was ever introduced. But if the original was "heard," the introduction of "seen" by imitation of the first line is easily explained. Another variant is found in a very large group of witnesses (but not Vaticanus or the Bodmer papyri): "*my* Father" is read in the first line of vs. 38, and "*your* father" is read in the second line. This creates an antithetic parallelism where line two is understood as a sarcastic reference to the descent of "the Jews" from the devil (see 44): "You are doing exactly what you have heard from your father." The insertion of the possessives is obviously a scribal attempt at clarification, but did these scribes understand the second line correctly? Bernard, Barrett, and Bultmann are among those who think so. However, it seems too early in this section of the discourse for the introduction of the theme of the devil as the father of the Jews; it makes the development in 41–44 senseless. Here Jesus is still trying to convince his audience to obey the real Father, God. The "you do" is an imperative command, not a sarcastic indicative as it is in vs. 41.

39. *Our father is Abraham.* The interpretation of this depends on the meaning of the second line of vs. 38. If the reference there is to the devil, then "the Jews" say this by way of protest. If the reference there is to Jesus' Father, then here the Jews are saying that they want nothing to do with his "father" for they have Abraham.

If you are . . . you would be doing. This awkward English is a careful rendition of the confused situation in the Greek. The witnesses are divided on three readings: (a) *Real condition:* "If you are . . . do." Codex Vaticanus and P[66] read an imperative in the apodosis. (b) *Contrary-to-fact condition:* "If you were . . . you would be doing." The Byzantine tradition supports this reading, which implies that "the Jews" are not Abraham's children. This seems to contradict vs. 37. (c) *Mixed condition,* as we have translated it. This is supported by P⁷⁵ and Codices Sinaiticus and Bezae. The idea is that the Jews are really Abraham's children, but are denying it by their actions.

The confusion in the witnesses is best explained by assuming that (*c*) was the original reading, and that (*a*) and (*b*) are attempts to iron out the mixed condition by making it consistent in both protasis and apodosis.

40. *I am a man.* This unqualified use of *anthrōpos* for Jesus without any implication of uniqueness is not encountered elsewhere in the NT (see Bernard, II, p. 311). Some theologians have been disturbed by its implications, perhaps because of a crypto-monophysitic strain in their thought. Actually, however, this verse has no great theological import, for "a man" here is simply a semitism for "someone" (BDF, § 301²).

Abraham did not do that. That Abraham would not kill a divine messenger may be a general inference from Abraham's character, or perhaps a specific reference to a scene like that of Gen xviii where he welcomed divine messengers.

41. *doing your father's works.* This is the first instance of the sarcasm that some would find above in vs. 38. Jesus is working on the principle that the son behaves like his father; and although "the Jews" should by right be Abraham's children, their actions betray that the devil is their father (44).

We were not born illegitimate. Literally "of fornication." The usual interpretation is that "the Jews" see in the hint that the devil is their father a charge that Abraham is not their father and that they are illegitimate. In this interpretation, their "we" is simply an answer to the "you [plural]" in Jesus' last statement. But there is another possibility: the Jews may be turning to an *ad hominem* argument against Jesus. He has been talking about his heavenly Father and about their father, but were there not rumors about his own birth? Was there not some question of whether he was really the son of Joseph? (See NOTE on i 45.) The Jews may be saying, *"We* were not born illegitimate [but you were]." There is an early witness to Jewish attacks on the legitimacy of Jesus' birth in Origen *Against Celsus* I 28 (GCS 2:79); and the *Acts of Pilate* II 3, has the Jews charging Jesus: "You were born of fornication."

42. *from God I came forth.* The phrase "from God" found its way into the Nicene creed in the expression "God from God." Theologians have used this passage as a description of the internal life of the Trinity indicating that the Son proceeds from the Father. However, the aorist tense indicates that the reference is rather to the mission of the Son, i.e., the Incarnation. "I came forth and am here" is all one idea. This is confirmed by the same aorist use of *exerchesthai* in xvii 8, where the parallelism shows that "came forth" refers to mission: "They have truly realized that I *came forth* from you, and they have believed that you *sent* me."

am here. The verb *hēkein* is attested in pagan religious usage; it refers to the coming of a deity who makes a solemn appearance. It appears again in I John v 20: "We know that God's Son was here."

Not on my own have I come. Same wording as vii 28; note once again that these Tabernacles discourses share common themes.

43. *hearing.* This is *akouein* with the accusative, a construction that usually refers to physical hearing, rather than to listening with understanding. They have become so obdurate that they cannot even hear him; they are deaf.

44. *The devil is the father.* The Greek can also be read: "the father of the devil"; and the Gnostics took it thus in their opposition to the God of the OT,

whom they regarded as the source of evil because He was responsible for the existence of matter.

you belong to. Literally "you are of"; see the contrast with "the man who belongs to God" in vs. 47.

He was a murderer from the beginning. This is probably a reference to the murder of Abel by Cain (Gen iv 8; I John iii 12–15). In NovT 6 (1963), 79–80, J. Ramón Díaz has pointed out that in the Palestinian Targum of Gen v 3 it is not specified that Cain was the son of Adam, but only that Eve was his mother: "Eve had borne Cain who was not like him [Adam]." This may be an early instance of the tradition that Cain was born of Eve and the evil angel Samael. If this tradition was in mind in vs. 44, we can see very clearly why Jesus says that the devil is the father of "the Jews," because they would kill Jesus, even as Cain, the devil's son, killed Abel. Dahl, *art. cit.*, offers abundant documentation for a reference to Cain. He probably carries the theory too far, however, in maintaining that the father of the Jews mentioned in 38(?), 41, and 44 is Cain and not the devil. He has to explain the clause under discussion here as a textual error or misunderstanding.

never based himself on truth. The implication that the devil was also a liar from the beginning is probably a reference to the deception by the serpent in Gen iii 4–5.

speaks his native language. The fact that Jesus speaks the truth has been stressed as an indication that he comes from the Father; so too the lie is indicative of diabolic origin.

the father of lying. Literally "the father of it/him," i.e., of the lie or of the liar.

45. *believe me.* The dative is used here rather than *eis* with the accusative (which refers to deep faith); the implication *may* be that "the Jews" do not show signs even of initial faith. This verse makes it unbelievable that these words have been addressed to "those Jews who had believed him," as vs. 31 indicates.

46. *Can any one of you convict me of sin?* In viii 7–9 the challenge of being without sin disqualified the scribes and Pharisees from stoning the adulteress, but there was no suggestion that Jesus was disqualified. Heb iv 15 is another witness of the NT tradition that Jesus was sinless. The background of the tradition may be that of the Suffering Servant of Isa liii 9 in whom there was *no deceit.* The Testament of Judah xxiv 1 says: "No sin will be found in him [the star from Jacob]"; but we cannot be certain if this was a Christian interpolation.

47. *belongs to God.* See NOTE on vs. 44.

hears the words of God. This criterion offered by Jesus is used in turn by his disciples in I John iv 6: "Anyone who has knowledge of God listens to us, while anyone who does not belong to God refuses to listen to us."

48. *a Samaritan.* Bernard, II, p. 316, suggests that Jesus is being associated with the Samaritans who refused to recognize the Jews as the exclusive children of Abraham. Bultmann, p. 225[6], sees in the expression a charge of heterodoxy. However, it may simply be tantamount to being "demented," i.e., having a demon of madness (see NOTE on vii 20). The story of Simon Magus in Acts viii 14–24 indicates that possession of a spirit and magical powers were greatly esteemed in Samaria, an attitude that is echoed in later traditions about Simon and Dositheus. In some patristic citations of vs. 48 (Mehlmann, *art. cit.*) the charge of being illegitimate ("born of fornication") is added; see NOTE on vs. 41.

49. *honor.* An interesting passage to be compared with the use of "honor" and "glory" in vss. 49–50 and 54 is that of II Pet i 17, which speaks of the Trans-

figuration as the moment when Jesus received honor and glory from the Father.

50. *One who does seek it and He passes judgment.* This may be an echo of Isa xvi 5: "A throne shall be set up in covenant love [*ḥesed*], and on it shall sit in fidelity ['*emet*] one who passes judgment and seeks out justice." In John, even though no object is expressed for "seeks," what God seeks is the glory of the Son.

51. *see death.* A Hebraism for "die" (Ps lxxxix 48; Luke ii 26). When the questioners pick up Jesus' words in the next verse, they cite him as saying "taste death."

52. *experience death.* Literally "taste death"; this idiom is not found in the OT, but it is the same as "see death." It is used elsewhere in the NT for physical death, and that is how "the Jews" misunderstand it here; but Jesus is referring to spiritual death. The *Gospel of Thomas,* saying ⅟1, seems to draw from John's usage: "Everyone who finds the explanation of these words will not taste death." (See NTS 9 [1962–63], 159.)

53. *Abraham who is dead.* Here John uses *hostis,* an indefinite relative. It may indicate that the antecedent is taken as a type, thus: "Abraham who nevertheless was a man who died" (BDF, § 293[2]). This could easily become causal, becoming the equivalent of "since he died." But in NT Greek such distinctions based on the precise use of relatives are tenuous.

pretend to be. Literally "make yourself."

54. *'our God.'* The textual witnesses betray considerable confusion as to whether one should read "your God" in indirect discourse, or "our God" in direct discourse. The latter seems less polished and thus more original; it is found in both Bodmer papyri.

55. *you do not know Him . . . I do know Him.* The first "know" is from *gignōskein;* the latter from *eidenai* (*oida*). See App. I:9. The affirmation that Jesus does *know* the Father is expressed both with *eidenai* (vii 29) and with *gignōskein* (x 15, xvii 25). Especially instructive for comparison are:
vii 28–29: "Him you do not know. I know Him."—*eidenai* in both parts.
xvii 25: "Though the world did not know you, I knew you."—*gignōskein* in both parts.

56. *rejoiced . . . glad.* It is strange that the first verb is stronger than the second, for we would expect the fulfillment to be stronger than the prospect. There is considerable versional and patristic evidence for reading "desired" in place of "rejoiced." This may stem from the cross-influence of Matt xiii 17 (=Luke x 24): "Many prophets and just men have *desired* to see what you see." But scholars like Torrey, Burrows, and Boismard suggest that the Greek variants of John represent a misunderstanding of an original Aramaic text. See Boismard, EvJean, pp. 48–49.

at the prospect of. This is literally a purpose clause, but there is a tacit idea of desire and hope; the purpose clause takes coloring from the main verb, "rejoiced" (ZGB, § 410). Others think that the *hina* which introduces the clause stands for *hote,* "when" (ZGB, § 429).

When he saw it. Up to the time of Maldonatus (16th century) exegetes were almost unanimous in assuming that this referred to a vision that took place during Abraham's life. More recently, however, the interpretation has gained ground that John means that after Abraham died, he saw Jesus' day. Bernard, II, p. 321, suggests that this might be a reference to the joy among the OT saints when the news reached Hades that Jesus was born. Yet, John's whole method of using the OT militates against this view. In xii 41 we are told that

Isaiah saw the glory of Jesus, and the reference is to an event in Isaiah's life, namely his initial vision in the Temple. If an incident in Abraham's life is meant, it may be the birth of Isaac which was the initial fulfillment of God's promises to Abraham, the first in a chain of actions that would ultimately lead to the coming of Jesus. This fits the theme of joy, for in Gen xvii 17 we are told that at the annunciation of Isaac's birth, Abraham fell to the ground and laughed (in scorn, but the rabbis took it as joy); see also Gen xxi 6. Jubilees xvi 17–19 says that Abraham was told that it was through Isaac that the holy people of God would be descendant, and that both Abraham and Sarah rejoiced at the news. There are later rabbinic traditions that Abraham saw the whole history of his descendants in a vision (Midrash Rabbah XLIV 22 on Gen xv 18); IV Ezra iii 14 says that God revealed to Abraham the end of times. Cavaletti, *art. cit.*, suggests in particular the tradition that Abraham saw the Temple rebuilt, and he connects viii 56 with ii 19 (see following NOTE, on viii 57 and ii 20). This would evoke the theme of resurrection (resurrected Jesus=rebuilt Temple) as a commentary on the statement in viii 51 about not seeing death.

57. *not even fifty years old.* We have seen that the reference to forty-six years in ii 20 has been implausibly interpreted as an estimation of Jesus' age (see NOTE there). Luke iii 23 says that Jesus was about thirty when he began the ministry. Irenaeus, following John, says that Jesus was not far short of fifty when he died (*Adv. Haer.* II 23:6; PG 7:785). Chrysostom and other witnesses read "forty" in the text of John viii 57, probably as an attempt to harmonize with Luke. For a full discussion see G. Ogg, "The Age of Jesus when He Taught," NTS 5 (1958–59), 291–98.

How can you have seen Abraham? Although the majority of witnesses favor this reading, there is good evidence, including P[75], for reading: "How can Abraham have seen you?" This is supported by Bernard, II, p. 321, and he explains how the translation we have chosen may reflect a mistake in copying. However, the second translation seems to be an adaptation to the wording of vs. 56. "The Jews" would be more likely to give priority to seeing Abraham rather than to seeing Jesus.

58. *before Abraham even came into existence.* Some Western evidence, including Bezae, omits the verb (*ginesthai*) and has simply: "Before Abraham I am." In this verse the distinction is obvious between *ginesthai*, which is used of mortals, and the divine use of *einai*, "to be," in the form "I AM." This same distinction was seen in the Prologue: the Word *was*, but through him all things *came into being*. In the OT the same distinction is found in the address to Yahweh in Ps xc 2: "Before the mountains *came into being* . . . from age to age you *are*."

59. *picked up rocks.* The Temple of Herod was not finished, and there would have been stones lying around among the building materials. For a stoning in the temple precincts see Josephus *Ant.* XVII.IX.3;✗216. A passage like this throws no light on the question of whether or not the Sanhedrin had the power of capital punishment; it is presented as a spontaneous act of indignation and one not likely to be restrained by the provisions of Roman law, if such a law existed.

temple precincts. At the end of the verse a late Greek tradition adds: "passing through their midst, and thus he got away." The first of these added phrases is from Luke iv 30; the second represents a misdivision of ix 1 (which is the next verse in John) and the transfer of the verb of motion from there to here. Despite the impression created by this scribal addition, there is no clear suggestion here that Jesus' escape was miraculous, as it was in Luke iv 30.

COMMENT

Literary Analysis

This third division of ch. viii shows far fewer parallels to previous passages of John than the first two divisions showed. There are signs of a few editorial insertions (see NOTES on vss. 31 and 35), but on the whole we have here a rather homogeneous discourse. The theme of Abraham holds it together, being introduced in vs. 33, continuing through 37, 39, 40, 53, 56, 57, and closing the discourse in 58. The technique of developing the discourse through objections on the part of "the Jews" reaches perfection here, and one can readily sense the increasing bitterness on both sides. In the early part of the discourse the Jews argue with Jesus, but as it goes on they hurl at him accusations of being illegitimate and possessed by a demon, and conclude by attempting to kill him. In the early part of the discourse Jesus pleads with the Jews to act like children of Abraham, but as it goes on he speaks more harshly, even accusing them of being the children of the devil. W. Kern, *art. cit.*, would break the discourse into three strophes which, with some adaptations, can serve us as convenient subdivisions for our discussion:

(1) 31–41a: "the Jews" claim to have Abraham as their Father. Notice how their objections in 33 and 39 balance one another.

(2) 41b–47 (Kern goes to 48): Jesus tells them that their real father is the devil.

(3) 48–59: the claims Jesus makes for himself, and comparison with Abraham.

At most, however, these subdivisions represent slight changes in the direction of the general thought, which is consistent.

COMMENT: DETAILED

(1) 31–41a: *Abraham and the Jews*

Dodd, *art. cit.*, has done much to clarify the background and purpose of this discourse in the Gospel and in NT thought. The insistence with which the people of Israel claimed Abraham as their father is traceable to the promise of God to Abraham that his descendants would be a blessing to the whole world and God's chosen ones (Gen xxii 17–18; Ps cv 6). In the course of time the sense of responsibility that accompanied the status of being a son of Abraham inevitably lost its sharpness, and for some it was replaced by a sense of automatic divine protection. In his *Dialogue with Trypho,* Justin charges that the Jews, as seed of Abraham, expected to receive the kingdom of God no matter what their personal lives had become (CXL 2; PG 6:797;

also StB, I, pp. 117 ff.). In the Lazarus parable we see the reflection of
a current belief that anyone who called on "father Abraham" would never
go to the place of eternal torture (Luke xvi 24), a belief that Jesus corrected. In his ministry Jesus reacted strongly against the claim that being
children of Abraham gave an automatic status of sanctity or privilege. John
the Baptist had warned that God could create a new generation of descendants for Abraham from the stones (Matt iii 7–10). Jesus warned that
strangers would come to sit with Abraham at the heavenly banquet table
while the children of the kingdom would be cast out (Matt viii 11–12). Perhaps Matt xxiii 9 was also directed against the presumption of the children
of Abraham: "Call no one on earth your father, for you have one Father
who is in heaven." Thus, at least the substance of Jesus' attack on the
Jewish claim to be children of Abraham as it is found in John viii fits in with
what we know to have been a theme traditionally associated with Jesus.

In the conflict of the Church with the Synagogue this theme was greatly
developed (and indeed this development has left its mark on some of the
Synoptic sayings cited above). In Paul we find a denial that the promise of
Abraham was directed to the Jews. Galatians iii 16 draws an exegetical
argument from the fact that the OT speaks of Abraham's offspring in the
singular (*sperma* in the Greek), an indication for Paul that it meant Jesus
Christ. So Paul can say to the Christians: "If you are Christ's, then you are
descendant from Abraham (iii 29)"; the Christians are Abraham's children
through his wife Sarah, a freewoman, and not through the slave girl Hagar,
as are all those who are slaves of the Law.

The themes of freedom and slavery and of being true descendants of
Abraham also run through John viii 31–41. The particular import of these
verses is seen if we remember that, in part at least, John was directed to
Jewish Christians who were hesitating between their obligations to the
synagogue and their ancestral customs on the one hand, and their belief in
Jesus on the other. It has even been suggested that the strange reference to
"those Jews who had believed in him" in vs. 31 was meant to refer to the
Jewish Christians, but the desire of these Jews in 37 to kill Jesus does not
fit in with the suggestion. Rather we think that the substance of the discourse is directed to "the Jews" in the ordinary Johannine meaning of the
word, i.e., those who are hostile to Jesus, but that many of the lines have a
secondary applicability to the situation of the Jewish Christians.

In particular, vs. 31 would clearly remind the Jewish Christians that what
distinguishes the true disciples of Jesus is abiding in his word, not any
special loyalty to the Law. The revelation that the Son of God has brought,
which is the truth, has set free those who believe in it (32, 36). Paul had
cried out, "Christ has set us free . . . do not submit again to a yoke of
slavery (Gal v 1)." Thus, for Paul slavery was servitude to the yoke of the
Law, and, tragically, the Law could not take away sin but only make sin
more dangerous (Rom vii 7 ff.). The progression of Paul's thought is summed
up in Rom viii 2: "The law of the Spirit of life in Christ Jesus has set me free
from the law of sin and death." John does not speak of slavery to the Law,

but goes directly to a slavery to sin (34). The Jewish Christians who received
the gospel message would, of course, understand that Jesus was speaking of
freedom and slavery on the spiritual level, but "the Jews" who are pictured
as Jesus' actual audience typically misunderstand and think that he is speaking on a political level. The nationalistic pride found in vs. 33 resembles the
magnificent boast of Eleazar to the besieged Jews at Masada (Josephus
War VII.viii.6;⚹323): "Long ago we determined to be slaves to neither
the Romans nor anyone else, save God." But Jesus says that they are not free
with the only freedom that concerns him, a freedom from sin. This is the
freedom of the true descendant of Abraham (*sperma* in the singular; see
Note on vs. 33), and is a freedom that can come only through the Son (36).
We have seen in the Note that vs. 35 is a later insertion into the discourse,
but perhaps its introduction was considered appropriate because it fitted into
the use of this discourse of John in polemic with the Jews. The theme in vs.
35 concerns the possibility of the slave's being dispossessed from the household. As we saw in the Matthean passages we cited above, the possibility
was held up to the Jews that they might lose their privileged place as
children of Abraham. In Gal iv 30 Paul describes how Abraham's son by
the slave woman was cast out in favor of his son by the free woman.

The phraseology of vs. 37 is more diplomatic than Paul's words. For
Paul only the Christians are the true descendants of Abraham. But the
Johannine Jesus admits that "the Jews" are descendant from Abraham as part
of his plan to get them to act like Abraham. Strangely enough, there is no
recourse here to Abraham as a man of *faith*, a theme that seems to have
been the common property of the early Church (Gal iii 6; Rom iv 3; James ii
22–23; Heb xi 8, 17). Rather, the stress in John is on doing *works* worthy
of Abraham, and only in the passing references to Jesus' word making no
headway (37) and his having spoken the truth (40) is there an oblique
reference to their lack of faith.

The mention of Jesus' Father in vs. 38 is countered with an implicit rejection by "the Jews" in 39. This causes Jesus to harden his attitude. In vs. 39
he is still insisting that they are children of Abraham (real condition in the
protasis), but by 41 he says that their works betray a demonic descent. This
variation in statement is trying to capture the same idea that Paul gives
expression to in Rom ix 7: "Not all who are descendant from Abraham are
children of Abraham." That spiritual characteristics were required to be
truly worthy of Abraham is also found in roughly contemporary Jewish
thought; *Pirqe Aboth* v 22 says: "A good eye, a lowly spirit, and a humble
mind are the marks of the disciples of Abraham our father."

(2) 41b–47: *The real father of "the Jews"—God or the devil?*

In vs. 41a, with Jesus' first hint that the devil is the father of "the Jews,"
the theme of Abraham slips into the background. It becomes clear that Jesus
is not challenging the purity of their descent from Abraham; he is challenging their status as God's people. Perhaps by implication their response

in 41b is a vilification of Jesus (see NOTE), but its main burden is to defend the purity of their religious status. In the OT unfaithfulness to Yahweh was often described as fornication or adultery, and the Israelites who engaged in false worship were called the children of fornication (Hos ii 4). Therefore, when in 41 the Jews deny that they are children of fornication, they are denying that they have wandered from the true path of the worship of God. In stressing that God is their father, they are reiterating the terms of the covenant with Moses whereby Israel became God's child (Exod iv 22) and Yahweh became Israel's father (Deut xxxii 6)—a theme reiterated constantly in the prophetic preaching (Isa lxiv 8; Mal ii 10). A passage that is particularly applicable here is Isa lxiii 16, addressed to Yahweh: "For you are our father. Even were Abraham not to recognize us, . . . you, Lord, are our father."

Jesus answers with a blunt denial. In vs. 39, by expressing himself in a conditional sentence with a "real" protasis, he admitted their claim to descent from Abraham (according to the flesh); in 42, by expressing himself in a conditional sentence that is entirely contrary to fact, Jesus totally denies that God is their Father. The criterion for filiation is once more the principle that the son should act like the father, and the actions of "the Jews" in hating Jesus shows that they are not God's children. It is interesting that in Gal iii 26, 29, we have Paul joining the question of being God's sons with that of being Abraham's descendants. Paul assures the Christians that they are sons of God through faith, thus by implication contrasting them with the Jews; but Paul does not go so far as to say that the Jews are the sons of the devil. If the statement that John reports to this effect (44) seems harsh, similar statements were attributed to Jesus in the Synoptic tradition. In speaking to the scribes and Pharisees about the type of convert they make, Jesus says: "When he becomes a proselyte, he becomes twice as much *a son of hell* as yourselves (Matt xxiii 15)." In the explanation of the Parable of the Weeds (Matt xiii 38–39), we are told that the weeds who are opposed to the sons of the kingdom are *the sons of the Evil One*. We should also note that the same thought is found elsewhere in the Johannine literature, for I John iii 8 says: "The man who acts sinfully belongs to the devil because the devil is a sinner from the beginning."

The stress on the devil's essential nature or what he was from the beginning pervades vs. 44; perhaps it is by contrast with viii 25 where Jesus stressed that he himself was what he had been telling them from the beginning. Here for the first time in the Gospel the fact that the devil is Jesus' real antagonist comes to the fore. This motif will grow louder and louder as the hour of Jesus approaches, until the Passion is presented as the struggle to the death between Jesus and Satan (xii 31, xiv 30, xvi 11, xvii 15). Thus, in seeking to bring about the death of Jesus which is the devil's main purpose, "the Jews" are doing the work of Satan. This is exemplified to the extreme in Judas; for, as he betrayed Jesus to death, Satan entered into him (xiii 2,

27). In emphasizing the essential nature of the devil as a sinner, a murderer, and a liar, Jesus is speaking in the tradition of the late OT period which traced all sin and death to the devil's work described in the early chapters of Genesis. Wis ii 24 says: "By the envy of the devil death entered the world"; Sir xxv 24 says: "Sin began with a woman [Eve], and because of her we all die." We pointed out in the NOTES on vs. 44 that the specific charge of lying is to be connected with Satan's deception of Eve, and the charge of murder to the story of Cain. It is possible that in the latter instance the charge is even wider, and that as in Wisdom of Solomon and Sirach the penalty of death brought by the first sin is meant. That the serpent of Gen iii was considered a murderer is seen in a 4th-century A.D. work, *Apostolic Constitutions* (VIII 7:5; Funk ed., I, 482).

We may pause for a moment to analyze the emphasis on lying in the last part of vs. 44. In Johannine dualism, lying is equivalent to darkness; it is part of the diabolic realm that is opposed to the truth and light of God. Thus, we are not to think here of occasional deception but of fundamental perversion. If Jesus Christ is the truth (xiv 6), the devil is the liar par excellence. In the Gospel the dualism of light/darkness is more common than that of truth/perversion; but in I John the latter form of dualism is frequent (i 6, 10, ii 4, iv 20, v 10). I John ii 22 asks, "Who is the liar? None other than he who denies that Jesus is the Christ. This is the antichrist, denying the Father and the Son" (also II John 7). This is very close to the thought in the division of John viii under consideration. A similar dualism is well known at Qumran where the spirit of truth is opposed to the spirit of perversion (also see NOTE on vs. 32). These are not only two great angelic leaders locked in battle (1QS iii 19), but also two ways of life in which men walk (1QS iv 2 ff.). So too in the Johannine literature: if in the Gospel truth and lying are personified in Jesus and Satan, in I John iv 1–6 the spirit of truth and the spirit of error are found in men; and in II John 4 and III John 3 Christians walk in truth. (See our article on John and Qumran in CBQ 17 [1955], 559–61.) Finally, we may note that the emphasis on lying in this third division in the discourse in ch. viii stands in contrast to the emphasis on truth in the first two divisions. There we heard that Jesus' witness can be *verified* (14), that his judgment is *valid* (16), that what he says reflects the *truthfulness* of the One who sent him (26).

Verses 45–46 help to remind the reader of Jesus' earlier words concerning truth. In particular, vs. 45 points up the radical opposition that exists between the sons of the father of lying and the truth. We might expect to have vs. 45 say that, even *though* Jesus told the truth, they did not believe him; but John actually says that they did not believe *because* he told the truth. In iii 20 we heard that the children of darkness hate the light; here the children of lying hate the truth. Jesus may plead with them plaintively (46), but they are radically incapable of hearing (47—see NOTE).

Verse 47 forms an inclusion with 41 and 42. The Jews claimed in 41 that God was their father; Jesus terminates his response to them in 47 with: "You do not belong to God." In 42 Jesus opened his response by pointing out that they did not love him even though he came forth from (*ek*) God; in 47 he says that the reason they do not hear him is because they are not from (*ek*) God. For a working out of this see Barrosse, TS 18 (1957), 557.

(3) 48–59: *The claims Jesus makes for himself and comparison with Abraham*

Jesus has said that "the Jews" are not the true children of Abraham (vss. 31–41a), nor the true children of God (41b–47); in the third and final subdivision of this section they answer by challenging his claims about who *he* is. Jesus has told the Jews that they are of the devil; now they say that he is the one who has the demon (48). Jesus says that he has nothing to do with a demon—that is ruled out by the honor that he gives the Father (49). We are not far removed here from the scene in the Synoptic tradition (Mark iii 22–25) where Jesus is accused of being possessed by the prince of demons. He answers by saying that he is casting out demons (and thus doing the work of God) and this is not the work of Satan. In the charges against Jesus of being illegitimate (vs. 41—see NOTE), of being a Samaritan and of being demented we have forerunners of the personal attacks on Jesus that became part of Jewish apologetics against Christianity. (Needless to say, there was a corresponding vilification of the Jews by Christian apologists.)

In Scene One of the Tabernacles discourses (vii 18) Jesus offered the fact that he was not seeking his own glory as a criterion that he was telling the truth. This is repeated here in vss. 50 and 54 with the added note that God seeks the glory of Jesus and that this glorification of Jesus will be accomplished through the judgment of vindication that the Father will pass. Later on, in the hour of Passion, death, resurrection, and ascension, which is the hour of judgment on the world (xii 31, xvi 11), we shall be told that the Son is glorified (xii 23, xiii 31, xvii 1). For some men this judgment that vindicates and glorifies the Son will be a judgment that leads to death and the realm of the devil, but not for those who keep Jesus' word (51). "Keeping" Jesus' word or commandment is a common Johannine theme (xiv 21, 23–24, xv 20, xvii 6; I John ii 5). It means to hear and obey, and so the promise in vs. 51 is very much like that of v 24: "The man who hears my word . . . possesses eternal life . . . he has passed from death to life." Yet, perhaps "keep" means just a bit more than "hear"; it echoes the notion of the word of Jesus which abides in the believer (see NOTE on vs. 31). The word of Jesus is the antidote to the sin and death which the devil brought into the world in the Garden of Eden. It is not at all unlikely that we should interpret the promise of immortality in vs. 51 in light of the murdering proclivities of the devil mentioned in 44; See A. M. Dubarle, "Le péché originel dans les suggestions de l'Evangile," RSPT 39 (1955), 603–14.

Jesus' statement is greeted by the Jews in vss. 52–53 with the misunderstanding that appears so often in John's narrative. Always thinking on the level of this world below, they understand his remarks in terms of deliverance from physical death, just as they had understood, mistakenly, his remarks about freedom in terms of political freedom (33). Their objection reintroduces the Abraham theme that dominated vss. 31–41. The Jews throw up the example of Abraham to Jesus much in the same way that the Samaritan woman (iv 12) had thrown up the example of Jacob to him: "Surely, you don't pretend to be greater than our father Jacob who gave us this well?" They demand to know who he pretends to be, thus reiterating their question of vs. 25. There Jesus answered them in terms of divinity, re-emphasizing in vs. 28 the divine *egō eimi* of 24; he can do no less here, and his response will terminate in 58 with another divine *egō eimi*.

To lead up to that solemn statement Jesus returns in vs. 54 to the theme of the glory which he shares with the Father. We have heard several times in these Tabernacles discourses of the failure of "the Jews" to know or recognize God (vii 28–29, viii 19). In vs. 55 this is worked in cleverly with the theme of lying so prominent in viii 44. But in his self-defense Jesus has not neglected the protest of the Jews concerning Abraham, and so in 56 Jesus insists that he is the real fulfillment of the history of Israel that began with the promise to Abraham. Once before (v 46) he had said that if the Jews believed Moses, they would also believe him, for it was of him that Moses wrote. Now he assures them that it was of him that Abraham had a vision. They had asked if he pretended to be greater than Abraham; he tells them that Abraham was but his forerunner, looking forward to his day. The thought that through its spokesmen the OT looked forward with joy to Jesus is also found in Matt xiii 17 (see NOTE on vs. 56) and Heb xi 13 ("These all died in faith, not having received what was promised, but having seen and greeted it from afar").

The climax of all that Jesus has said at Tabernacles comes in the triumphant proclamation by Jesus of the divine name, "I AM," which he bears (see App. IV). In viii 12 he had opened this third scene of the Tabernacles discourses with "*I am* the light of the world"; the concluding "I AM" of vs. 58 represents an inclusion. No clearer implication of divinity is found in the Gospel tradition, and "the Jews" recognize this implication. Leviticus xxiv 16 had commanded: "He who blasphemes *the name* of the Lord shall be put to death; all the congregation shall stone him." We are not certain what the legal definition of blasphemy was in Jesus' time; but in John's account the use of the divine name represented by *egō eimi* seems to be sufficient, for the Jews seek to carry out the command of Leviticus. In the view of the evangelist, however, they are simply proving that Jesus spoke the truth: they are murderers like their father! Jesus hides (*kryptein*) himself by slipping out of the temple precincts. This too may be an inclusion designed to hold together chs. vii and viii, for we remember that Jesus first came up to the Temple for Tabernacles in secret (*en kryptō:* vii 10).

Before we close this discussion, we may ask whether there is any likelihood that Jesus made such a public claim to divinity as that represented in vs. 58, or are we dealing here exclusively with the profession of faith of the later Church? As a general principle it is certainly true that through their faith the evangelists were able to clarify a picture of Jesus that was obscure during the ministry. However, it is difficult to avoid the impression created by all the Gospels that the Jewish authorities saw something blasphemous in Jesus' understanding of himself and his role. There is no convincing proof that the only real reason why Jesus was put to death was because he was a social, or ethical, reformer, or because he was politically dangerous. But how can we determine scientifically what the blasphemous element was in Jesus' stated or implied claims about himself? In the clarity with which John presents the divine "I AM" statement of Jesus, is he making explicit what was in some way implicit? No definitive answer seems possible on purely scientific grounds. We also mention the possibility that John is historically correct in showing that the Jewish authorities took umbrage at Jesus' claims long before that Sanhedrin trial when, on the night before Jesus' death, another *egō eimi* (Mark xiv 62) provoked the high priest to cry blasphemy and call for death.

Perhaps here we should re-emphasize that a chapter like John viii with its harsh statements about "the Jews" must be understood and evaluated against the polemic background of the times when it was written. To take literally a charge like that of vs. 44 and to think that the Gospel imposes on Christians the belief that the Jews are children of the devil is to forget the time-conditioned element in Scripture. (Esther ix with its reverse pogrom presents to thoughtful Jews a similar problem of time-conditioned religious attitudes.) Lest the picture seem too dark, we must remember that this same Fourth Gospel records the saying of Jesus that salvation comes from the Jews (iv 22).

BIBLIOGRAPHY

Cavaletti, S., "La visione messianica di Abramo (Giov. 8, 58)," BibOr 3 (1961), 179–81.

Charlier, J.-P., "L'exégèse johannique d'un précepte légal: Jean VIII 17," RB 67 (1960), 503–15.

Dahl, N. A., "Der Erstgeborene Satans und der Vater des Teufels (Polyk. 7:1 und Joh 8:44)," *Apophoreta* (Haenchen Festschrift; Berlin: Töpelmann, 1964), pp. 70–84.

Dodd, C. H., "A l'arrière plan d'un dialogue johannique," RHPR 37 (1957), 5–17 on viii 33–47.

Funk, R. W., "Papyrus Bodmer II (P66) and John 8, 25," HTR 51 (1958), 95–100.

Kern, W., "Die symmetrische Gesamtaufbau von Joh. 8, 12–58," ZKT 78 (1956), 451–54.

Mehlmann, John, "John 8,48 in Some Patristic Quotations," Bib 44 (1963), 206–9.

Smothers, E. R., "Two Readings in Papyrus Bodmer II," HTR 51 (1958), especially pp. 111–22 on viii 25.

34. AFTERMATH OF TABERNACLES:
—THE HEALING OF A BLIND MAN
(ix 1–41)

As a sign that he is the light, Jesus gives sight to a man born blind

IX 1 Now, as he walked along, he saw a man who had been blind from birth. 2 His disciples asked him, "Rabbi, who committed the sin that caused him to be born blind, he or his parents?" 3 "Neither," answered Jesus.

> "It was no sin on this man's part,
> nor on his parents' part.
> Rather, it was to let God's work be revealed in him.
> 4 We must work the works of Him who sent me
> while it is day.
> Night is coming
> when no one can work.
> 5 As long as I am in the world,
> I am the light of the world."

6 With that he spat on the ground, made mud with his saliva, and smeared the man's eyes with the mud. 7 Then Jesus told him, "Go, wash in the pool of Siloam." (This name means "one who has been sent.") And so he went off and washed, and he came back able to see.

8 Now his neighbors and the people who had been accustomed to see him begging began to ask, "Isn't this the fellow who used to sit and beg?" 9 Some were claiming that it was he; others maintained that it was not, but just someone who looked like him. He himself said, "I'm the one, all right." 10 So they said to him, "How were your eyes opened?" 11 He answered, "That man they call Jesus made mud and smeared it on my eyes, telling me to go to Siloam and wash. When I did go and wash, I got my sight." 12 "Where is he?" they asked. "I have no idea," he replied.

13 They took the man who had been born blind to the Pharisees. (14 Note that it was on a Sabbath day that Jesus had made the mud and opened his eyes.) 15 In their turn, the Pharisees too began to inquire how he had got his sight. He told them, "He put mud on my

---

13: *took.* In the historical present tense.

eyes; and I washed and now I can see." 16 This prompted some of the Pharisees to assert, "This man is not from God because he does not keep the Sabbath." Others objected, "How can a man perform such signs and still be a sinner?" And they were sharply divided. 17 Then they addressed the blind man again, "Since it was your eyes he opened, what have you to say about him?" "He is a prophet," he replied.

18 But the Jews refused to believe that he really had been born blind and had subsequently gained his sight until they summoned the parents of the man [who had gained his sight]. 19 "Is this your son?" they asked. "Do you confirm that he was born blind? If so, how can he see now?" 20 The parents gave this answer: "We know that this is our son and that he was born blind. 21 But we do not know how he can see now, nor do we know who opened his eyes. [Ask him.] He is old enough to speak for himself." (22 His parents answered this way because they were afraid of the Jews, for the Jews had already agreed that anybody who acknowledged Jesus as Messiah would be put out of the Synagogue. 23 That was why his parents said, "He is old enough. Ask him.")

24 And so, for the second time, they summoned the man who had been born blind and said to him, "Give glory to God. We know that this man is a sinner." 25 "Whether he's a sinner or not, I do not know," he replied. "One thing I do know: I was blind before, now I can see." 26 They persisted, "Just what did he do to you? How did he open your eyes?" 27 "I told you once and you didn't pay attention," he answered them. "Why do you want to hear it all over again? Don't tell me that you too want to become his disciples?" 28 Scornfully they retorted, "You are the one who is that fellow's disciple; we are disciples of Moses. 29 We know that God has spoken to Moses, but we don't even know where this fellow comes from." 30 The man objected, "Now that's strange! Here you don't even know where he comes from; yet he opened my eyes. 31 We know that God pays no attention to sinners, but He does listen to someone who is devout and obeys His will. 32 It is absolutely unheard of that anyone ever opened the eyes of a man born blind. 33 If this man were not from God, he could have done nothing." 34 "What!" they exclaimed. "You were born steeped in sin, and now you are lecturing us?" Then they threw him out.

35 When Jesus heard about his expulsion, he found him and said, "Do you believe in the Son of Man?" 36 He answered, "Who is he, sir, that I may believe in him?" 37 "You have seen him," Jesus replied, "for it is he who is speaking with you." [38 "I do believe, Lord," he said and bowed down to worship him. 39 Then Jesus said,]

17: *addressed.* In the historical present tense.

"I came into this world for judgment:
that those who do not see may be able to see,
and those who do see may become blind."

40 Some of the Pharisees who were there with him overheard this and
said to him, "Surely we are not to be considered blind too?" 41 Jesus
told them,

"If only you *were* blind,
then you would not be guilty of sin.
But now that you claim to see,
your sin remains."

NOTES

ix 1. *Now.* Literally "and"—a rather abrupt beginning.

as he walked along. This descriptive expression occurs only here in John but is
not an unusual introduction to a scene in the Synoptics: Mark i 16, ii 14; Matt
ix 27 (healing of the two blind men), xx 30 (healing of two blind men near
Jericho). It is doubtful whether this scene is in direct sequence to the preceding
scene, although, as the Gospel now stands, Jesus could be thought of as walking
away from the Temple. Yet he is certainly not in hiding (viii 59).

from birth. This is a Greek expression attested in LXX and the pagan writers
(BAG, p. 154). The more Semitic expression seems to be "from the mother's
womb" (Matt xix 12; Acts iii 2).

2. *disciples.* We have not heard of Jesus' disciples being with him since ch. vi
in Galilee. If these disciples are the Twelve, this is the first indication that they
came up to Jerusalem with Jesus. Or are they the obscure Judean disciples of
vii 3? Or are we dealing with a scene that was once independent and actually took
place in Jerusalem on another occasion?

who committed the sin? Despite the Book of Job, the old theory of a direct
causal relationship between sin and sickness was still alive in Jesus' time, as this
question and the similar one in Luke xiii 2 indicate. If an adult got sick, the
blame could lie in his own behavior. The problem of a baby born with an
affliction offered greater difficulty. Yet, Exod xx 5 offered a principle for the
solution: "I, the Lord your God, am a jealous God, visiting the iniquity of the
fathers upon the children to the third and fourth generation. . . ." Some of
the rabbis held that not only could the sin of the parents leave its mark on an
infant, but also the infant could sin in the mother's womb (StB, II, pp. 528–29).
For Jesus' attitude toward the relation of sin to sickness see NOTE on v 14.

3. *it was to let.* Jesus was asked about the cause of the man's blindness, but he
answers in terms of its purpose.

to let God's works be revealed in him. The rabbis spoke of God giving men
"punishments of love," i.e., chastisements which, if a person suffered them
generously, would bring him long life and rewards. But this does not seem to be
Jesus' thought here or in xi 4; rather, it touches upon God's manipulation of
history to glorify His name. A good example would be Exod ix 16, cited in
Rom ix 17, where God tells Pharaoh: "This is why I have spared you: to show

you my power so that my name may be declared throughout all the earth." That Jesus' works are really God's works is implied in Matt xii 28; Mark ii 7.

4. *We . . . me.* This is the reading of the better manuscripts, but some witnesses have attempted to level out the difference in person: "We . . . us," or "I . . . me." Bultmann, p. 251⁹, prefers the latter and suggests that "we" was introduced by the Christian community. Rather, the "we" is probably Jesus' way of associating his disciples with him in his work. That he desires this association is seen in iv 35–38; note, too, that in the introduction to ch. xi, which has much in common with the introduction to ch. ix, the use of the first person plural is frequent. As for the insistence that "we" must work while it is day, in xii 36 it is said that the disciples have the light and they are invited to become sons of light. Another instance of Jesus' associating the disciples with him in his speech is Mark iv 30: "To what shall *we* compare the kingdom of God?"

must work the works . . . while it is day. The same type of necessity is expressed in Luke xiii 32. Dodd, *Tradition*, p. 186, suggests that a statement of proverbial wisdom may underlie the Johannine saying and cites rabbinic examples.

5. *I am the light of the world.* The disciples are given this role in Matt v 14. Jesus' self-description may stem from Isa xlix 6, where the (Suffering) Servant is described as a light to the nations.

6. *With that.* In most of the Synoptic accounts of the healing of the blind there is a request on the part of the afflicted man.

he spat. Only John and Mark (vii 33: *healing a deaf mute;* viii 23: *healing a blind man*) record that Jesus used spittle. The Marcan spittle miracles seem to have been deliberately omitted by Matthew and Luke. The use of spittle was part of the primitive tradition about Jesus but left him open to a charge of engaging in magical practice. In the Mishnaic tractate *Sanhedrin* 10:1, Rabbi Aqiba (2nd century) is reported as cursing anyone who utters charms over a wound; the Tosephta adds spitting to the utterance of charms (Barrett, p. 296).

smeared. Or "anointed" (*epichriein*); this is the best attested Greek reading and is supported by both Bodmer papyri. Some scholars, e.g., Barrett, suspect that it was borrowed from vs. 11, and they prefer the reading of Codex Vaticanus: "he *put* mud *on* the man's eyes" (*epitithenai*). However, this reading could have been borrowed from vs. 15.

mud. Irenaeus, *Adv. Haer.* v 15:2 (PG 7:1165), sees here a symbol of man's being created from the earth; see the use of "clay" or "mud" in Job iv 19, x 9.

7. *wash in the pool.* An antecedent for such a directive may be found in II Kings v 10–13, where Elisha does not heal Naaman on the spot but sends him to wash in the Jordan. In Luke xvii 12–15 Jesus does not heal the lepers immediately but sends them off to the priests and they are healed on the way. As for Jesus' ability to cure at a distance, this has been shown in the healing of the royal official's son in iv 46–54.

Siloam. This pool, known in Hebrew as Shiloaḥ, was situated at the southern extremity of the eastern hill of Jerusalem, near the conjunction of the Kidron and Tyropean valleys. It was a repository for the waters from the spring of Gihon which were conducted to the pool by a canal. Mentioned in Isa viii 6, the water of Siloam was used in the water ceremonies and processions of Tabernacles. Rabbinic sources mention it as a place of purification (StB, II, p. 583).

"one who has been sent." The name "Shiloh" in MT of Gen xlix 10 was interpreted in a messianic sense in Jewish tradition of a later period. Had a

mystique developed around the not too dissimilar name "Shiloaḥ" on the basis of Isa viii 6? "Shiloaḥ" appears to be related to the root *šlḥ*, "to send"; but whether or not the derivation is valid is hard to say, for there is real similarity to Akk. *šiliḥtu*, the exit basin of a canal. In any case "Shiloaḥ" is not a passive participial form, as would be required by John's etymology. The evangelist is either following a different reading of the consonants (e.g., *šālūaḥ*, "sent") or exercising liberty in adapting the etymology to his purposes. Young, ZNW 46 (1955), 219–21, points out that in the apocryphal *Lives of the Prophets* there is the same etymology, along with a tradition of miracles associated with Siloam; however, this work may have been influenced by the Johannine story.

8. *used to sit and beg.* Mark x 46 describes Bartimaeus as a blind beggar who was sitting by the roadside.

9. *I'm the one.* Literally *egō eimi;* this is an instance of a purely secular use of the phrase.

11. *I got my sight.* The verb *anablepein*, literally "to see again," is used in vss. 11, 15, 18, with the wider connotation of receiving sight, for the man had never seen before.

13. *the Pharisees.* The interrogators are called Pharisees in vss. 13, 15, 16 (see also 40); in vss. 18 and 22, they are called "Jews," the more usual Johannine terminology. The variation is not sufficient indication that the descriptions of the interrogations come from different hands; so also Bultmann, p. 250[2], against Wellhausen and Spitta.

16. *This man is not from God.* The principle behind this judgment would be akin to Deut xiii 1–5 (2–6 MT): even a wonder worker must not be believed but be put to death if he tends to draw people aside from the way which God commanded.

he does not keep the Sabbath. First, since the man's life was not in danger, Jesus should have waited until another day to heal (see NOTE on vii 23). Second, among the thirty-nine works forbidden on the Sabbath (Mishnah *Shabbath* 7:2) was kneading, and Jesus had kneaded the clay with his spittle to make mud. Third, according to later Jewish tradition (TalBab *Abodah Zarah* 28b) there was an opinion that it was not permitted to anoint an eye on the Sabbath. Fourth, TalJer *Shabbath* 14d and 17f says that one may not put fasting spittle on the eyes on the Sabbath.

How can a man perform such signs? The principle that a sinner cannot work miracles is *not* universally attested in biblical tradition. Exodus vii 11 reports that the sorcerers of the Pharaoh were able to imitate Aaron's miracle. In Matt xxiv 24 Jesus admits that false messiahs and prophets will show great signs and wonders to lead astray even the elect.

sharply divided. The question of Jesus divides the Pharisees, even as it divided the crowd in vii 43.

17. *He is a prophet.* The only prophets who worked notable healing miracles were Elijah and Elisha (see also Isa xxxviii 21). Perhaps the similarity to Elisha's having Naaman wash in the Jordan is in mind. Yet, all that may be meant is that the man believes that Jesus has divine power and that "prophet" is the best-known category of such extraordinary men.

18. *[who had gained his sight].* This is omitted in P[66] and some minor witnesses. It is repetitious and awkward, but that may be why copyists omitted it.

21. *we do not know.* This is omitted by SB following minor versional and patristic evidence.

[*Ask him*]. P⁷⁵ adds considerable strength to the previous witnesses that omitted these words. They may be borrowed from vs. 23.

old enough to speak. Literally "He is old enough. He will speak for himself." Not the age of reason but the age of legal acceptability is meant.

22. *put out of the Synagogue*. Luke vi 22 says that the day will come when men will *cast out* the name of the disciples of Jesus as evil and *exclude* them; thus the possibility of some type of excommunication seems to be envisaged as the future fate of believers in Jesus. Unfortunately, we are not totally certain of the legislation concerning excommunication in the 1st century; see E. Schürer, II, ii 59–62. Some scholars would distinguish: (*a*) n⁻ᵉzîfāh: the minor ban of about a week's duration; (*b*) *niddūy* or *šammatâ:* a more formal banishment lasting thirty days—although this cut off association with fellow Israelites, seemingly it did not cut off participation in the religious services of the community; (*c*) *ḥērem:* the solemn curse or excommunication imposed by Jewish authorities, permanently excluding one from Israel. (These three categories are distinguished on the basis of later Jewish law.) John is referring to the exclusion of Jewish Christians from the synagogue at the end of the 1st century (see COMMENT), and thus the excommunication meant is closest to the last of the three types.

24. *Give glory to God*. This was an oath formula used before taking testimony or a confession of guilt (Josh vii 19; I Esdras ix 8). However, it is not impossible that a play on words is meant, for the blind man will give glory to God. Rom iv 20 says that Abraham grew strong in his faith as he gave glory to God; also Rev xix 7.

We know. We heard this "we" of learned Jewish authority on Nicodemus' lips in iii 2; it will be countered by the former blind man's "I know" in vs. 25.

25. *a sinner or not*. The man seems to know that the Law of the Sabbath has been broken, and he admits that the Pharisees are authorities on that subject. But, as his next words show, he is wondering if Jesus is not beyond the Law since he obviously did good in restoring sight.

27. *you didn't pay attention*. Literally "hear"; some witnesses read "believe," thus attempting to interpret the hearing. P⁶⁶ and some minor Western witnesses omit the negative, giving the connotation: "I told you and you heard me."

28. *disciples of Moses*. Barrett, p. 300, points out that this was not a regular title for rabbinic scholars, although it is used for the Pharisees in a *baraitah* in *Yoma* 4a. A later instance of the principle of thought involved here is found in the Midrash Rabbah VIII 6 on Deuteronomy where the Jews are warned that there is only one Law and Moses revealed it. There is not going to be another Moses who will come down from heaven with a different law.

29. *God has spoken to Moses*. Exodus xxxiii 11: "The Lord used to speak to Moses face to face"; also Num xii 2–8. Other instances of the argument concerning the relation of Jesus to Moses are seen in i 17, v 45–47, vii 19–23. It is interesting that Papyrus Egerton 2 joins John v 45 and ix 29 (see p. 230).

don't even know where this fellow comes from. In vii 27 the people of Jerusalem mistakenly thought they knew where Jesus came from, namely, Galilee (vii 41). Jesus' answer has always been to insist that he comes from above and from the Father, and it is this heavenly origin that "the Jews" do not know (viii 14). Here the Pharisees seem to be questioning his claim to be from God, since they contrast it with the known relation between Moses and God. Is there also a hint of illegitimacy (see NOTE on viii 41)?

30. *you don't even know.* The sarcastic astonishment of the former blind man resembles that of Jesus toward Nicodemus in iii 10.

31. *We know.* The man has adopted the "we" of the Pharisees (vs. 24), just as in iii 11 Jesus adopted the "we" of Nicodemus. Undoubtedly, such passages were used in the polemics between Jews and Christians.

God pays no attention to sinners. This is a common biblical principle, e.g., Isa i 15; I John iii 21. "Sinners" refers to those unwilling to reform.

devout and obeys His will. "Devout," *theosebēs,* is a common term in Hellenistic religious circles for describing piety; it occurs only here in the NT. "To do God's will" is a Hebrew description of piety (Bultmann, p. 256[2]).

32. *absolutely unheard of.* Literally "not heard from of old"—a rabbinic usage. No miraculous healing of a blind man is recorded in the protocanonical books of the OT; Tobias' sight was miraculously restored (Tob xi 12–13), but he was not born blind.

33. *If this man were not from God.* The same argument was used by Nicodemus in iii 2.

34. *born steeped in sin.* This is probably more than an instance of contempt for those who do not know or observe the Law (see NOTE on vii 49). It is an attribution of the man's congenital blindness to prenatal sin.

threw him out. This is not a formal excommunication but simply ejection from their presence.

35. *found him.* This is contrasted with the action of the Pharisees in driving him out, and it illustrates Jesus' promise in vi 37: "Anyone who comes to me I will never drive out." It may also reflect the Johannine theme of an analogy between Jesus and Wisdom. In Wis vi 16 Wisdom is described as going about in search of those who are worthy of her and graciously appearing to them in their paths.

Son of Man. Some later Greek witnesses and the Latin mss. read "Son of God"; but this is clearly the substitution of a more customary and complete formula of Christian faith, probably under the influence of the use of this passage in baptismal liturgy and catechesis. Why does Jesus present himself to the former blind man under the title of the Son of Man? Verses 39–41 have a theme of judgment, and judgment is a frequent setting for the figure of the Son of Man (see NOTE on i 51). We may recall Luke xviii 8: "When the Son of Man comes, will he find faith on earth?"—in John, the Son of Man finds faith in the former blind man. Also, in Matt viii 20 Jesus presents himself as the Son of Man to a prospective disciple.

36. *Who is he?* This question could reflect the man's ignorance of what the title means, but more likely it refers to the identity of the bearer of the title (see xii 34). The question is curious since the man already knows that Jesus is a prophet (17), has unique power (32), and comes from God (33).

sir. Or perhaps "Lord," since *kyrios* has both meanings. Yet, it seems appropriate to indicate a development from vs. 36 to vs. 38 in the use of the term.

37. *seen him.* For John this is the real purpose of the gift of sight; it enables the man to see and believe in Jesus.

38–39. [*I do . . . Jesus said*]. The bracketed words are omitted in Codex Sinaiticus, P[75], the OL, Tatian, Achmimic—a wide spread of early witnesses. As will be seen below, these verses contain some non-Johannine peculiarities. Perhaps we have here an addition stemming from the association of John ix with the baptismal liturgy and catechesis. Verse 38 describes a rather liturgical gesture.

38. *he said.* The Greek form *ephē* is rare in John (only i 23). However, some witnesses also read it in vs. 36, and its use here may be borrowed from there.

bowed down to worship him. This is the standard OT reaction to a theophany (Gen xvii 3), and John uses the same verb, *proskynein,* in iv 20–24 to describe the worship due to God (also xii 20). The action of bowing down to worship Jesus is not infrequent in the Synoptics, especially Matthew, but occurs only here in John.

39. *came into this world for judgment.* See p. 345. The attitude here is very much like that of iii 19–21.

may become blind. See the Isaian passage cited in xii 40. The line of distinction between the result of Jesus' ministry and its purpose is not drawn sharply because of the oversimplified outlook which attributes everything that happens to God's purpose. Matt xxiii 16 calls the Pharisees blind guides; also Matt vi 23: "If what is light be darkness for you, how deep is that darkness."

40. *Pharisees who were there with him.* Their presence seems a bit contrived in the setting pictured in vs. 35.

41. *your sin remains.* In Mark iii 29 it is said that he who blasphemes against the Holy Spirit never receives forgiveness. I John v 16 knows of a "sin unto death." For the aggravation of guilt see John xv 22. The theme of remaining is common in John, but here it is sin that remains rather than a gift of God.

COMMENT

Context and Construction

After the long and intricate discourses of vii–viii, ch. ix provides a pleasant interlude. How closely is ch. ix related to the Tabernacles setting of vii–viii? In itself the story is complete and could have a place anywhere in one of Jesus' visits to Jerusalem; for instance, there are many similarities with ch. iii (see NOTES on ix 24, 30, 33, 39). However, the intensity of the hatred of the Pharisees for Jesus makes the general setting of the Tabernacles pilgrimage quite appropriate. The pool of Siloam (vs. 7) played a role in the water ceremonies we discussed in relation to vii 37–38; and ix 4–5 develop the theme of light in the darkness which is also a Tabernacles theme, as we saw in discussing viii 12.

Nevertheless, the *immediate* connection of ch. ix with the feast and with what was said in viii is not assured. John gives no precise dating for the healing, and the next indication of time will be that of the feast of Dedication, three months after Tabernacles, in x 22. Thus, even if we would accept the present Gospel order and agree that the healing is related to the Tabernacles visit, there may be a considerable gap in time alluded to between viii and ix.

The internal construction of the story shows consummate artistry; no other story in the Gospel is so closely knit. We have here Johannine dramatic skill at its best. We have given an outline on p. 203, and we may analyze it here. Before narrating the miracle, the evangelist is careful to have Jesus point out the meaning of the sign as an instance of light coming into darkness. This is a story of how a man who sat in darkness was brought to see the light, not only physically but spiritually. On the other hand, it is also a tale of how those who thought they saw (the Pharisees) were blinding themselves to the light and plunging into darkness. The story starts in vs. 1 with a blind man who will gain his sight; it ends in vs. 41 with the Pharisees who have become spiritually blind.

After setting the scene for a theological understanding of the sign, the evangelist narrates the miracle with modest brevity (vss. 6–7), for his real interest is in the interrogations. In each of these the former blind man gives voice to statements that betray an ever deepening knowledge of Jesus. In the interrogation by the neighbors all that the man knows is that his benefactor was the *"man they call Jesus"* (11). Under the pressure of the more searching preliminary interrogation by the Pharisees the man is brought to confess that Jesus is a *prophet* (17). In the final interrogation by the Pharisees he becomes an ardent defender of Jesus' cause: what Jesus has done shows that he is *from God* (33). And then in climactic response to Jesus' own interrogation, the man comes to see Jesus as *the Son of Man* (37).

While the former blind man is gradually having his eyes opened to the truth about Jesus, the Pharisees or "the Jews" are becoming more obdurate in their failure to see the truth. In their preliminary interrogation they seem to accept the fact of the healing (15). While some are offended by the violation of the Sabbath rules, others seem willing to be convinced (16) and to hear the former blind man's own evaluation of Jesus (17). But in the second interrogation those who are the most hostile (the Jews) dominate the scene. They have begun now to doubt the very fact of the miracle by seeking to show through the man's parents that he never was blind. In the final interrogation of the man all interest in seeing where the truth lies has disappeared; they seek to trap the man by having him repeat the details of the miracle (27). No matter what he may say about the miracle, they shall refuse to accept Jesus' heavenly origins (29). Their legal procedure descends to the level of vilifying the witness (34). At the end of the story the Pharisees who sat in judgment on the miracle are judged guilty by Jesus (39, 41).

The care with which the evangelist has drawn his portraits of increasing insight and hardening blindness is masterful. Three times the former blind man, who is truly gaining knowledge, humbly confesses his ignorance (12, 25, 36). Three times the Pharisees, who are really plunging deeper into abysmal ignorance of Jesus, make confident statements about what they know of him (16, 24, 29). The blind man emerges from these pages in John as one of the most attractive figures of the Gospels. Although the Sabbath setting and the accusation against Jesus create a similarity between this miracle and the healing of the man at the pool of Bethesda in ch. v, this clever and voluble blind man is quite different from the obtuse and unimaginative paralytic of ch. v (see p. 209). The blind man's confutation of the Pharisees in vss. 24–34 is one of the most cleverly written dialogues in the NT.

The Value of the Story as Tradition

From the above remarks it should be obvious that the evangelist has contributed a great deal of his own artistry to the reporting of this scene. A miracle story has been shaped into an ideal tool at the service of Christian apologetics and into an ideal instruction for those about to be baptized (see below). But even when this is granted, we must still ask whether or not the fundamental story may represent historical tradition. What is at work here—adaptation of a primitive story through selection and emphasis, a vivid creation of the imagination, or imaginative reworking of Synoptic material?

The tradition that Jesus healed the blind is well attested in the Synoptic tradition. Such healing has no background in OT miracles, but the picture of the (spiritually) blind having their eyes (figuratively) opened was part of the prophets' picture of the ideal or messianic times (Isa xxix 18, xxxv 5, xlii 7). We list below the healings of the blind in the Synoptic tradition, with the proviso, however, that doublets may be involved.

(*a*) Healing of Bartimaeus who *sat and begged* near Jericho as Jesus was on the way to Jerusalem (Mark x 46–52; Luke xviii 35–43; Matt xx 29–34 [two blind men]).

(*b*) Two blind men in Galilee (Matt ix 27–31—a doublet of the preceding?).

(*c*) A blind mute in Galilee (Capernaum?)—this is according to Matt xii 22–23; but Luke xi 14 mentions only a mute and places the scene on the way to Jerusalem.

(*d*) A blind man healed in stages with the use of *spittle* at Bethsaida (Mark viii 22–26). In similar circumstances Matt xv 30 gives a summary which mentions healing the blind.

(*e*) *At Jerusalem,* in a summary connected with the cleansing of the Temple, Jesus is said to have healed the blind (Matt xxi 14).

In evaluating the similarity of John's account to those of the Synoptics, we should note that the apocryphal *Acts of Pilate* vi 2 says that a blind man, who is obviously Bartimaeus of (*a*) above, was *born* blind, and thus seemingly blends the Synoptic account with John's. Justin *Apol.* i 22:6 (PG 6:364) may also be blending the two traditions when he says that Jesus "cured the lame, the paralytics, and *those blind from birth* [plausibly reading *pērous* for *ponērous*]." Actually, the similarities between the various Synoptic accounts and John's account are rather few (notice *italics* above). John is certainly not dependent on any single Synoptic account, nor is there any convincing evidence that John is dependent on any combination of details from the various Synoptic scenes. The most striking and important features in John are not found in the Synoptic scenes, for example: *blind from birth; use of mud; healing through the water of Siloam; interrogation about the miracle; questioning of parents.* Of course, these strikingly different details are often the very points that serve the Johannine theological interests, and therefore one is hard put to prove scientifically that they were not invented for the sake of pedagogy. Some points that might be mentioned in favor of the primitive and authentic character of the Johannine story are the use of spittle, the brevity with which the miracle is narrated, the local information about the pool of Siloam, the acquaintance with the fine points of the Sabbath rules. In general, then, it seems that probability favors the theory that behind ch. ix lies a primitive story of healing preserved only in the Johannine tradition (so also Dodd, *Tradition*, pp. 181–88). The evangelist with his sense of drama has seen in this story an almost ideal example of a sign that might be used to instruct his readers and strengthen them in their belief that Jesus is the Messiah (xx 31), and has elaborated the tale with that goal in mind.

The Lessons Taught by the Story

(a) *Triumph of light over darkness.* The primary lesson that the evangelist meant to convey is the one we emphasized above when describing the construction of the chapter: the acting out of the triumph of light over darkness. Just as the OT prophets accompanied their spoken word by symbolic actions which dramatized their message, so also Jesus acts out here the truth he proclaimed in viii 12, "I am the light of the world." Not only the whole arrangement of the chapter, but also the very specific introduction in vss. 2–5 make this lesson clear. Dodd, *Tradition*, pp. 185–88, maintains that there is much in 2–4 that resembles what is found in the Synoptic statements of Jesus (see NOTES), and we note that vs. 5 resembles closely Matt v 14. Thus, the evangelist may have found the key to his understanding of the scene in traditional sayings of Jesus.

(b) *Apologetic lesson.* In addition to the light/darkness, sight/blindness drama, the evangelist had a second purpose in presenting this story to his readers: that of apologetics. In the preliminary interrogation of the man by the Pharisees (vss. 13–17) we hear some of the doubts that bothered the authorities about Jesus during his ministry. The problem of his violation of the Sabbath was certainly an authentic part of the early tradition about Jesus, and on the basis of Synoptic parallels this preliminary interrogation has every right to be considered as part of the healing story (Mark iii 1–6; Luke xiii 10–17). But, whereas in ch. v the Sabbath motif dominated the story of the healing of the paralytic, it is really only incidental in the development of ch. ix; for in the subsequent interrogations of the parents and of the man (18–23, 24–34) the Sabbath question fades into the background. In these interrogations the real issue is whether or not Jesus has miraculous power and, if he does, who he is.

Here we pass from the arguments of Jesus' ministry to the apologetics of Church and Synagogue in the era of spreading Christianity, and the evangelist shows us the prolongation into his own time of the debate over Jesus that had already begun to rage when Jesus was alive. In vss. 28–33 we have in capsule form the violent polemic between the disciples of Moses and the disciples of Jesus in the late 1st century. The same mentality is at work here that prompted the anachronistic designation of the authorities of Jesus' time

as "the Jews," for the "we" that is heard on the lips of the Pharisees is really
the voice of their logical descendants, that is, the Jews at the end of the 1st
century who have once and for all rejected the claims of Jesus of Nazareth
and who regard his followers as heretics. The "we" on the lips of the former
blind man is the voice of the Christian apologists who think of the Jews as
malevolently blinding themselves to the obvious truth implied in Jesus'
miracles.

In the parenthetical vss. 22–23 we seem to have the final development of
the apologetic use of this Johannine story. These verses may well represent
the hand of an editor bringing the story up to date, for they are somewhat
intrusive in the narrative. As we pointed out in the Introduction, they help
us to determine the earliest possible date for the Gospel in its present form
(p. LXXXV); for they refer to the attempt around A.D. 90 to drive out from
synagogues Jews who had accepted Jesus as the Messiah. It is quite possible
that during the ministry Jesus and his disciples met opposition in the synagogues and were handled roughly in the heat of debate (Luke iv 28–29).
But it is almost unbelievable that during Jesus' lifetime a formal excommunication was leveled against those who followed him. Matthew x 17
mentions being flogged in synagogues but only as part of the *future* fate
of Christian missionaries. Acts shows the apostles entering synagogues and
even the Temple itself without any suggestion that they have been excommunicated. Even the description of Jesus' followers in vs. 22 as those who
acknowledged that he was the Messiah is too formal for the ministry of
Jesus. Once again the Gospel is showing us the ultimate development of the
hostility that was incipient in Jesus' lifetime. The parents' fear of speaking
represents the dilemma of those practicing Jews who believe that Jesus is
the Messiah but who now (i.e., the end of the 1st century) find that they can
no longer profess this faith and remain Jews. Through the example of the
blind man in vs. 34, the Gospel appeals to them to allow themselves to be
excommunicated, for Jesus will seek them out as he sought out the blind man
in vs. 35 and bring them to complete faith.

(c) *A baptismal lesson.* The story of the man born blind appears seven
times in early catacomb art, most frequently as an illustration of Christian
Baptism (Braun, JeanThéol, I, pp. 149 ff.). Chapter ix served as a reading in
preparing converts for Baptism—see the interesting note in Hoskyns, pp.
363–65, on the use of John ix in the lectionaries or liturgical books of the
early Church. In particular, when the practice of three scrutinies or
examinations before Baptism developed (at least from the 3rd century on,
according to Braun, pp. 158–59), John ix was read on the day of the great
scrutiny. From what we can reconstruct of the ceremony as we know it at a
slightly later stage, when the catechumens passed their examination and were
judged worthy of Baptism, lessons from the OT concerning cleansing water
were read to them. Then came the solemn opening of the Gospel book and
the reading of John ix, with the confession of the blind man, "I do believe,
Lord" (38), serving as the climax. (See Roman Missal for Wednesday after
the Fourth Sunday of Lent.) After this the catechumens recited the creed.

It is also interesting to note that two of the gestures of Jesus in John ix, anointing and the use of spittle, later became part of the baptismal ceremonies (although the use of spittle is more directly related to Mark vii 34). We pointed out in the NOTE that the insertion of the bracketed words in vss. 38–39 may also be a sign of the baptismal use of this chapter.

Thus, there is no doubt that the Church found a baptismal lesson in the healing of the blind man. What evidence do we have from the Gospel itself that the baptismal interpretation may reflect the evangelist's own intent? John gives only two verses to the miracle itself (an indication that the account may be primitive, for the later tendency is to draw attention to the marvelous element in the working of the miracle). Although Jesus' gestures are described, it is emphasized that the man was healed only when he washed in the pool of Siloam. Thus, unlike the healing of the paralytic in ch. v, the story in ix illustrates the healing power of water. The Gospel pauses to interpret the name of the pool where this healing water was obtained, and the explanation that the name means "one who has been sent" clearly associates the water with Jesus. In John Jesus is the one who was sent by the Father (iii 17, 34, v 36, 38, etc.). Moreover, we must remember that it was the water from this same pool of Siloam that was used in the ceremony at Tabernacles, and Jesus had said by way of replacement in vii 37–38 that he was now the source of life-giving water.

Another indication that the evangelist intended sacramental symbolism in the narrative is the stress on the fact that the man was *born* blind (vss. 1, 2, 13, 18, 19, 20, 24). This comes to a climax in vs. 32: "It is absolutely unheard of that anyone ever opened the eyes of a man born blind." Since the man's physical blindness is so obviously contrasted with the sin of spiritual blindness (39), we may well suspect that the evangelist is playing on the idea that the man was born in sin (2, 34)—sin that can be removed only by washing in the waters of the spring or pool that flows from Jesus himself. We think that the symbolism of the Gospel was correctly interpreted by Tertullian when he opened his tract on Baptism with the words: "The present work will treat of our sacrament of water which washes away the sins of our original blindness and sets us free unto eternal life" (SC 35:64). Augustine exclaims: "This blind man stands for the human race . . . if the blindness is infidelity, then the illumination is faith. . . . He washes his eyes in that pool which is interpreted 'one who has been sent': he was baptized in Christ" (*In Jo.* XLIV 1–2; PL 35:1713–14).

That such symbolism would be understood by Christians of the NT period is indicated by the fact that "enlightenment" was a term used by NT authors to refer to Baptism (e.g., Heb vi 4, x 32—Hebrews is a work with many Johannine affinities). In the 2nd century Justin, *Apol.* I 61:13 (PG 6:421), tells us that the washing of Baptism was called enlightenment. Perhaps even the mention of "anointing" (*epichriein*="smearing" in 6, 11), the Greek root of which is related to "chrism" and "christen," may have baptismal significance. I John ii 20, 27, speaks of an anointing which comes from the

Holy One (Baptism?); and II Cor i 21–22 speaks of anointing and the giving of the Spirit.

Even the Pauline association of Baptism with the death of Jesus (e.g., Rom vi 3) may not be totally absent from John ix. In ix 3 we are told that the healing of the blind man is going to be a revelation of God's works, and vs. 4 is insistent that this work must be done now while it is day, for night is coming. Some have thought that this means that Jesus wishes to heal the man on this particular day even though it is the Sabbath. However, the same necessity of taking advantage of the day is found in xi 9–10, where there is no question of the Sabbath. Rather the necessity flows from the fact that death is already casting its dark shadow over Jesus' life. The same idea is found in Luke xiii 32: "Look! I cast out demons and effect cures today and tomorrow, and the third day I must finish my course." We heard in ch. viii that "the Jews" were trying to kill Jesus, and with this threat of imminent death in mind Jesus feels that he cannot delay his healing of the blind man through the waters of Siloam. We shall see in ch. xi that as Jesus' death draws closer, his life-giving activity increases. If we are correct in seeing baptismal significance in the healing of the blind man, this symbolism has as its background Jesus' approaching death.

35. AFTERMATH OF TABERNACLES:
—JESUS AS SHEEPGATE AND SHEPHERD
(x 1–21)

A figurative attack on the Pharisees

The Parable(s)

X 1 "Truly I assure you,
    anyone who does not enter the sheepfold through the gate,
    but climbs in some other way,
    is a thief and a bandit.
   2 The one who enters through the gate
    is shepherd of the sheep;
   3 for him the keeper opens the gate.

    And the sheep hear his voice
    as he calls by name those that belong to him
    and leads them out.
   4 When he has brought out [all] his own,
    he walks in front of them;
    and the sheep follow him
    because they recognize his voice.
   5 But they will not follow a stranger;
    they will run away from him
    because they do not recognize the voice of strangers."

6 Although Jesus drew this picture for them, they did not understand
what he was trying to tell them.

The Explanations: a. The gate

7 So Jesus said [to them again],
    "Truly I assure you,
    I am the sheepgate.
   8 All who came [before me]
    are thieves and bandits,
    but the sheep did not heed them.

9 I am the gate.
Whoever enters through me
will be saved;
and he will go in and out
and find pasture.
10 A thief comes
only to steal, slaughter, and destroy.
I came
that they may have life
and have it to the full.

b. The shepherd

11 I am the model shepherd:
the model shepherd lays down his life for the sheep.
12 The hired hand, who is not the shepherd
and does not own the sheep,
catches sight of the wolf coming,
and runs away, leaving the sheep
to be snatched and scattered by the wolf.
13 And this is because he works for pay
and has no concern for the sheep.

14 I am the model shepherd:
I know my sheep
and mine know me,
15 just as the Father knows me
and I know the Father.
And for these sheep I lay down my life.
16 I have other sheep, too,
that do not belong to this fold.
These also must I lead,
and they will listen to my voice.
Then there will be one sheep herd, one shepherd.
17 This is why the Father loves me:
because I lay down my life
in order to take it up again.
18 No one has taken it away from me;
rather, I lay it down of my own accord.
I have power to lay it down,
and I have power to take it up again.
This command I received from my Father."

19 Because of these words the Jews were again sharply divided. 20 Many of them were claiming, "He is possessed by a devil—out of his mind! Why pay any attention to him?" 21 Others maintained, "These are not the words of a demented person. Surely a devil cannot open the eyes of the blind!"

NOTES

x 1. *Truly I assure you.* Bernard, II, p. 348, maintains that the double "amen," which is what this clause represents, is never used abruptly to introduce a fresh topic. In iii 11 and v 19 it represents only a new stage in Jesus' comments on what has preceded.

sheepfold. There were several types. At times, the sheepfold was a square marked off on a hillside by stone walls; here it seems to be a yard in front of a house, surrounded by a stone wall which was probably topped with briars.

gate. Although *thyra* is the normal word for the door of a room (Matt vi 6), the translation "gate" seems more appropriate here for the opening in a stone enclosure.

bandit. *Lēstēs* has the sense of "robber" (Mark xi 17) but is also used in the Gospels to refer to guerrilla warriors and revolutionary banditti like Barabbas, who was involved in insurrection (Luke xxiii 19). Because some think that vs. 8 refers to messianic revolutionaries, the translation "bandit" seems the most comprehensive. The combination of "thief and bandit" appears in Obad 5.

3. *by name.* It seems that Palestinian shepherds frequently have pet names for their favorite sheep, "Long-ears," "White-nose," etc. (Bernard, II, p. 350).

those. Literally "the sheep."

leads them out. The verb *exagein* is used in some of the important shepherd passages of the OT (LXX): Ezek xxxiv 13; Num xxvii 17.

4. *brought out.* Literally "cast out" (*ekballein*). This is probably just a variant of *exagein*, but there may be a hint of the helplessness of the sheep. Sheep often have to be pushed through a gate.

[all]. Some manuscripts omit this word; some have it in a different word order.

walks in front of them. In shepherding there is occasionally a helper who brings up the rear of the flock.

5. *not follow a stranger.* Bernard, II, p. 350, suggests that we are to think that there were several flocks in the one sheepfold, so that there would be a process of separation when the shepherd came to call out his own flock. This is far from certain, and the Gospel never mentions the presence of other sheep in this fold.

6. *drew this picture.* Literally "spoke this parable." The Greek word is *paroimia* which often means "proverb," e.g., II Pet ii 22. In LXX *paroimia* (like the *parabolē*, which the Synoptics use) is used to translate *māšāl*, a broad Hebrew term that covers almost all types of figurative speech. *Paroimia* and *parabolē* are used synonymously in Sir xlvii 17; in general they do not differ greatly in meaning, although there may be more emphasis on the enigmatic in *paroimia*. The use of *paroimia* tends to increase in the later Greek versions of the OT.

See E. Hatch, *Essays in Biblical Greek* (Oxford: Clarendon, 1889), pp. 64–71; and F. Hauck, *paroimia*, TWNT, V, pp. 852–55. Although xvi 25 indicates that in Johannine thought Jesus' parables were not easily understood, the present passage leaves no doubt that Jesus spoke this way to make himself understood.

7. [*to them again*]. The manuscript tradition on the inclusion, omission, and order of these words is very confused.

the sheepgate. The Sahidic version reads "the shepherd," a reading that now receives its first Greek support from P[75]. Black, p. 193[1], follows Torrey in believing that the original "shepherd" became "gate" through a mistake in copying the underlying Aramaic. Actually, however, "gate" is the more unexpected and difficult reading; "shepherd" may well have been introduced by copyists in an attempt to make the explanation of the parable a consistent picture. That Jesus could not at the same time be both gate and shepherd (11, 14) would cause trouble.

8. *All*. This is omitted by Codex Bezae and some versional and patristic evidence. If "came before me" was understood as a reference to the OT period, then the statement that all (in the OT) were thieves and bandits probably seemed too drastic.

[*before me*]. Supported by Codex Sinaiticus and strong versional evidence, the omission of these words now has the backing of P[75]. Are the words an explanatory gloss interpreting the past tense, "came"? Or is the omission another reflection of the difficulty just mentioned above?

9. *the gate*. It is quite clear that here the image is that of the gate through which the sheep go in and out. Bishop, *art. cit.*, gives an interesting modern example of the shepherd's sleeping across the entrance to the fold and thus serving as both shepherd and gate to the sheep. In some of the offshoots of Islam, the title *Bāb* ("gate," e.g., to knowledge) has been applied to great religious leaders.

10. *A thief*. Literally "the thief"; the definite article is probably parabolic style, as "the sower" in Mark iv 3.

slaughter. Thyein is not the usual verb "to kill" (*apokteinein*) used elsewhere in John; it has the connotation of sacrifice and could well be a sly reference to the priestly authorities. See the related noun in Matt ix 13, xii 7.

and have it to the full. There is some evidence (P[66]*, Bezae) for the omission of this clause, an omission by haplography since the last two lines of vs. 10 both end in the Greek verb *echousin* ("have"). For a similar expression of the overflowing fullness brought by Christ see Rom v 20.

11. *model*. Or "noble"; perhaps "noble" would be more exact here and "model" more exact in vs. 14. Greek *kalos* means "beautiful" in the sense of an ideal or model of perfection; we saw it used in the "choice wine" of ii 10. Philo (*De Agric*, #6, 10) speaks of a *good* (*agathos*) shepherd. There is no absolute distinction between *kalos* and *agathos*, but we do think that "noble" or "model" is a more precise translation than "good" for John's phrase. In the Midrash Rabbah II 2 on Exod iii 1, David who was the great shepherd of the OT is described as *yāfeh rō'eh*, literally "the handsome shepherd" (see I Sam xvi 12).

lays down his life. This is a Johannine expression (xiii 37, xv 13; I John iii 16), as contrasted with "to *give* one's life" (Mark x 45). "To lay down life" is a rare expression in secular Greek, and John's usage may reflect the rabbinic Hebrew idiom *māsar nafšō*, "to hand over one's life." The suggestion that we should translate here "risks his life" (see Judg xii 3), while it may be suitable in this particular verse, is made difficult by the clear reference to death in vss. 17–18.

12. *leaving the sheep.* There is an interesting parallel in the early 2nd-century A.D. Jewish apocalyptic work IV Ezra (v 18): "Do not desert us as a shepherd does (who leaves) his flock in the power of harmful wolves."

13. *this is because.* This verse appears to be an explanatory addition.

14. *my sheep.* Jesus can say that the sheep are his because the Father has given men to him (vi 37, 44, 65, xvii 6–7).

15. *lay down.* There is strong early evidence for reading "give"; it may be original. "Give" is also a variant in vs. 11, but the evidence is stronger here.

16. *fold.* This term appeared in vs. 1 with a slightly different nuance. There the fold represented those whom Jesus was coming to save; here it represents the group in Israel who already believe in him. The distinction, however, does not seem to be as sharp or important as Bultmann, p. 292, would make it.

listen to my voice. This theme is found in viii 47, xviii 37 (see iii 29).

there will be. Or "they will be"; the evidence is evenly divided between the two readings, although it may be that the latter is a slightly more difficult reading.

one sheep herd, one shepherd. Although it is more customary today to speak of a *flock* of sheep, we are attempting to preserve here the closeness in the Greek between *poimnē* ("sheep herd, flock") and *poimēn* ("shepherd"). There is no other support for Jerome's reading of "one *fold,* one shepherd," although he seems to have been translating a Greek ms. that read *aulē* instead of *poimnē.* Bernard (II, p. 363), an Anglican, says that "one fold" is wrong ideologically as well as textually, since what Jesus wanted was one flock even if it lived in many folds. However, such an interpretation of the intention of the evangelist seems anachronistic; it belongs more to the modern concern with a divided Christianity and the "branch" theory of the Church.

17. *loves. Agapan*—see Note on v 20.

18. *has taken.* There are many witnesses, including P[66], for a present tense; but the aorist is the more difficult and, almost certainly, the more original reading. The past reference may be to the attempts on his life in v 18, vii 25, viii 59. However, there is also the possibility that this is another instance where John pictures Jesus during the ministry speaking in the past tense of his death and resurrection (see Note on iii 13).

have power. Bernard, II, p. 365, would interpret this as "I have authority" (see Note on "empowered" in i 12), but this is to overwork the technical meaning of *exousia.* The phrase is tantamount to "I can" (Lagrange, p. 283).

20. *possessed by a devil.* Literally "has a demon"—a phrase that we have translated in terms of his being "demented" (vii 20, viii 48). Thus, this charge and that of being "out of his mind" are two different ways of saying the same thing, since madness was thought to be the result of demonic possession (see Mark v 1–20).

21. *a demented person.* Again, literally "one who has a demon."

a devil cannot open the eyes of the blind. See Note on ix 16. It has been suggested that in this particular instance the general argument about the divine provenance of miracles is bolstered by a text like Ps cxlvi 8 which says that it is *the Lord* who opens the eyes of the blind.

COMMENT: GENERAL

Sequence

We have seen that Johannine stories, particularly those marking the major divisions in the Book of Signs, tend to look both forward and backward; they resume themes already seen and point forward to themes to come. This seems to be the case with the discourse on the sheepgate and the shepherd which, though it is not a major division of the book, does terminate the discourses at the feast of Tabernacles and introduce the discourse at Dedication. We believe that the understanding of the twofold direction of the discourse helps to solve many of the problems in its sequence that have disturbed commentators.

First, it seems quite clear that it is to be related to what has preceded in ch. ix. No new audience is suggested; and as the Gospel now stands, there is no reason to believe that Jesus is not continuing his remarks to the Pharisees to whom he was speaking in viii 41. Indeed, in x 21, after Jesus has spoken about the sheepgate and the shepherd, his audience recalls the example of the blind man, while others repeat the charges of madness that we have heard hurled at Jesus during the Tabernacles discourses.

Yet, there are two principal objections to connecting the discourse on the sheepgate and the shepherd to what has preceded. (a) There is an abrupt change of topic in x 1–18. The whole theme of ix was that of light; there was no reference to the imagery of sheep which dominates in x. This objection has considerable force and may mean that the evangelist has joined once independent discourses, but it really does not weaken the view that the evangelist envisaged the same audience for x as for the end of ix. And, although the imagery may have changed, the theme at the beginning of x seems to be an attack on the authorities (*the thieves and bandits; the careless gatekeepers; the strangers who are not known to the sheep; the cowardly hired hands*), and this was also the theme at the end of ix. In fact, the example of the blind man who refused to follow the guidance of the Pharisees and turned to Jesus is not unlike the example of the sheep in x 4–5 who will not follow a stranger but recognize the voice of their true master. (b) The second objection is chronological. The feast of Tabernacles takes place in September/October; the feast of Dedication, which is the next time indication (x 22), takes place in December. Thus, the Gospel places a span of three months between the incidents of ch. vii and those of x 22 ff. (Probably we are justified in assuming that the evangelist wishes us to think that the two feasts are in the same year.) Now, are we justified in relating x 1–21 to the earlier feast of Tabernacles when x 26–27, which is clearly dated at Dedication, mentions the theme of the sheep? In other words, x 26–27 presupposes the same audience as x 1–21. This is scarcely plausible if the words in x 1–21 were spoken months before at another feast. However, this objection is not so cogent as it might seem. We have noted that, while ix and x 1–21 are placed in the general context of Tabernacles, these chapters are not so tightly tied to the feast as are chs. vii–viii. (See p. 376.) Therefore, even if we take the present sequence literally, there is nothing to indicate that the incident in ix and the discourse in x 1–21 may not have taken place *between* Tabernacles and Dedication, and thus not be separated from the remarks in x 26–27 by three months. More important, we should give to this problem the same answer we gave to the gap that separated chs. v and vii, where over a year later (according to the strict Gospel chronology) Jesus was still talking about the healing of the paralytic on the Sabbath (vii 21–23 in reference to ch. v). The evangelist does not seem to have been preoccupied with the problems of how the audience hearing Jesus would have known of the earlier action or words; the evangelist is addressing gospel readers who have just read about the earlier actions and words.

Second, x 1–21 points forward and serves as a transition to the feast of Dedication, as shown by the relation of x 1–21 to 26–27, just mentioned above. Bruns, *art. cit.*, has argued very strongly for seeing the motifs of Dedication in the discourse on the sheepgate and the shepherd (although he goes too far in dissociating the discourse of ch. x from the themes of Tabernacles). The historical event of the rededication of the Temple by Judas Maccabeus (Note below on vs. 22) which was recalled in the feast was a reminder of the high priests, like Jason and Menelaus, who had betrayed their office by contributing to the Syrian desecration of the holy place. They may have sparked Jesus' references to the thieves, robbers, and hirelings who betrayed the flock. Moreover, Miss Guilding, pp. 129–32, has shown that, if her interpretation of the cycle of synagogue readings is correct, all the regular readings on the Sabbath nearest Dedication were concerned with the theme of the sheep and the shepherds. In particular, Ezek xxxiv, which, as we shall see, is the most important single OT background passage for John x, served as the *haphtarah* or prophetical reading at the general time of Dedication in the second year of the cycle.

If this interpretation of the twofold function of x 1–21 is correct, then we can scarcely believe that its position as a bridge between Tabernacles and Dedication was an accident. That an "either-or" approach in deciding the relationship of this passage in John to the two feasts mentioned in its context may be an aberration is suggested by the fact that the Jews themselves related the two feasts. For them Dedication was another Tabernacles, only celebrated in the month of Chislev (II Macc i 9). Moreover, our interpretation rules out the numerous rearrangements of ch. x, supported by scholars like Moffatt, Bernard, E. Schweizer, Wikenhauser, Bultmann, all designed to give a "better" chronological or logical sequence. Bernard, for instance, proposes this order: ch. ix, x 19–29, x 1–18, x 30–39—a thesis that presupposes that x 19–29 constituted one page of the manuscript of John which accidentally got out of order. This rearrangement brings the mention of the blind man in x 21 closer to ch. ix, and places the discourse on the sheepgate and the shepherd after the time indication about Dedication

in x 22. Bultmann's reconstruction is more elaborate; he expands Jesus'
remarks to the Pharisees in ix 39–41 by adding verses from viii and xii, and
then uses x 19–21 as the conclusion of these remarks. Bultmann's order for
the rest of ch. x is: 22–26, 11–13, 1–10, 14–18, 27–30, 31–39. Although
each rearrangement does contribute something toward smooth sequence, the
subjectivity that governs them is a drawback. In analyzing the structure of
parables and explanation, we shall see below that Bultmann violates the
deliberate plan that guides x 1–21. Thus, we agree with Dodd, Feuillet,
Schneider, and others in accepting the present order in John as a purposeful
arrangement and not a product of accident or confusion.

Parable and Allegory

There is an argument among scholars as to whether we should speak of
parable or allegory (or both) in John x. The distinction between *parable*
(a simple illustration or illustrative story having a single point) and *allegory*
(an expanded series of metaphors where the various details and persons
involved all have a figurative meaning) was used as the basis of critical
parable exegesis by A. Jülicher at the end of the last century. Jülicher
maintained that allegory was an artificial, literary device, and was never
used by a rustic preacher like Jesus who spoke in simple parables. The
Christian exegetes were the ones who interpreted Jesus' one-point parables
as if they were allegory. Thus, for instance, the explanation of the Parable
of the Sower (Mark iv 13–20), which gives an interpretation to the seed,
the birds, the soils, etc., is an allegorization which stems from early Christianity rather than from Jesus himself. Jülicher traced this process of allegorization into the patristic era, where it became elaborate indeed.

In "Parable and Allegory Reconsidered," NovT 5 (1962), 36–45 (NTE,
Ch. xiii), we have tried to show that, although Jülicher's theory continues to
have a considerable following, it is really a gross oversimplification. Jülicher
was correct in pointing out the dangers of overallegorizing in patristic exegesis, but he was wrong in drawing a sharp distinction between parable
and simple allegory in Jesus' own preaching. M. Hermaniuk, *La parabole
évangélique* (Louvain, 1947), has shown that the distinction between parable
and allegory, stemming from the precisions of Greek oratorical training, had
no foundation in Hebrew thought; for the one basic Hebrew term *māšāl*
covered all figurative illustrations: parable, allegory, proverb, maxim, simile,
metaphor, etc. Simple allegory was within the plausible range of Jesus'
preaching, as we can see from contemporary Qumran and rabbinic examples. A Jesus who spoke exclusively in what moderns define as parables
is a 19th-century critical creation.

Turning to the question of parable and allegory in John x, we hope to
show below that x 1–5 consists of several parables, while x 7 ff. consists
of allegorical explanations. The latter feature is not an *a priori* indication
that the material could not have come from Jesus himself. As we shall see,
some of the material in x 7 ff. may represent a later expansion of Jesus'

remarks. In the Synoptic Gospels also, most scholars recognize that in the explanations of parables (e.g., Mark iv 13–20; Matt xiii 37–43) there has been a certain expansion in the interests of early Christian catechesis; but, as we have tried to prove in our article cited above, underneath this catechetical expansion and application one finds traces of an explanation that may very well stem from Jesus himself. So too in John x, while not all the explanations of 7 ff. need come from the one time or the one situation, there is no reason to rule out the possibility that we may find among them the traces of Jesus' own simple allegorical explanation of the parables in x 1–5. It is important to note with Schneider, *art. cit.*, that the explanations are centered on three terms that appear in the parables of vss. 1–5: (*a*) the gate is explained in 7–10; (*b*) the shepherd is explained in 11–18; (*c*) the sheep are explained in 26–30. The recognition of this plan in ch. x is the decisive factor that, as we saw, militates against rearrangement of the verses. An effective way to see how simple an allegory we have in the explanation of the parables is to contrast what is said in the Gospel about the gate, the shepherd, and the sheep with the elaborate patristic allegories built around John x (see Quasten, *art. cit.*). Cornelius a Lapide, that 17th-century mirror of patristic exegesis, tells us that *the flock* is the Church, *the owner* of the flock is the Father, *the gatekeeper* is the Holy Spirit, etc. It is this type of developed allegory that is an anachronism on Jesus' lips.

COMMENT: DETAILED

Verses 1–5: The parable(s)

Cerfaux, *art. cit.*, has pointed out that the figures found in these verses appear frequently in the Synoptics. Mark vi 34 compares the crowds who come to hear Jesus to sheep without a shepherd. Jesus attacks the Pharisees' lack of care for outcasts with the Parable of the Lost Sheep in Luke xv 3–7. Thus, in having Jesus use the imagery of shepherding, and in having such parables continue the remarks addressed to the Pharisees in ix 41, the fourth evangelist is being quite true to the traditional picture of Jesus' ministry. It is worth noting also that these parables in John are related to the theme of those who *cannot see* in ix 40, while the first parable in Mark illustrates that some may see with their eyes but *not* really *perceive* (iv 12 and par.). Thus, the often stressed lack of sequence between John ix and x is not as obvious as might first seem.

(*a*) The point of the parable in x 1–3a is relatively clear: there is a proper way to approach the sheep, namely through the gate opened by the keeper. Any other approach is malevolent. Verses 1 and 2 mention entering through the *gate;* vs. 3a is the first mention of the *keeper*. O'Rourke, *art. cit.*, would see two different parables here; but he bases his judgment on an over-rigorous application of the principle that all parables can be reduced to two terms of comparison. John A. T. Robinson, *art. cit.*, treats 1–3a as only one parable but centers the imagery around the gatekeeper. He reminds us of Synoptic passages where Jesus uses both the imagery of the gatekeeper (Mark xiii 34) and the imagery of the coming of a thief (Luke xii 39) in order to inculcate watchfulness. Drawing on these comparisons, Robinson thinks that the parable in John is a warning to the authorities that they should fulfill their role as the watchmen for God's people, a frequent OT theme (Jer vi 17; Ezek iii 17; Isa lxii 6). This warning carries a tone of eschatological urgency, an urgency that is expressed elsewhere in the NT in terms of judgment standing at the gate (Mark xiii 29; Rev iii 20).

While this interpretation of the parable in x 1–3a is possible, it does seem that vss. 1 and 2 give more emphasis to the gate than Robinson allows. (Robinson's article should be modified by the remarks of P. Meyer, *art. cit.*) The explanation of the parable in 7–10 would also indicate that the real point in the parable is that of entering through the gate. If this is so, the attack on the Pharisees is not so much in terms of their not being watchful gatekeepers (3a), as in terms of their being thieves and bandits who do not approach the sheep through the gate. The fact that the feast of Dedication (near at hand, it would seem from x 22) might bring to mind the example of the bad high priests of Maccabean times who were truly thieves and bandits suggests that Jesus meant to include in his remarks the Sadducees as well as the Pharisees. In Mark xi 17–18 both the priests and scribes heard Jesus charge that God's house was being turned into a den of *bandits*.

(*b*) In 3b–5 the close relationship between the sheep and the shepherd is in sharper focus than in 1–3a. Here a wealth of OT background may be suggested. The figure of the true shepherd of the flock who leads the sheep out to pasture reminds us of the symbolic description of Joshua (who bears the same Hebrew name as Jesus) in Num xxvii 16–17: "Appoint a man over the congregation [LXX *synagogē*] . . . who shall lead them out and bring them in, that the congregation of the Lord may not be like sheep without a shepherd" (see also Mic ii 12–13). We may note in passing that Bruns, pp. 388–89, sees in the passage in Numbers an echo of the priestly ideal and ordination; should his observation be true, it would give another reason for thinking that Jesus was attacking the priests as well as the Pharisees in these parables. That Jesus thought of his ministry in terms of this passage in Numbers is suggested by Mark vi 34, where he pities the crowds that come to him because they are like sheep without a shepherd.

There are good Synoptic parallels which employ the imagery of a shepherd's care for his sheep to describe Jesus' relation to his followers (Matt xxvi 31; Luke xii 32, "little flock"). Dodd, *Tradition*, p. 384, points out that the individual knowledge that the shepherd has of the sheep when he calls them one by one (John x 3b) is quite similar to the individual care for the sheep exemplified in the Parable of the Lost Sheep (Luke xv 3–7).

Do vss. 3b–5 constitute a separate parable, or are they to be joined to 1–3a as a continuous parable? The fact that the Pharisees (and the priests?) are now attacked as shepherds who are strangers to the flock, rather than as the thieves and bandits (or as the careless gatekeepers) of 1–3a does suggest that we have another parable. Thus, 1–5 may consist of twin parables—a feature fairly common in the Synoptic tradition, e.g., Luke xv 3–10 (*lost sheep; lost coin*); xiv 28–32 (*man building a tower; king going to war*). The statement that the sheep will not follow shepherds whose voices are strange to them would be a particularly telling attack on the Pharisees of ch. ix whose admonitions the blind man had rejected.

Verse 6: *The reaction*

That the reaction to the parable(s) is a failure to understand is not surprising, for similar lack of comprehension greets the parables in the Synoptic tradition (Mark iv 13). The failure to understand causes Jesus to explain these parable(s) of the sheepgate and the shepherd, even as it caused him to explain the Parable of the Sower in the Synoptic tradition. The failure is not primarily an intellectual problem; it is an unwillingness to respond to the challenge of the parables. In the Synoptic Gospels that challenge is centered around the kingdom of heaven; in John it is centered around Jesus himself. The familiar Synoptic phrase, "The kingdom of heaven is like . . . ," has its Johannine parallel in "I am [*egō eimi*] . . ." (x 7, 9, 11, 14).

Verses 7–10: *Explanation of the gate*

Drawing on the imagery of the parable in vss. 1–3a, Jesus now explains: "I am the gate." However, this metaphorical identification is capable of at least two different interpretations.

(*a*) The first interpretation, found in vs. 8, sees Jesus as the gate whereby the shepherd approaches the sheep. This interpretation lies very close to the parable itself, for once again we hear of the thieves and bandits who avoid the gate. Does the statement, "All who came [before me] are thieves and bandits," refer to the Pharisees (and the priests) of Jesus' time? Bultmann, p. 286[4], denies this, for he insists that the coming referred to must be an eschatological coming in one of the great moments of salvation. He thinks that in the Gnostic source which he posits for John this was a condemnation of Moses and the prophets, but that in the Gospel it may have been reapplied to the divine saviors of the Hellenistic world. Other scholars see a reference to the false messiahs of Jesus' era, or even to the Qumran Teacher of Righteousness. It is true that there were a number of would-be national liberators before Jesus (Josephus *Ant*. XVII.x.4–8; ⨪269–84), but we are not certain that they claimed to be messiahs. Nevertheless, the term *lēstēs*, "bandit," would certainly fit such insurrectionaries (see H. G. Wood, NTS 2 [1956], 265–66). These suggestions are interesting, but in our opinion the Pharisees and Sadducees remain the most probable targets of Jesus' remarks. The unhappy line of priestly rulers and politicians from Maccabean times until Jesus' own day could certainly be characterized as false shepherds, thieves, and robbers who came before Jesus. And the

Pharisees too had soiled themselves in the political power struggle in the Hasmonean and Herodian periods. The strong language used in this explanation of the parable may well be compared with that of Matt xxiii, where Jesus attacks the unjust exercise of authority over the people by the scribes and Pharisees.

(b) The second interpretation of Jesus as the gate is found in vss. 9–10. Here he is the gate leading to salvation, a gate, not for the shepherd, but for the sheep. All must pass through the gate that is Jesus in order to be saved; he has come (10) to bring life to the sheep. This explanation has little to do with the parable of 1–3a, and we may have here an adapted saying of Jesus from another context. If vs. 10 is looked on as an isolated saying, its pattern is very close to that of Mark ii 17. The idea in 10 resembles that in John xiv 6: "I am the way; . . . no one comes to the Father except through me" (see also Rev iii 7–8). The concept of the gate of salvation is found in Ps cxviii 20: "This is the gate of the Lord; the righteous shall enter through it." At the end of the 1st century A.D., in the very period when the final form of the Gospel was being written, Clement of Rome (I Cor xlviii 3) was already applying this psalm verse to Jesus. Indeed, it is not too unlikely that Jesus may have used this Psalm to interpret his ministry, since the Synoptic tradition has him employing another simile from the same Psalm (Ps cxviii 22, "The stone which the builders rejected has become the chief cornerstone," cited in Mark xii 10 and par.). All the Gospels associate Ps cxviii 26, "Blessed be he who enters in the name of the Lord," with Jesus' entry into Jerusalem.

This interpretation of Jesus as the gate to salvation makes its appearance very early in patristic exegesis, for Ignatius (Phila ix 1) says: "He is the gate [thyra, as in John and Revelation] of the Father, through which enter Abraham and Isaac and Jacob and the Prophets and the Apostles and the Church." The reference to the OT figures may be Ignatius' way of getting around the difficulty of the sweeping condemnation of "all who came before me" in John x 8. There is a parallel to the Johannine picture of the gate to salvation in Matt vii 13 where Jesus speaks of the narrow door or gate (pylē) that leads to salvation. The 2nd-century Shepherd of Hermas (Similitude ix 12:3–6) seems to weave together the Johannine and Synoptic imagery: the door [pylē] into the kingdom of God is the Son of God; no man can enter otherwise than through the Son.

We must comment on the theme in vs. 9 that those who go in and out through the gate that is Jesus find pasture. We have heard previously that Jesus supplies the living water and the bread of life; now he offers the pasture of life, for vs. 10 makes it clear that in speaking of pasture, he is really speaking of fullness of life. This gift of life is opposed to the slaughter that is associated with the thief. (In the Tabernacles discourse in viii 44 we heard that the devil is a murderer, so the opposition between the thief and the shepherd is a reflection of the opposition between Satan and Jesus.) The thief comes to destroy; in iii 16 Jesus said that God gave the only Son so that everyone who believes in him may not be destroyed but may have eternal life (also vi 39). Since it seems that vss. 8 and 9–10 are two different explanations of Jesus as the gate (with 8 being closer to the parable of 1–3a), we need not think that the thieves and bandits of 8 (and 1), whom we identified as the Pharisees and the priests, need be the same as the thief of 10. The thief of 10 who comes only to steal, slaughter, and destroy is more like "the one who comes in his own name" of v 43, that is, a general representative of darkness who is a rival to the Son. This is an instance of the tendency of the historical enemies of Jesus' ministry to become more general figures of evil as the gospel message is preached in a later period and on a worldwide scale.

Verses 11–16: Explanation of the shepherd

The first parable in vss. 1–3a concerned the way to approach the sheep; therefore its explanation concerned the gate. The second parable in 3b–5 concerned the relation between the shepherd and the sheep; therefore its explanation concerns the shepherd. Just as we had two interpretations of "I am the gate" (7, 9), each with a different nuance, so we have two interpretations of the statement "I am the model shepherd" (11, 14), each with its own nuance. The recognition that each of the parables has its own explanation and that the explanations themselves go in different directions saves us from the oversimple patristic solution which would make one consistent allegory of all these themes and have Jesus as both the gate and the shepherd at the same time.

(*a*) In the first interpretation, found in vss. 11–13, Jesus is the model or noble shepherd because he is willing to die to protect his sheep. The theme of dying for the sheep appears rather abruptly, for there was no suggestion of this in the parable. (Meyer, p. 234, thinks that the gate of 7–10 is not so much the person of Jesus as it is his death, for that is what will bring life to the sheep [see xii 24]. This view, attractive as it is, seems to go beyond the text.) The association of death with being a shepherd is found in other sayings attributed to Jesus (Mark xiv 27; John xxi 15–19). The Synoptic Parable of the Lost Sheep pictures the trouble that a shepherd will take for a lost sheep; John's saying in vs. 11 extends the risk of the shepherd even to the point of death.

In vss. 12–13 the hired hand and the wolf come into the cast of this little scene. Since these figures did not appear in the parables of 1–5, it would seem that the interpretation of "I am the model shepherd" in 11–13 has really made use of a new parable. If this parable too is an attack on the Pharisees, they are now represented by the hired hand who betrays his flock. The imagery of the wolf appears in Matt x 16: "I send you like sheep in the midst of wolves." The symbolism of the shepherd protecting his flock from wolves became traditional in the early Church. In Acts xx 28–29 Paul instructs the elders or bishops of Ephesus to feed their flock because fierce wolves were coming who would not spare the sheep. The parallelism to John's parable is doubly interesting if John was written at Ephesus. See also I Pet ii 25, v 1–2.

(*b*) In the second interpretation, found in vss. 14–16, Jesus is the model shepherd because he knows his sheep intimately. (Verse 15, however, shows that the theme of death is not forgotten.) Since the close bond between sheep and shepherd is the theme of the original parable in 3b–5, this interpretation of Jesus as the shepherd is much closer to an explanation of the parable than the interpretation found in 11–13. That Jesus knows his sheep by name (3b) and that they recognize his voice (4) is commented on in vs. 14: "I know my sheep and mine know me." God's intimate knowledge of His people is proclaimed in the OT (e.g., Nah i 7) and the NT (I Cor viii 3; Gal iv 9; II Tim ii 19). Since Jesus' activity is always patterned on that of the Father (John viii 28), we are not surprised that he possesses intimate knowledge of his followers. Verse 16 stresses that the purpose of this knowledge is to bring these followers into union with one another (and, of course, with Jesus and his Father—xvii 21). That there are other sheep who do not belong to the fold introduces the Gentile mission (see also xi 52).

The question of the Christian mission to the Gentiles was a burning one in the early Church, and we may well wonder whether we are dealing in vs. 16 with a theme of Jesus' own ministry or a theme introduced by later Christian theologians. This is a complicated critical problem, well treated by J. Jeremias, *Jesus' Promise to the Nations* (London: SCM, 1958). It is true that the Church came to an affirmative decision on its mission to the Gentiles only after laborious consideration and much opposition. However, it is an oversimplification to claim that these indications of struggle and doubt preclude any directive on the subject from Jesus himself. All the gospel traditions include statements by Jesus pertaining to the conversion of the Gentiles (e.g., Matt viii 11; Mark xi 17; some of the parables), and it is not easy to explain all of these statements as later compositions. A plausible solution is that the Church came only slowly to understand the import of these figurative sayings of Jesus pertaining to the Gentiles—sayings which, because they were figurative, were not understood at the time of their utterance. Now, of course, in that process of understanding, the statements of Jesus took on greater scope. For instance, in John x 16, the evangelist is probably thinking of "this fold" in terms of the existing Church; but if the saying was originally spoken by Jesus, "this fold" must have had a much simpler meaning. In itself, is the reference to "a fold" during Jesus' ministry any more anachronistic than the reference to his followers as "a flock" (Luke xii 32; Matt xxvi 31, spelling out the implications of Mark xiv 27)? What has happened in John is that a simple parabolic expression has been applied by the evangelist to a later church situation; but then the context of Matt xviii has done exactly the same thing for the Parable of the Lost Sheep (xviii 12–14).

We must pause briefly to consider the OT background that lies behind

Jesus' claim to be the shepherd (see C. K. Barrett, JTS 48 [1947], 163–64).
Because the patriarchal civilization and that of Israel until well after the
conquest of Palestine was largely pastoral, the imagery of shepherding is
frequent in the Bible. Even when agriculture became dominant in Israel,
there remained a nostalgia for the pastoral. Yahweh might be pictured as
the tender of the vine and the planter of the seed, but He remained more
familiarly the shepherd of the flock (Gen xlix 24; Pss xxiii, lxxviii 52–53).
The Patriarchs, Moses, and David were all shepherds, and so "shepherd"
became a figurative term for the rulers of God's people, a usage common
throughout the ancient Near East. Impious kings were scathingly denounced
as wicked shepherds (I Kings xxii 17; Jer x 21, xxiii 1–2). In particular, Ezek
xxxiv is important background for John x. There God denounces the
shepherds or rulers who have not cared for the flock (His people) and
have plundered it, neglecting the weak, the sick, and the straying. "So they
were scattered for want of a shepherd and became food for all the wild
beasts . . . my sheep were scattered over all the face of the earth with
none to seek or search for them" (xxxiv 5–6). God promises that He will
take His flock away from these wicked shepherds, and He Himself will
become their shepherd. "I shall lead them out of the nations, and gather
them from the countries; I shall bring them to their own land and tend them
on the mountains of Israel . . . I shall feed them with good pasture . . .
I myself shall be the shepherd of my sheep . . . I shall seek the lost"
(xxxiv 11–16). God promises that He will judge between the sheep and the
goats, and will set His servant David (i.e., the anointed king) as the one
shepherd over the sheep. The chapter concludes: "And you, my sheep,
are the sheep of my flock, and I am your God." Obviously, much of what
Jesus says about shepherding both in John and the Synoptics reflects Ezek
xxxiv; in particular, Matt xviii 12–13=Ezek xxxiv 16; Matt xxv 32–33
=Ezek xxxiv 20.

Despite these OT similarities, Bultmann, p. 279, insists that many features
in the Johannine picture of the shepherd and the flock cannot be explained
from the OT. In John, Jesus is not a kingly shepherd as is the shepherd
of OT symbolism; there is stress on the gate, on thieves and bandits—
figures not found in the OT pastoral symbolism; and finally the OT puts
no stress on the *knowledge* which the shepherd has of the flock. For
Bultmann the tradition from which the Johannine picture comes is that of
the Mandeans. (See Introduction, p. LV.) Besides the difficulty of proving
the priority of the Mandean parallels, we suggest that Bultmann exaggerates
the differences between John and the OT background. In any use by
Jesus of OT figures there is originality; to deny OT background because a
new dimension or orientation has been given to OT ideas and symbols
is to fail to understand Jesus' relation to the OT. Therefore, the question
must not be whether Jesus' symbolism is exactly the same as that of Ezekiel
or of other parts of the OT, but whether there is enough similarity to
suggest that the OT supplied the raw material for his creative reinterpreta-

tion and the continuation of that reinterpretation in the preaching of the apostles.

Basically it would seem that Ezekiel's portrait of God (or the Messiah) as the ideal shepherd, in contrast to the wicked shepherds who plunder the flock and allow sheep to be lost, served as the model for Jesus' portrait of himself as the ideal shepherd, in contrast to the Pharisees, who are thieves who rob the sheep and hirelings who allow the sheep to be scattered. If the gate to the sheepfold does not appear in the OT passages, we have shown above that the picture of the gate to salvation does have OT precedents. As for *knowledge* of the flock, we have mentioned above that God's knowing his people is a common biblical theme. And since the knowledge of the flock in John is not purely intellectual but implies care and love, is it that remote from the picture of tender care for the flock in Ezek xxxiv 16 and Isa xl 11? If the knowledge of individual sheep in John is like the care for individual sheep in the Parable of the Lost Sheep, then we are indeed close to Ezekiel, where God says "I shall seek the lost." (It is worth noting that an early representation of the Johannine "Good Shepherd" shows him with the lost sheep on his shoulders.) True, the mutuality of knowledge between the shepherd and the sheep (John x 14) goes beyond the OT parallels; but could this theme be drawn from a common NT concept of intimacy (Matt xi 27; Luke x 22; Gal iv 9), rather than from distant Gnostic traditions? The imagery in the immediate Johannine context, like that of the gathering of the other sheep and that of the one shepherd (x 16), comes from Ezek xxxiv 23, 12–13. (See also Mic ii 12; Jer xxiii 3; Isa lvi 8.)

The unique feature in the Johannine picture of the shepherd is his willingness to die for the sheep. This is not found clearly in the OT, although in I Sam xvii 34–35 David risks his life against bear and lion for the sheep. It is not impossible that Jesus spoke more vaguely of risking one's life for the sheep (see NOTE on vs. 11) and that in the light of his death his remarks were reinterpreted in terms of deliberately laying down his life for the sheep (x 18). In the one instance in the Synoptics where Jesus relates shepherding and death (Mark xiv 27; Matt xxvi 31), he cites Zech xiii 7. Taylor, *Mark*, p. 548, judges that this quotation is authentic and that it shows that Jesus did reflect on the effect that his death would have on his little flock. Elsewhere in Johannine literature we find death associated with the image of the lamb—the Lamb of God slain to take away the sins of the world (Rev v 6; John i 29), the Lamb from whom flows life itself (Rev vii 17, xxii 1). This has much in common with the image of the shepherd who lays down his life so that others may have life to the full. The similarity suggests that we need not go outside the OT for the background of this particular aspect of the Johannine picture of the shepherd: it is a combination of elements from the OT descriptions of the shepherd and of the Suffering Servant (see pp. 60–61).

Verses 17–18: Laying down his life

These verses seem to lie somewhat outside the picture of the parable and its explanation, for they constitute a short commentary on the phrase in vs. 15, "I lay down my life," rather than on any element of the pastoral symbolism. Nevertheless, the fact that the evangelist or an editor has seen fit to join these verses to vs. 16, which mentions the gathering of other sheep, may mean that we are to understand that the other sheep will come to Jesus' flock only through Jesus' death and resurrection. We shall see in xii 20–23 that the coming of the Gentiles is intimately related to the glorification of Jesus through return to his Father.

Many commentators have tried to weaken the telic force of vs. 17, "I lay down my life *in order to* take it up again" (e.g., Lagrange, p. 283); they feel uneasy that Jesus would lay down his life with the calculated purpose of taking it up again. This is a failure to understand that in NT thought the resurrection is not a circumstance that follows the death of Jesus but the essential completion of the death of Jesus. In Johannine thought, in particular, the passion, death, resurrection, and ascension constitute the one, indissoluble salvific action of return to the Father. If Jesus is to give life through the Spirit, he must rise again (vii 39); and so resurrection is truly the purpose of his death. As we shall hear in xii 24, the grain of wheat must die, but it dies so that it may spring up again and bear fruit.

We note that in both vss. 17 and 18 it is Jesus himself who takes up his life again. The normal NT phraseology is not that Jesus rose from the dead but that *the Father* raised him up (Acts ii 24; Rom iv 24; Eph i 20; Heb xi 19; I Pet i 21—also see NOTE on ii 22). But since in Johannine thought the Father and the Son possess the same power (x 28–30), it really makes little difference whether the resurrection is attributed to the action of the Father or of the Son. This is a profound theological insight on which later Trinitarian theology would capitalize.

Verse 18 speaks of the divine command or commandment, and this is a theme that will recur frequently in the subsequent chapters. The "command" of the Father covers the same area as the "will" of the Father: it reflects the bond of love that exists between the Father and the Son; it involves the mission and obedient death of the Son; it brings life to men (xii 49–50, xiv 31). Those who follow the Son must also accept the divine commandment and let the love that it reflects be seen in their own lives (xiii 34, xv 12, 17); if the command of the Father led the Son to lay down his life for men, the acceptance of this command by Jesus' followers suggests a readiness on their own part to lay down their lives for one another (xv 13). Verse 18 describes both Jesus' death and his resurrection as commanded by the Father; this is conclusive proof that when Jesus lays down his life *in order to* take it up again, his motive is not one of self-seeking. It is the Father who willed that the death of Jesus should lead to resurrection and return to Himself.

Verses 19–21: Reaction of the Jews

The reaction to the parable(s) in vss. 1–5 was failure to understand; the reaction to the explanation of the parable(s) in vss. 7–18 is one of division. The verses that describe this division are a good transition to what follows at Dedication, for there some will challenge the messianic implications of Jesus' presentation of himself as the shepherd. At the same time these verses recall previous reactions to Jesus at Tabernacles, where there was also division (vii 12, 25–27, 31, 40–41, ix 16) and the accusation of madness (vii 20, viii 48).

BIBLIOGRAPHY

Bishop, E. F., "The Door of the Sheep—John x. 7–9," ET 71 (1959–60), 307–9.

Bruns, J. E., "The Discourse on the Good Shepherd and the Rite of Ordination," AER 149 (1963), 386–91.

Cerfaux, L., "Le thème littéraire parabolique dans l'Evangile de saint Jean," *Coniectanea Neotestamentica* 11 (1947; Fridrichsen Festschrift), 15–25. Also RecLC, II, pp. 17–26.

Feuillet, A., "La composition littéraire de Joh. ix–xii," *Mélanges Bibliques . . . André Robert,* pp. 478–93. In English in JohSt, pp. 129–47.

Jeremias, J., *"poimēn,"* TWNT, V, pp. 484–504.

Meyer, P. W., "A Note on John 10, 1–18," JBL 75 (1956), 232–35.

Mollat, D., "Le bon pasteur (Jean 10: 1–18, 26–30)," BVC 52 (1963), 25–35.

O'Rourke, J. J., "Jo 10, 1–18: Series Parabolorum?" VD 42 (1964), 22–25.

Quasten, J., "The Parable of the Good Shepherd: John 10: 1–21," CBQ 10 (1948), 1–12, 151–69.

Robinson, John A. T., "The Parable of the Shepherd (John 10. 1–5)," ZNW 46 (1955), 233–40. Also in TNTS, pp. 67–75.

Schneider, J., "Zur Komposition von Joh. 10," *Coniectanea Neotestamentica* 11 (1947; Fridrichsen Festschrift), 220–25.

36. JESUS AT DEDICATION:
—JESUS AS MESSIAH AND SON OF GOD
(x 22–39)

Jesus is consecrated in place of the temple altar

X 22 It was winter, and the time came for the feast of Dedication at Jerusalem. 23 Jesus was walking in the temple precincts, in Solomon's Portico, 24 when the Jews gathered around him and demanded, "How long are you going to keep us in suspense? If you are really the Messiah, tell us so in plain words." 25 Jesus answered,

"I did tell you, but you do not believe.
The works that I am doing in my Father's name
give testimony for me,
26 but you refuse to believe
because you are not my sheep.
27 My sheep hear my voice;
and I know them,
and they follow me.
28 I give them eternal life,
and they shall never perish.
No one will snatch them from my hand.
29 My Father, as to what He has given me, is greater than all,
and from the Father's hand no one can snatch away.
30 The Father and I are one."

31 When the Jews [again] got rocks to stone him, 32 Jesus protested to them, "Many a noble work have I shown you from the Father. For just which of these works are you going to stone me?" 33 "It is not for any 'noble work' that we are stoning you," the Jews retorted, "but for blaspheming, because you who are only a man make yourself God." 34 Jesus answered,

"Is it not written in your Law,
'I have said, "You are gods" '?

35 If it calls those men gods
   to whom God's word was addressed—
   and the Scripture cannot lose its force—
36 do you claim that I blasphemed
   when, as the one whom the Father consecrated and sent into the
   I said, 'I am God's Son'? |world,
37 If I do not perform my Father's works,
   put no faith in me.
38 But if I do perform them,
   even though you still put no faith in me,
   put your faith in these works
   so that you may come to know [and understand]
   that the Father is in me
   and I am in the Father."

39 Then they tried [again] to arrest him, but he slipped out of their
clutches.

Notes

x 22. *winter*. Or wintery weather—the month of December.

feast of Dedication. Hanukkah, or "Tabernacles of the month of Chislev" (II Macc i 9), was a feast celebrating the Maccabean victories. For three years, 167–164 B.C., the Syrians had profaned the Temple by erecting the idol of Baal Shamem (the oriental version of Olympian Zeus) on the altar of holocausts (I Macc i 54; II Macc vi 1–7). This pollution of the holy place by the "abominable desolation" (Dan ix 27; Matt xxiv 15) came to an end when Judas Maccabeus drove out the Syrians, built a new altar, and rededicated the Temple on the twenty-fifth of Chislev (I Macc iv 41–61). The feast of Dedication was the annual celebration of the reconsecration of the altar and Temple.

Dedication. The Gr. *Enkainia*, literally "renewal," is used to translate *Hanukkah* which means "dedication." These nouns and related verbs are used in the MT and LXX for the dedication or consecration of the altar in the Tabernacle of the Exodus days (Num vii 10–11), in the Temple of Solomon (I Kings viii 63; II Chron vii 5), and in the Second Temple (Ezra vi 16). Thus, the term is somewhat evocative of the consecration of all the houses of God in Israel's history.

23. *Solomon's Portico*. The outermost court of the Temple was surrounded by magnificent covered colonnades or cloisters on all four sides. These porticoes were open on the inside facing the Temple, but closed on the outside. The oldest portico, the one on the east side, was popularly associated with Solomon, the builder of the first Temple (Josephus *War* V.v.1;✳184–85; *Ant.* XV.xi.3; ✳396–401, XX.ix.7;✳221). While forming the boundary of the temple precincts, it was outside the temple proper, as the Western variant of Acts iii 11 makes clear ("As Peter and John came out [of the Temple] . . . the people stood astonished in the portico which is known as Solomon's").

24. *keep us in suspense*. Literally "take away our life [*psychē*—breath of

life]." The use of this expression for suspense is not well attested; perhaps it means, as in modern Greek, "annoy, bother." That John intends a play on the literal sense is not impossible (Hoskyns, p. 383). The idea would then be that, although Jesus lays down his own life for those who follow him (x 11, 15), he also provokes judgment and thus *takes away the life* of those who reject him (xi 48).

26. *not my sheep.* Good witnesses, including P[66], add: "as I told you."

29. *My Father, as to what He has given me, is greater than all.* The textual witnesses are divided on behalf of at least five different Greek readings, each giving a different grammatical construction. No reading is without difficulty; but besides the one above, the two most important are:

"My Father, who has given (them) to me, is greater than all."

"As for my Father, what He has given to me is greater than all."

The detailed reasons for our choice would require a long explanation based on the Greek text; they may be found in Birdsall, *art. cit.* The other readings seem to have developed in an attempt to smooth out the grammar of the original.

30. *The Father and I are one.* This was a key verse in the early Trinitarian controversies (see Pollard, *art. cit.*). On one extreme, the Monarchians (Sabellians) interpreted it to mean "one person," although the "one" is neuter, not masculine. On the other extreme, the Arians interpreted this text, which was often used against them, in terms of moral unity of will. The Protestant commentator Bengel, following Augustine, sums up the orthodox position: "Through the word 'are' Sabellius is refuted; through the word 'one' so is Arius."

31. *[again].* Some witnesses have "again"; others have "therefore"; others have both; still others have neither. "Again" may represent a scribal harmonization with viii 59.

32. *noble. kalos;* is this an echo of the noble or model (*kalos*) shepherd who lays down his life for his sheep (x 11)?

the Father. Some witnesses, including seemingly both Bodmer papyri, read "my Father."

33. *make yourself God.* Against the evidence of the vast majority of witnesses, P[66] gives evidence of reading the article before *theon* ("God"); for *ho theos* as "God, the Father" see i 1.

34. *in your Law.* Here "Law" refers to the OT in general and not only the Pentateuch, for it is a psalm that is being cited (same wide usage in xii 34; I Cor xiv 21). However, perhaps the Jewish interpretation of the psalm as referring to what God said at Sinai (where the Law was given) should be considered —see COMMENT. The "your" is omitted by some important witnesses, but not by either Bodmer papyrus. Both Barrett, p. 319, and Bultmann, p. 296[8], are inclined to favor omission, but such an omission may very well have been a scribal attempt to soften the seeming harshness of Jesus' attitude toward the OT and his tendency to dissociate himself from the Jewish heritage (see NOTE on vii 19). It is also possible that the "your" may have had an argumentative function, being equivalent to "the Law which even *you* admit."

35. *calls . . . gods.* Besides this instance where the judges were called gods, Jesus might also have cited Exod vii 1 where Moses was called god.

God's word was addressed. This expression connotes a divine call; we find it used for men like Hosea (i 1), Jeremiah (i 2), and John the Baptist (Luke iii 2).

the Scripture. The psalm cited in vs. 34, or Scripture in general?

lose its force. Literally *lyein* is "break, set aside"; it is passive here. Often this passage is assumed to reflect a reverence for the details of the Law (Scripture) which are not to be set aside (Matt v 17–18). Jungkuntz, pp. 559–60, points out that in reference to Scripture *lyein* is contrasted to *plēroun*, the passive of which means "to be fulfilled," and that therefore *lyein* means "to keep from being fulfilled." In rabbinic usage, *baṭṭēl*, which seems to be the Aramaic equivalent of *lyein*, means "to nullify, render futile." The use of *lyein* in John vii 23 means that a man receives circumcision even on a Sabbath so that the fulfillment of the Law will not be frustrated.

36. *consecrated. Hagiazein*, "to consecrate, sanctify," is used in LXX of Num vii 1 to describe Moses' consecration of the Tabernacle, whereas *enkainizein* (see NOTE on vs. 22 above) is used in Num vii 10–11 for the dedication of the altar. The two are synonyms. Numbers vii was a synagogue reading for the feast of Dedication (Guilding, pp. 127–28). Here the Father has consecrated Jesus; in xvii 19 Jesus says, "I consecrate myself"; vi 69 calls Jesus "God's Holy One [*hagios*]."

37. *put no faith.* Here and in the next verse the present imperative is used with a durative value.

38. *though you still put no faith.* Codex Bezae and the Latin read "though you do not wish to put faith."

[*and understand*]. This is the reading of the best witnesses; others substitute "and believe"; Bezae, OL, and OS have neither. "Know and understand" represent the aorist and present of the same verb *ginōskein;* some scribes may have found the expression pleonastic.

39. *Then.* Omitted in important witnesses but perhaps by homoioteleuton: *ezētoun oun.*

[*again*]. Missing in some important witnesses and in a different sequence in others. Like the "again" in vs. 31, this may represent a tendency to harmonize with the mention of previous attempts at arrest (vii 30, 32, 44, viii 20).

clutches. Literally "from their hand [singular]"; there are plural variants, probably because, while the Hebrew idiom tends to use the singular, the Greek idiom uses the plural. See NOTE on vii 44.

COMMENT

We come to the last of the series of feasts which began with chapter v: the Sabbath, Passover, Tabernacles, and now Dedication. As we stressed in treating x 1–21, the break between Tabernacles and Dedication is not so sharp as the break between the other feasts. At Dedication Jesus is in the temple precincts much as he was at Tabernacles (vii 14, 28); "the Jews" press him to tell who he is much as they did at Tabernacles (viii 25, 53); the question of the Messiah comes up again (vii 26, 31, 41–42, ix 22); and, of course, the attempt to arrest Jesus and to stone him, the charge of blasphemy, the triumphant answers in terms of unique relationship with the Father—all these are echoes of what happened at Tabernacles.

These similarities, which occur chiefly in the narrative portions of x 22–39, suggest that we may be dealing with some duplicate accounts of reactions to Jesus. The nicely balanced arrangement of this section also points to a carefully edited scene. There are two basic questions: Is Jesus the Messiah (24)? Does he make himself God (33)? Each receives an answer of approximately the same length (25–30, 34–38), an answer that ends on the theme of Jesus' unity with his Father. To each answer "the Jews" react unfavorably, first with an attempt to stone him, then with an attempt to arrest him.

Yet, as in all the Johannine scenes, we must not jump too quickly to a negative evaluation of the tradition here. It is hard to imagine why the setting at the feast of Dedication would or could have been invented. It was a relatively unimportant feast and not a pilgrimage feast. Although we may find a connection between the theme of the dedication of the Temple or an altar and the consecration of Jesus (vs. 36), the connection is not so obvious that the saying would have been responsible for the creation of the setting. Miss Guilding would suggest that the fact that shepherd readings were common at Dedication time in the synagogues prompted the chronological inventiveness of the evangelist. Yet, as we have insisted, the argument can be reversed: if Jesus really spoke in Jerusalem during the feast of Dedication, what topic would have been more natural than the readings the people had recently heard in the synagogues, or would soon hear? And there is one detail of local color that is very accurate. At this winter season, when the cold winds sweep in from the east across the great desert, we find Jesus in the east portico of the Temple, the only one of the porticoes whose closed side would protect it from the east wind (see NOTE on vs. 23).

As for the content of Jesus' discourse, this too shows traditional elements which cannot be easily discounted. As we shall see, the two questions implied in vss. 24 and 33 about Jesus' being Messiah and God (or Son of God) are exactly the questions that the Synoptic Gospels set in the framework of the trial of Jesus before the Sanhedrin. Jesus' answers and the charge of blasphemy are also found in the Synoptic trial scene. We have suggested before that in scattering these charges throughout a longer final ministry in Jerusalem, John may be giving the truer picture; for the Synoptic trial scene has the air of being a summary and a synthesis of oft-repeated charges. As for the almost rabbinic argument based on Scripture in vss. 34–36, although it could conceivably be the product of the Synagogue-Church debate, it was certainly not created in Gentile Christian circles, and in format it would have been perfectly at home in Jesus' ministry.

A plausible solution is that in the general setting and in the basic content of the discourse the evangelist is dealing with traditional material. But in giving form and movement to the scene, the evangelist has dealt imaginatively, supplying the standard controversy patterns that have run through the last chapters.

Verses 22–31: Jesus as the Messiah

The question that sets the topic for the first scene at the feast of Dedication is found in vs. 24: "If you are really the Messiah, tell us so in plain words." All the Synoptic accounts of the trial before the Sanhedrin have the high priest ask Jesus if he is the Messiah, but Luke xxii 67 is closest to

John: "If you are really the Messiah, tell us so." The answer of Jesus in the two is virtually the same: in John he says, "I did tell you, yet you do not believe"; in Luke he says, "If I tell you, you will not believe."

The demand that Jesus say plainly whether or not he is the Messiah makes particular sense in the present sequence in John, where Jesus has spoken of himself figuratively as a shepherd. As we have seen in the OT background, the shepherd was a frequent symbol for the Davidic king (see Ezek xxxiv 23), so that the messianic implications of Jesus' claim to be the shepherd were apparent to the Jewish authorities. Neither here nor in the Synoptics, however, does Jesus answer without qualification a direct question about his messiahship. Too often for the questioners "Messiah" had nationalistic and political overtones which Jesus would not wish to encourage. A good example of this is the picture of the warlike Messiah in Ps Sol xvii 21–25: he shatters unjust rulers; he breaks sinners into pieces with a rod of iron; nations flee before him. If subsequent Christian tradition has captured a valid insight into Jesus' thought by giving him the name of Messiah or Christ, it must still be recognized that his messiahship evinced an originality that changed the very content of the concept. Perhaps the best commentary on Jesus' attitude toward the question of whether or not he is the Messiah is found in John x 30 where his answer is epitomized in the statement: "The Father and I are one"—an answer that is affirmative in tone but not phrased in traditional terminology.

In vs. 25 Jesus begins his answer to the question about messiahship by recalling the works he is doing, foremost among which would be the healing of the blind man which "the Jews" themselves mentioned in x 21. It is interesting that in the Synoptic tradition when John the Baptist sends disciples to ask if he is the one who is to come, Jesus answers by recalling the works he has been doing on behalf of the blind, the lame, etc. (Matt xi 2–6). But, although we may presume that the reference to Jesus' works was not lost on John the Baptist, it fails to convince the Jews in John, for they are not sheep who hear the shepherd's voice.

This reference to sheep in vss. 26–27 recalls x 1–21 and effectively binds together the two parts of ch. x. As Schneider has pointed out, the explanations in x 7–10 and 11–16 of the pastoral parable(s) drew attention to the sheepgate and the shepherd but gave little attention to *the sheep*. Verse 4 had said that the sheep who belong to Jesus would hear him and follow, and we have this exemplified by contrast in vss. 26–27, where "the Jews" do not hear and follow because they are not sheep of the flock. As Chrysostom (*In Jo.* LXI 2; PG 59:338) puts it so well, if they do not follow Jesus, it is not because he is not a shepherd, but because they are not sheep. In x 1–21 we saw the Pharisees compared to thieves, bandits, and hirelings; now we are told that they are not among the sheep given to Jesus by the Father (see NOTE on 14). To hear the voice of Jesus one must be "of God" (viii 47), "of the truth" (xviii 37). While this dualistic separation of Jesus' audience into two groups is clearer in John than in the Synoptics, we should note that in Matt xvi 16–17 what enables Peter to recognize Jesus as Messiah and

Son of God (the two titles involved in John x 22–39) is the revelation Peter has *from the Father.* In Johannine terminology Peter and the other members of the Twelve are sheep given to Jesus by the Father, and so they hear his voice and know who he is (see also Matt xi 25). Those in John who do not hear are like those in the Synoptics who hear the parables but do not understand. Our point in stressing that John's thought has Synoptic parallels is to show the vulnerability of Bultmann's view (pp. 276 and 284) that the flock here resembles the community of the predestined of the Gnostic myth. Jeremias, *art. cit.* (see above, p. 400), seems to do more justice to the whole NT picture in maintaining that the flock here stands for Jesus' community —the community of his followers which after his death developed into the primitive Christian community (Acts xx 28–29; I Pet v 3; *I Clem* xliv 3, liv 2). There is in John an element of predestination as to who shall belong to the flock, but in this, John does not seem to vary from common NT teaching.

The reference to the sheep in vss. 26–27 leads in 28 to the thought of the wolves who snatch the sheep when the hireling guards the flock (x 12). However, Jesus is the model shepherd and no one will snatch from his hand the sheep that the Father has given him. This is because Jesus acts for the Father, and no one can snatch the sheep from the Father's hand (vs. 29). The statement of the Father's supreme power over men in 29 recalls OT statements that souls are in God's hands (Wis iii 1) and that no one can deliver from God's hand (Isa xliii 13). We note that vss. 28 and 29 make the same statement about Jesus and about the Father: no one can snatch the sheep from either's hand. This leads us to an understanding of the unity that is expressed in 30: it is a unity of power and operation. It was an affirmation such as found in 30 that ultimately led the 4th-century Church to the doctrine of the one divine nature in the Trinity, nature being essence considered as a principle of operation.

It seems worth while to pause for a moment to summarize what we have heard thus far in John about the relations between Father and Son. The Son comes from the Father (viii 42); yet the Father who sent him is with him (viii 29). The Father loves the Son (iii 35); the Son knows the Father intimately (viii 55, x 15). In his mission on earth, the Son can do only what he has seen the Father do (v 19), can judge and speak only as he hears from the Father (v 30). The Son was taught by the Father (viii 28) and has received from Him powers such as that of judgment (v 22) and of giving and possessing life (v 21, 26, vi 57). The Son does the will of the Father (iv 34, vi 38) and has received a command from the Father that concerns his death and resurrection (x 18). It will be noted that all these relationships between Father and Son are described in function of the Son's dealings with men. It would be the work of later theologians to take this gospel material pertaining to the mission of the Son *ad extra* and draw from it a theology of the inner life of the Trinity.

Returning to x 30, we find that the unity posited there also concerns men; for just as the Father and Son are one, so they bind men to themselves

as one—"that they may be one, even as we" (xvii 11). This unity that is communicated to believers is what prevents anyone from snatching them away
from either Father or Son. Paul puts it more lyrically in Rom viii
38–39: "Neither death, nor life, nor angels . . . nor anything else in all
creation will be able to separate us from the love of God in Christ Jesus,
our Lord."

Verses 32–39: Jesus as the Son of God

In the past, statements of Jesus intimately associating him with God have
provoked "the Jews" to want to kill him (v 17–18, viii 58–59), and this
reaction is all too true here (vs. 31). Jesus meets their violence by again
recalling the works he has been doing (32, as in 25); their objection, however, is not to his works (as it has been in the past to Sabbath miracles) but
to his blasphemous words. This is the first time (33) that the official charge
of blasphemy occurs in John, although it was presupposed in viii 59 (p. 367).
In the Synoptics (Mark xiv 64; Matt xxvi 65) a solemn charge of blasphemy
is leveled against Jesus at the trial after he has described his future position
as Son of Man sitting at the right hand of God. Once again we are handicapped by lack of evidence as to what constituted blasphemy according to
the Jewish law of this period (see Blinzler, *Trial*, pp. 127–33). The Gospels
seem to be in agreement that the basis of the Jewish charge of blasphemy
against Jesus involved more than his claim to be the Messiah; John is
more specific than the others in stating that it was his making himself God
or equal to God (v 18). Surely there is a great deal of Christian post-resurrectional insight involved in the Johannine estimation of the situation.
However, since neither here nor in v 19 ff. is there any denial by Jesus of the
Jewish estimate of the import of his words, we may be reasonably certain
that the evangelist believed that the estimate was substantially correct. In
Johannine thought the error was not in the description of Jesus as divine
("The Word was God"), but in the assertion that he was *making himself*
God. For John, Jesus never makes himself anything; everything that he is
stems from the Father. He is not a man who makes himself God; he is the
Word of God who has become man. That is why vs. 36 really answers the
Jewish charge: it was the Father who consecrated Jesus. Moreover, we
must be cautious in evaluating the Johannine acceptance of Jesus as divine
or equal to God. As we shall see below in discussing vs. 37, such a
description of Jesus is *not* divorced from the fact that Jesus was sent by
God and acted in God's name and in God's place. Therefore, although the
Johannine description and acceptance of the divinity of Jesus has ontological
implications (as Nicaea recognized in confessing that Jesus Christ, the Son of
God, is himself true God), in itself this description remains primarily
functional and not too far removed from the Pauline formulation that
"God was in Christ reconciling the world to Himself" (II Cor v 19).

We saw that the question of Jesus' messiahship in vs. 24 resembled the
question asked of Jesus by the high priest in the Synoptic trial, and in

particular Luke's form of the question and answer. Whereas Mark xiv 61 and Matt xxvi 63 have one question which mentions the Messiah, the Son of God (or of the Blessed), Luke xxii 67 mentions only the Messiah in his first question. Luke xxii 70 has a second question asked by the high priest, "Are you the Son of God?" Thus, again Luke is closest to John where the question of making himself God or Son of God (33, 36) is separated from that of being Messiah. P. Winter, *Studia Theologica* 9 (1955), 112–15, suggests that the Lucan tradition borrows from that of John; but while this is not impossible as regards details, the number of Johannine parallels to the Synoptic trial before the Sanhedrin suggests a more complicated situation (see our discussion in CBQ 23 [1961], 148–52, and the discussion below on pp. 441 ff.).

In response to the charge of "the Jews" that he is making himself God, Jesus answers with reasoning drawn from the OT. He cites a line from Ps lxxxii 6, although here as elsewhere in the NT not only the line cited but the rest of the verse and even the context are important for the argument. The whole verse reads: "I say, 'You are gods, sons of the Most High, all of you.'" Jesus is interested not only in the use of the term "gods" but also in the synonymous expression "sons of the Most High," for he refers to himself as Son of God in vs. 36.

The Psalm was understood as a castigation of unjust judges: although they have been given the title "gods" because of their quasi-divine function (judgment belongs to God—Deut i 17), they shall die like other men. The same exalted estimation of what a judge should be is implicit in the expressions whereby the people were told to submit themselves to the judges: "They shall appear before Yahweh" (Deut xix 17), or "be brought to God" (Exod xxi 6, xxii 9). Now the argument that Jesus draws seems to have two aspects. *First,* if there was a common practice in the OT to refer to men like the judges as "gods" and this was no blasphemy, why do the Jews object when this term is applied to Jesus? To a Western mind this argument seems to be a deceptive fallacy. The Jews are not objecting that Jesus is raising himself to the level of a god in the sense in which the judges were gods; they are objecting that he is making himself God with a capital "G." In other words, Jesus is glossing over the two different meanings that "god" has in his argument, one being an applied meaning, the other a proper meaning. Part of the solution of this difficulty may lie in recognizing that Jesus was arguing according to the rabbinic rules of hermeneutics, which were often different from modern attitudes. The presence of the word "gods" in the text was the important factor, regardless of difference of meaning. Some scholars, like Bultmann and Strathmann, seem to interpret Jesus' use of such an argument in terms of his meeting the Pharisees on their own level or of making a parody of their way of interpreting Scripture. However, we should beware of assuming that Jesus had other hermeneutic principles than those current in his time. The consistent pattern of his exegesis is not in harmony with modern hermeneutics even where he is not arguing with the Pharisees, for example, the citations attributed to him in the scene of the temptation by the devil (Matt iv 1–11). The citations used in his arguments with the Pharisees (Matt xix 4, xxii 41–45) are interpreted in much the same overliteral pattern that we find in John x 34–36, and it seems difficult to think that he was always adapting himself to principles he did not accept. If it is objected from a critical viewpoint that the use of some of these Scripture citations may actually stem from later Christian usage, it must still be observed that the tradition shows no signs of regarding such hermeneutics as unworthy of Jesus. Therefore, if there appears to be sophistry in John x 34–36, we are not certain that either the speaker or the audience would have had that impression.

But there is a *second* aspect to the argument that gives consolation to any who may remain distrustful. There is an aspect of the *a minori ad maius* ("from the lesser to the greater") or the *a fortiori* which was well known in rabbinic thought. The reason why the judges could be called gods was because they were vehicles of the word of God (vs. 35), but on that premise Jesus deserves so much the more to be called God. He is the one whom the Father consecrated and sent into the world and thus a unique vehicle of the word of God. Thus, there is some reason justifying the use of "god" in two different senses in the argument. Is there any suggestion in x 34–36 that Jesus is *the Word* of God? If the argument "from the lesser to the greater" were worked out in full detail, it might run thus: if it is permissible to call men gods because they were vehicles of the word of God, how much more permissible is it to use "God" of him who *is* the Word of God. This gives us the interesting *possibility* (but no more) of a foreshadowing of the title "Word" that became so prominent in the Johannine hymn that serves as the Prologue.

Others would press the argument in x 34–36 even further. Barrett, p. 319, and Dahl, CINTI, p. 133, draw on the rabbinic interpretation of Ps lxxxii 6. The occasion of the Psalm was thought to have been the Sinai revelation of the Law; the coming of this word of God to the Israelites made them gods or sons of the Most High. Against this background the argument of Jesus might be that, since the Sinai revelation ultimately bears witness to him (John v 46), how much more right has he to the title of God or Son of God? Hanson, *art. cit.*, gives a different twist to this background of the rabbinic interpretation of the Psalm. He holds that in Johannine thought the one who addressed the Jews at Sinai was the pre-existent Word of God, and thus we might translate vs. 35: "If the Law calls those men gods whom the Word of God addressed [at Sinai]. . . ." The *a fortiori* then would be the justice of applying the title God or Son of God to the human bearer of the Word of God. Jungkuntz, *art. cit.*, draws heavily on giving to vs. 35c the meaning that Scripture cannot be kept from fulfillment (see NOTE). The Psalm concerns the judges who received the title of gods; one of John's themes is that Jesus is the judge par excellence (see p. 345); Scripture thus finds its fulfillment in Jesus, who is par excellence worthy of the title given to judges. Moreover, since the judges were the forerunners of the Davidic kings and one of the most important attributes of the Davidic king was to be a just judge, Scripture also brings the concept of judge to fulfillment in the Messiah, the king-judge par excellence. Although none of these suggestions is capable of proof, they do show that Jesus' argument may have been more subtle and convincing than would first appear to Western eyes.

Moving on, we now turn attention to the use of the word "consecrated" in vs. 36. In the sequence of feasts that we have seen in Part Three, of the Book of Signs (chs. v–x), there has always been up to now a theme of replacement. On the Sabbath feast (ch. v) Jesus insisted that there could be no Sabbath rest for the Son since he must continue to exercise even on the Sabbath the powers of life and judgment entrusted to him by the Father. At Passover (vi) Jesus replaced the manna of the Passover-Exodus story by multiplying bread as a sign that he was the bread of life come down from heaven. At Tabernacles (vii–ix) the water and light ceremonies were replaced by Jesus, the true source of living waters and the light of the world. Now at the feast of Dedication, recalling in particular the Maccabean dedication or consecration of the temple altar, but more generally reminiscent of the dedication or consecration of the whole series of temples that had stood in Jerusalem (see NOTES on vss. 22, 36), Jesus proclaims that he is the one who has truly been consecrated by God. This seems to be an instance of the Johannine theme that Jesus is the new Tabernacle (i 14) and the new Temple (ii 21).

The statement that Jesus was consecrated by God would not have been anomalous in the framework of traditional Israelite thought. In the OT the term "consecrated" was applied to men set aside for important work or high office. It was used of Moses (Sir xlv 4), of Jeremiah (Jer i 5), of the priests (II Chron xxvi 18), and of others. Does the use of this term of Jesus (see NOTE on vs. 36) constitute a Johannine allusion to the priesthood of Jesus, a theme that is found in Hebrews (a work with parallels to John)? Hebrews v 5 stresses that Jesus was made a high priest by his Father, just as John stresses that the Father consecrated Jesus. In the Judaism of NT times the priests were the primary examples of men whose consecration had set them apart as "holy"; Jesus was the Holy One of God par excellence (vi 69). For another *possible* instance of the theme of Jesus as priest see COMMENT on xix 23 (in The Anchor Bible, vol. 29A).

In vs. 37 Jesus returns to the theme of works that we heard in vs. 25. Here the reference to works is especially appropriate: Jesus has just claimed to be the one sent by God; therefore God must stand behind the works that Jesus does. This is an instance of the Jewish concept of the šālîaḥ or deputy. In Jewish thought the officially commissioned envoy or deputy had the authority of the sender and was legally identifiable with the sender. This not only explains why Jesus' works are the Father's works but may also have a bearing on the whole argument of vss. 34–36, where Jesus, sent by God, does not deny the charge that he is presenting himself as God.

Along with xiv 11, vs. 38 has become a standard text justifying the Christian apologetic use of miracles; it is understood as showing that Jesus used miracles to show that he came from God. Now, of course, there is a probability that the apologetic interests of the early Church have had a certain influence on a text like vs. 38, and therefore we are not certain historically how much of Jesus' own outlook on his actions is represented in this verse. We must further insist that the emphasis on miracles in this verse is slightly different from the understanding that apologetic manuals propose. The works of Jesus in John (see App. III) are never purely external criteria invoked to prove a point. They are part of Jesus' ministry; they are signs that bring to understanding rather than proofs that convince; the response to them is one of faith rather than of intellectual acknowledgment.

This second part of the discourse at Dedication ends, even as did the first, with a statement of the unity that exists between Father and Son (vs. 38, compared with 30). We stressed in 30 that the unity was one of power and operation; that is why in 38 the *works* of Jesus can reveal this unity, for they are the common works of Father and Son stemming from a common source.

BIBLIOGRAPHY

Birdsall, J. N., "John x. 29," JTS 11 (1960), 342–44.

Hanson, A., "John's Citation of Psalm LXXXII," NTS 11 (1964–65), 158–62 on John x 33–36.

Jungkuntz, R., "An Approach to the Exegesis of John 10:34–36," *Concordia Theological Monthly* 35 (1964), 556–65.

Pollard, T. E., "The Exegesis of John x.30 in the Early Trinitarian Controversies," NTS 3 (1956–57), 334–49.

37. APPARENT CONCLUSION TO THE PUBLIC MINISTRY
(x 40–42)

Jesus withdraws across the Jordan to where his ministry began

X 40 Then he went back across the Jordan to the place where John had been baptizing earlier; and while he stayed there, 41 many people came to him. "John may never have performed a sign," they commented, "but whatever John said about this man was true." 42 And there many came to believe in him.

NOTES

x 40. *where John had been baptizing.* Bethany, as in i 28; see NOTE there.

stayed. If the imperfect is the correct reading here, this is the only use of that tense of *menein* in John. However, there are good witnesses, including P66 and P75, for the aorist which would then have to be taken in a complexive sense, as often in the Greek of the papyri.

41. *many people.* These are probably to be thought of as followers of John the Baptist, who came from their homes when they heard Jesus had returned to the area where John the Baptist had been active. That a colony of John the Baptist's disciples remained permanently in the area seems less likely, unless we are to think of a group like the Qumran community.

never . . . performed a sign. The Synoptics do not attribute miracles to John the Baptist, although Herod is said to have thought that Jesus who was working miracles was John the Baptist come back to life (Mark vi 14). The implication there is probably not that miracles were associated with John the Baptist, but that one who had come back to life would have marvelous powers.

whatever John said about this man was true. Yet, up to this time Jesus had not shown himself to be the Lamb of God who takes away the world's sin (i 29); nor had he baptized with a holy Spirit (i 33), for the Spirit had not yet been given (vii 39). Perhaps we are to think of these things as about to come true in the hour of Jesus' glory which will soon begin.

COMMENT

These verses supply a conclusion for Part Three of the Book of Signs, namely, chs. v–x; and, indeed, by their tone they seem to bring to an end the public ministry of Jesus. Jesus' last public words would then be the ringing challenge found in x 37–38. If, as we suggest, vs. 11 of the Prologue is descriptive of the public ministry ("To his own [land] he came; yet his own people did not accept him"), he now leaves the hostile land and people of Palestine to cross the Jordan. There he finds the faith that was lacking in his own land. Moreover, these verses form an inclusion with the opening scene of the ministry in i 19–28. The Gospel deliberately reminds us of the scene where John the Baptist was baptizing across the Jordan and where he bore witness to Jesus.

We shall see in treating chs. xi–xii that they have peculiarities which suggest that they are an editorial addition to the original gospel outline. For that reason we suggest that at one time the Johannine sketch of the public ministry came to a conclusion with x 40–42. (We should note, however, that other commentators, like Bultmann and Boismard, who think that ch. x was the original conclusion of the first part of the Gospel, have a different theory of the role of x 40–42. Bultmann treats these verses as the introduction to ch. xi; for Boismard x 22–39 should be followed by xi 47 ff.) Before chs. xi–xii were added to the gospel outline, we suggest that x 40–42 was followed by the opening of the Book of Glory in ch. xiii. The switch of locale from the Transjordan to Jerusalem would be no more violent than that between chs. v and vi. Moreover, the opening line of xiii would bear special meaning if it followed x 40–42 ("Jesus was aware that the hour had come for him to go across from this world to the Father"): when Jesus would cross the Jordan the second time, he would truly be going to his land, for he would be going to the Father. We remember that in the Synoptic picture of the (last) journey of Jesus to Jerusalem, he went into the regions beyond the Jordan before he went up to Jerusalem to die (Mark x 1; Matt xix 1). Now we have seen similarities between this Synoptic journey and John's picture of Jesus' going up to Jerusalem for Tabernacles (see p. 309). If x 40–42 was once followed by xiii, we would have a sequence in John that resembles another aspect of the Synoptic journey. One should note that just as the memory of John the Baptist is recalled here in John, so too is it recalled in the Synoptic account of Jesus' days in Jerusalem following his journey (Mark xi 27–33).

In any case, while the retirement of Jesus to the region beyond the Jordan had the practical purpose of seeking shelter from the hostility aroused in Jerusalem, it also served the theological purposes of the evangelist. Jesus was not to die by mob violence; he would die only when he was ready to lay down his life (x 18). When he would return to Jerusalem, he would do so of his own accord and with the certain knowledge that he was going up to die. It was only at the following Passover that the hour which the Father had appointed would come. But for the moment in a place still echoing with the cry of John the Baptist's witness and still bright with the light of his lamp (v 35), Jesus pauses and is greeted by faith. The darkness has not yet come.

T. F. Glasson, ET 67 (1955–56), 245–46, has noted an interesting point. The Johannine passages dealing with John the Baptist grow progressively shorter: i 19–36, iii 22–30, v 33–35, x 41. Does the evangelist intend to illustrate the principle enunciated in iii 30: "He [Jesus] must increase while I must decrease"? The emphasis that John the Baptist worked no miracles and that at the end his followers came in numbers to believe in Jesus may be part of the apologetic of the Fourth Gospel against sectarians of John the Baptist.

THE BOOK OF SIGNS

Part Four: Jesus Moves Toward the Hour of Death and Glory

OUTLINE

38. JESUS GIVES MEN LIFE:—THE STORY OF LAZARUS
(xi 1–44)

A sign that Jesus is the life

XI 1 Now there was a man named Lazarus who was sick; he was from
Bethany, the village of Mary and her sister Martha. (2 This Mary whose
brother Lazarus was sick was the one who anointed the Lord with
perfume and dried his feet with her hair.) 3 So the sisters sent to in-
form Jesus, "Lord, the one whom you love is sick." 4 But when Jesus
heard it, he said,

> "This sickness is not to end in death;
> rather it is for God's glory,
> that the Son [of God] may be glorified through it."

(5 Yet Jesus really loved Martha and her sister and Lazarus.) 6 And so,
even when he heard that Lazarus was sick, he stayed on where he was
two days longer.

7 Then, at last, Jesus said to the disciples, "Let us go back to Judea."
8 "Rabbi," protested the disciples, "the Jews were just now trying to
stone you, and you are going back up there again?" 9 Jesus answered,

> "Are there not twelve hours of daylight?
> If a man goes walking by day, he does not stumble
> because he can see the light of this world.
> 10 But if he goes walking at night, he will stumble
> because he has no light in him."

11 He made this remark, and then, later, he told them, "Our beloved
Lazarus has fallen asleep, but I am going there to wake him up." 12 At
this the disciples objected, "If he has fallen asleep, Lord, his life will
be saved." (13 Jesus had really been talking about Lazarus' death, but
they thought he was talking about sleep in the sense of slumber.) 14 So
finally Jesus told them plainly, "Lazarus is dead. 15 And I am happy for
your sake that I was not there so that you may come to have faith.
In any event, let us go to him." 16 Then Thomas (this name means

7: *said;* 8: *protested;* 11: *told.* In the historical present tense.

"Twin") said to his fellow disciples, "Let us go too that we may die with him."

17 When Jesus arrived, he found that Lazarus had [already] been four days in the tomb. 18 Now Bethany was not far from Jerusalem, just under two miles; 19 and many of the Jews had come out to offer sympathy to Martha and Mary because of their brother. 20 When Martha heard that Jesus was coming, she went to meet him, while Mary sat quietly at home. 21 Martha said to Jesus, "Lord, if you had been here, my brother would never have died. 22 Even now, I am sure that whatever you ask of God, God will give you." 23 "Your brother will rise again," Jesus assured her. 24 "I know he will rise again," Martha replied, "in the resurrection on the last day." 25 Jesus told her,

> "I am the resurrection [and the life]:
> he who believes in me,
> even if he dies, will come to life.
> 26 And everyone who is alive and believes in me
> shall never die at all.—

Do you believe this?" 27 "Yes, Lord," she replied. "I have come to believe that you are the Messiah, the Son of God, he who is to come into the world."

28 Now when she had said this, she went off and called her sister Mary. "The Teacher is here and calls for you," she whispered. 29 As soon as Mary heard this, she got up quickly and started out toward him. (30 Actually Jesus had not yet come into the village but was [still] at the spot where Martha had met him.) 31 The Jews who were in the house with Mary, consoling her, saw her get up quickly and go out; and so they followed her, thinking that she was going to the tomb to weep there. 32 When Mary came to the place where Jesus was and saw him, she fell at his feet and said to him, "Lord, if you had been here, my brother would never have died." 33 Now when Jesus saw her weeping, and the Jews who had accompanied her also weeping, he shuddered, moved with the deepest emotions.

34 "Where have you laid him?" he asked. "Lord, come and see," they told him. 35 Jesus began to cry, 36 and this caused the Jews to remark, "See how much he loved him!" 37 But some of them said, "He opened the eyes of that blind man. Couldn't he also have done something to stop this man from dying?" 38 With this again arousing his emotions, Jesus came to the tomb.

23: *assured;* 24: *replied;* 34: *told;* 38: *came.* In the historical present tense.

It was a cave with a stone laid across it. 39 "Take away the stone," Jesus ordered. Martha, the dead man's sister, said to him, "Lord, it is four days; by now there must be a stench." 40 Jesus replied, "Didn't I assure you that if you believed, you would see the glory of God?" 41 So they took away the stone. Then Jesus looked upward and said,

"Father, I thank you because you heard me.
42 Of course, I knew that you always hear me,
   but I say it because of the crowd standing around,
   that they may believe that you sent me."

43 Having said this, he shouted in a loud voice, "Lazarus, come out!" 44 The dead man came out, bound hand and foot with linen strips and his face wrapped in a cloth. "Untie him," Jesus told them, "and let him go."

39: *ordered, said;* 40: *replied;* 44: *told.* In the historical present tense.

NOTES

xi 1. *Lazarus.* The name *La'zār* is a shortened form of Eleazar; ossuary inscriptions show the name Eleazar to have been common in NT times. This man does not appear in the Synoptic tradition; but the fact that the name means "God helps" is not sufficient reason for thinking that he is a purely symbolic figure. We note that the evangelist does not explain Lazarus' name.

Bethany. Some would suggest a figurative play on this name, interpreted as reflecting *Bēt-'anyā*, "House of affliction"; see NOTE on the Bethany across the Jordan in i 28. However, the Bethany near Jerusalem is well attested as the place where Jesus resided when visiting Jerusalem (Mark xi 11, xiv 3); and therefore Bethany as the locale of John's story is plausible enough without a resort to symbolism. Bethany is probably to be identified with the Ananyah mentioned in Neh xi 32; the sequence of the towns mentioned before Ananyah (Anathoth and Nob) suggests that it should be localized just east of Jerusalem. See W. F. Albright, BASOR 9 (1923), 8–10. Today the town is called El 'Azariyeh, a name derived from "Lazarus."

Mary and her sister Martha. These two sisters, with Martha mentioned first (as in John xi 5 and 19), appear in the Synoptic tradition only in Luke x 38. The geographical sequence in which Luke mentions the incident concerning them, as part of Jesus' journey to Jerusalem, would suggest that their village was in Galilee or Samaria. However, the Lucan account of the journey to Jerusalem is an amalgamation of scenes, many of which Luke could not localize precisely, either chronologically or geographically. It is interesting that the Lucan story follows the Parable of the Good Samaritan which involves a man's journey from Jerusalem to Jericho—a journey which would bring him past the Bethany described in John. Thus, there may be some latent reminiscence in the Lucan sequence of the location of the village of Martha and Mary near Jerusalem. That John should identify Bethany as the village of Mary and Martha may indicate that the reader, who might not know of Lazarus, was expected to be familiar with the names of the two sisters. The OSˢⁱⁿ and, perhaps, Tatian read: "He was from Bethany, the brother of Mary and Martha."

2. *the one who anointed the Lord.* This verse is clearly a parenthesis added by an editor: it refers to a scene in ch. xii which has not yet been narrated; it uses the term "Lord," which John does not usually use of Jesus during the ministry when describing him in third person narrative. Bultmann, p. 302, thinks that this verse is a harmonization with the account of the anointing in Mark xiv 3–9; yet almost all the words come from the account in John xii 1–3.

3. *Lord.* Once again, this word could be translated as "Sir," but here believers are speaking.

the one whom you love. This description, which uses *philein,* "to love," is the basis for the suggestion that Lazarus is the anonymous "disciple whom Jesus loved" (*agapan* in xiii 23, xix 26, xxi 7, 20; *philein* xx 2). See discussion, p. xcv.

4. *[of God].* This is omitted or substituted for in two early papyri (P⁶⁶, P⁴⁵), the OL and Coptic versions. Here and v 25 are the only two places in John that Jesus uses the term "Son of God" directly of himself (x 36 involves the citation of a psalm; the Clementine Vulgate reads "Son of God" in v 28). In the COMMENT we shall see parallels between ch. xi and Jesus' words in ch. v.

through it. Presumably through the sickness, but grammatically the "it" could refer to God's glory.

5. *loved.* The verb here is *agapan,* as contrasted with *philein* in 3, 11 (*philos*), 36. There seems to be no great difference; see NOTE on v 20 and App. I:1. Jesus' love for Lazarus has already been affirmed in vs. 3, and is not really necessary here. Verse 5 seems to be a parenthetical insertion to assure the reader that Jesus' failure to go to Lazarus (6) does not reflect indifference. As vss. 5 and 6 now stand, they offer a paradox.

6. *heard.* This seems repetitious after the use of the same expression in vs. 4; it is probably resumptive.

7. *Then.* After two days Jesus acts. Some suggest a connection to the second Cana miracle which is also a life-giving miracle and takes place after Jesus remained in Samaria for two days (iv 40, 43); others suggest a resemblance to Jesus' own resurrection which took place on the third day (I Cor xv 4). All of this is dubious.

back. The *palin* is omitted in some early versions.

8. *Rabbi.* This is the last time that the disciples address Jesus with this title. "Rabbi" was also used in ix 2; notice the similarities between ix 2–5 and xi 8–10.

just now trying to stone you. Probably intended as a reference to x 31.

9. *the light of this world.* This means the sun, but on the theological level is a reference to Jesus (viii 12, ix 5).

10. *he has no light in him.* Codex Bezae reads: "It [i.e., the night] has no light in it"; but this is an attempt to simplify. The Jews evidently thought that light resided in the eye (Matt vi 22–23).

11. *to wake.* This expression is not used in secular Greek in the sense "to rouse from death," to the best of our knowledge.

12. *fallen asleep.* In Hebrew and in Greek, both secular and LXX, "to sleep" can be a euphemism for death, but the disciples fail to penetrate the reference. Bultmann, p. 304⁶, denies that this is an instance of Johannine misunderstanding which, by his definition, involves confusion of the heavenly and the earthly; this seems arbitrary.

his life will be saved. The disciples believe that restful sleep means that the crisis of the illness has passed. The passive of *sōzein,* "to save," can mean, on a purely secular level, "to recover from illness," but John is playing on the theme of spiritual salvation. P75 reads "he will get up."

15. *come to have faith.* This is an attempt to represent the aspect of a single act implicit in the aorist.

16. *Thomas.* There is not much evidence that Aram. *te'ōmâ* ("Twin"; Heb. *te'ōm*) was used as a personal name. "Thomas" may represent a transliteration; but BAG, p. 367, suggests that "Thomas" was a Greek name which, because it resembled the Semitic term, was adopted by Jews in Greek-speaking regions.

(this name means "Twin"). The Greek word for twin is *didymos,* and this is a well-attested Greek name. Some would even have us understand John to mean that the man was called *Te'ōmâ* in Aramaic ("Thomas" then would be the Greek way of giving his Semitic name, and not a Greek name) and Didymus in Greek: "Thomas, called Didymus." However, he is known in all the lists of the Twelve as Thomas, never as Didymus. John consistently explains the man's name (xx 24, xxi 2); for similar explanations see i 38, iv 25, xx 16. There is an interesting tradition that Thomas was the twin of Jesus, at least in appearance.

die with him. Some would see here an ironical truth, for in Pauline terminology all Christians have died with Christ (Rom vi 8; II Cor v 14).

17. *[already].* This is omitted in some important witnesses; in others it is found in different positions. It may be a scribal clarification.

four days. This detail is mentioned to make it clear that Lazarus was truly dead. There was an opinion among the rabbis that the soul hovered near the body for three days but after that there was no hope of resuscitation (StB, II, p. 544).

18. *just under two miles.* Literally "fifteen stadia" or 1¾ miles. This agrees with the location of El 'Azariyeh (see NOTE on vs. 1).

19. *many of the Jews.* The evangelist stresses the number who would be witnesses to the miracle.

to offer sympathy. Or "console," as we have translated in vs. 31. In a warm climate where embalming is not practiced, burial takes places on the day of death. This means that the mourning which precedes burial in our culture must follow burial in such lands. According to custom in Jesus' time, the sexes walked separately in the funeral procession, and after burial the women returned alone from the grave to begin the mourning which lasted for thirty days. This mourning included loud wailing and dramatic expression of grief. See StB, IV, pp. 592–607, for burial customs; also Edersheim, *Life and Times of Jesus* (New York, 1897), I, pp. 554–56; II, pp. 316–20.

20. *Jesus was coming.* To say that this contradicts the statement in vs. 17 that he had arrived is hypercriticism; description of simultaneous events is always awkward.

Mary sat quietly. Women in mourning sat on the floor of the house (see Ezek viii 14). From vs. 29 we gather that Mary had not been told of Jesus' arrival.

21. *Lord.* This is omitted in Codex Vaticanus and OSsin.

23. *rise.* The words used in vss. 23–25 are *anastasis* and *anistanai,* as in v 29, vi 39–45; the only time in John that a word from this root is used for the resurrection of Jesus is in xx 9, although that usage is frequent in Acts. The verb *egeirein* in the passive is the common term for the resurrection of Jesus in the Gospels.

25. *[and the life].* This is omitted in P45, some OL, OSsin, and sometimes in

Origen and Cyprian. Omission is really harder to explain than addition, unless the mention of resurrection alone in vs. 24 would have had some influence. On the other hand, however, the phrase does fit in logically with the flow of ideas— see COMMENT.

even if he dies. The aorist points to understanding this as a reference to physical death; it discourages the translation "even if he is dead [i.e., in sin]."

26. *everyone who is alive.* Does this refer to physical life or to spiritual life? Bultmann, Lagrange, and Hoskyns think that vs. 26 refers to physical life, and they understand the comparison between vss. 25 and 26 thus:

25: Belief, despite physical death, will lead to eternal life.

26: Physical life combined with belief will not be subject to death.

Bernard and others maintain that vs. 26 refers to spiritual or eternal life. The comparison would then be:

25: The believer, if he dies physically, will live spiritually.

26: The believer who is alive spiritually will never die spiritually.

One argument for this view is that one article governs the two participles "living and believing" in vs. 26, an indication that they are both on the same plane. Moreover, the verb "to live" is related to *zōē,* "life," the term which is John's standard word for eternal life. It seems, then, that this second view is the more convincing of the two. The life in both vs. 25 and 26 is spiritual or eternal life; death in 25 is physical, while death in 26 is spiritual. The same twofold use of death is found in vi 49–50.

in me. This goes with "believes" but may also be meant to go with "alive"; for two participles governing the same prepositional phrase see i 51. To be alive in Jesus would certainly mean to be alive spiritually, rather than physically.

27. *the Messiah, the Son of God.* This is quite like the Petrine confession in Matt xvi 16; contrast John vi 69.

he who is to come into the world. John vi 14: "This is undoubtedly the Prophet who is to come into the world"; see NOTE there. Martha seems to join different expectations here; we may compare this with the different titles given to Jesus in i 41, 45, 49.

28. *The Teacher.* Given as the Greek equivalent of rabbi in i 38 and xx 16, "Teacher" is used for Jesus in iii 2, 10, xiii 13, 14. In direct address in the present chapter, the sisters speak to Jesus as "Lord."

30. *not yet come into the village.* Jesus' remaining outside the town and the cautious whispering about his presence in vs. 28 suggest to some that there is an attempt to keep Jesus' presence from being too widely known. We recall the element of danger mentioned in vs. 8.

31. *thinking.* P[66] and many later manuscripts read "saying."

to weep there. This means to wail; see Mary Magdalen's behavior at the tomb of Jesus in xx 11, 15.

33. *shuddered, moved with the deepest emotions.* This translates two Greek expressions. The first, rendered by "moved with the deepest emotions," is the aorist middle of the verb *embrimasthai,* which also appears in vs. 38; here the verb is used with the expression *tō pneumati,* "in spirit," while in 38 it is used with *en heautō,* "in himself"—these are Semitisms for expressing the internal impact of the emotions. The basic meaning of *embrimasthai* seems to imply an articulate expression of anger. In LXX, the verb, along with its cognates, is used to describe a display of indignation (e.g., Dan xi 30), and this usage is also found in Mark xiv 5. The verb also describes Jesus' reaction to the afflicted (Mark i 43; Matt ix 30). In these latter instances does the verb express anger?

While it does not seem that Jesus would have been angry at the afflicted, he may very well have been angry at their illness and handicaps which were looked on as manifestations of Satan's kingdom of evil. (It should also be noted that the use of the verb in such Synoptic passages is associated with the stern command to keep the secret of what Jesus has done and of what he is.) Turning to the passage in John, we find that the Greek Fathers understood it in a sense of getting angry, while most of the early versions soften the emotion to one of being troubled. P[45], P[66], and Codex Bezae offer a reading which also softens the impact; they read "as if" before the verb. Modern translators offer such interpretations as "groan, sigh, chafe."

The second Greek expression, rendered by "shuddered," is *tarassein heauton*. *Tarassein*, usually intransitive (xiv 1, 27), implies deep disturbance; here, used with the reflexive, it means literally "he troubled himself." Note the expression *tarassein en pneumati* in xiii 21, which has elements of both the Greek expressions in the present passage. Black, pp. 174–78, suggests that these two Greek expressions are variant translations of the one original Aramaic expression which meant "to be strongly moved." Boismard, EvJean, pp. 49–51, agrees and offers examples from patristic citations of John where only one or the other Greek expression appears.

34. *come and see*. Jesus used these words in i 39. Lightfoot, p. 223, draws a dramatic contrast between Jesus' inviting men to come and see the source of light and life and the invitation extended by men to Jesus to come and see the abode of darkness and death. Such a contrast probably goes beyond the evangelist's intent.

35. *cry*. The weeping is caused by the thought of Lazarus in the tomb, but the verse is primarily intended to set the stage for vs. 36. In Luke xix 41 Jesus weeps over Jerusalem; Heb v 7 mentions his tears in what seems to be a reference to the Gethsemane scene.

37. *opened the eyes*. These Jews show no doubts about the reality of the miracle of healing the blind man, as did "the Jews" of ch. ix. This may well be another indication of different strata of Johannine tradition.

38. *arousing his emotions*. See NOTE on vs. 33.

a cave with a stone laid across it. Vertical shaft tombs were more common for private burial than horizontal cave tombs. The stone kept animals away. The burial place was outside the town because otherwise the living might contract ritual impurity from contact with the corpses of the dead.

39. *the dead man's sister*. The identification of Martha at this point in the story is strange; it suggests to Bultmann and others that Martha's role in the story in vss. 20–28 was secondary. This Gospel, however, does show a tendency to reidentify the dramatis personae. The identification is omitted in OL, OS[sin], and the late Codex Koridethi; yet, this may be an attempt to avoid the difficulty. The word for "dead man" used here is different from the word used in vs. 44; to some this would be another sign of a gloss.

four days. See NOTE on vs. 17.

a stench. The suggestion that decomposition would have begun does not contradict the picture of careful preparations implied in vs. 44. The oils and spices employed in Jewish burial practice prevented unpleasant odor for a while; but there was no real embalming, such as that practiced in Egypt, which prevented decomposition. The OS[sin] adds a sentence to Martha's exclamation: "Lord, why are they taking away the stone?"

40. *Didn't I assure you.* The words that follow are not a direct citation of anything that was said to Martha in this chapter but rather the general import of Jesus' remarks. See COMMENT.

41. *looked upward.* The gesture of looking up to heaven is a natural prelude to prayer, as seen in Luke xviii 13, where the publican does not feel worthy to make this gesture. The Synoptics mention that Jesus looked up to heaven before multiplying the loaves (p. 243, ✗11b above); John mentions this in the "priestly" prayer of xvii 1. A few Greek mss. read "up to heaven" instead of "upward" in the present verse.

42. *I say it.* The Greek verb is aorist, but this probably represents a too literal rendering of the Semitic perfect. With verbs of speaking, Hebrew often uses the perfect tense for an instantaneous action which is completed the very moment the word is spoken (see Joüon, *Grammaire de l'Hébreu Biblique,* § 112 f.). There is a poorly attested variant, "I do it," which is defended by Bernard, II, pp. 398–99.

standing around. This intransitive use is unique in NT Greek, and Bernard defends another reading: "standing by me." Again the textual support for his proposal is weak.

43. *shouted.* The verb *kraugazein* occurs only eight times in the whole Greek Bible, six of which are in John. In chs. xviii–xix it is used four times for the shouts of the crowd to crucify Jesus. Thus, a contrast might be drawn between the crowd's shout that brings death to Jesus and Jesus' shout that brings life to Lazarus. That the evangelist intended such a contrast is made dubious, however, by the use of the verb in xii 13, where the crowd shouts the praise of Jesus, albeit somewhat nationalistically.

44. *linen strips.* This is a rare Greek word, used for bedcovering in Prov vii 16; presumably we are to think of a type of bandage. The skeptical question of how Lazarus got out of the tomb if his hands and feet were bound is really rather silly in an account which obviously presupposes the supernatural. There may be a theological reason for mentioning the burial garments. In xx 6–7 we are told that Jesus' burial garments remained in the tomb, perhaps with the connotation that he would have no more use for them since he was never to die again. Therefore, some scholars suggest that it is because Lazarus will die again that he comes forth with his burial garments. There is no other evidence, however, that the future fate of the risen Lazarus comes into the evangelist's perspective.

his face wrapped in a cloth. In Jesus' burial, too, there is mention of a separate covering for the head (xx 7).

COMMENT: GENERAL

We have already suggested that at one stage in the formation of the Fourth Gospel the public ministry ended with what is now x 40–42, and that chs. xi–xii were a later addition to the plan of the Gospel. Besides the arguments offered on p. 414, we may now call attention to some features in xi and xii that support this suggestion. There is no doubt that the material of chs. xi–xii comes from Johannine circles, for it abounds in typically Johannine features (personalities like Thomas, Philip, and Andrew; *egō eimi* in xi 25; "misunderstanding" in xi 11–14; the theme of being "lifted up" in xii 32; many words of the Johannine vocabulary, etc.). Yet, in the use of the term "the Jews," these chapters differ noticeably from what we have seen in chs. i–x. In xi 19, 31, 33, 36, 45, xii 9, 11, the Jews are not the hostile Jewish authorities but the ordinary people of Judea and Jerusalem who are often sympathetic to Jesus and even believe in him. We saw this peculiarity in viii 31, a verse that gave every sign of being an editorial addition, and it is possible that chs. xi–xii are an addition made at the same stage of editing.

An even more compelling argument may be drawn from the sequence in which the Lazarus miracle now appears. It is placed between the winter feast of Dedication (x 22) and the spring feast of Passover (xi 55), with a suggestion in the latter reference that the miracle took place near the end of this three to four month interval. If we follow this sequence, we must suppose that Jesus left his retreat in the Transjordan (x 40), came up to Bethany, and then after the miracle withdrew again to Ephraim near the desert (xi 54). Subsequently he would return to Bethany six days before Passover (xii 1), only to go into hiding again after a single day's preaching in Jerusalem (xii 36). This complicated sequence is hard to reconcile with the Synoptic picture wherein before Passover Jesus came from the Transjordan through Jericho to Jerusalem, with Bethany as his domicile. We pointed out on p. 414 that it would be far easier to reconcile the sequence in John with that of the Synoptics if chs. xi–xii were not considered.

The problem of sequence becomes even more difficult when we realize that John makes the Lazarus miracle the direct cause of the death of Jesus, for it provokes a session of the Sanhedrin (xi 46–53) which reaches a decision to kill Jesus. The theme of the Lazarus miracle is also found in Jesus' triumphal entry into Jerusalem (xii 9–11). What makes all of this startling is that the Synoptics know nothing of Lazarus. They describe in much more detail than John the days preceding Jesus' death, the speeches that he made in the temple courts, and the session of the Sanhedrin; but they make no mention of the raising of Lazarus. How can such a discrepancy be explained if the Lazarus miracle happened in the sequence in which John has placed it?

Some scholars solve the problem by suggesting that the story of the raising of Lazarus is a fictional composition based on Synoptic material (see Richardson, p. 139). The Johannine account is supposed to have had its inspiration in the Lucan story of the raising of the son of the widow of Nain (vii 11–16), and the Johannine characters are thought to have been suggested by the Lucan story of Martha and Mary (x 38–42) and the Lucan Parable of Lazarus (xvi 19–31). In particular, the final line of the parable is significant, for to the suggestion that Lazarus should come back from the dead to warn the rich man's brothers, God says, "They will not be convinced even if someone should rise from the dead."

By way of general objection against such a proposal, we note that it presupposes an approach to the problem of Johannine tradition that we have not found successful elsewhere in the Gospel, namely, the suggestion that John does not contain independent historical tradition but is dependent on a reshuffling of Synoptic details. However, precisely because chs. xi–xii may have had a history of their own, the proposal needs detailed discussion. In his article W. Wilkens has subjected the Lazarus story to a penetrating literary analysis. He finds beneath the Johannine account a brief narrative of the raising of Lazarus of Bethany which is no harder to believe than the raising of the son of the widow of Nain, or the raising of Jairus' daughter (Mark v 22–43). That Jesus raised the dead is an important part of the Synoptic tradition (Matt xi 5), and we should not be surprised to find the same picture in the Johannine tradition. As for the proposal that the inspiration of the Johannine story came from the Lucan Parable of Lazarus, it is quite plausible that the direction of the borrowing was in the opposite direction, as Dunkerley, *art. cit.,* suggests. The Lucan parable could easily have come to an end with xvi 26, where the fate of Lazarus is contrasted with that of the rich man. The theme of the rich man's brothers and the resurrection of Lazarus (xvi 27–31) seems to be an afterthought, for there is no preparation for it in the narrative. We have seen many contacts between Lucan and Johannine tradition in some of which Luke may well have been influenced by an early (oral?) stage of the Johannine tradition, and the secondary ending of the parable may be another instance.

From the contents of the Johannine account, then, there is no conclusive reason for assuming that the skeleton of the story does not stem from early tradition about Jesus. What causes doubt is the importance that John gives to the raising of Lazarus as the cause for Jesus' death. We suggest that here we have another instance of the pedagogical genius of the Fourth Gospel. The Synoptic Gospels present Jesus' condemnation as a reaction to his whole career and to the many things that he had said and done. In the triumphal entry of Jesus into Jerusalem, we are told in Luke xix 37 that, much to the discontent of the Pharisees, the people were praising Jesus because "of *all the mighty miracles* they had seen." The Fourth Gospel is not satisfied with such a generalization. It is neither sufficiently dramatic nor clear-cut to say that all Jesus' miracles led to enthusiasm on the part of some and hate on the part of others. And so the writer has chosen to take *one miracle* and to make this the primary representative of all the mighty miracles of which Luke speaks. With a superb sense of development he has chosen a miracle in which Jesus raises a dead man. All Jesus' miracles are signs of what he is and what he has come to give man, but in none of them does the sign more closely approach the reality than in the gift of life. The physical life that Jesus gives to Lazarus is still not in the realm of the life from above, but it is so close to that realm that it may be said to conclude the ministry of signs and inaugurate the ministry of glory. Thus, the raising of Lazarus provides an ideal transition, the last sign in the Book of Signs leading into the Book of Glory. Moreover, the suggestion that the supreme miracle of giving life to man leads to the death of Jesus offers a dramatic paradox worthy of summing up Jesus' career. And finally, if a pattern of sevens had any influence on the editing of the Gospel (p. CXLII), the addition of the Lazarus miracle gave the seventh sign to the Book of Signs.

We suggest then that, while the basic story behind the Lazarus account may stem from early tradition, its causal relationship to the death of Jesus is more a question of Johannine pedagogical and theological purpose than of historical reminiscence; and this explains why no such causal connection is found in the Synoptic tradition. A miracle story that was once transmitted without fixed context or chronological sequence has been used in one of the later stages in Johannine editing as an ending to the public ministry of Jesus. As we mentioned in the Introduction (p. XXXVII), this addition may have occurred in the evangelist's second edition of his Gospel or, more probably, in the final redaction.

Within the story itself, the miracle has been made to serve the purposes of Johannine theology, but we cannot join Wilkens in the theory that by stripping off *all* the Johannine theology, one can arrive at the form the story possessed in early tradition. If Johannine theology had roots in the sayings of Jesus, and we believe that it did, we cannot be certain that the theological themes that now stand out clearly in John were not embryonic in the earliest form of the story. That there are traces of editing within the story is obvious in the parenthetical additions found in vss. 2 and 5 and in the duplications we shall point out below. However, we remain skeptical whether such observations enable us to make as detailed a reconstruction as Wilkens has attempted.

We may notice one final effect that the present sequence of the Gospel has produced. In xi 37 the Jews associate the healing of the blind man (ch. ix) with the Lazarus story, and we suspect that the writer intended such an association. There are some interesting parallels in format between the two stories (see NOTE on vs. 8). In ch. ix the healing of the blind man was a dramatization of the theme of Jesus as the light; the raising of Lazarus in xi is a dramatization of the theme of Jesus as the life (xi 25). The two themes of light and life were mingled in the Prologue in describing the relationship of the Word to men (i 4). Just as the Word gave life and light to men in the creation, so Jesus the incarnate Word gives light and life to men in his ministry as signs of the eternal life that he gives through enlightenment gained from his teaching (and from Baptism).

COMMENT: DETAILED

Verses 1–6: Setting

The story deals with characters of whom only Luke in the Synoptic tradition shows any knowledge. Since the Synoptic tradition contains little remembrance of Jesus' ministry in Judea, the failure to mention Judeans like Martha, Mary, and Lazarus is not too startling. There is little real proof for the thesis that Martha and Mary were not mentioned in the original form of the story (Wilkens) and that the brother-sister relationship between Lazarus and the two women is artificial. Behind such a thesis there often lies the questionable assumption that Luke's vague localization of the home of the two women in Galilee is correct (see NOTE on vs. 1). It is an interesting coincidence that the names Lazarus, Martha, and Mary have all appeared on ossuaries of the 1st century A.D. found in the Jerusalem area, and in one instance all three names have been found in one tomb quite close to Bethany (BA 9 [1946], 18).

There is frequent emphasis on the love that Jesus has for the family. If Bethany was Jesus' lodging place when he came to Jerusalem (and this is attested in the Synoptic tradition), then it is not too unreasonable to suggest that it was at this home that he stayed and that its occupants were truly his close friends. But John takes what may be a true reminiscence and uses it with theological purpose; for Lazarus, the one whom Jesus loves, is probably being held up as the representative of all those whom Jesus loves, namely the Christians. This is seen when we compare "our beloved [*philos*] Lazarus" of xi 11 with the title "beloved [*philoi*]" that III John 15 uses for the Christians. Just as Jesus gives life to his beloved Lazarus, so will he give life to his beloved Christians.

The symbolic importance of the miracle is made clear from the beginning. We were told in the story of the healing of the blind man (ix 3) that the blindness was for the purpose of having God's works revealed in him. So in xi 4 we are told that Lazarus' sickness is for God's glory, since God's glory will be evident only when the Son is glorified. Such a statement has several Johannine plays on words. The reason why the sickness is *not to end in death* is because Jesus will give life, that is, physical life as a sign of eternal life. This miracle will *glorify* Jesus, not so much in the sense that people will admire it and praise him, but in the sense that it will lead to his death, which is a stage in his glorification (xii 23–24, xvii 1).

The paradox created by the editorial addition of the parenthetical vs. 5 is an interesting one. Out of love Jesus did not go to help the sick Lazarus, for he would be of more help to Lazarus when Lazarus was dead. Evidently the author wishes us to think that Lazarus died immediately after the sisters sent the message. The day that it took for the message to come to Jesus, plus the two days that Jesus remained on after he got the message (6), plus the day that it took Jesus to go to Bethany—these are the four days of vs. 17. For the possible theological and apologetic motives behind the mention of these days see NOTES on vss. 7 and 17. We may note that the sisters' message to Jesus (3) is the same type of discreet suggestion that we encountered in ii 3: it presents a situation in which Jesus can help without formally requesting him to do anything. Neither at Cana nor here is Jesus moved by the suggestion. As Bultmann, p. 303, puts it, "Jesus' works have their own hour."

Verses 7–16: Should Jesus go up to Judea?

The discussion of whether Jesus should go to Judea seems to run in two strains: **(a)** Verses 7–10 and 16 are concerned with his going up to die, and there is no mention of helping Lazarus in these verses. The function of these verses is to tie in the general story with what has happened in the preceding chapters, namely, the several attempts to stone Jesus (especially x 31) and his taking refuge by leaving Judea and going into the Transjordan (x 40). The theme of light and darkness in xi 9–10 is related to ix 4, where there is the same emphasis on taking advantage of the light. The light of the world mentioned in xi 9 is also found in viii 12, and each passage expresses antipathy to walking in the dark. The urgency of these passages is not unlike that of Jer xiii 16: "Give glory to the Lord your God before it grows dark, before your feet stumble on the darkening mountains." If these verses in xi, especially 7–8, were added as part of an editorial attempt to make the Lazarus story fit into its present sequence, we may have the explanation of why "the Jews" in vs. 8 has its more usual meaning of hostile authorities, a meaning that it does not have in the rest of the chapter. The fear of the disciples in vs. 8 and the suggestion in 16 that Jesus is going up to die have parallels in the Synoptic tradition. In Mark x 32, as Jesus starts up to Jerusalem from the Jordan valley, the disciples follow Jesus, but they are filled with fear about what is going to happen. In x 34 Jesus tells them that he is going to die. Thomas' anticipation that the disciples may die with Jesus (John xi 16) is not without parallel in the Synoptic tradition, for Mark viii 34–35 invites the disciple to lose his life for Jesus' sake. For a distant Synoptic parallel to John xi 10 see NOTE.

(b) Verses 11b–15, while they have the same theme of going up to Jerusalem, introduce the possibility of helping Lazarus. The disciples misunderstand Jesus' reference to Lazarus' sleep (i.e., death) and to a journey to wake him (i.e., raise him). Such a play on words is not strange to the Synoptic tradition; for in Mark v 39, after the daughter of Jairus has died, Jesus tells the crowd, "The child is not dead, but asleep." The misunderstanding of the disciples in John leads Jesus to explain (14) and to divulge once more the theological purpose of what is happening (15). The explanation is the same as in vs. 4; but, while in 4 the relation of the miracle to God is emphasized (*glorification*), in 15 the relation of the miracle to the disciples is emphasized (*belief*). This last sign of Jesus has much in common with the first: "What Jesus did at Cana . . . revealed his *glory* and his disciples *believed* in him" (ii 11). The two aspects of the miracle are brought together in xi 40 where Martha is told that *belief* in Jesus will lead her to see the *glory* of God.

Verses 17–27: Martha greets Jesus

The duplication that we found in vss. 7–16 seems to continue through 17–33; for 20–27 tell us how Martha came out from the house to greet

Jesus, while 28–33 tell us how Mary came out from the house to greet Jesus. The two accounts are very similar, and both women utter the same greeting (21, 32). Many critics think the Martha incident was added later (so Bultmann, Wilkens), because the Johannine theology of the Martha account is more developed. (We have mentioned above the further critical judgment that both stories, first Mary, then Martha, were added.) However, granting that the role of one woman has now spread to the other, we are not so certain that the incident was first centered around Mary. Of the two, Mary is the better known; and we can see why, if Martha originally had a role, an editor might feel impelled not to slight Mary. However, if Mary had the original role, why would an editor feel impelled to give a longer role to the less important Martha? In comparing vss. 20–27 and 28–33, we find that Mary's part is unimaginative and merely repeats what we heard in Martha's part, and this is what we would expect if a role for Mary was an afterthought. A study of vs. 2, which is clearly an editorial addition, suggests that later editing gave prominence to Mary. Also, if the Lazarus story once circulated separately, among its latest features should be those which tie it into its present context. The emphasis on Mary provides the bridge between the Lazarus story of xi and the story of the anointing at Bethany in xii 1–9. Certainly the Johannine theology in vss. 20–27 shows development, but why could not such development have taken place even if a brief account of Martha's going to meet Jesus were part of the original story?

Taking the Martha and Mary incidents as they now appear in the Gospel, we find that the two women are true to the portrait painted of them in Luke x 38–42. There Martha is busy serving, while Mary sits at the Lord's feet listening to his words. In John, Martha rushes out to meet Jesus, while Mary *sits* quietly at home. But when Mary hears that the Teacher has come, she hastens out and falls *at his feet*. Obviously there is some cross-influence between the Lucan and Johannine portraits of the two women, but the direction of the influence is not easy to trace.

Throughout the incident involving Martha we see that she believes in Jesus but inadequately. In vs. 27 she addresses him with lofty titles, probably the same titles used in early Christian professions of faith; yet 39 shows that she does not as yet believe in his power to give life. She regards Jesus as an intermediary who is heard by God (22), but she does not understand that he is life itself (25).

We saw that the message sent by the two sisters to Jesus (vs. 3) was quite similar in style to the delicate suggestion offered to Jesus by his mother in the Cana scene (ii 3). So also Martha's statement in 22, "Whatever you ask of God, God will give you," has a certain resemblance to Mary's instruction to the waiters in ii 5: "Do whatever he tells you." In each there is the same half-expressed hope that Jesus will act despite the seeming impossibility of the situation. Yet we have no indication of the direction of Martha's hope or that she thought that Jesus would or could bring Lazarus back from the grave. The force of "even now" in vs. 22 is disputed;

but 39 makes it clear that Martha expected no immediate return from the grave. Bultmann, p. 306, is correct when he says that vs. 22 is more a confession than a request.

Jesus' answer in vs. 23 is misunderstood by Martha as one of the ejaculations of general comfort that it was customary for the Jews to utter at the time of death. She joins him in professing the doctrine of the resurrection of the body, advocated by the Pharisees against the Sadducees (Mark xii 18; Acts xxiii 8). Although this doctrine came into Israelite theology at a late period (it first appears in the early 2nd century B.C. in Dan xii 2), it was widely accepted even by the common people in Jesus' time. In the 1st century A.D. it would become part of the official prayers of Judaism as the second of the *Eighteen Benedictions:* "You, O Lord, are mighty forever for you give life to the dead." However, Martha's general understanding of the resurrection on the last day is scarcely adequate in the present situation, for in Johannine realized eschatology the gift of life that conquers death is a *present* reality in Jesus Christ (25–26).

In the NOTE on vs. 26 we have mentioned various ways of understanding vss. 25–26. In our opinion the most satisfactory exegesis is that of Dodd, *Interpretation*, p. 365. There are two principal ideas. First, Jesus says, "I am the *resurrection.*" This is the direct answer to Martha's profession in 24 and (without excluding the final resurrection) tells her of the present realization of what she expects on the last day. This statement is commented on in the second and third lines of 25. Jesus is the resurrection in the sense that whoever believes in him, though he may go to the grave, shall come to eternal life. "Life" in 25c is that life from above which is begotten through the Spirit, and it conquers physical death. Second, Jesus says, "I am the *life.*" This statement is commented on in vs. 26. Whoever receives the gift of life through belief in Jesus will never die a spiritual death, for this life is *eternal* life. We notice that, as usual with the "I am" statements which have a predicate, the predicates "resurrection" and "life" describe what Jesus is *in relation to men*—they are what Jesus offers to men. We have seen the concepts of resurrection and life joined before: in vi 40 and 54 the aspect of resurrection that was emphasized was one of final eschatology; in v 24–25 it was one of realized eschatology.

In response to Jesus' presentation of himself as the resurrection and the life, Martha confesses him under a series of frequent NT titles (see NOTES on vs. 27). We are probably to understand her outlook in much the same way that we understood that of the Samaritan woman in ch. iv. There Jesus presented himself as the source of living water, but the woman could understand him only as a prophet (iv 19). Ultimately Jesus had to send her off to call her husband in order to lead her to deeper faith. So here in xi, in order to make Martha understand that he has the power to give life now, he will act out a drama of the gift of life by raising Lazarus. He does not reject her traditional titles, but he will demonstrate the deeper truth that lies behind them. The evangelist in xx 31 shows how the traditional titles must be understood in terms of Jesus' power to give life to men: ". . . that you may have faith that Jesus is the Messiah, the Son of God, and that, through this faith, you may have life in his name." If we may oversimplify, Martha's difficulty is that she does not realize the full force of "the one who is to come into the world"; she does not fully understand that the light and the life have already come into the world.

Verses 28–33: Mary greets Jesus

As we have insisted, this scene really does not advance the action; vs. 34 could easily follow vs. 27, and no one would know the difference. The only dissimilarity between Mary's greeting to Jesus and that of Martha is that Mary falls at Jesus' feet (32). Some would see in this the suggestion of a livelier faith on Mary's part, but it is noteworthy that Mary of Bethany is always pictured at Jesus' feet (Luke x 39; John xii 3). We may observe that prostration at Jesus' feet is a Lucan (viii 41, xvii 16) rather than a Johannine trait—perhaps another indication that it is the Mary incident that is secondary.

Verse 33 requires comment, for both here and in 38 Jesus exhibits a strong display of emotion. (It is possible that vs. 33 and 38 are duplicate accounts.) We have given a long NOTE on the difficulty of translating the Greek, but let us discuss the possibility that Jesus was indignant or angry, rather than moved by sympathy (Lagrange, Bernard) or sorrow. Hoskyns and Bultmann are among the commentators who think that he was angry because Mary and the Jews showed a lack of faith. This suggestion is not implausible for vs. 38, because the question in 37 can be taken as a manifestation of insufficient faith. But the weeping in vs. 33 scarcely indicates lack of faith, since Jesus himself cried (35). A better explanation of the anger of Jesus in 33 would be the reason offered for similar displays of anger in the Synoptic tradition (see NOTE), namely, that he was angry because he found himself face to face with the realm of Satan which, in this instance, was represented by death. It is interesting that two other occasions on which the verb *tarassein* is employed (John xiv 1, 27) describe the reaction of the disciples in face of the imminent *death* of Jesus; and in xiii 21 the verb is used to describe how Jesus was moved at the thought of being betrayed by Judas into whose heart *Satan* had entered. Chrysostom (*In Jo.* LXIII 2; PG 59:350) suggests that we have here in John the same emotion that, according to the Synoptics, came over Jesus in the Garden of Gethsemane (Mark xiv 33)—emotional distress prompted by the imminence of death and the struggle with Satan.

Verses 34–44: The raising of Lazarus

Verses 34–40 set the stage for the miracle by describing Jesus' sorrow before he comes to the tomb and the opposition to his command to open the tomb. This setting of the stage gives the author an opportunity to remind us of the themes that have run through the chapter so that we shall not miss the final significance of the miracle. Verse 36 recalls that Lazarus is the beloved (Christian?). Verse 37 calls forth the memory of the blind man, so that Jesus as the light and Jesus as the life will be juxtaposed. Verse 40 unites the theme of belief of which Jesus spoke to Martha in 25–26, and the theme of glory of which we heard in 4. It is fitting that glory be mentioned here; for it not only gives an inclusion within the chapter, but also, as we have mentioned, forms an inclusion with the Cana miracle (xi 40 and ii 11), thus bringing together the first and last of the signs. Moreover, the theme of glory serves as a transition to the Book of Glory, which is the second half of the Gospel.

The words of Jesus in vss. 41–42 have offered difficulty to commentators. John presents these words as a prayer, and this evaluation receives confirmation from several details. Before he speaks, Jesus looks upward, a gesture which is a prelude to prayer (see NOTE). Jesus' first word is "Father," a translation of the Aram. *'abbâ*, which was Jesus' characteristic but unusual way of addressing God in prayer, for example, Luke xi 2; Mark xiv 36 (on the use of *'abbâ* see TS 22 [1961], 182–85). Jesus' prayer in vs. 41 opens with thanksgiving, as do the classic Jewish prayers. Yet, the explanation of why Jesus is praying (vs. 42) has struck many as strange. Loisy, p. 353, writes with a certain brutality: "The Johannine Christ prays to expound the theses of the evangelist. In appearance, he would be praying for the gallery, since he speaks to his Father only to arouse faith in his own person and in his divine mission." For those who think in this manner, Jesus is not praying, for he is not asking for anything from the Father. However, the prayer of petition is not the only form of prayer. If prayer is a form of union with God, then the Johannine Jesus is always praying, for he and the Father are one (x 30).

One of the most basic prayers of Jesus in the Synoptic tradition is that the Father may bring about the accomplishment of His will (Matt vi 10; Mark xiv 36). The life of the Johannine Jesus is a perpetual "Your will be done," because Jesus does nothing on his own (v 19). His very food is to do the will of the Father (iv 34). It is this prayerful attitude that is summed up in xi 42: "I knew that you always hear me." His is a supreme confidence in the Father because he always does what is pleasing to the Father (I John iii 21–22). He knows that whatever he asks is according to the Father's will and that, therefore, he is heard (I John v 14). He demands this same confidence in the prayer of his followers (xiv 12–13, xv 16, xvi 23, 26).

In vss. 41–42 Jesus rejoices because the fact that his prayer is heard leads the crowd to faith, but this is neither arrogance nor showmanship. Because his prayer is heard, they will see a miraculous work which is the work of the Father. Through the exercise of the power of Jesus which is the power of the Father, they will come to know the Father and thus receive life themselves. Jesus will gain nothing for himself; he wishes only that his audience will come to know the Father who has sent him (42c; also xvii 20–21). Perhaps the crowd that is present does not even hear his words; but they can see his prayerful attitude as he raises his eyes to the Father, and thus the prayer leads them to believe in the source of his power. In the OT Elijah had prayed (I Kings xviii 37): "Hear me, O Lord, that this people may know that you, O Lord, are God." Jesus' prayer to his Father expresses the same idea, but with supreme confidence. "It is for God's glory" (xi 4).

Having thus prepared the people for the import of the sign, Jesus calls Lazarus forth from the grave. With characteristic brevity John does not dwell on the details of the miracle—it is covered in two verses (43–44) —for the marvelous is not important. What is crucial is that Jesus has given (physical) life as a sign of his power to give eternal life on this earth (realized eschatology) and as a promise that on the last day he will raise the dead (final eschatology). The latter motif is obvious in the clear reminiscences of v 26–30 which are found in ch. xi. (We remember that v 26–30 is a duplicate in terms of final eschatology of what was said in v 19–25 in terms of realized eschatology.) The parallels are so close that some have suggested that ch. v was the original locus of the Lazarus story. We may note the following parallels (see also NOTE on vs. 4):

xi 17: "Lazarus is *in the tomb*.

43: Jesus shouts in a loud *voice*, "Lazarus, *come out!*"

25: "I am the *resurrection* and the *life*."

v 28–29: "An hour is coming in which all those *in the tombs* will hear his *voice* and will *come forth*—those who have done what is right unto the *resurrection of life*."

Thus, in many details ch. xi acts out the promise of ch. v.

BIBLIOGRAPHY

Dunkerley, R., "Lazarus," NTS 5 (1958–59), 321–27.
Wilkens, W., "Die Erweckung des Lazarus," TZ 15 (1959), 22–39.

39. MEN CONDEMN JESUS TO DEATH:
—THE SANHEDRIN
(xi 45–54)

Jesus is condemned to die and withdraws to Ephraim

XI 45 This caused many of the Jews who had come to visit Mary and had seen what Jesus did, to put their faith in him. 46 But some of them went to the Pharisees and reported what he had done. 47 So the chief priests and the Pharisees gathered together the Sanhedrin. "What are we going to do," they said, "now that this man is performing many signs? 48 If we let him go on like this, everybody will believe in him; and the Romans will come and take away our holy place and our nation."

49 Then one of their number who was high priest that year, a certain Caiaphas, addressed them: "You have no sense at all! 50 Don't you realize that it is more to your advantage to have one man die [for the people] than to have the whole nation destroyed?" (51 It was not on his own that he said this; but, as high priest that year, he could prophesy that Jesus was to die for the nation—52 and not for the nation alone, but to gather together even the dispersed children of God and make them one.) 53 So from that day on they planned to kill him.

54 For this reason Jesus no longer moved about openly among the Jews, but withdrew to a town called Ephraim in the region near the desert, where he stayed with his disciples.

NOTES

xi 45. *many of the Jews who.* Bernard, II, pp. 401–2, insists that the Greek means: "many of the Jews, i.e., those who had come . . ."—a translation which suggests that all the Jews who had come to Mary believed in Jesus. Such a translation probably puts too much reliance on the exactness of agreement of the participle in Koine Greek. The indication in vs. 46 is that some of the Jews *who had been there* did not believe, and this is the way Codex Bezae interprets vs. 45.

Mary. The fact that only Mary is mentioned here encourages those who think that the character of Martha was a later addition to the Lazarus story. It is just as plausible, however, that this is an instance of the memory of the more famous Mary (who anointed Jesus) overshadowing that of Martha.

seen. The verb is *theasthai,* which often connotes perceptive visions. See App. I:3.

46. *the Pharisees.* Only in vs. 54 are the hostile Jewish authorities called "the Jews," and that verse has no necessary connection with the meeting of the Sanhedrin. In ix 13 and 18 the Pharisees and the Jews are alternate titles.

47. *the chief priests and the Pharisees.* Is this a mistake? The Pharisees had no authority to convene the Sanhedrin. The three estates of the Sanhedrin were the priests, the elders, and the scribes. Yet, most of the scribes were Pharisees, and we may well suspect that the Sanhedrin would not have moved against Jesus if the Pharisees were not opposed to him. John would have been more exact in speaking of priests and *scribes* (Mark xiv 43, 53); but, as we have stressed, John does not attempt to be precise about the Jewish groups that existed before the destruction of the Temple. The Judaism of the Pharisees survived, and it was this Judaism that presented the challenge to Christianity when the Fourth Gospel was being written. Thus, the reference to the Pharisees is more a question of simplification than of error.

gathered together. The same verb is used in vs. 52, and there may well be an intentional contrast between the two gatherings: the Sanhedrin is gathered to kill Jesus; God's dispersed children are gathered that they may be given the gift of life. See also vi 12–13.

the Sanhedrin. Although we have had implicit references to this body (e.g., vii 45 ff.), this is the only occurrence of the proper name in John.

What are we going to do. We interpret this question as deliberative with a rare use of the present tense (BDF, § 366⁴). Bernard, II, p. 403, and Barrett, p. 338, are among those who take it as a rhetorical question, "What are we doing now?", expecting an answer of "Nothing." In other words, for them it is tantamount to "Why are we doing nothing?" However, Schlatter, pp. 256–57, and Lagrange, p. 313, cite good rabbinic parallels for the construction: "What am I to do now that . . . ?"

many signs. In the present Johannine chronology Jesus had performed two major signs in less than six months (the blind man in ix; Lazarus in xi).

48. *everybody will believe in him.* There is patristic evidence, e.g., Augustine, Chrysostom, Cyril of Alexandria, for the omission of this phrase (Boismard, RB 60 [1953], 350–51). It may be related to xii 11.

holy place . . . nation. Chrysostom reads "nation . . . city," and it is not impossible that the "holy place" refers to Jerusalem, the place chosen by Yahweh to put His name (Deut xii 5). More probably, however, the holy place is the Temple (John iv 20; Acts vi 13, vii 7). II Macc v 19 mentions the nation and the place (i.e., Temple) together.

49. *high priest that year.* This formula will be found again in vs. 51 and xviii 13. It has been used by many scholars (e.g., Bultmann, p. 314²) to show that the author did not know Palestinian customs, for they interpret it to imply a belief that the high priest was changed each year, as were the pagan high priests in Asia Minor. Actually the Jewish high priest traditionally held office for life (Num xxxv 25), although in Jesus' time the term of office depended on Roman favor. Caiaphas was high priest from A.D. 18 to 36. The discussion of whether or not the evangelist is guilty of error here is to some extent dependent on the validity of the indication in xviii 13 that Annas was high priest (see The Anchor Bible, vol. 29A).

That statement is either grossly erroneous, or betrays an intimate knowledge that the deposed high priest Annas was still exercising influence and in fact could still be called high priest. If the latter alternative is chosen, then we can scarcely think that the possessor of such knowledge would be mistaken about the elementary question of the term of office. Indeed, aside from the problem of xviii 13, it would be surprising to find that the OT indications of a life term were unknown to this Gospel writer, who has shown considerable knowledge of the OT. Perhaps the whole problem is a false one, as pointed out by Bernard, II, p. 404, and others who see another implication in "high priest that year." The genitive expression thus translated need not mean "for that year" but can be a temporal genitive (BDF, § 186²) meaning "in that year." (The fact that the genitive expression is separated from the noun it governs by the participle "being" gives support to this suggestion.) The idea, then, would be that he was high priest that *fateful* year in which Jesus died—John is underlining not the limit of the term but its synchronism. This suggestion is as old as Origen (*In Jo.* xxvɪɪɪ 12; PG 14: 708ᶜ).

Caiaphas. Probably derived from a Semitic name like *Qayyafâ,* the name appears as Caiphas in Western tradition. This son-in-law of Annas was deposed shortly after Pilate was removed as procurator, and it is quite possible that he held his office through a financial understanding with Pilate. The casual way in which he is introduced here and the bluntness of his address to his confreres may indicate that this was not an official session of the Sanhedrin with the high priest presiding. At least, it seems to be more informal than the session described in Mark xiv 55 ff. at which Jesus was tried. Josephus, War II. vɪɪɪ.14;⚹166, gives an interesting confirmation of how bluntly the Sadducees spoke. We note that neither Mark nor Luke mentions Caiaphas in the trial of Jesus; Matt xxvi 3 mentions him at a preliminary session of the Sanhedrin, and xxvi 57 mentions him at the final trial (as does John xviii 24).

50. *to your advantage.* So the best witnesses, but there is respectable support for "to *our* advantage." It is tempting to join Codex Sinaiticus and some patristic evidence and omit the pronominal adjective, but this omission may be under the influence of xviii 14.

[*for the people*]. This is omitted by some early Latin patristic evidence, Augustine, Chrysostom, Theodoret, and some Ethiopic witnesses. Normally this would not be sufficient basis for putting it in brackets, but the redemptive theology that the phrase seems to imply does seem strange on the lips of Caiaphas. The word for "people" appears in John only in this verse and in its reiteration in xviii 14. The development of Caiaphas' statement, found in the parenthetical observations of vss. 51–52, mentions only "nation." Thus, there is reason for treating the phrase as a gloss. Otherwise, if the phrase was part of the original text, we should probably understand *hyper,* not in the sense "for, in behalf of" (normal in John), but in the sense "in place of."

51. *that year.* There is some evidence for omitting either "that" (P⁶⁶; Bezae) or the whole phrase (P⁴⁵; OSˢⁱⁿ; OL).

52. *children of God.* The only other occurrence of this in the Gospel is in the Prologue (i 12), but it is frequent in the Johannine Epistles. Not all men but only those whom the Father has given to Jesus are God's children (viii 42); and so the dispersed children of God are the Gentiles destined to believe in Jesus. Jer xxxi 8–11 associates the gathering of the dispersed (Jews) with God's fatherhood, and that association may lie behind John's expression.

and make them one. Literally "gather together *into one.*" See the "one sheep herd" of x 16.

53. *planned.* The reading "planned together" in many late manuscripts probably reflects the influence of Matt xxvi 4 and shows that the scribes associated the Matthean and Johannine accounts of the preliminary sessions of the Sanhedrin.

54. *Ephraim.* There is no certain identification of this town. Codex Bezae reads *Samphourin,* but this may be a corruption of Semitic *šēm 'efrayīm* ("whose name is Ephraim"). P⁶⁶* omits "town," and thus the region becomes Ephraim. Some would identify it with Eṭ-Ṭaiyibeh, a town some twelve miles northeast of Jerusalem, whose ancient name was Ophrah (Josh xviii 23) or Ephron (Josh xv 9). II Sam xiii 23 mentions the town of Ephraim, but the location is vague (near Bethel, like the Ephraim of Josephus *War* IV.ix.9;⚔551?—if so, it may be Eṭ-Ṭaiyibeh). W. F. Albright, AASOR 4 (1922–23), 124–33, argues that the Ephraim of John was not Eṭ-Ṭaiyibeh but Ain Sâmieh, slightly to the northeast and lower in a valley. Eṭ-Ṭaiyibeh, being some three hundred feet higher than Jerusalem, is very exposed and rather cold for a sojourn in February and March, especially if we remember that Jesus had no permanent shelter. (Albright's argument is tied in with Johannine chronology.) There are no villages between Sâmieh and the Jordan valley, and so it is literally on the edge of the desert.

stayed. The Greek ms. witnesses are about evenly divided between two readings, one from the verb *menein,* "to stay," and the other from *diatribein,* "to spend some time" (see iii 22).

COMMENT

This session of the Sanhedrin, which according to John's chronology took place several weeks before Passover (xi 55, xii 1), is not attested in the Synoptic tradition. This fact, plus certain seeming inaccuracies about the role of the Pharisees in the Sanhedrin and the term of office of the high priest, has led many critics to regard xi 45–53 as a theological construction based on material borrowed from the Synoptics. As usual, we believe that a more nuanced judgment is called for. We have indicated in the NOTES on vss. 47 and 49 that the "inaccuracies" are not so clear-cut as might first seem. Moreover, the Synoptic tradition does give some evidence of a session of the Sanhedrin before the final session that sentenced Jesus to death. Mark xiv 1–2 and Luke xxii 1–2 speak simply of the plotting of the chief priests and scribes two days before Passover, but in Matt xxvi 1–5 this seems to become a preliminary session of the Sanhedrin. We pointed out in the NOTES on vss. 49 ("Caiaphas") and 53 that there are points of similarity between the Johannine and Matthean scenes, and we note that in both these scenes the session of the Sanhedrin decides to kill Jesus. Now, obviously, there is a chronological difference, but we are simply calling attention to the possibility and, indeed, likelihood of sessions of the Sanhedrin before the final trial.

And we should remember that the final trial before the Sanhedrin as described in the Synoptic Gospels probably represents a collection of charges that were made at various periods (for traces of scattered elements resembling those of the trial see discussions of John i 51, ii 19, x 24–39). In many ways (see CBQ 23 [1961], 148–52, or NTE, pp. 198–203) the Johannine picture which gives a wider distribution to these charges is really more plausible. It is interesting, for instance, that the theme of the destruction of the Temple which plays an important part in the final Synoptic trial (Mark xiv 57–58) also appears in this session in John (vs. 48: "take away our holy place") but in a different and more realistic way. Thus, the likelihood of the presence of historical material in John's scene cannot be decided on the basis of conformity with Synoptic tradition, for one cannot presuppose that the Synoptic material pertaining to the sessions of the Sanhedrin is absolutely reliable.

The introduction to the scene in John relates the session of the Sanhedrin to the Lazarus miracle, and this creates the paradox that Jesus' gift of life leads to his own death. Here, of course, we are dealing with the theological outlook of the Gospel. The Lazarus miracle, like so many of Jesus' deeds and sayings, creates a division among men who judge themselves by their reaction to Jesus. The fact that some are believing in his signs forces the Jewish authorities to act (vs. 47). This agrees with what is found in Mark xi 18 where, after the cleansing of the Temple, we are told: "The chief priests and scribes . . . sought a way to destroy him . . . because all the crowd was astonished at his teaching." The basic point that seems to lie behind all these Gospel statements is that the enthusiasm that Jesus aroused disturbed the Jerusalem authorities.

C. H. Dodd, *art. cit.*, has analyzed the literary character of the scene in John and has successfully shown that it fits into one of the common formats of early stories about Jesus. It is a pronouncement story, that is, a story preserved in the Christian community because it contained a pregnant saying. The account in John leads up to the all-important saying in vs. 50: "It is more to your advantage to have one man die [for the people] than to have the whole nation destroyed." We see in the parenthetical comment of vss. 51–52 why this pronouncement was so important to early Christian circles, namely, because it was regarded as an unconscious prophecy of the salvific nature of Jesus' death. In his own mind Caiaphas was giving voice to a common-sense maxim of political expediency. He was anxious to get rid of Jesus lest, as one more in a series of revolutionaries, this troublemaker provoke the Romans to action against the Jews. But to the perceptive ear of the Christian theologian he was echoing a traditional saying of Jesus himself: "The Son of Man came . . . to give his life as a ransom for many" (Mark x 45). Caiaphas was right; the death of Jesus would save the nation from destruction. Yet Caiaphas could not suspect that Jesus would die, not in place of Israel but on behalf of the true Israel. We can see that such an unconscious prophecy on the lips of a Jewish high priest would make an effective argument in the Jewish-Christian circles to whom (in part) the Fourth Gospel was addressed.

Verse 52 expands the scope of the prophecy to include the Gentiles as well, and we have insisted that the Fourth Gospel also had as its purpose the encouragement of Gentile Christians. Since the Christian community is the true Israel, the true flock of Jesus (x 16), the OT imagery of gathering the dispersed children of Israel (Isa xi 12; Mic ii 12; Jer xxiii 3; Ezek xxxiv 16) can now be used for all those who become part of that community. And the author confirms Caiaphas' judgment—this conversion of the Gentiles will be the further effect of Jesus' *death*. Later on in John xii 32 Jesus himself will say, "When I am lifted up from the earth, I shall draw *all men* to myself." In I John ii 2 we shall be assured, "He is a propitiation for our sins, and not only for our sins, but also for those of the whole world."

Yet, we should note that if vs. 52 hints at the universality of salvation, it also stresses the communal aspect of that salvation. Many writers have commented on Johannine individualism (e.g., C. F. D. Moule, NovT 5 [1962], 171–90), for John does not mention the Church. But do we not have here a true concept of the Church since the dispersed children are to be gathered and made *one?* They are to become one with that true nation of Israel, that true people, who would be spared through Jesus' death. In the words of x 16, the other sheep who have not been part of the fold are to come and be part of the one sheep herd. Many have commented that the Pauline concept of the Church as the body of Christ probably sprang from the thought of the unity created by eating the eucharistic body of Christ (I Cor x 17). It is scarcely accidental that John's description of redeemed Jews and Gentiles gathered into one echoes the terminology of the eucharistically oriented multiplication of the loaves (vi 13) where the fragments are *gathered together*. The passage of the *Didache* (ix 4) cited on p. 248 joins echoes of John vi 13 and xi 52, and thus implicitly shows that the related themes of Johannine ecclesiology and sacramentalism are no figments of the modern imagination.

The introduction of the theme of the gathering of the Gentiles and their union with Israel into a context related to the death of Jesus is not Johannine innovation. It is implicit in the Parable of the Wicked Tenants which the three Synoptic Gospels associate with the period before the final Passover. There (Mark xii 7–10) the killing of the son is what causes the vineyard to be given to others. Nor is this theme out of place in a passage where Caiaphas has just spoken of the danger to the "holy place," that is, the Temple. As we know from ii 19–21, Jesus' death will lead to the replacement of the Jerusalem Temple with the temple of his body. In the OT the Gentiles are often pictured by the prophets as streaming toward the holy hill of the Temple (Isa ii 3, lx 6; Zech xiv 16); Isa lvi 7 characterizes the Temple as "a house of prayer for all nations." When through Jesus' death his body becomes the new temple, naturally he serves as the focus for gathering together the Gentiles. Caiaphas foresees the Roman destruction of the holy place; but he does not foresee that in the new temple that will replace it all the prophetic dreams of the gathering of the nations will be fulfilled. See Braun, *art. cit.*

The unique feature of this pronouncement story in John is that the key saying is not on the lips of Jesus but on the lips of his enemy. The principle of unconscious prophecy was accepted in Judaism (examples in StB, II,

p. 546). In particular, the gift of prophecy was associated with the high priesthood. Josephus, *Ant.* XI.viii.4;※327, tells how the high priest Jaddua received an enlightenment that Alexander the Great would spare Jerusalem. Even high priests whose lives were far from perfect had the privilege, for example, Hyrcanus in *Ant.* XIII.x.7;※299. Therefore, John's outlook on the powers of Caiaphas was very much at home in 1st-century Judaism. The particular Christian aspect is found in the emphasis that Caiaphas was gifted because he was high priest *that* fateful *year* of salvation. We also note that there is nothing strange in Caiaphas' fear of Roman destruction of Jerusalem. In the Synoptic tradition Jesus himself suggests this fate for Jerusalem (Mark xiii 2; Luke xxi 20), and at least the possibility of such a Roman move must have been proposed often.

There is nothing in the Synoptic tradition that resembles Jesus' withdrawal to Ephraim in John xi 54. The very obscurity of the reference makes it likely that we are dealing with a historical reminiscence. It is a transitional fragment in John, and we cannot depend on its present position as representing its original chronological sequence. At least in its use of "the Jews," vs. 54 is certainly distinct from the normal pattern of ch. xi. The similarity to the withdrawal in x 39–40 suggests the possibility of duplicate accounts.

■ ■ ■

With ch. xii John will begin narrating events that have clear parallels in the Synoptic tradition of the last week of Jesus' life. It might be well before we enter that material to give a list of the parallels already seen in the Synoptic and Johannine accounts of the (final) Jerusalem ministry. We base the Synoptic parallels on Mark.

Mark		*John*
xi 18	Worried opposition of priests and scribes (Pharisees).	xi 47
xi 30–33	Last mention of John the Baptist.	x 40–42
xii 1–11	Responsibility of Israel's leaders for death of Jesus and God's choice of a new people.	xi 46–52
xii 12	Attempt to arrest Jesus.	x 39
xii 18–27	Jesus affirms the resurrection of the dead.	xi 1–44
xii 31	Commandment of love.	(xiii 34–35)
xii 38–40	Attack on the scribes (Pharisees).	ix 40–x 18
xii 43	Teaching at the treasury.	viii 20
xiii 1–2	Destruction of the Temple.	xi 48

BIBLIOGRAPHY

Braun, F.-M., "Quatre 'signes' johanniques de l'unité chrétienne," NTS 9 (1962–63), especially pp. 148–50 on xi 47–52.

Dodd, C. H., "The Prophecy of Caiaphas (John xi 47–53)," NTPat, pp. 134–43.

40. WILL JESUS COME TO JERUSALEM FOR PASSOVER?
(xi 55-57)

Transitional Passage

XI 55 Now the Jewish Passover was near; so many people from the country went up to Jerusalem to purify themselves for Passover. 56 They were on the lookout for Jesus; and people around the Temple were saying to one another, "What do you think? Is there really a chance that he'll come for the feast?" 57 The chief priests and the Pharisees had given orders that anyone who knew where Jesus was should report it so that they could arrest him.

NOTES

xi 55. *Passover.* This is the third Passover mentioned in John. At the first Passover (ii 13) Jesus had observed the regulation which made Passover a pilgrimage feast (a role originally held by the feast of the Unleavened Bread, now combined with Passover) and had gone up to Jerusalem. At the second Passover (vi 4) he apparently remained in Galilee.

many people. The number of Passover pilgrims seems to have varied between 85,000 and 125,000 (J. Jeremias, ZDPV 66 [1943], 24–31). If we add this to the population of Jerusalem (25,000), there were over 100,000 participants at Passover in Jerusalem. Josephus, *War* VI.ix.3;⁂422–25, gives the extraordinary figure of over 2,500,000, derived from the count taken by Cestius in the 60s.

to purify themselves. Num ix 10 forbids the unclean man to participate in the regular Passover service (see II Chron xxx 17–18). In particular, there would have been a need for those who lived in contact with Gentiles to purify themselves. For instance, Gentiles often buried their dead near their houses, and this would make their Jewish neighbors subject to the seven-day purification commanded by the laws governing defilement from corpses (Num xix 11–12). Josephus, *War* I.xi.6;⁂229, mentions that the countryfolk purified themselves at Jerusalem before a feast; see also Paul's behavior in Acts xxi 24–27.

for Passover. Literally "before Passover"; Chrysostom, the OS, and a few Greek witnesses omit this phrase, which may be an explanatory gloss.

57. *orders.* There is respectable evidence for reading the singular.

so that. The conjunction used (*hopōs*) occurs only here in the Johannine writings.

COMMENT

These verses constitute a transition to the following scenes. The similarity of vss. 56–57 to vii 11, 13, suggests than an editor may be reusing traditional material from a variant account to create the transition. The material in vs. 55, however, betrays an immediate knowledge of Jewish customs. Verse 57 is probably to be understood in terms of an arrest at an opportune time and place. The authorities certainly knew where Jesus was when he entered Jerusalem (xii 12); yet they did not arrest him, for it was not opportune.

41. SCENES PREPARATORY TO PASSOVER AND DEATH:—THE ANOINTING AT BETHANY
(xii 1–8)

Jesus' body is anointed for death

XII 1 Six days before Passover Jesus came to Bethany, the village of Lazarus whom Jesus had raised from the dead. 2 There they gave him a dinner at which Martha served and Lazarus was one of those at table with him. 3 Mary brought in a pound of expensive perfume made from real nard and anointed Jesus' feet. Then she dried his feet with her hair, while the fragrance of the perfume filled the house. 4 Judas Iscariot, one of his disciples (the one who was going to hand him over), protested, 5 "Why wasn't this perfume sold? It was worth three hundred silver pieces, and the money might have been given to the poor." (6 It was not because he was concerned for the poor that he said this, but because he was a thief. He held the money box and could help himself to what was put in.) 7 To this Jesus replied, "Leave her alone. The purpose was that she might keep it for the day of my embalming. [8 The poor you will always have with you, but you will not always have me.]"

4: *protested*. In the historical present tense.

NOTES

xii 1. *Six days before Passover*. Since for John Passover will be Friday-evening/Saturday, the Bethany scene seems to be dated Saturday-evening/Sunday. The reference to the next day in vs. 12 points to Saturday evening as the occasion of the dinner. We must presume that the Sabbath had come to an end, or Martha could not be serving at table. Some have thought that the meal was connected with the Habdalah service which brought the Sabbath to a close, but we simply do not know enough about the customs of the time to make any judgment. P66* alone reads "five days" instead of "six days."

the village of Lazarus. Literally "where Lazarus was." It is strange to find Bethany identified here when it played such a role in the previous chapter. But if, as we have suggested, the Lazarus story was brought into its present chronological sequence rather late, and if at one time it was separate from the story of the anointing, then there might have been need to identify Bethany.

whom Jesus had raised from the dead. An editorial gloss, as the repetition of the name Jesus indicates.

2. *they gave.* The subject is not identified; it may be equivalent to a passive: "a dinner was given." The OS^sin makes Lazarus the host, but the description of him as one of those at table would suggest that he was a guest. The Synoptic tradition (Mark xiv 3) speaks of the house of Simon the leper, and Sanders, *art. cit.,* would make Simon the father of Lazarus, Mary, and Martha.

3. *expensive.* In John *polytimos;* in Mark xiv 3 *polytelēs,* "valuable."

perfume. Or "ointment"; the Greek word *myron* normally refers to a perfume or ointment made of myrrh. Either as dried powder or liquid, *myron* was made from the gummy resin that exudes from a low shrubby balsam tree which grows in west-central South Arabia and in northern Somaliland. It was used as incense, in cosmetics, perfume, medicines, and in burial preparations. (See G. W. van Beek, BA 23 [1960], 70–94.) However, John's use of *myron* (also Mark xiv 3) is more generic, in the general sense of "perfume," for this *myron* is not of myrrh but of nard.

made from real nard. The word we translate "real" is the adjectival form *pistikos,* a word of uncertain meaning that appears in the NT only in the Marcan and Johannine accounts of the anointing. Among suggested translations are: "genuine"; "*spike*(nard)"; "mixed with *pistachio* oil." *Pistikos* is literally "faithful"; in Aramaic *qušṭâ* is often found with "nard" and *qušṭâ* also means "faith." Thus, *pistikos* may be an overliteral translation—see Köbert, Bib 29 (1948), 279. There is also the possibility that *pistikos* is a corruption of *tēs staktēs;* stacte is an oil from the storax shrub.

nard. Also known as spikenard, this is a fragrant oil derived from the root and spike (hair stem) of the nard plant which grows in the mountains of northern India. P^66* and Codex Bezae omit "nard"; perhaps the scribe felt the difficulty in having *myron* of nard.

4. This verse is introduced by "then" or "but" in various witnesses, but these are probably scribal attempts at smoothness.

Judas Iscariot. Elsewhere (see NOTE on vi 71) Judas is identified as the son of Simon. This has led Sanders, *art. cit.,* to make Judas the elder brother in the family of Lazarus, Mary, and Martha (see above on vs. 2). In what must remain a classic statement (p. 41), he describes Judas as a "masculine Martha gone wrong"!

5. *It was worth.* We have supplied these words; the Greek has simply: "sold for 300 silver pieces."

three hundred silver pieces. Mark xiv 5 speaks of *more* than 300 silver pieces; this is just the opposite of the phenomenon encountered in discussing John vi 7 where Mark (vi 37) speaks of 200 denarii and John of more than 200 denarii. The denarius served as a day's wage (Matt xx 2), so this was a pound of expensive perfume indeed.

6. *not . . . concerned for the poor.* The same expression was used in x 13 to describe the hireling who "has no concern for the sheep."

money box. Originally the Greek word described a case for musical reeds; then it came to mean a box, chest, or coffer. It is used as "money box" in II Chron xxiv 8, 10.

help himself to. Literally "lift [what was put in]."

7. *Leave her alone.* This is clearly the meaning in Mark xiv 6; but in John it could be connected to the following clause: "Allow her to . . ."

The purpose was that she might keep. In the best Greek witnesses this is an elliptical purpose clause: "in order that she may keep." Another reading with weaker attestation seeks to avoid the difficulty: "She has kept." This second reading, while not original, is probably the correct *interpretation*. The idea is not that she is to keep the perfume for some future use, but that (unknowingly) she was keeping it until now to embalm Jesus. We have tried to indicate this by supplying the words: "The purpose was." This interpretation would agree with the scene in Mark xiv 3 where the woman breaks the jar so that there is no perfume left, and thus there can be no question of keeping some for future use. It also explains Judas' indignation—all the valuable perfume has been used. If John meant that Mary was to keep some of the perfume for the future embalming of Jesus, we would expect to hear of this later. We do not; Mary of Bethany has no role in the burial preparation of Jesus' body; and indeed the extraordinary amount (about 100 lbs.) of burial spices brought by Nicodemus (xix 39) would seem to exclude any significant role that the few remaining drops of Mary's pound of perfume might have. Other suggested translations are:

Boismard: Keep it for the day of my embalming. (*hina* plus subjunctive= imperative)

Torrey: Should she keep it till the day of my embalming?

Barrett (as a possibility): Let her keep it in mind on the day of my embalming.

8. This verse is word for word identical with Matt xxvi 11; Mark xiv 7 has the verse but with an extra clause: "and whenever you wish, you can do good for them." This verse in John is omitted by witnesses of the Western group (Bezae, OL, OS[sin]); and the fact that it agrees with Matthew instead of with Mark suggests that it was a later scribal addition copied from the more traditional Matthew.

The poor you will always have. Deut xv 11: "The poor will never be lacking in the land."

you will not always have me. This contrast fits in well with rabbinic theology. There were two classifications of "good works" (the expression in Mark xiv 6): those that pertain to mercy, e.g., burial; those that pertain to justice, e.g., almsgiving. The former were looked upon as more perfect than the latter. See J. Jeremias, ZNW 35 (1936), 75–82.

COMMENT

Comparison with Synoptic Anointings

The Synoptic tradition knows of two scenes where a woman anoints Jesus. Mark xiv 3–9 and Matt xxvi 6–13 tell of an anointing of Jesus at Bethany by an unnamed woman just before his death. (Matthew's account is totally dependent on Mark's and need not be considered for our purposes.) Luke does not have this scene, but in vii 36–38 tells of an anointing of Jesus in Galilee by a sinner woman. No one really doubts that John and Mark are describing the same scene; yet, many of the details in John are like those of Luke's scene. Are all the evangelists describing the same incident, or were there two incidents? Does John have any original material, or is the Johannine account merely an imaginative reshuffling of Synoptic material? A table comparing details is of value:

Mark xiv 3–9	John xii 1–8	Luke vii 36–38
2 days before Passover	6 days before Passover	during the ministry
Bethany	Bethany	Galilean setting
house of Simon (leper)	not specified	house of Simon (Pharisee)
unnamed woman	Mary of Bethany	sinner woman
with alabaster jar	with a pound	with alabaster jar
valuable perfume	expensive perfume	perfume
made from real nard	made from real nard	
		weeps on feet
		dries them with hair
pours perfume on *head*	anoints *feet*	anoints *feet*
	dries them with hair	
some (disciples) angry	Judas angry	Jesus criticizes Simon (44 ff.)
value: more than 300 denarii	value: 300 denarii	
Jesus defends woman	Jesus defends Mary	Jesus forgives woman (50)
"Leave her alone"	"Leave her alone"	
"Poor always with you"	"Keep perfume for burial"	
"Has anointed for burial"	"Poor always with you"	
"To be told in whole world"		

Any solution offered for the origins of John's account must explain the clear parallels to both of the Synoptic scenes. Dodd, *Tradition,* pp. 162–73, has a helpful discussion but posits one basic incident behind all three accounts. A more workable solution is that of P. Benoit as presented by Legault, *art. cit.,* a solution that posits two basic incidents as follows: (1) An incident in Galilee at the house of a Pharisee. A penitent sinner enters and weeps in Jesus' presence. Her tears fall on his feet, and she hastily wipes them away with her hair. There is no anointing with perfume in this scene. The (scandalous) action of loosening the hair in public fits the character of the woman and helps to explain the Pharisee's indignation. This incident is the backbone of Luke's narrative. (2) An incident at Bethany at the house of Simon the leper where a woman (named Mary), as an expression of her love for Jesus, uses her expensive perfume to anoint Jesus' head. The positing of two incidents has the advantage of respecting the totally different nature and purpose of the Lucan scene from that of Mark and John. The very strong element of sinfulness and forgiveness that is essential to the Lucan story is totally missing in the Bethany account. Now, starting with these two different incidents, we can see how in oral tradition they might become confused and the details of one might pass to the other.

Luke, who does not narrate the anointing in Bethany, presents us with a story of the first incident but with much admixture of detail from the second incident. Anointing has been introduced; and since the first incident mentioned Jesus' feet, the anointing is associated with the feet. Such an anointing seems pointless. People anointed the face that their person might have a pleasant fragrance, but the anointing of feet is really unparalleled. (Legault, p. 138, points out the weaknesses of the parallels usually advanced.) A further detail in Luke's account that may have come from the second incident is the name Simon, which appears only when Jesus begins to speak to the Pharisee (Luke vii 40). Up to that time the host is simply one of the Pharisees, and this may represent the original form of the first incident.

Mark (and Matthew) seems to represent an almost pure form of the second incident. There are no names in the Marcan account except that of Simon. The Johannine identification of the woman as Mary of Bethany and of the protesting disciple as Judas is hard to evaluate. It may well represent historical information preserved in the Fourth Gospel alone, but other scholars would regard it as part of a later tendency to identify unknown characters with known characters. (But for what, then, was Mary of Bethany known, if she did not anoint Jesus?—see xi 2.) In giving the value of the perfume as *more* than three hundred silver pieces, Mark seems to represent a more developed form of the tradition than John's flat three hundred silver pieces.

John's account represents a form of the second incident into which have been incorporated details from *the Lucan form* of the first incident. If Luke's anointing of the feet is anomalous, the woman's action becomes even more extraordinary in John when she proceeds to wipe off the perfume she has just applied! Luke's description of the wiping away of tears makes sense; but since the Johannine account does not mention tears, the action of wiping has now been transferred to the perfume. The letting down of hair, not inappropriate in the first incident, is out of character for the virtuous Mary of Bethany. Such a confused transferral of details can best be explained on the level of contact during the oral stage of transmission. We have seen and will see other instances of cross-influence between Luke and John going in both directions. With the exception of details that have come from the Lucan account, John's account is remarkably like that of Mark. That Mark and John both use the unique expression "perfume made from real nard" (see Note) cannot be by coincidence; but does one draw from the other, or are they both dependent on a common source? The small differences that surround the details in which they are most alike (Mark has *valuable* perfume in contrast to John's *expensive* perfume; Mark has *more* than 300 denarii) suggest the latter. Now, if both John and Mark reproduce for us a source that is common to them, it is by no means certain that Mark represents that source in a more original form than does John, once the Lucan elements have been stripped away. We shall discuss comparative details below, but we suggest that the account of the incident at Bethany that underlies the present Johannine narrative gives evidence in some points of being close to the earliest tradition about that incident.

Before we conclude this comparison, we wish to make two observations. *First,* granting that the final Johannine form of the story represents a somewhat confusing amalgamation of details from two originally separate incidents, we must nevertheless realize that the strange picture of anointing Jesus' *feet* was preserved for a reason—as we shall see below, it suits Johannine theological purpose. Even though he was almost certainly not an eyewitness of the scene, the writer must have been as aware as are we at a distance of two millennia that one does not normally anoint feet nor wipe off perfume.

Second, the crisscrossing of details from two different incidents that we have described did not cease with the publication of the written Gospels. In the popular mind, under the influence of the Lucan picture of a sinful woman, the woman of Bethany (Mary, according to John) was soon characterized as a sinner. Then, for good measure, this sinful Mary of Bethany was identified with Mary of Magdala from whom seven devils had been cast out (Luke viii 2) and who went to the tomb of Jesus. And so, for instance, the Catholic liturgy came to honor in a single feast all three women (the sinner of Galilee, Mary of Bethany, Mary of Magdala) as one saint—a confusion that has existed in the Western Church, although not without demur, since the time of Gregory the Great.

John's account

John's account of the anointing is dated six days before Passover, while Mark's account of the Bethany scene seems to be dated two days before Passover. We say "seems" because no date appears in the actual Marcan account of the anointing (xiv 3–9) but only in the context (xiv 1). More than likely Mark xiv 1–2 was originally joined to xiv 10, and the account of the anointing is an interpolation. Nevertheless, even if the date of "two days before Passover" does not govern the scene of the anointing, Mark and Matthew place the scene considerably after Jesus' entrance into Jerusalem (Mark xi 1–10), while John places it before the entrance. No decision on which localization is correct seems possible. Boismard has suggested that in mentioning "six days before Passover" John is establishing a week at the end of the ministry to form an inclusion with the week at the beginning of the ministry (see p. 106); and Barrett, p. 342, also seems to favor this solution. However, in this Johannine account of the end of the ministry there is no insistent counting of days such as we found in ch. i.

John's story of the Bethany anointing identifies many of the participants (Lazarus, Martha, Mary, Judas), although it does not mention the one character whom Mark identifies, Simon the leper. Since we regard the present localization of the Lazarus story as secondary, we suspect the mention of Lazarus and Martha to be an editorial attempt to tie chs. xi and xii together. It is obvious that they have no important role in the scene of the anointing. The mention of Lazarus in vs. 1 is awkward (see NOTE), and the picture of Martha serving at table may represent the influence of the similar picture of Martha in Luke x 40. There is a better chance that the characters of Mary and Judas were originally part of the story and that their names were lost in the Synoptic tradition.

We may pause for a moment to discuss the role of Judas in John's story. That an intimate disciple like Judas would betray Jesus required some explanation, and the Gospels offer two general solutions. The first and probably more primitive explanation of Judas' evil actions is that he was the tool of the Prince of Evil. Luke xxii 3 and John xiii 2, 27, tell us that Satan entered into Judas, while John vi 70 calls Judas a devil. The second explanation, not necessarily opposed to the first, is that Judas betrayed Jesus for love of money. While in the Marcan account of the betrayal (xiv 11; also Luke xxii 5) the idea of giving money to Judas seems to be a proposal of the chief priests, Matt xxvi 15 has Judas demanding money. The picture of Judas' cupidity was naturally painted in darker and darker tones as the story was retold. John's portrait of Judas in xii 4–6 is even more hostile than that of Matthew, for John presents Judas as a thief.

Yet, even if this presentation represents a development, John may well be giving us historical information not preserved in the other Gospels by reporting that Judas kept the common funds. This information lends plausibility to the dialogue in xiii 27–29 and explains the place of honor that Judas had near Jesus at the Last Supper (see NOTE on xiii 23 in The Anchor Bible, vol. 29A). The Synoptic Gospels seem to imply that Judas could be in possession of thirty pieces of silver without causing suspicion, and this would be explicable if he had the common funds. It is not impossible that the Johannine identification of the disgruntled disciple at Bethany as Judas was part of the popular tendency to present Judas in a hostile light. Yet, neither is it impossible that precisely because he handled money for the group, Judas *was* the disciple who did raise a protest at Bethany, and that again this remembrance was lost in the Synoptic tradition.

John does not report the praise of Mary of Bethany that is found in Mark xiv 9: "Wherever the Gospel is preached in the whole world, what she has done will be told in memory of her." If John were dependent on Mark, the omission of this praise would be hard to understand, since xi 2 presumes that Mary was well known precisely because she anointed Jesus. It has been suggested that the Johannine parallel to the Marcan saying is found in xii 3, where we are told that the fragrance of the perfume filled the house. The Midrash Rabbah on Eccles vii 1 says: "The fragrance of a good perfume spreads from the bedroom to the dining room; so does a good name spread from one end of the world to the other." If this rabbinic comparison was known at the time when the Fourth Gospel was written, then there is indeed a parallel between the Marcan and Johannine ideas. Bultmann, p. 317, insists that, besides indicating the amount of perfume used, the statement in vs. 3 about the fragrance filling the house had a symbolic meaning; but he sees the symbolism in terms of *gnosis* filling the world.

The theological import of the anointing in both John and Mark is directed toward the burial of Jesus (John xii 7; Mark xiv 8), and there is no evidence that the story was ever narrated in Christian circles without such a reference. If we have understood vs. 7 correctly (see NOTE), Mary's action constituted an anointing of Jesus' body for burial, and thus unconsciously she performed a prophetic action. And indeed this may explain why the rather implausible detail of the anointing of the *feet* was kept in the Johannine narrative— one does not anoint the feet of a living person, but one might anoint the feet of a corpse as part of the ritual of preparing the whole body for burial. At the end of ch. xi the Sanhedrin decided to kill Jesus, and now Mary's action prepares Jesus for death. Hoskyns, p. 408, points out that in the present Johannine sequence the gift of life to Lazarus meets with two reactions. The session of the Sanhedrin is the supreme expression of refusal to believe; the anointing by Mary is a culminating expression of loving faith. In each there is an unconscious prophecy of Jesus' death.

Barrett, p. 341, and others have suggested that the anointing by Mary is a royal anointing, and that John has moved this anointing to its present position so that it might constitute a preparation for Jesus' entry into Jesusalem as an anointed king. However, there is no hint of this motif in the text of the anointing; and, as we shall see in the next scene, Jesus does not really accept the royal acclamations of the crowd. If John meant to signify the anointing of Jesus as king, then one would have expected the anointing of the head, not of the feet. Some scholars are uneasy about the theory that the anointing at Bethany served as the embalming of Jesus (vs. 7) because xix 39 implies an embalming on the day of Jesus' burial. Yet, since the embalming at Bethany is only on a figurative level, it does not create an obstacle to a real future embalming. In Mark the (figurative) embalming motif is even clearer at Bethany than it is in John; yet Mark xvi 1 depicts the women coming to the tomb on Easter morning to embalm Jesus.

BIBLIOGRAPHY

Legault, A., "An Application of the Form-Critique Method to the Anointings in Galilee and Bethany," CBQ 16 (1954), 131–41.

Sanders, J. N., " 'Those whom Jesus loved' (John xi. 5)," NTS 1 (1954–55), 29–41—a treatment of the family circle at Bethany.

42. SCENES PREPARATORY TO PASSOVER AND DEATH:—THE ENTRY INTO JERUSALEM
(xii 9–19)

Jesus' reaction to the acclamation of the crowds

XII 9 Now the large crowd of the Jews found out that he was there and came out, not only because of Jesus, but also to see Lazarus whom he had raised from the dead. 10 The chief priests, however, planned to kill Lazarus too, 11 because on his account many of the Jews were going over to Jesus and believing in him.

12 The next day the large crowd that had come for the feast, having heard that Jesus was to enter Jerusalem, 13 got palm fronds and came out to meet him. They kept on shouting:

> "Hosanna!
> Blessed is he who comes in the Lord's name!
> Blessed is the King of Israel!"

14 But Jesus found a young donkey and sat on it. As the Scripture has it:

> 15 "Do not be afraid, O daughter of Zion!
> See, your king comes to you
> seated on a donkey's colt."

(16 At first, the disciples did not understand this; but when Jesus had been glorified, then they recalled that it was precisely what had been written about him that they had done to him.)

17 And so the crowd which had been present when Jesus called Lazarus out of the tomb and raised him from the dead kept testifying to it. 18 This was [also] why the crowd came out to meet him: because they heard that he had performed this sign. 19 At that the Pharisees remarked to one another, "You see, you are getting nowhere. Look, the world has run off after him."

NOTES

xii 9. *the large crowd.* The presence of the article is awkward, especially since the style of the Greek word order is poor. The difficulty of the reading has caused many textual witnesses to omit the article. At first glance there seem to be three crowds in this section: (*a*) the crowd (vs. 17) of those who saw Jesus raise Lazarus and who now believe in Jesus; (*b*) the large crowd (vs. 9) of those who heard about this miracle and who got to Bethany before Jesus left for Jerusalem; (*c*) the large crowd (vss. 12, 18) of those who heard about the miracle and who come out to meet Jesus as he enters Jerusalem. Part of this confusion seems to have been introduced when vss. 9–11 and 17–19 were added as editorial framework to the basic narrative of 12–16. This basic narrative had only one "large crowd" of the Jews—a stylized "crowd" like that of vi 2, a Greek chorus giving voice to sentiments of misunderstanding. This crowd came to meet Jesus. But the editorial additions have introduced another crowd that accompanies Jesus. (Despite the awkwardness, [*a*] and [*b*] are seemingly to be identified, for the summary picture in 17–18 includes only two crowds.)

the Jews. Here and in vs. 11 the Jews are clearly distinct from the Jewish authorities, a phenomenon that we saw in ch. xi as well.

Lazarus. The Lazarus motif with persistent identification ("whom he had raised from the dead") is mentioned only in the editorial framework (vss. 9–11, 17–19), not in the basic narrative of the entrance into the city.

10. *planned to kill.* Echo of xi 53.

11. *on his account.* Abbott, JG, § 2294ᵃ, suggests: "for the sake of [seeing] him." However, it is difficult to make a precise distinction here between motive and cause, as Abbott does.

many of the Jews were going over. Although the words "many" and "of the Jews" are separated in Greek, the expression is partitive (Abbott, JG, § 2041). Some would prefer: "Many were leaving the Jews," understanding a genitive of separation. This is difficult to justify grammatically (BDF, § 180; *hypagein* normally takes *apo*), and implies a different use of the Jews than in vs. 9.

going over. This could mean to Bethany, but more likely means going over to Jesus' side.

12. *The next day.* From that mentioned in xii 1, and thus, seemingly, a Sunday. It is from John that we get both elements in "Palm Sunday." How literally we are to accept the chronological sequence is hard to judge.

the large crowd. Once again many witnesses omit the difficult definite article. On the size of the festal crowd see NOTE on xi 55.

13. *palm fronds.* John's description, involving two words for palm (*baion; phoinix*) is precise, albeit somewhat tautological; the same expression is found in the Testament of Naphthali v 4. The question has been raised as to whether palm trees grew in Jerusalem so that the branches would have been easily available. Lagrange, p. 325, suggests that they grew in the warmer eastern valley through which Jesus passed; and I Macc xiii 51 seems to suggest that palm was available in Jerusalem in the second month of the year, thus not too long after Passover. However, there is recent evidence to the contrary. A letter of Simon

Bar-Kochba (Ben Kosiba), written from near Jerusalem, ordered a lieutenant to get palm from En Gedi and bring it to the Jerusalem area, probably for the celebration of Tabernacles (see Yadin, BA 24 [1961], 90). Even today most of the palm for Palm Sunday is brought to Jerusalem from Jericho. Because of John's mention of palm, some have suggested that the entrance into Jerusalem really took place before the feast of Tabernacles when a great amount of palm was brought from the Jordan valley to build huts and to be carried in the processions (Lev xxiii 40; Neh viii 15). According to all the Gospels, the refrain chanted by those who witnessed the entrance of Jesus was taken from Ps cxviii, a Psalm that was part of the Tabernacles liturgy (but also sung at Passover and Dedication). Likewise, Zech ix 9, cited in Matthew and John, can be related to the Tabernacles context of Zech xiv 16. Indeed, Zech xiv 4, set in a context of Tabernacles, prophesied that God was to appear from the Mount of Olives, and Jesus was making his entry into Jerusalem by way of this Mount. For other arguments see J. Daniélou, MD 46 (1956), 114–36; T. W. Manson, BJRL 33 (1951), 271–82. The theory that Jesus entered Jerusalem at Tabernacles rather than at Passover is interesting, but beyond the possibility of proof.

kept on shouting. The Scripture citation that follows is the only OT quote in the Gospel that is not prefixed or followed by a formula of introduction such as, "The Scripture says. . . ." The omission of such a formula is more common in the Synoptics; but Freed, p. 332, is scarcely correct in using this as an argument to prove John's dependency here on the Synoptics. To have the crowd shout such a formula would obviously have been awkward.

Hosanna. This is a transliteration of Aram. *hōšaʻ-nâ*, Heb. *hōšīʻā-(n)nâ*, meaning "Save (—please)." This was used as a prayer for help; in particular at Tabernacles it was a prayer for rain (J. Petuchowski, VT 5 [1955], 266–71). But it was also used as an acclamation or greeting (II Sam xiv 4). The fact that the Gospels do not translate the Hebrew term, as does LXX, probably indicates that in this usage "Hosanna" is not a prayer of petition but a cry of praise. Luke xix 37 correctly speaks of praising God. "Hosanna" probably had already entered into the prayer formulae of the Christian community. See Freed, *art. cit.*, and bibliography cited there.

he who comes in the Lord's name. The original idea of the Psalm (cxviii 26) was almost certainly: Blessed in the Lord's name is he who comes, i.e., the pilgrim who comes to the Temple (see II Sam vi 18). However, in the NT "he who is to come" is taken as a title for Jesus (Matt xi 3, xxiii 39; John i 27, vi 14, xi 27). In John "he who comes in the Lord's name" has particular significance, since according to xvii 11–12 the Father has given Jesus the divine name (*egō eimi?*).

Blessed is the King of Israel. Literally "and the King of Israel." This is not from the psalm; see NOTE on vs. 15.

14. *young donkey.* In comparing the terminology used in the Gospels for this animal, we must distinguish between (1) the OT citation, Zech ix 9, which appears in Matthew and John, and (2) the description of the animal in the general narrative of Jesus' entry into Jerusalem which is found in all the Gospels.

(1) Zech ix 9 gives two descriptions ([a] and [b] below) in poetic parallelism of the animal on which the king will enter into Jerusalem; LXX translates freely:

(a) MT *ḥamōr*, "donkey"; LXX *hypozygion*, "beast of burden"; Matthew *onos*, "donkey."

(*b*) MT *'ayir ben-'ªtōnōt*, "a colt, the foal of she-asses";

LXX *pōlos neos*, "a new colt";

Matt *pōlos huios hypozygiou*, "a colt, the foal of a beast of burden." (Note: *pōlos* is used for a young animal, more often a horse's colt; but when the context specifies, it is also used for the young of other animals—see W. Bauer, JBL 72 [1953], 220–29.) In citing Zechariah, Matthew in general follows LXX, but the Matthean terminology for the animal seems to be almost a literal translation from MT with some use of LXX words. The citation of Zechariah in John xii 15, on the other hand, is unique. For John the king is *seated* (not riding or mounted as in MT, LXX, Matthew) on a *pōlos onou*, "a donkey's colt"—only one description, combining (*a*) and (*b*).

(2) In the description of the animal as part of the narrative of the entry:

■ Mark xi 2 and Luke xix 30 speak of a colt (*pōlos*) on which no man has ever sat—therefore *new*, as in the LXX of (*b*);

■ Matt xxi 2, 7, speak of *two* animals, "a she-donkey and a colt with her" (*onos* and *pōlos*—vocabulary taken from the Matthean form of the Zechariah citation) and says that Jesus sat on them (*sic*);

■ John xii 14 speaks of a "young donkey" (*onarion*, a diminutive of *onos*—not the vocabulary of the Johannine form of the Zechariah citation).

15. *Do not be afraid, O daughter of Zion.* Unlike the rest of this verse this is not part of the citation of Zech ix 9, which reads, "Rejoice greatly, O daughter of Zion." This, then, may be another example of a compound citation in John (see NOTE on vii 38 in § 29, p. 323). The Greek words "Do not be afraid" occur frequently in LXX of Isaiah, e.g., xl 9; but the full expression that John uses resembles most closely MT (not LXX) of Zeph iii 16: "Do not be afraid, O Zion ['O daughter of Zion' occurs in iii 14]." The import of this passage in Zephaniah is to assure Jerusalem that "the King of Israel, the Lord" (iii 15) is in her midst. This may well be the source of "the King of Israel" which John xii 13 has added to the citation of the psalm.

16. *the disciples.* Many witnesses have "his disciples," but the possessive is found in different word orders and is probably a scribal clarification.

understand. Literally "know" (*ginōskein*); but the Codices Bezae and Koridethi have the almost synonymous verb *noein* ("understand") which may be original.

they had done to him. Actually *the disciples* had not done anything that was part of the OT prophecies. Only in the Synoptic tradition did they get the donkey and put Jesus on it, and thus unconsciously do to him "these things that had been written about him." Bernard, II, p. 427, thinks that John is implicitly recalling the Synoptic picture. Perhaps, however, the "they" should be taken more generally and understood as equivalent to a passive ("was done to him").

17. *the crowd.* See NOTE on vs. 9.

when Jesus called Lazarus. There is strong Western support, plus P[66], for reading "that" instead of "when," thus: "The crowd which was with him began to testify that he had called Lazarus. . . ." This reading makes good sense and removes any obstacle to identifying the crowd in vs. 17 with that in vs. 9. However, it is probably wiser to opt for the more difficult reading.

kept testifying. Presumably we are to understand that the eyewitnesses had begun their testimony by convincing those of whom vs. 9 speaks (and who are now part of this crowd).

18. [*also*]. This word is found in different positions or is omitted in some very early Greek witnesses. However, the problem of the various crowds may have been responsible for the omission.

19. *You see.* This can be translated as an imperative.

the world. There is good evidence in the Western tradition for reading "all the world" or "the whole world." "All the world" is a Semitic idiom, like the French *tout le monde,* for "everyone." Luke xix 39 reports indignation among the Pharisees at the enthusiasm with which Jesus was acclaimed.

COMMENT

Verses 9–11: Transition

In order to keep alive the Lazarus motif in the story of the acclamation of Jesus as he entered Jerusalem, the writer has supplied a transitional framework both before and after the story of the entry. The result is not entirely a happy one. If vs. 12 were placed after vs. 8, one would have a good sequence; and indeed the confusion of the various crowds would disappear (see NOTE on vs. 9). There is little or no original material in vss. 9–11. Verse 10 is a reworking of xi 53 and serves to remind us of the malevolent plotting that is continuing behind the scene. In their determination to reject the gift of life, the authorities would destroy not only the giver but also the recipient. Verse 11 can be understood against the background of the struggle between the Synagogue and the Church in the late 1st century. It is a tacit invitation to those Jews who believe in Christ to follow the example of their compatriots who had already left Judaism to follow Jesus.

Verses 12–16: The Acclamation of Jesus as He Enters Jerusalem

Relation to the Synoptic accounts. The account of Jesus' entry into Jerusalem appears in all three Synoptics; and some scholars, like Freed, *art. cit.,* maintain that John's narrative is simply a theological rewriting of the Synoptic account and that differences can be explained in terms of adaptation to John's theology. We tend to agree with D. M. Smith's refutation of Freed's position; see also Dodd, *Tradition,* pp. 152–56.

The Synoptic versions of the incident are found in Mark xi 1–10; Matt xx 1–9; and Luke xix 28–38, and betray minor variations among themselves. The following important points of comparison with John may be made.

(1) THE ANIMAL(s): Unlike the Synoptics, John has no introductory information about the sending of two disciples to find a donkey's colt in Bethphage. Only after the procession has begun does John (vs. 14) tell us that *Jesus* found a young donkey. There is no particular reason to doubt the Synoptic picture, and in this instance the Johannine description could be a theological adaptation to emphasize that sitting on the donkey was Jesus' reaction to the crowd's acclamation. However, the fact that the

Johannine vocabulary for the animal differs from that of the Synoptics (see NOTE on vs. 14) does suggest the other possibility of variation within early traditions of the story.

(2) THE CROWD(s): John speaks of several (two or three) crowds of the Jews, with some accompanying him and some coming out to meet him. As we have stated, part of this picture of confused enthusiasm stems from the editor's binding of this incident with the Lazarus story. The Synoptics do not have a group coming out to meet Jesus, but there are disciples who escort Jesus from Bethany to Jerusalem. Luke xix 37 has a multitude of disciples; Mark xi 9 has some who go before Jesus and some who follow him; only Matt xxi 9 speaks of these as crowds. We have already called attention (p. 429) to the parallel in theme between John's emphasis on the Lazarus miracle as the cause of enthusiasm and Luke xix 37 where the disciples praise God with a loud voice for all the mighty works that they have seen.

(3) THE ACTIONS OF THE CROWD: The Synoptics mention that the disciples spread their garments on the donkey and also on the road; John does not mention this. In Mark and Matthew, those accompanying Jesus cut leaves and branches and spread them on the road; in John, the people who come out to meet Jesus get palm fronds (presumably to carry in their hands). In these details, then, John's description is less spectacular than that of the Synoptics. To a certain extent the action described by John resembles one of the standard processions of Tabernacles or Dedication where the people carried the *lulab* of myrtle, willow, and palm (see p. 327).

(4) THE SHOUT OF THE CROWD (Ps cxviii 25–26): **(a)** *Hosanna.* Found in Mark, Matthew, John (Luke simply mentions their *praising* God). Matt xxi 9 adds "to the son of David," which is not part of the psalm. **(b)** *Blessed is he who comes in the Lord's name.* The same in Mark, Matthew, John (Luke has "the king" in place of "he"). Freed, p. 332, makes the point that "Blessed" is found nowhere else in John. Yet, since all the Gospels are citing LXX at this point, this word does not prove Johannine dependence on the Synoptics. **(c)** Mark adds another blessing: "Blessed is the coming kingdom of David our father." John adds: "Blessed is the King of Israel." Matthew and Luke do not have this feature. None of the Gospels follows the psalm, "We bless you from the house of the Lord." **(d)** The Synoptics add a final "Hosanna" or "Glory in the highest" which John does not have.

By way of evaluation, it will be noted that John is close to the Synoptics only in (*a*) and (*b*) where *all* are close to the psalm. John's form of (*c*) could be an imaginative rearrangement based on Mark's "kingdom of David" or Luke's mention of "the king" in (*b*), but this possibility is scarcely compelling.

(5) THE SCRIPTURAL CITATION: Both Matthew and John cite Zech ix 9. Matt xxi 5 cites it on the occasion of Jesus' order to the disciples to go to Bethphage and get the animal(s); John xii 15 cites it on the occasion of Jesus' getting the donkey. For the dissimilarity between the two citations, see the NOTE. There is no firm evidence to support Freed's contention

(pp. 337–38) that John is adapting Matthew's form of the citation. The vocabulary describing the animal could conceivably be a combination of the two Matthean descriptions, but it also could stem from a direct translation and combination of the Hebrew terms in MT. Certainly John's understanding of the passage is different from Matthew's (two animals).

(6) There is nothing in the Synoptics resembling John xii 16.

When we weigh the similarities and dissimilarities in these six points of comparison, we find that in part of (1), (2), part of (3), and (6), John's variants could be explained as deliberate variants of the Synoptic tradition, variants guided by a theological motif. But in these instances it is equally probable that John is giving us a theological adaptation of a tradition similar to that of the Synoptics, but not the same. The situation in (4) and (5) and the vocabulary variants mentioned in the NOTE on vs. 14 tip the scales in favor of the latter suggestion.

Interpretation of the Scene. In the Synoptics this represents the first time during the ministry that Jesus comes to Jerusalem; the entry is followed by the cleansing of the Temple. This fact, combined with the references to David both in Mark and Matthew, seems to give the scene the aspect of the triumphal entry of the messianic king who has come to claim his capital and his Temple (see Taylor, *Mark,* pp. 451–52, for various other possible interpretations). In John the context is markedly different. Jesus has been at Jerusalem many times; and while this entry provokes enthusiasm, the explanation for the enthusiasm lies in the Lazarus miracle. Indeed, to be precise, it is not specifically stated that Jesus *entered* Jerusalem, although that is implied; and, of course, there is no subsequent cleansing of the Temple. Thus, we must seek a different interpretation of the scene in John.

We notice that John places the greeting with palm and the acclamation from Ps cxviii at the very beginning of the narrative, and this is important for the interpretation of what Jesus does. Although the carrying of palms can be associated with Tabernacles or Dedication (see NOTE on vs. 13), Farmer, *art. cit.,* has argued convincingly that this gesture was evocative of Maccabean nationalism and that it was as a symbol of nationalism that the palm appeared on the coins of the Second Revolt (A.D. 132–135). When Judas Maccabeus rededicated the temple altar after its profanation by the Syrians (164 B.C.), the Jews brought palms to the Temple (II Macc x 7: *phoinix*—one of the two words John uses). When his brother Simon conquered the Jerusalem citadel (142 B.C.), the Jews took possession of it carrying palm fronds (I Macc xiii 51: *baion*—the only occurrence in LXX of this other word used by John). In the Testament of Naphthali v 4, where there occurs the same expression for palm fronds that John uses, the fronds are given to Levi as a symbol of power over all Israel. On the basis of this background, the action of the crowd in John's scene seems to have political overtones, as if they were welcoming Jesus as a national liberator. This suggestion may receive some confirmation in the statement that the crowd "came out *to meet* him [*eis hypantēsin*—vs. 13]." This was the normal Greek expression used to describe the joyful reception of Hellenistic sovereigns into a city. For instance, Pergamum came out to meet Attalus III; Antioch came out to meet Titus (Josephus *War* VII.v.2;※100)—so A. Feuillet, JohSt, pp. 142–43.

The line that John xii 13 adds to the citation from Ps cxviii 26 also smacks of nationalism. The crowd evidently interprets *"he who comes* in the Lord's name" as the *King of Israel.* The juxtaposition of these two titles is also found in the crowd scene of vi 14–15. There the people designate Jesus as "the Prophet *who is to come* into the world," and Jesus recognizes that this means they will attempt to make him king. We may remember, too, that the Hosanna shouted by the crowds in xii 13 was used in addressing kings (II Sam xiv 4; II Kings vi 26).

Only after the crowd has thus expressed its nationalistic conceptions does Jesus get the donkey and sit upon it. The adversative conjunction that begins xii 14 suggests that this is in reaction to the enthusiastic greeting. The large crowd (vs. 12) has misunderstood the Lazarus miracle and the gift of life, even as another large crowd (vi 2) in Galilee misunderstood the multiplication of the loaves, the bread of life, and tried to make Jesus king. The Sanhedrin had reacted to the Lazarus miracle with a malevolent resolution to kill Jesus; Mary of Bethany had reacted to it with gratitude and love; now the crowd reacts with nationalistic misunderstanding. Jesus seeks to dispel this misunderstanding with a prophetic action that the disciples will not understand until after his death and resurrection (vs. 16).

That mounting the donkey was a prophetic action is seen in the citation of Zech ix 9. How does this prophecy interpret the action? It is not an action designed to stress humility, for John omits the line of Zechariah cited by Matthew, namely, "humble and riding on a donkey." In fact, it seems as if the Zechariah part of the citation is really only materially valuable to John inasmuch as it portrays a king seated on a donkey (but see below for the relevance of the context in Zechariah). What is important for John is the line placed first in vs. 15 which is seemingly from Zeph iii 16 (see NOTE). The Zephaniah passage tells Israel that Yahweh is in her midst as the "King of Israel," but the portrait of the king is not a nationalistic one. To Jerusalem, filled with the presence of Yahweh, will stream people from *all over the earth* to seek refuge (iii 9–10). Yahweh will save Israel from her enemies; in particular He will save the lame and gather the outcast (iii 19). This passage throws light on how the Johannine Jesus would have the crowd interpret the Lazarus miracle. It is a gift of life for people all over the earth, not a sign of nationalistic glory for Israel. They should not be acclaiming him as an earthly king, but as the manifestation of the Lord their God who has come into their midst (Zeph iii 17) to gather the outcast.

This universalistic interpretation of Jesus' action in xii 14 fits in well with the context in John xi–xii. In xi 52 John interpreted Caiaphas' unconscious prophecy to mean that Jesus would save not only Israel, but the Gentiles as well. In xii 19 the Pharisees use a hyperbole which, by Johannine irony, is truer than they suspect: "The *world* has run off after him." The whole scene of entry leads to the climactic moment when the Gentile Greeks come to Jesus in xii 20. Jesus relates this to his being lifted up so that he can draw *all men* to himself (xii 32). The Sanhedrin would have Jesus die in place of Israel (xi 50); the crowd shouts for him as King of Israel (see NOTE on "shouted" in xi 43). But the only anointing that Jesus receives is an anointing for death (xii 7); the only crown he will wear is the crown of thorns (xix 2); the only robe he will wear is the cloak of mockery; and when thus anointed and robed, he stands before his people and is presented as their king, the crowd will *shout,* "Crucify him!" (xix 14–15). Thus, they will lift him up to draw all men.

Returning to the OT citation that is the key to the Johannine emphasis in this scene, we find the same universalism in the context of Zech ix 9. There, the very next verse says that the king who came on the donkey ". . . shall command peace to the Gentiles, and his dominion shall be from sea to sea." Appropriately, ix 11 associates all this with the blood of the covenant. And finally, if we turn to another work of the Johannine school (Rev vii 9), we find a similar picture of how Jesus Christ should be acclaimed. There we find another *large crowd from every nation carrying palms* and crying out in praise of the salvation brought by the slain Lamb.

In summation, while there may be an element of nationalism in the Synoptic description of the acclamation of Jesus, this is clearer in John; and Jesus' entering Jerusalem on a donkey is a prophetic action designed to counteract that nationalism. It is an affirmation of a universal kingship that will be achieved only when he is lifted up in death and resurrection. The peculiar Johannine order of events (acclamation, followed by Jesus' reaction in selecting a donkey) and details (palms—see NOTE for difficulty) are ordered to this theological purpose. If there was, as we suspect, an independent Johannine narrative of the entry, parallel to the Synoptic form, nevertheless this narrative has in its order and details been heavily adapted to fit the writer's theological insight. In xii 16 we are told that this theological insight was not gained at the time of the entry, but only after the resurrection. It is interesting that in ii 22 we have a similar statement pertaining to the cleansing of the Temple and Jesus' identification of his body as the temple. Is this repetition an echo of the fact that these two scenes were once joined in John even as they are in the Synoptics?

Verses 17–19: Transitional Conclusion

In this part of the editorial framework, matching vss. 9–11, the Lazarus motif is brought back. The crowd associated with the Lazarus miracle is now brought to meet the crowd associated with the entry into Jerusalem. Notice the artistic balance between vss. 9–11 and 17–19: both begin with the theme of the crowd and the Lazarus miracle; both end by emphasizing the hostility of the authorities, chief priests, and Pharisees. Verse 11 stresses that many Jews are coming to believe in Jesus; 19 stresses that the whole world is going after him. In vs. 19 the Pharisees strike the same note of despair that they sounded along with the priests in xi 47–48; and like Caiaphas, although less dramatically, they speak in prophecy. The "world" has run off after Jesus, but in a wider sense than they intend.

BIBLIOGRAPHY

Farmer, W. R., "The Palm Branches in John 12, 13," JTS N.S. 3 (1952), 62–66.

Freed, E. D., "The Entry into Jerusalem in the Gospel of John," JBL 80 (1961), 329–38.

Smith, D. M., "John 12, 12 ff. and the Question of John's Use of the Synoptics," JBL 82 (1963), 58–64.

43. SCENES PREPARATORY TO PASSOVER AND DEATH:—THE COMING OF THE HOUR
(xii 20–36)

The coming of the Greeks marks the coming of the hour

XII 20 Now among those who had come up to worship at the feast there were some Greeks. 21 They approached Philip, who was from Bethsaida in Galilee, and made a request of him. "Sir," they said, "we would like to see Jesus." 22 Philip went and told Andrew; then both Philip and Andrew came and told Jesus. 23 Jesus answered them:

"The hour has come
for the Son of Man to be glorified.
24 I solemnly assure you,
unless the grain of wheat falls to the earth and dies,
it remains just a grain of wheat.
But if it dies,
it bears much fruit.
25 The man who loves his life
destroys it;
while the man who hates his life in this world,
preserves it to live eternally.
26 If anyone would serve me,
let him follow me;
and where I am,
my servant will also be.
The Father will honor
anyone who serves me.
27 Now my soul is troubled.
Yet, what should I say—
'Father, save me from this hour'?
No, this is just the reason why I came to this hour.
28 'Father, glorify your name!'"

22: *went, told, told;* 23: *answered.* In the historical present tense.

Then a voice came from the sky:

> "I have glorified it
> and will glorify it again."

29 When the crowd that was there heard it, they said that it was thunder; but others maintained, "It was an angel speaking to him." 30 Jesus answered, "That voice did not come for my sake, but for yours.

> 31 Now is the judgment of this world.
> Now will the Prince of this world be driven out.
> 32 And when I am lifted up from the earth,
> I shall draw all men to myself."

(33 This statement of his indicated what sort of death he was going to die.) 34 To this the crowd objected, "We have heard from the Law that the Messiah is to remain forever. How can you claim that the Son of Man must be lifted up? Just who is this Son of Man?" 35 So Jesus told them:

> "The light is among you only a little while longer.
> Walk while you have the light,
> or the darkness will come over you.
> The man who walks in the dark
> does not know where he is going.
> 36 While you have the light,
> keep your faith in the light,
> and so become sons of light."

After this speech Jesus left them and went into hiding.

Notes

xii 20. *Now . . . there were some.* For this style in opening a narrative see iii 1.

Greeks. Hellēnes or Gentiles (in this instance, proselytes), not *Hellēnistai* or Greek-speaking Jews. See NOTE on vii 35. Only the understanding that the first Gentiles have come to Jesus explains his exclamation that the hour has come (vs. 23).

21. *Bethsaida in Galilee.* See NOTE on i 44. Some have thought that Galilee is mentioned here because of its association with Gentiles (Matt iv 15, citing Isa ix 1).

to see Jesus. "To see" may have the sense of "to visit with, to meet" (BAG, p. 220, *eidon* ⚹6), as in Luke viii 20, ix 9. Yet, in the Johannine theological context "to see" may well mean "to believe in."

23. *answered them.* Does the "them" refer to Philip and Andrew or to the

Greeks? Really, Jesus' response is a comment on the whole scene rather than a direct answer to either group.

glorified. The mention of "glory" so soon after the acclamation with palms has an interesting parallel in Luke xix 38, where during the entry into Jerusalem the multitude shouts, "Glory in the highest."

24. *the grain*. A parabolic use of the article (Luke viii 5, 11: "the sower . . . the seed").

wheat. *Sitos* can mean "wheat," in particular, or "grain," in general. It is used in the Parable of the Weeds in Matt xiii 25.

falls to the earth. Literally "falling into the earth, dies"; the emphasis is on dying.

remains just a grain of wheat. Literally "remains alone." The verb *menein* (see App. I:8) in John is used of persons, the Spirit, love, joy, wrath, and the word.

25. *loves . . . hates*. Semitic usage favors vivid contrasts to express preferences. Deut xxi 15; Matt vi 24; Luke xiv 26 are more examples of this.

his life. *Psychē* has sometimes been translated "soul," but Jewish anthropology did not contain the dualism of soul and body which this translation might suggest. *Psychē* refers to physical life; it can also mean one's self (Heb. *nefeš*). In x 15 it refers to life, and that seems to be the meaning here as well.

destroys. *Apollynai* can mean "to lose" or "to destroy"; the latter seems to provide a better contrast with "preserves." Some manuscripts have a future tense here, but this is a harmonization with the Synoptics, which all use the future in their form of this statement—see COMMENT.

to live eternally. Literally "unto eternal life"; this is *zōē*, the life that the believer receives from above.

26. *If anyone*. While the saying has Synoptic parallels (see COMMENT), this particular type of indefinite condition is Johannine. Other Johannine features in the Greek of this verse are chiasm and the use of the possessive pronominal adjective.

Father will honor. We have heard of the honor that men pay to Jesus or to the Father (v 23, viii 49), but here we have an example of the reciprocity in the eternal life promised in John.

27. *soul*. *Psychē* as in vs. 25, but here the danger of dualistic misinterpretation does not seem so great. We could translate this, "*I* am troubled"; but when the emotions are involved, "soul" helps to express the sentient aspects of man.

save me. There is a reference in Heb v 7 to Jesus' anguish before death: "Jesus offered up prayers and supplications to Him who was able *to save* him from death." This resembles the tradition found in John, for the Synoptic narratives of the agony do not use the verb "to save."

this is just the reason. Some would translate as a question: "Was it for this reason that I came to this hour [i.e., to be saved from the hour]?"

28. *your name*. There is respectable evidence for reading "your Son," but this is probably the cross-influence of xvii 1. Codex Bezae adds here a clause from xvii 5.

a voice came from the sky. Bernard, II, p. 438, suggests that this is a *bath qōl* ("a daughter of the voice"—a type of inferior divine inspiration, the offspring of God's word that had formerly come to the prophets, but now was heard no more in Israel in its pristine force). This rabbinic term, however, really does not fit the NT picture where the voice of God is looked on as a supreme manifestation, e.g., at the baptism of Jesus. The closest parallel would be in the Testament of Levi xviii 6–7: "The *skies* shall be opened, and sanctification shall come upon him from the Temple of glory with *the Father's voice,* as from Abraham to Isaac; and the *glory* of the Most High shall be uttered over him."

have glorified it/and will glorify it. With neither tense of the verb is the object expressed.

29. *thunder.* In the OT, whether naïvely or poetically, thunder was described as the voice of God (I Sam xii 18). Does John wish us to think that thunder accompanied the voice, or that the sound of the voice was mistaken for thunder? The alternative suggestion that an angel was speaking favors the latter. Neither suggestion from the crowd indicates that the voice was understood (see Acts ix 7, xxii 9).

angel speaking. For angelic voices from heaven see Gen xxi 17, xxii 11. The theory that this verse in John forms an inclusion with the mention of angels in i 51 seems unlikely.

31. *Prince of this world.* This is a Johannine term for Satan (xiv 30, xvi 11), but perhaps it also occurs in I Cor ii 6–8 where Paul speaks of the doomed princes or powers of this world. In II Cor iv 4 Paul speaks of the hostile "god of this world"; Eph ii 2 speaks of "the prince of the power of the air," and Eph vi 12 speaks of "the world rulers of this darkness." Ignatius of Antioch uses the Johannine term several times in his writings. The Hebrew equivalent, *śar ha'ōlām,* is found in rabbinic writings as a reference to God, not to Satan. Barrett, p. 355, concludes that John is seemingly not in close contact with Jewish thought at this point. However, the modified dualism implied in John's portrait of a struggle between the Prince of this world and Jesus is very close to the Qumran picture of a struggle between the angel of darkness and the prince of lights (see CBQ 17 [1955], 409 ff., or NTE, pp. 109 ff.).

driven out. There is respectable evidence in the versions for reading "cast down." The fact that "cast [driven, thrown] out" is the more normal Johannine vocabulary (vi 37, ix 34, xv 6) raises the possibility that the better-attested reading is the product of a scribal tendency toward conformity.

32. *from the earth.* There is strong patristic evidence, but virtually no manuscript evidence, for the omission of these words. See RB 57 (1950), 391–92.

I shall draw. See NOTE on vi 44 for possible relation to Jeremiah. Such a relation would give a background of divine covenant love to the lifting up of Jesus and its effects.

all men. There is interesting attestation, including P66, for a neuter plural reading which would make the lifting up of Jesus effective on all things. However, BDF, § 138¹, suggests that it is simply a neuter used for a general masculine reference.

33. *indicated.* The verb is *sēmainein,* related to *sēmeion,* "sign." The sign is found in the expression that Jesus uses: "lifted up" is the sign of the crucifixion. There is nothing in this passage that would support the thesis that Jesus' death was itself a sign; rather, as part of being lifted up, Jesus' death belongs to the glorious realization of God's plan, not to the signs of that realization.

sort of death. The parenthetical explanation relates being lifted up to being crucified; this will be clear in xviii 31–32, which indicates a Roman punishment. That crucifixion does not exhaust the concept of being lifted up was shown on p. 146. It is possible that the editor who inserted vs. 33 is thinking that crucifixion not only lifted up the body of Jesus, but also outstretched his arms to draw men. See a similar reference to the crucifixion of Peter in xxi 19.

34. *from the Law.* As we mentioned in the NOTE on x 34, "Law" can refer to the whole OT. But even with this latitude, it is difficult to find a particular passage that says that the Messiah is to remain forever. Barrett, p. 356, seems inclined to settle for the common messianic teaching of the Scriptures, rather than an individual passage. It is true that there are many passages that concern the eternal rule of the Davidic line or king (Pss lxxxix 4, cx 4; Isa ix 7; Ezek xxxvii 25), and other passages that concern the eternal rule of the (or a) Son of Man (Dan vii 14; En xlix 1, lxii 14). But there is no text that says that the Messiah *remains* forever. In fact, "remains forever" is an expression that the OT applies to Yahweh, His justice, truth, praise, etc. Van Unnik, *art. cit.,* has come up with the best suggestion made so far. He points to Ps lxxxix 36, which says that David's "seed remains forever." This is a Psalm that is interpreted messianically both in the NT (Acts xiii 22; Rev i 5, iii 14) and in rabbinic sources (StB, IV, p. 1308; Midrash Rabbah xcvii on Genesis, Soncino ed., p. 901). Although vs. 36 speaks of the "seed," vs. 51 speaks of the "anointed" (messiah).

who is this Son of Man. Actually it is the crowd and not Jesus who mentioned the Son of Man. Is this a request to identify the Son of Man by giving the name of the person who is the Son of Man? Or is this a request about his nature and relationship to the Messiah? See COMMENT.

35. *among you.* Literally "in you"; in Acts iv 34 "in" means "among." The "with you" of the standard Byzantine text is a scribal clarification imitating Johannine style.

darkness will come over you. This verb, *katalambanein,* appears as "overcome" in i 5; see NOTE there.

The man who . . . This saying is almost identical with I John ii 11.

36. *went into hiding.* So also after Tabernacles (viii 59).

COMMENT

The mention of the feast in vs. 20 binds this scene to the general context of Passover, which has served as background from xi 55 on. There is a minimum of factual setting. One may presume that the intent of the writer was to situate the scene immediately after the entry of Jesus into Jerusalem, and, indeed, in the temple precincts where Jesus was wont to teach. From the viewpoint of thought sequence, the scene is an ideal conclusion to chs. xi–xii. Chapter xi began by announcing that the purpose of the Lazarus miracle was "that the Son [of God] may be glorified through it." Now the hour for this glorification has come (xii 23). The Lazarus miracle began a chain of actions pointing toward Jesus' death; now the hour has come for Jesus to be lifted up in crucifixion (xi 32–33). The Lazarus miracle pointed to Jesus as the resurrection and the life (xi 25); now begins that hour in which Jesus will be lifted up in resurrection and draw all men to himself to give them life (xii 32, 24). We saw in chs. xi–xii a series of universalistic references pointing out God's intent to save the Gentiles; now the Gentiles come to Jesus (xii 20–21) to see him. Truly this is a climactic scene.

Verses 20–22: The coming of the Greeks

The theological import of this scene is relatively clear from what we have said about universalism. Jesus had said that he would lay down his life and that other sheep not belonging to the fold would join his flock. The appearance of Gentiles wishing to see (believe in?) Jesus indicates that it is time for him to lay down his life. However, it seems that the theological import has so dominated the writer's interest that he has abbreviated his picture of what happened to the point of making it enigmatic. We may guess that these Gentiles approached Philip, who bore a Greek name and came from a predominantly Gentile area, because he spoke Greek. Why Philip should consult Andrew is not clear, except that these two disciples work as a team in John (vi 5–8). The *coming* of the Gentiles is so theologically important that the writer never tells us if they got to see Jesus, and indeed they disappear from the scene in much the same manner that Nicodemus slipped out of sight in ch. iii. The very awkwardness of all this suggests that a poorly known incident from early tradition has been used as the basis for theological adaptation. There is nothing intrinsically improbable in the basic incident.

Verse 23 (27–28): The hour of glorification

Many times in this Gospel we have heard Jesus state that his hour (or time: vii 6, 8) had not yet come (ii 4, vii 30, viii 20), i.e., the hour of Jesus' return to his Father through crucifixion, resurrection, and ascension. (See App. I:11.) Now, and consistently in the next chapters (xiii 1, xvii 1), we are told that the hour has come. Evidently the coming of the Greeks has indicated this; and Jesus, whose life could not be taken away from him involuntarily (x 17–18), is ready for the hour of laying down his life and taking it up again. In vs. 27 he resists the temptation to ask his Father to save him from the hour; rather he rejoices at the opportunity for glorifying his Father that the hour will offer.

Since vss. 27–28 pick up the themes of the hour and of glory that are found in 23, it is not unlikely that at one time 23, 27–28 were a unit. In CBQ 23 (1961), 143–48 (NTE, pp. 192–98), we showed that, although John does not describe an agony in Gethsemane such as found in the Synoptic tradition, there are elements scattered through John that parallel the Synoptic agony scene. Some of those elements are present in this section of ch. xii (see also COMMENT on xiv 30–31, xviii 11): (a) In the Synoptics it is only in the agony scene that "the hour" becomes a technical expression for the passion and death of Jesus (Mark xiv 35; Matt xxvi 45; see NOTE on "time" in John vii 6). An impressive parallel to John xii 23 is found in Mark xiv 41: "The hour has come." (b) John xii 27, "My soul is troubled [*tarassein*]," is parallel to Mark xiv 34, "My soul is sorrowful [*perilypos*]." Both reflect Ps xlii 5: "Why are you sorrowful [*perilypos*], my soul, and why do you trouble [*syntarassein*] me?" (c) John xii 27, "Father, save me from this hour," is parallel to Mark xiv 35–36: "He prayed that, if it were possible, this hour might pass from him. . . . 'Father . . . remove this cup from me.'" In both instances Jesus recognizes that this is not the Father's will. (d) There is a further, very tenuous comparison possible between the voice from the sky that some people think is an angel (John xii 29) and the angel in the garden mentioned in some manuscripts of Luke (xxii 43).

We need not jump to the conclusion that John presents us with a dismembered form of the Synoptic agony scene. It is quite probable that Jesus underwent an experience of agony in the face of death as described in the Synoptic scene, for this is not the type of incident that the primitive Church would invent about its glorified master. Yet, since there were no witnesses to report the prayer of Jesus during the agony (the disciples were asleep at a distance), the tendency would be to fill in the skeletal framework of the Gethsemane scene with prayers and sayings uttered by Jesus at other times. Therefore, the Johannine picture where such prayers and sayings are scattered *may* actually be closer to the original situation than the more organized Synoptic scene.

Verse 24: The Parable of the Seed that Dies

Verse 23 is now separated from vss. 27–28 by a series of sayings that constitute a magnificent commentary on the theme of death and life. Although the present sequence is the product of editorial rearrangement, the writer has employed some sayings of Jesus, passed down in Johannine circles, which have a good claim to represent early tradition.

Verse 24 has been the subject of study by Rasco, *art. cit.*, and Dodd, *Tradition*, pp. 366–69. In both format and symbolism it represents a short parable very similar to the Synoptic parables. It has its peculiar Johannine features: (*a*) the double "amen," which we translate as "I solemnly assure you"; (*b*) the verb *menein*, "to remain"; (*c*) the use of *pherein* in the expression "to bear fruit," as contrasted with the more common Synoptic verbs *poiein* or *dounai*. Yet, for instance, there are good Synoptic parallels for a parable beginning with a condition (Matt v 13; Mark iii 24); and we get a perfect parallel to John's contrasting conditions in Matt vi 22–23. As for the symbolism, the Synoptics have a parable about *a grain* of mustard (Mark iv 30–32) and several parables dealing with wheat or grain in general, for example, the Sower and the Seed in Mark iv 1–9, and the Grain Growing by Itself in Mark iv 26–29.

The general meaning of the Johannine parable is clear from the context: Jesus is speaking of death as the means of gaining life. Indeed, in its present sequence after the coming of the Greeks, it is meant to refer to *Jesus'* death as the means of bringing life to all men (xii 32). The details of the parable need not be allegorized, for example, the falling (in)to the earth is not a reference to the Incarnation. We should note that the contrast to dying and bearing fruit is one of not dying and thus remaining unproductive. We might have expected an alternative of the seed rotting away; however, the parable is concerned not with the fate of the grain but with its productivity—it either remains barren or bears fruit. This fruit is to be understood in the same sense as in iv 36, where the context of sayings about harvest showed that the fruit consisted in the people who were coming to Jesus and thus to God.

What is the peculiar feature of this parable is the insistence that only through death is the fruit borne. Some point out that there is no similar message in any Synoptic parable, and that even in the Synoptic predictions of the passion where we hear that the Son of Man *must* die (Mark viii 31; also Luke xxiv 26), there is no emphasis on the fruitful results of that death. Mark x 45, ". . . to give his life as a ransom for many," comes to mind, but this is certainly very far from the parabolic genre. As for the imagery of bearing fruit, we can suggest a possible Synoptic parallel that has its roots in the OT. There are no good OT parallels for John's parable, although Isa lv 10–11 is interesting. However, the expression "much fruit" is used in the Greek of Dan iv 12 (both LXX and Theodotion) to describe the great tree of Nebuchadnezzar's dream. This same OT verse is used in the Synoptic Parable of the Mustard Seed (Mark iv 32), where we are told that the tree that grows from the little grain of mustard is so great that the birds of the air can nest in it. Taylor, *Mark,* p. 270, comments that, because in Daniel the tree symbolizes the protection that a great empire gives to its subject peoples, it is reasonable to suppose that the Synoptic parable of the kingdom contemplates the Gentile nations. Thus, in John and the Synoptics, we have two parables concerning the productivity of a grain (of wheat, of mustard); both contemplate the coming of the Gentiles to God, and both may well be drawing on the imagery of Dan iv 12. If we recall once more that the Synoptic picture of the kingdom has much in common with the Johannine picture of Jesus, we can see how much at home the basic Johannine parable is among the traditional parables of Jesus.

We should mention that others have sought wider afield for the background of this Johannine parable. Some, like Holtzmann, draw a comparison with the mystery religions where the annual cycle of death and rebirth was dramatized with an ear of grain. However, the automatic and immutable character of this cycle would form a poor background for John's conception of the death and resurrection of Jesus in which Jesus' free choice of the time and conditions is heavily emphasized. Dodd, *Interpretation,* p. 372[1], suggests that John's Hellenistic readers would be aware of that symbolism whereby there is in man a divine seed which has come down from above and is destined to return to its source. But is this not far from John's idea that Jesus' death enables others to come to God? The Valentinian parallel that Dodd cites about the Heavenly Man who must die in order that other seeds may find their way into the Pleroma may be influenced by John, rather than constituting an independent parallel. A better parallel is found in I Cor xv 35 ff. where Paul speaks of the seed that does not come to life unless it is sown; he mentions the resurrection of the body in light of this figure. The image is not exactly the same as John's, and Loisy's suggestion (p. 371) that John may have borrowed from Paul is unwarranted. Here, as elsewhere, Paul's figurative language may have been influenced by an oral tradition of Jesus' parables (see D. M. Stanley, CBQ 23 [1961], 26–39).

Verse 25: On loving and hating life

It has often been suggested that this verse is a Johannine variation on a Synoptic saying, but Dodd, *art. cit.*, has now shown that the situation is more complicated. There are five sayings reported in the Synoptic Gospels on this theme; when analyzed, the sayings fall into three basic patterns: (*a*) Mark viii 35; Luke ix 24; (*b*) Matt x 39 and, in part, xvi 25; (*c*) Luke xvii 33. Let us now compare these patterns in terms of the alternative attitudes toward one's life that are offered:

1. Destroying life:
(*a*) Whoever wishes to save (*sōzein*) his life will destroy (*apollynai*) it.
(*b*) The man who finds (*eurein*) his life will lose (*apollynai*) it.
(*c*) Whoever seeks to gain (*peripoieisthai*) his life will lose (*apollynai*) it.
We note that the Synoptic patterns for the subject vary between a general participle in (*b*) and the indefinite relative in (*a*) and (*c*); these probably represent two different ways of rendering the Aramaic original into Greek. There is a variation in the verb of the protasis ("save, find, gain") but with no important over-all difference of meaning. The Greek verb in the apodosis is always the same but seems to be used in its different meanings of "lose" and "destroy."

2. Preserving life:
(*a*) But whoever destroys (*apollynai*) his life for my sake will save (*sōzein*) it.
(*b*) And the man who loses (*apollynai*) his life for my sake will find (*eurein*) it.
(*c*) And whoever loses (*apollynai*) [it] will keep it alive (*zōogonein*).
We notice that while (*a*) and (*b*) use the same verbs as in 1, simply reversing them, (*c*) introduces a new verb into the apodosis. In (*a*) and (*b*) there is an explanatory phrase in the protasis, namely, "for my sake" (or "for the Gospel" in important witnesses of Mark viii 35); there is no such phrase in (*c*) and, indeed, no object for the verb of the protasis. In (*b*) and (*c*) "and" introduces the sentence, while in (*a*) "but" is used.

By way of general comparison, (*a*) and (*b*) have much in common, the principal difference being that of vocabulary. The vocabulary in (*c*) betrays Lucan elegance. On the other hand, the omission of the phrase in 2 (*c*) looks very primitive. No single pattern represents the original form of the saying.

Let us now turn to John's form of the alternative attitudes toward life:
1. The man who loves (*philein*) his life destroys (*apollynai*) it;

2. and the man who hates (*misein*) his life in this world preserves (*phylaxein*) it to live eternally.

John's pattern, although it too consists in antithetic parallelism with balanced members, is as different from any one of the Synoptic patterns as they are different among themselves. It is closest to Synoptic pattern (*c*) in that it uses more than two basic verbs—four verbs, compared to the three in (*c*) —yet the Johannine verbs are simple verbs without the Lucan elegance of (*c*). John's verb "preserve" is equivalent to the "save" of (*a*). Like (*a*) and (*b*), John adds in 2 an explanatory phrase in the protasis ("in this world" as compared to the Synoptic "for my sake"), but John also matches this with an explanatory phrase in the apodosis, "to live eternally." These phrases represent the familiar Johannine contrast between the life of this world and eternal life (see App. I:6). Like (*b*), John uses the general participle, rather than the indefinite relative, for the subject of 1. From all this we would agree with Dodd that there is no real proof for treating the Johannine form of the saying as an adaptation of a Synoptic pattern. Underlying John xii 25 is an independent variant of a saying attributed to Jesus, a variant comparable in every way with the variants represented in the Synoptic tradition. Dodd even suggests that John's form is in some ways closer to the original Aramaic saying than is any of the Synoptic patterns.

The basic contrast in the Johannine form of the saying is between loving and hating one's life. This pair of opposites is well attested biblically, as we see in a comparison of Luke xiv 26, "If one does not *hate* his father and mother . . . and even *his own life* . . . ," with the Matthean form of the same saying, "He who *loves* father or mother more than me . . ." (Matt x 37). John condemns the love of one's life in this world; elsewhere we find condemnations of love of darkness (iii 19) and love of glory among men (xii 43). In Johannine dualism these three elements—darkness, this world, and human glory—are but different facets of the realm of evil; and a love of any one of them represents an unwillingness to love Jesus above all.

In stressing the need to hate one's life in this world in order to live eternally, vs. 25 repeats in non-parabolic form the theme of vs. 24, that is, the need of dying in order to live. Here, however, the theme is applied in a different way. In vs. 24 Jesus had to die in order to bring others to life; now we see that the follower of Jesus cannot escape death any more than his master but must pass through death to his own eternal life. We might say that vs. 25 explains the way in which the new grain produced by the seed of 24 gains a life of its own. It should be noted that one group of the above-mentioned Synoptic forms of this saying (Mark viii 35 and par.) is found immediately after Jesus' first prediction of his death (Mark viii 31) and a stress on the necessity of each disciple's carrying the cross (Mark viii 34). Thus, this Synoptic interpretation of the saying lies close to John's.

Verse 26: The following of Jesus

We have just mentioned that the Marcan parallel (viii 35) to John xii 25 on preserving and destroying life is immediately preceded (viii 34) by the statement: "If anyone wishes to come after me, let him deny himself, take up his cross, and follow me." This is the parallel for John xii 26. Thus, both the Synoptic and Johannine traditions join these two sayings, but in inverse order. In both traditions the saying about following Jesus is a call for a willingness to imitate Jesus in suffering and death.

The Synoptic tradition speaks of one who would *come after* Jesus; John speaks of one who would *serve* Jesus. Dodd, *Tradition*, p. 353, thinks that the Johannine verb *diakonein* may represent a later adaptation of the saying to the Church situation. The Synoptic Gospels speak of Jesus' "service" to others (Luke xxii 27) and of the need that his disciples should "serve" other men (Mark ix 35), but they do not refer to the disciples as the servants of Jesus. Yet, while Dodd may be correct, we note that the women who *followed* Jesus were said to have *served* him (Mark xv 41; see Luke x 40). Therefore, it is not impossible that John's form of this statement is ancient.

In the last part of vs. 26 Jesus shows his servants what they will receive for following him, namely, they will be with him and the Father will honor them. This is another way of saying what was said in vs. 25 about preserving life to live eternally, for eternal life is related to being with Jesus in the Father's love.

We have stated that the sayings of vss. 24–26 which represent an insertion between 23 and 27–28 are nevertheless a splendid commentary on the meaning that the hour of Jesus' death and resurrection will have for all men. A demonstrative action joining the themes of these sayings is found in the life of Ignatius of Antioch in whose writings we seem to have the earliest echoes of Johannine thought. Ignatius went to a martyr's death, willing to hate his life in this world in order to live eternally, and thus gave an example of how a servant should follow Jesus. As he did so, he cried out, "I am God's grain" (*Romans* iv 1).

Verses 27–30: The hour of glorification (resumed from vs. 23) and the Father's voice

In this scene so parallel to the agony in the garden, we see the true humanity of the Johannine Jesus. No less than in the Synoptics, the Johannine Jesus is fearful in the face of the awful struggle with Satan (vs. 31) that the hour of his passion and death entails. If in the agony he struggles with the human preference that the cup of suffering pass him by (Mark xiv 36), so in John he struggles with the temptation to cry out to his Father to save him from the hour. But he triumphs in each scene by submitting himself to the Father's will or plan. The prayer (28), "Father, glorify your name," is really a plea that God's plan be carried out; for the name that the Father has entrusted to Jesus (xvii 11, 12) can only be glorified when its bearer is glorified through death, resurrection, and ascension. Only then will men come to realize what the divine name "I AM" means when applied to Jesus (viii 28). Verse 28 gives us the Johannine form of the petition in the Lord's Prayer, "Hallowed be your name." (This petition, properly translated as, "May your name be sanctified," is not a request for men to praise God's name, but a request for God to sanctify His own name—see TS 22 [1961], 185–88. The first three petitions in the Lord's prayer are synonymous, and the first petition has the same general import as the third: "Your will be done," or "May your will come about." As we have pointed out, the parallel in the agony for John's "Glorify your name" is in the "Your will be done" of Matt xxvi 42.)

Jesus' submission to God's plan for making His name glorified in Jesus is met with a reassuring answer from the Father. This is the first time in John that the Father has spoken from heaven, since there was no voice from the sky in the Johannine account of the baptism of Jesus and there is no Johannine account of the Transfiguration. Yet, as Bultmann, p. 327[7], points out, this scene in John incorporates some of the motifs that the Synoptics have embodied in the scene of the Transfiguration. In the sequence in Mark, the Transfiguration (ix 2–8) follows Jesus' first prediction of his death (viii 31) and is intended as an anticipation of the majesty (or "glory" in Luke ix 32) of the resurrected Christ. The voice of the Father that speaks from the sky acknowledges Jesus as the Son. So also in John, after the stress on the death of Jesus in xii 24–25, the voice of the Father from the sky promises that the divine name will be glorified again, that is, in the lifting up of Jesus (vs. 32).

The two tenses of the verb "glorify" in the divine answer (vs. 28) are puzzling. What is the exact reference for the past (aorist) and future tenses? We may distinguish three solutions:

(a) It is unlikely that we have here a reference to the pre-existent and the post-resurrectional glory of Jesus. Although Jesus does speak of the glory he possessed before the world existed (xvii 5), this is scarcely a glorification of the divine name. Such a glorification involves a revelation of that name to men.

(b) The aorist tense, if complexive, may be a reference to all the past glorifications of the divine name through the miracles that Jesus had worked during the ministry. The future tense may be a reference to all the glorification that will come about through the death, resurrection, and ascension. This suggestion finds support in passages like ii 11 and xi 4 that mention glorification in relation to signs.

(c) Thüsing, pp. 193–98, puts forward another plausible suggestion. The aorist refers to the whole ministry of Jesus, including the hour. Facing the hour which has now come, Jesus has prayed that the Father will accomplish the glorification of His name through the Son. The past tense used by the heavenly voice means that God has heard the prayer and accomplished that glorification in the hour now begun. There is a similar usage in xvii 4 where, after saying that the hour has come, Jesus continues, "I glorified [aorist] you on earth by accomplishing the work you gave me to do." This glorification is completed on the cross when Jesus can say, "It is finished" (xix 30). The future glorification of the divine name will be accomplished by the exalted Christ who, as vs. 32 assures us, will draw all men to himself. Boismard relates this passage in John to xiii 31–32. Whether or not the two passages were ever joined, the verses in xiii constitute a remarkable commentary on what has just been said. "Now has the Son of Man been glorified, and God has been glorified in him. God will, in turn, glorify him in Himself and will glorify him immediately." Here too the present hour is included in the glorification already accomplished, and the future glory is in exaltation with the Father.

The purpose that Jesus (vs. 30) allots to the heavenly voice is puzzling. In xi 41–42 we heard Jesus speaking to the Father with the purpose of leading the bystanders to belief. Yet, if in the present instance there is not the least indication that the crowd understood the voice, how was it for their sake? Is vs. 30 to be connected to 31 in the sense that the very sound from heaven constitutes a threat of judgment? Or does its obvious synchronization with Jesus' preaching signify for the crowd that God approves of Jesus?

Verses 31–34: The lifting up of Jesus and the problem of the Son of Man

In these last words that Jesus speaks during the public ministry (31–32, 35–36), the atmosphere of dualistic division returns once again. The hour brings condemnatory judgment to the Prince of this world but life to those who are drawn by Jesus; the last few hours of the light that is Jesus emphasize the surrounding darkness that is closing in. There is an interesting parallel in the Lucan scene of the agony where Jesus says to those who have come to arrest him (xxii 53): "This is your hour and the power of darkness."

The hour that brings glory to Jesus brings expulsion to his great enemy. The variant in vs. 31 (see Note) would contrast the lifting up of Jesus with the casting *down* of the Prince of this world. (This might be compared to Rev xii 5, 8–9, where the catching up of the messianic child to heaven is paralleled by Satan's being cast down from heaven; also see Luke x 18.) However, the ordinary reading of vs. 31 is not a reference to Satan's expulsion from heaven but to his loss of authority over this world. This inference seems to be contrary to the statement of I John v 19: "The whole world is in the power of the Evil One." Perhaps we can say that the victorious hour of Jesus constitutes a victory over Satan in principle; yet the working out of this victory in time and place is the gradual work of believing Christians. Even in the Christian life there is a tension between a victory already won (I John ii 13) and a victory still to be won (I John v 4–5). To suggest that the Fourth Gospel is so much in the atmosphere of realized eschatology that the writer expects no further victory over evil than that won in the victorious hour of Jesus' life is to reduce him to a hopeless romantic who cannot recognize existing evil in the world. There are other NT references to Jesus' victory over the power of death (Heb ii 14) and over the powers and principalities (Col ii 15); yet these do not rule out the expectation of a future expansion of this victory.

In the third Johannine reference (vs. 32) to the lifting up of Jesus, we find both the salvific aspect of that lifting up (first reference: iii 14–15) and the aspect of judgment (hinted at in the second reference: viii 28). We have pointed out (p. 146) that the Johannine usage of "being lifted up" was probably suggested by the description of the Suffering Servant in Isa lii 13. Both the themes of death and glory which surround the present reference of Jesus' being lifted up are also found in that Servant hymn. The Greek of Isa lii 13 has the Servant lifted up "and glorified immediately"; and Isa liii describes his death.

This is the only one of the three references to the lifting up of Jesus that does not mention the Son of Man, yet the crowd in vs. 34 seems to imply that Jesus had spoken of the Son of Man. Bultmann, p. 269, would join xii 34 to viii 28, so that the objection of the crowd follows the second of the three references and one that does mention the Son of Man. However, this suggestion is not a major improvement, for viii 28 does not say that the Son of Man *must* be lifted up, as the statement of the crowd in xii 34 would imply. Gourbillon, *art. cit.*, has an even more imaginative solution. He points out that it is the first of the three references (iii 14) that fits best the implications of xii 34, for it does state, "The Son of Man must be lifted up." Gourbillon thinks that the whole passage iii 14–21 would fit very well between xii 31 and 32. Since iii 19–21 has the theme of light and darkness, the introduction of this theme in xii 35–36 would not be so abrupt. Moreover, the judgment theme in iii 17–19 would follow xii 31 very well. If Jesus had just said (iii 14) that the Son of Man must be lifted up, the opening of xii 32 would give a very smooth sequence: "And when I am lifted up. . . ." These are interesting observations, and it is perfectly possible that at one stage in the history of the Johannine tradition these passages were a unit. Once again, though, we must hesitate before the obvious impossibility of conclusive proof.

In vs. 34 the crowd also mentions the Messiah, although Jesus has not used that title. This is another indication that the acclamation of Jesus with palms is to be interpreted as a nationalistic messianic gesture. It is interesting that vs. 34 establishes a relationship between the Messiah and the Son of Man. Elsewhere in John we have seen two different expectations about the Messiah (p. 53): one in terms of a Davidic Messiah born at Bethlehem (vii 42); the other in terms of a hidden Messiah, close to the expectations of a hidden Son of Man in Enoch (vii 27, i 26). Is the crowd identifying the two expectations here, or is it speaking of the hidden Messiah? Indeed, it is even difficult to determine whether the crowd itself is making the juxtaposition of Messiah and Son of Man, or is presupposing that Jesus identifies them. We get a similar juxtaposition on Jesus' lips in the Synoptic scene of the trial before Caiaphas (Mark xiv 61–62) when the high priest asks Jesus if he is the Messiah and Jesus answers in terms of the Son of Man.

It is possible that a discussion like that of vs. 34 would have had meaning to certain groups of Jews during Jesus' lifetime, especially those influenced by the thought of Enoch. But the Fourth Gospel probably has in mind here the Jewish arguments against Jesus at the end of the 1st century. This may be an early formulation of the debate found in Justin *Trypho* xxxii 1 (PG 6:541, 544). There Trypho objects that Jesus cannot have been the Messiah or the Son of Man because he did not establish the great kingdom and eternal rule of which the OT speaks. Justin answers in terms of the exaltation of Jesus in the Father's presence. These are the very themes found in John xii 32–34.

Verses 35–36: The departing presence of the light

Jesus does not answer the crowd's questions directly. Instead of speaking about the Son of Man or the Messiah, he insists on the short duration of his own stay as the light. If this seems to have little relation to the Son of Man, we may remember that ch. ix, which began with Jesus as the light of the world (ix 5), ended with an identification of Jesus as Son of Man (ix 35–37). It is noteworthy too that the Isaian picture of the Suffering Servant, which, as we saw, provided background for the concept of being lifted up in glory, also offers background for the image of Jesus as the light. Isa xlix 5–6 speaks of the servant as the light to the nations, just as John portrays Jesus as the light in the context of the coming of the Greeks.

By introducing the theme of light and darkness, Jesus directs his discussion with the crowd from the intellectual realm to the moral realm, much as he did with the Samaritan woman when she began to speak of the Messiah. The crowd ponders about the nature and identity of the Son of Man; but it is more important that they face up to the judgment that is associated with the Son of Man, the judgment of coming to the light and walking in it lest they be swallowed up in darkness. And this is of immediate import, for they shall be able to come to the light only a little while longer. As we pointed out in the NOTE on viii 12, there are good Qumran parallels for the expression "to walk in light or in darkness" as a metaphor for a good or bad way of life. The expression "sons of light" (36) is one of the standard Qumran descriptions for the community, even as John uses it to describe those who believe in Jesus (also I Thess v 5; Eph v 8). This terminology was particularly apt in Christian circles, where "enlightenment" was a term for Baptism (p. 381).

Thus, Jesus ends his ministry to the Jews on a note of challenge. If the hour has come, this means that it is time for the light to pass from the world. The power of darkness is closing in for the final struggle. The moment of judgment has come. To illustrate dramatically the theme of the passing of the light, Jesus now hides himself. The next time the crowds look upon him, they will look upon a man of suffering (xix 5, 37) whom they have rejected. It is worth noting that the last words of the ministry in Mark xiii 35–37 are also words of urgent appeal: the servants must watch lest the master suddenly come and find them asleep. John emphasizes that the master *has* come, and they have turned away. Jesus' going into hiding in this second ending of the ministry is parallel to his withdrawing beyond the Jordan (x 40) in the first ending of the ministry.

BIBLIOGRAPHY

Dodd, C. H., "Some Johannine 'Herrnworte' with Parallels in the Synoptic Gospels," NTS 2 (1955), especially pp. 78–81 on xii 25. Now in *Tradition*, pp. 338–43.

Gourbillon, J.-G., "La parabole du serpent d'airain," RB 51 (1942), 213–26.

Rasco, A., "Christus, granum frumenti (Jo. 12, 24)," VD 37 (1959), 12–25, 65–77.

van Unnik, W. C., "The Quotation from the Old Testament in John 12:34," NovT 3 (1959), 174–79.

THE BOOK OF SIGNS

Conclusion: Evaluation and Summation of Jesus' Ministry

44. AN EVALUATION OF JESUS' MINISTRY TO HIS OWN PEOPLE
(xii 37–43)

XII 37 Even though Jesus had performed so many of his signs before them, they refused to believe in him. 38 This was to fulfill the word of Isaiah the prophet:

> "Lord, who has believed what we have heard?
> To whom has the might of the Lord been revealed?"

39 The reason they could not believe was that, as Isaiah said elsewhere,

> 40 "He has blinded their eyes
> and numbed their minds,
> for fear they might see with their eyes
> and perceive with their minds
> and so be converted,
> and I shall heal them."

41 Isaiah uttered these words because he had seen his glory, and it was of him that he spoke.

42 Nevertheless, there were many, even among the Sanhedrin, who believed in him. Yet, because of the Pharisees they refused to admit it, or they would have been put out of the synagogue. 43 They preferred by far the praise of men to the glory of God.

NOTES

xii 38. *This was to fulfill.* Literally a *hina* subordinate clause. Grammatically it could be consecutive; yet, as vs. 39 makes clear, the basic thought is not that the unbelief resulted in the fulfillment of the prophecy, but that the prophecy brought about the unbelief. In this mentality where the OT prophecies had to be fulfilled, *hina* clearly has telic force. See NOTE "fulfilled" on xiii 18.

what we have heard. Literally "our report," i.e., the report we have received.

the might. Literally "the arm."

39. *could not believe.* There is a tendency among the Greek patristic commentators to soften this to "would not believe."

40. *numbed.* The verb *pōroun,* often translated "to harden," means "to make

dull or obtuse" (also Mark vi 52). The two Bodmer papyri have increased the evidence for reading *pēroun*, an almost synonymous verb.

minds. Literally "heart." The heart was looked on as the seat of mental, as well as physical, life.

for fear. This is a negative purpose clause (*hina mē*). To soften the harsh impact of God's preventing sight, some commentators have suggested that *hina* is causal here: "because they did not see." However, the existence of causal *hina* in NT Greek is still disputed (ZGB, § 412–14), and to posit it here does not seem to do justice to the force of the passage.

perceive. Noein (LXX *synienai*).

be converted. Strephein (LXX *epistrephein*); this really has the sense of a middle voice: "turn themselves."

I shall heal. The three preceding verbs have been subjunctive, but now the mood shifts to the future indicative (also LXX). See BDF, § 369[3].

41. *because. Hoti* is the best attested reading, but there is considerable support for *hote*, "when." In this instance there would not be much difference in meaning.

his glory . . . of him. Evidently these two pronouns have the same antecedent, and the second one can logically refer only to Jesus. Because of the difficulty of the statement that Isaiah saw Jesus' glory, some Greek witnesses have corrected "his" to "God's."

42. *Sanhedrin.* Literally "authorities"; see iii 1, vii 26, 48.

43. *preferred . . . to.* Literally "loved more than." The comparative particle *ēper*, supported by P[66*] and P[75], occurs in the NT only here, and is probably to be preferred to the reading *hyper* ("over"), despite the relatively strong attestation of the latter. It is not impossible, however, that the latter is a Semitism (*'al*).

the praise of men . . . the glory of God. Doxa is used twice, but with two different connotations (see NOTE on v 41, 44). The *glory* of God was probably suggested by the Isaian scene in vs. 41.

COMMENT

Verses 37–39: The OT citations

At the close of his narrative of the ministry of Jesus, the writer stops to evaluate. The only honest evaluation possible is that expressed in the Prologue (i 11): "To his own he came; yet his own people did not accept him." But why? That this question haunted primitive Christianity we see in Rom ix–xi. The standard NT answer is in terms of OT prophecy, in particular Isa vi 10. God had told Isaiah that his message would fall on deaf ears, and that whatever he did would remain unseen by willfully blind eyes. The NT authors found that this was true, not only in Isaiah's ministry but also in Jesus' ministry, which was the fulfillment of Isaiah's ministry. This explanation seems unsatisfactory to the modern reader who knows that OT prophetic messages were directed primarily to the contemporary situation and not to a distant future. But the explanation must be understood in the hermeneutic mentality of NT times. The concept that people had to disbelieve ("could not believe" in vs. 39) Jesus' word and deed because the OT said they would disbelieve must not be misunderstood on a psychological plane. This is an explanation on the plane of salvific history. It does not destroy human freedom, for vs. 42 makes it quite clear that men were free to accept Jesus. John's summation is not a statement of determinism but an implicit appeal to believe.

In vs. 37 the writer introduces his evaluation by echoing the last part of Deuteronomy (xxix 2–4). There Moses begins his third and final address by reminding the people that, although the Lord had *performed signs before them* in Egypt, the Lord still had not given them the mind to comprehend, or the eyes to see, or the ears to hear. (This primitive thought shows no theoretical awareness of secondary causality or divine permissiveness as regards what is related to salvation. The Lord causes these things directly; and so if they did not see or hear, it was because the Lord had caused them not to see or hear.) In exactly the same way, the Gospel tells us, Jesus had performed signs, and yet they had refused to believe.

The reason for this refusal lies in the Lord's causality, for His words in the OT had to be fulfilled. Both of the texts from Isaiah (liii 1, vi 10) that John cites are quoted elsewhere in the NT, and the writer is almost certainly drawing on stock texts or testimonies used by the Christians to explain and defend Jesus Christ.

The citation of Isa liii 1 in vs. 38 is verbatim the text of LXX. We have seen in our study of xii 20–36 that much of the terminology John uses to describe the hour of Jesus' being lifted up in glory has its background in the Suffering Servant hymns of Deutero-Isaiah. It is interesting, then, that in vs. 38 the writer turns to this same source to explain the failure of the Jewish people to accept Jesus, for Isa liii is the song par excellence of the Servant as rejected and despised. Notice that the passage very nicely covers the whole of Jesus' ministry, both his words ("what we have heard") and his works or signs (what has been effected by the Lord's might or "arm" —this expression is used in Deut v 15 in describing God's agency in the signs of the Exodus).

In vs. 40 John cites Isa vi 10, the classical OT passage used in the NT to explain Israel's failure to believe in Jesus. Paul's last words in Acts (xxviii 26–27) consist of this citation: it is his explanation of why the Jews have not accepted the gospel he preached. (The citation of a similar passage from Isa xxix 10 in Rom xi 8 shows us that Luke in Acts has not misinterpreted Paul's mind.) Isa vi 10 also appears in the Synoptic Gospels (implicitly in Mark iv 12; Luke viii 10; explicitly in Matt xiii 13–15) as an explanation of why the people have not understood the parables of the kingdom. If we recall once again the relation between the kingdom in the Synoptics and the person of Jesus in John, we can see the similarity between the failure to understand the parables of the kingdom and the failure to accept Jesus. It is interesting that, while the Synoptics put the citation of Isa vi 9–10 on Jesus' own lips, John clearly presents it as a Christian explanation of what happened.

Perhaps no other OT citation in John illustrates so well the difficulty of determining whether the source of John's OT citations was MT, LXX, or some other Greek rendering of MT. While the other NT citations of Isa vi 10 are close to LXX, John's form is quite distinct.

> MT: *Make* [imperative] the heart of this people fat, and make their ears heavy, and shut their eyes, for fear that they see with their eyes, and hear with their ears, and understand with their heart, and convert and *be healed.*

> LXX (Matthew, Acts): The heart of this people *has been* rendered dull [passive]; and with their ears they hear only with difficulty; and they have closed the eyes, for fear that they see with the eyes, and hear with the ears, and understand with the heart, and be converted and *I shall heal* them.

> John: *He has* blinded their eyes and numbed their heart, for fear that they see with the eyes, and perceive with the heart, and be converted and *I shall heal* them.

We have italicized some important differences. The rendition in LXX and Matthew has softened the initial imperative of the MT to a less offensive passive, so that it is no longer the prophet who hardens the hearts of the people. Also, in this rendition at the end of the verse, God enters directly to heal the people. In John's rendition it is God who has blinded the eyes of the people—an attribution that must be understood in light of the above-mentioned failure to distinguish secondary causality. Perhaps this emphasis in John is an adaptation of the text to its new context in the Gospel. John omits the phrase "of this people" found both in the MT and LXX, and several verbs used by John are different from those used in LXX and Matthew (see NOTE on vs. 40). More important, at the beginning John does not follow the order of Isaiah (heart, ears, eyes) in listing the organs affected; rather John omits "ears" and speaks of the eyes before the heart (mind). It is not impossible that, as several other times, John is blending OT citations, and that the quotation from Isaiah has been influenced by the quotation from Deut xxix 3–4 which lies behind vs. 37. In Deuteronomy it is God who acts on the heart and the eyes and ears of the people. In the last words of the Isaiah citation, "I shall heal them," John stands with LXX against the MT.

Verse 41: Isaiah's vision of Jesus' glory

If vs. 40 was a citation of Isa vi 10, this next verse recalls Isaiah's initial vision of the Lord upon a throne in vi 1–5. There are two things to note in John's reference. First, John seems to presuppose a text where Isaiah sees God's *glory*, but in both the MT and LXX of Isaiah it is said that Isaiah saw the Lord Himself. This has led many commentators to suggest that John is following the tradition of the Targum (or Aramaic translation) of Isaiah where in vi 1 Isaiah sees "the glory of the Lord" and in vi 5 "the glory of the *shekinah* of the Lord." The possibility of

John's use of Targums has already been discussed in relation to i 51 (p. 90) and vii 38 (p. 322), and the Johannine citation of a Targum for the Isaiah text may have been determined by the frequent stress in this Gospel that no one has ever seen God.

Second, John supposes that it was the glory *of Jesus* that Isaiah saw. This is not unlike the supposition in viii 56 that Abraham saw Jesus' day (see NOTE there). There are several possible ways to interpret this. If we accept the suggestion of a citation of a Targum, then the statement that Isaiah saw the *shekinah* of God may be interpreted in light of the theology of i 14 where Jesus is the *skekinah* of God (p. 33). The belief that Jesus was active in the events of the OT is attested in I Cor x 4, where Jesus is pictured as the rock which gave water to the Israelites in the desert (also Justin *Apol.* i 63 [PG 6:424], where Jesus appears to Moses in the burning bush). In later patristic interpretation Isaiah was thought to have hailed the three divine persons with his "Holy, holy, holy" (Isa vi 3), and Jesus was identified as one of the seraphs who appeared with Yahweh. Another possible interpretation of John xii 41 is that Isaiah looked into the future and saw the life and glory of Jesus. This is certainly the thought found in the vision section of the *Ascension of Isaiah* (this part of the apocryphon is of 2nd-century Christian derivation). Sir xlviii 24–25 says that through his powerful spirit Isaiah foresaw the future and foretold what should be until the end of time.

Verses 42–43: The half-hearted belief of some among the Sanhedrin

If John has interpreted in terms of Isaiah the general failure to believe, a special mention is given to those in the Sanhedrin who believe but will not profess their faith publicly. The writer's disapproval of their behavior is so emphatic that clearly he is thinking of an abuse of his own time. The mention of the synagogue excommunication indicates that vss. 42–43 are directed to Jews at the end of the 1st century who believe in Jesus but are afraid to confess this faith. As for the information that Jesus had followers among the members of the Sanhedrin, John speaks elsewhere of Nicodemus (iii 1, vii 50); all the Gospels mention Joseph of Arimathea, who was a member of the Sanhedrin (Mark xv 43); and Luke xviii 18 mentions a young member of the Sanhedrin. Acts vi 7 tells us that in the early days of the Jerusalem church "a great many of the priests were obedient to the faith" (also Hebrews seems to be addressed to converted priests—see iii 1). This statement in John about authorities who believed in Jesus is only an apparent contradiction of vii 48, where the Pharisees deny that any of the authorities believe in him. In xii 42 the writer makes clear that the Pharisees did not know about these believers.

In the present order of the Gospel where chs. xi–xii seem to have been appended to the public ministry, this evaluation in xii 37–43 constitutes the end of the Book of Signs—a rather pessimistic ending, for the signs of Jesus have not brought many to belief. Yet this evaluation corresponds to the evaluation at the end of the Book of Glory in xx 30–31, where it becomes clear that the signs of Jesus did, after all, accomplish their purpose. If these signs failed to convince the Jews, they are written here in the Gospel to confirm the belief of the Christians and bring life to those who believe.

45. AN UNATTACHED DISCOURSE OF JESUS USED AS
A SUMMARY PROCLAMATION
(xii 44–50)

XII   44 Jesus proclaimed aloud:

"Whoever believes in me
is actually believing, not in me,
but in Him who sent me.
45 And whoever sees me
is seeing Him who sent me.
46 As light have I come into the world
so that no one who believes in me
need remain in darkness.
47 And if anyone listens to my words without keeping them,
it is not I who condemn him;
for I did not come to condemn the world
but to save the world.
48 Whoever rejects me and does not accept my words
already has his judge,
namely, the word that I have spoken—
that is what will condemn him on the last day,
49 because it was not on my own that I spoke.
No, the Father who sent me
has Himself commanded me
what to say and how to speak,
50 and I know that His commandment means eternal life.
So when I speak,
I speak just as the Father told me."

NOTES

xii 45. *sees*. *Theōrein* (see App. I:3), a verb that often implies sight with spiritual depth. Cf. xiv 9: "Whoever has seen [*horan*] me has seen the Father."

47. *listens to my words*. Here *rēma* is the object of the verb "to listen, hear," as also in viii 47. Some ten other times *logos* or *phōnē* ("voice") serve as object.

without keeping them. There is respectable evidence (P⁶⁶ᶜ; Bezae) for omitting the negative. The resultant "and keeps them" gives a laudatory cast to the verse.

48. *rejects.* The verb *athetein* occurs only here in John. It occurs five times in Luke—one-third of its NT occurrences.

accept my words. For a similar expression in the Synoptics see Matt xiii 20.

already has his judge. Literally "has that which [or him who] judges him." We recall the two shades of meaning, "judge, condemn," in the Johannine use of *krinein* (see NOTE on iii 17).

49. *not on my own.* Literally "of [*ek*] myself"; thirteen other times in John the preposition used is *apo*.

I spoke. "I came" is a weakly attested variant. Bultmann, p. 263, thinks that originally the first line of vs. 49 went with the last line of 50, and that everything in between is the evangelist's commentary.

50. *means.* Literally "is."

when I speak. Literally "whatever I speak." Cf. viii 28: "I say only those things that the Father taught me."

COMMENT

The discourse that Jesus gives in these verses is clearly not in its original context; for, since Jesus has gone into hiding (xii 36), this discourse has no audience or setting. One solution, adopted by Bernard and others, has been to transfer vss. 44–50 to a place between xii 36a and 36b. Bultmann sees 44–50 as part of a long discourse on light consisting of viii 12, xii 44–50, viii 21–29, xii 34–36, x 19–21. Needless to say, there is no real proof for these ingenious proposals. Boismard, "Le caractère," points out that this discourse has some peculiarities in style (see NOTES) and suggests that this passage of Johannine material may have had its own history of transmission. The fact that xii 46–48 is very much like iii 16–19 (see above, p. 147) makes it quite plausible that, in part, xii 44–50 is a variant of material found elsewhere in John but preserved by a different disciple. In the final redaction of the Gospel this independent discourse was probably added where it would cause the least disarrangement (we came to a similar solution for iii 31–36). Actually, the redactor's judgment was a good one, for this little discourse, which now comes at the end of the Book of Signs, nicely summarizes Jesus' message.

The clauses in vss. 44 and 45 form a very neat pair: *belief* in Jesus is belief in Him who sent Jesus; *seeing* Jesus is seeing Him who sent Jesus. We shall find still a third statement to this effect in xiii 20 (a verse strangely out of place): "Whoever receives anyone I shall send receives me; and *whoever receives [lambanein] me receives Him who sent me.*" There is little difference in these three statements, since believing in, seeing, and receiving Jesus are all basically the same action. There is still another form of the statement in Matt x 40: "Whoever receives you receives me; and whoever receives [*dechesthai*] me receives Him who sent [*apostellein*—John uses *pempein*] me." Since this Matthean parallel is closest to John xiii 20, we shall reserve detailed comment until there (The Anchor Bible, vol. 29A); but we should remember that we have already seen that Matt x 38–39 is parallel to John xii 25–26.

Having stressed his close relationship to the Father, Jesus turns in vss. 46 ff. to his mission among men. Much of what we have said in reference to the closely parallel verses in iii 16–19 is applicable here. If 46 holds out the offer of light to those who believe in Jesus, 47–48 apply to those who do not keep or accept his words and thus reject him. The condemnation in 47 of those who listen to Jesus' words (*akouein* with the genitive, which usually implies understanding) and still do not keep them (*phylassein*) resembles the criticism in Matt vii 26 of "everyone who hears [*akouein* with the accusative] these words of mine and does not *do* them." See also James i 22. The Johannine "keep" is not really different from the Matthean "do," since both verbs mean observance (cf. the use of *phylassein* in Mark x 20 for observing the Ten Commandments; Heb. *šmr* has the same range of meaning). If there is a Matthean parallel for the first part of John xii 47, there is a parallel for the second part of 47 in some manuscripts of Luke ix 56, "For the Son of Man did not come to destroy the souls of men but to save them."

We pointed out in the NOTE the Lucan character of the verb "to reject" which appears in vs. 48, for example, Luke x 16, "Whoever rejects me rejects Him who sent me." This is the Lucan equivalent of Matt x 40, cited above as a parallel to John xii 44–45. Thus, in this typically Johannine discourse there are many individual sayings with Synoptic parallels. Another feature of vs. 48 is that it has elements of both realized and final eschatology. The realized eschatology appears in the first part of the verse which states that whoever rejects Jesus and does not accept his words is judged by the word that Jesus has spoken. This forms an interesting contrast with the final eschatology of what is said in Mark viii 38 (Luke ix 26): "Whoever is ashamed of me and of my words . . . of him the Son of Man will also be ashamed when he comes in the glory of his Father with the holy angels." But final eschatology appears in John xii 48 in the reference to the last day in the last line of the verse (which Bultmann, p. 262[7], naturally attributes to the Ecclesiastical Redactor). It should be noted that the last part of vs. 48 is offered as an explanation of the first part—an indication that the sharp contradiction drawn today between realized and final eschatology was not so apparent in NT times.

In vss. 48 ff. we have many echoes of Deuteronomy, as has been pointed out by M. J. O'Connell, "The Concept of Commandment in the Old Testament," TS 21 (1960), 352. (We also saw similarities to Deuteronomy in xii 37.) The thought that God will punish the failure of His people to hear the words of His messenger is, of course, an ancient one. But we call particular attention to Deut xviii 18–19 where God speaks of the Prophet-like-Moses: "I shall put *my words* in his mouth, and he will speak to them all that *I command him*. And *whoever does not hear the words* which the prophet will speak in my name, I shall take vengeance on him." We may note several points of comparison between John and Deuteronomy, following Boismard, "Les citations." In vss. 47–48 John uses the verbs "to listen to" and "to accept" to describe the reaction that the hearers should have to Jesus' words. The MT of Deuteronomy has the verb "to hear, listen to," while the Aramaic Targum (pseudo-Jonathan) has the verb *qᵉbal*, which means both "to accept" and "to hear." (Boismard would use this as another proof that John cites Targums, but the evidence here is tenuous.) In vss. 47–48 John uses *rēma* for "word" (see NOTE) as does LXX of Deuteronomy. The passage in Deuteronomy also seems to be reflected in vss. 49–50. God will put His words in the mouth of the Prophet-like-Moses; similarly Jesus does not speak on his own but only what the Father has commanded him to speak. Again, the theme of *command* runs through both passages. In the MT of Deuteronomy it is God who takes vengeance on the man who refuses to hear; in the Targums (Neofiti I, Pseudo-Jonathan) it is God's *memra* or word that takes vengeance. The latter offers a parallel to John (48) where the word that Jesus has spoken is the agent of condemnation.

Not all the parallels to Deuteronomy are centered on Deut xviii 18–19. Indeed, this same thought that the words of Jesus will condemn those who refuse to accept them is quite like passages in Deuteronomy (xxxi 19, 26) where Moses says that his words and laws will be a witness against the people if they do evil. This is especially interesting if we remember John v 45, which said that Moses would accuse the Jews of not believing in Jesus.

In John xii 49–50 the stress on the commandment that Jesus has received from the Father becomes very strong. This commandment (see App. I:5) affects not only what Jesus has spoken (vs. 49) but also his actions, for x 18 spoke of a command from the Father in relation to Jesus' death and resurrection. Of course, this command is not imposed on Jesus from without; it is but another facet of the oft-repeated theme that Jesus and the Father have the same will (v 30, vi 38). And this commandment that Jesus has received from the Father affects men. As xii 50 makes clear, it involves eternal life for men; and this is because the words and deeds of Jesus that the commandment directs are themselves the source of eternal life (vi 68, x 10). Here too we are in the atmosphere of Deuteronomy, where "commandment" sets the pattern by which Israel is to fulfill its vocation as the holy people of God. Deut xxxii 46–47 says that the commandment of God given through Moses is a principle of life for the people; man lives by every word that proceeds from the mouth of God (Deut viii 3). We also find an echo of the relation of divine commandment to life in the Synoptics. In Luke x 25–28 when a scribe asks Jesus what he must do to inherit eternal life, he is told that if he keeps the command of God written in the Law he will live.

In John, however, it is very clear that the command of God that means eternal life is more than any OT commandment. It is the word of God spoken through Jesus that now sums up the covenant obligations of the believer. In v 39 Jesus had criticized the inadequateness of searching the OT Scriptures in which the Jews thought they had eternal life. Now Jesus spells out in a positive manner that it is in his word that men do have eternal life. And so, in its own way, this short discourse of Jesus, placed as a summary statement at the end of the public ministry, is the Christian form of what Moses proclaimed "when he had finished speaking all these words to Israel" (Deut xxxii 45–47):

Take to heart all the words which I have now given you . . .
that your children may be careful to do all the words of this Law;
for this is no trivial matter for you,
but it means your very life.

BIBLIOGRAPHY

Boismard, M.-E., "Le caractère adventice de Jo., XII, 45–50," SacPag, II, pp. 188–92.
——"Les citations targumiques dans le quatrième évangile," RB 66 (1959), especially pp. 376–78 on xii 48–49.

APPENDIXES

APPENDIX I: JOHANNINE VOCABULARY

It is not our purpose here to cover all the words important for Johannine thought, nor to treat in depth the theological implications of Johannine vocabulary. Such an investigation would constitute a book in itself. Rather, we have selected a few of the more crucial words whose peculiar Johannine import must be understood if one is to understand John, and we have discussed them very briefly to acquaint the reader with the problems involved. In other words, this appendix is an introduction to Johannine vocabulary and its theological ramifications. For further reading, consult works like: E. A. Abbott, *Johannine Vocabulary* (London: Black, 1905), and E. K. Lee, *The Religious Thought of St. John* (London: SPCK, 1950).

The following words are treated in this appendix:

(1) *agapē, agapan; philein*="love" ("beloved," "friend")
(2) *alētheia, alēthēs, alēthinos*="truth," "true," "real" ("verified," "valid")
(3) *blepein; theasthai; theōrein; idein; horan*="see" ("catch sight of," "look at")
(4) *doxa*="glory," "honor"
(5) *entolē*="command," "commandment"
(6) *zōē*=(eternal) "life"
(7) *kosmos*="world"
(8) *menein*="remain," "abide," "stay," "dwell on"
(9) *pisteuein*="believe" ("have faith," "come to faith," "put faith")—with note on *eidenai* and *ginōskein*="know," "realize"
(10) *phōs; skotia*="light"; "darkness"
(11) *hōra*="hour"

(1) *agapē, agapan; philein*="love" ("beloved," "friend")

FREQUENCY OF OCCURRENCE

	Synoptic	John	I II III John	Rev	Total Johannine	Total NT
agapan	26	36	31	4	71	141
agapē	2	7	21	2	30	116
philein	8	13		2	15	25

It is quite obvious that Johannine usage prefers the use of verbs for the concept of "love," and, in particular, prefers *agapan* to *philein*. The ratio of the use in the Gospel of the verb *agapan* to the noun *agapē* is especially interesting when contrasted with Pauline usage which gives more stress to the noun (75 times to 33 for the verb). John's concept of love seems to give more stress to the active element.

Are *agapan* and *philein* synonymous? In his famous *Synonyms of the New Testament*, Trench drew a distinction between the two. *Agapan* (=*diligere* in the Vulg.) means strong love, but love that is reverential and reasoned; *philein* (=*amare* in the Vulg.) refers to stronger and more intimate love. Thus, according to Trench, in John xxi 15–17 Jesus asks Peter twice, "Do you love [*agapan*] me?" But Peter in his response keeps insisting that he loves (*philein*) Jesus more intimately. When Jesus asks Peter for the third time, "Do you love [*philein*] me?", he is conceding Peter's claim of passionate affection. Westcott, however, although he also distinguishes the two verbs, interprets the scene in another way. In his view, Peter answers in terms of *philein* because he does not venture to claim that he has attained to the higher love of *agapan*. Evans, *art. cit.*, thinks that the verb *agapan* implies a certain superiority, for it connotes the satisfaction of a superior with an inferior. In his view, Peter's refusal to use *agapan* is an expression of humility. (Naturally, since the differentiation is in the Greek, these writers are really discussing the mentality of the author rather than that of the historical figures in the scene.) Thus, even those who distinguish the two verbs are not in agreement on which one expresses the higher form of love.

More emphasis has been placed in recent years on *agapan*, since Anders Nygren wrote his masterful *Agapē and Eros*. Nygren exalts *agapē* as the unique love made possible through Jesus—a spontaneous, unmerited, creative love, opening the way to fellowship with God and flowing from God to the Christian and from the Christian to his neighbor. Spicq, *art. cit.*, thinks of Johannine *agapan*-*agapē* as representing an outgoing, effect-producing, gift-giving love. It is a love that is restless until it shows itself, as in the statement, "God loved [*agapan*] the world so much that He gave the only Son" (John iii 16; I John iv 9). And in Jesus this love pressed on to find its culminating effectiveness in dying and rising for men: "He now showed his love for them to the very end" (John xiii 1). It is a love even to the point of death (xv 13). Thus God's whole saving relationship to men can be expressed by the statement, "God is love" (I John iv 8, 16). The ideal Christian is presented in terms of love as the Beloved Disciple.

Theories like that of Spicq are very attractive; but one must recognize that a careful study of the Johannine uses of *agapan* and *philein* shows that the verbs are often used interchangeably, so that scholars like Bernard, Bultmann, and Barrett are not at all convinced that the verbs are not synonymous. (We may add also that LXX uses both verbs to translate Heb. '*āhēb*.) We may cite the following examples of interchangeability:

- the Father loves the Son: *agapan* in iii 35; *philein* in v 20.
- the Father loves the disciples because they love Jesus: *agapan* twice in xiv 23; *philein* twice in xvi 27.
- Jesus loves Lazarus: *agapan* in xi 5; *philein* in xi 3.
- there is a special disciple whom Jesus loves: *agapan* in xiii 23; *philein* in xx 2.
- Christians are referred to as *agapētoi*, "beloved," in III John 2, 5, 11; they are called *philoi*, "friends," in III John 15 (twice).

It is not impossible that the variation in these examples may sometimes represent different strains in Johannine material or different stages in Johannine editorship. But certainly there does not seem to be any significant difference in meaning. Bernard, II, pp. 702–4, examines John xxi 15–17 and finds none of the interplay that Trench finds. One should also note that *agapan* need not refer to exalted love, for it can be used to describe a preference for darkness (John iii 19), and a preference for human praise (xii 43). *Philein*, in similar manner, is used for the selfish love of one's own life (xii 25) and for the world's love of its own (xv 19). Thus, we must be very careful about sweeping generalizations concerning the usage and the difference of these verbs in John. The fact that there was so much synonymous parallelism in Hebrew poetry seems to have created almost a predisposition for employing interchangeable synonyms.

BIBLIOGRAPHY

Barrosse, T., "The Relationship of Love to Faith in St. John," TS 18 (1957), 538–59.

Cerfaux, L., "La charité fraternelle et le retour du Christ (Jo., xiii 33–38)," ETL 24 (1948), 321–32. RecLC, II, pp. 27–40.

Evans, T. E., "The Verb 'agapan' in the Fourth Gospel," SFG, pp. 64–71.

Spicq, C., "Notes d'exégèse johannique. La charité est amour manifeste," RB 65 (1958), 358–70.

————Agapē (Paris: Gabalda, 1959), especially III, pp. 111–357 on the Johannine writings.

Šuštar, A., "De caritate apud Joannem," VD 28 (1950), 110–19, 129–40, 193–213, 257–70, 321–40.

(2) *alētheia, alēthēs, alēthinos*="truth," "true," "real" ("verified," "valid")

FREQUENCY OF OCCURRENCE

	Synoptic	I II III	Total	Total
	Synoptic	John	John	Rev	Johannine	NT
alētheia	7	25	20		45	109
alēthēs	2	14	3		17	26
alēthinos	1	9	4	10	23	28

Quite obviously these are favorite Johannine terms, and the adjectives are almost proper to John.

Bultmann, TWNTE, I, pp. 232 ff., and Dodd, *Interpretation*, pp. 170 ff., distinguish carefully between a Hebrew concept of truth and a Greek concept. In the Hebrew OT *'emet* is related to the root *'mn*, "to be firm, solid"; and thus *'emet* is the essential solidity of a thing, or that which makes it trustworthy and reliable. God is absolutely true in this sense of being worthy of confidence and of being faithful to His promises. Words are true if they are solidly founded. A man's life is true if it is faithful to God's ways. Thus, there is a moral element in the Hebrew concept of "truth." The Gr. *alētheia* has the basic meaning of non-concealment; it describes what is unveiled. Thus, truth is a fact or a state of affairs insofar as it is seen or expressed; and for the Greek truth and reality are closely related. In particular, in a Platonic system of thought, "truth" describes the world of ultimate reality in contrast with the world of shadows. In Philo the term is related to gnosis. The Greek concept, then, is intellectual rather than moral. Although LXX uses *alētheia* to translate *'emet*, sometimes the translators saw fit to employ *pistis*, "faith," "fidelity," as being closer to the meaning of *'emet*.

Both Dodd and Bultmann maintain that the Johannine use of "truth" is closer to the Greek idea. Bultmann, TWNTE, I, p. 245, says that in John *alētheia* denotes "divine reality" and this can be related to Greek dualism. But since this divine reality is revealed to men and offers the possibility of life, the Johannine use of "truth" is closest to the Gnostic redeemer myth. Dodd, p. 177, says: "The use of the term *alētheia* in this Gospel rests upon common Hellenistic usage in which it hovers between the meanings of 'reality,' or 'the ultimately real,' and 'knowledge of the real.'"

In evaluating this claim, we must note that all recognize that some passages in John reflect Hebrew usage. In the NOTE on i 14 we saw that *charis* and *alētheia* echo the OT phrase involving *ḥesed* and *'emet*. Expressions like "act in truth" (see NOTE on iii 21; also I John i 6) and "walk in truth" (II John 4; III John 3) reflect Hebrew usage. Dodd (pp. 174–75) himself points out OT parallels for John iv 23–24 and xvii 17. The Semitic background has been greatly enlarged by the Qumran discoveries; and as we shall see in App. V (in vol. 29A), these scrolls give us the first extra-Johannine examples of "the spirit of truth" (John xiv 17, xv 26, xvi 13; see COMMENT on iv 24).

Making allowance for these passages, we must now ask whether the most characteristic Johannine use of *alētheia* for heavenly reality is a reflection of direct Hellenistic influence. De la Potterie, "L'arrière-fond," has argued impressively against the thesis of Dodd and Bultmann. He points out that, while in the apocalyptic and sapiential literature of the OT "truth" often refers to simplicity of heart and correct moral behavior, "truth" also serves as a synonym of *wisdom*. Prov xxiii 23 puts the command to buy truth in parallelism with the command to buy wisdom; the sage in Sir iv 28 tells his disciples to strive even to the death for truth. Moreover, "truth" is associated with "mystery" or God's hidden plan of salvation, so that to know the truth is to know the plans of God (Wis vi 22). The "book of truth" in Dan x 21 is a book in which are inscribed the designs of God for the times of salvation. Wis iii 9 promises those who trust in Yahweh an understanding of truth. At Qumran too, besides having a moral tone, "truth" is connected with mysteries. "The mystery [*swd*] of truth" appears (1QH i 26–27, x 4–5, xi 4) as does "the mysteries [*rzy*] of His Wisdom" (1QpHab vii 8). The Qumran psalmist (1QH vii 26–27) thanks God because, "You have given me an understanding of your truth and have made me know your marvelous mysteries." The equation of truth with wisdom and mysteries means that in the Semitic background of the NT there is a strain where truth refers to heavenly reality as does wisdom. We need not go beyond this Semitic background to find truth used in reference to God's plan of salvation which is revealed to men.

Thus, De la Potterie thinks that many of the Johannine passages which Dodd and Bultmann would trace to a Greek or Gnostic background are really the heir of the apocalyptic and sapiential association of truth with wisdom and mysteries. For instance, John xvii 17 says, "Your word is truth"; the expression "word of truth" occurs in OT sapiential passages, e.g., Ps cxix 43; Eccles xii 10. In Johannine usage truth is not seen by contemplation as in Hellenistic usage, but is heard (John viii 40). In the OT Wisdom speaks to men, and either God or the angels tell men mysteries, so that men hear the truth.

Blank, *art. cit.*, maintains that the essential aspect of truth in John is that it is associated with the revealer. The statement that Jesus is the truth (xiv 6) may well be a reflection of the theme that Jesus is incarnate Wisdom (Introduction, VIII:D). Furthermore, if we remember that in Pauline thought Jesus is the expression of the mystery, i.e., God's mysterious plan of salvation (Col i 27; Eph iii 4), the Johannine identification of Jesus as the truth may reflect a heritage that joins mystery and truth. In general, then, we think that De la Potterie's theory merits consideration. It fits very well with our thesis that the primary influence on John was Judaism, and not Gnosticism nor Hellenistic thought (Introduction, IV).

We must also comment briefly on the Johannine use of the two adjectives *alēthēs* and *alēthinos*. *Alēthinos* implies exclusivity in the sense of "the only real," as compared with the putative or would-be. It is used in a contrast between the heavenly and the earthly, or between the NT reality and the OT type. Thus, in i 9 Jesus is the real light while John the Baptist is not. In vi 32 Jesus' revelation is the real bread from heaven when contrasted with the manna in the desert which the crowds think was bread from heaven. In xv 1 Jesus, and not the Israel of the OT, is the real vine.

Alēthēs means "true, despite appearances," and does not necessarily imply a contrast with something putative. Thus, in vi 55, despite appearances, Jesus' flesh is truly food. In the sense of "truthful," "verified," *alēthēs* is applied to testimony which contains statements difficult to believe (x 41, xix 35, xxi 24). In v 32 and viii 14 we are told that Jesus' testimony is true, despite the circumstance that he is his own witness.

BIBLIOGRAPHY

Blank, J., "Der johanneische Wahrheits-Begriff," BZ 7 (1963), 164–73.
de la Potterie, I., "L'arrière-fond du thème johannique de vérité," StEv, I, pp. 277–94.
————"La verità in S. Giovanni," RivBib 11 (1963), 3–24.

(3) *blepein; theasthai; theōrein; idein; horan*="see"
("catch sight of," "look at," "notice," "observe")

There are forms from five verbs used in John to express sight, but it is difficult to decide how many of these forms represent distinct verbs in the evangelist's mind. *Blepein* is used only in the present and imperfect; *horan* is used only in the future and the perfect; *idein* (*eidon*) is used only in the aorist. Can these three verbs be thought of as supplying different tense expressions of the one verbal concept? Most authors recognize that at least *horan* and *idein* must be treated together.

FREQUENCY OF OCCURRENCE

	John	I II III John	Rev	Total NT
blepein	17	1	13	
theasthai	6	3		22
theōrein	24	1	2	58
idein (*eidon*)	36	3	56	
horan	31	8	7	114

Only with the verbs indicated does Johannine usage represent an important percentage of NT usage.

We have made no attempt in the translation to find a different English word to correspond to each of these Greek verbs. However, Phillips, *art. cit.*, following Abbott, *Vocabulary*, § 1597–1611, thinks that a rather consistent shade of meaning can be established for each verb. Beginning from the most material form of sight and progressing to the highest form of insight, he would arrange the Greek verbs thus: *blepein, theōrein, horan* (*idein*), *theasthai;* the last verb would be followed by *pisteuein*, "to believe," a verb which describes the full appreciation of the real, heavenly truth. Let us discuss the meaning suggested for each verb:

(a) *blepein*. Both Abbott and Phillips characterize this as the verb of material sight or ocular vision. It is used in ch. ix to describe the sight the blind man regained. In xiii 2 the disciples *look at* one another in puzzlement; in xx 1 Mary *sees* that the stone has been moved away from the tomb (also xxi 9). Thus, in many instances *blepein* has no special significance.

However, in ix 39 *blepein* does take on a spiritual dimension: Jesus came into the world for judgment, "that those who do not see may be able to see." Here the Gospel is speaking of spiritual insight; yet the verb may have been chosen by way of contrast with its use for physical sight throughout the rest of the chapter. In v 19 *blepein* is used for a very exalted form of sight, namely, the Son's seeing what the Father is doing. Thus, there are exceptions to Phillips' thesis that *blepein* is the lowest verb on the scale of sight.

(*b*) *theōrein*. According to Phillips and Abbott, this means to look at with concentration, to behold. It implies more expenditure of time than *blepein*. This greater intensity of sight carries with it a certain depth of understanding, but not to any great degree. This interpretation of *theōrein* does seem valid for a number of instances where the verb is used to describe the seeing of signs—a sight which leads to the acceptance of Jesus as a wonder-worker or a marvelous man, but which does not constitute full faith. (See App. III.) Jesus is obviously not satisfied with the faith that springs from seeing (*theōrein*) in ii 23, iv 19, and vi 2. It is clear in vi 19 that seeing Jesus on the water does not lead to real understanding.

Yet there are other instances where *theōrein* seems to represent the deepest and most perceptive sight. This verb is used in vi 40, which promises eternal life to everyone who looks upon the Son and believes in him. In xvii 24 it is used for the full sight of Jesus' glory, presumably in heaven.

In still other instances *theōrein* seems to mean no more than physical sight, much in the manner of *blepein*. In xx 12 Mary observes the two angels at the tomb, and in xx 14 she sees Jesus standing there—in neither instance is there any spiritual insight. That the world cannot see the Paraclete (xiv 17) is an inability which stems partially from the physical invisibility of the Spirit. See also I John iii 17.

(*c*) *horan*, together with *idein*. It has been suggested that these verbs describe sight accompanied by real understanding. Phillips suggests the translation "perceive," for intuitive intelligence is involved. It is claimed that these verbs are used for seeing the resurrected Jesus where real faith is the result (xx 8, 25). An example is the statement at the Last Supper (xvi 16): "There is just a little while before you lose sight of me [*theōrein*=physical sight], and again a little while before you see me [*horan*, i.e., with the eyes of faith after the resurrection]." Other good examples of perceptive sight are i 50, 51, iii 11, 32, xi 40, xiv 7, 9, xix 35, 37, xx 29. At first impression another example might be i 34 which uses *horan* to describe how John the Baptist saw the Spirit descend upon Jesus, but almost the same statement is found in i 32, which uses *theasthai*. Are not these verbs just variants in different redactions of the same scene?

Moreover, there are clear instances where *horan* is used for sight without any real perception. In iv 45 it is used for seeing signs and recognizing Jesus as a wonder-worker (=*theōrein*). In vi 36 still less perception is indicated. *Idein* (*eidon*) is used for merely physical sight in i 39, v 6, vi 22, 24, vii 52, xii 9; I John v 16; III John 14. It is used for an inadequate sight of signs (=*theōrein*) in iv 48, vi 14, 30.

(*d*) *theasthai*. The root meaning of this verb suggests connection with the theater, and so Abbott, *Vocabulary*, § 1604, would translate it as "contemplate." Phillips thinks that it means to look at some dramatic spectacle and in a measure to become a part of it. This meaning may hold true in i 14, "We have seen his glory," and perhaps in iv 35, "Look at the fields; they are ripe for the harvest." In I John i 1 there does seem to be a progression from *horan* to *theasthai*: "Something we have seen [*horan*] with our own eyes, something we have actually looked at [*theasthai*]."

Yet, in other instances like i 38 and vi 5, *theasthai* seems to refer to mere physical sight. In xi 45 *theasthai* is used for seeing a sign and coming to (seemingly) adequate faith (=*horan*); and as we pointed out above under (*c*), *horan* and *theasthai* in i 34 and i 32 respectively seem to be interchangeable. The same interchangeability is found in the statement that no one has seen God in John i 18 and I John iv 12.

By way of conclusion, we may say that there certainly are different types of sight in John. At most there may be a tendency to use one verb rather than another for a specific form of sight, but the consistency is not remarkable. Those scholars who think that the verbs are synonymous have almost as many texts to prove their point as do the scholars who would attribute specific meanings to the verbs.

BIBLIOGRAPHY (see also under *pisteuein*)

Phillips, G. L., "Faith and Vision in the Fourth Gospel," SFG, pp. 83–96.

(4) *doxa*="glory," "honor"

FREQUENCY OF OCCURRRENCE

	Synoptics	I John	II III John	Rev	Total Johannine	Total NT
doxa	23	18		17	35	165

Of the Synoptic occurrences, 13 are in Luke; so among the Gospels Luke and John share a predilection for this word. In Johannine use there is a *doxa*, "praise," "honor," that can be gained on a purely natural level, but Jesus despises this (v 41, vii 18). The only *doxa* that is worth while is that which is given to God (vii 18, xii 43). And this *doxa* or praise that men give to God is only a recognition of the *doxa* or glory that God possesses.

The concept of the glory of God in OT thought offers important background for Johannine use. In the OT there are two important elements in the understanding of the glory of God: it is a *visible* manifestation of His majesty in *acts of power*. While God is invisible, from time to time He manifests Himself to men by a striking action, and this is His *kābōd* or glory. Sometimes the action is in the realm of nature, e.g., a thunderstorm. Sometimes it takes place in history. In Exod xvi 7–10 Moses promises the people: "In the morning you shall see the glory of God." He is referring to the miracle of the manna to be performed by God. God's glory is in the cloud whereby His presence becomes visible to the Israelites in their desert wanderings (Exod xvi 10), and also in the fire (Exod xxiv 17).

Since Jesus is the incarnate Word of God, he is an embodiment of divine glory (i 14). The two elements of *kābōd* are present in him. He represents the visible divine presence exercising itself in mighty acts. More than the Synoptics, John insists that this *doxa* was visible during the ministry and not only after the resurrection. It is true that John does not describe the Transfiguration which for the Synoptics is really the only manifestation of glory during the public ministry (Luke ix 32). Yet John does stress that the divine *doxa* shone through Jesus' miraculous signs (ii 11, xi 40, xvii 4).

The whole NT agrees that the resurrected Jesus was the vehicle of *doxa* because the resurrection was the mighty act of God par excellence. Since John conceives of passion, death, and resurrection as the one "hour," John sees the theme of glory throughout the whole hour. In fact, the hour is the time for the Son of Man to be glorified (xii 23, 28, xiii 32, xvii 1). Jesus prays in the midst of the hour: "So now glorify me, Father, in your presence with that glory which I had with you before the world existed" (xvii 5).

(5) *entolē*="command," "commandment"

FREQUENCY OF OCCURRENCE

	Synoptics	I John	II John	III Rev	Total Johannine	Total NT
entolē	16	11	18	2	31	68

The related verb *entellesthai* occurs three times in John.

For Paul *entolē* is the characteristic mark of the Mosaic Law, as we see in Rom vii. In vii 8 Paul says that sin found an opportunity in the *entolē*. Yet both Paul (Rom xiii 9–10) and the Synoptics (Matt xxii 36–40) recognize that Jesus, without dispensing from the essential commandments of the Old Law, subsumed them under an *entolē* or commandment of love.

Five times (4 singular; 1 plural) John uses *entolē* in reference to the Father's command to Jesus. Another five times (2 singular; 3 plural) *entolē* pertains to Jesus' command to the disciples. The same variation is found with the verb *entellesthai;* compare xiv 31 with xv 14, 17. The frequency of the term *entolē* in the Last Discourse may be accounted for by the recognition that this is the portion of the Gospel where Jesus speaks intimately with his disciples. Moreover, the Last Discourse is a leave-taking much like the final patriarchal speeches in the Pentateuch which also involve last commands (see too Matt xxviii 20).

Let us first discuss the use of *entolē* for the Father's command to Jesus. In xii 49–50 the Father has commanded Jesus what to say and how to speak; in xiv 31 the Father has commanded Jesus what to do, especially in face of his approaching death struggle with the Prince of this world; in x 18 the command that Jesus has received from the Father covers his laying down his life and his taking it up again. Thus, Jesus' whole ministry comes under the Father's command—his words; his deeds; and especially that most important of his deeds, his passion, death, and resurrection. And because Jesus has fulfilled and lived out this command, he remains in the Father's love (x 17). It is obvious, then, that the command given to Jesus concerns his relations to men, i.e., his mission. And this command has an effect on men: "I know that His commandment means eternal life" (xii 50).

We turn now to the use of *entolē* for Jesus' command to his disciples. Just as Jesus' own life lay under the Father's command, a command given in love and lived out in loving acceptance, so also the believer who comes to Jesus and would be his disciple must live his life under Jesus' commandment. Once again the obligation of this commandment is one of love, patterned on the love that binds Father and Son: "You will remain in my love if you keep my commandments, just as I have kept my Father's commandments and I remain in His love" (xv 10). Indeed, the substance of the command that Jesus gives finds its expression in the love of his followers, one for the other (xiii 34, xv 12, 17). What is new about this commandment is neither the substance of it nor the intensity demanded, but rather its christological motivation which raises it to a way of life patterned on Jesus' life. The command that Jesus received from the Father specifically touched on his death for men; the love commanded among Christians must be modeled on this example (xv 12–13). And the *entolē* is not only modeled on Jesus' example, but is even undertaken in a spirit of love for him (xiv 15, 21).

How are we to interpret this command to love one another? Does it mean that there is no other obligation in the Christian life, or does it mean that the many moral obligations of the Christian life are to be imbued with love as their inspiration and unifying factor (as in Matt xix 18–19)? Perhaps the variation between plural and singular in the use of *entolē* indicates that the latter is closer to Jesus' intent. (This variation will have to be discussed in more detail in commenting on I John in The Anchor Bible, vol. 30.) The commands (plural in xv 10) that Jesus received from the Father concerned his whole way of life. So also the commandments given by Jesus are a way of life wherein the essential of the commandment is the spirit of love that radiates into that life. In stressing the relation between commandment and way of life, we may note that xiv 21 and 23 clearly equate keeping Jesus' commandments and keeping his word. (*Tērein*, "keep," governs *entolas* [always plural] 9 times in the Johannine writings, while it governs *logon* or *logous*, "word[s]," 8 times.) If the command that covers Jesus' ministry means eternal life for men (xii 50), so also the words that he speaks to men mean life for them (vi 63). It is interesting that the same verb *didonai*, "give," which is constantly used of the salvific gifts in the Gospel (*living water; bread of life; God's word*), is used in xiii 34 of Jesus' giving the command to his disciples. In summation, we may say that in John Jesus' *entolē* to his disciples covers a way of life that leads to man's salvation; it is lovingly given, accepted in love, and lived in love in imitation of Jesus.

In an article in CBQ 25 (1963), 77–87, entitled "The Ancient Near Eastern Background of the Love of God in Deuteronomy," W. L. Moran has shown that love is closely related to the covenant concept in Deuteronomy. In a similar vein, in his article, "The Concept of Commandment in the Old Testament," TS 21 (1960), 351–403, an article intended as a prolegomenon to a study of *entolē* in John, M. J. O'Connell has pointed out how deeply the Johannine concept of commandment is rooted in the OT, especially in Deuteronomy, which is Moses' "Last Discourse" to his people. For the author of Deuteronomy, writes O'Connell (p. 364), "The *entolē* expresses the fact that the life-giving will of the personal God lays claim to the whole of man's being, a claim which man is to affirm for himself with inward love and reverence as well as with outward conformity to God's precepts. The *entolē* has for its inmost significance to unite man to God, to make him 'follow Yahweh.'" As O'Connell points out, the OT offers remarkable background for the Johannine concepts of the *entolē* as a revelation of what God is, of the intimate association of *entolē* and love, and of the identification of *entolē* with words given by God to be spoken to others.

(6) *zōē*="life" ("eternal life")

FREQUENCY OF OCCURRENCE

	Synoptics	I John	II III John	Rev	Total Johannine	Total NT
zōē	16	36	13	17	66	135

Obviously "life" is a favorite Johannine theological word; and, as Filson, *art. cit.*, has pointed out, the Fourth Gospel may be called the Gospel of life, for xx 31 enunciates as the chief purpose for which the Gospel was written: "that you may have life in his name." In particular, the expression *zōē aiōnios,* "eternal life," occurs seventeen times in John and six times in I John. (*Aiōn,* "age," "aeon," "segment of time," is the Greek rendering of Heb. *'ōlām,* a period of time without visible beginning or end.)

Even without the qualifying adjective *aiōnios, zōē* in John does not refer to natural life. Rather *psyche* is used for that life to which death is a terminus (xiii 37, xv 13). Yet, of course, it is natural life which must have originally suggested the use of "life" as a symbol for a special gift of God. Natural life is man's most treasured possession; "life" is therefore a good symbol to indicate the most precious of divine gifts lying beyond man's reach. Since man thinks analogically of God, it was appropriate to speak of God's "life" on the analogy of man's life; and God's greatest act of friendship to man was described in terms of man's receiving a share in God's life. The relation of this symbolism to that of becoming God's children is obvious.

Bultmann, TWNTE, II, pp. 870–72, sees strong Gnostic influence on the Johannine concept of life. Dodd, *Interpretation,* pp. 144–50, gives OT and rabbinic parallels for John, but also cites Platonic and Hermetic parallels as examples of the world of Greek philosophic thought into which John has brought the Semitic concept of eternal life. Feuillet, *art. cit.,* insists more strongly on the differences between John's concept of life and that found in Plato and the *Hermetica.* These views reflect different theories of Johannine origins as discussed in Introduction, IV.

The Hebrew expression which underlies the Gr. *zōē aiōnios* occurs once in the protocanonical OT, at Dan xii 2 where it is said that the just who are dead awake to *hayyē 'ōlām,* "the life of the eternal age." The rarity of the expression is explained by the fact that only in the very late era of OT thought is there explicit attestation of a belief in a life that transcends death (although the roots of the concept in Israelite theology may be older than hitherto believed). This was expressed in two ways in the books of the 2nd and 1st centuries B.C.: in Daniel and II Macc xii 43–44 (and in Pharisaic theology) it was expressed in terms of the resurrection from the dead; in Wis iii 2–4, v 15 it was expressed in terms of the immortality of the soul after physical death.

What was the attitude at Qumran? Josephus, *War* II.viii.11;⁣154, says that the Essenes believed in the immortality of the soul, but this belief is not clear in the Qumran texts. Rather, as part of their expectation of an imminent divine intervention, the theologians of Qumran based their hopes on the New Jerusalem which would be realized in their times. 1QS iv 7 says that at the divine visitation all the sons of light who walk in the spirit of truth will have "eternal joy in life without end [*hayyē nēṣaḥ*—a more biblical form of *hayyē 'ōlām*]." In other words, the sectarians seem to mean that the messianic days will continue forever on earth. CDC iii 20 says that those who remain faithful to the community are destined to "life without end." However, the expectations at Qumran were not exclusively futuristic, for the sectarians thought of the community as already possessing some of the benefits of this bliss-to-come. The Qumran documents teach clearly that the community shares the fellowship of the angels (1QS xi 7) who are the sons of God. H. Ringgren, *The Faith of Qumran* (Philadelphia: Fortress, 1963), pp. 85, 128, comments on the life of this heavenly-earthly fellowship and quite properly compares it to the Johannine approach to eternal life in terms of realized eschatology.

In other Jewish writings, the concept of *hayyē 'ōlām* developed in two different ways. In rabbinic thought "eternal life" is contrasted with "temporal life," and the principle of distinction is one of duration. Gradually in the Talmud *hayyē 'ōlām* came to mean "everlasting life," i.e., one that is not only of indefinite duration, but has no end; see Dodd, *Interpretation*, pp. 144–45. On the other hand, in apocalyptic writing like Enoch and IV Ezra there was a tendency to distinguish two ages, "This Age," and "The Age to Come." Life in these two ages would differ not only quantitatively (duration), but qualitatively. There would be a different kind of life in the *hayyē 'ōlām*.

With this background in mind, let us turn to what John means by "eternal life." This is the life by which God Himself lives, and which the Son of God possesses from the Father (v 26, vi 57). The Son has a specific orientation toward men, for he is the divine Word spoken with the purpose of giving eternal life to men (i 4; I John i 1–2) and it is for this purpose that the Son has come among men (x 10; I John iv 9). As far as men are concerned, Jesus is life (xi 25, xiv 6; Rev i 18); his words are spirit and life (John vi 63). Belief in him is the only way in which men can receive God's life (iii 16, v 24, xx 31). How is this life communicated? Natural life is given when God breathes His spirit or breath into the dust of the earth (Gen ii 7); so eternal life is given when Jesus breathes forth God's Holy Spirit upon his disciples (John xx 22). The Spirit is the life-giving force (vi 63), and the Spirit can only be given after Jesus has conquered death (vii 39). The communication of this gift of the Spirit to future generations is associated with the living waters of Baptism which beget a man anew (iii 5, iv 10, 14, vii 37–39) and which have their headwaters in the water that flowed from the side of the crucified Jesus (xix 34). This eternal life given to men by the life-giving Spirit is nourished by the body and blood of Jesus in the Eucharist (vi 51–58).

There can be no doubt then that for John "eternal life" is qualitatively different from natural life (*psychē*), for it is a life that death cannot destroy (xi 26). Indeed, the real enemy of eternal life is not death but sin (I John iii 15, v 16). In the line of apocalyptic thought sketched above, for John "eternal life" is the life of the Age to Come given here and now. We pointed out in the Introduction, VIII:C, that the dominant interest in John is one of realized eschatology. There is a real similarity between the eternal life that Jesus offers here below through the living waters of Baptism and the life at the end of time when the New Jerusalem descends from heaven and through its streets flows the water of life from the throne of the Lamb (Rev xxii 1). In the Gospel eternal life and divine sonship are gifts already in the possession of the Christian (although there is room for future perfection when even physical death is no more—v 28–29).

Since the difference between divine life and natural life is primarily qualitative, the best translation of *zōē aiōnios* is "eternal life," rather than "everlasting life," a translation which would put the emphasis on duration. But we do not imply that there is no connotation of "everlasting" in John's understanding of this life. If death cannot destroy it, obviously it has no definite terminus. In vi 58 we hear, "The man who feeds on this bread will *live forever*." But, unlike the Platonic and Hermetic concepts of life, the Johannine concept of eternal life is not without relation to time. The eternal life of the Christian has come through the action of the Son of God who became man in time. One can possess this eternal life only if one is a branch on the vine which is Jesus (xv 5). Even the most "gnostic" statement in the Gospel, "Eternal life consists in this, that they know you the only true God, and the one whom you sent, Jesus Christ" (xvii 3), is rooted in a historic event in a way in which Gnostic thought is not. Here "know" means to be in a vital and intimate relationship with the Father and Jesus, and such a relationship comes through faith in Jesus and hearing his words. John never suggests that this relationship can come through ecstatic contemplation of the divinity, as in the *Hermetica*, nor through a mystic vision of God, as in the mysteries.

The emphasis on life is much clearer in John than in the Synoptics. Yet once again we may suspect that the fourth evangelist is not inventing a theme but capitalizing on a theme that was in the tradition of Jesus' words as far back as we have evidence. In Mark ix 43 (also Matt xxv 46) Jesus speaks of entering into life after the resurrection of the body. In a passage found in Mark x 17 and in a variant form in Matt xix 16 (which may represent "Q"), a man asks Jesus what he must do to inherit or have "eternal life." The language of "enter life," "inherit life," is similar to the language that the Synoptics use of the kingdom (Matt xix 24, xxv 34). Luke xviii 29–30 clearly associates eternal life and the kingdom of God. The fourth evangelist, who reports little concerning the kingdom, seems to have taken an expression associated with the kingdom, namely, "life" or "eternal life," and have made it a main theme of the Gospel. The greater adaptability of the theme of life to his emphasis on realized eschatology was undoubtedly a factor in the choice. The fact that the OT portrays Wisdom as leading men to life (Prov iv 13, viii 32–35; Sir iv 12; Bar iv 1) and immortality (Wis vi 18–19) was probably another factor, for Wisdom motifs are important in this Gospel (Introduction, VIII:D).

BIBLIOGRAPHY

Feuillet, A., "La participation actuelle à la vie divine d'après le quatrième évangile," StEv, I, pp. 295–308. Now in English in JohSt, pp. 169–80.

Filson, F. V., "The Gospel of Life," CINTI, pp. 111–23.

Mussner, F., *ZOE, Die Anschauung vom "Leben" im vierten Evangelium unter Berücksichtigung der Johannesbriefe* (Munich: 1952—*Theologische Studien,* I 5).

Simon, U. E., "Eternal Life in the Fourth Gospel," SFG, pp. 97–109.

(7) *kosmos*="world"

FREQUENCY OF OCCURRENCE

	Synoptics	I John	II III John	Rev	Total Johannine	Total NT
kosmos	14	78	24	3	105	185

What we would call "the universe" is described in Hebrew as "heaven and earth"; only in late Hebrew did *'ōlām,* "age," come to mean "world." Greek, however, found in *kosmos,* "world," a word to give expression to the Hellenic appreciation of the order in the universe. If LXX adopted this term, it could do so in fidelity to the Hebrew thought found in Genesis that in the beginning God put order into the heavens and the earth. In i 3, 10, xvii 5, 24, John is heir to biblical thought in recognizing the creation of the world by God and, in particular, by God's word (see App. II).

But "the world" can mean more than the physical universe, for it often refers to that universe inasmuch as it is related to man. "The world" sometimes bears the nuance of a creation capable of response. Gen i 26 describes man as the culmination of God's creation; Gen ii shows animate creation at man's service;

Sir xvii 2 says that God granted men authority over the things upon earth. Thus, the world finds its expression in man who was created in the image and likeness of God. It receives its orientation from man—either through him it praises God, or through his sin it is directed to evil. Biblical thought does not hesitate to attribute natural blessings to man's observance of God's commands, and natural catastrophes to man's sins (Deut xxviii 39–40).

Besides referring to the universe under man's direction, "the world" can refer even more directly to the society of men (see NOTE on i 10). What we call "mankind" or "men" may be called "the world."

Now, in studying these uses of "world" which involve man, we must remember that in biblical thought Adam's sin had an evil effect on the world. Darkness may not have overcome the light, but before the coming of Jesus darkness was the prevalent atmosphere of the world (John i 5). In Rom viii 22; Gal iv 3, Paul sees creation in bonds and yearning for liberation. Satan is the Prince of this world (John xii 31, xiv 30, xvi 11).

Yet, it is clear in Johannine thought that the world has not become evil in itself, but rather is evilly oriented and dominated. John iii 16 says that God loved the world and did not want it to perish. Especially in the first half of the Gospel (chs. i–xii) there are many references that show God's benevolence and salvific intent toward the world. Jesus was sent by the Father to save the world (iii 17, x 36, xii 47) and to give life to the world (vi 33, 51). He is the Saviour of the world (iv 42; I John iv 14; see also John vi 14, xi 27) and the Lamb of God who takes away the sin of the world (i 29). He has come into the world as the light of the world (viii 12, ix 5) to give witness to the truth (xviii 37). Hidden in the darkness there were some selected by God who came out of the darkness into the light shining in Jesus. But for the others who preferred darkness, the coming of the light into the world only hardened their orientation toward evil and thus provoked their self-condemnation (iii 19–20).

The reaction of those who turned from Jesus was one not simply of rejection, but also of opposition. And so, as the ministry advances and particularly in the second half of the Gospel, "the world" is rather consistently identified with those who have turned against Jesus under the leadership of Satan, and a strong note of hostility accompanies the use of "the world." Jesus' coming has become a judgment on the world (ix 39, xii 31) and on the sons of darkness who inhabit it (xii 35–36; I John ii 9–10). So strong is the influence of the Prince of this world that I John v 19 exclaims that the whole world is in the power of the Evil One. Jesus and his followers cannot be of this world, for the world has now become incompatible with faith in Jesus and love for him (John xvi 20, xvii 14, 16, xviii 36; I John ii 15). The Spirit which Jesus sends is also incompatible with the world and hostile to it (John xiv 17, xvi 8–11). In short, the world hates Jesus and his followers (vii 7, xv 19, xvi 33; I John iii 13).

In the struggle between Jesus and the world, Jesus overcomes the world in his hour of passion, death, and resurrection (xvi 33) and casts down the Prince of this world (xii 31). However, the working out of this victory against the world must continue after Jesus' departure. Jesus sends his followers out into the world (xvii 18), and their faith in him is to overcome the world (I John v 4–5). Their purpose is to make the world believe in Jesus and come to know his mission from the Father (John xvii 21, 23). Before their challenge, the world with all its allurements is passing away (I John ii 17).

BIBLIOGRAPHY

Benoit, P., "Le monde peut-il être sauvé?" *La Vie Intellectuelle* 17 (1949), 3–20.
Braun, F.-M., "Le 'monde' bon et mauvais de l'Evangile johannique," *La Vie
    Spirituelle* 88 (1953), 580–98; 89 (1953), 15–29.

(8) *menein*="remain," "abide," "stay," "dwell on"

FREQUENCY OF OCCURRENCE

	Synoptics	I John	II III John	Rev	Total Johannine	Total NT
menein	12	40	27	1	68	118

John likes to use *menein* to express the permanency of relationship between
Father and Son and between Son and Christian. Yet John does not make use
of the many compounds of *menein* (*epimenein* appears in the story of the
adulteress) that are frequent in the other NT writings (55 times).

In the OT permanence is a mark of God and what pertains to Him, as contrasted with the temporary and transitory aspect of man. In the words of Dan
vi 26, "He is the living God enduring [*menōn*] forever." Wisdom too is enduring
in herself and renews all things (Wis vii 27). In the NT, citing from the OT,
the word of God abides forever (I Pet i 25). This atmosphere of the permanence
of the divine had its influence on the Johannine predilection for *menein*. The
crowds in xii 34 cite as an axiom, "The Messiah is to remain forever"; and since
John presents Jesus as the Messiah and as the Son of God, all that pertains to
Jesus must be permanent and remain forever. The Spirit was given to the prophets
for a time, but the Spirit remains on Jesus (i 32). The man who imitates Jesus
by doing God's will endures forever (I John ii 17). See also John vi 27, xv 16.

But the Johannine use of *menein* is more complicated; for the study of this
verb, especially in the formula *menein en,* introduces us to the whole problem
of the Johannine theology of immanence, i.e., a remaining in one another that
binds together Father, Son, and the Christian believer. We hear in John that
just as the Son is in the Father, and the Father is in the Son (xiv 10–11), so is
the Son to be in men, and men are to be in the Father and the Son (xvii 21,
23). The verb here is *einai en,* "to be in," but this is synonymous with *menein
en,* except that *menein* has the added note of permanence. *Menein* is used for
this indwelling more frequently in the Epistles. The use of *menein* for reciprocal
indwelling gives the possibility of a secondary, spiritual meaning to the more
ordinary uses of *menein,* e.g., John i 39 where the disciples stay with Jesus.

Before we analyze the Johannine concept of mutual indwelling, we may ask
about the background of such an idea. The OT picture of God's dwelling in the
Tabernacle or the Temple in the midst of Israel is no real help, for in John it
is a question of God's dwelling in an individual. Perhaps a better parallel may
be found in the frequent passages in the OT where God's spirit or word is given
to a prophet. Also there is a passage like Wis vii 27 where we are told that Wisdom is enduring in herself, dwells among men, and passes into holy souls. The
idea of being "in God" is found in the Hellenistic world. Dodd, *Interpretation,*
pp. 187–92, discusses union with God in Philo and the *Hermetica,* singling out,
in particular, instances where being in God implies ecstasy or a pantheistic approach. None of the Johannine passages appears to be a reference to ecstatic
experience, and John's union is not one of identity between God and man. Chris-

tians are one with one another on the pattern of the oneness of Father and Son (xvii 21), but John never suggests that they become the Father and the Son.

The closest NT parallel to Johannine immanence is the frequent Pauline formula "in Christ" and its counterbalancing formula "Christ in us." Exegetes are not agreed on the precise import of the Pauline formula, but many would associate it with Paul's concept of the body of Christ. Paul's unity formula does not have the same patterning on the Father-Son relationship that is characteristic of Johannine immanence theology. However, there is a partial parallel between the Pauline thought that the Spirit of God dwells (*oikein*—Rom viii 9) in the Christian and the Johannine thought that the Paraclete remains with or in the disciple of Jesus (xiv 16–17).

Perhaps it is not possible to find sufficient background for the Johannine concept of immanence without connecting it to other theological points already discussed, e.g., eternal life, realized eschatology. This is suggested by the fact that the Johannine writings use *menein* and its synonyms not only for the indwelling of the Father and the Son in the Christian, but also for the indwelling of divine attributes, gifts, and powers. Notice the equivalences in the following.

These are said to abide or remain in the Christian:	*The Christian is said to abide in or belong to these:*
God's or Jesus' word(s): v 38, xv 7; I John ii 14, 24.	Jesus' word: viii 31.
eternal life: I John iii 15.	light: I John ii 10; see John xii 46.
divine love: I John iii 17.	love: John xv 9–10; I John iv 16.
truth: I John i 8; II John 2.	truth: I John iii 19.
divine testimony: I John v 10.	teaching of Christ: II John 9.
divine anointing: I John ii 27.	
divine seed: I John iii 9.	

Turning now to the Johannine usage of *menein* for the divine indwelling, we may note that Pecorara, pp. 162–64, has carefully analyzed the seven different meanings of *menein* in John, but he concentrates on the two dominant meanings: "to remain on in something" and "to be intimately united with someone." It is the latter that particularly interests us here. Passages like John vi 56 and xv 4–5 treat of the abiding or remaining of Jesus in the Christian and of the Christian in Jesus. I John iv 15–16 (iii 24?) speaks of the mutual indwelling of God the Father and the Christian, while John xiv 23 and I John ii 24 speak of Father and Son and the Christian. From xiv 10–11 and xvii 21, 23, there can be no doubt that the intimate indwelling of Father and Son is being transferred through the Son to the Christian. And this is quite understandable for, as we saw on p. 407, what John says about the relationship and unity of the Father and the Son is always oriented toward men. The mutual indwelling of the Father and the Son is not a static but a dynamic relation (Dodd, *Interpretation*, p. 194).

The fact that the relationship between Jesus and his disciples is patterned on the Father-Son relationship is also given expression in what John says about life and love (see our treatment above). Indeed, common indwelling, life, and love are but different facets of the basic unity binding Father, Son, and believer (xvii 11, 21, 23). Divine indwelling is an intimate union that expresses itself in a way of life lived in love. If we understand this truth, we shall avoid the mistaken identification of John's concept of indwelling with an exalted mysticism like that of a Teresa or of a John of the Cross. To remain in Jesus, or in the Father, or in

one of the divine attributes or gifts is intimately associated with keeping the
commandments in a spirit of love (John xv 10; I John iv 12, 16), with a struggle
against the world (I John ii 16–17), and with bearing fruit (John xv 5)—all
basic Christian duties. Thus, indwelling is not the exclusive experience of chosen
souls within the Christian community; it is the essential constitutive principle
of all Christian life.

BIBLIOGRAPHY

Pecorara, G., "De verbo 'manere' apud Joannem," *Divus Thomas* 40 (1937),
159–71.
Schnackenburg, R., "Zu den joh. Immanenzformula," *Die Johannesbriefe* (2 ed.;
Freiburg: Herder, 1963), pp. 105–9.

(9) *pisteuein*="believe" ("have faith," "come to faith," "put faith")—
   with note on *eidenai; ginōskein*="know," "realize"

FREQUENCY OF OCCURRENCE

	Synoptics	John	I II III John	Rev	Total Johannine	Total NT
pisteuein	34	98	9		107	241

It is worth noting that the noun for "faith," *pistis*, never occurs in the Gospel
(once in I John; 4 times in Revelation); this is another example of the Johannine
preference for verbs and action that we saw with *agapan*. In the rest of the NT
pistis occurs 243 times, thus more than the verb. In App. III, "Signs and Works,"
we shall discuss the various stages in the genesis of faith in John, as well as
the relation of believing to seeing; here we are concerned primarily with the use
and meaning of *pisteuein*.

Phrases involving the participial expression *ho pisteuōn*, "the believer," or "the
one who believes," are almost proper to John (e.g., iii 15, 16, 18) when compared
with the rest of the NT—an exception is Acts xiii 39. For John, being a believer
and being a disciple are really synonymous, for faith is the primary factor in
becoming a Christian. The frequency of *pas*, "all, every," in the construction is
indicative of this also. That John prefers the verb *pisteuein* to the noun shows
that the evangelist is not thinking of faith as an internal disposition, but as an
active commitment. The double "Amen" (see NOTE on i 51) with which Jesus
prefaces his important statements is a call for a believing reliance on him and
on his word.

The particular nuance of the Johannine concept of believing is seen in the
predilection for the preposition *eis* after *pisteuein*, "believe in[to]" (36 times in
John; 3 in I John; 8 elsewhere in NT). There is no real parallel for this usage
in LXX or in secular Greek. Some have found a Semitic parallel in the Dead Sea
Scrolls (1QpHab viii 2–3) where a word of the root *'mn*, "fidelity, faith," is
followed by the preposition *b^e* to describe the relation that the observers of the
Law (the community) have to the Teacher of Righteousness (their leader). But
it is not certain whether the passage is speaking of "their fidelity to him" or of
"their belief in him."

With the exception of I John v 10, *pisteuein eis* is used in the Johannine writings for belief in(to) a person: twice it governs the Father; 31 times it governs
Jesus; 4 times it governs the name of Jesus. There is the same demand to believe in Jesus as there is to believe in God (John xiv 1). A frequent synonym

is to "come to" Jesus (parallelism in vi 35, vii 37–38), and this synonym gives us another proof of the dynamic nature of the Johannine concept of belief. Thus, *pisteuein eis* may be defined in terms of an active commitment to a person and, in particular, to Jesus. It involves much more than trust in Jesus or confidence in him; it is an acceptance of Jesus and of what he claims to be and a dedication of one's life to him. The commitment is not emotional but involves a willingness to respond to God's demands as they are presented in and by Jesus (I John iii 23). This is why there is no conflict in John between the primacy of faith and the importance of good works. To have faith in Jesus whom God sent is *the work* demanded by God (vi 29), for to have faith implies that one will abide in the word and commands of Jesus (viii 31; I John v 10).

Although there are various stages in the development of faith (see App. III), in general John uses *pisteuein eis* for true, salvific faith. Exceptions are found in ii 23–24 and xii 42–43, and these warn us that we must not draw too sharp a distinction between the various constructions with *pisteuein*. In an article of which we have seen only a summary, T. Camelot, RSPT (1941–42), 149–55, studies these constructions and minimizes the distinction between *pisteuein eis* and a rival construction, *pisteuein* with the dative, which occurs some 20 times in the Gospel and twice in I John. Nevertheless, this latter construction does have differences of emphasis. *Pisteuein* with the dative is used for believing both in someone (Moses, Jesus, the Father) and in something (the word, Scripture). The element of commitment to a person is less obvious here, and the simple acceptance of a message seems to be the dominant idea. Sometimes, therefore, *pisteuein* with the dative is used by the evangelist to describe a faith which in his judgment is not satisfactory (vi 30, viii 31?). *Pisteuein* also occurs with *dia*, "believe on account of." This expression covers the grounds of faith, e.g., the words or works of Jesus (iv 41, 42, xiv 11). See the NOTE on iii 15 for another possible usage. Of course, many times *pisteuein* is used absolutely without any object, and this construction has various shades of meaning. For excellent tables illustrating almost every aspect of the Johannine usage of *pisteuein*, see Gaffney, *art. cit.*

It is worthy of note that in the Gospel most of the uses of *pisteuein* (74 out of 98) occur in chs. i–xii or the Book of Signs. This division of frequency agrees with the thesis that in the Book of Signs Jesus is presenting to men the choice of believing, while in the Book of Glory (chs. xiii–xx) he is speaking to those who already believe and, thus, is presuming faith. It is true that in xiv 10 Jesus decries the inadequacy of the faith of the disciples and that he tries to increase their commitment (xiv 1), but the groundwork of faith has been laid. The emphasis on the response of the disciples in the Book of Glory is in terms of love which is the perfection of the commitment of the believer.

■ ■ ■

To a certain extent "knowing" and "believing" are interchangeable in John. The last lines of xvii 8 put in parallelism the *knowledge* ("realize"=*ginōskein*) that Jesus came forth from the Father and the *belief* that Jesus was sent by the Father. A comparison of xiv 7 and 10 shows the similarities between the two verbs "to know" (*ginōskein* and *eidenai*) and the verb "to believe." If "to come to" is synonymous with the active element in the concept of believing, "to know" is partially synonymous with the receptive element in believing. We stress that the semantic area covered by these verbs is only partially the same; for while

Jesus may be said to know the Father (x 15), he is never said to believe in the Father. Only Jesus knows the Father directly, but through him that knowledge is offered to men (xiv 7).

The two verbs "to know" occur with the following frequency:

| | I | II III | |
	John	John	Rev
ginōskein	56	26	4
eidenai (*oida*)	85	16	12

Once again showing a preference for verbs, the Johannine writings never use the noun *gnōsis,* "knowledge." De la Potterie, *art. cit.,* has made a strong case for distinguishing between the two verbs. In his view *ginōskein* refers to the acquisition of knowledge; it covers the field of experiential knowledge which a man has gained through long effort. *Eidenai* (*oida*), on the other hand, does not mean "to come to know," but simply "to know"; it refers to immediate certitude possessed with assurance. Spicq, *Dieu et l'homme,* p. 99[1], maintains the same type of distinction: *ginōskein* refers to knowledge through instruction, while *eidenai* refers to knowledge through vision (*oida* and *eidon,* "I saw," are related). Basically the same idea is found in Abbott, *Vocabulary,* §§ 1621–29, who translates *ginōskein* as "to acquire knowledge about," and *eidenai* as "to know all about."

There is some basis for the distinction. *Ginōskein* is preferred by John for the knowledge that Jesus acquires by human means, e.g., iv 1, vi 15. However, it is not always easy to be certain that the evangelist means us to think that Jesus did acquire knowledge by human means. For instance, in v 5 Jesus knows that the cripple has been sick a long time; in xvi 19 he knows that the disciples want to question him. Are these instances of ordinary knowledge, or of the divine ability to read men's hearts (ii 25)? We must be careful of circular reasoning in studying such uses of *ginōskein.* A good example of deep spiritual knowledge gained by experience is found in Peter's use of *ginōskein* in vi 69: "We are convinced that you are God's Holy One."

We may also concede that *eidenai* is frequently used for the intuitive knowledge that Jesus has of the Father and of the things of God. However, the distinction breaks down when we realize that *ginōskein* is used in many of the same instances where *eidenai* is used. Note the following instances:

- Jesus knows the Father: *eidenai* in vii 29, viii 55; *ginōskein* in x 15, xvii 25.
- Jesus knows all things or all men: *eidenai* in xvi 30, xviii 4; *ginōskein* in ii 24.
- "If you knew me, you would know my Father too": *eidenai* in both parts in viii 19; *ginōskein* and *eidenai* in xiv 7.
- The world or sinners do not know the Father or Jesus: *eidenai* in vii 28, viii 19, xv 21; *ginōskein* in i 10, xvi 3, xvii 25; I John iii 1, 6.

The proponents of distinction have elaborate explanations for the instances when either verb is used in a way that seems to violate the meaning proposed for it. However, there are so many exceptions that it is probably best to come to the same decision here that we reached about the attempts to distinguish the various verbs "to love" and "to see." John may tend to use one verb in one way and the other verb in another way, but it is really a question of emphasis and not of sharp distinction. The evangelist is not so precise as his commentators would make him.

BIBLIOGRAPHY

Barrosse, T.—See under (1) *agapē*. . . .

Bonningues, M., *La Foi dans l'Evangile de saint Jean* (Brussels: Pensée Catholique, 1955).

Braun, F.-M., "L'accueil de la foi selon S. Jean," *La Vie Spirituelle* 92 (1955), 344–63.

Cullmann, O., *"Eiden kai episteusen," Aux sources de la tradition chrétienne* (Mélanges Goguel; Paris, 1950), pp. 52–61.

Decourtray, A., "La conception johannique de la foi," NRT 81 (1959), 561–76.

de la Potterie, I., *"Oida et ginōskō,* les deux modes de la connaissance dans le quatrième évangile," Bib 40 (1959), 709–25.

Gaffney, J., "Believing and Knowing in the Fourth Gospel," TS 26 (1965), 215–41.

Grelot, P., "Le problème de la foi dans le quatrième évangile," BVC 52 (1963), 61–71.

Grundmann, W., "Verständnis und Bewegung des Glaubens im Johannes-Evangelium," *Kerygma und Dogma* 6 (1960), 131–54.

Hawthorne, G. F., "The Concept of Faith in the Fourth Gospel," *Bibliotheca Sacra* 116 (1959), 117–26.

Leal, J., "El clima de la fe en la Redaktionsgeschichte del IV Evangelio," EstBib 22 (1963), 141–77.

Vanhoye, A., "Notre foi, œuvre divine, d'après le quatrième évangile," NRT 86 (1964), 337–54.

(10) *phōs; skotia*="light"; "darkness"

FREQUENCY OF OCCURRENCE

	Synoptics	I John	II III John	Rev	Total Johannine	Total NT
phōs	15	23	6	4	33	73
skotia	3	8	6		14	17

The other NT works tend to use *skotos* for "darkness"—of the 30 times only 2 are Johannine. Many of the NT uses of "light" and "darkness" refer simply to physical phenomena; here we are concerned with symbolic use. The dualistic contrast between light and darkness is preponderantly Johannine, although it appears occasionally in other NT works (Luke xi 35; II Cor vi 14; Eph v 8; I Thess v 4; I Pet ii 9).

Light is a natural phenomenon that lends itself to symbolism. With its clarity and warmth, it is obviously something desirable and good, while darkness is spontaneously feared as evil. As E. Achtemeier, *art. cit.*, has shown, the OT made good use of this symbolism (Job xxx 26). Life was associated with sunlight, while the realm of death was pictured as gloomy darkness (Job x 21; Ps cxliii 3). Ps xlix 19 says that the man who dies will nevermore see the light. Yet, in the OT light and darkness remain only poetic symbols for good and evil.

From the writings at Qumran we now know that in pre-NT times this symbolism had taken on new dimensions, for in the Dead Sea Scrolls light and darkness have become two moral principles locked in struggle for domination over mankind. For each principle there is a personal angelic leader created by God, namely, the prince of lights (presumably Michael) and the angel of darkness (Belial). Light is the equivalent of truth; darkness, of perversion; and men walk in one or the other way. According to their acceptance or rejection of the community's interpretation of the Law, they become sons of light or sons of darkness. Ultimately God will destroy evil, and then wickedness will disappear before justice, as darkness before light. This modified dualism ("modified" because the principles are created) is much closer to the atmosphere of the Fourth Gospel than anything in the OT.

In Johannine thought God is light and in Him there is no darkness (I John i 5). The Word who is God (John i 1) comes into the world as the light of the world (viii 12, ix 5) bringing life and light to men (i 4, iii 19). The coming of this light was made necessary by man's sin which brought darkness over the world, a darkness which has been striving to overcome the light left to sinful man (John i 5). Thus, for John the leader of the forces of light is the uncreated Word—a significant difference from Qumran theology—while the leader of the forces of darkness is the Prince of this world (Luke xxii 53 speaks of "the Power of Darkness").

By way of response to the coming of the light, men line up as sons of light or sons of darkness according to whether they come to the light radiant in Jesus or turn away. All this has been documented by references above when we discussed *kosmos*. Here we would only note that while at Qumran the acceptance of the Law separated the sons of light and the sons of darkness, for John it is the acceptance or rejection of Jesus. As we have mentioned, toward the end of the ministry and in the last days of Jesus' life, the term "world" is increasingly employed for those who turn away from Jesus, and so "world" and "darkness" practically become synonymous. Darkness becomes most intense at the moment when Jesus is handed over to death by Judas at Satan's instigation (xiii 27); then John dramatically comments, "It was night" (xiii 30). It was still dark on Easter morning when Mary came to the tomb (xx 1), but this was all changed by Jesus' resurrection.

As faith in Jesus begins to overcome the world (I John v 4), I John ii 8 exclaims, "The darkness is lifting and the real light is already shining." Christians must walk in this light by their pure way of life and by their love for one another (I John i 6–7, ii 9–10). Ultimately in the heavenly Jerusalem there will come a day when light will have triumphed completely and there will be no darkness. "And the city has no need of sun or moon to shine upon it, for the glory of God is its light and its lamp is the Lamb. . . . And there shall be no night there" (Rev xxi 23–25).

BIBLIOGRAPHY

Achtemeier, E., "Jesus Christ, the Light of the World. The Biblical Understanding of Light and Darkness," Interp 17 (1963), 439–49.

Fenasse, J. M., "La lumière de vie," BVC 50 (1963), 24–32.

Weisengoff, J. P., "Light and Its Relation to Life in Saint John," CBQ 8 (1946), 448–51.

Note: Much of the literature on the Dead Sea Scrolls discusses dualism between light and darkness, and its relation to John. See the discussion by this writer in CBQ 17 (1955), 405–19 (now in NTE, pp. 105–20).

(11) *hōra*="hour"

Although the frequency of this word in John (26 times) is not extraordinary for a Gospel, the special connotation given to "the hour" in John is noteworthy. In the other Gospels *hōra* almost always refers to the hour of the day, but John frequently uses the word to designate a particular and significant period in Jesus' life. We can best determine the content of "the hour" by lining up (*a*) the passages which say that it has not come or is still coming, and (*b*) the passages which say that it has come.

(*a*)   ii 4: "My hour has not yet come"—Cana.

     iv 21: "An hour is coming when you will worship the Father neither on this mountain nor in Jerusalem"—to the Samaritan woman.

     iv 23: "An hour is coming and is now here when the real worshipers will worship the Father in Spirit and truth."

     v 25: "An hour is coming and is now here when the dead shall hear the voice of God's Son, and those who have listened shall live."

     v 28–29: "An hour is coming in which all those in the tombs shall hear his [the Son of Man's] voice and come forth."

vii 30, viii 20:   Failure of an attempt to arrest Jesus "because his hour had not yet come."

     xvi 2: "An hour is coming when anyone who puts you to death will think he is paying homage to God." See also xvi 4.

     xvi 25: "An hour is coming when I shall no longer speak to you in figurative language, but will tell you plainly about the Father."

     xvi 32: "An hour is coming—indeed has already come—when you will be scattered each on his own."

(*b*)   xii 23: "The hour has come for the Son of Man to be glorified"—at Jerusalem. Before this the Sanhedrin has laid plans to kill him (xi 53); he has been anointed by Mary with perfume for the day of his embalming (xii 7); and Gentiles have asked to see him (xii 21).

     xii 27: Jesus does not ask his Father to save him from this hour, for he has come to this hour with a definite purpose.

     xiii 1: The Last Supper opens with Jesus "aware that the hour had come for him to pass from this world to the Father."

     xvii 1: "Father, the hour has come; glorify your Son."

We may begin by distinguishing the instances where "hour" is used with the definite article or a possessive pronominal adjective ("the hour; my hour; his [Jesus'] hour") from those where "hour" has no article ("an hour"). The former instances clearly refer to a special period in Jesus' life, a period best defined in xiii 1—the hour of return to the Father. This return is accomplished in passion, death, and resurrection; it stretches from Palm Sunday to Easter Sunday. We receive a warning that this hour is to include Jesus' arrest and death in vii 30 and viii 20. The first time that Jesus says that the hour has come (xii 23) is after his triumphal entry into Jerusalem. At this moment the Sanhedrin has already decided to kill him; he has been anointed for death; and the coming of the Gentiles indicates to Jesus that the divine plan of salvation is going into effect. Since this salvation cannot be accomplished except through his death and resurrection, Jesus knows with certainty that the hour is at hand. That the hour also includes the resurrection and ascension to the Father is seen in xii 23 and xvii 1 which put glorification as the goal of the hour.

Turning now to the passages which speak of "an hour," we may ask if these are related to "the hour" of Jesus. It seems that these passages apply the effects of Jesus' hour to those who believe in him. For instance, there are four passages that say, "An hour is coming." In iv 21 this coming hour will see a change in the worship of God, with both Jerusalem and Gerizim losing significance; in v 28–29 it will bring the resurrection of the body; in xvi 2 it will involve persecution; in xvi 25 it will bring a clear understanding of Jesus' words (through the Paraclete?). Evidently the reference of the coming hour is to the period after the resurrection when belief in Jesus has spread. The effects to be produced in this coming hour do not have the same immediacy, but then none of Jesus' statements about future events have clear chronological perspectives.

There are three more references to "an hour" which say both that it is coming and that it "is now here" or "has already come." The combination of the two temporal indications would suggest an inchoative or anticipated effect of Jesus' hour upon the disciples. In iv 23 this coming and yet present hour is one of worshiping the Father in Spirit and truth; in v 25 it involves the gift of eternal life to those spiritually dead. Although the gift of the Spirit and hence the gift of life was not made until after the resurrection (vii 39, xx 22), the work of Jesus during his ministry already offered to those who believed in him an anticipation of these heavenly gifts. The resurrected Jesus, after all, acted in continuity with what he had already begun during his ministry. And so during the ministry the effects of the hour may be said both to be coming and to be already here. The third passage and one spoken at the Last Supper is xvi 32 which concerns the scattering of the disciples, presumably at the death of Jesus. Since this Supper is part of the hour, John can properly say, "An hour . . . has already come." However, since the particular effect of being scattered will take place after the Supper and at a time later in "the hour," John can properly say, "An hour is coming."

Is this concept of "the hour" of Jesus exclusively Johannine? The Synoptics use "the hour" for the time when the disciples will undergo persecution (Mark xiii 11 and par.) and for the hour of the coming of the Son of Man (Matt xxiv 44, xxv 13—see John v 28–29). These passages have parallels in the Johannine reference to "an hour." More important is the absolute Synoptic use of "the hour" for the passion of Jesus. In the Garden of Gethsemane in Mark xiv 35, Jesus prays to the Father that "if possible *the hour* might pass from him" (cf. John xii 27); and in Mark xiv 41 (Matt xxvi 45), he tells the disciples that "*the hour* has come" because his betrayer has arrived. Thus, there is a trace in the Synoptic tradition of a concept of Jesus' hour much like John's concept. Yet, here as elsewhere, the Fourth Gospel has made a major theme of something that appears only incidentally in the other Gospels.

In two passages John uses *kairos*, "[appointed] time," as a synonym for "hour." In vii 6, 8, Jesus announces: "It is not yet time for me," and "The time is not yet ripe for me." These verses resemble the use of "hour" in ii 4, vii 30, viii 20. It is extremely interesting that in Matt xxvi 18, in a setting just before the Last Supper, Jesus says, "My time [*kairos*] is at hand."

APPENDIX II: THE "WORD"

The difficulty of determining the background of the first verse of the Fourth Gospel, "In the beginning was the Word," is illustrated dramatically in Goethe's *Faust* (Pt. I, lines 1224–37). When Faust begins to translate the NT into German, he starts with the Prologue, only to find that "Word" is an inadequate translation. His alternate suggestions come from a strange combination of Greek and German philosophy: "In the beginning was the Thought [*der Sinn*]"; or "In the beginning was the Power [*die Kraft*]." At the end, enlightened by the spirit, Faust triumphantly proclaims the real translation: "In the beginning was the Act [*die Tat*]." Modern investigations into the background of the Johannine use of "the Word" are as varied, if not as romantic. For references in what follows the reader's attention is called to the Bibliography given for the Prologue.

We may begin by pointing out that "the word" was a name used by the early Christians for the good news preached by the apostles (Mark iv 14, 15; Acts viii 25), a preaching which was an extension of the ministry of Jesus. Our problem is to account for the progression to the personified use of "Word" as a title for Jesus in the Prologue. Two other passages in the Johannine writings should be considered. In Rev xix 11–16 the divine warrior called Faithful and True, and bearing a divine name which no one knows but himself, comes down to smite the nations. This King of kings and Lord of lords is called "the *Word* of God." The background for the scene is found in Wis xviii 15 where the destroying angel of the Exodus is described as God's almighty word which came down from heaven. In describing the bearer of judgment as the word of God, both Revelation and Wisdom of Solomon are playing on the theme that the word of God is a sword of judgment over men. The other passage is in the Prologue of I John i 1: the subject which "was from the beginning" is "the *word* of life of which we are speaking." Here Jesus is looked on as the revealing word which gives life to men, a word which is passed on to men by those whom he sent forth. Neither of these examples from Revelation and I John are sufficient to explain the personification of "the Word" in the Prologue to John; but perhaps they may keep us from going too far afield in our search for background, as if the use in the Prologue were entirely unique in the Judaeo-Christian heritage.

A. *Suggested Hellenistic Background*

Was the Greek world the source of the *logos* theology of the Prologue? We should distinguish between two possibilities: first, that the idea of the *logos* came from the Hellenistic world of thought; second, that the basic components of the idea of "the Word" came from a Semitic background, and when this idea was translated into Greek, *logos* was chosen to express it because of the connotations this term had in the Hellenistic world. J. A. T. Robinson inclines toward the second possibility, as do many others. However, since subjective intention in the author's choice of words is always difficult to prove, we shall concentrate on the source of the idea of a personified Word of God. The following examples of the use of *logos* in the Hellenistic world are significant: (1) It was at Ephesus, the traditional site of John's Gospel, that Heraclitus in the 6th century B.C. first introduced *logos* into Greek philosophical thought. Striving to explain the continuity amid all the flux that is visible in the universe, Heraclitus resorted to *logos* as the eternal principle of order in the universe. The *logos* is what makes the world a *kosmos*. (2) For the Stoics the *logos* was the mind of God (a rather pantheistic God who penetrated all things), guiding, controlling, and directing all things. (3) Philo used the *logos* theme (over 1200 times in his works) in his attempt to bring together the Greek and Hebrew worlds of thought. For Philo the *logos*, created by God, was the intermediary between God and His creatures; God's *logos* was what gave meaning and plan to the universe. It was almost a second god, the instrument of God in creation, and the pattern of the human soul. However, neither the personality nor the pre-existence of the *logos* was clear in Philo (see Bernard, I, p. cxl), and the Philonian *logos* was not connected to life. (4) In the later Hermetic literature the *logos* was the expression of the mind of God, helping to create and order the world. (5) In the Mandean liturgies we hear of "the word of life," "the light of life," etc. These may be distant echoes of borrowings from Christian thought. (6) As for the more general field of Gnosticism, "the Word" occurs in the newly discovered *Gospel of Truth*, e.g., in xvi 34–37: "The Word who came from the *plērōma* who is in the thought and mind of the Father, the Word who is called the Saviour." It is plausible that this Valentinian Gnostic use has been influenced by John, since the *Gospel of Truth* is considerably later than John.

In evaluating some of these examples, one must remember that the Gospel of John and some of these Hellenistic works had a common heritage in the Wisdom Literature of the OT (which certainly influenced Philo and some of the Gnostic Odes), and that parallels can therefore be traced back to Semitic roots. Again the parallels between the Prologue and the Hellenistic literature are often on a surface level, e.g., the *logos* is related to creation. The deep blending in the Prologue of motifs from Gen i–iii ("In the beginning," creation, light, life, darkness against light) and from the Sinai theophany (tent or Tabernacle, glory, enduring love) suggests that the basic imagery of the hymn comes from the OT. The activity of "the Word" in creation, in the world, and above all in the history of salvation indicates that this concept is closer to the dynamic implications of Heb. *dābār* than to the intellectual abstraction implicit in the philosophical usages of the Gr. *logos*. When one reads the hymn of the Prologue and compares it to the Hellenistic parallels suggested above, one realizes the truth of Augustine's remark (*Confessions* VII 9; CSEL 33:154) that while he had found the equivalent of most of the Christian doctrines in the pagan authors, there was one thing he had never read in them—that the Word became flesh. The basic theme of the Prologue is strange to the Hellenistic parallels that have been offered; and so let us see if a better background may be found in biblical and Jewish thought.

B. *Suggestions for a Semitic Background*

There is no one Semitic parallel that explains completely the Prologue's use of "the Word," but taken together the following points do offer considerable background against which such usage would be quite intelligible.

(1) "The word of the Lord" (*debar YHWH; logos kyriou*). We have mentioned Heb. *dābār*. This means more than "spoken word"; it also means "thing," "affair," "event," "action." And because it covers both word and deed, in Hebrew thought *dābār* had a certain dynamic energy and power of its own. When in the prophetic

books of the OT we hear that "the word of the Lord" came to a particular prophet (Hos i 1; Joel i 1), we need not think simply of informative revelation. This word challenged the prophet himself; and when he accepted it, the word impelled him to go forth and give it to others. This was a word that judged men. For the Deuteronomist the word is a life-giving factor (Deut xxxii 46–47), and for the Psalmist (cvii 20) the word of God has the power to heal people. Wis xvi 26 says that the word (*rēma*) of the Lord preserves those who believe in Him, just as the word (*logos*) of God healed those bitten by the serpents in the desert (xvi 12—see John iii 14). We see here many of the functions ascribed to the Word in the Prologue: the OT "word of the Lord" also came, was accepted, was empowered, and gave life. Moreover, the word of God was also described in the OT as a light for men (Pss cxix 105, 130, xix 8). That other NT writers saw the similarity between the prophetic word and Jesus Christ may be seen in Heb i 1–5, a little hymn not without resemblances to the Prologue: "In many and various ways God *spoke* of old to our fathers by the prophets; but in these last days He has *spoken to us by a Son*."

The "word of the Lord" also had a creative function in the OT even as has the Word of the Prologue. We saw that the Prologue imitates Gen i, and there creation takes place when *God says*, "Let there be light. . . ." According to Ps xxxiii 6, "By the word of the Lord the heavens were established"; and in Wis ix 1 Solomon begins: "O God of my Fathers . . . who have made all things by your word." Thus there is good OT background for the statement of John i 3 that through the Word all things came into being. While Hebrew thought did not personify the "word of the Lord," we must remember that in Hebrew outlook a word once spoken had a quasi-substantial existence of its own. There are several passages in the OT where the word of God exercises independent functions which are almost personal. The first is Isa lv 11 (this chapter of Isaiah forms the background for the Bread of Life discourse in John vi): using the comparison of the rain and snow which come down from heaven and make the earth fruitful, God says, "So shall my word [*dābār; rēma*] be that goes forth from my mouth; it shall not return to me empty. Rather it shall accomplish what I want and prosper in the things for which I sent it." (See also Ps cxlvii 15, 18.) We have here the same cycle of coming down and returning that we encounter in the Prologue. A second passage is Wis xviii 15, cited above as background for the use of "the Word of God" as a title in Rev xix 13. It is interesting that the destroying angel can be spoken of as the word of God, for the activities of the angel border on the personal. The last passage that may be cited as attributing personal activities to the word of God is the LXX of Hab iii 5. In the great theophany, as God comes from Teman, a *logos* (the LXX translation reflects Heb. *dābār*, but the MT reads *deber*, "plague") goes forth before His face into the earth; and much of the action that follows may be understood as the work of this word.

Perhaps we should add that, while we have concentrated on the biblical doctrine of the divine word, this concept of a creative word of God is not confined to Hebrew thought. It is found in the Near East as far back as the 3rd millennium B.C. See W. F. Albright, *From the Stone Age to Christianity* (Anchor ed., 1957), pp. 195, 371–72.

(2) *Personified Wisdom*. In *Interpretation*, pp. 274–77, Dodd gives two lists of parallels for the Prologue's use of "the Word," one from the Wisdom Literature of the OT, the other from Philo. By any standard the former is far more impressive, even if we leave aside the probability that parallels between John and

Philo may be the result of common dependence on the Wisdom Literature. Since the Fourth Gospel presents Jesus as Wisdom who has come to call men, reveal truth to them and give life to them (see Introduction, VIII), it is not surprising to find an echo of this thought in the Prologue. Indeed the Prologue brings together strains from both the Prophetic and the Wisdom Literature of the OT. The title, "the Word," is closer to the prophetic "word of the Lord"; but the description of the activity of the Word is very much like that of Wisdom. Moreover, the treatments of personified Wisdom in Proverbs, Sirach, and Wisdom of Solomon are worked into poetic or hymnic units (Prov i 20–33, viii–ix; Sir xxiv; Wis vii 22 ff.; Bar iii 9 ff.), and these Wisdom poems offer a parallel in general literary form to the Johannine hymn to the Word.

Spicq, *art. cit.,* has carefully studied the introductions that mark the five divisions of the collected proverbs of Sirach, introductions that deal with Wisdom. He finds it remarkable that not only are the functions of Wisdom and the Word quite similar, but also the order in which the functions are presented is roughly the same.

In comparing Wisdom and the Word we may begin by noting that Wisdom is never called the word of God. However, in Sir xxiv 3 Wisdom says, *"From the mouth* of the Most High I came forth . . . in the highest heavens I dwelt"; and Wis ix 1–2 puts God's word and God's Wisdom in parallelism. Prov viii 22–23 says of Wisdom, "The Lord created me *at the beginning* . . . from of old I was poured forth, at first, before the earth was created." Thus, while unlike the Word Wisdom was created, it existed at the beginning before the creation of the world. Sir i 1 affirms that Wisdom comes from the Lord and remains with (*meta*) Him forever, just as the Prologue states that the Word who was with (*pros*) God is ever at the Father's side (i 18). The relation of Wisdom to God is difficult to define. If Proverbs and Sir xxiv 9 say that God created Wisdom, Wis vii 25–26 says that Wisdom is an aura of the might of God, a pure *effusion of the glory of the Almighty* (compare John i 14), the refulgence of eternal *light.* Thus, while Hebrew thought would not say that Wisdom was God, as the Prologue says that the Word was God, nevertheless Wisdom is divine. The Prologue does not speculate on how the Word proceeds from the Father, other than to identify the Word as God's only Son (*monogenēs*). It is interesting that Wis vii 22 applies the adjective *monogenēs* to Wisdom in the sense of "unique." The hymn in Heb i 1–5, which we have seen to have affinities with the Prologue, describes to some extent how the Son proceeds from the Father. This hymn can find no better language for the purpose than to draw from the descriptions of Wisdom in the OT, particularly in the Book of Wisdom, for Hebrews says that the Son is the reflection of the glory of God, and the representation of His being.

Wisdom like the Word was an active agent in creation. Wis ix 9 tells us that Wisdom was present when God made the world, and vii 22 calls Wisdom "the artificer of all." In Prov viii 27–30 Wisdom describes how it aided God in creation, serving as God's craftsman. Wisdom is also similar to the Word in being light and life for men. Eccles ii 13 says, "I saw that wisdom is more profitable than folly, even as light is more profitable than darkness." (See also Prov iv 18–19.) In Prov viii 35 Wisdom says, "He who finds me, finds life"; and Bar iv 1 promises that all who cling to Wisdom will live.

The Prologue says that the Word came into the world, only to be rejected by men, especially by the people of Israel. Wisdom also came to men; e.g., Wis ix 10 records Solomon's prayer that Wisdom be sent down from heaven to be with him and work with him. Prov viii 31 says that Wisdom was delighted to be with men. There were foolish men who rejected Wisdom (Sir xv 7); and En xlii 2 says plaintively, "Wisdom came to make her dwelling place among the children of men and found no dwelling place." Bar iii 12 addresses itself to Israel in particular: "You have rejected the fountain of wisdom."

The Word set up his tent or tabernacle among men; so Sir xxiv 8 ff. says that Wisdom set up her tabernacle in Jacob (Israel). If some have seen the glory (*doxa*) of the Word filled with covenant love (*charis*), Wisdom is like a tree spreading out its branches of *doxa* and *charis* (Sir xxiv 16).

Thus, in the OT presentation of Wisdom, there are good parallels for almost every detail of the Prologue's description of the Word. The Prologue has carried personification further than the OT did in describing Wisdom, but that development stems from the Incarnation. If we ask why the hymn of the Prologue chose to speak of "Word" rather than of "Wisdom," the fact that in Greek the former is masculine while the latter is feminine must be considered. Moreover, the relation of "Word" to the apostolic kerygma is a relevant consideration.

(3) Jewish speculation on the Law (Torah). See G. F. Moore, *Judaism* (Harvard, 1927), I, pp. 264–69; StB, II, pp. 353–58; Boismard, *Prologue*, pp. 97–98. In later rabbinical writings the Law is pictured as having been created before all things and as having served as the pattern on which God created the world. The "in the beginning" of Gen i 1 was interpreted to mean "in the Torah." This idealization of the Law probably had its beginning in the last pre-Christian centuries. Sir xxiv 23 ff. gives evidence of the identification of Wisdom with the Torah. Bar iv 1, having spoken of personified Wisdom, says: "This is the book of the commandments of God, and *the Law* that will endure forever." In many instances Torah and "the word of the Lord" are almost interchangeable, e.g., in the parallelism of Isa ii 3, "Out of Zion shall go forth the Law, and out of Jerusalem the word of the Lord." Thus, the speculation on the Law has much in common with the other themes that we have cited as background for the Prologue's use of "the Word."

In particular, we may note the following parallels with the Prologue. Prov vi 23 says that the Torah is a light. The passage in Ps cxix 105 which says that God's *word* is a light is set in the context of praise of the Law; and indeed some LXX manuscripts read "Law" in place of "word." Testament of Levi xiv 4, in a passage very much like John i 9, speaks of "the Law which was given to enlighten every man." (There are Christian interpolations in Testament of Levi, however.) While the Prologue says that the Word was the source of life, the rabbis maintained that the study of the Law would bring one to the life of the age to come (*Pirqe Aboth* vii 6). While the Prologue stresses that Jesus Christ is the unique example of God's enduring love (*ḥesed* and *'emet*), the rabbis taught that the Law was the supreme example (Dodd, *Interpretation*, p. 82). John i 17, with its contrast between the Law and Jesus Christ, may indicate that, in part, the Johannine doctrine of the Word was formulated as a Christian answer to Jewish speculation on the Law (see also John v 39).

(4) The Targumic use of *Memra*. When John cites Scripture, as we have seen, sometimes the citation is taken from neither the Hebrew nor LXX, but from the Targums or Aramaic translations. In these Targums, *memra*, Aramaic for "word," has a special function. (The cautions expressed by G. F. Moore in "Intermediaries in Jewish Theology," HTR 15 [1922], especially pp. 41–55, are still important.) The *Memra* of the Lord in the Targums is not simply a translation of what we

have spoken of as "the word of the Lord"; rather it is a surrogate for God Himself. If in Exod iii 12 God says, "I will be with you," in the Targum Onkelos God says, "My *Memra* will be your support." If in Exod xix 17 we are told that Moses brought the people out of the camp to meet God, in Targum Onkelos we are told that they were brought to the *Memra* of God. If Gen xxviii 21 says, "Yahweh shall be my God," Targum Onkelos speaks of the *Memra* of Yahweh. This is not a personification, but the use of *Memra* serves as a buffer for divine transcendence. If the Aramaic expression for "word" was used in the Targums as a paraphrase for God in His dealings with men, the author of the Prologue hymn may have seen fit to use this title for Jesus who pre-eminently incorporated God's presence among men. The personification of the Word would, of course, be part of the Christian theological innovation.

In sum, it seems that the Prologue's description of the Word is far closer to biblical and Jewish strains of thought than it is to anything purely Hellenistic. In the mind of the theologian of the Prologue the creative word of God, the word of the Lord that came to the prophets, has become personal in Jesus who is the embodiment of divine revelation. Jesus is divine Wisdom, pre-existent, but now come among men to teach them and give them life. Not the Torah but Jesus Christ is the creator and source of light and life. He is the *Memra*, God's presence among men. And yet, even though all these strands are woven into the Johannine concept of the Word, this concept remains a unique contribution of Christianity. It is beyond all that has gone before, even as Jesus is beyond all who have gone before.

Before we close we may ask about one more point: Is the revelation of God in the Word formulated against a background of God's previous silence, as Jeremias, *art. cit.* (see Bibliography to the Prologue), pp. 88–90, has suggested? Heb i 1–2 contrasts God's *speaking* through a Son with His speaking through the prophets; but we must remember that in Jewish estimation no prophet had spoken in the land for centuries. Ps lxxiv 9 says: "There is no longer any prophet." Passages like I Macc iv 41–50, xiv 41; Testament of Benjamin ix 2, show a nostalgic longing for a new prophet. In the rabbinic exegesis of Gen i 1–3 it was maintained that before God spoke there was silence. Is the Prologue presenting God's Word as once more coming forth from the divine silence? Certainly such a picture would appeal to the Hellenistic world where, as we know from the magical papyri and from the hymns to "silence," silence was a mark of the *Deus absconditus*. There are several relevant indications. In the quasi-personification of the divine word in Wis xviii 14, discussed above as part of the background for the Johannine use of "the Word," God's almighty word leaped down from heaven "when *silence* encircled all things." Secondly, Ignatius of Antioch, who seems to offer an early echo of Johannine thought, speaks in *Magn* viii 2 of God, "who manifested Himself through Jesus Christ His Son, who is His Word proceeding *from silence*." However, the emphasis on silence may be Ignatius' own contribution rather than stemming from John, for Ignatius puts a similar stress on the Incarnation wrought in silence in Eph xix 1. Thus, the suggestion that the Word broke God's silence is an attractive hypothesis, but one without adequate proof.

APPENDIX III: SIGNS AND WORKS

When we compare the presentation of the miracles of Jesus in the Fourth Gospel with the presentation in the Synoptic Gospels, there are some obvious differences. Some of these differences are relatively superficial. *First,* there is a difference in the number of the miracles, for John narrates fewer miracles than do the Synoptics. For instance, some 200 of the 425 verses of Mark chs. i–x deal directly or indirectly with miracles, a statistic which means that almost one half of the Marcan narrative of the public ministry concerns the miraculous. John describes only seven miracles (see p. CXLII) each carefully selected to encourage the faith of the reader (xx 30–31). *Second,* there is a difference in the circumstances accompanying the miracles. In the Synoptic tradition there is much more attention to the marvelous aspect of the miracles and the enthusiasm they produce —the crowds pressing around Jesus with their sick and pleading for help; the awe at the sight of the miracle; the excited reports of what has been done, passing from town to town. This vivid coloring of the miracle has faded in John; here the miracles are narrated with discretion (ii 8–9), and detailed descriptions of the marvelous are avoided. Thus, John does not share some of the features that the Synoptic narratives have in common with the pagan stories of miracles attributed to the wonder-workers of the Hellenistic world.

When we consider the kind of miracles narrated in John, we find little difference from the Synoptic narratives. Three of the seven Johannine miracles are also found in the Synoptic tradition, namely, the curing of the royal official's son (iv 46–54), the multiplication of the loaves (vi 1–15), the walking on the sea (vi 16–21). Another three of the Johannine miracles are of the same type of miracle found in the Synoptic tradition, namely, the curing of a paralytic (v 1–15), the curing of a blind man (ix), the raising of the dead (xi). Only the changing of water to wine (ii 1–11) has no exact parallel in the Synoptic tradition (see the COMMENT on the Cana scene in § 6).

It is when we come to the question of the function of the miracles that we encounter a major difference between the Synoptics and John. Let us begin with the Synoptic Gospels, where the miracles are primarily acts of power (*dynameis*) accompanying the breaking of the reign of God into time. The miracles worked by Jesus are not simply external proofs of his claims, but more fundamentally are acts by which he establishes God's reign and defeats the reign of Satan. Many of the miracles attack Satan directly by driving out demons. Many more heal sickness which is associated with sin and evil. The raising of men to life is an assault on death which is Satan's peculiar realm. Even the nature miracles, like the calming of the storm, are an attack on the disorders introduced into nature by Satan. For details, see our article cited in the bibliography, pp. 186–99.

The function of miracles as acts of power accompanying the reign of God dominates the Synoptic outlook, but there are a few miracles that do not seem to fit into this picture. In these instances, the primary purpose of the miracle seems to be one of symbolism. The multiplication of the loaves seems to be a pedagogical echo of OT themes, e.g., God's feeding of Israel in the desert; Ezekiel's promise that God Himself would pasture the flock (cf. Ezek xxxiv 11; Mark vi 34). Thus, this miracle symbolizes the fulfillment of OT prophecies. The miraculous catch of fish in Luke v 1–11 is symbolic of the great number of people to be caught by the disciples as fishers of men. The withering of the fig tree (Mark xi 12–14, 20–21) is a prophetic symbol of the rejection of Judaism.

There are more miracles that are primarily acts of power, but secondarily have a symbolic role. The healing of the sick and the raising of the dead may have a secondary symbolism of fulfilling the OT prophetic picture of the day when the Lord would comfort His people by giving life to the dead, sight to the blind, etc. (Isa xxvi 19, xxxv 5–6, lxi 1–3). In his response to the emissaries of John the Baptist (Matt xi 2–6) Jesus calls on this symbolism of fulfillment to show that he is the one who was to come. In Mark viii (cf. 22–26 in the setting of 11–21 and 27–30) the opening of the eyes of the blind is used to symbolize growth in faith. Symbolism of the conversion of the Gentiles colors the healing of the centurion's boy in Matt viii 5–13, and the healing of the daughter of the Syrophoenician woman in Matt xv 21–28.

Turning from the Synoptic Gospels to John, we find a different emphasis in the function of the miracles. John does not speak much of the reign or the kingdom of God, and therefore does not present the miracles as acts of power (*dynameis*) helping to establish the kingdom. Perhaps the closest that John comes to the Synoptic concept of the miracle as *dynamis* is in v 19: "The Son has no power [*dynamis*] to do a thing by himself—only what he sees the Father doing"—this statement is in explanation of the miracle of healing the paralytic on the Sabbath. In implicit harmony with the Synoptic tradition, John thinks of the Son acting with the power of the Father in performing his miracles, and John considers these miracles to be an integral part of the ministry or "work" of Jesus. That the emphasis is different, however, is seen in the fact that John makes no apparent connection between the miracles and the destruction of the power of Satan. The complete absence of exorcisms in John is notable. John, of course, speaks of a hostility between Jesus and Satan (xiv 30, xvi 33); indeed, Johannine thought is more dualistic than that of the Synoptics, but the miracles are not seen as weapons in the struggle. A possible exception is the Lazarus miracle where Jesus' emotion in the face of death (see NOTE and COMMENT on xi 33) may represent anger at the power of Satan.

In John the primary function of the miracles seems to be one of symbolism, a function that we found primary for a few miracles in the Synoptics and secondary for many more. Perhaps the best approach to understanding the Johannine concept of the function of the miracles is through the vocabulary used for the miracles of Jesus. Jesus himself consistently refers to them as "works" (17 times Jesus employs the singular or the plural of *ergon;* only in vii 3 do others speak of his "works"). Other characters in the Gospel and the editor refer to Jesus' miracles as "signs," a term that Jesus does not use of his miracles.

The works of Jesus

The term "works" is used on two occasions in the Synoptics to describe Jesus' miracles (Matt xi 2; Luke xxiv 19). Thus, if the term is an authentic one on the lips of Jesus, it is another instance of John's stressing vocabulary preserved only incidentally in the Synoptic tradition. OT background for the use of the term may be found in the work or works of God accomplished on behalf of His people, beginning with creation and continuing with salvation history. The use of *ergon* for creation is quite prominent in LXX (Gen ii 2); and in salvation history the Exodus offers a special example of the works of God (Exod xxxiv 10; Pss lxvi 5, lxxvii 12; also Deut iii 24 and xi 3 where "works" is a variant reading). It is interesting against this background of the Exodus that in Acts vii 22 Stephen calls Moses "a man mighty in words and *works*." By the use of the term "works" for his miracles Jesus was associating his ministry with creation and the salvific works of his Father in the past: "My Father is at work even till now, and so I am at work too" (John v 17). So close is the union of Jesus and the Father in the works of the ministry that the Father Himself may be said to perform Jesus' works (xiv 10).

The concept of "work" in John is wider than that of miracles; in xvii 4 Jesus can sum up his whole ministry as a work. Not only are Jesus' miracles works; his words are works too: "The *words* that I say to you are not spoken on my own; it is the Father, abiding in me, who performs the *works*." (xiv 10). That words and works are companions in John may be seen from the Johannine custom of having a miraculous work followed by an interpretative discourse. (The great works of God in the OT are also often followed by an interpretation, e.g., the song of Exod xv after the crossing of the sea.) *Word* reminds us that the value of the miracle is not in its form but in its content; the miraculous *work* reminds us that the word is not empty, but an active, energetic word designed to change the world.

The signs of Jesus

The word "sign" is used of miracle in the Synoptic Gospels, but not in the same way as in John. We may distinguish two uses of "sign" in the Synoptics and a third use in Acts. **(a)** "Sign" is used in an eschatological setting, in reference to the signs of the last times and of the parousia (Matt xxiv 3, 24, 30). In Matt xxiv 24 the combination "signs and wonders" is used to refer to the prodigies of the false prophets (see also II Thess ii 9; Rev xix 20). The eschatological use of "signs" stems from the prophetic books and the apocalyptic seers of the OT (Dan iv 2[iii 99H], vi 28), and is frequent in Revelation. Josephus, *War* VI.v.3;⚹288–309, refers to the miraculous events connected with the fall of Jerusalem as "signs and wonders." **(b)** "Sign" is used when non-believers demand a miracle of Jesus as an apologetic proof (Matt xii 38–39, xvi 1–4; Luke xxiii 8; I Cor i 22). This usage probably stems from the occasional OT use of "sign" as a divine mark of credibility, e.g., Tob v 2 (Sinaiticus): "What sign can I give him [that he may believe that you sent me as your representative]?" In a similar way the Pharisees demand Jesus' credentials. This use of sign in the Synoptics has a pejorative connotation, for Jesus refuses to give such signs since they are requested by an evil and faithless generation. **(c)** In Acts "signs and wonders" have become a simple description of the miracles of Jesus and of the apostles. This usage may reflect the influence of Septuagintal language on Luke; however, the expression appears in Paul too (Rom xv 19; II Cor xii 12). (For a history of this combined description see McCasland, *art. cit.*) In Acts ii 22 Jesus is called a man attested by "mighty works, wonders, and signs"—a text that equates the standard Synoptic term for miracle, *dynamis* ("mighty work") with *teras* ("wonder") and *sēmeion* ("sign"). The expression "signs and wonders," as well as "signs" alone, is used for the miracles of the apostles in Acts ii 43, iv 30, v 12, vi 8, etc.

How does the Johannine use of sign match the three uses of sign given above? Let us begin with the use in (*b*). In John ii 18 and in vi 30 those who do not believe demand a sign, and these instances are approximately the same as the Synoptic usage. Partially akin to the usage in (*b*) are the instances in John where people come to believe in Jesus because of signs, but this belief is not satisfactory (ii 23–25, iv 48, vi 26). It is a belief in signs as credentials of the supernatural, but shows no understanding of what the sign tells about Jesus and his relation to the Father. Nevertheless, such inadequate believers have taken one step on the road to salvation; they are quite different from the willfully blind who refuse to see the signs at all (iii 19–21, xii 37–41). Those who demand signs in the Synoptic tradition (Matt xvi 1–4) are closer to the willfully blind.

The most characteristic Johannine use of "sign" is as a favorable designation for a miracle, and this use is not unlike (*c*) above. The evangelist refers to what happened at Cana as the first of Jesus' signs (John ii 11), and to the healing of the official's son at Cana as the second of the signs (iv 54). He says that John the Baptist worked no sign (x 41), while Jesus performed many (xx 30). It is interesting, however, that John shows no favor toward the combination "signs and wonders." It appears only in iv 48: "Unless you people can see signs and wonders, you never believe." Such a statement reflects the Johannine distrust of the marvelous element in the miracle.

Sēmeion, "sign," is a somewhat narrower term than *ergon*, "work"; while both are used for miracles, *sēmeion* is not used of the whole ministry of Jesus. Yet, even words may be signs, e.g., in xii 33 (xviii 32) and xxi 19 there is a statement which serves as a sign (*sēmainein*) of how Jesus or Peter is to die. Similarly Philo uses the verb *sēmainein* for the symbolic significance of OT passages, although, of course, in John an element of prophecy is included in such symbolic statements. Except for the summary statement in xx 30, the Johannine use of "sign" is confined to chs. i–xii, whence the designation "The Book of Signs." With ch. xiii and "the hour," John passes from sign to reality.

Are there non-miraculous signs in John? Every use of *sēmeion* refers to a miraculous deed; but Dodd, for instance, suggests that the evangelist considered actions such as the cleansing of the Temple as signs. It is possible that he did; the Jews did not, however (ii 18). The fact that the cleansing of the Temple is followed by ii 23, which mentions that Jesus did many *signs* in Jerusalem, does not really prove that the cleansing is a sign. We saw that ii 23–25 is simply an editorial transition to ch. iii. Moreover, iv 54 would seem to indicate that there was no sign in the period between the two Cana miracles. Another candidate for a non-miraculous sign might be iii 14–15, where the raising up of the Son of Man is compared to the elevation of the serpent in the Exodus narrative. The comparison is drawn from Num xxi 9, where (LXX) it is said that Moses set the serpent on a *sēmeion*.

We have not discussed the relation of the Johannine sign to the use in Synoptic grouping (*a*), the eschatological use of sign. John does not use sign to refer to miracles or prodigies marking the final intervention of God at the end of time or the second coming of the Son of Man. Perhaps the very fact that the evangelist uses sign to designate the miracles worked by Jesus during the ministry is a reflection of the theology of realized eschatology that dominates the Gospel. There were already signs of the last times in the ministry of Jesus. This thought is not too far from that enunciated in Matt xii 39, 41, i.e., that no sign will be given except the sign of Jesus' own preaching. Matt xvi 3 says that the signs of the times are already present if the Pharisees could only interpret them.

What is the background for the Johannine use of "sign," since that use is somewhat different from the use in the Synoptics and Acts? R. Formesyn, *art. cit.,* shows that there is little in common between John and the pagan Hellenistic writings in the use of *sēmeion,* and that John is much closer to the terminology of LXX. In particular, we suggest that just as the Exodus story gave the background for the Johannine use of *ergon,* so also it supplies background for the Johannine use of *sēmeion.* This suggestion receives confirmation from the frequency of Exodus motifs in John: the Tabernacle (i 14); the paschal lamb (i 29, xix 36, COMMENT on xix 14, 29, in The Anchor Bible, vol. 29A); the bronze serpent (iii 14); Jesus and Moses (i 17, v 45–47); the manna (vi 31 ff.); the water from the rock (vii 38–39). In the account of the Exodus, we are told that God multiplied signs through Moses (Exod x 1; Num xiv 22; Deut vii 19); yet the people refused to believe. In Num xiv 11 God asks, "How long will they not believe in me despite all the signs which I have performed among them?" This is very much like John xii 37, "Even though he had performed so many of his signs before them, they refused to believe in him." In the next verse John answers the problem with a reference to the arm ("might") of the Lord (Isa liii 1) which had been at work in these signs. Deut vii 19 speaks of "signs, the wonders, the mighty hand, the outstretched arm." John xx 30 ends the Gospel on the note of the signs Jesus had performed before his disciples, just as Deut xxxiv 11 ends on the note of the signs and wonders that Moses had performed before Israel. Num xiv 22 connects God's glory to His signs; so also Jesus' signs showed his glory (ii 11, xii 37, 41).

In summary, the two Johannine terms for miracles, "works" and "signs," share as a background the OT description of God who acts on behalf of man. While both *ergon* and *sēmeion* occur in LXX accounts of the Exodus, the Synoptic term *dynamis* is rare (a variant in Exod ix 16; also Deut iii 24—elsewhere *dynamis* refers to an army or host). The term "work" expresses more the divine perspective on what is accomplished, and so is a fitting description for Jesus himself to apply to the miracles. The term "sign" expresses the human psychological viewpoint, and is a fitting description for others to apply to the miracles of Jesus.

■ ■ ■

After this discussion of the Johannine vocabulary for the miracles, we may return to the question of the function that the miracles have in Johannine thought. John presents the miracles as a work of revelation which is intimately connected with salvation. In the OT story of the Exodus the physical deliverance accomplished by God's work on behalf of His people is in primary focus (a deliverance with spiritual overtones, of course). In John the reference to spiritual deliverance is primary, and the symbolic element is stronger. And, as we have said, this primary emphasis on the symbolic possibilities of the miracle differentiates John from the Synoptics. This does not mean that the material action, like healing, can be dispensed with, but simply that there is little emphasis on the material results of the miracle and great emphasis on the spiritual symbolism. If Jesus heals the official's son and grants him life (iv 46–54), the explanation that follows this miracle and that of Bethesda makes it clear that the life which Jesus communicates is *spiritual* life (v 21, 24). If Jesus restores the blind man's sight, the interchange that follows (ix 35–41) shows that Jesus has given him spiritual sight and reduced the Pharisees to spiritual blindness. If Jesus gives life to Lazarus, the remarks of Jesus (xi 24–26) show that the restoration of physical life is important only as a sign of the gift of eternal life.

The Johannine sign with its symbolism is not unlike the prophetic symbolic action of the OT, as Mollat, *art. cit.,* has pointed out. Often the prophet performed an action that graphically portrayed God's coming judgment or God's intervention in the life of Israel, e.g., Isa xx 3; Jer xiii 1–11; Ezek xii 1–16. The prophetic action, however, was purely a sign since it accomplished nothing of itself (although in the Hebrew understanding of prophetic dynamism, there may have been more of a connection between the prophetic action and the events that followed than is apparent to the modern mind). In the realized eschatology of John, the signs of Jesus not only prophesy God's intervention but already contain it. The physical health, sight, and life are gifts which contain an anticipation of spiritual life and faith. The prophetic aspect of the signs of Jesus consists in this: the spiritual life and sight which have been attached to physical miracles will be poured forth without such intervention once Jesus has been glorified and the Spirit has been given. Thus, the miracle is a sign, not only qualitatively (a material action pointing toward a spiritual reality), but also temporally (what happens before *the hour* prophesying what will happen after the hour has come). That is why, as we have explained, the signs of Jesus are found only in the first book of the Gospel (chs. i–xii).

The prophetic element in the miraculous sign is what allows the Johannine narrative of the miracle to bear so often a secondary sacramental significance (see Introduction, VIII:B). Once Jesus has returned to his Father in crucifixion, resurrection, and ascension, the sacraments are the great means of pouring out spiritual life, for from the side of the crucified Lord come the Eucharist and Baptism (xix 34, vii 38–39). These sacraments are the efficacious signs of the post-ascensional period, even as the miracles were the efficacious and prophetic signs of the period before the hour had come. Well does Fitzer, *art. cit.,* pp. 171–72, remark, "The miracle is to be understood as the sign of the presence of God in Christ. The sacrament is to be understood as the sign of the presence of Christ in the Church."

The various reactions of men to signs

In App. I:9 when we discussed the Johannine concept of believing, we postponed the treatment of the various stages of faith until we should treat the signs of Jesus. These stages of faith are closely related to the reactions of men to the signs of Jesus. P. Riga, *art. cit.,* compares the signs in John to the parables of the Synoptic Gospels. Both signs and parables have an enigmatic element which divides the audience. Some are prompted by the gift of faith to penetrate this enigma and to come to the revelation behind the sign or the parable; others cling blindly to an exclusively materialistic understanding. There are several ways of presenting the various stages of reaction (see the articles by Grundmann and Cullmann in the Bibliography of App. I:9); but it seems convenient to distinguish four stages, the first two of which are unsatisfactory, and the latter two, satisfactory. (a) The reaction of those who refuse to see the signs with any faith, e.g., Caiaphas who counsels the Pharisees to kill Jesus even though they admit that Jesus is performing many signs (xi 47). This is the reaction of people who refuse to come to the light (iii 19–20); it would have been better for them if their eyes were physically incapable of sight (ix 41, xv 22). Their willful blindness can only be explained as the fulfillment of the lack of faith predicted in the OT. (b) The reaction of those who see the signs as wonders and believe in Jesus as a wonder-worker sent by God. Jesus regularly refuses to accept a type of belief based on signs (ii 23–25, iii 2–3, iv 45–48, vii 3–7); indeed, the Gospel seems to indicate that a certain acceptance of signs is not real belief (vii 5). What is unsatisfactory about this acceptance of signs? Grundmann seems to hold that all faith in signs is insufficient, because faith must have *the word* as its true basis. However, this opinion does not do justice to the frequent correlativity between word and miraculous work or sign; nor does it solve the instances to be cited in (*c*) below where faith in signs seems to receive approval. Haenchen, *art. cit.*, seems to come closer to solving the problem when he distinguishes between signs as proofs of the divine power of Jesus and signs as revelation of the Father acting through Jesus. (Haenchen suggests that in the tradition used by the evangelist the miracles were signs in the first sense; and that the evangelist employed them in the second sense.) In other words, it is not sufficient to be impressed by the miracles as wonders wrought by the power of God; they must also be seen as a revelation of who Jesus is, and his oneness with the Father. **(c)** The reaction of those who see the true significance of the signs, and thus come to believe in Jesus and to know who he is and his relation to the Father. Such a faith, which seems to be satisfactory, is the culmination of several of the narratives of the miracles of Jesus (iv 53, vi 69, ix 38, xi 40). It is this understanding of a sign that enables the believer to see that Jesus is the manifestation of God's glory (ii 11). In this sense the works that Jesus performs give testimony for him (v 36), and Jesus can challenge men to put faith in his works (x 38—note that this verse is not simply a challenge to believe in the miracles as credentials of Jesus, but to believe in the works as manifesting the oneness of the Father and the Son). At the Lazarus miracle Jesus thanks the Father (xi 41–42) for this sign that will lead people to believe in him as the resurrection and the life. We may note that there are substages within this satisfactory reaction to signs: the disciples who believed at Cana (ii 11) are still growing in faith in vi 60–71 and xiv 5–12. Full salvific faith in Jesus is a gift of God which, like the gift of the Spirit, can come only after the resurrection. This is seen in the fullest profession of faith in the Gospel (xx 28). **(d)** The reaction of those who believe in Jesus even without seeing signs. This is praised by Jesus in xx 29. Such disciples believe on the word of those who were with Jesus (xvii 20), and Jesus blesses them and prays that they may see his glory (xvii 24). It is rather idle to speculate as to whether those who did see the signs of Jesus and came to faith through them were inferior to those who would come to faith without signs. A faith not based on signs became a necessity when the period in which Jesus worked signs came to an end. That John did not mean to exclude the miracles of the Twelve (see Acts) and their usefulness for the spread of the faith is suggested by xiv 12 where Jesus promises: "The man who has faith in me will perform the same works I perform. In fact, he will perform far greater than these." The next verse indicates that these works performed by the believer are related to the glorification of the Father in the Son. Nevertheless, in exalting a faith that has no dependence on miraculous sign, John is appealing to the life-situation of the Church of his time where sacrament has largely replaced miracle as the vehicle of symbolic revelation.

BIBLIOGRAPHY

Brown, R. E., "The Gospel Miracles," BCCT, pp. 184–201. Also in NTE, Ch. x.
Cerfaux, L., "Les miracles, signes messianiques de Jésus et oeuvres de Dieu, selon l'Evangile de saint Jean," *L'Attente du Messie* (Recherches Bibliques, I), pp. 131–38. Also RecLC, II, pp. 41–50.

Charlier, J.-P., "La notion de signe (*sēmeion*) dans le IVᵉ Evangile," RSPT 43 (1959), 434–48.

Fitzer, G., "Sakrament und Wunder im Neuen Testament," IMEL, pp. 169–88.

Formesyn, R., "Le sèmeion johannique et le sèmeion hellénistique," ETL 38 (1962), 856–94.

Haenchen, E., " 'Der Vater, der mich gesandt hat,' " NTS 9 (1962–63), 208–16.

McCasland, S. V., "Signs and Wonders," JBL 76 (1957), 149–52.

Menoud, Ph.-H., "La signification du miracle selon le Nouveau Testament," RHPR 28–29 (1948–49), 173–92.

———"Miracle et sacrement dans le Nouveau Testament," *Verbum Caro* 6 (1952), 139–54.

Mollat, D., "Le semeion johannique," SacPag, II, pp. 209–18.

Riga, P., "Signs of Glory. The Use of *'Sēmeion'* in St. John's Gospel," Interp 17 (1963), 402–24.

See also under *pisteuein*, "believe," in App. I:9.

APPENDIX IV: *EGŌ EIMI*—"I AM"

Johannine Usage

The Gr. *egō eimi*, "I am," can be simply a phrase of common speech, equivalent to "It is I" or "I am the one." However, it also has had a solemn and sacral use in the OT, the NT, Gnosticism, and pagan Greek religious writings. Bultmann, p. 167[2], has classified four different uses of the formula: **(a)** *Präsentationsformel*, or an introduction, answering the question, "Who are you?" Thus, "I am Socrates"; or in Gen xvii 1, "I am El Shaddai." **(b)** *Qualifikationsformel*, or as a description of the subject, answering the question, "What are you?" Thus, "I am a philosopher"; or in Ezek xxviii 2, the king of Tyre says, "I am a god." **(c)** *Identifikationsformel*, where the speaker identifies himself with another person or thing. Bultmann cites a saying of Isis, "I am all that has been, that is, and that will be." The predicate sums up the identity of the subject. **(d)** *Rekognitionsformel*, or a formula that separates the subject from others. It answers the question, "Who is the one who . . . ?" with the response, "It is I." This is an instance in which the "I" is really a predicate.

Now keeping in mind this spectrum of usage, extending from the banal to the sacral, let us consider the use of *egō eimi* in John. Grammatically we may distinguish three types of use:

(1) The absolute use with no predicate. Thus,

    viii 24: "Unless you come to believe that I AM, you will surely die in your sins."

    viii 28: "When you lift up the Son of Man, then you will realize that I AM."

    viii 58: "Before Abraham even came into existence, I AM."

    xiii 19: "When it does happen, you may believe that I AM."

There is a natural tendency to feel that these statements are incomplete; for instance, in viii 25 the Jews respond by asking, "Well, then, who are you?" Since this usage goes far beyond ordinary parlance, all recognize that the absolute *egō eimi* has a special revelatory function in John. According to Daube, *art. cit.*, p. 325, T. W. Manson has proposed that the formula really means, "The Messiah is here." The meaning is suggested for Mark xiii 6 (Luke xxi 8): "Many will come in my name, saying I am"—here Matt xxiv 5 supplies a predicate, "I am the Messiah." However, there is not much in the context of the Johannine passages that would incline us to think that Jesus is speaking of messiahship. A more common explanation, as we shall see below, is to associate the Johannine use with *egō eimi* employed as a divine name in the OT and rabbinic Judaism.

(2) The use where a predicate may be understood even though it is not expressed.

    vi 20: The disciples in the boat are frightened because they see someone coming to them on the water. Jesus assures them, *"Egō eimi;* do not be afraid." Here the expression may simply mean, "It is I, i.e., someone whom you know, and not a supernatural being or a ghost." We shall point out, however, that divine theophanies in the OT often have this formula: Do not be afraid; I am the God of your ancestors. As we have said in the COMMENT on § 21, in vi 20 John may well be giving us an epiphany scene, and thus playing on both the ordinary and sacral use of *egō eimi*.

xviii 5: The soldiers and police who have come to the garden across the Kidron to arrest Jesus announce that they are seeking Jesus, and Jesus answers, *"Egō eimi."* This means, "I am he"; but the fact that those who hear it fall to the ground when he answers suggests a form of theophany which leaves men prostrate in fear before God. Once again John seems to be playing on a two-fold use of *egō eimi*.

(3) The use with a predicate nominative. In seven instances Jesus speaks of himself figuratively.

vi 35, 51: "I am the bread of life [living bread]."
viii 12 (ix 5): "I am the light of the world."
x 7, 9: "I am the [sheep]gate."
x 11, 14: "I am the model shepherd."
xi 25: "I am the resurrection and the life."
xiv 6: "I am the way, the truth, and the life."
xv 1, 5: "I am the [real] vine."

(On the borderline of this group of "I am" statements would be two others: viii 18, "I am one who gives testimony on my behalf"; and viii 23, "I am of what is above." See the NOTES on both verses.) In discussing these "I am" statements in the light of the four possible formulas given above, Bultmann thinks that, as they now stand in the Gospel, five of the seven belong to his group (*d*). This means that Jesus is saying, *"I* am the bread, the shepherd, etc., and this predicate is not true of some other person or thing. Zimmermann, p. 273, agrees that the use is exclusive; the accent is on the "I" and the predicate is only a development —thus, this type of "I am" sentence is related to the absolute use in (1). Those who think that the "I am" sentence with a predicate came from proto-Mandean sources hold that in the Gospel Jesus is contrasting his claim to be the bread, the shepherd, etc., with that of the claimants put forward by the proto-Mandeans.

A more obvious contrast is suggested by the Gospel context. "I am the bread" is found in a context where the crowd suggests that manna given by Moses was the bread from heaven (vi 31). The statement at the feast of Tabernacles, "I am the light," was probably by way of contrast with the festal lights burning brightly in the court of the women at the Temple. The double claim, "I am the gate" and "I am the shepherd," was probably by way of contrast with the Pharisees mentioned at the end of ch. ix (see p. 388).

Bultmann thinks that two of the "I am" statements, xi 25 and xiv 6, belong to group (*c*) of the "I am" formulas where the predicate identifies the subject. Thus, these statements are not primarily a contrast with another's claim to be the resurrection, the life, the way, and the truth. In our opinion, not only is this correct, but it is also probable that the five statements that Bultmann attributes to (*d*) have features that belong to (*c*) as well. The stress in all of these "I am" statements is not exclusively on the "I," for Jesus also wishes to give emphasis to the predicate which tells something of his role. The predicate is not an essential definition or description of Jesus in himself; it is more a description of what he is in relation to man. In his mission Jesus is the source of eternal life for men ("vine," "life," "resurrection"); he is the means through whom men find life ("way," "gate"); he leads men to life ("shepherd"); he reveals to men the truth ("truth") which nourishes their life ("bread"). Thus, these predicates are not static titles of autodoxology but a revelation of the divine commitment involved in the Father's sending of the Son. Jesus is these things to men because he and the Father are one (x 30) and he possesses the life-giving power of the Father (v 21). Jesus' statement, "I am the truth, the light, . . ." must be related to similar statements about the Father's relation to men: "God is Spirit" (iv 24); "God is light" (I John i 5); "God is love" (I John iv 8, 16).

There are other indications that the predicate cannot be neglected in these statements. The discourses associated with the "I am" statements explain the predicate; this is clear in the explanations of the bread, the gate, the shepherd, and the vine. Moreover, there is much to be said for the parallelism that some scholars would establish between this class of "I am" statements and the Synoptic parables that begin with "The kingdom of heaven [God] is like . . ." (see J. Jeremias, TWNT, V, p. 495; L. Cerfaux, RecLC, II, pp. 17–26). We refer the reader to the discussion above on p. cx. Certainly in the Synoptic parables the force of the comparison is centered around an explanation of the symbol to which the kingdom is compared.

Finally, it should be noted that there are "I am" statements with a nominal predicate in Revelation as well as in John. But, while in John the predicates are adaptations of OT symbolism (bread, light, shepherd, and vine are all used symbolically in describing the relations of God to Israel), the predicates in Revelation are frequently taken directly from OT passages. Note the following examples: Rev i 8: "I am the Alpha and the Omega"; i 17: "I am the first and the last, and the living one" (cf. Isa xli 4, xliv 6, xlviii 12); ii 23: "I am the one who searches mind and heart" (cf. Jer xi 20).

The Background of Johannine Usage

There are many pagan examples of a sacral use of "I am," e.g., in the Isis magical formulas, the Hermetic corpus, and the Mithraic liturgy. Convenient examples may be found in Bernard, I, p. cxix; Barrett, p. 242. We have already mentioned the existence of Mandean parallels. Many scholars, like Norden and Wetter, have suggested that the background of the Johannine formula is found in such pagan religious usage—a usage which passed from the Oriental world into the Greek world. However, as Zimmermann has pointed out, it remains difficult to find pagan parallels to John's absolute use of *egō eimi,* a use which is the most important for understanding this formula in John. The magic texts that read simply "I am" are not examples of an absolute use, for a name is to be supplied by the user of the text. Of course, the question of the background of the Johannine *egō eimi* is but a small facet of the larger question of influences on the religious thought of the Fourth Gospel that we discussed in the Introduction, IV. The Gnostic and Hellenistic parallels for the "I am" formula are not so convincing as to change the general position adopted there, namely, that the most likely place to look for Johannine background is in Palestinian Judaism.

The OT offers excellent examples of the use of "I am," including the only good examples of the absolute use. Zimmermann begins his study of the OT formulas with a treatment of the passages containing the statement, "I am Yahweh," or "I am God," for the absolute use of "I am" is a variant of this statement. In Hebrew the statement contains simply the pronoun "I" (*'anī*) and the predicate "Yahweh" or "God" (*'ēl; 'elōhīm*), without a connecting verb. LXX uses *egō kyrios, egō theos,* but sometimes supplies the connecting verb *eimi.* The statement has various uses. It may be used as God tells who and what He is, much in the manner of Bultmann's group (*a*) of the "I am" formulas (Gen xxviii 13;

Ezek xx 5). These instances where God presents Himself to man are often designed to reassure man, and so may be accompanied with a directive not to fear (Gen xxvi 24). Another use of "I am Yahweh" occurs when God wishes to give a foundation for accepting His statement (Exod vi 6, xx 1, 5; Lev xviii 5). The formula assures the hearer that what is stated has divine authority and comes from God. Thus, this use is revelatory in a limited way.

A use that is more closely associated with revelation is where God promises, "You shall know that I am Yahweh." This knowledge of Yahweh will be gained through what He does (Exod vi 7, vii 5). Many times what God does will help or save; other times it is God's punishing judgment that will cause men to know that He is the Lord. This OT use offers interesting parallels for class (1) of the Johannine "I AM" statements. There Jesus says that men will come to know or believe that "I AM." In John viii 24 this is related to God's punishing judgment; in viii 28 it is related to the great salvific action of death, resurrection, and ascension.

The most important use of the OT formula "I am Yahweh" stresses the unicity of God: I am Yahweh and there is no other. This use occurs six times in Deutero-Isaiah, as well as in Hos xiii 4 and Joel ii 27. The Heb. *'anī YHWH* in Isa xlv 18 is translated in LXX simply as *egō eimi*. In this use which stresses unicity a Hebrew alternate for *'anī YHWH* is *'anī hū* ("I [am] He"), and the latter expression is always translated in LXX as *egō eimi*. Now, as the formula stands in the Hebrew text of Isaiah, it is clearly meant to stress that Yahweh is the only God. We pointed out in discussing the banal use of *egō eimi* that it normally means "I am he" or "I am the one," and so it is quite appropriate as a translation for *'anī hū*. Nevertheless, since the predicate "He" is not expressed in the Greek, there was a tendency in LXX for the formula to stress not only the unicity of God but also His existence.* We see this same tendency at work in LXX translation of Exod iii 14, the all-important text for the meaning of "Yahweh." If we understand "Yahweh" as derived from a causative form (see F. M. Cross, Jr., HTR 55 [1962], 225–59), the Hebrew reads, "I am who cause to be," or perhaps more originally in the third person, "I am 'He who causes to be.'" But LXX reads, "I am the Existing One," using a participle of the verb "to be," and thus stressing divine existence.

There is even evidence that the use of *egō eimi* in LXX of Deutero-Isaiah came to be understood not only as a statement of divine unicity and existence, but also as a divine name. The Hebrew of Isa xliii 25 reads, "I, I am He who blots out transgressions." LXX translates the first part of this statement by using *egō eimi* twice. This can mean, "I am He, I am He who blots out transgressions"; but it can also be interpreted, "I am 'I AM' who blots out transgressions," a translation which makes *egō eimi* a name. We have the same phenomenon in LXX of Isa li 12, "I am 'I AM' who comforts you." In Isa lii 6 the parallelism suggests a similar interpretation: "My people shall know *my name;* in that day (they shall know) that I am He who speaks." LXX can be read, "that *egō eimi* is the one who speaks"; and thus *egō eimi* becomes the divine name to be known in the day of the Lord. Dodd, *Interpretation*, p. 94, cites rabbinic evidence from the

---

* This whole discussion is predicated on the more usual view that the *hū* in the Heb. *'anī hū* is the pronoun "he," so that literally we have in Hebrew "I He" with the copula understood. The Gr. *egō eimi* would then give a slightly different thrust than the Hebrew. But some scholars think that *hū* had simply the force of a copula, and that the Hebrew meant exactly the same as the Greek. See W. F. Albright, VT 9 (1959), 342.

2nd century A.D. where the passage is taken to mean, "In that day they shall know that 'I AM' is speaking to them." Dodd gives other passages to show that not only the Greek form *egō eimi,* but also the Hebrew form *'anī hū* served as a divine name in the liturgy. A variant form *'anī wᵉhū,* "I and he," was also used, and Dodd thinks that it indicated the close association or quasi-identification of God and His people. (For possible relevance to John, see NOTE on viii 16.) Daube, *art. cit.,* points out the stress on the formula "I am" in the Passover *Haggadah* where God is emphasizing that He and no other delivered Israel: "I and not an angel . . . I and not a messenger; I Yahweh—this means, I AM and no other."

Against this background the absolute Johannine use of *egō eimi* becomes quite intelligible. Jesus is presented as speaking in the same manner in which Yahweh speaks in Deutero-Isaiah. In viii 28 Jesus promises that when the Son of Man is lifted up (in return to the Father), "then you will know that *egō eimi.*" In Isa xliii 10 Yahweh says that He has chosen His servant Israel, "that you may know and believe me and understand that *egō eimi.*" John draws attention to the implications of divinity in the use of *egō eimi* by Jesus. After the use in viii 58, the Jews try to stone Jesus; after the use in xviii 5, those who hear it fall to the ground.

The use of "I AM" as a divine name in late Judaism may explain the many Johannine references to the divine name that Jesus bears. In his ministry Jesus made known and revealed the Father's name to his disciples (xvii 6, 26). He came in the Father's name (v 43) and did his works in the Father's name (x 25); indeed, he says that the Father has given him His name (xvii 11, 12). The hour that brings the glorification of Jesus means the glorification of the Father's name (xii 23, 28). After this hour has come, believers can ask for things in Jesus' name (xiv 13, xv 16, xvi 23). In the name of the glorified Jesus the Father sends the Paraclete (xiv 26). The great sin is to refuse to believe in the name of God's only Son (iii 18). What is this divine name that has been given to Jesus and that he glorifies through his death, resurrection, and ascension? In Acts and Paul (e.g., Philip ii 9) the name given to Jesus at which every knee should bend is the name *kyrios* or "Lord"—the term used in LXX to translate "Yahweh" or "Adonai." While John too uses the title *kyrios* for Jesus (xx 28; see also NOTE on iv 11), it is quite possible that John thinks of *egō eimi* as the divine name given to Jesus. If this name is to be glorified through the hour of the death and resurrection, John viii 28 says, "When you lift up the Son of Man, then you will know that 'I AM.'"

We have seen that the absolute use of "I am" in John is the basis for other uses, in particular for the use in class (3) with a nominal predicate. If the background of the use in class (1) is the OT and Palestinian Judaism, we may well suspect the same for class (3). We have already mentioned that most of the nominal predicates used in John are adaptations of OT symbolism. The OT offers examples where God uses the formula "I am" with a nominal predicate descriptive of God's action on behalf of men, e.g., "I am your salvation" (Ps xxxv 3); "I am the Lord, your healer" (Exod xv 26). See also the OT parallels cited above for the "I am" statements found in Revelation. Occasionally a verbal formula offers a semantic parallel to a Johannine "I am" statement, e.g., "I kill and make alive" (Deut xxxii 39) compared with John's "I am the life." As further OT background for Johannine usage we may mention the first person discourses of Wisdom in Proverbs and Sirach. Although Wisdom does not speak in the "I am" formula, the habit of having Wisdom speak in an "I style" (Prov viii; Sir xxiv) may in part explain John's preference for having Jesus say, "I am the vine," instead of "The kingdom of God is like a vineyard."

The Synoptic Usage

Is the phrase "I am" on the lips of Jesus a Johannine creation, or are there examples of this use in the Synoptic tradition as well? We are interested primarily in the "I am" sayings without a predicate.

There are three Synoptic passages where "I am" is used in a way very similar to the examples we saw under class (2) of Johannine usage, i.e., no predicate is expressed, although it may be understood; and the evangelist seems to play on both a banal and a deeper use of *egō eimi*.

    Mark xiv 62; Luke xxii 70: When Jesus is asked by the high priest if he is the Messiah, the son of the Blessed One, he answers, *"Egō eimi."* This may be simply an affirmative, "I am." Yet, his answer provokes the charge of blasphemy—a charge that would be more understandable if Jesus were claiming a divine name rather than simply affirming messiahship.

    Matt xiv 27 (Mark vi 50): As Jesus comes walking across the water, he says to the disciples in the boat, *"Egō eimi;* do not be afraid." This is the same use we saw in John vi 20. That Matthew intends more than a simple "It is I" is suggested by the profession of faith elicited from the disciples (Matt xiv 33), "Truly, you are God's Son!"

    Luke xxiv 36 (some witnesses): After the resurrection Jesus appears to his disciples and says, *"Egō eimi;* do not be afraid." Once again this may simply mean, "It is I" (see xxiv 39); but the post-resurrectional context suggests a revelation of the Lordship of Jesus.

There is one example of an "I am" statement in the Synoptic Gospels which approaches close to the absolute Johannine usage of class (1). When speaking of the signs of the last days, Jesus warns, "Many will come in *my name*, saying *egō eimi"* (Mark xiii 6; Luke xxi 8). Some would supply a predicate, e.g., "I am he, i.e., Jesus or the Messiah." Matt xxiv 5 does supply a predicate, "I am the Messiah." However, the context does not clearly suggest the predicate; and the juxtaposition of *egō eimi* and "my name" does bring us very close to Johannine usage.

Thus, John's absolute use of "I am" in classes (1) and (2) may be an elaboration of a use of "I am" attributed to Jesus in the Synoptic tradition as well. Once again, rather than creating from nothing, Johannine theology may have capitalized on a valid theme of the early tradition. There are no explicit Synoptic parallels to class (3) of John's "I am" sayings, but this class is, as we have seen, a possible variation on the Synoptic parabolic theme.

BIBLIOGRAPHY

Daube, D., "The 'I Am' of the Messianic Presence," *The New Testament and Rabbinic Judaism* (London: Athlone, 1956), pp. 325–29.

Schulz, S., *Komposition und Herkunft der Johanneischen Reden* (Stuttgart: Kohlhammer, 1960), pp. 70–131.

Schweizer, E., *Ego Eimi* (Göttingen: Vandenhoeck, 1939).

Zimmermann, H., "Das absolute *'Egō eimi'* als die neutestamentliche Offenbarungsformel," BZ 4 (1960), 54–69, 266–76.